CONTEMPORARY ACCOUNTING
A STRATEGIC APPROACH FOR USERS

CONTEMPORARY ACCOUNTING
A STRATEGIC APPROACH FOR USERS

PHIL HANCOCK
PETER ROBINSON
MIKE BAZLEY

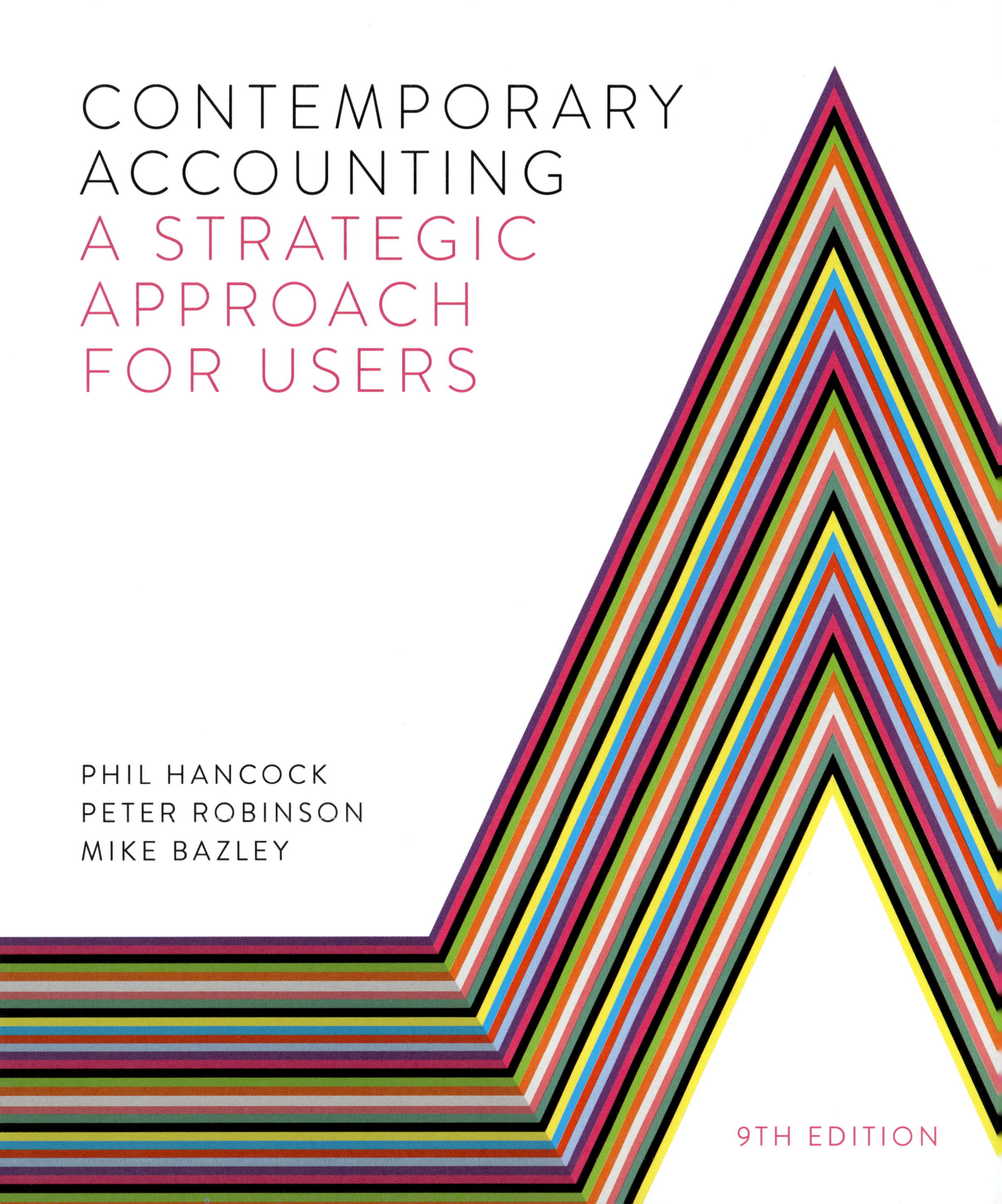

9TH EDITION

Contemporary accounting: a strategic approach for users
9th Edition
Phil Hancock
Peter Robinson
Mike Bazley

Publishing manager: Dorothy Chiu
Publishing editor: Geoff Howard
Developmental editor: Gregory Hazelwood
Senior project editor: Tanya Simmons
Art direction: Danielle Maccarone
Cover design: Neil Keighley
Text design: Aisling Gallagher
Permissions/Photo researcher: Janet McKeown
Editor: Angela Tannous
Proofreader: Penelope Goodes
Indexer: Julie King
Cover: Neil Keighley (Ektavo)
diaCritech

Any URLs contained in this publication were checked for
currency during the production process. Note, however, that
the publisher cannot vouch for the ongoing currency of
URLs.

For product information and technology assistance,
in Australia call 1300 790 853;
in New Zealand call 0800 449 725

For permission to use material from this text or product, please email
aust.permissions@cengage.com

National Library of Australia Cataloguing-in-Publication Data
Phil Hancock
Contemporary accounting: a strategic approach for users
9th ed.
9780170261999 (pbk)
Includes index.
Accounting--Australia--Textbooks. Accounting--Australia--Problems,
exercises, etc.
Other Authors/Contributors: Peter Robinson. Mike Bazley
657.0994

Cengage Learning Australia
Level 7, 80 Dorcas Street
South Melbourne, Victoria Australia 3205

Cengage Learning New Zealand
Unit 4B Rosedale Office Park
331 Rosedale Road, Albany, North Shore 0632, NZ

For learning solutions, visit cengage.com.au

Printed in China by China Translation & Printing Services.
1 2 3 4 5 6 7 18 17 16 15 14

BRIEF CONTENTS

CONTENTS

BRIEF CONTENTS

1 INTRODUCTION TO ACCOUNTING 1

2 TYPES OF ORGANISATIONS AND THE FINANCIAL REPORTING FRAMEWORK 29

3 ETHICS AND CORPORATE GOVERNANCE — 73

4 WEALTH AND THE MEASUREMENT OF PROFIT — 89

5 PRESENTATION OF FINANCIAL POSITION AND THE WORKSHEET 107

6 PRESENTATION OF FINANCIAL PERFORMANCE AND THE WORKSHEET 150

10 FINANCIAL STATEMENT ANALYSIS — 301

13 PERFORMANCE MEASUREMENT AND THE BALANCED SCORECARD 408

14 COSTS AND COST BEHAVIOUR 444

15   BUDGETS   499

18 CAPITAL INVESTMENT DECISIONS 600

APPENDICES

PREFACE

Contemporary Accounting, 9th edition, provides an introduction to accounting for students at universities and other higher education institutions. With the nature and extent of topic coverage, the text meets the needs of students completing a first course in accounting. Thus, the text is well suited to fulfilling the requirements of a one-semester unit in accounting for students enrolled in undergraduate accounting and non-accounting majors or MBA or equivalent post graduate qualifications. The book provides an excellent overview of the accounting function in business for non-accounting majors, and the approach taken to financial accounting provides a solid foundation on which accounting majors can better understand the bookkeeping function. Supplementary materials are available for instructors who want more material on double-entry bookkeeping to support the concepts covered in the book. Where relevant, the implications of different accounting policy choices for managers and other external decision makers are discussed.

The objective of this textbook is to convey an understanding of accounting without introducing unnecessary technical terminology and procedures. Building on basic concepts, it provides a clear understanding of financial statements, their uses and limitations. Accounting terms and concepts are defined in accordance with official pronouncements. Given that Australia has adopted International Financial Reporting Standards (IFRS) for use by all reporting entities in the private and public sectors, the IFRS and relevant pronouncements on the conceptual framework issued by the International Accounting Standards Board (IASB) provide the conceptual basis of *Contemporary Accounting*. Where required, these concepts and regulatory requirements are used to analyse various issues in accounting.

Where appropriate, extracts from annual reports are provided to illustrate contemporary accounting practices. Also included are extracts from the 2013 Woolworths Limited Annual Report. This report appears in Appendix 1 and students are invited to refer to it frequently throughout the text.

Worksheets, based upon the balance sheet equation, are used to introduce accounting techniques and principles such as duality. The in-chapter worked examples and end-of-chapter questions provide students with an understanding of concepts such as assets, liabilities, equity, income, revenues and expenses, and allow them to see how financial statements are prepared. This approach avoids the problems often experienced by students in trying to understand debits and credits.

The text covers financial accounting in Chapters 1 to 11, and these chapters focus on the development of accounting information relevant to the decision-making needs of external users. Chapters 12 to 18 examine the decision-making needs of internal users (i.e. managers) and provide an introduction to core management accounting topics. In each chapter learning objectives and key concepts are identified and highlighted. Review exercises are included and solutions are provided at the end of each chapter. Additional review questions and problems are provided at the end of each chapter. The problems are presented in order of difficulty. The more difficult problems are primarily intended for use in MBA courses (and these are indicated in each chapter) but instructors of undergraduate courses may also find them useful. The ethics case studies are intended for all students and are well suited to in-class group discussions. We recommend that students refer to the comprehensive glossary as they work through the book.

Contemporary Accounting has been presented in a manner that students find easy to read. The response to the first eight editions of this book has been very positive. However, there are major changes in the 9th edition of the book. These changes have been made in response to comments from past and current users of the book, and also in response to changes that have occurred in education, the business world and the accounting profession.

A NEW APPROACH

With the unfortunate passing of Mike Bazley, Peter Robinson has joined with Phil Hancock as an author of *Contemporary Accounting*. On the basis of feedback received and the introduction of a new author, a thorough review of the text has been undertaken. While the main elements of the text, including the conceptual approach and the use of the worksheet, have been retained, the strategic role of accounting information has been given a greater emphasis.

The main changes to each chapter are outlined below:

- Chapter 1 includes the new G4 version of the Global Reporting Initiative and provides an expanded discussion on agency theory and costly contracting.
- Chapter 2 provides the discussion of group or consolidated accounts, which was covered in Chapter 11 in the 8th edition. Some material on the standard setting process has been removed. An example has been added to illustrate the difference between cash and accrual accounting.
- Chapters 3 and 4 are similar to the 8th edition.
- Chapter 5 has been amended so that it now commences with a discussion about business activities and introduces the worksheet to record transactions.
- Chapter 6 presents a more simplified discussion of the statement of changes in equity.
- Chapter 7 is a new chapter on statement of cash flows, following the coverage of the other three financial statements. It includes much of the content on cash flow statements from Chapter 11 of the 8th edition.
- Chapter 8 is a new chapter on accounting for assets. It covers receivables, inventory, property, plant and equipment, and intangible assets. It incorporates the material from chapters 7, 8 and 9 of the 8th edition but in much less detail.
- Chapter 9 is a new chapter on accounting for liabilities. It covers accounts payable, accruals, provisions, taxation and financial liabilities such as hire purchase, leases, bank overdrafts and long-term loans and debentures. It also covers equity as a source of funds.
- Chapter 10 covers financial statement analysis and is similar to Chapter 13 of the 8th edition.
- Chapter 11 reviews how worksheet transactions can be recorded using debits and credits, and is similar to Chapter 13 of the 8th edition.
- Chapter 12 draws upon the material previously covered in Chapter 14 of the 8th edition and introduces management accounting as a source of information used by managers to make resource allocation decisions. New features in Chapter 12 include the use of the value chain concept to illustrate the range of activities undertaken by a firm, and more detailed coverage of Michael Porter's five forces analysis and generic competitive strategies.
- Chapter 13 examines the material on performance measurement covered in Chapter 20 of the 8th edition. This material provides a strategic analysis of performance measurement, including the use of different financial and non-financial performance measures and the use of the balanced scorecard as a comprehensive performance management framework.
- Chapter 14 provides a more integrated and comprehensive examination of costs, including the nature and behaviour of costs, direct and indirect costs, product and period costs, and the allocation of overhead costs using traditional volume and activity-based cost allocation models. It combines material previously covered in Chapters 16 and 17 of the 8th edition.
- Chapter 15 is based on Chapter 19 of the 8th edition, and examines the nature and purpose of budgets with a detailed practical illustration of the development of a master budget. The material on budgets is extended to cover the nature and purpose of projected financial statements.

- With the discussion of cost behaviour now appearing in Chapter 14, Chapter 16 provides a more focused examination of cost-volume-profit analysis, previously covered in Chapter 17 of the 8th edition.
- Chapter 17 incorporates the material previously covered in Chapter 18 of the 8th edition, and examines short-term decision making with and without resource constraints, as well as key management accounting concepts such as sunk, opportunity and relevant costs.
- Chapter 18 examines long-term decision making (i.e. capital investment projects), previously which was covered in Chapter 15 in the 8th edition. The revised chapter provides additional commentary on different types of capital investment decisions, dealing with uncertainty and post-implementation audits.

   Additional within textbook resources included are as follows:

- Appendix 1 provides an extract from the Annual Report of Woolworths Limited for the year ending 30 June 2013. Reference is made to the Woolworths financial report throughout the financial accounting section of the 9th edition, enabling readers to examine the financial report of a real company. Most of the financial accounting chapters include end-of-chapter questions relating to the report. These questions are intended to encourage student interest in reading published financial reports and becoming familiar with the contents.
- Updated Recent newspaper articles are used to illustrate the various topics discussed in many chapters. These articles provide a real-world context for the subject matter discussed, as well as stimulating student interest in accounting as a field of professional practice.

RESOURCES GUIDE

FOR THE STUDENT

As you read this text you will find a number of features in every chapter that enhance your study of accounting, and will enable you to relate these concepts to real-world accounting applications.

Learning objectives introduce each chapter and give a clear outline of what you will be studying. The learning objectives are also referenced by margin icons to enhance your learning experience.

Key concept boxes bring special attention to important points and provide precise definitions of key accounting concepts.

Case studies help you to relate accounting to the real-world business environment.

Each one has a clearly marked **Commentary** section that outlines the discussion in the case.

Stop and think exercises progressively reinforce your understanding of key concepts, and provide you with the opportunity to reflect and revise important concepts.

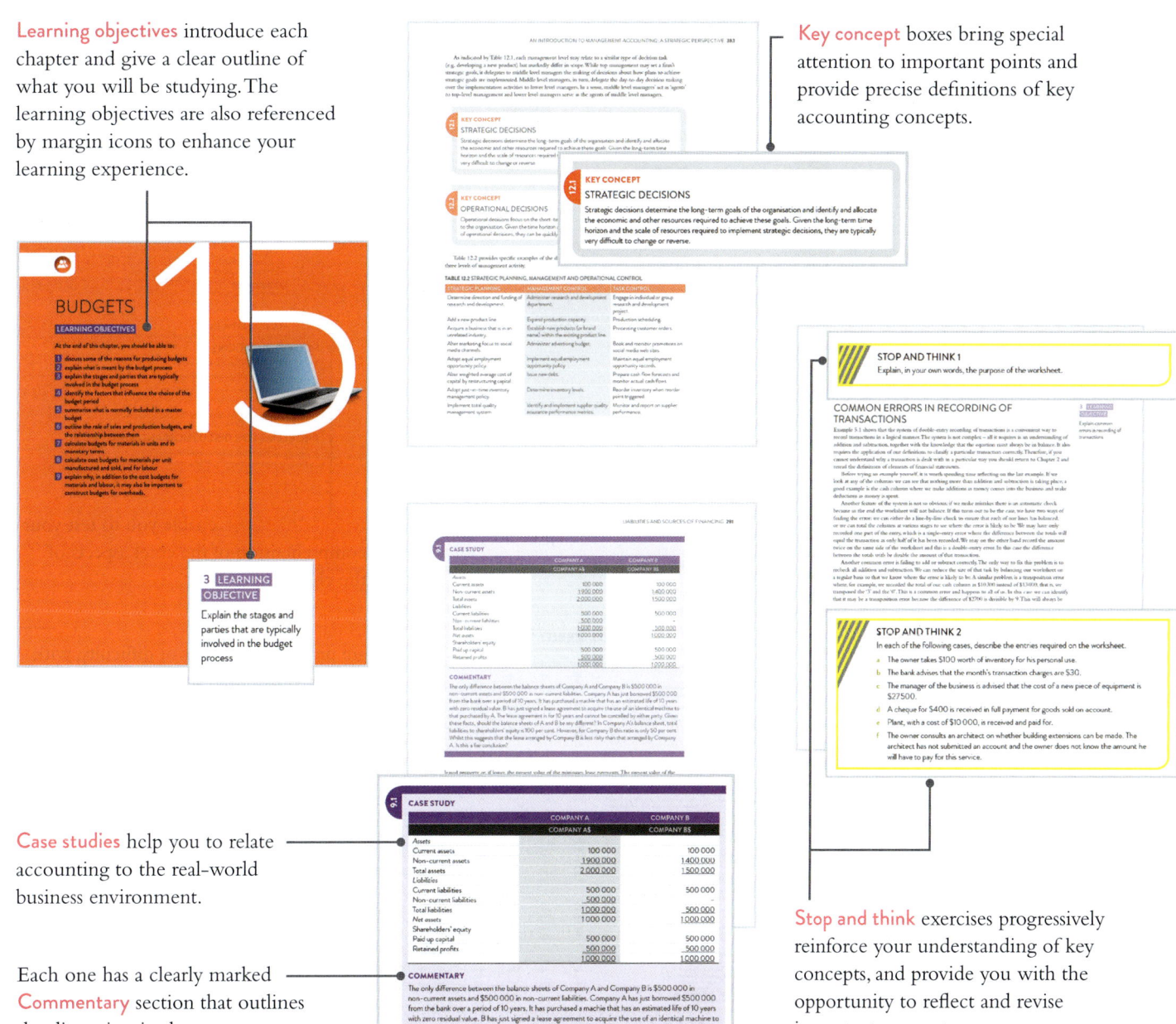

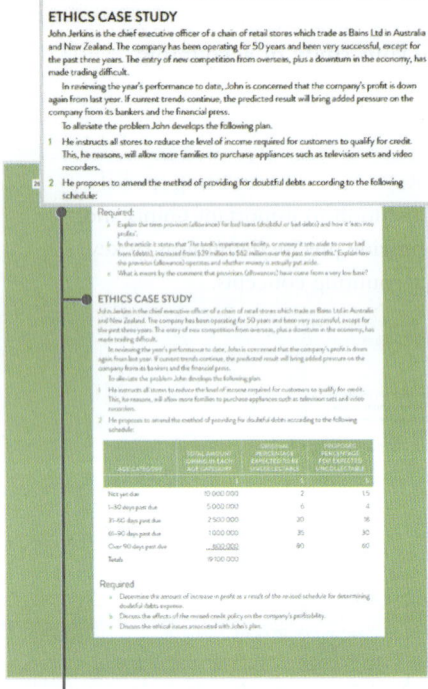

Worked examples provide you with a step-by-step guide to approaching important concepts.

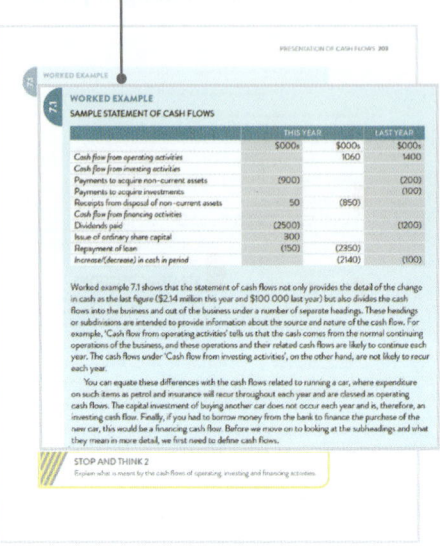

The summary reviews the chapter's main points and reflects its learning objectives to consolidate your understanding of key concepts and issues.

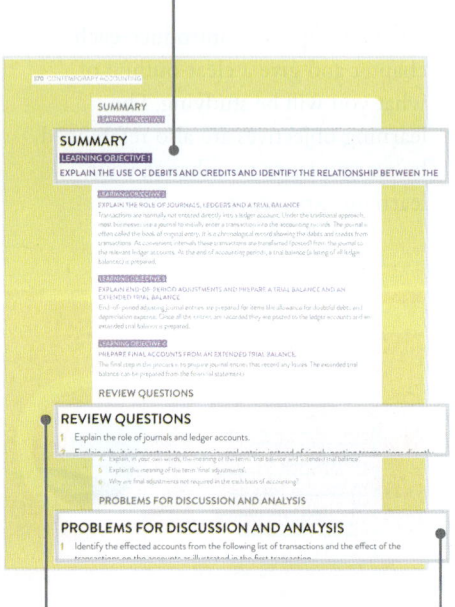

Ethics case studies provide you with real-world examples and dilemmas toyou're your understanding of ethics in accounting.

At the end of the chapter, you will find several learning tools to help you review the chapter's key concepts and extend your learning.

Review questions enable you to test your comprehension of the chief aspects of the chapter.

Problems for discussion and analysis are presented in order of difficulty, with more difficult questions labelled as suitable for postgraduate students.

WOOLWORTHS LTD 2013 ANNUAL REPORT

Extracts from the Woolworths Ltd Annual Report 2013 are included in the appendix. The margin icon on the left highlights when references to these extracts are made in the financial accounting section of this text so you to acquire an appreciation of and become familiar with the financial report of a real company. Questions relating to this report can be found in the end-of-chapter sections.

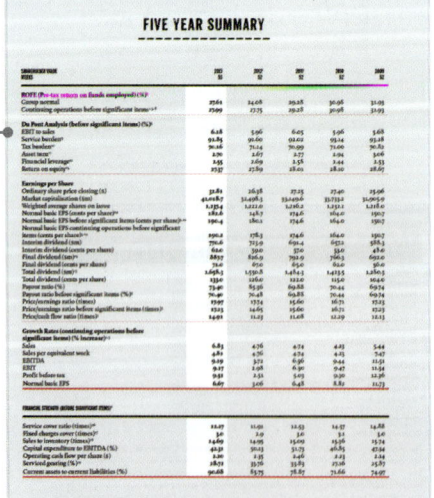

ETHICS AND CORPORATE SOCIAL RESPONSIBILITY

Throughout the text you will find the ethics and corporate social responsibility margin icon to indicate the discussion of issues relating to ethics, and corporate social responsibility.

CENGAGENOW

The ninth edition of Contemporary Accounting has a dedicated CengageNOW study tool that integrates the material in the text with myriad review opportunities. You can test your understanding of chapter concepts, concentrate your revision on your weakest areas and then verify your progress using the latest technology.

For updates and news relating to *Contemporary Accounting*, please go to http://login.cengagebrain.com/.

GOT IT ACCOUNTING

Also available from Cengage Learning is Got It Accounting so you can get key accounting concepts locked down. This unique revision model sorts through eight key topics to make sure you really have 'got it' in time to pass your first assessment. Buy it now from https://gotit.net.au for less than the price of a cup of coffee.

FOR THE INSTRUCTOR

Cengage Learning is pleased to provide you with a selection of resources that will help you prepare your lectures. These teaching tools are available on the companion website, accessible via http://login.cengage.com.

SOLUTIONS MANUAL

The solutions manual provides instructors with suggested solutions to all the end-of-chapter questions in the text.

POWERPOINT PRESENTATIONS

Chapter-by-chapter PowerPoint presentations cover the main concepts addressed within the text and can be edited to suit your own requirements. Use these slides for student handouts or to enhance your lecture presentations and to reinforce the key principles of your subject, or for student handouts.

ARTWORK

The digital artwork files of graphs, tables, and exhibits from the book can be used in a variety of media. Add them into your course management system, use them within student handouts or copy them into lecture presentations.

CENGAGENOW

CengageNOW
for the ninth edition of *Contemporary Accounting* is a powerful and fully integrated online teaching and learning system that provides you with flexibility and control. This complete digital solution offers a comprehensive set of digital tools to power your course:

- Integrated e-book
- Personalised study plans, which include a variety of revision tools (animated examples, quizzes, games) for students to use as they master the chapter materials
- Assessment options, which include the full test bank
- Course management tools, including the grade book
- WebCT and Blackboard integration.

EXAMVIEW TEST BANK

ExamView®

ExamView test bank helps you to create, customise and deliver tests in minutes for both print and online applications. The quick test wizard and online test wizard guide you step by step through the test-creation process. With ExamView's complete word-processing abilities, you can add an unlimited number of new questions to the bank, edit existing questions and build tests of up to 250 questions using up to 12 question types. You can export the files into Blackboard or WebCT, publish tests online or print them in hard copy.

ABOUT THE AUTHORS

Phil Hancock is a Winthrop Professor of Accounting and the Associate Dean of Teaching and Learning for the Business School at the University of Western Australia. Phil has extensive experience in the regulation of corporate financial reporting, management and international accounting in both the educational and private sectors. Phil was Chair of the Accounting Learning Outcomes Working Party, which was responsible for drafting the threshold learning standards for graduates of bachelor and master degrees in accounting in 2010. Phil is a Fellow of CPA Australia and the Institute of Chartered Accountants, and the Accounting and Finance Association of Australia and New Zealand (AFAANZ). In 2013 Phil was awarded the Outstanding Contribution to Accounting and Finance Education by AFFANZ. He is a member of the Western Australian Divisional Council for CPA Australia, and a member of the Financial Reporting panel of the CPA Program. As a teacher, Phil has held senior positions at the University of Western Australia, Edith Cowan University and Murdoch University, where he was an Associate Professor in Accounting before moving to the University of Western Australia.

Peter Robinson has taught at all West Australian universities, spending more than 20 years with each of Curtin University and the University of Western Australia (UWA). Peter has also held teaching appointments with the University of New South Wales (UNSW), the University of Texas at Austin, and the University of South Africa. Peter has taught the breadth of the accounting curriculum at undergraduate and post graduate level with strategic management accounting and public sector financial management being his more recent areas of teaching specialisation.

Peter has also been an active contributor to the development and delivery of study materials used by candidates seeking admission to the Institute of Chartered Accountants in Australia and CPA Australia; to the professional development of managers and senior executives in the for-profit, not-for-profit and public sectors both in Australia and internationally; and has regularly consulted with clients in these sectors upon a wide range of financial and performance management topics. Apart from Peter's undergraduate and post graduate studies in accounting with Curtin, UWA and UNSW, he has a Master of Education (UWA). Over the past five years, Peter has contributed, as reviewer, presenter of professional development material to high school teachers, and as chief examiner in 2011 and 2012, to the development and delivery of Western Australia's Certificate of Education Accounting and Finance course of studies for senior secondary school students in Years 11 and 12. Peter is a Fellow of CPA Australia.

Mike Bazley (1931–2013) was the inspiration behind the first edition of this book, which now enters its 9th edition. The success of this text is a tribute to Mike's perseverance, as many of the publishers he initially approached were not particularly interested in his idea of adapting the UK text *Accounting in Business Context*. However, Thomas Nelson, now Cengage Learning, finally agreed and in 1991 the first edition was published. Sadly Mike Bazley passed away in February 2013. Mike was an excellent teacher and highly regarded by the students he taught, an outstanding work colleague, a valued friend and a true gentleman to all that he met. He is deeply missed by his family and many friends and former colleagues.

Mike Bazley was born in the United Kingdom where, having undertaken national service, he joined a medium-sized company and worked his way to joint managing director. In 1969, Mike migrated to Australia and began his period of employment at the University of Western Australia, which eventually led him to taking up a lectureship in 1977 in UWA's then Department of

Accounting and Finance. He subsequently took up a position with Murdoch University where he was Dean of Studies and Chair of the School of Commerce and Senior Lecturer. In addition to his academic work, he also consulted for the West Australian state government, conducted public seminars and contributed to various academic and professional publications. Mike was a Fellow of CPA Australia. Having retired in 1995, Mike still continued to take great interest in the development of this text. We dedicate the 9th edition of this text to Mike in recognition of his prior contributions over the past 20-plus years and the very substantial and positive influence that he had on its development.

ACKNOWLEDGEMENTS

We wish to express our appreciation and gratitude to the following people who have contributed in some way to the development of this book: Professor Alan Davison for his support and encouragement; Professor Christine Jubb for helpful suggestions on the content of the 6th edition; the reviewers, who provided useful suggestions for the 9th edition; Colette Larsen and Lesley Murrish, for the unenviable task of typing many drafts of the very first edition of the book; and to Pam Bazley and Jenny Hancock for their patience, and for proofreading early versions of the first edition.

We also acknowledge our debt to Aidan Berry and Robin Jarvis, the authors of *Accounting in Business Context* published in the UK. This book was originally based on the British text, although the two books are now significantly different. Responsibility for the opinions expressed and for any errors in this book is entirely our own.

Phil Hancock
Business School
University of Western Australia

Peter Robinson
Michael Bazley

Cengage Learning would also like to thank the following reviewers for their incisive and helpful feedback:
- Paul Blayney (University of Sydney)
- Dr Leo Langa (UWA)
- DR Marcus Craig Rodrigs (University of Newcastle)
- Matt Dyki (Univeristy of Melbourne)
- Philip Colquhoun (Victoria University of Wellington)
- Peta Stevenson-Clarke (RMIT University).

1

INTRODUCTION TO ACCOUNTING

INTRODUCTION

This chapter discusses the role of accounting, its uses and its users. It will also give you an appreciation of the role of accounting within a business organisation and in its dealings with others. We introduce some ideas about the ways accounting helps managers to meet business objectives by, for example, providing the information necessary to make a decision about buying or renting premises. The ways that the size and type of the organisation affect its accounting will be discussed. For example, in a small family restaurant the accounting requirements are much less complex than in a large business such as Woolworths Limited.

Also, while there are many shareholders who rely upon published financial statements for information about the financial performance and position of Woolworths, this is not the case with a small family restaurant. In this chapter we discuss the information required by the internal stakeholders, like managers, and those external to the organisation, like shareholders. The information provided to managers is referred to as management accounting while the information provided to external users is called financial accounting. We discuss the relationships and linkages between management and financial accounting. Another function of accounting worthy of mention is tax accounting, where information is provided to the government for the purpose of levying taxes.

Another factor that both affects and is affected by accounting is the commercial environment. The commercial environment can influence accounting through government legislation such as the adoption of a new corporations act or through the introduction of a goods and services tax (GST). Accounting can also be affected by changes in technology. For instance, developments in information technology have allowed accounting information to be provided more quickly and efficiently, enabling different decisions to be made than might otherwise have been the case. In addition to accounting in the business sector, we also briefly discuss accounting in the public and not-for-profit sectors. Finally, we look at the limitations of accounting information. As with most sources of information, there are imperfections. From this brief résumé we can see that the accounting activity interacts with all levels of business.

Accounts are normally seen as a series of figures. These figures are, in fact, a convenient way of summarising and reporting information that would be indigestible in narrative form. If you were asked to provide a report that gives details of the value of everything you own, it would be simpler to use figures to represent the value rather than words. The value of some things (e.g. good health, lead-free petrol or an academic qualification) is difficult to express or analyse in numerical terms, but this has not stopped people assigning a monetary value to them.

In order to understand the role and importance of accounting in the context of business organisations, we need to decide what 'accounting' means. If you were to look up the word 'account' in *Roget's Thesaurus* you would be directed to words such as 'report' and 'narration'. It is also referred to as commercial arithmetic, double-entry bookkeeping and so on. These alternatives imply totally different things: a report is something that conveys information for a particular purpose, while commercial arithmetic implies a mechanical exercise following agreed rules or principles.

Besides problems about what accounting can and should document, other issues need to be considered; for example, whether a numerical format is the best format for presenting the information. We also need to consider who the report is for and what its purpose is. For instance, you may give different accounts of your car's condition to a prospective buyer and to a mechanic. In both cases the description could be true, but the prospective buyer may be given general details about the car's performance while the mechanic is told about the car's problems. So we can see that the question of defining accounting has many facets: what you report, how you report, who you are reporting to and for what purpose. We shall look at these issues in more detail later in this chapter. First, let us get a better idea of how accounting is generally understood by examining some definitions from the accounting literature.

WHAT IS ACCOUNTING?

1 **LEARNING OBJECTIVE**

Explain what is meant by the term 'accounting'

There are a number of definitions of 'accounting' and they have changed over time in response to the changing accounting environment. One definition that has stood the test of time is that given by the American Accounting Association in *A Statement of Basic Accounting Theory* (also known as *ASOBAT*), which defines accounting as:

> the process of identifying, measuring and communicating economic information to permit informed judgement and decisions by users of the information. [1966, page 1]

First, this definition states the purpose of accounting. Second, it states that accounting has a number of components – some technical (such as measuring the data), some analytical (such as identifying the data) and some that require further information (such as the communication of this economic information to users: who are these users and what form does this information take?). Finally, the definition implies that the information has value in the decision-making process. The definition assumes that economics concerns any situation in which a choice must be made involving scarce resources.

Another definition was offered by the American Institute of Certified Public Accountants (AICPA) in the 1973 Trueblood Report (*Objectives of Financial Statements*), which looks to the role of accounting in decision making. The report lists 12 objectives that emphasise this decision-making process. They can be summarised as follows:

* to provide information, through financial statements, for the making of economic decisions
* to provide information for predicting, comparing and evaluating the effectiveness of management's use of scarce resources
* to provide information to predict and evaluate the going concern of an entity
* to provide information on earnings, cash flows, profitability and the financial position of the entity.

The usefulness of accounting information for decision making is reinforced by accounting concepts (known as the conceptual framework or the *Framework*), discussed in more detail in Chapter 2.

The conceptual framework gives us a clue to the fact that accounting is closely related to other disciplines (we are recording economic data) and it also gives us some clue as to the uses of accounting information; that is, for reporting on what has happened and as an aid to decision making and control of the business or organisation ('the entity').

A definition from the *Macmillan Dictionary of Accounting* (Parker 1986) states:

> accounting, in broad terms, is the preparation and communication to users of financial and economic information. The information ideally possesses certain qualitative characteristics. Accounting involves the measurement, usually in monetary terms, of transactions and other events pertaining to accounting entities. Accounting information is used for stewardship, control and decision making.

This suggests that accounting information has a key role in the running of a successful organisation.

The use of accounting information for business decision making is also brought out clearly in the definition given by the American Accounting Principles Board in 1970:

> Accounting is a service activity. Its function is to provide quantitative information, primarily financial in nature, about economic entities that is intended to be useful in making economic decisions, in making reasoned choices among alternative courses of action. (*APB 4*)

The fact that accounting is described as a service activity reinforces the point made earlier: in order to understand the usefulness of accounting, we need to know who uses it and for what purpose.

2 LEARNING OBJECTIVE

Explain the difference between management accounting, financial accounting and tax accounting

For what purpose is accounting information used?

Accounting information can be used on at least two levels: that of the individual and that of the organisation (or entity). At the individual level, people can use accounting information to help them control the level of their expenditure, to assist in planning future levels of expenditure, to help them raise additional finance (through, for example, mortgages or hire-purchase) and decide the best way to spend their money. So we can see that for the individual, accounting can have three functions: planning, controlling and decision support.

At the level of the entity, accounting is used to control the activities of the organisation, to plan future activities, to assist in raising finance, and to report the activities and success of the entity to interested parties and to the government to determine taxes payable.

An entity also uses accounting in planning, controlling and decision making (which are all internal activities or functions). The major difference between the two levels is that in the case of an entity, accounting also has an external function: providing information to people outside the entity. This external function is usually met through the provision of financial statements or financial reports, and is often referred to as **financial accounting**. The external users require the information that is contained in the financial statements to use in the decision-making process, or to evaluate what management has done with money invested in the business. The financial statements must be prepared in accordance with Generally Accepted Accounting Principles (GAAP). For individuals, the main external users are likely to be banks and the government for tax purposes.

Organisations also must report their activities to the government for the purposes of paying tax. The preparation of the activities of the organisation must be in accordance with the tax rules as specified in the tax legislation. This arm of financial accounting is often called tax accounting, where the objective is to report the activities of the organisation in compliance with the tax rules so that the organisation pays the minimum amount of tax to the government. The tax rules and GAAP rules are not always identical and thus accounting profit differs from taxable income. Hence the reference to 'two sets of books', which does not mean an organisation is engaged in deceit or misrepresenting its state of affairs.

Besides meeting the needs of external users, the system that produces the financial accounting reports and tax returns also meets some of the needs of internal users. One need is to analyse the results of past actions. This requires information on actual outcomes. These can then be evaluated against the projected outcomes, and reasons for differences can be identified so that appropriate actions can be taken. This is only one of a number of needs that managers have. Their other needs are met through different reports that are based upon information provided by the internal **accounting system**.

The internal accounting system, which may be in addition to the system that underpins the external financial reporting system, is often referred to as the **management accounting** function. The major difference between financial accounting and management accounting is that management accounting is primarily directed towards providing information of specific use to managers.

It is important to realise that the financial statements prepared for external users in accordance with GAAP provide a summary of the outcomes of the decisions made by managers. The two types of accounting are therefore interconnected and this can best be demonstrated by the following example. In 1999, Woolworths introduced its *Project Refresh* strategy, which focused on improving business processes and efficiencies throughout its supply chain. The supply chain can be described as movement of a product or raw material (apples) from its original source (fruit grower) to the customer (you). We discuss the supply chain and its management in more detail in Chapter 14. As a result of *Project Refresh*, Woolworths achieved significant reductions in costs of goods by several billion dollars. The very successful strategy, initially tracked and recorded through the management accounting system, was reported to the external users (shareholders) through increased profits in the published financial statements. While we cover financial accounting in Chapters 1 to 11 and management accounting in Chapters 12 to 18, it is important to keep in mind that the two are connected and interdependent.

Financial accounting information, which is often less detailed, has many users apart from managers. This leads us to the question posed below.

Who uses accounting information?

3 LEARNING OBJECTIVE

Identify the main users of accounting information, and the main purposes for which the information is used

Whether accounting information relates to the activities of an individual or to a business entity, its users can be placed in two broad categories:
* those inside the entity, such as managers or, in the case of a small business, the owner
* those outside the entity, including banks, analysts, the government, tax authorities, investors, creditors and trade unions.

INTERNAL USERS

The major internal user of accounting information is the management of an entity. For a small entity this is likely to be the owner, or a small number of individuals in the case of a partnership. However, many businesses are much larger and are owned by numerous individuals or groups of individuals, as is the case with large entities such as Woolworths, National Australia Bank or Woodside Limited.

Often the major investors themselves are owned by others, as is the case with the major financial institutions. In such a situation, it is extremely unlikely that the actual owners would or could take an active part in the day-to-day running of the entity. Consider the chaos if all the people who bought shares in Woolworths tried to take an active part in the day-to-day running of that business. Instead, these owners or shareholders delegate the authority for the day-to-day running to a group of directors and managers.

These directors and managers are involved in the routine decision-making activities of the entity and their information needs are equivalent to that of the small business owner. These needs are normally met by unpublished reports of various kinds, usually based on information provided through both the financial accounting system and the management accounting system. The exact nature of the reports varies from entity to entity. A department store may require information about the profitability of each of its departments, whereas a factory producing a small number of different products is likely to require information about the profitability of each product.

The form of each report will also vary according to its purpose. If the purpose of the report is to assist management, it needs to show the past transactions and performance, probably measured against some predetermined standard. For planning purposes, though, a forecast of what is likely to happen in the future is more important.

These different forms of reports and ways of grouping information are normally referred to under the heading of 'management accounting'.

As stated earlier, management accounting is the focus of the second part of this book. At this stage it is worth briefly summarising the different categories of management accounting reports. To do this we need to make some generalisations about the needs of managers and to categorise those needs. In practice, of course, there is a certain amount of overlap between the categories but we need not concern ourselves with this at present. The broad categories that we have referred to in terms of the needs of managers are as follows.

STEWARDSHIP

Stewardship is when managers need to protect the entity's economic resources (normally referred to as assets) from, for example, theft, fraud and wastage.

PLANNING

Managers need to plan activities so that finance can be raised, marketing and promotional campaigns set up and production plans made.

CONTROL

Managers need to control the activities of the entity. This includes measures such as setting sales targets, managing human resources, and ensuring that there are sufficient raw materials to meet the demands of production and sufficient goods in stock to satisfy customer demand. It will also include identifying where targets can be set.

DECISION MAKING

Managers need to make specific decisions. For example, should we produce the item ourselves or buy it in? How much will it cost to produce a particular item? How much money will we need in order to run the entity?

Rather than getting deeply involved at this stage, let us first look at the other broad area we identified – the needs of users outside the entity: the external users. We shall be returning to the needs of internal users in more detail in Chapter 12.

STOP AND THINK 1

What are the needs of internal users? Can you identify any other needs of internal users? If so, can you suggest how these would be met?

EXTERNAL USERS

We need to establish who the external users are. The potential users can be divided into three groups, as follows:

- *resource providers*: employees, lenders (those who lend money to the entity; for example, bankers), creditors, suppliers (those who supply the entity with goods and services) and, in the case of business entities, investors (that is, shareholders – the owners of the entity)
- *recipients of goods and services*: those who benefit from the provision of goods and services by the reporting entity; that is, customers
- *parties performing a review or oversight function*: government, trade unions and special interest groups acting on behalf of the general public; for example, Greenpeace.

These groups are normally provided with information by means of published financial statements prepared in accordance with GAAP, except for governments which as stated earlier receive information about a organisation's activities based on tax rules. In order to decide to what extent the financial statements meet the needs of the external users and to understand more fully the importance of accounting, we shall briefly discuss the needs of the external users listed above.

OWNERS AND SHAREHOLDERS

In the case of small entities the owners are likely to be actively engaged in the day-to-day operations of the entity. In these small entities, the owners' needs are often met by the management accounting information and reports.

1.2 KEY CONCEPT

FINANCIAL ACCOUNTING

Financial accounting can be thought of as the part of the accounting system that tries to meet the needs of various external user groups. It does this by means of an annual report, which includes a statement of comprehensive income (and possibly an income statement), a statement of financial position (sometimes called a balance sheet), a statement of changes in equity, a statement of cash flows, notes to the financial statements, information required by law and any additional information the entity wishes to supply.

As the entity grows, however, it is likely that the owners will become divorced from its immediate and routine operations. Therefore, the owners will not have access to the management accounting information, which in any case may be too detailed for their requirements. This is the case in organisations listed on a stock exchange. (A listed or quoted organisation is one whose shares are traded in an open market where demand and supply govern the price of the share.) It is also the case in a number of other types of entities, such as public sector and not-for-profit entities, where the functions of management are carried out by people on behalf of the major stakeholders/owners.

In all these cases, the owners/major stakeholders need to know:
* whether the entity has done as well as it should have done
* whether the managers have looked after, and made good use of, the resources of the entity.

In order to evaluate whether the entity has done well and whether resources have been adequately used, it is necessary to compare the results of different entities. Information of this type is normally based on past results, and under certain conditions it can be provided by financial statements.

Owners/major stakeholders also need to know how the entity is going to fare in the future. Financial accounting is unlikely to provide this information for a variety of reasons, in particular because it is largely, if not exclusively, based on the past. Past results may be taken into account as one piece of information among many when one is trying to predict the future, but in a changing world it is unlikely that past results will be repeated because conditions will have changed.

Although there are limitations concerning the usefulness of the information in annual reports, they are often the only form of report available to an owner/major stakeholder who is not involved in the day-to-day activities of the business. Such users therefore have to base their decisions on this information, despite its inadequacies. For example, students can study the financial statements of various universities to see how much money they spend on resources such as the library and computing before deciding which university to choose for their courses.

In practice, the shareholder's involvement in this process of making comparisons (in the case of a listed organisation) is likely to be fairly indirect. This is because most of the information contained in the annual report has already been looked at by the owner's professional advisers – accountants, stockbrokers or financial analysts. The investor and owner are likely to base their decision on the professional advice they receive, rather than relying upon their own interpretation of the information. This is not to say that they will rely exclusively on expert information or that they will not use the information provided in the annual reports to assist with their decision. The reality is likely to be a mixture, the balance of which will depend on the degree of financial sophistication of the shareholders or owners. The less sophisticated they are, the more reliance they will have to place on their expert advisers. For example, a shareholder – who is, after all, a part-owner – may seek accounting advice when attempting to understand the accounting information contained in the annual report, to decide whether to sell his or her shares.

LENDERS

People and organisations lend money in order to earn a return on that money. They are, therefore, interested in whether the entity is making sufficient profit to provide them with their return (usually in the form of interest). This information is normally provided in the statement of comprehensive income or an income statement. Lenders are also interested in ensuring that the entity will be able to repay the money it has borrowed; therefore they need to ascertain what resources an entity controls and what it owes. This information is normally provided in the statement of financial position (also called the balance sheet).

Research has shown that, in practice, bankers use a mixture of different approaches to arrive at a lending decision. The choice of approach is related to the size of the entity. In the case of smaller entities, the security-based approach predominates. This approach emphasises the availability of economic resources to meet repayments in the event of business failure, and the emphasis is clearly on the statement of financial position or balance sheet. However, with very large businesses the approach towards a lending decision is more likely to be the 'going concern' variety where the emphasis is on the profitability of the entity.

SUPPLIERS OF GOODS

Goods can either be supplied on the basis that they are paid for when they are supplied, or that they will be paid for at some agreed date in the future. In each case the supplier will be interested to know whether the entity is likely to stay in business and whether it is likely to expand or contract. Both these needs relate to the future; therefore, they can never be adequately met by information in the annual report because this relates to the past.

Suppliers of goods who are not paid immediately will be interested in assessing the likelihood of getting paid. This assessment is partially helped by the annual report: the balance sheet shows what resources are controlled by the entity and what is owed, and also gives an indication of the liquidity of the controlled resources. However, the balance sheet has limited usefulness for predicting the future. Often the information is many months out of date by the time it is made public, because in most cases it is only published annually.

CUSTOMERS

Like suppliers, customers are interested in an entity's ability to survive and, therefore, carry on supplying them with goods. For example, if you are assembling cars you need to be sure that the suppliers of components are not about to go bankrupt. The importance of this has increased with the introduction of techniques such as just-in-time management. (Briefly, this means that inventories of parts at the production centre are kept to a minimum, reducing the cost of storage space and parts. Parts are delivered to the production centre just in time, before the inventories run out.) We discuss inventories in more detail in Chapter 8. The customers in this situation need to see that the entity is profitable, that it has sufficient resources to pay what it owes, and that it is likely to remain in business and supply components efficiently and on time. Some of these information needs are met, at least partially, by the financial statements.

EMPLOYEES

Employees depend on the survival of the entity for their wages and therefore are interested in whether the entity is likely to survive. In the long term, an entity needs to make a profit in order to survive. The statement of comprehensive income or income statement may assist the employee in assessing the future viability of the organisation. The employee may also be interested in ascertaining how well the entity is doing, compared with other similar entities, for the purposes of wage negotiations – although the accounts are only useful for this purpose if certain conditions are met (these are explored later in this book). The accounts can also be used internally for wage negotiations because they provide evidence of the organisation's level of profitability and ability to pay.

THE GOVERNMENT

The government uses accounting information for a number of purposes, the most obvious of which is the levying of taxes. For this purpose it needs to know how much taxable income has been made. The profit an organisation reports to shareholders in its statement of comprehensive income or income statement is based on the application of GAAP, which we will discuss in Chapter 7. However, the profit upon which an organisation is assessed for tax purposes is based on the application of the tax rules and regulations and is the domain of tax accounting. While these rules are often identical to accounting rules, there are instances where they differ. For example, a government may exempt certain income from taxation as an incentive to participants in that industry. This was the case with the gold industry in Australia for many years. Exempt income was not included in gold producers' calculations of their taxable income; however, as it was still income, it was included in their income statements for reporting to shareholders. The government also uses accounting information to produce industry statistics for purposes such as regulation.

In certain cases, the government is both owner and customer (e.g. some state energy commissions) or public watchdog (e.g. the Environmental Protection Authority). It can combine any one of these roles with other roles, such as regulatory authority (e.g. Australian Securities and Investments Commission). The government uses accounting information for all these purposes.

THE GENERAL PUBLIC

The general public requires many different types of information about entities in both the public and private sectors. Much of this information is not supplied directly by financial statements. For example, the public might be interested in a organisation's environmental performance, which we expand upon in the next section, or its stance on fair trade issues.

This summary shows that the users of accounting information and the uses to which it can be put are many and varied. It is clear that accounting information has effects both within organisations and in the wider commercial environment in which entities operate and in which we live. It should also be clear that this wider environment can use accounting as a tool for entity control. Before going on to consider in detail the impact of accounting upon the commercial environment and vice versa, we should first consider the limitations of accounting information in order to put its potential impact in context.

STOP AND THINK 2

Who are the main users of accounting information? What are some of the main purposes for which that information is used and which accounting reports are they likely to use?

INTEGRATED REPORTING

Traditionally, organisations, particularly listed organisations, have pursued the maximisation of profit as their major objective. In accounting, reporting on financial performance has been their central focus and is the central focus in this book. However, in the twenty-first century there has been a growing concern about the ability of the world's resources to be able to meet the needs of future generations if not properly managed. The 2007 banking crisis caused a rethinking of the capitalist model and its focus on short-term outcomes. Sustainability and sustainable development are now important issues on the world agenda, but what is meant by the term 'sustainable development'?

The following definition is the one used by Dantes (2005):

> The concept of meeting the needs of the present without compromising the ability of future generations to meet their needs. The terms originally applied to natural resource situations, where the long term was the focus. Today, it applies to many disciplines, including economic development, environment, food production, energy, and social organisation. Basically, sustainability/sustainable development refers to doing something with the long term in mind.

> Dantes, 2005. Akzo Nobel, viewed 30 July 2014,
> www.dantes.info/Projectinformation/Glossary/Glossary.html

In this section we examine the concept of integrated reporting, which involves organisations reporting on all activities relevant to value creation. Such reporting includes financial information but also includes information on strategy, environmental, social, governance and other value-relevant activities in an integrated report. The International Integrated Reporting Committee (IIRC) was an outcome of a Sustainability Forum meeting on 17 December 2009 initiated by Prince Charles of the United Kingdom.

Many organisations have for some years provided additional information in relation to environmental and social issues beyond what is required in financial statements. The practice of publishing various types of corporate social reports is largely voluntary and has emerged with the increasing concern about sustainable development. There are a variety of names for this type of report. These include: environmental report, corporate social report, sustainability report, social impact report, stakeholder impact report, corporate social responsibility report and triple bottom line report.

A triple bottom line (TBL) report refers to the publication of economic, environmental and social information in one report. Integrated reporting is extending the TBL to include information about governance, strategy and any other relevant information about how an organisation creates value. The target audience for an integrated report is the providers of financial capital while for a sustainability report it is a broader range of stakeholders who want to know about an organisation's environmental and social impacts and how it is managing them.

The three components of a TBL are the environmental, social and economic activities of the organisation. Some organisations, such as mining organisations, have certain mandatory reporting obligations and conditions, such as restoring the land to its original condition after they have finished mining operations. However, such mandatory obligations only apply in certain industries and, in general, most organisations providing information about social and environmental issues do so on a voluntary basis.

A TBL report has three components, as noted below.

- *Environmental*: disclosures about many issues associated with the environment and the organisation's activities within this area. These may include issues to do with air, water, land, natural resources, flora, fauna and human health (e.g. greenhouse gas emissions, water contamination and workers' safety).
- *Social*: disclosures about many social issues such as the diversity of the organisation's employees, treatment of minorities, employment conditions for employees and community activities (e.g. criticism of Nike's 'sweatshop' production operations in Asian countries).
- *Economic*: the more traditional financial data and, for this reason, likely to contain more quantitative data than the previous two components.

As stated above, an integrated report adds information about governance and strategy to the TBL with the understanding that these areas are often linked. Argyle Diamonds' workforce policy for its mines workers is a good example:

> Commitment to Indigenous economic development in the region is more than a motherhood statement for Argyle. In 2000, 11 per cent of Argyle's workforce were living in the Kimberley and five per cent were Aboriginal. As a result of these stark statistics, a decision was made to localise the workforce to help ensure the benefits of the business were kept in the region. In December 2009, 71 per cent of our workforce was local and 26 per cent were Indigenous. These percentages had dropped slightly by December 2010 – to 68.1 per cent local and 24.7 per cent indigenous.
>
> Argyle Diamonds, 2010, p. 26

Having a local workforce is a cheaper alternative than the 'fly-in, fly-out' workforce and has a number of social benefits for the region, including the employment of a large number of Indigenous people.

The IIRC began a pilot program in 2011 so as to underpin the development of a framework for integrated reporting. There are over 90 organisations involved in the pilot including organisations like Coca Cola and National Australia Bank. (For more information go to www.theiirc.org.)

STOP AND THINK 3

Explain the meaning of an integrated report.

THE GLOBAL REPORTING INITIATIVE (GRI)

While the Integrated Report is a relatively new concept and the Framework is still evolving, sustainability reports have been around for some time. The most widely cited benchmark in the determination of what should be included in a sustainability report is the Global Reporting Initiative (GRI) – an institution based in the Netherlands. The GRI was established through the United Nations Environment Program with the objective of enhancing the quality, rigour and utility of sustainability reporting. In 2002, the GRI released the *Sustainability Reporting Guidelines*. In 2006 it released *G3*, containing revisions to the 2002 version and in 2013 G4 was published. The GRI identified a series of trends that added momentum to the need for techniques that enhanced an organisation's ability to more consistently and comprehensively report on the economic, environmental and social dimensions of its activities, products and services.

The GRI indicators were created through a process of stakeholder dialogue. In G4 there are two options described as *core* and *comprehensive*. The *core* option contains the essential components of a sustainability report. The *comprehensive* option contains all the parts of the *core* and has additional disclosures about the organisation's strategy, governance and ethics. The guidelines discuss principles for deciding on the report content and report quality.

The content principles upon which the GRI guidelines are based are:
- *materiality* – the report should cover topics and indicators relating to the organisation's significant environmental, social and economic performance, which enable users to make an informed assessment
- *stakeholder inclusiveness* – the report should engage stakeholders in the development of reports
- *completeness* – the TBL report should include all material information
- *sustainability context* – the TBL report should attempt to place information in a larger context of ecological or social limits.

5 LEARNING OBJECTIVE

Identify the Global Reporting Initiative (GRI) and explain, in broad terms, the GRI approach to sustainability reports

The quality principles upon which the GRI guidelines are based are:

- *balance* – the report should describe both positive and negative aspects of the organisation's performance
- *reliability* – information should be gathered, compiled and reported in such a manner that is capable of being verified by an external party
- *accuracy* – there should be a low margin of error
- *comparability* – consistency should be maintained in the preparation of the report to enhance comparability
- *clarity* – the report should be meaningful to as wide a range of users as possible
- *timeliness* – the report should be available on a regular basis so that information is not meaningless.

In the GRI, each of the three areas (economic, environmental and social) are detailed, and if there are applicable measurement methods these are also specified. Under the environment theme, the GRI has specified, in detail, 34 indicators for organisations to report on. The headings in the environment area are: materials; energy; water; biodiversity; emissions, effluents and waste; products and services; compliance; transport; overall; supplier environmental assessment; and environmental grievance mechanisms.

In the social area, there are 47 indicators under the following headings: employment; occupational health and safety; labour management/relations; training and education; diversity and equal opportunity; equal remuneration for women and men; supplier assessment for labour practices; labour practices grievance mechanisms; investment; non-discrimination; freedom of association; child labour; forced or compulsory labour; security practices; Indigenous rights; supplier human rights assessment; human rights grievance mechanisms; local communities; anti-corruption; public policy; anti-competitive behaviour; compliance; supplier assessment for impacts on society; grievance mechanisms for impacts on society; customer health and safety; products and services labelling; marketing communications; and customer privacy and compliance.

Finally, in the financial area there are nine indicators under the following headings: direct economic value generated and distributed; financial implications and other risks and opportunities for the organisation's activities due to climate change; coverage of defined benefit plan obligations; financial assistance received from government; ratios of standard entry-level wage compared to local minimum wage at significant locations of operation; proportion of senior management hired from the local community at significant locations of operation; development and impact of infrastructure investments and services supported; significant indirect economic impacts including the extent of impacts; and the proportion of spending on local suppliers at significant locations of operation.

What then are the main differences between an integrated report and a sustainability report? The two are closely related – especially if an organisation chooses the *comprehensive* option in the GRI's *G4* – as both provide information about an organisation, its governance and its economic performance as well as many aspects of its social and environmental impacts. It is argued that the objective is different as the integrated report is aimed at providers of financial capital and provides such users with details about how its strategy, governance, performance and prospects lead to the creation of value over time. On the other hand, the sustainability report is aimed at a broad range of stakeholders with the objective of providing information about the economic, social and environmental impacts of its operations. Will organisations provide two separate reports? Only time will tell but it is unlikely given the similarity between the two and the costs involved in preparing two separate reports.

STOP AND THINK 4

What is the GRI?

There are various awards given for the quality of reporting by organisations in both sustainability and corporate governance. The Association of Chartered Certified Accountants (ACCA) conducts annual awards in several countries. Not all organisations produce a separate report because many organisations choose to disclose environmental and social information in the annual report. Of course, there are also organisations that disclose very little information about social and environmental matters.

Limits on the usefulness of accounting information

6 LEARNING OBJECTIVE

Identify the limitations of accounting information

It has to be stressed that accounting is only one of a number of sources of information available to decision makers. Other sources of information might be just as important as, if not more important than, the information contained in the accounts that are available to decision makers – for example, integrated and sustainability reports.

To give you a flavour of what we are talking about, research into bankers' lending practices (referred to earlier) shows that a banker's personal interview with a client is as important as financial information. This is probably because accounting generally reports only on financial items (i.e. those items that can be expressed in financial, or monetary, terms) whereas the information that bankers are trying to derive from the interview is more qualitative (i.e. an impression of the ability of the applicant to run a successful business). It is also possible that the information that accounting provides is only of secondary importance; this would be the case where new technology has made the precise costing of a product irrelevant because the product is obsolete due to the change in technology.

In general, financial accounting information relates to the past, whereas the decisions that need to be taken normally relate to the future. Therefore, unless the past is a reasonable predictor of the future, financial statements will have some (albeit limited) value for this purpose. In the real world, because of the impact of such factors as changes in technology, innovations, fashions and inflation, the past is unlikely to be a very good predictor of the future. Of course we are not referring here to management accounting, which as we will see in Chapters 12 to 18 is very much focused on improving the future performance of an organisation.

Besides these problems, there is also the question of what is and what is not included in the financial accounts. For instance, some items (which it is generally agreed should be included in financial reports) are difficult to measure with any accuracy; therefore, the figures become subjective. A good example of this problem is an unfinished building. How do we decide on a figure to represent something that is only half-complete? Another example is the problem of deciding how long something is going to last. A car, for instance, loses value the older it gets. A business might decide that a car ceases to be useful to it after four or five years, but this is to some extent an arbitrary decision because there are many older cars that still serve a useful purpose.

In addition to the problem of deciding how long things will last or what stage of completion has been reached, certain items are difficult to quantify in terms of value and are not easily included in financial reports. For example, the value of a football club is dependent on its ability to attract supporters; this, in turn, is dependent on its ability to succeed, which is dependent on the abilities of the players, and so on. However, it is difficult to decide what value to place on a player because this value will vary according to, for example, the player's fitness. Even so, football clubs in the Australian Football League do attempt to quantify the value of their players. In the United Kingdom, Europe and the United States, basketball, baseball, soccer and gridiron teams also follow this practice.

In addition to the questions raised above, there are many factors concerned with the natural and commercial environment that need to be taken into account but cannot be adequately included in accounts, although they may be quantifiable in monetary terms. Examples are the potential market for the product, tariff restrictions, export subsidies and environmental issues. If information about these factors were included in the annual reports of a business, a loss of competitive advantage could result.

Finally, we have to deal with the fact that accounting information is expressed in monetary terms and assumes that the monetary unit is stable over time. This is patently not the case. Although there has been much discussion of the problems of accounting in times of inflation, no agreed solution has yet been found.

We can conclude that, while accounting provides some information that is useful to decision makers, it is important to bear in mind that:

- the information is only a part of that which is necessary to make effective decisions
- accounting is an inexact science and depends on a number of judgements and estimates
- the end result of the accounting process can only be as good as the inputs, and in times of rising prices some of these inputs are of dubious value
- accounting systems can be counterproductive; for example, the maximisation of a division's profit may not always ensure the maximisation of the profit of the entity.

Nevertheless, it is clear that accounting is vital to the running of a healthy and prosperous entity and, arguably, it is also an essential prerequisite for a prosperous economy. It will therefore be useful to look at accounting in the wider context of an entity and its regulatory environment. We will now examine how the accounting function interacts with and is different from other business functions. We will also examine the various factors that influence the choice of an accounting system – including regulatory and environmental considerations.

STOP AND THINK 5

What are the limitations of accounting information?

7 LEARNING
OBJECTIVE

Discuss the factors that
influence the choice
of accounting systems
for different types of
organisations

Accounting as a business function

Theoretically, the accounting department, like the personnel department, operates in an advisory capacity only – providing information for managers to make decisions. In practice, however, the financial elements controlled by the accounting function and the information it generates are so central to the operation of the entity that the influence of accounting is often pervasive. Although accounting is essential to the smooth running of the business, it does not have as direct an impact as, for example, the buying department or the production line. Its effects are generally subtler, although they may in certain instances be very obvious. For example, if the accounting information indicates that expenses are too high, this may have dramatic repercussions in other functional areas. Training and recruitment budgets may be immediately frozen, affecting the work of the personnel department and other operating departments, and possibly reducing both staffing and skills. Alternatively, a decision may be taken to stop expenditure on a current advertising campaign, therefore having a direct effect on the work of the marketing department.

Accounting can have unintended effects, too. For example, if sales representatives are judged solely on their sales this may lead them to sell goods to customers who are unlikely to pay in order to achieve the sales targets that have been set. It can also be a very dangerous tool if used in the wrong way. For example, targets could be set to achieve cost savings on a production line with no account taken of the effect on quality or employee safety.

The importance of accounting within a business should not be underestimated. It provides the basic information by which managers and owners can judge whether the business is meeting its objectives. Its importance is shown by the high salaries that accountants can command and by the prevalence of accountants on the boards of directors of our major public organisations.

Accounting is also different from other business functions in that it is not only a function but also an industry. The accounting industry sells accounting and other advisory services to other businesses and is itself a major employer of graduate labour.

CHOICE OF ACCOUNTING SYSTEMS

Accounting is used within business to evaluate alternative strategies – such as making a component or buying it in from a supplier. Therefore, it shapes business plans and activities. At the same time, accounting is itself a function of the type of activity that a business engages in and of the strategies a business adopts. In other words, the accounting system not only influences business strategies but is itself influenced by the goals, size and structure of the organisation. For example, the accounting system that is appropriate for a local builder who does one job at a time and who can clearly identify the amount of time and materials being used on that job is not appropriate for a manufacturing plant that uses one building and many machines to produce multiple products all at the same time. In the latter case, a much more sophisticated system of accounting is required to identify the materials used and the labour inputs for a specific product. Accounting systems are variable and depend on the type of activities a business engages in, and on the levels of activity.

Clearly, the organisation's goals will have a major impact on the accounting system it uses. For example, developing an accounting system with the primary purpose of measuring profit would be wholly inappropriate for a not-for-profit entity such as a government or public sector entity. Similarly, the requirements, in terms of accounting reports, will be very different in the cases of a workers' cooperative, a profit-oriented organisation and the Department of Education and Training. The cooperative's members are likely to be more interested in their pay and their share of the surplus generated than in the entity's profitability. Shareholders in an organisation, on the other hand, are likely to be more interested in judging overall profitability and comparing that with alternative investments. In the case of the Department of Education and Training it may be that the owners, that is, the general public, are primarily interested in the service they have received rather than the department's profitability.

Furthermore, the way in which an organisation is structured determines the type of accounting system that is needed. If a brewery operates all of its hotels by putting managers into them, it will need an accounting system that allows for the payment of regular salaries and bonuses based upon achieving preset targets. These targets are normally set in terms of barrelage so the brewery will need to know what the normal barrelage of each hotel is, the mark-up on items such as spirits and soft drinks, and the approximate mix of sales in order to ensure that its managers are not misappropriating the profits. If, though, it establishes its organisation so that each publican is a tenant of the brewery, a different accounting system will be required, because the publicans are not paid a salary or bonus – their remuneration comes from the profits they make from selling the beers, wines and spirits.

We have already alluded to the effect the size of an organisation has on its accounting system. The larger and more disparate the organisation is, the greater the need for organisational controls. These are achieved through a system of accountability that makes managers responsible for the performance of their divisions and provides reports that can be used by senior managers to evaluate the performance of their subordinates and of the organisation as a whole.

As we have already mentioned, it is vital that the accounting system is tailored to the needs of the organisation. If it is not, management may be unable to control the organisation and may have dysfunctional effects. Frequently, in the case of a small business, little accounting information is available on a day-to-day basis. This may be because the operations are sufficiently simple not to warrant much information, but is more likely to be because the owner does not have the skills to produce the information, and the costs of hiring the necessary expertise are perceived as outweighing the potential benefits. It is often the case in small businesses that the only time detailed accounting reports are produced is at the end of the financial year to meet the needs of the tax collector or when the bank demands them as a prerequisite to granting a loan or extending an overdraft.

REGULATORY AND ENVIRONMENTAL CONSIDERATIONS

In general, the environmental aspects of a business that interact significantly with accounting are: the state, technology and labour. Accounting is also affected by, and affects, the economy. For example, a country such as Zimbabwe, which suffers from hyperinflation out of necessity, uses costs other than original costs in its accounting reports because the value of the monetary unit in which accounting information is expressed changes so quickly. We have already discussed the potential uses of accounting information by employees and their organisations, such as trade unions. We have also mentioned different forms of organisation such as not-for-profit organisations. In the case of most small not-for-profit organisations, there is no requirement for the publication of accounting information, whereas for organisations, the form and content of their annual reports is laid down by legislation in the *Corporations Act 2001*.

The *Corporations Act* specifies Australian Accounting Standards (referred to as AASB Accounting Standards) for organisations that are reporting entities; the setting of these standards is discussed in Chapter 2. All public sector reporting entities must also comply with all Australian Accounting Standards, except in cases where the Treasurer's Instructions vary or amend a standard. A similar situation prevails in most Western countries, although the importance of legislation in relation to accounting standards varies from country to country. Similarly, reporting requirements are different in non-capitalist countries where the importance afforded to the income statement is considerably less.

Developments in technology have also had a major impact upon the function of accounting. These have allowed accountants to free themselves from the mundane tasks of recording and to become more involved in decision support and strategic issues. At another level, new technology has imposed and is still imposing challenges to accounting thought. Systems that were appropriate in a labour-intensive environment are found to be lacking in the age of flexible manufacturing systems, such as just-in-time management and computer-controlled manufacturing environments.

STOP AND THINK 6
What are the major objectives for a useful accounting system?

8 LEARNING OBJECTIVE

Explain what is meant by the term 'economic consequences' and relate this to the choice of accounting policies

ECONOMIC CONSEQUENCES OF ACCOUNTING INFORMATION

The development of accounting standards is the responsibility of the appropriate accounting standard-setting board. We discuss the development of accounting standards in Chapter 2. The selection of appropriate accounting policies for an entity is the responsibility of management. Where an accounting standard exists, the policies must comply with the standard. In some cases the standard allows a choice of policies and in other cases no standard exists. In these instances, the management of an entity can choose the most appropriate accounting policy.

As we will see in Chapter 2, the primary objective in selecting particular accounting standards is to provide useful information to the users of financial statements. As preparers of financial statements incur costs in complying with accounting standards, the standard setters attempt only to impose requirements where the expected benefits exceed costs.

Managers do not necessarily adopt the same objectives when they select appropriate accounting policies for their organisation. Earlier in this chapter we commented that there would be chaos if all the people who bought shares in Woolworths tried to take an active part in the day-to-day running of that business. Instead, these owners or shareholders delegate the authority for the day-to-day running to a group of directors and managers through contractual arrangements. Jensen and Meckling (1976) believe that contracts between two parties (such as shareholders and management) result in an agency relationship. They define an agency relationship as 'a contract under which one or more (principals) engage another person (the agent) to perform some service on their behalf which involves delegating some decision-making authority to the agent.' (Jensen and Meckling, 1976, p. 309). Thus, in a contract between shareholders and managers, shareholders are the principals and managers are the agents.

Many of these contracts are written. They include formal contracts between equity (or share) holders and the organisation's management (e.g. the memorandum and articles of association, management compensation schemes, and employee share ownership schemes), debt holders and management (e.g. debenture trust deeds) and less formal contracts in the form of the organisation's business structure (e.g. the hierarchical managerial chain of command and creating divisions serve to define the nature of interactions between managers). While all types of contracts are vital to the survival of an organisation, the contracts between shareholders and managers and debt holders and managers/shareholders have attracted the most attention in the accounting research literature and can affect the wealth of managers and organisations through:

- compensation plans
- debt contracts
- political costs.

Compensation plans

Many entities reward their managers through a fixed salary and an annual bonus. The bonus may be determined as a percentage of net profit. The bonus scheme, it is argued, provides an incentive to managers to increase net profit. Increases in net profit are in the best interests of shareholders. Therefore, the bonus scheme is intended to align the interests of managers more closely to those of shareholders.

However, a consequence of the bonus scheme is that managers may also be motivated to increase reported profit by the appropriate selection of profit-increasing accounting policies. Therefore, this strategy may increase reported profit when the underlying profitability of the entity has not increased. This has been described as a cosmetic increase in profits rather than a real increase in profits.

Some spectacular corporate collapses – such as Gourmet Food Holdings (including the Rosella brand) and the Hastie Group in Australia, and Lehman Brothers and Enron in the USA – raised considerable public outcry about many issues including the use of share options as part of the remuneration packages for corporate executives. The 2008–9 Global Financial Crisis (GFC) saw a number of banks collapse amid allegations of excessive lending motivated by greed. There is a view that the use of share options creates incentives for managers to do almost anything to keep reporting large profits so that the price of the organisation's shares continues to rise. In turn, this increases the value of the manager's share options. Such high-profile corporate collapses have led to considerable debate about the appropriateness of using share options as part of executive remuneration, given the highly publicised impact of such a policy on financial reporting. At the G-20 meeting in London in April 2009, finance ministers and central bank governors expressed a view that there should be some regulation of executive compensation. To date there has been no legislation in Australia to limit executive compensation. However, listed organisations now have to submit a remuneration that key executives report to the Annual General Meeting of shareholders.

Debt contracts

Many lenders require a contract before lending money to a borrower. Such contracts may impose certain restrictions on the borrower. For example, a new loan contract may contain a clause stating that if the borrower's level of debt exceeds a certain level the loan must be immediately repaid in full. The measurement of the level of debt may be based on the total liabilities figure as reported in the borrower's statement of financial position or balance sheet. Another common clause in debt contracts relates to the number of times the net profit covers interest expense. We will look at these and other ratios in Chapter 10.

These clauses in the debt contracts are based on accounting numbers as reported in the organisation's financial statements. Therefore, if an entity is approaching the limits of a clause in a debt contract, there are incentives for managers to select accounting policies that allow the entity to avoid being in violation of the debt contract.

Political costs

Political costs refer to the costs imposed on an entity by regulation, taxation and closer public scrutiny of its affairs. Some accountants argue that bigger organisations, like News Corporation, are subject to more political costs. Size is often measured in terms of net profit, total assets and total sales. These are all numbers determined by the application of accounting policies. Therefore, there are incentives for managers of large entities to select profit-decreasing accounting policies.

Another argument suggests that incentives exist for other types of businesses, such as telephone or electricity organisations, to choose profit-decreasing accounting policies. This choice is made at a time when the organisation wishes to increase the charges for its service. It is politically more acceptable to increase charges when reported profits have decreased.

Therefore, political costs create incentives for managers of large organisations to select accounting policies that decrease reported profits. This is clearly the reverse of the argument under compensation plans, in which the manager's self-interest prevails. With political costs, the interests of the organisation prevail. Ultimately, if the large organisation attracts lower political costs, its managers will be rewarded.

The dual reason for selection of accounting policies

The selection of appropriate accounting policies may be based on the objective of providing useful information to users, or it may be based on economic consequences. These two objectives need not be mutually exclusive and, as you read the following chapters, you should consider the role of both these objectives in the selection of accounting policies. Shareholders and lenders may initiate strategies to mitigate the incentives for managers to select accounting policies based on economic consequences. In this event, the selection of accounting policies is more likely to be based on the objective of providing useful information to users.

In the next section we briefly discuss the important issue of ethics in business and accounting.

1.1 CASE STUDY

SIA PROFIT DUE TO DEPRECIATION

By Paul Thompson

I REFER TO your article 'SIA hints net profit may be above $200m' by Andrea Tan (*BT*, April 20). First, may I say that, for the sake of the hardworking staff, I certainly hope it is true. They would then

Laurent Fievet/AFP/Getty Images

stand a good chance of getting previously implemented wage cuts restored. Second, may I bring to investors' attention – if they are not already aware – that SIA is engaging in earnings management, much like their peers in Europe and North America.

SIA's earnings management makes it difficult for me to get excited about the mildly bullish sentiment surrounding SIA. While things are indeed looking up for SIA, it is worth noting that the primary reason it stands any chance of making any profit at all for the year ended March 31, 2002 boils down to what some might call an accounting sleight of hand.

I hold SIA in high regard. SIA is a high-flier in the world of aviation. It offers impeccable service, far better than any other flag carrier I have flown in. It is also one of the world's most profitable airlines and, unlike many like the big US flag carriers and British Airways, it appears to have avoided a free fall into financial losses – and it has averted slashing staff numbers (the latter achievement is especially commendable).

The main reason, however, it has managed to steer clear of reporting losses for the past financial year (announcement is due in early May but SIA, for sure, already knows the score) is through a timely change in its accounting policy on the depreciation of fixed assets.

Depreciation is a major expense for airlines whose balance sheets are bulging with an expensive aircraft fleet. In its half-year report issued last October, soon after the terrorist attack on the World Trade Center, SIA said: 'Commencing this financial year, the company changed its depreciation rate for passenger aircraft, spares and spare engines from 10 years to 20 per cent residual value to 15 years to 10 per cent residual value. This is to bring it more in line with airline industry practice. Aircraft depreciation charge was $133 million lower as a result.'

In other words, SIA's policy change for the six months to Sept 30, 2001 caused expenses to be lower by $133 million and hence profit higher by the same figure. For the full year, the effect is likely to be double – that is, a boost to profits by some $266 million.

I do not doubt SIA when it says that this policy change aligns itself with industry practice. In fact, in 1999, I compared the depreciation policy of SIA with BA and found it to be more conservative. But the fact remains that had it not made this change, SIA would almost certainly be reporting a loss for the year to March 31, 2002 in the next few weeks.

Paul Thompson, *Business Times Singapore*, 25 April 2002.
Business Times Singapore © Singapore Press Holdings Limited. Reproduced with permission.

COMMENTARY

Although this article is not recent, it is an excellent example of the impact of accounting policy choice on an organisation's reported profits. It shows how Singapore Airlines (SIA) was able to increase reported profit by a change in accounting policy. The organisation stated that the aim of this change was not to boost earnings for the year, but rather to align its depreciation policy with those of other airlines.

A recurring theme in this book is how the choice of accounting policies will impact an organisation's reported results and may be explained by the existence of contracts, as well as the objective of providing useful and relevant information to users. By the time you complete the chapters on financial accounting, you will better appreciate how the choice of accounting policies affects an organisation's financial statements.

While SIA changed the way it accounts for the depreciation of its aircraft, the value of the aircraft did not change. Does this change in profit, resulting from a change in an accounting rule, make SIA more valuable? The answer is no, and consequently there should be no change in the value of SIA's shares based on this higher reported profit.

STOP AND THINK 7

What are the economic consequences of accounting policy choice?

9 LEARNING
OBJECTIVE

Identify career
opportunities for
accountants

Careers in accounting

Accountants are employed in many different areas in both the private and public sectors. This section provides only a brief overview of the different careers for accountants.

ACCOUNTING FIRMS

Most accounting firms operate as a sole proprietorship or a partnership. The most significant firms are large firms like PricewaterhouseCoopers, Ernst & Young, KPMG and Deloitte. Large firms provide services in the areas of auditing and assurance services, tax, management consulting, and insolvency and administration.

Accountants in accounting firms work in public accounting. They are members of the Institute of Chartered Accountants in Australia, CPA Australia or the Institute of Public Accountants.

INDUSTRY AND COMMERCE

All organisations, both large and small, employ accountants to perform many different duties. These duties include the preparation of financial statements for external reporting purposes. Large and medium-sized organisations also employ accountants in internal auditing. The internal auditor's role is to ensure that the internal controls in the organisation are adequate to safeguard the organisation's assets. Large and medium-sized organisations also often employ tax accountants to do all the work involved with income tax, payroll tax, Goods and Services Tax and other indirect taxes. They also employ cost accountants, whose job is to generate information about the behaviour of costs, to help establish budgets and to generally assist management in controlling costs and establishing appropriate prices for the organisation's products.

NOT-FOR-PROFIT ENTITIES

The not-for-profit (NFP) sector includes all levels of government, health, education, social services, culture and recreation, charities, business and professional associations, and others such as religious groups. Excluding the government sector, the NFP sector in Australia represented $43 billion to the gross domestic product (GDP) in 2006–7, which is the latest available figure (http://www.acnc.gov.au). As a result of its size, this sector employs many accounting graduates. Accounting for profit and NFP entities is very similar, although the absence of a profit motive does result in some differences.

The government employs many accountants, who work in all areas at the local, state and federal levels. Accountants can be found doing similar work to their private sector counterparts: preparing financial reports, auditing, tax work and cost accounting. Departments such as the Treasury and the Auditor-General's Office employ many accountants, and all departments employ some accountants to carry out all types of accounting work.

PROFESSIONAL MEMBERSHIP

The two major professional accounting bodies in Australia are the Institute of Chartered Accountants in Australia (ICAA) and Certified Practicing Accountants Australia (CPAA). The Institute of Public Accountants (IPA) is another professional organisation in Australia, for accountants 'recognised for their practical, hands-on skills and a broad understanding of the total business environment' (www.ipaa.com.au).

The three bodies have different categories of membership. University graduates are initially admitted as associates. They must then complete a professional program and have three years' practical experience before advancing in their membership. Finally, a public practice certificate is required for all principals in public accounting firms.

SUMMARY

LEARNING OBJECTIVE 1

EXPLAIN WHAT IS MEANT BY THE TERM 'ACCOUNTING'

In this chapter we have tried to give an idea of what accounting is and how it pervades both the internal workings of organisations and the external commercial environment. It can be seen at one level as a functional area of business and at an external level as an important determinant of business survival through its effect on groups such as shareholders, lenders and employees.

LEARNING OBJECTIVE 2

EXPLAIN THE DIFFERENCE BETWEEN MANAGEMENT ACCOUNTING, FINANCIAL ACCOUNTING AND TAX ACCOUNTING

Management accounting is prepared for internal users and is largely unregulated. Financial accounting results in financial statements prepared for external users in accordance with GAAP. Tax accounting involves the preparation of tax returns where the objective is to report the activities of the organisation in compliance with the tax rules so that the organisation pays the minimum amount of tax to the government.

LEARNING OBJECTIVE 3

IDENTIFY THE MAIN USERS OF ACCOUNTING INFORMATION, AND THE MAIN PURPOSES FOR WHICH THE INFORMATION IS USED

There are many users of accounting information and they include internal users (managers) and external users (shareholders, lenders, suppliers, customers, employees, government and the general public). We have shown that there is no perfect accounting report that will meet the needs of all users, and that the needs of users vary. For example, in the case of a small business the owner may wish to show a low profit to reduce the potential tax bill, but may need to show a high profit in order to persuade a banker to lend his or her business money.

LEARNING OBJECTIVE 4

IDENTIFY WHAT IS MEANT BY THE TERM 'INTEGRATED REPORTING'

An integrated report provides information on how an entity creates value through all of its activities and details its strategy and governance and includes information about environmental and social impacts.

LEARNING OBJECTIVE 5

IDENTIFY THE GLOBAL REPORTING INITIATIVE (GRI) AND EXPLAIN, IN BROAD TERMS, THE GRI APPROACH TO SUSTAINABILITY REPORTS

The Global Reporting Initiative (GRI) is based in the Netherlands and was established through the United Nations Environment Program with the objective of enhancing the quality, rigour and utility of sustainability reporting. In 2013, the GRI released the *G4 Sustainability Reporting Guidelines*.

The GRI guidelines allow organisations to choose a *core* or *comprehensive* option. Both options require the disclosure of a number of indicators across environmental, social and financial areas. The *core* option has some information about governance and ethics while the *comprehensive* option requires significantly more disclosures in these two areas.

LEARNING OBJECTIVE 6

IDENTIFY THE LIMITATIONS OF ACCOUNTING INFORMATION

We have shown that accounting will be useful only if it is used correctly and if its limitations are understood. Financial accounting is based on past information and only includes those elements that meet the definition and recognition criteria for assets, liabilities, income, expenses and equity. These definitions and recognition criteria are discussed in Chapter 2.

LEARNING OBJECTIVE 7

DISCUSS THE FACTORS THAT INFLUENCE THE CHOICE OF ACCOUNTING SYSTEMS FOR DIFFERENT TYPES OF ORGANISATIONS

The factors that influence the choice of an accounting system include the size of the organisation, the type of business activity being undertaken and whether it is simple or complex, the structure of the organisation and whether the organisation is for-profit or not-for-profit.

A failing business will still fail even though it has an excellent accounting system; on the other hand, potentially successful businesses have been allowed to go bankrupt because the accounting system did not give any warning signs or gave them notice too late to allow management to take action to rectify the situation.

LEARNING OBJECTIVE 8

EXPLAIN WHAT IS MEANT BY THE TERM 'ECONOMIC CONSEQUENCES' AND RELATE THIS TO THE CHOICE OF ACCOUNTING POLICIES

The economic consequences of accounting policies can influence a manager's choice of accounting policies. Accounting numbers are used in various contracts and this, it is argued, creates incentives for managers to choose accounting policies based on their impact on the numbers in the contracts. Managerial compensation and debt contracts create incentives for managers to favour profit-increasing accounting policies. Political costs create incentives for managers of large organisations to favour profit-decreasing accounting policies.

LEARNING OBJECTIVE 9

IDENTIFY CAREER OPPORTUNITIES FOR ACCOUNTANTS

Accountants work in many areas and in many types of organisations. Accountants work in public accounting firms providing various services including audit and assurance, taxation, an advisory service, and insolvency and administration. Accountants work in large, medium and small organisations preparing financial statements and all types of information for internal decision making by managers. Accountants also work in not-for-profit entities, which include all levels of government and other areas such as health, education and social services.

REVIEW QUESTIONS

1 For what purposes is accounting information used:
- by the individual
- by the entity or organisation?

2 Examples were given of certain limitations of accounting information. Can you give examples of your own?

PROBLEMS FOR DISCUSSION AND ANALYSIS

1 Refer to the 2013 Woolworths financial statements in Appendix 1.

   a What is the name of the auditing firm?

   b Does Woolworths include shares as part of the remuneration for employees?

   c Do these shares affect the determination of net profit for Woolworths?

2 Discuss what information you believe would be useful to the following groups of report users:

   a employees

   b investors

   c regulators

   d suppliers of goods and services

   e customers.

3 Should there be a legal requirement for organisations to produce a sustainability report or should it continue to be a voluntary practice?

4 The following are two definitions of triple bottom line (TBL) reporting:

   » *In the purest sense, the concept of TBL reporting refers to the publication of economic, environmental and social information in an integrated manner that reflects activities and outcomes across these three dimensions of a organisation's performance.* (Group of 100, 2003)

   » *The external reporting on the economic, social and environmental performance and impacts of an entity can have four potential purposes:*

     i *to improve the efficient operation of entities in achieving their legal purpose, e.g. highlighting areas of an entity's negative economic, social and environmental impacts and also increasing transparency and strengthening accountability for users*

     ii *to help meet the preferences of present and future investors, consumers, employees, creditors, suppliers and insurers*

     iii *to inform stakeholders with no direct ownership, investment or consumption interests*

     iv *as a significant public policy tool to maximise human welfare over time* (Institute of Chartered Accountants in New Zealand, 2002).

   Required

   a Compare and contrast the two definitions.

   b Critically evaluate both definitions.

5 Discuss the major differences between a triple bottom line report and an integrated report. Which one do you believe provides more useful information for shareholders? Other stakeholders?

6 If you work for an accounting firm, whose perspective should you take – the firm's, the client's, the user's or your own?

7 You own and run a small supermarket. What accounting information do you need, and how often?

8 You are the manager of a small local band which are offered $1000 for a three-hour performance. What financial (accounting) issues do you have to consider before accepting or rejecting the offer?

9 It was pointed out that accounting information is only a part of the input to the decision-making process. In order to expand your understanding of the role of accounting information, for the situation outlined below, identify:

a the accounting information that would be relevant

b any other information that would be relevant.

Head & Co. is in the business of making navigation equipment and wishes to diversify into the production of hang-gliders. The business is based in Sydney but the owners may be willing to move. The owners have little knowledge about the market for hang-gliders, but feel that there is money to be made in that field.

10 You are considering buying a small retail store selling electrical equipment. The selling agent is very enthusiastic. What non-financial information should you be requesting?

Note to instructors: the following problems are considered more suitable for use in postgraduate courses. However, undergraduate courses may also find them useful.

11 Tom was left some money in his mother's will and decided that he should give up his job and go into business for himself. While the lawyers were still sorting out his mother's estate, he started looking around for a suitable business. After a short time, he identified a small boat-building business that he felt was worth investing in. He was still uncertain about how much his mother had left him but thought that it was probably between $80 000 and $100 000. The boat-building business was for sale for $200 000 and so, assuming that he could finance the remainder, he engaged an accountant to check the books of the business and report back to him. As proof of his good faith, he deposited $2000, which he had in savings, with the business agents.

The report from the accountant confirmed his initial impression that the business was worth investing in, so he paid the accountant's modest fee of $1000 in full. At this stage he discussed his plans more fully with his bank manager, who was duly impressed with the professional approach taken by Tom.

The bank manager pointed out that Tom had no business experience and, therefore, was a high risk from the bank's point of view. However, in view of their long-standing relationship, the bank was prepared to take a chance and said that it would lend Tom 40 per cent of the purchase price.

On the basis of this, Tom signed a conditional agreement to buy the boat-building business. A short time after this he received a letter from his lawyers stating that his inheritance from his mother amounted to only $60 000. He could not raise the additional finance to purchase the boat-building business and so withdrew from the agreement, recovered his $2000 deposit and purchased a yacht with the intention of doing charter work to the Caribbean.

Required

Discuss the point at which, in your opinion, the accounting process should begin, giving reasons for your point of view. Pay particular attention to the dual needs of Tom as an owner and as a manager.

12 The No-Returns Rubber Company is considering setting up a new manufacturing plant that will produce rubber arbuthnots to be used in the manufacture of nuclear-powered frisbees. Discuss what information the managers are likely to require in order to make an informed decision about the viability of this project. Factors to be taken into account should include financial issues, health and safety considerations, and also the possible social and legal issues that may arise from the manufacture of non-biodegradable substances, such as rubber arbuthnots and nuclear items. Discuss how you think these considerations can be incorporated into a costing of the project.

13 Scasboro Beach is a beautiful beach in Bondavia. The surrounding residential area is very attractive because of the beach and the lovely views out to the ocean. After a great deal of negotiation, the Coastal Development Company obtained a permit from the local shire council to erect a 12-storey five-star hotel, which would encroach onto the lovely beach and sand dune area. Prior to this approval, the highest building permitted at Scasboro Beach was three storeys.

Construction began immediately. At this time a legal challenge to the hotel was lodged by a local ratepayers' association and environmental groups. They wanted the permit declared void because the planned structure would obstruct the views of existing property owners and cause damage to sand dunes in the area.

After the Coastal Development Company had invested $500 000 in the Scasboro Hotel project, a court hearing was held with the plaintiffs, which ordered demolition of the site as well as total restoration of the area. This would cost approximately $200 000. The company lost an appeal to a higher court.

Required

a Discuss how you might measure the economic value (using your understanding of what economic value means) of the project before the decision of:

   i   the lower court
   ii the higher court.

b What problems do you envisage in making such measurements?

c What losses were sustained and who sustained the losses in this case?

(Adapted from R.G. May, G. Mueller and T.H. Williams, *A New Introduction to Financial Accounting*, Prentice-Hall, 1975, Chapter 1, Exercise 1–2.)

14 At the beginning of time there was a small dwelling of cave men and women who elected themselves a leader called Ugg. Ugg's responsibilities were to restore peace and order in the dwelling, which had become unsettled due to a recent outbreak of stealing.

Ugg was a very intelligent cave man and he began thinking that if every cave person accounted for their belongings, then less stealing would happen. Furthermore, if cave people paid him some kind of 'due' in respect of their belongings, thieves would be deterred because the more belongings a cave person had, the more in dues he or she would have to give Ugg. Ugg decided to call this due the 'rock tax'.

The next day Ugg announced the rock tax to the dwelling. He explained to the cave people his thoughts from the previous day and asked for grunts of approval for the rock tax. These outweighed the grunts of disapproval so he then proceeded to outline the rock tax guidelines. These were:

1 one large brown fur equalled 50 morsels of meat

2 one small brown fur equalled 30 morsels of meat

3 one large black fur equalled two large brown furs

4 one small black fur equalled three small brown furs

5 for every 10 morsels of meat, one large rock had to be given to Ugg, which would help to build a wall around the whole dwelling. The tax would be paid once every 300 days commencing from the next day.

Ugg also said that he would personally check every cave to make sure truthful accounts were given.

Two of the oldest members of the dwelling, Thug and Olga, thought Ugg's rock tax was the best announcement they had ever heard and proceeded to add up their furs and morsels. Thug calculated he had six large brown furs, two small brown furs and five small black furs in addition to the 34 morsels of meat he had stored in his rock-fridge. Thug had exchanged three small brown furs for his rock-fridge some 400 days ago. Olga counted two large brown furs, 10 large black furs and nine small black furs in her rock-cabin. She also counted 22 meat morsels in her rock-fridge. Olga had exchanged one large black fur for the rock-fridge 200 days ago.

Required

Imagining you lived in this dwelling, calculate:

   a   the amount of tax that Thug and Olga should give Ugg

   b   how Thug and Olga would pay their tax to Ugg.

SUGGESTED ANSWERS TO STOP AND THINK EXERCISES IN THE CHAPTER

1   Identified in the text is the need for information to enable management to carry out its duties and responsibilities in terms of stewardship, planning, control and decision making. The second part of the question should provoke a number of different answers, perhaps related to the market for the internal user's product, competition or the economic situation. We have found that by encouraging the students to think about the alternative information needs, and the sources from which information can be derived, they are better able to see accounting in a wider context.

2   In general, for external users, the accounting reports that are normally used are the annual report or statements. Where specific reports, such as the balance sheet or income statement, are mentioned in the body of the text, these are shown below.

Management	Various reports including specialist reports to help run the business profitably
Owners	Annual report to help assess if management is doing a good job and protecting their investment
Lenders	Statement of comprehensive income, income statement and statement of financial position or balance sheet to assess if the loan can be repaid and, in the event of loan repayment problems, if there is adequate security
Suppliers	Statement of comprehensive income, income statement and statement of financial position or balance sheet because they are interested in issues that are similar to those of lenders
Customers	Statement of comprehensive income, income statement and statement of financial position or balance sheet to determine if the entity will continue to operate – particularly if the customer has a long-term contract
Employees	Profitability, therefore statement of comprehensive income and income statement to help assess ability of the entity to continue to operate
Government	Statement of comprehensive income and income statement to assess payment of taxes
The public	Annual report to assess the entity's impact on areas like the environment and to assess the entity's social policies and so on.

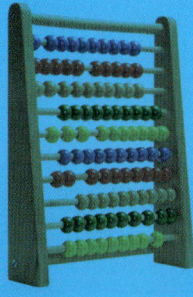

3   An integrated report provides information on how an entity creates value through all of its activities and details its strategy and governance and includes information about environmental and social impacts.

4   The Global Reporting Initiative (GRI) is based in the Netherlands and was established through the United Nations Environment Program with the objective of enhancing the quality, rigour and utility of sustainability reporting. In 2013, the GRI released the *G4 Sustainability Reporting Guidelines*. The GRI guidelines allow organisations to choose a *core* or *comprehensive* option. Both options require the disclosure of a number of indicators in environmental, social and financial areas. The *core* option has some information about governance and ethics while the *comprehensive* option requires significantly more disclosures in these two areas.

5   The limitations are as follows:

   a   The information is only a part of that which is necessary to make 'effective decisions'

   b   Accountancy is, as yet, an inexact science and depends on a number of judgements, estimates etc.

   c   The end result of the accounting process can only be as good as the inputs, and in times of rising prices some of these inputs are of dubious value

   d   Accounting systems can be counterproductive; for example, the maximisation of a division's profit may not always ensure the maximisation of entity profit.

6   Once again, a number of alternative answers are acceptable here. However, the final summary should include the following in relation to the major objectives for a useful accounting system: the provision of information that is useful in terms of meeting the needs of users, and information that is presented in a timely manner and in a format that is appropriate and understandable.

7   Economic consequences refer to the financial impact on an organisation from a particular accounting policy. For example, an accounting policy that requires all mining organisations to expense all exploration and development expenditure incurred would result in large losses for organisations not yet in production. Hence, this may make it difficult to attract investors to buy the organisation's shares, despite its future prospects.

2

TYPES OF ORGANISATIONS AND THE FINANCIAL REPORTING FRAMEWORK

LEARNING OBJECTIVES

At the end of this chapter, you should be able to:

1. identify the factors that influence the preparation of financial statements
2. identify three forms of business arrangement: a sole trader, a partnership and a company
3. identify the characteristics of a sole trader
4. explain the advantages and disadvantages of a partnership
5. explain the advantages and disadvantages of a company
6. identify the major differences between the statement of comprehensive income and balance sheet of a company and those of a partnership or sole trader
7. explain the main characteristics of the financial statements of a public company and the role and meaning of consolidated financial statements
8. explain the current framework for standard setting in Australia
9. explain the influence of accounting standards, the *Corporations Act 2001* and the Australian Securities Exchange Listing Rules on financial reporting requirements

10. explain what is meant by a conceptual framework
11. identify the role of a conceptual framework
12. explain the terms 'reporting entity', 'general-purpose financial statements', 'qualitative characteristics', and explain the objective of general-purpose financial reporting
13. explain the terms 'assets', 'liabilities', 'equity', 'income', 'revenue' and 'expenses'
14. identify the role of the audit and the auditor in financial reporting
15. explain what is meant by the term 'expectation gap'
16. explain the concept of audit independence and why it is so important.

Note to instructors: Instructors who defer consideration of this chapter until later in the course should be aware that the following terms, defined in this chapter, are used throughout the text: 'assets', 'liabilities', 'expenses', 'income', 'revenue' and 'equity'. These terms are restated in Chapters 5 and 6.

INTRODUCTION

In Chapter 1 we discussed the objectives of accounting and the influences of users on financial reporting. We also discussed the limitations of accounting information and the role of accounting in business, its effect on business, and some of the factors that influence accounting. The impact of accounting policies on management compensation and debt contracts was also mentioned.

The types of financial statements prepared by entities will depend on a number of factors including the type and size of the organisation. At the simplest level a small sole trader and the local football club may well only prepare a statement of cash receipts and payments with a statement of the bank balances at year end. For large public companies like Woolworths there are four main financial statements as listed below:

- Statement of profit or loss and other comprehensive income (referred to as the statement of comprehensive income) or the income statement and the statement of comprehensive income – the income statement reports income and expense items and profit or loss for a period of time. Income and expenses are determined using accrual accounting, which is explained later in this chapter but for now we can say income and expenses may not equal cash received and paid. Large entities like Woolworths also have to report items of other comprehensive income, which are added to profit (loss) to determine total comprehensive income for the same period. These statements are explained in detail in Chapter 6.
- Statement of financial position (balance sheet) – this statement reports the assets, liabilities and equity at a point in time. It is like a snapshot of a business at a point in time and is also based on accrual accounting and is explained in detail in Chapter 5.
- Statement of changes in equity – this statement reports the total changes to the equity for a period of time which arise from transactions with owners such as when a company pays a dividend to shareholders and is explained in detail in Chapter 6.
- Statement of cash flows – as the first statements are based on accrual accounting this statement reports all the inflows and outflows of cash for a period of time. This statement is explained in detail in Chapter 7.

In this chapter we consider different forms of organisations. We then examine the financial reporting framework that influences the preparation of financial statements for different types of organisations. The most extensive regulations exist for companies – in particular for listed public companies. Their financial reports must comply with various professional, statutory and securities exchange requirements. Other types of business organisations – such as not-for-profit and public sector entities – may be subject to various regulatory requirements, and in some cases must also comply with accounting standards. Organisations such as small private companies, partnerships or sole proprietorships are subject to much less regulation.

We also examine the process used for the establishment of accounting standards and the parties involved in the standard-setting process. The objective of financial reporting and the qualitative characteristics of financial information are also considered. We explain the definitions of key terms such as 'assets', 'liabilities', 'equity', 'income', 'revenue' and 'expenses' from the International Accounting Standards Board (IASB) *Conceptual Framework* are explained. Finally the role of the external auditor in financial reporting is discussed.

TYPES OF ORGANISATIONS

Organisations can be classified as either for-profit entities or not-for-profit entities. Common types of for-profit entities are sole proprietorships, partnerships and companies.

There are also not-for-profit and public sector organisations. In addition, there are other, less common forms such as cooperatives, friendly societies and provident societies. Each of these organisational forms requires slightly different accounts. This is because the needs of the users are slightly different or because of other factors, such as the requirements of legislation or other regulations (e.g. those imposed by a stock exchange). Rather than attempting to deal with all the different forms of organisation, we concentrate our discussion on simple forms of organisation: the sole trader, the partnership and the limited company.

There are distinct differences in the presentation of final accounts, relating to the structure, size, patterns of ownership and goals of an organisation. These influences operate at the organisational level, as explained in Chapter 1. Other influences that operate in the commercial context are legal requirements such as the reporting requirements of the *Corporations Act*, the *Partnership Act* and case law. These will be discussed in some detail here. Other influences, such as stock exchange listing requirements, are briefly discussed later in this chapter. We begin by discussing the smallest and most common form of business organisation: the sole trader.

The sole trader

A one-owner business is a common form of business organisation, and is simple to set up. All that is required is a business bank account. Because it is so simple and because it has no recognition in law, there are no formal guidelines for the format of the accounts. The fact that the business and the owner are not seen as separate legal entities can be a problem if the business gets into difficulties: the owner is liable for all the debts of the business and might have to sell personal possessions, such as the family home, to meet them. In addition, this form of organisation relies heavily on the owner for finance and this can cause problems if the business expands. Owners tend to have limited funds at their disposal. These problems can be alleviated or solved by, for example, introducing a partner into the business. Alternatively, the owner may set up a company, which limits his or her liability.

3 LEARNING OBJECTIVE

Identify the characteristics of a sole trader

FINANCIAL STATEMENTS OF A SOLE TRADER

A sole trader is not required to prepare all four financial statements but if the business did prepare an income statement and a balance sheet the following are examples of how they might look.

PHIL'S BUSINESS
INCOME STATEMENT FOR THE YEAR ENDING 30 JUNE 20X9

	$	$
Sales		45 000
Cost of goods sold		31 000
Gross profit		14 000
Rent	1 200	
Van expenses	1 000	
Van depreciation	1 000	3 200
Profit for the year		10 800

PHIL'S BUSINESS
BALANCE SHEET AS AT 30 JUNE 20X9

	$	$	$	$
Assets				
Current assets				
Cash	14 500			
Prepaid	300			
Inventory	4 000			
Total current assets		18 800		

	$	$	$	$
Non-current assets				
Van (at cost)	5 000			
Less Accumulated depreciation	(1 000)			
Total non-current assets		4 000		
Total assets			22 800	
Liabilities				
Current liabilities				
Accounts payable	2 000			
Total current liabilities		2 000		
Non-current liabilities	NIL	NIL		
Total liabilities			2 000	
Net assets				20 800
Equity				
Capital	10 000			
Profit and loss	10 800			
Total equity				20 800

4 LEARNING OBJECTIVE

Explain the advantages and disadvantages of a partnership

Partnerships

A partnership is a relationship that exists between two or more people to carry on a business in common with a view to profit. As an organisation, a partnership offers certain advantages and disadvantages compared to the sole trader. A partnership is not regarded as a legal entity separate from the partners who comprise it.

ADVANTAGES

The advantages of forming a partnership include the following.
* *Ease of formation.* A partnership can be easily formed between two or more persons: all they have to do is agree to form a partnership. The partnership agreement is usually in writing, although a verbal agreement can be sufficient to constitute a partnership.
* *Limited rules and regulations.* Unlike a company, a partnership is not subject to the requirements of the *Corporations Act.* The partners are not required to prepare financial statements which comply with accounting standards unless the partnership is a reporting entity. Therefore, the partnership only prepares an income statement and not a statement of comprehensive income.
* *Provision of capital and expertise.* A partnership is often formed to raise more capital than is possible for a sole trader. It may also be formed to bring together the different skills of the partners; for example, an accountant and an engineer.
* *Income tax.* There may be income tax advantages in forming a partnership since it is not a separate legal entity. A partnership is not taxed, as is the case for a company. However, the individual partners pay income tax on their share of partnership profits.

DISADVANTAGES

Disadvantages of the partnership form of organisation include the following.
* *Limited life.* A partnership can end at any time through, for example, the death of a partner, withdrawal of a partner, bankruptcy of a partner, incapacity of a partner, or admission of a new partner. However, the end of the partnership does not signify the end of the partnership business: it may continue under a new partnership for many years.
* *Unlimited liability.* As each partner is personally liable for all debts of the partnership, there is unlimited liability with all partnerships. Partners in accounting firms normally purchase professional indemnity insurance because of this risk.

- *Mutual agency*. As each partner is an agent of the partnership, he or she has the authority to enter contracts on behalf of the partnership provided such contracts are within the scope of normal operations.

FINANCIAL STATEMENTS OF A PARTNERSHIP

A partnership is not likely to prepare all four financial statements as most partnerships are not required to, hence they also have a great deal of flexibility in how they prepare their financial statements. Let us now look at an income statement and a balance sheet for a partnership.

ADAM & SMITH PARTNERSHIP
INCOME STATEMENT FOR THE YEAR ENDED 30 JUNE 20X7

	$	$
Sales		100 000
Cost of goods sold		60 000
Gross profit		40 000
Expenses		20 000
Profit		20 000
Distributions		
Salary		
Adam	6 000	
Smith	4 000	10 000
		10 000
Profit share		
Adam	5 000	
Smith	5 000	10 000

A comparison of the income statement of the sole trader, Phil, with that of the partnership reveals that the main difference is the distribution statements for the partnership. This statement shows that Adam and Smith were each paid a salary for services provided to the partnership, and the remaining profit was then shared equally.

StockLite/Shutterstock.com

ADAM & SMITH PARTNERSHIP
BALANCE SHEET AT 30 JUNE 20X7

	$	$	$	$
Assets				
Current assets				
Cash	10 000			
Inventory	10 000			
Total current assets		20 000		
Non-current assets				
Land and building	100 000			
Total non-current assets		100 000		
Total assets			120 000	
Liabilities				
Current liabilities				
Accounts payable	20 000			
Total current liabilities		20 000		
Non-current liabilities	NIL	NIL		
Total liabilities			20 000	
Net assets				100 000
Partners' equity				
Capital accounts				
Adam	40 000			
Smith	40 000			
Total capital accounts		80 000		
Current accounts				
Adam	11 000			
Smith	9 000			
Total current accounts		20 000		
Total partners' equity				100 000

A comparison of the balance sheet of Phil the sole trader with that of Adam and Smith reveals a difference in the equity part of the statements. The balance sheet for the partnership shows a balance for each partner under the headings of capital and current accounts. The current **account** reveals the partners' entitlement to profit, salary, interest, drawings and other, more short-term transactions. The capital account records the capital contributed by the partners. As current and capital items might be treated differently for legal purposes, it is useful to record them separately in the accounts.

5 LEARNING OBJECTIVE

Explain the advantages and disadvantages of a company

Companies

Unlike the partnership and the sole trader, a company is recognised as a separate legal entity quite distinct from its owners. The debts incurred in the normal course of business are those of the company. In the case of a default in payment, it is the company that is sued rather than the owner. The fact that the owners might also be the managers and the only employees is irrelevant: in the eyes of the law all these roles are different.

Companies can be:
• private (proprietary)
  • limited by shares
  • unlimited with share capital

- public
  - limited by shares
  - limited by guarantee
  - unlimited with share capital
  - no liability.

LIMITED-BY-SHARES COMPANIES

This class of company restricts the liability of members (shareholders) to a specified amount. For a limited company, the shareholders' liability is restricted to the amount paid for the share. Limited-by-shares companies include those found in the following list.

- *Proprietary companies or private companies.* These must have a minimum of one shareholder and normally have a maximum of 50 shareholders. A proprietary company must have the word 'Proprietary' or 'Pty' before the word 'Limited' or 'Ltd' as part of its name. These companies are often family companies and have fewer legal formalities than public companies, but they are unable to approach the general public to raise money.
- *Small or large proprietary companies.* A small proprietary company is one that meets at least two of the following criteria:
  - sales of less than $25 million
  - assets of less than $12.5 million
  - fewer than 50 employees.

    A small proprietary company does not generally have to prepare audited financial statements. All other proprietary companies are large and are required to lodge audited financial statements with the Australian Securities and Investments Commission (ASIC), unless granted an exemption.
- *Public companies.* A public company must have at least 50 non-employee shareholders and there is no maximum number for its shareholders. Usually, ownership of these companies is widespread. A public company can invite the public to subscribe to its shares or debentures and can be listed, which means that its shares are traded on a stock exchange, or unlisted. A public company must have the word 'Limited' or 'Ltd' as part of its name and is subject to many more rules and restrictions under the *Corporations Act* than are proprietary companies.

COMPANIES LIMITED BY GUARANTEE

Companies that are limited by guarantee are public companies whose shareholders undertake to provide a guaranteed amount of money in the event of the company being liquidated. This type of company does not have a share capital and, as such, does not raise initial capital. It is not, therefore, suitable for trading purposes. This form of company is often used for sporting clubs and not-for-profit charitable organisations.

UNLIMITED LIABILITY COMPANIES

Shareholders of an unlimited liability company are liable for all the debts of the company. For this reason such companies are not common in Australia, although some mutual funds are organised in this way. An advantage of this type of company is that there are no restrictions on the return of capital to shareholders.

NO-LIABILITY COMPANIES

This category is restricted to mining companies. The words 'No Liability' or 'NL' must be part of the company's name. Shareholders in these companies are not required to contribute the unpaid value of shares if the company is liquidated.

ADVANTAGES OF COMPANIES

The advantages of the company form of organisation are:

- *limited liability*: shareholders are liable only for the value of their shares
- *more capital*: a company has the potential to raise substantial amounts of capital, which is not possible for sole traders or partnerships
- *ease of transfer of ownership*: shareholders can buy and sell shares without affecting the operations of the company
- *no mutual agency*: shareholders cannot enter into contracts that would bind the company
- *professional management*: a company is managed by a board of directors and a managing director, while the shareholders maintain ownership. It is therefore possible to hire the best managerial talent available
- *continuous existence*: a company has an indefinite life and does not cease to function each time a shareholder sells shares, dies or goes bankrupt
- *separate legal entity*: unlike a sole trader or a partnership, a company is a separate legal entity. Therefore it can buy and sell property, sue and be sued, enter into contracts, hire and dismiss employees, be responsible for its debts and pay tax.

DISADVANTAGES OF COMPANIES

Disadvantages of the company structure include the following.

- *Taxation*. A company is a separate legal entity and is required to pay company tax, which is not the case for a sole trader or a partnership. However, provided shareholders receive their profits as franked dividends, the taxing of companies might not be a significant disadvantage, and, depending on income levels, could be an advantage.
- *Regulation*. A company is subject to more government intervention in the form of rules and regulations. This is particularly true for public companies. For example, they are required to produce accounts annually and to have them audited by a recognised firm of auditors, which can be expensive. A copy of the audited accounts must be lodged with ASIC, where it is available for inspection by the public. The form of these accounts is also subject to the *Corporations Act*, which requires that a company's accounts should consist of the company's balance sheet, the company's statement of comprehensive income (or statement of comprehensive income and income statement), the directors' report, the auditor's report and a directors' statement. In addition to these general requirements, there are detailed requirements, particularly in accounting standards, covering the content of the actual accounts. Such requirements are more onerous for companies that are required to prepare general-purpose financial reports.
- *Limited liability*. While generally an advantage, it may be a disadvantage for a small company if its ability to borrow money is restricted by the fact that its members have limited liability.
- *Separation of ownership and control*. This can also act as an advantage or a disadvantage. Managers might have incentives to make decisions that are not in the best interests of all shareholders. The *Corporations Act* contains provisions intended to discourage managers from behaving in this manner.

STOP AND THINK 1

Explain the differences between a partnership and a company. Under what circumstances would you expect either to be used?

6.1

WORKED EXAMPLE

FINANCIAL STATEMENTS OF A PRIVATE COMPANY

Unlike the sole trader or a partnership, a large private and all public companies are required to prepare all four financial statements, and many companies like Woolworths must also comply with all accounting standards. We only illustrate the statement of comprehensive income and the balance sheet.

JACK PTY LTD
STATEMENT OF COMPREHENSIVE INCOME FOR THE YEAR ENDING 30 JUNE 20X4

	NOTES	20X4		20X3	
		$000	$000	$000	$000
Sales	1		60 000		45 000
Cost of sales			40 000		30 000
Gross profit			20 000		15 000
Distribution costs	2	3 000		2 500	
Administration costs	2	11 000	14 000	9 000	11 500
Profit before taxation			6 000		3 500
Taxation	3		2 600		1 400
Profit after taxation			3 400		2 100
Other comprehensive income					
Unrealised gain (loss) on revaluation of properties			15 000		6 000
Total comprehensive income for the year			18 400		8 100

JACK PTY LTD
BALANCE SHEET AT 30 JUNE 20X4

	NOTES	20X4		20X3
		$000	$000	$000
Assets				
Current assets				
Cash at bank		3 500		2 000
Debtors		11 000		4 000
Inventory	7	10 000		7 000
Total current assets			24 500	13 000
Non-current assets				
Equipment	5	10 000		11 000
Land and buildings	6	70 000		56 000
Total non-current assets			80 000	67 000
Total assets			104 500	80 000
Liabilities				
Current liabilities				
Creditors		4 000		3 000
Taxation	3	2 600		1 400
Dividends	4	1 600		1 100
Total current liabilities			8 200	5 500

	NOTES	20X4		20X3
		$000	$000	$000
Non-current liabilities				
Total liabilities			8 200	5 500
Net assets			96 300	74 500
Capital and reserves				
Share capital	8	70 000		64 000
Retained profits	9	5 300		4 500
Reserves	10	21 000		6 000
Total capital and reserves			96 300	74 500

Clearly, to go through these requirements in great detail is outside the scope of an introductory text. Instead we have included in the previous section the statement of comprehensive income and a balance sheet for Jack Pty Ltd, a private company. (The financial statements for Woolworths, a publicly listed company, are in Appendix 1.) The financial statement highlights areas of difference between the accounts of the limited company and those of the other forms of organisation considered (see the accounts for Phil's business on pages 31–32 and Adam and Smith partnership on pages 33–34.

6 LEARNING OBJECTIVE

Identify the major differences between the statement of comprehensive income and balance sheet of a company and those of a partnership or sole trader

STATEMENT OF COMPREHENSIVE INCOME

The first difference is in the title of the statement: the fact that Jack is a proprietary limited company must be stated, and the new title does this. In addition, the statement contains comparative figures for the previous year, as well as references to a number of notes. These notes contain greater detail than can be shown on the face of the statement, and so are an integral part of the analysis of the accounts of a company. This will be discussed in more detail in Chapter 10. We can see that down to 'Gross profit' the format is familiar. However, we then find that expenses are classified into broad categories. These categories are laid down in AASB 101 *Presentation of Financial Statements*. The other difference is that the statement is called a statement of comprehensive income. We discuss statements of financial performance in detail in Chapter 6.

It is from the point at which the profit is shown that the real differences arise. The most striking of these is that taxation is included in the statement of comprehensive income. This is because the company is recognised as a separate entity for legal and tax purposes and its profits are liable to corporation tax. In contrast, the sole trader and the partnership are not separate legal or taxable entities: their profits are not taxed as such, but only as they form part of the income of the owner.

BALANCE SHEET

We now look at the balance sheet of a proprietary limited liability company and the differences that arise.

The format uses the current/non-current classification. AASB 101 allows companies to choose an alternative format in which assets and liabilities are listed in order of liquidity. Most banks list assets and liabilities in order of liquidity and do not use the current/non-current classification. We discuss balance sheets in detail in Chapter 5.

As you can see, the top part of the balance sheet is similar to those we have encountered before, except for the inclusion of dividends and taxation and the fact that a lot of the detail is included in the notes to the statements. For example, Note 6 would contain details of non-current assets bought and sold during the year, as well as the depreciation to date, and that charged during the year.

The lower part of the balance sheet is somewhat different in that the owners' equity is referred to as share capital. This might consist of different types each carrying different voting rights, and so on. This would only be apparent if we looked at the detail contained in the notes. Similarly, there may be different types of reserves, such as a revaluation reserve for revalued assets such as land and buildings. Jack has a revaluation reserve and more details are provided in the statement of changes in equity.

STOP AND THINK 2

Describe how the choice of organisational form determines the format of the final accounts.

FINANCIAL STATEMENTS FOR A PUBLIC COMPANY

The statements presented for Jack Pty Ltd above are for a private company and are simpler than those for a public company. Woolworths is a public company and its financial statements illustrate the usual format of each statement. Refer to the Woolworths financial report in Appendix 1. Note that the statements are headed 'consolidated'.

Most major companies, such like Woolworths, operate in a parent–subsidiary (or controlled entity) relationship for a variety of reasons. In fact, such companies often control many companies. Consolidated financial statements report the results and financial position of the combination of the parent entity and the other entities it controls. The preparation of these accounts is called consolidation, and the terms 'group' and 'consolidated' accounts are used and are interchangeable. In these accounts, the parent entity and its controlled entities are grouped to constitute an economic entity. It does not have the status of being a legal entity; it does not have the legal rights and obligations of a company.

Consolidated financial statements are useful to the management and shareholders of the parent entity in judging how well the parent has achieved its goals. They are also critical in reporting the financial position of the economic entity. For example, the collapse of Enron revealed billions of dollars in debt hidden in 'special purpose entities'. It is important that users are fully aware of all the debts of an entity when assessing issues like solvency and the going concern test. The collapse of Enron also caused losses for many employees who may have made different decisions about investing in the company they worked for had they been aware of its level of debt.

The purpose of consolidated financial statements is to give a view of the parent entity and its controlled entities as if they were one entity – the economic entity – so that, on the balance sheet, the accounts receivable represent the customers of the parent entity and all its controlled entities. Similarly, the consolidated statement of comprehensive income shows total revenue from sales made by the parent entity and all its controlled entities. In preparing consolidated financial statements, similar accounts from the individual statements of the parent entity and its controlled entities are combined. However, some accounts result from transactions between the parent entity and a controlled entity. If consolidated financial statements are to represent the position and results of an economic entity as a whole, then any transactions between members within the economic entity must be eliminated.

The consolidated financial statements are prepared by combining similar accounts from the separate statements of the parent entity and its controlled entities after elimination of all transactions between members of the economic entity.

In many cases, a parent entity owns 100 per cent of all its subsidiaries. However, there are also many instances when a parent entity will own enough to gain control of another entity, but not 100 per cent. For example, if a parent only owns 90 per cent of a controlled entity it means that other shareholders own 10 per cent of the shares in that controlled entity. Such shareholders are described as 'outside equity

7 LEARNING OBJECTIVE

Explain the main characteristics of the financial statements of a public company and the role and meaning of consolidated financial statements

KEY CONCEPT

2.1

CONSOLIDATED FINANCIAL STATEMENTS

Consolidated financial statements provide information about the performance, financial position and cash flows of an economic entity.

interest' in accounting standards as they are shareholders outside the shareholders of the parent entity. Outside equity interests are reported in consolidated financial statements based on their interest in the relevant controlled entity or subsidiary. For example, in the above case the outside shareholders represent 10 per cent of the net assets of the controlled entity at balance date. The outside equity interest is also entitled to 10 per cent of the profit/loss of the controlled entity for the period. Outside equity interest is not a liability in the consolidated statements but represents part of the equity of the net assets of the economic entity.

An examination of Woolworths financial report shows that all the statements have the word 'consolidated' in the title representing the economic entity of Woolworths Limited and all its subsidiaries as listed in Note 28 (see Appendix 1).

An examination of Note 32 of the Woolworths financial statements (available at www.woolworths limited.com.au) reveals the balance sheet and the statement of comprehensive income for the parent entity Woolworths Limited. This information would only be of use to users like creditors and lenders who deal with the parent entity, and the accounts show these are not large items.

Lenders to Cellarmaster Wines Pty Ltd have a claim against Cellarmaster, even though it is a 100 per cent controlled entity of Woolworths Limited. However, the existence of a cross guarantee of the debts of Cellarmaster as detailed in Note 29 of the Woolworths accounts means such creditors are interested in the financial position of the Woolworths group as revealed in the consolidated statements.

Not-for-profit entities (NFPEs) operate in many areas in our society including education, health, community services, leisure, religion and charities. The aim of a NFPE is to use its resources in an efficient manner to best achieve the objectives for which it was formed, rather than pursuing a profit for its owner(s).

8 **LEARNING**
OBJECTIVE

Explain the current framework for standard setting in Australia

In this book we concentrate on accounting from the viewpoint of private sector, for-profit companies. However, much of what is covered in the book is also relevant for entities in the not-for-profit (NFP) sector. In some chapters we also include examples from the NFP and public sectors. The remainder of this chapter examines the various influences that affect the preparation of financial reports for companies. The factors that may influence and regulate the preparation of the financial statements for most companies are accounting standards, accounting concepts and the *Corporations Act*. The Securities Exchange Listing Rules impose additional reporting obligations for listed public companies.

THE FRAMEWORK FOR SETTING ACCOUNTING STANDARDS

Accounting standards have a major influence on the financial statements that companies must prepare. The Australian Accounting Standards Board (AASB) sets accounting standards that must be applied in all general-purpose financial statements for both the private and public sectors in Australia. Australia has sector-neutral accounting standards, which means there is only one set of accounting standards for both the for-profit and not-for-profit sectors. We will talk more about this later.

Financial Reporting Council

The standard-setting arrangements also involve the Financial Reporting Council (FRC) which has oversight responsibility for the AASB and the Auditing and Assurance Standards Board (AUASB). There are 17 members of the FRC (plus the chairperson) comprising key stakeholders from professional accounting bodies, the business community, government, and regulatory agencies such as the Australian Securities and Investments Commission (ASIC). Members are appointed by the federal Treasurer.

Australian Accounting Standards Board

There are 14 members of the AASB, including a full-time chairperson. The AASB's responsibilities, as specified in section 227(1) of the *Australian Securities and Investments Commission Act 2001*, include the following:

- to develop a conceptual framework, not having the force of an accounting standard, for the purpose of evaluating proposed accounting standards
- to develop and issue accounting standards that have the force of law
- to formulate accounting standards for other purposes
- to participate in, and contribute to the development of a single set of accounting standards for worldwide use.

The AASB follows due process in the development of accounting standards and holds in public all meetings that relate to technical matters. The AASB has its own dedicated technical staff responsible for the preparation of papers for the AASB to consider as it develops accounting standards.

COMPLIANCE WITH ACCOUNTING STANDARDS

In accordance with the *Corporations Act*, compliance with the accounting standards and interpretations issued by the AASB is mandatory for all companies preparing general-purpose financial statements. Other jurisdictions such as state governments may also adopt AASB standards and make compliance with such standards mandatory. The Australian Securities and Investments Commission (ASIC) is responsible for enforcing compliance with the *Corporations Act*.

STOP AND THINK 3

Discuss the framework in Australia for setting standards for the accounting profession.

THE POLITICAL NATURE OF ACCOUNTING STANDARD SETTING

In Chapter 1 we discussed the choice of accounting policies and their economic consequences. The standard-setting body selects accounting standards based on the objective of providing useful information to the users of financial statements. Managers, however, may choose accounting policies based on the economic consequences for themselves and their organisations.

The due process used by the AASB provides managers with an opportunity to lobby the standard setters. They can attempt to influence its deliberations, particularly with reference to standards that are relevant to their company. The Group of 100 is an association of the chief financial managers from Australia's 100 largest companies. The group is active in making submissions to the standard setters. The decision by the FRC that forced the AASB to adopt International Financial Reporting Standards

9 LEARNING OBJECTIVE

Explain the influence of accounting standards, the *Corporations Act 2001* and the Australian Securities Exchange Listing Rules on financial reporting requirements means that Australians who want to influence the standard-setting process now need to influence the deliberations of the IASB. Given the size of the Australian capital market, this is a difficult task.

The Group of 100's agenda for lobbying the standard setters may be to ensure that financial statements provide useful information. Alternatively, its reasons could be motivated by contracts like bonuses for senior management that include accounting numbers as discussed in Chapter 1.

In any event, this interest in the standard-setting process means that standard-setting bodies have to achieve their stated objectives within a process that is quite political.

INTERNATIONAL ACCOUNTING STANDARDS

The International Accounting Standards Board (IASB) consists of members from a number of countries. It is based in London and began operations in January 2002, replacing the International Accounting Standards Committee (IASC). All standards issued by this board prior to 2002 are referred to as International Accounting Standards (IAS). All new standards issued by the IASB from January 2002 are called International Financial Reporting Standards (IFRS).

The term 'International Financial Reporting Standards' includes:
- International Financial Reporting Standards
- International Accounting Standards
- interpretations issued by the International Financial Reporting Interpretations Committee or the former Standing Interpretations Committee.

The mission of the IASB is to 'develop in the public interest, a single set of high quality, understandable and international financial reporting standards (IFRSs) for general-purpose financial statements (GPFS)'. The 15 board members are selected on their technical skills and accounting knowledge rather than on country or regional representation.

Although such standards do not override national standards, the IASB hopes that its activities will result in more uniform worldwide accounting standards. Where a country does not have a standard-setting authority, it can adopt the IAS (IFRS). From 1 January 2005, Australia adopted the IFRS. As a result, Australia has now issued all IASB standards, but only after subjecting them to due process. The impact of this decision means that Australia is now locked into IFRS and any changes that the IASB makes to IFRS must be replicated in Australia.

To allow users to distinguish the previous IAS from new IFRS, the following numbering system has been adopted by the AASB.
- AASB 1 = IFRS 1, AASB 2 = IFRS 2, so the same number applies to the new standards issued by the IASB
- AASB 101 = IAS 1, AASB 102 = IAS 2, so the original number of the IAS plus 100 allows users to identify AASB standards that are equivalent to IASC standards.

The same numbering policy applies to the adoption of Interpretations of IFRS and IAS for application in Australia.

In addition, some original Australian accounting standards like AASB 1031 *Materiality* have been retained for use because there is no equivalent IFRS or IAS. These standards are identified with numbering from 1000. It is estimated that in 2013 over 150 countries now use IFRS in some ways. There is a view that international harmonisation of accounting standards will facilitate the flow of capital across national borders. This has potential benefits for investors and for companies wishing to list their shares in other countries.

THE *CORPORATIONS ACT*

It is not our intention in this section to cover the requirements of the *Corporations Act* in detail. They are dealt with in courses on company law and company accounting.

Most companies are required to prepare financial statements in accordance with applicable accounting standards. These statements must show a true and fair view of the company's financial position and results for the period. Compliance with applicable accounting standards issued by the AASB is mandatory for all companies that are reporting entities under section 298 of the *Corporations Act*.

The *Corporations Act* also requires the following to be included with a company's financial statements:
- the directors' report
- the directors' statement
- the auditor's report.

The directors' report

The directors' report must include information such as directors' names, activities of the company, profit or loss for the year, amount of dividends, review of operations and other matters in relation to the company.

The directors' statement

The directors' statement, or declaration, states whether, in the opinion of the directors:
- the statements of comprehensive income and position present a true and fair view
- the company is able to pay its debts as they fall due
- the financial statements comply with accounting standards.

The reference to the ability of the company to pay its debts is an important statement about the solvency of the company and is clearly intended to reassure users such as employees, shareholders, creditors and lenders. There have been cases where directors of companies have been found guilty of making this statement when the company could not in fact pay its debts.

Shutterstock.com

The auditor's report

The auditor's report is prepared by an external auditor and is meant to reassure shareholders that they can rely on the financial statements prepared by the company. The auditor is required to form an opinion about the financial statements. The auditor's report must state whether the financial statements:

- comply with the requirements of the *Corporations Act*
- provide a true and fair view of the state of affairs of the company
- are in accordance with applicable accounting standards.

This is discussed in more detail later in this chapter.

10 LEARNING
OBJECTIVE

Explain what is meant
by a conceptual
framework

SECURITIES EXCHANGE INFLUENCE ON FINANCIAL REPORTING

Public companies in Australia that have their shares listed on a securities exchange must comply with the listing requirements of the ASX.

The Listing Rules impose additional requirements on listed companies. These rules require companies to provide:

- half-yearly reports
- a preliminary final statement
- additional details to the annual report
- additional details for mining exploration companies.

If companies do not comply with these they are likely to be delisted, so that their shares can no longer be traded on a securities exchange.

ACCOUNTING CONCEPTS

Accounting standards, the *Corporations Act* and the Australian Securities Exchange Listing Rules impose certain requirements on, and provide guidance for, companies as they prepare their financial statements. Public sector and NFP entities may also need to comply with legislative requirements or Treasurer's Instructions. However, not all accounting transactions can be specifically dealt with in an accounting standard, or the law, or in the Listing Rules. Accounting standards establish procedures on how to account for certain transactions and events, as well as providing detailed disclosure requirements. For example, cash flow statements must be prepared in accordance with AASB 107 *Statement of Cash Flows*.

The role of accounting concepts is to provide general guidance on issues, such as the definition of assets, liabilities, income, expenses and equity, in order to help accountants resolve specific problems as they arise.

In Australia, the due process followed for developing accounting concepts was the same as that followed for accounting standards. Four Statements of Accounting Concepts (SACs) were issued in Australia from 1990 to 1995. Because Australia issues accounting standards based on IFRSs, the AASB adopted the International Accounting Standards Board (IASB) *Framework* for the preparation and presentation of financial statements. However, it retained SAC 1 *Definition of the Reporting Entity* and SAC 2 *Objective of General-Purpose Financial Reporting* because the IASB *Framework* does not deal adequately with the objective of financial reporting or the reporting entity. In September 2010 the IASB and the FASB issued the first two chapters of a revised conceptual framework. The document includes the remaining parts of the previous framework, which have yet to be revised. The new document is called the *Conceptual Framework for Financial Reporting*. The first two chapters cover the objective of general-purpose financial reporting and the qualitative characteristics of useful financial information. In July 2013, the IASB issued a discussion paper on the conceptual framework dealing with the elements of financial statements, measurement and presentation, and disclosure. At the time of writing this edition, the AASB was in the process of approving the two new chapters for for-profit entities and retaining the content of the earlier Framework (2009) for not-for-profit entities. This is because the new chapters of the IASB conceptual framework are directed at for-profit entities only. Given that our focus in this book is for-profit entities, we use the two chapters as detailed in the IASB *Conceptual Framework* in this edition. However, the differences are not significant and in relation to the definitions and recognition criteria for the elements of the financial statements, they are the same.

Members of the accounting profession in Australia must comply with accounting standards under the Accounting Professional and Ethical Standards (APES) 205 *Conformity with Accounting Standards*. Even though the *Conceptual Framework* is not mandatory like accounting standards, it is listed in AASB 108 *Accounting Policies, Changes in Accounting Estimates and Errors* as relevant in accounting policy choice and therefore has some legal status.

What is a conceptual framework?

A conceptual framework is an attempt to develop some basic concepts of accounting to help accountants determine how transactions should be accounted for. As we indicated in Chapter 1, the preparation of financial statements involves many decisions about how to record transactions. To assist with this process, rule-making or standard-setting bodies have been established in most Western countries – in Australia this is the AASB. Standard-setting bodies are responsible for developing standards (rules) that help accountants to record transactions that could be described as difficult.

One might expect standards to be based on an underlying theory, but in practice they were determined on an ad hoc basis until the late 1980s. In recent years, standard-setting bodies have been concerned with developing a conceptual framework to provide the theory from which accounting standards can then be developed. For example, in 1978 the Financial Accounting Standards Board (FASB) in the USA defined the conceptual framework as:

> a coherent system of interrelated objectives and fundamentals that is expected to lead to consistent standards and that prescribes the nature, function and limits of financial accounting and reporting.

The IASB developed the IASB *Conceptual Framework*, which:

> sets out the concepts that underlie the preparation and presentation of financial statements for external users.

2.2 KEY CONCEPT

THE CONCEPTUAL FRAMEWORK

The *Conceptual Framework* sets out the concepts that underlie the preparation and presentation of financial statements for external users.

> **2.3** **KEY CONCEPT**
>
> ## GENERAL-PURPOSE FINANCIAL REPORT (GPFR)
>
> A GPFR provides information about the financial position of a reporting entity, which is information about the entity's economic resources and the claims against the reporting entity. Financial reports also provide information about the effects of transactions and other events that change a reporting entity's economic resources and claims. Both types of information provide useful input for decisions about providing resources to an entity.
>

> **2.4** **KEY CONCEPT**
>
> ## GENERAL-PURPOSE FINANCIAL STATEMENTS (GPFS)
>
> GPFS include:
>
> » a statement of comprehensive income
>
> » a statement of financial position or balance sheet
>
> » a statement of changes in equity
>
> » a statement of cash flows
>
> » notes to the financial statements.

Therefore, the *Conceptual Framework* attempts to establish concepts or ideas that determine how financial reports are prepared for general users. It is an attempt to establish the foundations for the preparation of general-purpose financial reports. Basic questions such as those in the following list are addressed.

- What entities should prepare general-purpose financial reports?
- Who are the users of general-purpose financial reports?
- What are assets, liabilities, income, expenses and equity?
- How should these items be measured and displayed?

In the following sections of this chapter we examine the *Conceptual Framework* and its development. The definitions of 'assets', 'liabilities', 'income', 'expenses' and 'equity' used throughout this book are also explained.

11 LEARNING OBJECTIVE

Identify the role of a conceptual framework

OBJECTIVES OF A CONCEPTUAL FRAMEWORK

Why develop a conceptual framework? In this section we briefly discuss some of the possible reasons for standard-setting bodies expending considerable time and resources on developing a conceptual framework.

FEWER ACCOUNTING STANDARDS

A conceptual framework enables the resolution of accounting problems without the need to issue an accounting standard every time an issue arises. This should result in fewer accounting standards and help to minimise what some see as the problem of 'standards overload' associated with preparing general-purpose financial reports that must comply with a large number of accounting standards.

MORE CONSISTENCY

Some new accounting standards will still be required. However, because they will all conform to the framework, there will be greater consistency.

IMPROVED COMMUNICATION

The various conceptual framework projects have already led to improved communication among accountants and between the standard-setting bodies and their constituents. All parties are now using common definitions for items such as assets, liabilities, income, expenses and equity.

DEFENCE AGAINST POLITICISATION

A set of concise and well-defined concepts should enhance the credibility of financial reporting and enable the standard-setting bodies to defend particular accounting standards on the basis that they are consistent with the appropriate framework. The setting of accounting standards will always be a political process to some extent. However, a conceptual framework should reduce the ability of lobby groups to influence the standard-setting process to achieve objectives that are not in the public interest.

STOP AND THINK 4

Discuss the reasons why it is desirable to have a conceptual framework.

THE *CONCEPTUAL FRAMEWORK*

In the next few sections we highlight major concepts from the *Conceptual Framework* with regard to private-sector entities. You should be aware that these concepts also apply to public sector and not-for-profit entities. We use many of these concepts throughout this book.

DEFINITION OF THE REPORTING ENTITY

In Australia, SAC 1 dealt with the issue of defining a reporting entity. As previously mentioned, SAC 1 is being retained until the IASB issues more detailed guidance on the definition of a reporting entity. Accordingly, we use the definition from SAC 1 in this 9th edition.

12 LEARNING OBJECTIVE

Explain the terms 'reporting entity', 'general-purpose financial statements', 'qualitative characteristics', and explain the objective of general-purpose financial reporting

KEY CONCEPT

2.5

REPORTING ENTITY

Reporting entities are entities (including economic entities) in respect of which it is reasonable to expect the existence of users dependent on general-purpose financial reports for information that will be useful to them for making and evaluating decisions about the allocation of scarce resources.

(AASB *Conceptual Framework*, SAC 1, para. 40)

The above definition highlights that for an entity to be a reporting entity, there must be a demand from users for general-purpose financial statements (other than users such as banks who receive special-purpose financial reports). Identifying users is critical and is considered in the next section.

When an entity is identified as a reporting entity in Australia, it is required to prepare general-purpose financial reports in accordance with accounting standards. If an entity is deemed not to be a reporting entity, it does not have to comply with accounting standards when preparing financial reports – this does not apply to a disclosing entity. A small family business is not likely to be a reporting entity and is therefore not required to spend money on preparing detailed general-purpose financial reports. If Mum and Dad run the family business, they normally know how the business is performing and do not require general-purpose financial reports.

In June 2010 the AASB issued AASB 1053 *Application of Tiers of Australian Accounting Standards* which applies from 1 July 2013. The standard aims to reduce the reporting burden on small and medium-sized entities. While all reporting entities are still required to prepare GPFS only 'publicly accountable entities' will be required to comply with all accounting standards. Publicly accountable entities are defined in the standard and include entities that invite the public to buy their equity or debt. Non-publicly accountable reporting entities can elect to follow the reduced disclosure regime.

STOP AND THINK 5

Why is the reporting entity concept important?

THE OBJECTIVE OF GENERAL-PURPOSE FINANCIAL REPORTING

General-purpose financial reporting provides financial information about the entity that existing and potential investors, lenders and other creditors can use to help them make decisions about providing resources to the entity. Those decisions could involve buying, selling or holding equity instruments, and providing or settling loans and other forms of credit. This is the objective as stated in paragraph OB 22 of Chapter 1 of the new IASB *Conceptual Framework*. The analysis of financial statements is considered in Chapter 10.

KEY CONCEPT

2.6

OBJECTIVE OF GENERAL-PURPOSE FINANCIAL REPORTING

The objective of general-purpose financial reporting is to provide financial information about the reporting entity that is useful to existing and potential investors, lenders and other creditors in making decisions about providing resources to the entity. Those decisions involve buying, selling or holding equity instruments and providing or settling loans and other forms of credit.

(IASB *Conceptual Framework*, 2010, para. OB 2). Copyright © IFRS Foundation. All rights reserved. Reproduced by Cengage Learning Australia with the permission of the IFRS Foundation ®. No permission granted to third parties to reproduce or distribute.

In order to achieve the objective, financial statements must be prepared on an accrual basis, not a cash basis. 'Accrual' refers to transactions being recognised when they occur and not when cash is paid or received. Under cash accounting the trigger for entry into the accounting records is the payment or receipt of cash. With accrual accounting the trigger is the provision or receipt of goods or services. This often occurs simultaneously, like buying food at a Woolworths store. Where goods are sold on credit, accrual accounting is used to record the transaction, not cash accounting. If a business purchases a machine with an expected life of 10 years, it is an expense in the year of acquisition in cash accounting. In accrual accounting the cost is spread over 10 years.

We use the following example to illustrate the difference between cash and accrual accounting. XYZ Ltd purchases a lease (or builds a factory on leasehold land) for $100 000, which has five years to run. The lease generates net cash revenues of $35 000 per annum for XYZ. XYZ incurs no other expenses.

If XYZ Ltd used cash accounting for years 1–5 the results would be

ITEM	YEAR 1	YEAR 2	YEAR 3	YEAR 4	YEAR 5	5-YEAR TERM
Cash revenue	$35 000	$35 000	$35 000	$35 000	$35 000	$175 000
Cash expenses	($100 000)	$0	$0	$0	$0	($100 000)
Profit/(Loss)	($65 000)	$35 000	$35 000	$35 000	$35 000	$75 000
Cumulative result	($65 000)	($30 000)	$5 000	$40 000	$75 000	$75 000

If XYZ Ltd used accrual accounting for years 1–5 the results would be

DETAILS	YEAR 1	YEAR 2	YEAR 3	YEAR 4	YEAR 5	5-YEAR TERM
Cash revenue	$35 000	$35 000	$35 000	$35 000	$35 000	$175 000
Accrual expenses	($20 000)	($20 000)	($20 000)	($20 000)	($20 000)	($100 000)
Surplus/ (Deficit)	$15 000	$15 000	$15 000	$15 000	$15 000	$75 000
Cumulative result	$15 000	$30 000	$45 000	$60 000	$75 000	$75 000

Accrual accounting provides a better measure of performance (but not cash flow) as the $100 000 outlay at the beginning benefits all five years and this is how it should be reported.

KEY CONCEPT

2.7

ACCRUAL ACCOUNTING

The method of accounting whereby revenues and expenses are identified within a specified period of time and are recorded as incurred, along with acquired assets, without regard to the date of receipt or payment of cash.

> **2.8** **KEY CONCEPT**
>
> ## GOING CONCERN
>
> The assumption that the entity will continue to operate into the foreseeable future and is not in the process of liquidation. Financial statements are prepared on this basis.

QUALITATIVE CHARACTERISTICS OF FINANCIAL INFORMATION

What qualities should financial information possess to be included in general-purpose financial reports? Paragraph QC 4 of Chapter 3 of the IASB *Conceptual Framework* states that: 'If financial information is to be useful it must be relevant and faithfully represent what it purports to represent. The usefulness of financial information is enhanced if it is comparable, verifiable, timely and understandable.' The fundamental characteristics are *relevance* and *faithful representation*.

Financial information is *relevant* if it is capable of making a difference to a user's decision – whether it is actually used is irrelevant. Financial information can be capable of making a difference in two main ways. It may confirm what the user expected. For example, the Reserve Bank makes decisions about the cash interest rate in Australia on the first Tuesday of each month. Investors are always predicting what the decision might be ahead of the Reserve Board's announcement. When the actual announcement is made it either confirms market expectations or, on some occasions, is contrary to market expectations. The second way financial information can make a difference is when it has predictive value. For example, the movement in the Dow Jones Index in the USA is often a predictor of what is likely to happen to the Australian share market when it commences trading on the next day.

For financial information to *faithfully represent* what it purports to, it must be *complete*, *neutral* and *free from error*. *Complete* information means that all relevant financial information that users require to understand a transaction is available. *Neutral* information is presented without bias so that it is not slanted towards a particular view that the preparer would like the user to take. For example, when a football fan is explaining why an umpire's decision was not fair they are likely to explain the event in a biased manner. *Free from error* does not mean it is perfectly accurate but rather that there are no errors in describing the transaction or in the process used to present financial information about the transaction. For example, an estimate of the fair value of an asset will faithfully represent the value if the process used to obtain the estimate, such as assumptions used, are accurately described and the limitations made clear to users.

Information must be both *relevant* and *faithfully represented* if it is to be useful to users of GPFS. Some information, such as forecasts of future profits, may be relevant but cannot be *faithfully* represented with an acceptable degree of reliability to be included in general-purpose financial reports. Conversely, some information may be *faithfully represented*, such as the historical cost of an asset 20 years ago, but is it of relevance to users? We look at different measurement attributes in Chapter 4 and should keep in mind the qualitative characteristics when considering the advantages and disadvantages of each attribute.

In addition to being a *relevant* and *faithful* representation, information must also pass the materiality test. This means that if the information is not likely to affect the user's decision adversely, the information is immaterial and need not be separately disclosed in the general-purpose financial report. In other words, we can ignore it for decision-making purposes.

The *Conceptual Framework* also states that *comparability*, *verifiability*, *timeliness* and *understandability* are qualitative characteristics that enhance the usefulness of information that is *relevant* and *faithfully represented*. As we will see in Chapter 10, when analysing financial statements it is important for users to be able to *compare* the general-purpose financial statements of different entities. It is important that independent observers are able to *verify* that the information is a *faithful* representation of the transaction. General-purpose financial statements should be prepared on a *timely* basis. It is of no use to a punter in 2014 to be told which horse won the 2013 Melbourne Cup. The same applies to financial information about a reporting entity. However, for large organisations there is inevitably a delay of two to three months from the balance date until the release of the general-purpose financial statements. The information should be *understandable* to users who have a reasonable knowledge of accounting and who are prepared to diligently study the information in financial statements. Such a user is sometimes described as a 'sophisticated' user.

> ## 2.9 KEY CONCEPT
> ## QUALITATIVE CHARACTERISTICS
> General-purpose financial reports should provide all the financial information that is *relevant* and can be *faithfully represented* subject to the constraint that the benefits of providing the information exceed the costs of providing the information. The information is enhanced by *comparability*, *verifiability*, *timeliness* and *understandability*.

The *Conceptual Framework* states that *relevant* and *faithfully represented* information should be disclosed to users subject to a cost/benefit constraint. The balance between benefits and costs is difficult and requires the exercise of judgement. The intent is that entities should not be required to provide information if the costs of providing the information are expected to exceed any benefits that may flow from the provision of such information. One of the problems is that often those who enjoy the benefits do not incur the costs. However, it is a general guide to standard setters that they should consider the costs and benefits to entities before imposing additional reporting obligations on them.

Financial statements should also report the substance and economic reality of a transaction and not merely its legal form. For example, A purports to sell an item to B but at the same time enters into an arrangement with B whereby A guarantees to purchase the item back from B in one month. Furthermore, A continues to use and enjoy the benefits from the item. The form of the transaction suggests a sale, but the substance of the arrangement is that A is borrowing money from B and using the item as collateral and no sale should be recognised by A. The objective of companies that enter into transactions of this type may be to increase reported profits and so mask underlying problems.

Traditionally, accountants have tended to overstate liabilities, understate assets, recognise unrealised losses and defer unrealised gains. This approach is known as conservatism and the *Conceptual Framework* does not regard conservatism as a required or appropriate qualitative characteristic in deciding the type of information to be disclosed in general-purpose financial reports.

DEFINITION AND RECOGNITION OF THE ELEMENTS OF FINANCIAL STATEMENTS

13 LEARNING OBJECTIVE

Explain the terms 'assets', 'liabilities', 'equity', 'income' and 'expenses'

Definitions and recognition criteria for assets, liabilities, income, expenses and equity are found in Chapter 4 of the *Conceptual Framework*. The guidance is identical to paragraphs 47 to 98 of the AASB *Framework* as the IASB is still completing the revisions to these paragraphs. Changes to definitions of some of the elements are almost certain to occur, but for the 9th edition of this book we continue to use the current definitions and make mention of the proposed definitions as at the time of writing. Each of these elements is discussed in turn and the definitions are identified as key concepts to be used in later chapters.

ASSETS

Before an item qualifies for inclusion in the financial statements (in this case the statement of financial position or balance sheet) it must not only meet the definition of an asset, it must also pass certain recognition criteria. First, it must be *probable* that the future economic benefits will eventuate and it must be possible to *reliably measure* the cost or some other value of the asset. Only when an item satisfies the definition and meets both recognition criteria will it qualify for inclusion on the balance sheet.

2.10 **KEY CONCEPT**

ASSETS

An asset is a resource controlled by the entity as a result of past events and from which future economic benefits are expected to flow to the entity.

(IASB *Conceptual Framework*, para. 4.4a). Copyright © IFRS Foundation. All rights reserved. Reproduced by Cengage Learning Australia with the permission of the IFRS Foundation ®. No permission granted to third parties to reproduce or distribute.

An asset is recognised in the balance sheet only when it is probable that the future economic benefits will flow to the entity, and it must be possible to reliably measure the cost or other value of such benefits.

The essential characteristics of an asset from the above definition include the following.

- *Future economic benefits*. This is the essence of assets and the clear implication in the term 'future economic benefits' is that for an item to be an asset there must be some clear expectation that some benefit will be derived from the item by the entity, either now or in the future, and that this benefit does not depend on physical form. This implies that the item must have some specific usefulness to the entity. An item that has no specific usefulness to the entity is not an asset. This is particularly important in times of rapidly changing technology as it suggests that the question of what is and what is not an asset can only be decided on the basis of its usefulness to the entity. For example, it is fairly obvious that a gold mine full of unmined gold is an asset for a mining business. However, there will come a point when all the gold has been removed and all that is left is a hole in the ground. The hole in the ground is no longer useful to the mining entity and ceases to be an asset. On the other hand, a hole in the ground could have future economic benefits for a different entity; for example, a rubbish disposal business.
- *Control*. Many definitions of assets imply that in order to be an asset something must be owned. In reality, most assets are owned, but the assertion that ownership is a precondition for the recognition of an asset by an entity is not correct. The entity must have the capacity to control the future economic benefits. While control often arises from legally enforceable rights, the absence of legal ownership does not automatically deny the existence of control. An example of this is a non-cancellable lease, where the lessee has control over the economic benefits embodied in the goods but the lessor maintains legal title to the goods. Thus, the lessor can resume possession of the goods, but only if the lessee is unable to meet the lease payments. On the other hand, the fact that an individual or entity owns an item does not necessarily mean that there is any future benefit to be obtained. For example, an old car that has been ordered off the road by the police may cease to be an asset, and in fact, unless it can be driven to the salvage yard, may become a liability.
- *Past events*. Only present abilities to control future economic benefits are assets. A decision at balance date to buy a new machine next year does not itself create an asset. However, if the entity has entered into an irrevocable contract to acquire the machine then a right might have been obtained and an asset created as a result of the contract. The signing of the contract is, in effect, the past event.

LIABILITIES

As is the case with assets, an item that meets the definition of a liability must also satisfy the criteria for recognition before being admitted to the balance sheet. It must be probable that settlement of the liability will be required and the amount required can be reliably measured.

2.1

CASE STUDY

HERNANDEZ THE LATEST TO COMMIT TO UNITED WITH FIVE-YEAR DEAL

By Daniel Taylor

Javier Hernandez has agreed a new five-year contract that moves him into Manchester United's higher bracket of earners and continues the club's policy of ensuring all their more valuable players are confirmed as long-term assets.

Hernandez's agreement follows the announcement on Monday that Tom Cleverley had signed a new four-year deal, meaning United have tied 13 players to contract extensions in the past year. Daniel Welbeck, who has two years to run on his current deal, has also been offered new terms though Dimitar Berbatov's position continues to look vulnerable.

Daniel Taylor, *The Guardian*, 13 October 2011. Copyright Guardian News & Media Ltd 2011.

Corbis/BPI/Matt West

COMMENTARY

The article raises the interesting question of whether a football player is an asset. The report suggests that the club sees the signing of Hernandez as a way of shoring up its long-term assets – the more valuable players. Consider whether a football player meets the definition of an asset. Manchester United controls the services of a player because of the contract it has with him. The future economic benefits relate to the value of the player's services and his resale value by way of the transfer payment, which clubs receive in the English football system when a player moves to another club. If transfer payments did not exist, as is the case in the Australian Football League, then a significant component of the future economic benefit is removed. Of course, the value of the playing service remains. The past event would be the signing of the contract.

Before being recorded on the balance sheet, an item that meets the definition of an asset must also satisfy the recognition criteria. It must be probable that the future economic benefits will flow to the entity and there must be a cost or other value that can be reliably measured. If the club had to pay an amount to secure the services of a player, as in the case of English football, then this amount would be what could be used to report the value of the player. The probability of the economic benefits flowing to the club depends on a number of issues, including a player's age, risk of injury, performance on the field, and so on.

While it is common practice for some sporting clubs to report players on balance sheets, it is not common practice with most entities to report their staff. Study the Woolworths balance sheet in Appendix 1 to see if you can locate any value for employees.

The essential characteristics of a liability from the above definition include the following.

- *Present obligation.* This means that a transaction or event in the past has created an obligation that has not yet been satisfied. As with assets, the word 'legal' is not used in the definition of a liability. The view adopted is that legal obligations alone do not give rise to liabilities. There may be other social or moral reasons that create a present obligation. For example, an entity may decide to rectify faults in one of its products even though the warranty period has expired. The entity is not legally obliged to rectify the faults, but the decision to do so imposes an obligation on the entity and the sacrifices required to honour the obligation constitute a liability.
- *Outflow of economic benefits.* The obligation must result in the entity having to sacrifice economic benefits in the future to discharge the obligation.
- *Past events.* Only present obligations to sacrifice economic benefits in the future are liabilities. An obligation that may arise in the future is not a liability.

In the Discussion paper on the *Conceptual Framework* issued by the IASB in 2013, changes are proposed to the definitions of assets and liabilities. The proposed definitions being considered are:

- An asset of an entity is a present economic resource controlled by the entity as a result of past events.
- A liability of an entity is a present obligation of the entity to transfer an economic resource as a result of past events. (IASB 2013, para. 2.11. Copyright © IFRS Foundation. All rights reserved. Reproduced by Cengage Learning Australia with the permission of the IFRS Foundation ®. No permission granted to third parties to reproduce or distribute.)

We use the current definitions in this 9th edition as any changes to these definitions will not be finalised while this edition is in print.

EQUITY

The definition of equity within the IASB *Conceptual Framework* is similar to that adopted by the Financial Accounting Standards Board in the USA. It is a residual definition whereby the identification of equity is dependent on the recognition of assets and liabilities. Consequently, unlike the other four elements of financial statements, the definition of equity does not require recognition criteria.

EXPENSES

Before expenses are recognised in the income statement, it must be probable that the decrease in economic benefits has occurred and that the amount can be reliably measured.

KEY CONCEPT

EXPENSES

Expenses are decreases in economic benefits during the accounting period in the form of outflows or depletions of assets or incurrence of liabilities that result in decreases in equity other than those relating to distributions to equity participants.

(IASB Conceptual Framework, para. 4.25b). Copyright © IFRS Foundation. All rights reserved. Reproduced by Cengage Learning Australia with the permission of the IFRS Foundation ®. No permission granted to third parties to reproduce or distribute.

An expense is recognised in the income statement only when it is probable the decrease in economic benefits has occurred and the amount can be reliably measured.

INCOME

As with the other elements, income is recognised in the financial statements only when it is probable that the inflow, or other enhancement, or decrease in liabilities has occurred and can be reliably measured.

KEY CONCEPT

INCOME

Income is increases in economic benefits during the accounting period in the form of inflows or enhancements of assets or decreases of liabilities that result in increases in equity, other than those relating to contributions from equity participants.

(IASB Conceptual Framework, para. 4.25a). Copyright © IFRS Foundation. All rights reserved. Reproduced by Cengage Learning Australia with the permission of the IFRS Foundation ®. No permission granted to third parties to reproduce or distribute.

Income is recognised in the income statement only when it is probable the inflow or other enhancement has occurred and the amount can be reliably measured.

The definition of income is consistent with that of expenses, and does not differentiate gains from other revenues. In Australia we previously used the term 'revenue' for what the IASB calls 'income'.

The IASB uses the term 'revenue' in International Accounting Standard (IAS) 18 *Revenue*, as defined in Key concept 2.15, and because of the adoption of IFRS in Australia, we now use the same definition. Revenue is, in fact, a subset of income but is not defined as a separate element in the *Conceptual Framework*.

KEY CONCEPT

REVENUE

Revenue is the gross inflows of economic benefits during the period arising in the course of the *ordinary activities* of an entity when those inflows result in increases in equity, other than those relating to contributions from equity participants.

(AASB 118, para. 7)

2.16 KEY CONCEPT

THE INTERRELATIONSHIP BETWEEN INCOME, REVENUE AND GAINS

In accordance with IASB definitions and terminology:

» income = revenue + gains

» revenue = inflows from ordinary activities

» gains = all other inflows.

MEASUREMENT OF THE ELEMENTS OF FINANCIAL STATEMENTS

One of the recognition criteria outlined in the *Conceptual Framework* is that an element must have a cost or other value that can be reliably measured. It is probably the most difficult area, but one which is critical to the accounting process. The IASB *Conceptual Framework* deals with measurement in paragraphs 4.54 to 4.56.

The four bases of measurement outlined in paragraph 4.54 of the IASB *Conceptual Framework* are:

- historic cost
- current cost
- realisable (settlement) value
- present value.

Each of these methods is discussed in detail in Chapter 4. We also add fair value to this list as it is a method of measurement that is now used in many accounting standards. The *Conceptual Framework* states that while historic cost is the most common measurement method, it is normally used in combination with other measurement bases. The IASB discussion paper issued in 2013 addresses the issue of measurement of the elements of financial statements.

14 LEARNING OBJECTIVE

Identify the role of the audit and the auditor in financial reporting

External audits

Users of GPFS wish to be assured that the information contained in these statements represents a true and fair assessment of the economic activities of the entity being reviewed. As mentioned earlier in this chapter, the person who audits general-purpose financial statements is the auditor. The auditor is seen as an *independent* external observer who is called upon, in the case of a company, to express an opinion that the reports provide a 'true and fair' representation of the company's financial status.

It is important to stress here that the directors of public companies, not auditors, are responsible for the preparation and presentation of a company's general-purpose financial statements. The purpose of an external audit is to add credibility to the reports presented by the directors. Most large companies also have an *internal auditor* who is responsible for making sure that correct processes are being followed.

2.17 KEY CONCEPT

EXTERNAL AUDIT

The external audit aims to provide assurance to absentee owners (shareholders) that the financial statements of the company provide a true and fair view of the company's financial position, performance and cash flows.

An efficient internal audit process can reduce the time required by the external auditor, thus helping to reduce the cost of the external audit.

All companies, except small private companies and some large private companies, must have their accounts audited as required by the *Corporations Act*. Other entities, such as banks, insurance companies, credit unions, building societies and some unions, are also required to be audited under separate legislation. In fact, many not-for-profit organisations, for whom there is no statutory requirement to do so, choose to present audited accounts to show users that their accounts can be relied upon. Examples of not-for-profit organisations include sporting organisations, clubs and societies. All public sector entities have their financial statements audited by the Auditor-General's office.

The external auditor, as noted above, does not prepare general-purpose financial statements; this is the responsibility of the company's directors. The auditor's task is to review the accounting systems used to prepare the reports, to check on the accuracy of certain transactions (particularly those involving large dollar amounts) and to state that the accounts have been prepared in accordance with the *Corporations Act* and applicable accounting standards, and that they provide a true and fair view of the entity. For annual reports, all reporting entities are required to obtain an audit opinion as to the truth and fairness of the GPFS. For interim reports, entities can choose whether they provide a full audit opinion or an audit review. An audit review does not involve a detailed audit, so the auditor is not able to express an audit opinion, only a statement about the GPFS.

You should now read the independent audit report prepared by Deloitte for the Woolworths 2013 financial report (Appendix 1).

THE AUDITOR

A person who is appointed as a company auditor is required, under the *Corporations Act*, to meet certain requirements. Briefly, the auditor must:
- have the appropriate tertiary qualifications and have completed a prescribed course in auditing or have other qualifications or experience that ASIC considers equivalent to both requirements
- meet one of the following practical experience requirements
  - satisfy all the components of an ASIC-approved competency standard
  - have the level of practical experience that is prescribed in the Corporations Regulations or experience that ASIC considers equivalent

- satisfy ASIC that he/she is capable of performing the duties of an auditor and is otherwise a fit and proper person to be registered as an auditor.

The shareholders at an annual general meeting appoint the auditor, though in practice, management usually provides the name of an auditor for approval by shareholders.

The auditor is required to form an opinion on the GPFS of a company, to determine whether proper records have been kept, and to report to shareholders. The auditor must also inform ASIC of any suspected wrongdoing by management or any non-compliance with applicable accounting standards.

The auditor can be removed only by special notice, given at the annual general meeting, and the commission must be informed. The commission has the power to stop an auditor from resigning or being removed from office.

Besides the statutory requirements noted above, the auditor is bound by professional obligations, which cover:
- independence, integrity, confidentiality and ethical considerations
- conformity with accounting and auditing standards, auditing guidelines and statements of auditing practice.

15 LEARNING OBJECTIVE

Explain what is meant by the term 'expectation gap'

THE EXPECTATION GAP

As discussed previously, the directors of a company are responsible for preparing the accounts, and the auditors are responsible for seeing that those accounts have been prepared according to statutory and professional requirements. Are auditors responsible for detecting fraud or illegal acts? The law requires auditors to exercise due care when forming their opinion; it does not require them to detect fraud, though if a suspicion is aroused it must be acted upon.

During the past decade the auditing profession has been criticised for not fulfilling what is seen as its role. This criticism has arisen, in part at least, because a number of companies have failed after being given an unqualified opinion by an auditor. The difference between what an auditor is required to do and what is expected by users is known as the expectation gap.

The reporting of fraud and illegal acts, whether actual or suspected, is a requirement of the *Corporations Act*. The problem the auditor faces is that it is often extremely difficult to detect a well-organised fraud, particularly where more than one party is involved. An auditor does not check every transaction of a business, but instead selects a sample to test. While the sampling methods are based on statistical methodologies, the reality is that the auditor does not check every transaction. For this to happen, the cost of an audit would be prohibitively high.

Therefore, the auditor uses a sampling method to test certain transactions so that he or she can be reasonably assured that the financial statements provide a true and fair view of the entity. This is not a guarantee that every error in the financial statements of a business has been detected. This in part explains

KEY CONCEPT

2.18

EXPECTATION GAP

The expectation gap describes the difference between the role performed by the auditor and the role that shareholders expect of the auditor.

STOP AND THINK 6

Are auditors required to check the accuracy of financial statements? Should they be?

why there is an expectation gap. The audit profession continues to grapple with the problem of fraud and illegal acts and professional pronouncements continue to be updated.

INDEPENDENCE

16 LEARNING OBJECTIVE

Explain the concept of audit independence and why it is so important

The *Corporations Law Economic Reform Program (CLERP 9)* included a number of changes to the *Corporations Act*, one of which related to the relationship between an auditor and his/her client and the independence of the auditor. These amendments resulted from concerns about the lack of audit independence in high-profile company failures such as Enron.

The auditor in Enron was providing a range of services to the client, not just audit. Other services related to tax, corporate finance, accounting, IT and an internal audit. In many cases like Enron, the fees received for non-audit services far exceed the audit fee. The concern here is that the auditor may be reluctant to be critical of the company because he or she relies on the other fees he/she receives. Consequently, companies in Australia are now required to disclose the fees they pay to auditors for all the services carried out in addition to the audit. They must also provide a statement as to why any additional fees have not compromised the independence of the audit. Auditors must make a declaration about their independence (see Appendix 1).

One of the other issues in the Enron case involved the appropriateness of ex-partners of Arthur Andersen (Enron's auditor) serving as directors on the Enron board. It was felt that such persons would not be truly independent directors. This also had the potential to affect the independence of the auditor because the former audit partner's firm was still engaged to do the audit. In Australia there is a two-year ban on former audit partners taking up positions as directors on the boards of former clients.

There is also a requirement for an automatic rotation of an audit partner after five years. The reason for this requirement relates to audit independence. There is a view that after being in charge of an audit for five years, the partner would be very familiar with the client and this might potentially impair his/her independence. ASIC has power to provide some relief to this requirement but only in limited circumstances. The professional accounting bodies have a professional standard that deals with professional independence. It provides a guide to issues associated with independence. This professional standard has also been revised and reissued in response to events like the failure of Enron.

2.19

KEY CONCEPT

AUDITOR INDEPENDENCE

Auditor independence means that the auditor must be independent of the client for whom the audit is conducted so that he/she is able to express a truly objective opinion about the financial statements.

It is essential that external auditors maintain independence from audit clients so that they can properly fulfil their duties and give unbiased opinions about firms' financial statements. Failure to maintain this independence, whether real or perceived, can only harm the image of the profession. It also serves to reinforce the expectation gap as a non-independent auditor is more likely to overlook events and transactions, as was the case in Enron. Moreover, when a company fails, shareholders have the right to ask, 'How could the auditor not see that something was seriously wrong?'

STOP AND THINK 7

Should auditors be allowed to provide non-audit services to an audit client?

SUMMARY

IDENTIFY THE FACTORS THAT INFLUENCE THE PREPARATION OF FINANCIAL STATEMENTS

While the chapter's emphasis was on companies in the private sector, much of what was discussed also applies to the public and not-for-profit sectors. As the financial reports of companies are the most regulated, most of the discussion related to issues affecting companies. The major influences on financial reporting for companies in Australia are:

- the IASB *Conceptual Framework*
- accounting standards
- the *Corporations Act*
- securities exchange listing requirements.
    For public sector and NFP entities there will be other influencing factors, like the relevant state legislation.

IDENTIFY THREE FORMS OF BUSINESS ARRANGEMENT: A SOLE TRADER, A PARTNERSHIP AND A COMPANY

A sole trader is a business run by one person and a partnership involves two or more parties. Neither of these forms of business is a separate legal entity. A company, however, is a separate legal entity.

IDENTIFY THE CHARACTERISTICS OF A SOLE TRADER

A one-owner business is a common form of business organisation, and is simple to set up. All that is required is a business bank account. Because it is so simple and because it has no recognition in law, there are no formal guidelines for the format of the accounts, except in the situation where the sole trader is a reporting entity.

EXPLAIN THE ADVANTAGES AND DISADVANTAGES OF A PARTNERSHIP

The advantages of forming a partnership (as a form of organisation) are:

- ease of formation
- limited rules and regulations
- provision of capital and expertise
- more favourable tax position.
    The disadvantages of a partnership include:
- limited life
- unlimited liability
- mutual agency.

EXPLAIN THE ADVANTAGES AND DISADVANTAGES OF A COMPANY

The advantages of companies as a form of organisation are:

- separate legal entity
- limited liability

- ease of transfer of ownership
- no mutual agency
- professional management
- continuous existence.
    Disadvantages of the company structure include:
- taxation
- regulation
- limited liability
- separation of ownership and control.

LEARNING OBJECTIVE 6

IDENTIFY THE MAJOR DIFFERENCES BETWEEN THE STATEMENT OF COMPREHENSIVE INCOME AND BALANCE SHEET OF A COMPANY AND A PARTNERSHIP OR SOLE TRADER

There are many differences between the financial statements of a company and either a partnership or a sole trader. For example, the balance sheet for a company contains shareholders' equity, which includes paid-up capital, retained profits and reserves. A sole trader or partnership does not need to prepare a statement of comprehensive income but a partnership may prepare a statement of partner's capital accounts. In addition, unlike a partnership or a sole trader, a company is required to pay taxation.

LEARNING OBJECTIVE 7

EXPLAIN THE MAIN CHARACTERISTICS OF THE FINANCIAL STATEMENTS OF A PUBLIC COMPANY AND THE ROLE AND MEANING OF CONSOLIDATED FINANCIAL STATEMENTS

Public companies prepare financial statements that have a shareholder's equity section, and many prepare consolidated financial statements that report the results and financial position of the combination of the parent entity and the other entities it controls.

LEARNING OBJECTIVE 8

EXPLAIN THE CURRENT FRAMEWORK FOR STANDARD SETTING IN AUSTRALIA

The FRC has oversight responsibility for both accounting and auditing standards in Australia. It is responsible for the appointment of all members (except the chairperson) to the AASB and the AUASB. The AASB is responsible for establishing accounting standards in Australia. The AUASB is responsible for establishing auditing standards.

LEARNING OBJECTIVE 9

EXPLAIN THE INFLUENCE OF ACCOUNTING STANDARDS, THE *CORPORATIONS ACT 2001* AND THE AUSTRALIAN SECURITIES EXCHANGE LISTING RULES ON FINANCIAL REPORTING REQUIREMENTS

The government-appointed AASB produces accounting standards that, under the *Corporations Act*, are mandatory for all companies that are reporting entities. The AASB sets accounting standards for all entities in both the private and public sectors. These standards are now the equivalent of IFRSs. The AASB has a full-time chair and employs a number of technical staff.

In addition to accounting standards, interpretations and accounting concepts also influence the preparation of external financial reports. The external financial reports prepared by companies are also influenced by certain requirements within the *Corporations Act*. In particular, the requirements of AASB standards, the directors' report, the directors' statement and the auditor's report influence the external financial reports prepared by companies. For this reason, a number of companies expend considerable resources to provide input to the standards-setting process.

For listed public companies, the Listing Rules of the Australian Securities Exchange require companies to present half-yearly reports, preliminary final statements and additional details in their annual reports. Under the *Corporate Law Reform Act 1994*, disclosing entities are also required to prepare yearly and half-yearly accounts and comply with continuous disclosure requirements.

LEARNING OBJECTIVE 10

EXPLAIN WHAT IS MEANT BY A CONCEPTUAL FRAMEWORK

A conceptual framework is a series of concepts or ideas that determine how financial reports are prepared for general users. It is an attempt to establish the foundations for the preparation of general-purpose financial reports.

LEARNING OBJECTIVE 11

IDENTIFY THE ROLE OF A CONCEPTUAL FRAMEWORK

The proposed benefits of having a conceptual framework include:

*   a reduction in the number of accounting standards required
*   more consistency in accounting standards
*   improved communication among parties involved in the preparation of general-purpose financial reports
*   the provision of a defence against the actions of lobby groups.

LEARNING OBJECTIVE 12

EXPLAIN THE TERMS 'REPORTING ENTITY', 'GENERAL-PURPOSE FINANCIAL STATEMENTS', 'QUALITATIVE CHARACTERISTICS', AND EXPLAIN THE OBJECTIVE OF GENERAL-PURPOSE FINANCIAL REPORTING

A reporting entity is an entity where there are dependent users who rely upon a general-purpose financial report to assist in economic decision making. General-purpose financial statements must include:

*   a statement of comprehensive income
*   a statement of financial position (balance sheet)
*   a statement of changes in equity
*   a statement of cash flows
*   notes to the financial statements.

The two principal qualitative characteristics are *relevance* and *faithful representation* of the information. *Verifiability*, *timeliness*, *understandability* and *comparability* enhance the relevance and faithful representation of information. The qualitative characteristics are subject to a cost/benefit constraint.

The objective of general-purpose financial reporting is defined as providing information to assist users in making decisions about the resources of the entity.

LEARNING OBJECTIVE 13

EXPLAIN THE TERMS 'ASSETS', 'LIABILITIES', 'EQUITY', 'INCOME', 'REVENUE' AND 'EXPENSES'

An asset is a resource that is controlled by the entity as a result of past events and from which future economic benefits are expected to flow to the entity. A liability is defined as a present obligation of the entity arising from past events, the settlement of which is expected to result in an outflow from the entity of resources embodying economic benefits. Assets and liabilities are only recognised in the balance sheet when it is probable that the future benefits will flow to the entity (asset) or resources will flow out of the entity (liability) and the amount can be reliably measured. Equity is the residual interest in the assets of the entity after deducting all its liabilities.

Income is increases in economic benefits during the accounting period in the form of inflows or enhancements of assets, or decreases in liabilities that result in increases in equity (other than those relating to contributions from equity participants). Revenue is defined in AASB 118 as the same as income except the inflows are from an entity's ordinary operations. Thus, income includes revenues and other gains.

Expenses are decreases in economic benefits during the accounting period in the form of outflows or depletions of assets or the incurrence of liabilities that result in decreases in equity (other than those relating to distributions to equity participants).

LEARNING OBJECTIVE 14

IDENTIFY THE ROLE OF THE AUDIT AND THE AUDITOR IN FINANCIAL REPORTING

Auditors are there to give some assurance as to the truth and fairness of financial statements but cannot guarantee that they are absolutely correct and free of errors. They provide an audit opinion in the case of annual reports or an audit review in the case of half-yearly reports.

LEARNING OBJECTIVE 15

EXPLAIN WHAT IS MEANT BY THE TERM 'EXPECTATION GAP'

The expectation gap describes the difference between the actual and the perceived role of the auditor and the audit process.

LEARNING OBJECTIVE 16

EXPLAIN THE CONCEPT OF AUDIT INDEPENDENCE AND WHY IT IS SO IMPORTANT

Audit independence is concerned with ensuring that auditors are able to give an independent opinion with regard to the financial statements of an audit client. The concern is that auditors may be reluctant to be critical of clients when they rely on other fees that are received from them or they have a close relationship with a client's management.

REVIEW QUESTIONS

1   Explain the difference between a sole trader and a partnership.

2   Why is it advantageous to set up a business as a limited company?

3   What are the differences between a sole trader and a limited liability (limited by shares) company?

4   Explain the differences between a limited liability (limited by shares), an unlimited liability, and a no-liability company.

5　Why do you think that mining companies are allowed to set up as no-liability companies?

6　Discuss the advantages and disadvantages of a partnership.

7　What do you think the phrase 'it's only a $2 company' means?

8　Discuss the various influences on external financial reporting for companies in Australia.

9　What are consolidated financial statements? What is their purpose?

10　Explain what is meant by the term 'controlled entity'.

11　Why might a company invest in another company?

12　What is a conceptual framework of accounting?

13　In your own words, define a reporting entity.

14　Discuss who uses general-purpose financial statements and why they require such statements.

15　Discuss the difference between control and ownership in terms of the definition of an asset.

16　'The conceptual framework approach to setting accounting standards is not about defining ideal accounting practices but about legitimising current practice, maintaining social and economic status and staving off attempts by the government to control standard setting.' Discuss.

17　What is your understanding of the term 'conservatism'?

18　Give some examples, other than those in the text, of financial information that can be faithfully represented but is irrelevant and relevant financial information which cannot be faithfully represented.

19　What is the purpose of an external audit?

20　What is meant by the expectation gap in relation to auditing?

21　Do you think that public financial statements would present a 'true and fair' view if they were not audited?

22　You are considering investing in two similar types of private companies. One has an unqualified audit report and the other has no audit report. How important is this to you in making your decision?

PROBLEMS FOR DISCUSSION AND ANALYSIS

1　Refer to the Woolworths financial report for 30 June 2013 in Appendix 1.

  a　On what basis are the accounts prepared?

  b　Who are the auditors of Woolworths Limited?

  c　How much does Woolworths pay for the audit and for other services? Is there an issue for audit independence? (You will need to access the entire annual report to answer this question. Go to www.woolworthslimited.com.au.)

2　Use your own words to express your understanding of these terms:

  a　an asset

  b　a liability

  c　equity

  d　an expense

  e　income.

3 Partners Mike and Phil share profits and losses in proportion to their fixed capital balances. The following balances were taken from the partnership's books as at 30 June 20X9:

	$
Cash	3 000
Accounts receivable	12 500
Inventory	8 400
Plant	100 000
Accumulated depreciation	3 000
Creditors	8 600
Capital: Mike	36 320
Capital: Phil	54 480
Sales	210 000
Cost of goods sold	163 000
Selling expenses	7 316
Depreciation expense	4 322
Financial expenses	1 827
General expenses	12 035

a On the basis of the above figures, calculate the profit for the period.

b What was the amount of profit/loss allocated to each partner?

4 Steve Hill and Lee Down formed a partnership, investing $250 000 and $200 000 respectively. Determine their participation in the year's profit of $150 000 under each of the following independent assumptions:

a no agreement concerning division of profit

b profit to be divided in the ratio of original capital investment

c interest at the rate of 10 per cent allowed on original investments and the remainder divided in the ratio of 2:3

d salary allowances of $65 000 and $70 000 respectively, and the balance divided equally

e allowance of interest at the rate of 10 per cent on original investments, salary allowances of $65 000 and $70 000 respectively, and the remainder divided equally.

5 Andrew Glen and Norman Dale have decided to form a partnership. They have agreed that Glen is to invest $150 000 and Dale is to invest $220 000. Glen will work full-time in the business, and Dale is to work half-time. The following plans for the division of profit are being considered:

a equal division

b in the ratio of original investments

c in the ratio of time devoted to the business

d interest of 10 per cent on original investments and the remainder in the ratio of 5 : 3

e interest of 10 per cent on original investments, salary allowances of $110 000 to Glen and $40 000 to Dale, and the remainder equally

f plan (e) except that Glen is also to be allowed a bonus equal to 20 per cent of the amount by which profit exceeds the salary allowances.

Required

For each plan, determine the division of the profit under each of the following assumptions:

i Profit of $276 000

ii Profit of $162 000.

Present the data in table form, using the following column headings:

	$276 000		$162 000	
Plan	Andrew Glen	Norman Dale	Andrew Glen	Norman Dale

6 Give three examples of a liability. How do your examples meet the criteria listed in Key concept 2.11? Do not use examples from the text.

7 Give three examples of an asset. How do your examples meet the criteria listed in Key concept 2.10? Do not use examples from the text.

8 ABC Ltd is being sued by a client for $100 000. The company's legal advisers say that there is only a 35 per cent chance of an unfavourable outcome. At the end of the financial year, the case has still to go to court. Should the $100 000 be reported as a liability?

9 Vanessa raised a $15 000 000 loan to fund the exploration that lead to the discovery of a deposit of silver.

a Does the deposit of silver meet the definition of an asset to Vanessa according to the AASB Framework? Why?/Why not?

b Under what circumstances may the deposit of silver be recognised in the balance sheet of Vanessa according to the AASB Framework?

c Does the loan meet the definition and recognition criteria of a liability to Vanessa during the term of the loan, according to provisions of the AASB Framework?

10 a Refer to Case study 2.1. Do you believe a football player should be recognised as an asset on Manchester United's balance sheet? What about a player who plays for the local community football club?

b Go to the website for the Liverpool Football Club at www.liverpoolfc.tv/. Review the club's annual report and explain how the club accounts for its players.

11 Most of the major airlines offer 'frequent traveller' specials where travellers can receive free flights, upgrades from economy to first or business class, or free accommodation packages. Some airlines have been trying to gain more market share by giving double-kilometres credit for each flight. How should the airlines account for frequent flyer points that have been issued to travellers but not yet redeemed? Are they a liability?

12 Why do you think companies take an active interest in the standard-setting process of the accounting profession?

13 Given that general-purpose financial reports are aimed at providing information that is 'useful to existing and potential investors, lenders and other creditors in making decisions about providing resources to the entity', discuss to what extent these users are represented in the due process.

14 Discuss and explain the different reporting requirements for public and private companies. Why do you think some private companies are exempted from regulatory standards?

15 You are discussing the financial position of a company with a friend. The friend is considering buying shares in the company and comments, 'I can't rely on the audit report as it does not guarantee the financial statements are correct'. Your friend knows you have just completed an accounting subject and asks you for your opinion about the value of the audit report. What would you say to your friend?

16 Roy Dorro is running a small accounting practice with annual fees of $100 000. He is approached by the CEO of a company that has just established premises in Roy's area. The CEO wants Roy to conduct the annual audit for the company and has indicated that a fee of $50 000 would be provided for the audit. Should Roy have any concerns about audit independence if he were to accept the engagement?

17 Examine the following cases for Ruliable Ltd and indicate whether you believe the company should recognise a liability.

   a Potential costs due to the discovery of a possible defect related to one of its products. It is probable that claims will be made and the costs can be reliably estimated.

   b There is a potential claim for damages to be paid from a lawsuit filed this year against another company. It is probable that the proceeds from the claim will be paid by Ruliable next year.

   c The company has a policy whereby it overhauls its major machinery every five years. This has been its practice for the last 25 years. At the balance date, the machinery had been overhauled three years previously.

18 For the current year ended 30 June, the results of operations of Hawkeye Corporation and its wholly owned subsidiary, Radar Enterprises, are as follows:

	HAWKEYE CORPORATION		RADAR ENTERPRISES	
	$	$	$	$
Sales		8 150 000		750 000
Cost of inventory sold	5 000 000		440 000	
Selling expenses	800 000		75 000	
Administrative expenses	600 000		35 000	
Interest expense (revenue)	(30 000)	6 370 000	30 000	580 000
Profit		1 780 000		170 000
Other comprehensive income		0		0
Total comprehensive income		1 780 000		170 000

During the year, Hawkeye sold inventory to Radar for $80 000. The inventory was sold by Radar to non-affiliated companies for $120 000. Hawkeye's interest revenue was realised from a long-term loan to Radar.

a   Determine the amounts to be eliminated from the following items in preparing a consolidated statement of comprehensive income for the current year:

i   sales

ii   cost of inventory sold.

b   Determine the consolidated profit.

19   Given the simplified balance sheet of Bazz Ltd and Lee Ltd, prepare a worksheet for the consolidation of the accounts of the parent company (Bazz Ltd) and its subsidiary (Lee Ltd). From your worksheet, prepare the consolidated balance sheet.

The following items need to be taken into consideration:

• Bazz Ltd acquired all the shares of Lee Ltd for $320 000 on the morning of 30 June 20X1.

• All assets and liabilities are stated at their fair values.

• Lee Ltd owed Bazz Ltd $10 000 for goods purchased on 15 June 20X1.

BAZZ LTD LEE LTD
BALANCE SHEET AT 30 JUNE 20X1

	BAZZ LTD	LEE LTD
	$	$
Assets		
Current assets		
Bank	180 000	50 000
Accounts receivable	100 000	150 000
Total current assets	280 000	200 000
Non-current assets		
Plant and equipment (net of depreciation)	300 000	300 000
Investment in Lee Ltd	320 000	–
Total non-current assets	620 000	300 000
Total assets	900 000	500 000
Liabilities		
Current liabilities		
Accounts payable	400 000	180 000
Total liabilities	400 000	180 000
Net assets	500 000	320 000
Equity		
Paid-up capital	400 000	300 000
Retained profits	100 000	20 000
Total equity	500 000	320 000

20 Bev and Daniel want to buy a business of their own. Bev is a schoolteacher and Daniel has worked in the public service and has a degree in commerce. They decide to buy a delicatessen, and choose one close to their home. The shop has been there for several years, but has not been a great success. Bev and Daniel will have to borrow a large amount of money to finance the purchase.

Required

You have been asked to advise the following:

a What form of organisation should they adopt for the business, a partnership or a company?

b Will the choice of organisation affect the availability of finance for their business? Explain.

c What skills will Bev and Daniel need to manage the business?

d How can they raise the required finance? What security do you think they will need to provide?

(Adapted from R. Craven, I. Urquhart and R. Woolley, *Case Studies in Accounting*, 3rd edn, VCTA Publishing, 1985, Case 3–3 and p. 36.)

21 The Magic Lawn Corporation is a family-owned company that produces and sells lawn care products. The company has recently developed a new product that enhances the water retention properties of all types of lawn. The potential for this product is unlimited, but in order to capitalise on its potential, the company needs a substantial injection of cash into the business. At present, the family owns all 10 000 shares of $1 value that have been issued. The shareholders' section of the most recent balance sheet is as follows:

	$
10 000 $1 value shares fully paid	10 000
Retained profits	2 990 000
	3 000 000

Following are the options that are being considered by the family in order to raise the additional cash:

a a five-year bank loan for $3 million – interest rate 10 per cent, payable annually in arrears; principal to be repaid at the end of five years

b converting to a public company and issuing 600 000 shares at an estimated market price of $5. Family members will have priority in the purchase of shares

c the issue of 600 000, 6 per cent, $5 cumulative preference shares to an investment company. The shares will be redeemable at the discretion of the Magic Lawn Corporation.

There are two important issues for the company:

i The company has always been family owned and they are concerned about losing control of the company.

ii The company has always had cash flow problems. Options (a) and (c) both involve regular cash payments for interest or dividends.

Write a report to the family outlining the advantages and disadvantages of each option. The tax rate for companies is 30 per cent. Interest is tax-deductible but dividends are not.

22 Bob Strongarm and Phil Hannock are partners in a consulting business. In the last three years, Bob's share of partnership profits has been $15 000, $20 000 and $30 000. He has been offered $80 000 for his share of the partnership. Bob decides that if his total share of profits over the next three years is less than $100 000 he will sell. The following schedule sets out some estimates of profits for the next three years:

SCHEDULE

	TOTAL PARTNERSHIP PROFITS		
	YEAR 1	YEAR 2	YEAR 3
Optimistic estimate	75 000	85 000	95 000
Most probable estimate	55 000	65 000	75 000
Pessimistic estimate	45 000	55 000	65 000

Bob and Phil currently share profits as follows: Bob receives a salary of $20 000, Phil's salary is $15 000, and the remainder is split with Bob getting 60 per cent.

Required

Calculate Bob's share of the profits over the next three years if his optimistic estimate is correct.

a Calculate Bob's share of the profits over the next three years if his most probable estimate is correct.

b Calculate Bob's share of the profits over the next three years if his pessimistic estimate is correct.

c If the probabilities are 20 per cent that the optimistic estimate will be correct, 60 per cent that the most probable estimate will be correct, and 20 per cent that the pessimistic estimate will be correct, should Bob sell for $80 000?

d Discuss the other factors Bob should consider when deciding whether or not to sell.

23 Tom has been employed at New Incentives Ltd for six months, after recently graduating from university with a degree in accounting. It is his first job after trying to find employment for six months. Tom's boss has asked him for a favour in preparing the income statement for the year. She wants Tom to include in income, cash received for services to be provided next year. She also wants him to record as an asset, cash paid for advertisements that were screened on television two weeks before the end of the accounting period. Tom is aware that management is to be paid bonuses based on the net profit for the period.

Discuss

a how the transactions should be reported according to your understanding of the IASB *Conceptual Framework*

b what Tom should do.

SUGGESTED ANSWERS TO STOP AND THINK EXERCISES IN THE CHAPTER

1   A company allows funds to be raised from members of the public. Therefore, it provides greater access to funds than a partnership. However, companies are subject to more rules and regulations and these rules are increasing in the wake of the collapse of companies like HIH, Enron and WorldCom. Shareholders in a limited company are only liable for the amount paid on their shares, whereas partners may be jointly and severally liable for all partners' debts. A company is a separate legal entity whereas a partnership is not.

2   An organisation's form (i.e. sole trader, partnership or company) determines the format of the final accounts in the following ways:
    – Sole traders: final accounts contain one or more owners' accounts.
    – Partnerships: final accounts contain current and capital accounts.
    – Companies: reports are governed by statutes, and are subject to accounting standards and audits.

3   Accounting standards are prepared and issued by the Australian Accounting Standards Board (AASB). These standards are legal standards and must be followed by all corporate reporting entities and disclosing entities pursuant with the *Corporations Act*. Members of the accounting bodies in Australia must also follow these standards when preparing accounts for other types of entities. AASB standards must be approved by federal Parliament, which has veto power. From 1 January 2005 the standards issued by the AASB have been equivalent to the IFRSs, as issued by the IASB.

4   There will be less of a need to develop accounting standards on every issue; hence, there should be fewer accounting standards.
    – Those accounting standards still required should be more consistent than is the case at present.
    – Using the same definitions for basic concepts such as assets and liabilities should improve communication among accountants, the standard setters and the constituents.
    – Standard-setting bodies should develop standards that are consistent with the conceptual framework. Hence, standard setters will be more accountable. At the same time they will be able to better resist the lobbying efforts of parties with vested interests on certain issues.

5   The reporting entity concept allows entities that do not have users who are dependent on general-purpose financial statements to avoid the unnecessary costs involved in the preparation of such statements. These costs are incurred in complying with all accounting standards and concept statements. An example is a family company where the family members do not need general-purpose financial statements to tell them how their business is performing because of their close involvement in its running. While AASB 1053 adopts a publicly accountable criterion in deciding whether an entity applies full IFRS or reduced disclosures, the reporting entity concept is important in deciding if the entity prepares GPFS.

6   Auditors are required to give an opinion as to the truth and fairness of financial statements, and whether they comply with accounting standards and the *Corporations Act*. In so doing, they give some assurance that there are no material errors. However, immaterial errors can slip through the audit. It is the director's responsibility to prepare the financial statements; therefore, the auditors should not be expected to guarantee that they are 100 per cent accurate.

7   This is a difficult and controversial question. In the USA the *Sarbanes-Oxley Act 2002* places restrictions on the type of services, other than auditing, that an audit firm can provide to an audit client. The approach in Australia involves some restrictions and more disclosure about the fees an auditor derives from the provision of other services to an audit client. The real issue is auditor independence, and some argue that an auditor can provide other services and still be independent due to professionalism. Others disagree and, partially as a result of what happened with Enron, argue for restrictions on the amount and type of other services an auditor can provide to audit clients.

CENGAGENOW

Go to http:\\login.cengagebrain.com to link to CengageNOW, your online study tool. First take the Pre-Test for this chapter to get your Personalised Study Plan, and then:

- revise your understanding of the key terms related to the financial reporting framework by completing the online crossword
- follow the links to financial reporting requirements and accounting standards
- explore the frameworks and policy statements of ASIC, AASB and IASB.

   After you have completed the activities in your Personalised Study Plan take the Post-Test to determine what concepts you have mastered and what you still need work on.

3

ETHICS AND CORPORATE GOVERNANCE

LEARNING OBJECTIVES

At the end of this chapter, you should be able to:

1 discuss the importance of ethics in accounting, and business in general

2 explain what is meant by ethical behaviour

3 identify the factors that should help determine appropriate ethical behaviour for accountants

4 explain what is meant by the term 'corporate governance'

5 identify the eight ASX Corporate Governance Council principles

6 discuss the issues associated with the role of the board of directors in corporate governance

7 discuss the issues associated with the role of the audit committee in corporate governance

8 identify the approaches to enforcing corporate governance requirements in Australia and the USA.

INTRODUCTION

The early part of the twenty-first century will be remembered in the world of business for the very high-profile collapses of companies such as Enron and Lehman Brothers among others in the USA, Vivendi and Parmalat in Europe, and the Hastie Group and Centro among others in Australia. The sub-prime lending debacle precipitated the Global Financial Crisis which resulted in unprecedented problems with the world's financial system. This caused governments in many countries to intervene to guarantee bank loans and acquire shares in many banks. The failure of such high-profile companies and banks raises serious concerns about many issues, including ethical behaviour, regulation of financial institutions, transparency of financial reporting, the appropriateness of accounting standards and corporate governance.

In this chapter we look at the issue of ethics and ethical behaviour in business. We examine different views of ethical behaviour and discuss the consequences of unethical behaviour. We then discuss corporate governance and explain what is meant by internal and external corporate governance. We examine issues associated with the role of boards of directors and the audit committees as part of corporate governance. We highlight the corporate governance requirements in Australia and other countries.

1 LEARNING OBJECTIVE

Discuss the importance of ethics in accounting, and business in general

ETHICS IN BUSINESS AND ACCOUNTING

Figures show that corporate fraud costs billions of dollars each year, as shown by the collapse of companies in the US, Italy and Australia. How does a large public company like Centro collapse, resulting in the loss of billions of dollars? How do we solve problems of corporate fraud and embezzlement?

Dr Rushworth Kidder, president of the Institute for Global Ethics in the USA, argues that this will not happen if companies adopt codes of ethics and create departments responsible for monitoring these codes. Employees should receive training about the codes of ethics and be required to follow them.

2 LEARNING OBJECTIVE

Explain what is meant by ethical behaviour

What are ethics?

Much has been written on business or professional ethics, but very few writers have attempted to define this term, perhaps believing that it needs no definition. What do we mean by *ethics*?

If we go back several thousand years we see that the word is derived from the Greek *e-thikos* (from 'ethos', meaning custom or usage). As employed by Aristotle, the term included the concepts of character and disposition. 'Relating to morals' is the way the *Macquarie Dictionary* defines ethics. From this it would appear that ethics is concerned with moral behaviour, and by 'moral' we mean the part of human behaviour that is formed primarily by national culture, parental influence, peer groups and religion.

A review of some of the literature on ethics provides interesting insights into this important area. Some writers refer to business ethics, which suggests that a particular set of ethics exists for business. This, in fact, is totally untrue as ethics apply to all parts of life and to think that you discard one set of ethics and adopt another as you enter the office is false. Ethics are like your skin – they go everywhere with you.

Even though it may appear difficult to define ethics, Dr Michael Josephson, in an essay entitled 'The need for ethics education in accounting' (1992), attributed the following characteristics to an ethical person.

- *Honesty and integrity.* Honesty is obviously important – what we should really be referring to is complete honesty or perhaps not being dishonest. For example, a six-year-old student, when asked by his teacher if he had eaten any of the chocolates she had left on her desk, replied 'No'. In fact he had taken the chocolates but had not eaten any. It could be argued that he did not actually lie, but he was still dishonest. Integrity refers to having the courage of one's convictions and acting on principle. Furthermore, it is important to have good principles. A serial killer who believes all prostitutes are evil is acting in accordance with his own convictions, but he is not a person of integrity.
- *Promise keeping.* This refers to fulfilling a commitment.

- *Fidelity or loyalty.* This refers to the need to be loyal, but loyal to who or what? The problem of conflicting loyalties is often the cause of ethical problems. In a company an employee could be loyal to an immediate boss, the general manager, the board of directors or the shareholders. The company itself exists in law but it is the people within a company that give it life. In a family relationship, for example, one person can be a mother, a wife, a daughter, a sister, a daughter-in-law, a sister-in-law, an aunt, a cousin and a niece. These different roles invariably lead to situations where being loyal to one party may involve disloyalty to another.
- *Fairness.* Again, this is a subjective term and what is fair to one party may be unfair to another. Consider an umpire in a football game. When he awards a penalty against one side, the supporters of that side often consider the decision unfair while the supporters of the side awarded the penalty consider the decision to be fair.
- *Caring.* Caring for others is perhaps best summed up by the rule 'Do unto others as you would have them do unto you.'
- *Respect.* You may not care for everyone, but you should give them respect.
- *Responsibility.* This refers to complying with the laws of the country and being part of a community.
- *Excellence.* We try to do our jobs as well as we possibly can. For example, we expect a surgeon about to remove our appendix to be competent at doing this.
- *Accountability.* To be ethical you must be accountable for your actions.

WHAT CAUSES UNETHICAL BEHAVIOUR?

Why do we have problems with fraud and embezzlement? Why do people not behave in an ethical manner? Josephson (1992) identified the following five reasons.
- *Self-deception.* This refers to the mistaken belief that because it is business, somehow it does not matter. Phrases such as 'everybody does it' or 'to get along, go along' reflect self-deception. A common example is cheating on one's income tax return based on the assumption that everybody else does. Just imagine what the streets of a city would be like if everybody dumped rubbish on the street because 'everybody does it'.
- *Self-indulgence.* A common defence for unethical behaviour is the assertion that it was done for someone else's benefit when in fact it was for the benefit of the individual who was being unethical.
- *Self-protection.* Many examples of fraud start from one incident and grow from there.
- *Self-righteousness.* The assertion that one is right no matter what others think is an example of self-righteousness. No doubt Adolf Hitler believed he was right.
- *Faulty reasoning.* This refers to not correctly estimating the costs of being ethical versus being unethical. Generally the costs of being ethical ('I will lose my job') are overestimated while the costs of being unethical ('I won't get caught' or 'I will repay this later') are underestimated. In his paper, 'Why I compromised my professional code of ethics' (1992), McKinley L. Tabor recounts the costs to his life of unethical behaviour. The costs included imprisonment, loss of family and friends, loss of respect, and other costs, all of which were in excess of what he embezzled from his employer.

Ethics and accounting

What is the relationship between business and ethics? Are ethics good for business? The answers to such questions depend on how we assess what is good for business. If we use short-term profitability as a measure, it may be that, on some occasions, doing what is ethical may not lead to short-term profitability. It may well improve long-term profitability, but if you are not in the company for the long haul, why bother being ethical? This raises issues about the objectives of business. Does the goal of profit maximisation conflict with ethical behaviour? Is there a conflict between self-interest and ethical behaviour? In Chapter 1 we introduced agency theory which explains the reason for contracts which

3 LEARNING OBJECTIVE

Identify the factors that should help determine appropriate ethical behaviour for accountants try to align the interests of shareholders and managers. Such contracts may in fact be the reason some managers engage in unethical behaviour.

Two frameworks developed by ethicists that are relevant to our discussion are *utilitarianism* and *deontology*. Utilitarianism judges the moral correctness of an action based entirely on its consequences. The action that should be pursued is the one where the favourable consequences to all parties outweigh the unfavourable consequences. The consequences to all parties that will be affected must be included.

In deontology the underlying nature of the action determines its correctness. There are two types of deontologists. Some feel the action itself is the only thing to be considered – lying, for example, is always unacceptable. Other deontologists believe that, for example, the nature of the action and its consequences in a particular situation should be considered. Therefore, in particular circumstances, lying may be acceptable.

Given the enormous costs of fraud and embezzlement, the potential gains to society of ethical behaviour are significant. The difficulty lies in developing an appropriate code of ethical behaviour that is adhered to by all people in business.

Business or professional behaviour is governed by sets of rules laid down by controlling bodies, and members of organisations or the profession are expected to follow these rules. In some professions, 'ethics' has come to mean these rules. For example, professional ethics should be regarded as 'standards of professional conduct (the ethics of lawyers)' (Statsky, 1985).

The financial problems of companies like Enron and HIH in the late 1990s and early 2000s can be attributed, in part, to some accountants substituting 'the rules' for genuine 'ethical behaviour'. In 2013 it was alleged that Leighton Holdings paid millions of dollars in kickbacks to win contracts in Iraq and other countries. For example, it was acceptable to follow the requirements of the *Corporations Act*, even when, by following the strict letter of the law, one was able to gain an unfair advantage that did not reflect the spirit of the law.

Business or professional ethics is a marrying of the rules of society with the moral principles by which a society is judged. The question of business ethics is well illustrated in this story by W. Albrecht (1992).

> There was once a very wealthy man who loved his money so much that he did not have many friends. In fact, he had only three friends. First, he had a lawyer friend who helped him structure his transactions to take advantage of other people. Second, he had an accountant friend who helped him count his money. And third, he had a minister of religion to whom he went every Sunday to confess the fact that he had taken advantage of others during the week. When he got old and was about to die, he called his three friends together and said, 'I have been wealthy all my life and I cannot stand going to the grave poor. I am going to give you each an envelope with $50 000 in it. I want you to promise me that when I die you will go to my casket and each deposit the envelope in the casket'. They all promised that they would.
>
> A short time later the rich man died. As the three friends passed by the casket, each deposited an envelope. The casket was sealed and the body was buried. Not long after, the minister developed a guilty conscience; he called the other two and said, 'We have to meet and talk about this'. When they met he said, 'You know, I thought about the poor members of my congregation. I thought about that money rotting down there in the grave and I just could not do it. I only put $25 000 in and I kept $25 000 to help the poor'. Then the lawyer said, 'If you really want to know the truth, he had asked me for free legal advice so often that I felt he owed it to me, so I kept $25 000 and only put $25 000 in'. Finally, the accountant said, 'You know I cannot believe you would do that. I cannot believe you would both be unethical. I want you to know that in my envelope was a cheque for the full $50 000'.

From Albrecht, W.S. (ed.), *Ethical Issues in the Practice of Accounting* © 1992 Cengage Learning.

As this is a text about accounting, let us look at three of several choices available to the accountant.

- He could have put an empty envelope in the grave, as his friend only asked him to deposit the envelope. This would have been following the letter of the request but not the spirit.
- He could have done what he did in the story. Here he followed the letter of the request and some would say a small measure of the spirit of the request. Of course, we know the cheque will never be cashed and that the accountant is $50 000 better off. Is the accountant guilty of stealing the money?
- He could have carried out his friend's wishes to the full, following the letter and the spirit of the request, and deposited the full $50 000 in cash in the casket.

As a professional person, the accountant was obliged to carry out, in full, the wishes of his client and friend regardless of his personal feelings or beliefs. Business or professional ethics mean just that: clever or smart alternatives are not acceptable.

Remember, one of the characteristics of an ethical person referred to by Josephson (1992) was promise keeping. All three individuals should not have promised to put the envelope in the casket if, in fact, they knew they could not do it. The lawyer should have asked for his unpaid time to be paid by the wealthy friend. The minister should have asked the friend to consider donating to the church. The accountant did not comply with the spirit of his friend's request and all three acted unethically.

As noted earlier, a lack of ethics contributed in some way to the gains made by some of the high-flyers involved in companies like Enron and HIH in the late 1990s and early 2000s. In 2013 allegations of corruption were made against Leighton Holdings in Australia. The Global Financial Crisis again highlighted issues around ethical behaviour and good governance. However, many individuals and organisations have since paid a very high price for being unethical.

Because they offer so many services to the general public and the business community, professional accountants should always conduct their business in an ethical manner. Major professional accounting bodies in all countries have developed codes of professional ethics to help members deal with the range of situations they encounter in their professional lives. A CPA Australia survey on professional ethics asked respondents to rank various types of ethical issues. The results showed that the issues of greatest concern were:

- client proposal for tax evasion (83.3 per cent)
- client proposal to manipulate financial statements (80.2 per cent)
- conflict of interest (79.3 per cent)
- presenting financial information in the most proper manner so as not to deceive users (76.3 per cent)
- failure to maintain technical competence in the discharge of duties (71.3 per cent)
- coping with a superior's instructions to carry out unethical acts (70.6 per cent).

In Australia, the major professional accounting bodies have now adopted the Code of Ethics for Professional Accountants as developed by the Accounting Professional and Ethical Standards Board (APESB). The full code can be viewed at www.apesb.org.au/issued-standards.

The rules of the professional bodies are intended not only to guide but, in some ways, to provide protection from the above types of ethical dilemmas for accountants. However, there are always some who are tempted to move around the rules for personal gain, and in the long run the profession and society are the losers. When dealing with accountants, individuals expect, and deserve to receive, conduct that will enhance the status of all who belong to that profession. Ethics in business and accounting are a matter of judgement based on rules and moral obligations.

To highlight the importance of ethics we have included a case study involving an ethical dilemma at the end of each chapter, starting with this chapter.

STOP AND THINK 1

How do you think you will handle your future ethical problems? Can you do anything now to make it easier to handle your future concerns?

Many believe that good corporate governance is one of the main ways of minimising divergent behaviour by senior executives as seen in some of the company failures referred to earlier in this chapter. Better corporate governance, should (some argue) increase the fear of being caught. We discuss corporate governance in the next section.

CORPORATE GOVERNANCE

What is meant by 'corporate governance'?

4 LEARNING OBJECTIVE

Explain what is meant by the term 'corporate governance'

Corporate governance is not a new concept but it has come into prominence in the wake of concerns about why and how the Hastie Group, Centro, Parmalat, Enron and WorldCom collapses happened. The result has been a major focus by regulators and governments on reviewing laws and regulations that govern corporations.

What do we mean by 'corporate governance'? The following definitions assist in understanding the concept.

> The system of relations between the shareholders, Board of Directors and management of a company, as defined by the corporate charter, by-laws, formal policy and rule of law.
>
> Investor Protection Association, Executive Office, 2006

> Corporate governance is about promoting corporate fairness, transparency and accountability.
>
> J. Wolfensohn, President of the World Bank, as quoted by an article in *Financial Times*, June 21, 1999

In Chapter 2, we looked at different forms of business organisation, including sole traders, partnerships and companies. As discussed in Chapter 1 the company is a separate legal entity and is often managed by professionals on behalf of its owners (shareholders). Corporate governance refers to the procedures and processes put in place because the company is managed by parties, normally on behalf of the owners. This separation of owners from management gives rise to agency problems, some of which were discussed in Chapter 1 in respect of the economic consequences and the choice of accounting policies. The board of directors is part of the process of corporate governance.

3.1

KEY CONCEPT

CORPORATE GOVERNANCE

Corporate governance consists of mechanisms such as the board of directors and audit committees that exist to provide some assurance to absentee owners that the management personnel of a company are accountable for their actions and minimise agency costs in respect of their management.

Good governance is not only relevant to companies and the for-profit sector, but also for the not-for-profit sector where a large number of volunteers, often without management experience, find themselves sitting on management committees. Good governance is critical for such organisations. Therefore, although we use the term 'corporate governance', most of the principles can be applied to the not-for-profit sector. For example, the board of directors in a not-for-profit entity may be called the management committee.

One of Wolfensohn's definitions above mentions fairness, transparency and accountability. All these terms are commonly used in financial reporting with accountability being an important objective.

The key concept definition above relates to what could be called *internal* corporate governance. *External* corporate governance refers to the discipline of the marketplace where a company, if it is listed on a stock exchange, is subject to the scrutiny of the share market. Companies can be taken over and managers replaced, and this threat acts as an incentive for managers to behave more in a manner that is in the best interests of shareholders. We use the term 'corporate governance' as it refers to *internal* corporate governance.

 **STOP AND THINK 2**

What is meant by the term 'corporate governance'?

ISSUES IN CORPORATE GOVERNANCE

In this section we discuss the ASX Corporate Governance Council *Corporate Governance Principles and Recommendations* published in August 2007, with amendments in 2010, and we consider the role of the board of directors and the audit committee.

5 **LEARNING**
OBJECTIVE

Identify the eight ASX
Corporate Governance
Council principles

THE ASX CORPORATE GOVERNANCE COUNCIL

The ASX Corporate Governance Council issued the *Corporate Governance Principles and Recommendations* in August 2007, and companies have been expected to comply with them since 2008. In addition, some amendments were made in 2010. This is the second edition of the corporate governance principles and recommendations following the first edition in 2003. There are eight principles, and a number of best-practice recommendations accompanying each principle. Listed companies are expected to comply with the principles and recommendations, and if they don't comply, they are expected to explain why (known as an 'if not, why not' approach).

The eight principles are listed on pages 10 to 12 of the ASX Corporate Governance Council's *Corporate Governance Principles and Recommendations with 2010 Amendments*.

> *Principle 1:* Lay solid foundations for management and oversight – Recognise and publish the respective roles and responsibilities of board and management.
>
> *Principle 2:* Structure the board to add value – Have a board of an effective composition, size and commitment to adequately discharge its responsibilities and duties. The chairperson should be an independent director.
>
> *Principle 3:* Promote ethical and responsible decision-making – Actively promote ethical and responsible decision-making for example, by establishing a code of conduct.
>
> *Principle 4:* Safeguard integrity in financial reporting – Have a structure to independently verify and safeguard the integrity of the company's financial reporting. Establish an audit committee is one recommendation.
>
> *Principle 5:* Make timely and balanced disclosure – Promote timely and balanced disclosure of all material matters concerning the company.
>
> *Principle 6:* Respect the rights of shareholders – Respect the rights of shareholders and facilitate the effective exercise of those rights.
>
> *Principle 7:* Recognise and manage risk – Establish a sound system of risk oversight and management of internal control.
>
> *Principle 8:* Remunerate fairly and responsibly – Ensure that the level and composition of remuneration is sufficient and reasonable and that its relationship to corporate and individual performance is defined.

Some of the recommendations associated with the eight principles include the following:
- The board should have a majority of independent directors.
- 'Independent' means a director cannot have been a substantial supplier or shareholder, or an employee of the company or its professional advisers, within the last three years.
- The chief executive officer (CEO) should not be the chairman. However, there is no restriction on the CEO being on other boards.
- No limit exists on the number of directorships.
- There should be an audit committee with at least one member with accounting or finance skills.
- There should be separate nominations and remuneration committees.

Full details of the best-practice principles can be found at www.asx.com.au/governance/corporate-governance.htm.

We now consider, in detail, the board of directors and the audit committee.

BOARD OF DIRECTORS

In most countries, it is a legal requirement for companies to have a board of directors. As stated above, other types of entities, such as not-for-profit entities, also have governing bodies charged with a range of responsibilities. The role of the company board is to represent the interests of shareholders and its responsibility is to create value for shareholders. The board is accountable to the shareholders. It is responsible for reviewing the performance of the CEO and senior management, and for rewarding the senior executive team. It must also ensure that the company meets all its legal and statutory obligations, and that the major risks confronting the company are managed.

6 LEARNING OBJECTIVE

Discuss the issues associated with the role of the board of directors in corporate governance

3.2

KEY CONCEPT

BOARD OF DIRECTORS

The board is an important corporate governance mechanism and its role is to represent shareholders and to create value for shareholders.

The following list outlines some issues in relation to company boards that have been addressed in the wake of high-profile company collapses.
- *Number of independent directors on boards.* In the case of Enron, many of the directors were not really independent as some of the non-executive directors had been previous auditors of the company. The argument supporting the use of independent non-executive directors is that they are more able to defuse agency conflicts between internal managers and absentee owners. However, others disagree and argue you need directors who understand the company's business.
- *Duality of leadership.* Should the CEO be chairman of the board or should the chairman come from the non-executive directors? If the roles are combined, some argue that the board's capacity to fulfil its duties is impaired.
- *Size of the board.* Some research suggests that the size of the board affects the performance of the firm.
- *Qualifications of directors.* A board should consist of directors with the appropriate skills to allow the board to discharge its duties.

- *Number of board memberships of directors.* There is a view that some directors belong to too many boards and do not have the necessary time to properly carry out their duties.
- *Length of service.* Should directors be required to step down after a certain period of time to prevent apathy, and also to prevent directors becoming too familiar with senior management?

Researchers have also been actively studying many questions concerning corporate governance. A number of studies have attempted to test whether companies with good corporate governance perform better in terms of profitability and share market performance. The results of studies are contradictory, in that some show a positive relationship while others report a negative relationship. However, a meta study by Finegold, Benson and Hecht (2007) suggests there is a need to look at the performance of boards more broadly than just financial performance. For example, increasing the number of independent directors may improve the social and environmental performance of companies. A study by Carter, Simpkins and Simpson (2003) found a positive relationship between the value of a firm and the number of female and minority group directors. One of the 2010 amendments to the ASX principles relates to policies to achieve greater gender diversity on boards.

7 LEARNING OBJECTIVE

Discuss the issues associated with the role of the audit committee in corporate governance

THE AUDIT COMMITTEE

An audit committee is a subcommittee of the board of directors and is another important corporate governance mechanism. The audit committee may be charged with various duties including:
- overseeing the appointment of and relationship with the external auditor
- overseeing the appointment of and relationship with the internal auditor
- reviewing compliance with regulations and accounting standards
- reviewing internal control procedures
- overseeing the company's risk management practices
- reviewing the company's financial statements and recommending them to the board for approval. The board has to sign off on the financial statements and certify that they represent a true and fair view of the company.

It is one matter to require the formation of an audit committee and another to specify its role and powers. The above roles are extensive and are not necessarily carried out by all, or even some, audit committees. As audit committees are a relatively recent phenomenon, their roles are still evolving. An important issue for all audit committees is whether the audit committee should have its own funding so it is not reliant upon management. If it is reliant upon management for funding it may not be able to effectively conduct its duties.

> **3.3 KEY CONCEPT**
>
> ## AUDIT COMMITTEE
>
> An audit committee is a subcommittee of the board of directors and part of the corporate governance of a company. Its roles vary according to the company but, in general, the role of the audit committee is to ensure that the financial statements have been reliably prepared and verified.

The major thrust for the creation of audit committees is to add credibility to the financial reporting process. The critical issue relates to how independent the audit committee is, as this influences its effectiveness. Ian Ramsay (2001) prepared a report for the federal government of Australia following the problems with HIH, One.Tel and others. In his report, Ramsay made the following comments about audit committees.

- An effective audit committee must not only exist and be independent, it must actually meet and be active.
- Audit committee members must be independent.
- Each member should be financially literate or should, within a reasonable period of time after appointment, become financially literate.

Research on the issue of audit committees supports the notion of benefits accruing to shareholders if a company has an audit committee. Companies committing accounting fraud are less likely to have audit committees (Dechow, Sloan & Sweeney, *Accounting Fraud*, 1996). Moreover, Klein (2000) reports that there is greater incidence of accounting fraud when an audit committee's independence declines and when the financial and accounting expertise of committee members is low.

STOP AND THINK 3
What is the role of the audit committee?

Enforcement of corporate governance

8 LEARNING OBJECTIVE

Identify the approaches to enforcing corporate governance requirements in Australia and the USA

The response of government to company failures has been somewhat different in the USA and Australia. The USA adopted what is described as a 'black letter law' approach through the passing of the *Sarbanes-Oxley Act* in 2002. This is an extensive legislative response to corporate failures and has many requirements including:
- the establishment of a Public Company Accounting Oversight Board with responsibility for overseeing the work of audit firms
- significant new rules relating to auditor independence
- a ban on the provision of many non-audit services to audit clients
- the requirement that the lead audit or coordinating partner and the reviewing partner rotate off the audit every five years
- the external auditor reporting directly to the audit committee
- the condition that the CEO, controller, CFO, chief accounting officer or person in an equivalent position cannot have been employed by the company's audit firm during the one-year period preceding the audit.

In Australia, the legislative response to company failures came through the federal government's Corporate Law Economic Reform Program (CLERP). *CLERP 9* (so named because it is number nine in the series) resulted in a number of changes (but not on the scale of the *Sarbanes-Oxley Act*) including the following:
- Audit committees are now compulsory for the top 500 companies.
- Requirements have been stipulated in relation to auditor independence.
- The employment and financial relationships between an auditor and client are subject to increased restrictions.
- The provision of non-audit services is subject to increased disclosure requirements.
- Auditing standards have been made legal, similar to accounting standards.
- There is to be automatic rotation of the audit partner every five years. This means that a partner in an accounting firm cannot be in charge of the audit of the same client for more than five years.

As stated earlier in this section, the approach in Australia has been largely based on a 'best practice' approach. A 'best practice' approach really places the onus on companies to adhere to good corporate governance principles, as issued by bodies like the Australian Securities Exchange. Companies should disclose their compliance with the principles in their annual report or explain why they do not follow 'best practice' if they do not. Companies now make extensive disclosures about corporate governance and how they comply with the ASX principles. For an example see pages 88 to 108 of the 2013 annual report for Woolworths Limited at www.woolworthslimited.com.au.

While research generally does not support a strong link between board composition and financial performance, some studies support a link between governance practices and investment risk. Other studies show a relationship between board composition and social and environmental performance. The problem for investors is how to measure governance practices across a large number of companies operating in many countries in a cost-effective way. As an outcome of this demand, a number of agencies have emerged offering ratings on the corporate governance of companies in many different countries. The Institutional Shareholders Services (ISS) located in the USA, Governance Metrics International (GMI) and Reputex in Australia offer such services.

Monkey Business Images/ Shutterstock.com

STOP AND THINK 4

Outline the approaches taken in Australia in relation to corporate governance as a result of high-profile company failures that have occurred here.

SUMMARY

LEARNING OBJECTIVE 1

DISCUSS THE IMPORTANCE OF ETHICS IN ACCOUNTING, AND BUSINESS IN GENERAL

The issue of ethics in accounting and business is extremely important. Ethics is concerned with morals and appropriate behaviour. Many large company failures have been involved in fraudulent activities the costs of which have been well publicised in the media. In addition to these high-profile failures, there are many other cases of fraud each year and the cost to the economy is enormous.

LEARNING OBJECTIVE 2

EXPLAIN WHAT IS MEANT BY ETHICAL BEHAVIOUR

It is difficult to define ethics, but 10 characteristics of ethical behaviour are:

» honesty
» integrity
» promise keeping
» fidelity or loyalty
» fairness
» caring
» respect
» responsibility
» excellence
» accountability.

Ethics go everywhere with you; they are not something you adopt just for the workplace. The important principle is that business and professional people should act in an ethical manner at all times.

LEARNING OBJECTIVE 3

IDENTIFY THE FACTORS THAT SHOULD HELP DETERMINE APPROPRIATE ETHICAL BEHAVIOUR FOR ACCOUNTANTS

Accountants are no different to anyone else and the 10 characteristics of ethical behaviour discussed in the previous section apply equally to them. Accountants also have a professional code of ethics, and this should help them deal with ethical dilemmas and guide them with regard to what constitutes appropriate ethical behaviour.

LEARNING OBJECTIVE 4

EXPLAIN WHAT IS MEANT BY THE TERM 'CORPORATE GOVERNANCE'

Corporate governance consists of mechanisms (such as boards of directors and audit committees) that provide some assurance to absentee owners that the management team of a company is accountable for its actions, and to minimise agency costs in relation to that management.

LEARNING OBJECTIVE 5

IDENTIFY THE EIGHT ASX CORPORATE GOVERNANCE COUNCIL PRINCIPLES

» Principle 1: Lay solid foundations for management and oversight
» Principle 2: Structure the board to add value

- » Principle 3: Promote ethical and responsible decision making
- » Principle 4: Safeguard integrity in financial reporting
- » Principle 5: Make timely and balanced disclosure
- » Principle 6: Respect the rights of shareholders
- » Principle 7: Recognise and manage risk
- » Principle 8: Remunerate fairly and responsibly.

LEARNING OBJECTIVE 6

DISCUSS THE ISSUES ASSOCIATED WITH THE ROLE OF THE BOARD OF DIRECTORS IN CORPORATE GOVERNANCE

The board is an important corporate governance mechanism and its role is to represent shareholders and create value for shareholders.

Issues addressed in relation to boards of directors in the wake of the company collapses include:

- » the number of independent directors on boards
- » duality of leadership
- » size of boards
- » qualifications of directors
- » the number of board memberships of directors
- » length of service.

LEARNING OBJECTIVE 7

DISCUSS THE ISSUES ASSOCIATED WITH THE ROLE OF THE AUDIT COMMITTEE IN CORPORATE GOVERNANCE

An audit committee is a subcommittee of the board of directors and is another important corporate governance mechanism. Duties assigned to audit committees include:

- » reviewing the company's financial statements and recommending them to the board for approval
- » overseeing the appointment of and relationship with the external auditor
- » overseeing the appointment of and relationship with the internal auditor
- » reviewing matters in relation to compliance with regulations and accounting standards
- » reviewing internal control procedures
- » overseeing the company's risk management practices.

LEARNING OBJECTIVE 8

IDENTIFY THE APPROACHES TO ENFORCING CORPORATE GOVERNANCE REQUIREMENTS IN AUSTRALIA AND THE USA

Government's responses to company failures differ in the USA and Australia. The USA has adopted what is described as a 'black letter law' approach, which represents the mandatory requirements, by passing the *Sarbanes-Oxley Act* in 2002. Australia made some changes to law through *CLERP 9*. However, the main approach has been that of best practice, with the ASX Corporate Governance Council's *Principles of Good Corporate Governance*.

REVIEW QUESTIONS

1 What challenges face business in relation to ethical behaviour? Are they different for accountants?

2 Is there a conflict between self-interest and ethical behaviour?

3 What is the role of a board of directors?

4 What issues are important for boards of directors in relation to their corporate governance role?

PROBLEMS FOR DISCUSSION AND ANALYSIS

1 Visit the Woolworths website (www.woolworths.com.au) and critically review the statement on corporate governance. What do you consider are the strengths and weaknesses of corporate governance at Woolworths?

2 In fewer than 100 words, detail your understanding of the word 'ethics'.

3 It is difficult to get hard facts about the cost of corporate fraud but estimates range from $1 billion to $5 billion per annum in Australia. Is it possible to regulate against fraud?

4 You have been hired by Jim's Towing Service, a sole proprietorship, to prepare the tax return for the business. Upon checking the bank statements and the cash books of the business you discover that Jim has not included in the revenue any cash received when customers paid cash. Only the amounts received from insurance companies have been included in the revenue. Discuss what you should do.

5 Michael P. Cockley is a young accountant who has just commenced practising in the Perth suburb of Nedlands. He is currently trying to build up his practice which specialises in giving taxation advice and preparing clients' taxation returns.

One of Michael's clients is Leslie Raby, a rather testy ex-navy officer. Captain Raby has only just come to Michael after falling out with another accountant. Amanda Trefrey, the former accountant, merely mentioned that there had been 'personality clashes and communication problems'.

As he looks at Raby's taxation assessment, Michael notices that it differs materially from his estimate and the difference is very much in his client's favour. In checking Raby's file, it becomes clear to Michael that the Taxation Office has made an error. Further, there is a strong likelihood that this error will result in a permanent advantage to his client. Raby's tax return was a full and proper disclosure and had been correctly prepared. It is unlikely that the error made by the Taxation Office will ever be discovered. In discussions with his client, it becomes apparent to Michael that Raby is aware of the error and the monetary gains that will accrue to him if this error is overlooked.

Discuss the following questions.

a What should Michael do under the circumstances?

b If nothing is said about the client standing to gain from the error made by the government department and he keeps the money, is the 'oversight' any different from stealing?

c What responsibility does Michael have? Should he act independently of the captain's wishes?

(Adapted from Paul H. Northcott, *Ethics and the Practising Accountant: Case Studies*, Australian Society of Certified Practising Accountants, 1993.)

6 Jan Skully is the founder and chairperson of Extraordinary Products Ltd. The company has performed well in the past, but over the last year the share price has steadily declined. As Skully owns a majority of the shares, she decides to do something to protect her investment. She secretly channels $200 million from other companies she owns into the purchase of additional shares in Extraordinary. These new shares are used by the other companies as security for the loans taken out to raise

the necessary cash to purchase the shares in Extraordinary. A year later Jan Skully dies and the transactions are uncovered and revealed in the press, and the price of Extraordinary's shares plummet.

Discuss:

    a whether the transactions were unethical

    b how the scheme could have been prevented.

7 Should corporate governance practices be enshrined in legislation or is it best to allow companies to self-regulate and choose their own appropriate corporate governance structures?

8 Discuss the advantages and disadvantages of having a majority of independent directors on a board. Why do you believe a requirement for independent directors to hold separate meetings is being seriously considered?

9 Why is it important for audit committees to have their own funding independent of management? Should any members of the management team attend meetings of the audit committee? Give reasons.

ETHICS CASE STUDY

It was reported in the press in November 2013 that ASIC was investigating Leighton Holdings over alleged corporate offences linked to claims the company paid hundreds of millions of dollars in bribes to win contracts in Iraq and other countries. The allegations include the payment of kickbacks in order to secure contracts. Similar allegations have been made about a subsidiary of the Reserve Bank on the ABC show *Four Corners* in 2013.

Required

One argument for the payment of bribes and kickbacks is that is the way business works in some countries.

    a Do you agree with this argument?

    b Discuss the ethical issues surrounding such transactions.

    c If found guilty of paying such bribes, should the offenders serve a prison sentence?

    d The GRI requires reporting of anti-corruption actions including risk assessment of the potential for corruption and training of staff about anti-corruption policies. Do you think such actions and disclosures would assist to minimise the prospects of the payment of such bribes and kickbacks?

SUGGESTED ANSWERS TO STOP AND THINK EXERCISES IN THE CHAPTER

1 Students should demonstrate an understanding of the issues involved with ethics and appreciate the real costs of being unethical.

2 Corporate governance refers to the rules and procedures that are adopted within a company to provide assurances to absentee owners (shareholders) that the management of the company is accountable for the ways in which it manages the company.

3 The audit committee can have several tasks, but its main role is to ensure that the financial statements are reliable, provide a true and fair view of the company and are not biased by the company's management team.

4 Australia has made some legislative changes through *CLERP 9*, but the main approach has involved best practice regulations with the ASX Corporate Governance Council's Principles of Good Corporate Governance and Best Practice Recommendations.

WEALTH AND THE MEASUREMENT OF PROFIT

LEARNING OBJECTIVES

At the end of this chapter, you should be able to:

1 identify what is meant by the terms 'wealth' and 'profit'

2 explain the meaning of historic cost

3 explain the replacement cost method of measurement

4 explain the economic value method of measurement

5 explain the net realisable value method of measurement

6 explain the fair value method of measurement.

INTRODUCTION

In Chapter 1 we established that there are a number of different users of accounting information. Each user requires different information for different purposes. However, some items of information are required by most users. They want to know the resources and obligations of an entity and how it is performing.

In Chapter 2 an asset was described as an economic resource controlled – but not necessarily owned – by an entity. The information about an entity's resources and obligations could be termed the worth of the entity, or its wealth. This measure of wealth or worth relates to a point in time. The other information required by most users concerns the way the entity has performed over a period of time. This performance during a period can be measured as a change in wealth over time. If you increase your wealth you have performed better, in financial terms, than someone whose wealth has decreased over the same period of time. The measurement of the change in wealth over time is referred to in accounting terminology as 'profit measurement'. Profit in some countries is sometimes referred to as income. We use the term 'profit' in this chapter to represent the increase in wealth, as the term 'income' was used in Chapter 2 to represent the sum of revenues and gains.

In this chapter we look at the ways accountants can measure wealth and profit, and discuss the merits of the alternatives available. We also examine, in some detail, the way in which the choice of a measurement system affects the resultant profit and wealth measures. To do this we need to start by defining profit and wealth, because these two ideas are directly linked.

PROFIT AND WEALTH

1 LEARNING OBJECTIVE

Identify what is meant by the terms 'wealth' and 'profit'

A definition of profit that is widely accepted by accountants is based on the definition of an individual's income (profit) put forward by the economist Sir John Hicks (1946), who stated:

> Income [profit] is that amount which an individual can consume and still be as well off at the end of the period as he or she was at the start of the period.

This definition is shown in Figure 4.1.

FIGURE 4.1 PROFIT OR LOSS IS DETERMINED BY MEASURING WEALTH AT DIFFERENT POINTS IN TIME

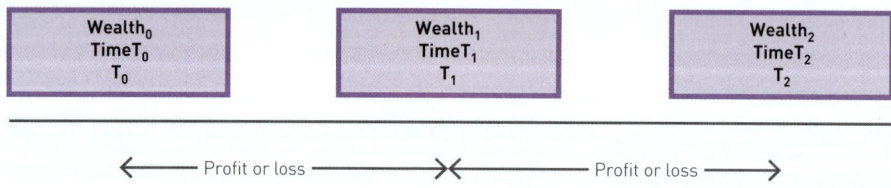

By referring to the diagram, we can arrive at the profit or loss for a period by measuring wealth at time T_0 and subtracting that figure from our measurement of wealth at the end of the period, at time T_1. Similarly, the profit or loss for a second period can be measured by subtracting the wealth at time T_1 from the wealth at time T_2.

It should also be clear from Figure 4.1 that wealth is static and represents a stock at a particular point in time. Thus, $wealth_0$ is the stock of wealth at time T_0, $wealth_1$ is the stock of wealth at time T_1 and $wealth_2$ is the stock of wealth at time T_2.

If we look at the way in which profit is depicted in Figure 4.1, it is apparent that profit is a flow over time. To measure the profit earned over a period of time, it is necessary to measure the stock of wealth at the start and end of that period.

KEY CONCEPT

WEALTH

Wealth is a static measure and represents a stock at a particular point in time. This stock can change over time. So, the wealth measured at the start of a period will not necessarily be equal to the wealth measured at the end of the period. The difference between the two is the profit or loss for that period of time.

KEY CONCEPT

PROFIT

Profit represents the difference between the wealth at the start of the period and at the end of the period. Unlike wealth, which is essentially a static measure, profit is a measure of flow which summarises activity over a period.

To summarise, we have shown that we can express the profit for the first period, from time T_0 to time T_1, as:

$$\text{profit for period}_1 = \text{wealth}_1 - \text{wealth}_0$$

Similarly, we can express the profit for the second period, the period between time T_1 and time T_2, as:

$$\text{profit for period}_2 = \text{wealth}_2 - \text{wealth}_1$$

We have also established that the profit or loss is derived by measuring the wealth of an individual, or an entity, at two points in time. Now let us look in more detail at what we are trying to measure and how we can measure it.

We start by examining the case of an individual because this is simpler and more in line with your own experience. The underlying arguments and principles are just the same for an entity but the degree of complexity increases. Let us suppose that we asked an individual to measure his or her wealth; that is, the sum of possessions less debts.

WORKED EXAMPLE

ALEXIA

Alexia came up with the following list of assets and told us that she owed nothing.

AT THE START OF THE YEAR: T_0	AT THE END OF THE YEAR: T_1
A new Toyota Corolla	A one-year-old Toyota Corolla
One new dress	The same dress
Five shirts	The same five shirts
Four pairs of jeans	Five pairs of jeans
One surfboard	One surfboard
$400 cash	$500 cash

While the lists above might accurately reflect the assets Alexia controls and what she owes, we cannot easily see whether she is better or worse off at the end of the year than she was at the start. With the benefit of our own knowledge of the world, we could perhaps say that she must be worse off because everything is one year older. This, however, assumes that the value of her possessions decreases with time. In many cases that is a reasonable assumption, but clearly there are cases where the value increases. For example, would our attitudes towards the value of her possessions change if the car was a 1957 FJ Holden? Leaving that question aside for a moment, you may have noticed that as soon as we started to discuss the measurement of wealth we also started talking of the more abstract concept of value.

This raises two questions: one relates to value, which we shall discuss in more detail later; the other relates to the way in which we assign value. In the case of the lists of possessions in our example, the easiest item to deal with in terms of value is the cash. This is because it has already had a value assigned to it with which we are all familiar: a monetary value. On the face of it, therefore, it seems that if we assigned a monetary value to each of the items in the list we would have solved part of our problem. In fact, it is not as easy as that because we all know that the value of money is not stable; we only have to listen to our grandparents or even our parents talking about what money used to buy to realise that the value of money has decreased over time.

If we leave the problem of the changing value of money aside and use money as a measure of value, then we have no problem with the value of the cash in the bank, but what of the other items? What is the value of the car, for example? Is it worth less because it is one year older, and, if so, how much less? The same line of argument can be applied to the dress, the shirts and the surfboard. However, in the case of the jeans we do not even know whether they are the same jeans; clearly, there must be at least one pair that has been acquired during the year, since Alexia had five pairs at the end of the year compared with four at the beginning. In addition we have yet to establish whether the age of the items is important for the purposes of arriving at a value. In order to decide on that question, we first need to look at the possibilities available to us.

We shall limit our discussion to the most common possibilities. Although numerous alternatives are put forward, many are combinations of those defined later in this chapter. The important point to note at this time is the relationship between wealth and profit and the way in which a change in the measurement of one affects the other. This will be explored in more detail later, using our example of Alexia.

ALTERNATIVE SYSTEMS OF VALUATION

We will first deal with those alternatives that relate to cost and then discuss those that are based on some concept of value. We start with historic cost and after that discuss replacement cost.

Historic cost

2 LEARNING OBJECTIVE

Explain the meaning of historic cost

Historic cost is the cost incurred by the individual or entity in acquiring an item measured at the time of the originating transaction. It is extremely important because it underpins most current accounting practice. For example, we know that the historic cost of this textbook to you will be different from the historic cost to the bookshop. This difference is what keeps the bookshop in business. But let us take our example a stage further. Let us assume that at the end of the year you no longer need this textbook and decide to sell it. In this situation you will probably find that the book is no longer worth what you paid for it and, therefore, the historic cost is no longer a fair representation of the book's worth or your wealth.

In order to tackle this problem, when measuring your wealth at the end of the year you could write the historic cost down to some lower figure to represent the amount of use you have had from the book. Accounting follows a similar process and the resulting figure is known as the written-down historic cost. It can be described as the historic cost after an adjustment for use. The adjustment for use is commonly referred to as depreciation, and there are several ways to arrive at a depreciation figure. This concept is discussed in Chapter 8.

KEY CONCEPT

4.3

HISTORIC COST

The historic cost is the cost incurred by the individual or entity in acquiring an item – measured at the time of the originating transaction.

The problem with historic cost and written-down historic cost is that, as the value of money and goods changes over time, they are likely to be only a fair representation of value at a particular point in time – at the time of the original transaction. At any other time, the historic cost of an item would only be a fair representation of its worth if the world were static; that is, with no innovation, for example. Clearly this is not the case and so we should look for alternative measures. One such alternative is an item's replacement cost. This is certainly more up-to-date and allows for the changes that take place in a non-static world.

STOP AND THINK 1

In your own words, explain the meaning of 'historic cost'.

Replacement cost

The replacement cost (also known as 'current cost' in the *Conceptual Framework* discussed in Chapter 2) of an item is the amount that would have to be paid at today's prices to purchase the same or a similar item. It is often very relevant, as those who have had cars written-off will know. In those cases, the amount that the insurance company pays you often bears no relationship to what it would cost to replace your car, perhaps because yours was better than average or had just had a new engine installed. The first problem that arises in using replacement cost is that you have to want to replace the item. You might not want to replace a textbook that you used at school because it is no longer of use to you. Even if you do want to replace the item, you may find that it is difficult to identify the replacement cost. Think of a unique item such as Leonardo da Vinci's *Mona Lisa*!

3 LEARNING OBJECTIVE

Explain the replacement cost method of measurement

KEY CONCEPT

4.4

REPLACEMENT COST

The replacement cost is the amount that would have to be paid at today's prices to purchase an item similar to the existing item.

Even if you could replace an item with an exact replica, you might not wish to do so. You might wish to obtain a newer version or one with extra functions. The most obvious example of this is the replacement of computer equipment, which is constantly expanding in power while its size and price are generally decreasing. This leads us to the same problem that we had with historic cost: the replacement cost of a computer does not take into account the age of the machine that we actually own. The solution is the same as for historic cost: estimate the effect of usage and arrive at a written-down replacement cost.

As we can see, there are distinct problems in using either historic cost or replacement cost. In a number of situations these two types of costs are unlikely to be useful measures of value or wealth. Historic cost is unlikely to be useful when prices change, whatever the reason for that change. Replacement cost, while overcoming that problem by using up-to-date costs, is itself irrelevant if there is no intention of replacing the item.

Before reading the next sections on measurement methods other than cost, it is worth spending a few minutes thinking of the situations in which historic cost and replacement cost are appropriate and those situations when they are unlikely to be suitable. Any measure is useful only if it is appropriate. For example, while the acceleration of a car may be important in certain circumstances, it is irrelevant for an emergency stop. Similarly, the historic cost or replacement cost of a motor car is unlikely to be useful if we want to sell the car, because the selling price will be governed by other factors. The alternatives to these cost-based measures are measures related to worth. However, as we will see, these measures also have their own set of problems.

Economic value

The economic value (referred to as 'present value' in the *Conceptual Framework* discussed in Chapter 2) of an item is the value of the expected earnings from using the item discounted at an appropriate rate to give a present-day value. For an example of what is meant by the terms 'present value' and 'discount rate', consider the following: a person deposits $100 in a bank at a fixed interest rate of 10 per cent compounded annually for five years. At the end of five years the $100 would have grown to $161.51 (assuming no taxes or charges). The present value of $161.51 discounted at 10 per cent per annum produces a figure of $100. Discounting is the opposite of compounding. Compounding asks: how much will I have after x periods at y interest rate? Discounting asks: what is the present value of a sum to be received in x periods given y interest rate? Chapter 18 has more detailed information on the time value of money and capital investment decisions.

KEY CONCEPT

ECONOMIC VALUE

Economic value is, or would be, an ideal measure of value and wealth. Economic value is the value of the expected future earnings from using the item in question discounted at an appropriate rate to give a present-day value.

The problem is not in defining the measure of economic value but in actually estimating future earnings. This implies knowledge of what is going to happen; problems to do with foreseeing technological change, global economic changes and so on, make the estimation of future earnings difficult. Even if we assume that we can make reliable forecasts, we are left with the question of finding an appropriate rate at which to discount the estimated future earnings. The trouble here is that each individual might want to use a different rate depending on his or her circumstances. For example, a very wealthy person like Bill Gates might not be too worried if he sees money returned in a year rather than immediately, but if you have no money to buy food the situation is entirely different. We should not reject this measure because of such problems. With the use of mathematical techniques relating to probability, it is still a useful tool in decision making. In fact, underlying techniques such as net present value are normally used in investment appraisal decisions.

Net realisable value

Net realisable value (NRV) is the estimated proceeds of sale less, where applicable, all further costs to the stage of completion and less all costs to be incurred in marketing, selling and distribution to customers. On the face of it, such a measure should be easily obtainable, but in practice the amount for which an item can be sold varies with the circumstances of the sale. These circumstances are not always connected with the item for sale but can depend on such things as the location of the property: for example, an ice works would have more value in the tropics than in Antarctica, all other things being equal. The problems of arriving at the net realisable value are apparent in the second-hand car market where there is a trade price and a range of retail prices. Another good example is the housing market, where independent valuations can differ by as much as $40 000 on a property worth between $110 000 and $150 000.

5 **LEARNING OBJECTIVE**

Explain the net realisable value method of measurement

KEY CONCEPT

NET REALISABLE VALUE

The net realisable value is an alternative measure of value to economic value. The net realisable value is defined as the estimated proceeds of sale, less (where applicable) all further costs to the stage of completion and less all costs to be incurred in marketing, selling and distribution to customers.

4.6

Besides the problem of arriving at a value, other factors affect the net realisable value. For example, if you are in financial difficulties you may be prepared to accept less than the market value in order to get a quick sale. The value in the latter situation is known as the forced sale value and is the most likely value where circumstances are unfavourable to the seller. Further, one is assuming that there is a buyer who is willing to buy, otherwise the property is valueless relative to converting it into cash. On the other hand, if the market conditions are neutral between buyer and seller, then the net realisable value is likely to be the open market value.

STOP AND THINK 2
In your own words, explain what is meant by the net realisable value method of measurement.

4.1

WORKED EXAMPLE

ALEXIA (CONTINUED)

It should be clear from the preceding sections that plenty of alternative measurement methods are available, and that each has its own problems. If you remember, the starting point for this discussion was that we wanted to establish whether Alexia was better off at the end of the period than she was at the start. Did she make a profit? The problem is not one of finding a concept of profit, it is one of measurement: most of these concepts rely either on a measurement of a future amount or on the measurement of wealth.

We have already pointed out that to measure a future amount is extremely difficult in the real world because of the effects of uncertainty. This leaves us with the alternative of measuring wealth and to the problem of finding the most appropriate measure. As we have seen, all the measures put forward so far have inherent difficulties, and it may be that the solution lies in combining two or more of these to obtain the best measure. For the purposes of this introductory text it is unnecessary to examine this area in greater depth. Before leaving this area, let us reconsider the example based on the wealth of Alexia and assign some values to see what effect the choice of measure has.

	YEAR T_0		
DESCRIPTION	REPLACEMENT COST $	HISTORIC COST $	NET REALISABLE VALUE $
Toyota Corolla	13 500	13 500	10 500
Dress	200	210	30
Shirts	75	75	10
Surfboard	180	180	100
Jeans	400	400	60
Cash	400	400	400

If you study the figures carefully you will notice that the only figure common to all three columns is the cash figure. Apart from the cost of the dress, the replacement cost and the historic cost for all other items are also identical. In reality, this is always the case at the time when the goods are bought, but it is unlikely to be so at any other time. In this example, the fact that the replacement cost of the dress is different from the historic cost indicates that the dress was bought when the price of dresses was higher than it was at the start of the year in question. In other words, the point in time at which we are measuring is different from the date of acquisition and, as we said, in these circumstances the replacement cost is likely to differ from the historic cost.

You will also notice that the net realisable value is lower than the historic cost and the replacement cost, even though some of the items were clearly new at the start of the year. Once again, this is obviously the case in most situations because personal goods that are being resold are effectively second-hand goods, even if they have not been used. The situation for a business entity is not necessarily the same because sometimes the goods are bought not for use but for resale; for example, by a retailer or wholesaler. In these cases the net realisable value of the goods bought for resale should be higher than the cost – otherwise the retailer would not stay in business very long.

Let us now look at Alexia's situation at the end of the year and assign some values to the items owned at that time. We will then be in a position to measure the increase in wealth, or profit, and to use this as a basis for discussion of the problems of measurement we referred to earlier.

❯

	YEAR T₁		
DESCRIPTION	REPLACEMENT COST $	HISTORIC COST $	NET REALISABLE VALUE $
Toyota Corolla	10 000	13 500	8 000
Dress	270	210	27
Shirts	80	75	5
Surfboard	180	180	90
Jeans	400	400	30
Cash	500	500	500

You will notice that (disregarding the cash) the figures have changed in all cases, except for historic cost where they are the same as at the start of the year. This highlights one of the problems with this measure: it tells us only what an item costs, not necessarily what it is worth today.

Let us look more closely at the car. As you can see, the replacement cost is lower than at the start of the year. This is because the car we are replacing at the end of the year is a one-year-old model rather than a new model. There is also a problem in using replacement cost for items such as the dress. It may be unlikely that you would want to purchase a year-old dress, whereas there is a ready market for second-hand cars. You will also see that the replacement cost is higher than the net realisable value. This is because costs would be incurred in selling the car, and the amount that you would receive would be reduced by these costs.

Let us now look at what we get in terms of our measures of wealth and profit, starting with historic cost.

	HISTORIC COST	
DESCRIPTION	YEAR T₀ $	YEAR T₁ $
Toyota Corolla	13 500	13 500
Dress	210	210
Shirts	75	75
Surfboard	180	180
Jeans	400	400
Cash	400	500
	14 765	14 865

We can now measure the profit under historic cost as we have a figure for wealth at the start and end of the year. Thus, using the formula:

$$\text{wealth at } T_1 - \text{wealth at } T_0 = \text{profit}$$

we get:

$$\$14\,865 - \$14\,765 = \$100$$

The figures at T₁, and therefore the profit, would be different if we used written-down cost. Remember, written-down historic cost is the reduction in the cost of an asset to reflect the use of the asset.

Let us look at what would happen if we used replacement cost rather than historic cost.

DESCRIPTION	REPLACEMENT COST	
	YEAR T_0 $	YEAR T_1 $
Toyota Corolla	13 500	10 000
Dress	200	270
Shirts	75	80
Surfboard	180	180
Jeans	400	400
Cash	400	500
	14 755	11 430

We can now measure the profit under replacement cost as we have a figure for wealth at the start and end of the year. Thus, using the formula:

$$\text{wealth at } T_1 - \text{wealth at } T_0 = \text{profit}$$

we get:

$$\$11\,430 - \$14\,755 = \$3\,325 \text{ loss}$$

In other words, according to the replacement cost figures, Alexia is $3 325 worse off at the end of the year than she was at the start.

Finally, let us see what the situation would be if we were using the net realisable value to arrive at our measures of wealth.

DESCRIPTION	NET REALISABLE VALUE	
	YEAR T_0 $	YEAR T_1 $
Toyota Corolla	10 500	8 000
Dress	30	27
Shirts	10	5
Surfboard	100	90
Jeans	60	30
Cash	400	500
	11 100	8 652

We can now measure the profit under net realisable value as we have a figure for wealth at the start and the end of the year. Thus, using the formula:

$$\text{wealth at } T_1 - \text{wealth at } T_0 = \text{profit}$$

we get:

$$\$8\,652 - \$11\,100 = \$2\,448 \text{ loss}$$

Once again, using net realisable value as the basis for measuring wealth we find that Alexia is worse off at the end of the year than she was at the start.

You might well be wondering at this point which is the correct answer. This takes us back to the question of who is to use the information and for what purpose it is being used. Clearly this varies from case to case; however, at the moment, it is important for you just to understand that differences arise depending on the valuation method adopted. Alexia is clearly worse off at the end of the year than she was at the start since she no longer has a brand-new car, so you may feel that replacement cost or net realisable value are the better alternatives. However, you must bear in mind that we are trying to measure the amount that can be spent while maintaining wealth; there is a hidden assumption that Alexia wants to maintain the wealth she had at the start.

This might not, in fact, be the case. Alexia might, for example, have been banned from driving, which could mean that she does not want to replace her car. The net realisable value would be more useful in this case, because she would probably want to sell the car. However, although she has lost her driving licence she still needs to go out – even if only to buy food – and needs to wear clothes, so to value these on the assumption that they are going to be sold is not a defensible position.

CURRENT ACCOUNTING PRACTICE

Historic cost is the measurement method commonly adopted in most countries. This is specifically stated in paragraph 4.55 of the IASB *Conceptual Framework*, as mentioned in Chapter 2. However, the *Conceptual Framework* acknowledges that other bases of measurement like net realisable value, present value and current cost are also used for certain types of assets in certain cases. Accounting standards like AASB 116 *Property, Plant and Equipment* require all items of property, plant and equipment to be initially recognised at cost. However, AASB 116 allows entities to choose cost or fair value subsequent to the date of acquisition if they so choose. Other accounting standards like IFRS 9 *Financial Instruments* require the use of fair value for most types of financial assets. The use of fair value allows entities to report changes in the value of non-current assets since the date of acquisition. AASB 102 *Inventories* requires inventories to be valued at the lower of cost and net realisable value for profit-making entities. NFP entities are permitted to use the lower of replacement cost and net realisable value for donated inventory as there is no cost.

Fair value

Fair value is the price that would be received to sell an asset or paid to transfer a liability in an orderly transaction between market participants. The market value of an asset traded in a liquid market such as Woolworths shares is its fair value. However, where there is no liquid market (such as for the shares of an unlisted company) then the fair value needs to be derived in some other way. This could be the market value of a similar item. For example, the fair value of a house could be based on recent selling prices for houses of a similar size and condition in the same area.

Much has been written about the increased use of fair value by standard setters. Indeed some have argued that the turmoil experienced in share markets around the world as a result of the sub-prime lending crisis in 2009, was more severe due to the use of fair values for many types of financial assets. They argue that the requirement to write financial assets such as financial instruments held for trading to fair value and to add this change to profit (loss) for the period (called mark-to-market accounting in the USA) contributed to the decline in share prices. The contrary view is that information about fair values is extremely important for investors trying to assess the worth of shares held in financial institutions. Clearly the issue about the use of fair values, and the requirement to increase or decrease the value of some assets based on movements in fair value – and to report the changes in profit (loss) – remains a heated issue for standard setters.

The IASB has been working on the accounting standards dealing with financial instruments and the use of fair value. It is building a single new standard IFRS 9 *Financial instruments* which it first issued in November 2009 and then expanded in October 2010. As a result of the reclassification, an entity could

6 LEARNING OBJECTIVE

Explain the fair value method of measurement

change from fair value to the amortised cost method for some financial instruments. In September 2011 the IASB issued IFRS 13 *Fair value measurement*, which provides guidance on how to measure fair value.

KEY CONCEPT

4.7

FAIR VALUE

The price that would be received to sell an asset or paid to transfer a liability in an orderly transaction between market participants at the measurement date. (AASB 13, 2011, para. 9)

Bloomberg via Getty Images

STOP AND THINK 3

What is the difference between fair value and net realisable value?

You should now read the Woolworths financial report in Appendix 1 and observe that Note 1(B) (page 110) states that the company uses the historic cost basis except for:

- available-for-sale financial assets
- derivative financial instruments
- financial instruments held for trading
- financial assets valued through other comprehensive income
- other financial liabilities that are measured at revalued amounts or fair values.

CONCLUSION

We have seen that there are a number of alternative ways of measuring a person's wealth and that each has its own problems. One common objection to both replacement cost and net realisable value is that they are subjective, which is true in many cases. This is one reason why accounts are still prepared using historic costs or modified historic costs, even though, as we have seen in the simple example of Alexia, this can lead to irrelevant information being produced and wrong decisions being taken. Another reason often cited for retaining historic cost in the accounts is that it is a system which is based on what was actually spent, and owners of entities need to know what money has been spent on. But to what extent can the advantage of historic cost make up for its deficiencies as a measure of wealth and, therefore, as the basis for profit measure? To compensate for the deficiencies of historic cost, fair value is now required for many types of financial assets and liabilities. This has prompted some to argue that the use of fair value compounded the falls on share markets as a result of the Global Financial Crisis. This question is and has been the subject of much debate which will continue for many years to come. For our purposes we need to be aware of the problems associated with using each of the alternatives, because they might well result in different decisions being taken.

SUMMARY

LEARNING OBJECTIVE 1

IDENTIFY WHAT IS MEANT BY THE TERMS 'WEALTH' AND 'PROFIT'

Wealth is a static measure and represents a stock at a particular point in time. This stock can change over time. Thus, the wealth measured at the start of a period will not necessarily be equal to the wealth measured at the end of the period. The difference between the two is the profit or loss for that period of time.

Profit represents the difference between the wealth at the start of a period and at the end of the period. Unlike wealth, which is essentially a static measure, profit is a measure of flow that summarises activity over a period.

LEARNING OBJECTIVE 2

EXPLAIN THE MEANING OF HISTORIC COST

The historic cost is the cost incurred by the individual or entity in acquiring an item – measured at the time of the originating transaction.

LEARNING OBJECTIVE 3

EXPLAIN THE REPLACEMENT COST METHOD OF MEASUREMENT

The replacement cost is the amount that would have to be paid at today's prices to purchase an item similar to the existing item.

LEARNING OBJECTIVE 4

EXPLAIN THE ECONOMIC VALUE METHOD OF MEASUREMENT

Economic value is, or would be, an ideal measure of value and wealth. The economic value is the value of the expected future earnings from using the item in question discounted at an appropriate rate to give a present-day value.

LEARNING OBJECTIVE 5

EXPLAIN THE NET REALISABLE VALUE METHOD OF MEASUREMENT

The net realisable value is an alternative measure of value to economic value. It is defined as the estimated proceeds of sale, less (where applicable) all further costs to the stage of completion and less all costs to be incurred in marketing, selling and distribution to the customer.

LEARNING OBJECTIVE 6

EXPLAIN THE FAIR VALUE METHOD OF MEASUREMENT

The fair value is the price that would be received to sell an asset or paid to transfer a liability in an orderly transaction between market participants at the measurement date.

REVIEW QUESTIONS

1 Profit is normally seen as a flow over time, whereas wealth can be described as a stock at a point in time. Explain in your own words what is meant by the terms 'wealth' and 'profit' and the difference between a stock and a flow.

2 Wealth can be measured in a number of different ways. List the options discussed in this chapter, together with any drawbacks or problems that were identified with their use.

3 In certain situations we said that written-down costs could be used as an alternative measure. Explain in your own words the difference between cost and written-down cost and suggest when the latter would be more appropriate.

4 What effect, if any, do rapid changes in technology have on the appropriateness of each of the different ways of assigning a cost or a value to an item?

PROBLEMS FOR DISCUSSION AND ANALYSIS

1 Refer to the Woolworths 2013 annual report in Appendix 1.
   a How does Woolworths measure inventories?
   b How does Woolworths measure property, plant and equipment?
   c Note 1(M) refers to 'Impairment'. What does this mean?

2 Make a list of all your possessions and all your debts (that is, all your assets and liabilities) so that you can determine your own wealth. What values did you use for your possessions? Explain why you selected these values. You may also like to calculate your wealth one year ago. Did your wealth increase or decrease in the past year?

3 One hears of large sums of money being exchanged between soccer clubs in Europe. How do you think a club arrives at a figure of, say, 10 million Euro for a player?

4 A Ford Laser was purchased by Totem Ford for $10 000 and later sold in new condition to Spike Buzley for $12 000. One year later, Spike crashed the car and was told by the Royal Automobile Club it would cost $4000 to repair. Spike was advised that his car would be worth $1000 if repairs were not made, and could be sold for $7000 if the repairs were made. Spike was alarmed to hear this because Totem Ford were now selling new Ford Lasers for $13 000.

   At the time Spike decides to have his car repaired, what would be:
   a the historic cost
   b the replacement cost
   c the net realisable value?

5 Two sisters went into business buying and selling beds. Details of their transactions are as follows.
   They initially bought 400 beds at $200 each. At the end of six months they had sold 300 of the 400 beds for $300 each. Unfortunately, during that time the bed manufacturer, which was their only source of supply, had increased the price of each bed to $240. To make matters worse, a discount store had opened in the area and it was selling the same beds for $280 each. The sisters found that, on average, over the six months they had incurred costs for advertising and so on which amounted to $20 for each bed that was sold.
   a On the basis of the information provided, calculate what the sisters' wealth was at the start of the six months and at the end of the six months, and what profit had been made. Calculations should be made using historic cost, replacement cost and net realisable value.
   b Having calculated the profit for the first six months, discuss whether the profit figure is a useful benchmark for measuring the performance of the business, and also whether it is useful as a guide to future profitability.

6 Jean owns a shop that used to sell clothes. Given the location, she believes she would make more money running a restaurant on the same premises. She has obtained planning permission for the

change of use and bought some of the equipment needed, but has not yet started trading. She makes a list of the items that the business owns:

» freehold shop
» hanging display rail for clothes
» a two-year-old car which is essential for the business
» new restaurant tables and chairs
» a cash register
» a quantity of fashion garments that were not sold in the closing-down sale.

Under certain circumstances, only one of the various methods of valuation is appropriate. Giving brief reasons for your choice, suggest the most appropriate value to be placed on each of the above items.

You may find that you need more information or have to make some assumptions. This is normal, but you should state any assumptions that you are making.

7 If the persons or things listed below were crucial to your entity and had to be insured:

a How would you initially value them?

b How would you value them 12 months after the initial date of acquisition (or accession)?

 i an elite football player

 ii a 2011 Holden Commodore car

 iii a building of heritage value – for example, the Sydney Opera House

 iv the Prime Minister

 v a block of land

 vi the trademark 'Coca-Cola'.

Note: Assumptions may need to be made; please state any assumptions that you make.

8 On 1 July 20X1, the KLT Company purchased a very specialised item of machinery. KLT is the only company in Australia producing a special instrument used in the medical industry; hence, the new machinery has no resale value other than its scrap value. The following is a list of various values at 30 June 20X2 for the machine under different valuation methods discussed in this chapter.

	$
Historic cost	1 000 000
Net realisable value	10 000
Replacement cost	1 250 000

Required

From the values listed (or any other value you believe is relevant) discuss which one the following users would consider as most relevant for their purposes:

a a banker considering lending funds to KLT with the specialised machinery as security

b a shareholder in assessing the value of the company's shares

c management in assessing the performance of the company.

Note to instructors: The following problems are considered more suitable for use in MBA courses. However, undergraduate courses may also find them useful.

9   Michelle Computers Ltd has had a difficult year owing to increasing costs associated with keeping its hardware and software up to date in the face of rapidly improving technology. As company accountant, you are aware that the company is overstocked with out-of-date virus software which the board of directors wishes to have valued at cost. 'After all,' the managing director tells you, 'you accountants follow the historic cost convention.'

   a   Should the software be valued at cost? If not, what value should be placed on it?

   b   The directors are responsible for the final accounts. What action, if any, should you take?

   c   If historic cost is used, will it affect the income statement?

10 Merlin's Magic Supply Company Ltd lists the following assets and liabilities at time periods T_0 and T_1:

	HISTORIC COST		REPLACEMENT COST		NET REALISABLE VALUE	
	T_0	T_1	T_0	T_1	T_0	T_1
Cash	1 000	2 000	1 000	2 000	1 000	2 000
Land	10 000	10 000	12 000	14 000	12 000	14 000
Inventory	1 500	2 250	1 500	2 500	1 500	2 500
Trade creditors	1 000	1 500	1 000	1 500	1 000	1 500
Trade debtors	1 200	1 750	1 250	1 750	1 150	1 650

   a   From the different valuation methods discussed in this chapter, calculate the most appropriate change in net worth of the company if it is:

      i   a small trading company

      ii a superannuation plan

   with supporting arguments for your decision.

   b   If you were liquidating this company at time T_1, what value would you place on it? Explain your assumptions.

11 AASB 141 *Agriculture* requires companies with biological assets like grape assets to measure the fair value at the end of each reporting period and report gains and losses as part of profit or loss for the period.

   Required

   a   Do you think the change in the value of grape assets should be included in its profit? Give reasons.

   b   Why do you think the standard setters require fair value to be used for assets like grapes and sheep instead of historic cost?

12 In August 2005, Western Australia's biggest meat processor, E G Green & Sons, suspended trading with debts estimated at $20 million. The company was at that time facing either (i) liquidation; or (ii) trading out of difficulty and continuing as a going concern.

   a   Identify five of the major groups of stakeholders which would be directly impacted by the suspension in the entity's operations.

b What method(s) of valuing the firm's non-monetary assets may have been appropriate under both scenarios? Support your discussion by identifying the reasons for your choice of methods.

ETHICS CASE STUDY

Jane, the accountant for Salisbury Ltd, received the following memo from her boss concerning a machine recently purchased from a competitor.

> Dear Jane,
>
> Due to the problems faced by our competitor, I have negotiated to purchase their plant and equipment, which is only 12 months old, for $500 000. The plant and equipment is worth at least $1 000 000. Therefore, I want you to record the plant and equipment at $1 000 000 and the difference between this and the cash paid should be included in profit for the period.
>
> Signed, Ted Johnson

Jane is aware that it has been a difficult year for Salisbury Ltd and it is likely to report a loss for the period. If the company reports a loss it will be in default of a contract with the bank and there is a risk the bank will stop the company's overdraft facility. Accounting standards require that assets be initially recorded at cost. Salisbury Ltd intends to use the plant and equipment, and has no intention of selling it.

Discuss

a the appropriate way to record the transaction

b what Jane should do.

SUGGESTED ANSWERS TO STOP AND THINK EXERCISES IN THE CHAPTER

1 Your answer should relate to what was paid for an item at the date of acquisition.
2 Your answer should include what an item can be sold for less the costs of selling it.
3 A major difference between fair value and net realisable value is that the expected costs to sell an item are deducted to determine NRV but are not deducted for fair value. Also, fair value involves an orderly market and willing market participants to the transaction whereas NRV does not.

CENGAGENOW

Go to http:\\login.cengagebrain.com to link to CengageNOW, your online study tool. First take the Pre-Test for this chapter to get your Personalised Study Plan, and then:

» revise your understanding of the key terms related to wealth and the measurement of profit by completing the online crossword
» explore IFRS requirements on fair value
» link to the AASB Conceptual Framework.

After you have completed the activities in your Personalised Study Plan take the Post-Test to determine what concepts you have mastered and what you still need work on.

5

PRESENTATION OF FINANCIAL POSITION AND THE WORKSHEET

LEARNING OBJECTIVES

At the end of this chapter, you should be able to:

1. appreciate that financial statements are a summary of transactions and explain the format and purpose of the worksheet used to record the transactions

2. analyse and classify balance-sheet-only transactions onto a worksheet

3. explain common errors in single- and double-entry recording of transactions

4. explain the meaning and purpose of the balance sheet

5. identify the requirements an item must satisfy to be recognised as an asset on a balance sheet

6. explain the distinction between current and non-current assets

7. identify the requirements an item must satisfy to be recognised as a liability on a balance sheet

8. explain the distinction between current and non-current liabilities

9. explain the meaning of 'equity'

10. explain and apply the balance sheet equation

11. explain and apply some common balance sheet ratios

12. identify the limitations of a balance sheet

13. discuss the factors that influence the format of a balance sheet.

INTRODUCTION

In Chapter 1 we discussed the objectives of accounting reports and the influences users exert on financial reporting. We also discussed the limitations of accounting information and the role of accounting in business, its effect on business and some of the factors influencing accounting. In Chapter 4 we examined some possible approaches to measuring profit from the point of view of both the economist and the accountant. We now look more specifically at the ways in which accountants measure wealth and profit.

We suggested that the problem facing accountants is that of finding an appropriate basis for the measurement of wealth. An additional problem is that in the real world a system that only measures wealth and derives profit from it cannot cope with the complexity of today's entities. Consider a large retailing group such as Woolworths: should it have to carry out a valuation of everything owned by the business – for example, all its premises, vehicles and stocks – on one day of the year? The costs of such an operation would make it prohibitively expensive, even if it were logistically possible. For companies such as BHP Billiton, where operations are carried out on a worldwide basis, these logistical problems would be even greater. Such a system also makes it very difficult for the managers or owners to make decisions on a day-to-day basis because they would have information at hand only once a year. Because of these problems with annual valuation systems, we need to find separate ways of measuring wealth or financial position and profit or financial performance.

Bloomberg via Getty Images

The measurement of financial performance will be dealt with in detail in Chapter 6. In this chapter we concentrate on the problem of measuring financial position, and the way in which accountants approach it. We look in some detail at the use of the statement, which purports to measure wealth.

The name used by the IFRS has varied from balance sheet to statement of financial position. In the relevant standard IAS 1 *Presentation of financial statements*, the name used from 2009 is statement of financial position, but entities can choose other names like balance sheet. In the 9th edition of this text we continue to use balance sheet, as indeed does Woolworths, but you should be aware that you will see both names used in practice.

We examine the statement and its component parts, such as assets and liabilities, the format in which this statement is normally presented and the way in which that is influenced by the type of entity, regulations and the needs of users.

Before we look at the balance sheet we need to appreciate that business activities result in transactions which form the basis for what is recorded in the accounting records, which in turn form the basis for the financial statements. We use a worksheet in chapters 5 to 10 to record accounting transactions and in Chapter 11 we show how to move from a worksheet to debits and credits.

BUSINESS ACTIVITIES AND THE WORKSHEET

We now introduce the **worksheet** as a tool for recording information to facilitate the preparation of financial statements like the balance sheet and the statement of comprehensive income to be discussed in Chapter 6. In this chapter we use simple examples to illustrate the principles involved for application to a balance sheet. In Chapter 6 we extend the worksheet to incorporate the statement of comprehensive income. These principles are the same no matter how complex the business is. It is normally the number of transactions that is the problem rather than their complexity. Most large and some small businesses require sophisticated recording systems to deal with the thousands of transactions that take place during the year. This is one of the major uses of computers in business today. Computers not only provide a vehicle for recording accounting transactions, but the more sophisticated systems also analyse the data and produce reports such as balance sheets, statements of profit or loss and other comprehensive income, and other reports tailored to meet the particular needs of users or managers of businesses. For our purposes, however, we do not need to introduce a high level of sophistication to understand the principles involved. We can set up a perfectly adequate double-entry recording of transactions system using a spreadsheet. We refer to our manually produced spreadsheet as a worksheet and we use it to illustrate the basics of double-entry recording of transactions. The worksheet is set out in the form of a balance sheet equation with columns headed as appropriate. We use the following simple data to illustrate the worksheet.

5.1

WORKED EXAMPLE

BEETLE

Beetle started up a small business selling pet food and the first transactions were as follows:

- Open a business bank account and deposit $10 000 of Beetle's own money.
- Buy a van for $4000 cash.
- Buy some inventory for $6000 cash.
- Get a bank loan of $12 000. (For the purpose of this example we assume the loan will be a current liability.)
- Buy some equipment for $8000 cash.

Each of these transactions has been entered on the worksheet (version 1) and you should look at it while reading the description of what has been done.

Before looking at the transactions in detail, let us briefly discuss the way in which the worksheet has been set up. One column identifies and describes the transaction. In our case, this is the number of the transaction taking place. You could include a fuller description, e.g. providing the date, the invoice number, the name of the suppliers involved or whatever is appropriate.

1 **LEARNING OBJECTIVE**

Appreciate that financial statements are a summary of transactions, and explain the format and purpose of the worksheet used to record the transactions

BEETLE WORKSHEET: VERSION 1

2 **LEARNING OBJECTIVE**

Analyse and classify balance-sheet-only transactions onto a worksheet

	ASSETS				= LIABILITIES + EQUITY	
TRANSACTION	CASH	VAN	INVENTORY	EQUIPMENT	LOANS	CAPITAL
1	10 000					10 000
2	−4000	4000				
3	−6000		6000			
4	12 000				12 000	
5	−8000			8000		
Balance	4000	+ 4000	+ 6000	+ 8000	= 12 000	+ 10 000

After the column containing the description, there are columns for each asset purchased and these are followed by columns for the liabilities and owners' equity. Thus, in effect, we have across the top of our worksheet the balance sheet equation:

$$\text{assets} = \text{liabilities} + \text{owner's equity (or equity)}$$

Let us now examine each of the transactions in turn and see how they have been entered into our double-entry worksheet.

Transaction 1

In the case of this transaction, Beetle expects to get a future benefit; therefore, we have an asset. So we have made a column for cash and entered the amount paid into the bank account. On the other side of our worksheet we have made a column entitled Capital (part of equity) and have entered in that column the amount that the owner has put into the business. It should be noted that if we were to total up our worksheet we would have the figures for the balance sheet at that point in time, and this is true at every stage, as long as all transactions up to the statement date have been recorded.

Transaction 2

For this transaction we have opened another column in which we have recorded the van as an asset because it will give a future benefit. We have also deducted the amount paid for the van from the cash column. In other words, Beetle has exchanged one asset (cash) for another (a van). The worksheet, if totalled now, would still balance and would correctly record that the business owns a van that cost $4000 and has $6000 in the bank.

Transaction 3

Next, Beetle used some of his cash to purchase pet food. We therefore need to record that the asset Cash is reduced by $6000 and that there is a new asset, Inventory, which cost $6000. We have classified the inventory as an asset because we have assumed that Beetle will get a future benefit from it.

Transaction 4

In this transaction Beetle borrowed some money and put it in the bank. The amount in the bank is therefore increased by the amount of the loan ($12 000). On the other side of the worksheet we open a column in which we record the fact that the business has a liability; that is, it has an obligation to another entity to pay cash (in this case, $12 000). Once again, if we were to total up our worksheet at this point we would find that it balanced.

Transaction 5

This transaction involves using one asset, our cash, to purchase another asset, equipment. Once again, the equipment can be viewed as an asset of the business as the business is going to get some future benefit. All that is needed is to open a column for the new asset and show that it cost $8000 and reduced the amount Beetle has in the bank by the same amount.

From the worksheet it should be obvious that every transaction involves two entries. For example, when the owner pays in the money an entry is made in the cash column and one is made in the owner's equity column. If all columns are totalled, the worksheet will always balance. If either of these points is not clear it is important that you look again at what has been done so that you understand both before moving on.

You might have noticed that in the worksheet all transactions are those that only affect the balance sheet. We will introduce another column for a statement of comprehensive income in Chapter 6.

Explain, in your own words, the purpose of the worksheet.

COMMON ERRORS IN RECORDING OF TRANSACTIONS

3 LEARNING OBJECTIVE

Explain common errors in single- and double-entry recording of transactions

Example 5.1 shows that the system of double-entry recording of transactions is a convenient way to record transactions in a logical manner. The system is not complex – all it requires is an understanding of addition and subtraction, together with the knowledge that the equation must always be in balance. It also requires the application of our definitions to classify a particular transaction correctly. Therefore, if you cannot understand why a transaction is dealt with in a particular way you should return to Chapter 2 and reread the definitions of elements of financial statements.

Before trying an example yourself, it is worth spending time reflecting on the last example. If we look at any of the columns we can see that nothing more than addition and subtraction is taking place; a good example is the cash column where we make additions as money comes in to the business and make deductions as money is spent.

Another feature of the system is not so obvious: if we make mistakes there is an automatic check because in the end the worksheet will not balance. If this turns out to be the case, we have two ways of finding the error: we can either do a line-by-line check to ensure that each of our lines has balanced, or we can total the columns at various stages to see where the error is likely to be. We may have only recorded one part of the entry, which is a single-entry error where the difference between the totals will equal the transaction, as only half of it has been recorded. We may, on the other hand, record the amount twice on the same side of the worksheet and this is a double-entry error. In this case the difference between the totals will be double the amount of that transaction.

Another common error is failing to add or subtract correctly. The only way to fix this problem is to recheck all addition and subtraction. We can reduce the size of that task by balancing our worksheet on a regular basis so that we know where the error is likely to be. A similar problem is a transposition error where, for example, we recorded the total of our cash column as $10 300 instead of $13 000; that is, we transposed the '3' and the '0'. This is a common error and happens to all of us. In this case we can identify that it may be a transposition error because the difference of $2700 is divisible by 9. This will always be

In each of the following cases, describe the entries required on the worksheet.

a   The owner takes $100 worth of inventory for his personal use.

b   The bank advises that the month's transaction charges are $30.

c   The manager of the business is advised that the cost of a new piece of equipment is $27 500.

d   A cheque for $400 is received in full payment for goods sold on account.

e   Plant, with a cost of $10 000, is received and paid for.

f   The owner consults an architect on whether building extensions can be made. The architect has not submitted an account and the owner does not know the amount he will have to pay for this service.

the case if we simply transpose two figures; for example, 45 as 54 or 97 as 79. Notice that the difference is divisible by 9 but it does not necessarily have the number 9 in the difference. The difference between 97 and 79 is 18, which is divisible by 9.

A more extensive worksheet application is demonstrated in Chapter 6 after we introduce the statement of comprehensive income. We now examine the balance sheet and the role of the balance sheet as one of the four primary financial statements.

4 LEARNING OBJECTIVE

Explain the meaning and purpose of the balance sheet

DEFINITION OF THE BALANCE SHEET

In the case of an individual, we have said that his or her wealth or financial position can be measured by simply listing the economic resources he/she controls – assuming, of course, that he/she does not owe anybody money. To some extent the same can be said for an entity, although the level of complexity is greater. The way in which this listing is achieved is similar to that for an individual, and the resulting statement is called a balance sheet or statement of financial position. You should note that the balance sheet relates to a position at a point in time. It is because of this that the analogy with a snapshot is often found in accounting textbooks.

5.1 KEY CONCEPT

THE BALANCE SHEET

The balance sheet is a statement, at one point in time, which shows all the resources controlled by the entity and all the obligations due by the entity.

The balance sheet equation derived from this definition is ASSETS = LIABILITIES + EQUITY.

This definition of a balance sheet is not intended to be comprehensive, it merely provides us with an outline of what we are referring to. Although an entity does not exist in the same way as a person, for accounting purposes (and for some legal purposes) an entity is presumed to exist in its own right and is treated as a separate entity from the person or persons who own or operate it. In broad terms, it is possible to account for any unit that has a separate and distinct existence. It may be that this is a hotel, for example, or a group of hotels, or a more complex entity such as Hilton International Hotels. This idea of a separate entity is often referred to in accounting literature as the business entity principle. It applies equally to entities that are not commonly referred to as businesses, such as charitable organisations, clubs and societies. The question of whether the entity should be accounted for separately relates not only to the legal situation but also to whether it can be seen to have a separate existence.

5.2 KEY CONCEPT

THE BUSINESS ENTITY PRINCIPLE

The business entity principle states that transactions, assets and liabilities that relate to the entity are accounted for separately. It applies to all types of entities, irrespective of the fact that the entity may not be recognised as a separate legal or taxable entity.

When we are looking at large public companies, such as Woolworths or Telstra, the application of this principle and the reasons for it are self-evident. However, they are less clear with smaller entities, such as the corner newsagent or a second-hand car business. If, for example, you decided to set yourself up as a car dealer, for accounting purposes the cars purchased by you as a car dealer and the money earned as a result of that activity would be treated separately from your own personal car and money. This allows the tax authority to tax you separately on the profits from your business and it also helps you to determine the value of your business should you wish to sell it or take in a partner. The important point to remember is that for each business entity it is possible to account separately and, therefore, to draw up a balance sheet at a point in time. We now examine the balance sheet in more detail.

THE PURPOSE OF THE BALANCE SHEET

The purpose of a balance sheet is to communicate information about the financial position of an entity at a particular point in time. This is why the IASB prefers to use the name statement of financial position as this is exactly what it is. The statement summarises information contained in the accounting records in a clear and intelligible form. If the items contained in it are summarised and classified in an appropriate manner it can give information about the financial strength of the entity and indicate the relative liquidity of its assets. It also gives information about the liabilities of the entity, that is, what economic resources the entity is obliged to provide to other entities as a result of past transactions. The combination of this information can assist users to evaluate the financial position of the entity. It is an important statement when assessing the going concern of an entity, which we discussed in Chapter 2 (see Key concept 2.8). It should be remembered, however, that financial statements are only one part of the information needed by users; therefore the importance of this accounting statement should not be overemphasised.

> **5.3 KEY CONCEPT**
>
> ## LIQUIDITY
>
> Liquidity refers to the ease with which assets can be converted to cash in the normal course of business.

In most entities, a balance sheet is prepared at least once a year, though it can be done more or less frequently. Convention dictates that a normal accounting period is a year, and tax laws and other legislation are set up on that basis. Because the balance sheet represents the financial position at one point in time, its usefulness is limited: the situation may have changed since the last statement was prepared. For example, if you prepare a balance sheet in December and consult it in October it will be 10 months out of date. To extend our snapshot analogy, we can picture a business as a movie and a balance sheet as a still shot from that movie.

ELEMENTS OF THE BALANCE SHEET

5 LEARNING OBJECTIVE

Identify the requirements an item must satisfy to be recognised as an asset on a balance sheet

We need to know what a balance sheet contains. We have already said that it is similar to an individual's own measurement of wealth or financial position. If you consider how you would measure your own financial position, you will realise that you need to make a list of the economic resources you control (assets) and take away the economic resources due to other entities (liabilities). For an entity, this listing of assets and liabilities at a particular point in time is the entity's balance sheet. We discussed assets and liabilities in Chapter 2 and we restate the definitions in this chapter. The recognition criteria are then discussed before we look at the classification of assets and liabilities in subcategories.

Assets

We can find many definitions of assets, although most of them refer to legal ownership rights and so do not accord with contemporary accounting thought. Assets are not defined in the *Corporations Act*, so in Chapter 2 we defined a useful working description in Key concept 2.8 from the *Conceptual Framework* and restate this here in Key concept 5.4. This definition is in line with contemporary accounting thought and similar to that adopted by other standard-setting bodies.

Before an item can be considered as an asset for inclusion in the balance sheet it must not only meet the definition of an asset, it must also pass certain recognition criteria. First, it must be probable that the future economic benefits will eventuate and second, the asset must possess a cost or other value that can be measured reliably. Only when an item satisfies the definition and meets both recognition criteria will it qualify for inclusion on the balance sheet.

KEY CONCEPT 5.4

ASSETS

An asset is a resource controlled by the entity as a result of past events and from which future economic benefits are expected to flow to the entity.

(IASB *Conceptual Framework*, para. 4.4a). Copyright © IFRS Foundation. All rights reserved. Reproduced by Cengage Learning Australia with the permission of the IFRS Foundation ®. No permission granted to third parties to reproduce or distribute.

An asset is recognised in the balance sheet only when it is probable that the future economic benefits will flow to the entity and it must be possible to reliably measure the cost or other value of such benefits.

PROBABLE FUTURE ECONOMIC BENEFITS

The clear implication in the term 'future economic benefits' is that for an item to be an asset there must be a clear expectation that the entity will derive some benefit, now or in the future, and that this benefit does not depend on physical form. It must also be probable that those benefits will flow to the entity. Probable is defined as more likely than less likely.

MEASUREMENT

The second recognition criterion is that an asset must be capable of reliable measurement. The normal measure used is the dollar (a monetary unit). The problem is: on what basis do we measure? Some items that may lead to future economic benefits are extremely difficult to measure. For example, consider the worth of a brand such as Coca-Cola, which obviously has future economic value to the entity. The problem facing accountants, once they have decided that there is a future benefit, is how to measure that benefit in monetary terms. In the above example it would be impossible to isolate the effect these items have in monetary terms. Therefore, we do not include them in the balance sheet as assets, even though the business is clearly getting a benefit from them. (However, if another entity acquired Coca-Cola, it would recognise an asset for the amount paid for the brand.) Other examples of items which are clearly of benefit, but which are not included for accounting purposes, are a good location, a highly motivated workforce or a reputation for excellent service. You will remember from Chapter 1 that we discussed this problem in the context of the limitations of accounting information. Intangible assets present particular measurement problems and we discuss intangible assets in Chapter 8.

CONTROL BY THE ENTITY

While it may seem patently obvious that the benefits of assets should accrue to the entity – that is, be received by the entity at some point in time – it is vital in many cases to be able to separate the assets of the entity from those of the owner. For example, a factory building is likely to be an asset to an entity because the benefits from its use are likely to accrue to the entity. However, if the entity is a corner shop with residential accommodation, it is somewhat less clear which part of the building is an asset of the business and which is not. In practice it may well be that some of the goods held for resale are physically stored in part of the residential accommodation. There is unfortunately no general rule that can be applied and each case must be considered on its merits. The process of distinguishing between the assets of the owner and those of the business is merely an application of the business entity principle, referred to earlier, which states that the business should be viewed as separate from the owner and, therefore, accounted for separately.

STOP AND THINK 3

What are the deficiencies, if any, in the following definition of an asset? 'Assets are the things a business owns.'

Categories of assets

6 LEARNING OBJECTIVE

Explain the distinction between current and non-current assets

For accounting purposes, assets are normally separated (as far as possible) into subcategories. The reasoning behind this is that financial statements should provide information that is useful for making economic decisions. This is the objective of financial reporting, as stated in Key concept 2.6. These decisions can be made more precisely if some indication is given regarding the nature of the entity's assets. The categories used in Australia are current and non-current assets. In some countries the terms 'fixed assets' or 'long-term assets' are used instead of 'non-current assets'.

CURRENT ASSETS

Some accounting texts suggest that current assets are those that are part of the entity's operating cycle; they are also known as circulating assets. Other texts suggest that current assets are those that are converted into cash within an accounting period.

Before continuing our discussion, we need to know what is meant by the term 'operating cycle'.

THE OPERATING CYCLE

It is easier to understand the term 'operating cycle' if we look at one or two examples. In the case of a shop selling clothes, the operating cycle consists of buying garments and selling them for cash. In the case of an assembly business, the operating cycle involves more processes such as buying components, and then going through the process of assembly, selling and the collection of cash from a sale. Thus, the operating cycle has no fixed time period but depends on the nature of the business. It may, in fact, extend over a number of years. This is the case with property development, shipbuilding and heavy construction industries. The fact that the operating cycles are of different lengths is not vital because, in general terms, those assets that are part of the operating cycle are similar and are likely to be items such as inventory, cash in the bank, and so on. This means that, in general terms, these assets are likely to be liquid (refer to Key concept 5.3).

5.5

KEY CONCEPT

OPERATING CYCLE

Operating cycle is defined as the time between the acquisition of materials entering into a process and its realisation in cash or an instrument that is readily convertible into cash.

(AASB 101, para. 68)

THE REALISATION PERIOD

Some accounting texts suggest that what distinguishes current assets from other assets is whether or not they will be realised in the form of cash in the current accounting period. By convention, an accounting period is normally one year, though it can cover any period we care to use. If we applied this test strictly we would find that in many cases, such as that of a shipbuilder, something that is part of the operating cycle will not in fact be realised in the form of cash within a year.

In Australia, the realisation period is normally one year, unless the operating cycle is longer, in which case the operating cycle is used.

5.6

KEY CONCEPT

CURRENT ASSETS

Current asset means an asset that:

» is expected to be realised, or is held for sale or consumption, in the normal course of the entity's operating cycle

» is held primarily for trading purposes or for the short term and is expected to be realised within 12 months of the reporting date

» is cash or a cash-equivalent asset unless it is restricted from being exchanged or used to settle a liability for at least 12 months after the reporting date.

(AASB 101, para. 66)

CLASSIFICATION OF CURRENT ASSETS

Examples of current assets include cash, accounts receivable, short-term investments, inventories and prepaid expenses. These assets should be classified according to either their nature (such as accounts receivable which represent amounts owing from third parties) or their function (such as short-term investments which represent assets being held for sale).

NON-CURRENT ASSETS

Most texts refer to non-current assets as fixed assets. The term 'fixed assets' has been in use in accounting literature for decades and is still in use in a number of countries. Non-current assets generally include those assets that were acquired with the intention of retaining them for the purpose of generating income over a number of years. Items that meet this classification include land and buildings, machinery, vehicles, plant and equipment.

The term 'non-current asset' is now applicable in Australia as it is used in the International Financial Reporting Standards. Although the term is not defined in the *Corporations Act*, it is required to be used as a heading in the balance sheet to signify all assets other than current assets. The definition given in Key concept 5.7, which fits intuitively with the requirements of the *Corporations Act*, is used in accounting standards. As you can see, it is all-encompassing.

KEY CONCEPT

NON-CURRENT ASSETS

Non-current assets are all assets other than current assets.

(AASB 101, para. 66)

Depending on their nature, other items could be classed as either non-current or current assets. Examples are loans made to others over a period of years, a mortgage, or a long-term investment in the shares of another entity. All these could be classed as current assets if they met the definition within the time constraint. For example, a long-term loan with only 12 months left of its term would be reclassified from a non-current asset to a current asset.

Examples of non-current assets include plant and equipment, furniture and fixtures, motor vehicles, land and buildings, long-term receivables and intangibles. As with current assets, non-current assets are also classified according to their nature or function.

Having looked at what constitutes an asset, and at the way in which assets are divided into two classes on the balance sheet, we can now turn to the other part of the statement: what economic resources are owed to other entities. In accounting terminology, these are the liabilities.

STOP AND THINK 4

Explain, in your own words, the difference between non-current assets and current assets and why it is important to classify assets into subgroups.

Liabilities

As with the term 'assets', there are several definitions of liabilities, most of which refer to amounts owed by an entity. The *Corporations Act* does not define the term 'liabilities'. To be consistent with our approach to assets, we will use the definition cited in Key concept 2.11 and revisited here.

7 LEARNING OBJECTIVE

Identify the requirements an item must satisfy to be recognised as a liability on a balance sheet

KEY CONCEPT

LIABILITIES

Liabilities are defined as a present obligation of the entity arising from past events, the settlement of which is expected to result in an outflow from the entity of resources embodying economic benefits.

(IASB *Conceptual Framework*, para. 4.4b). Copyright © IFRS Foundation. All rights reserved. Reproduced by Cengage Learning Australia with the permission of the IFRS Foundation ®. No permission granted to third parties to reproduce or distribute.

A liability is recognised in the balance sheet only when it is probable that settlement of the liability will be required and it is possible to reliably measure the amount required.

As with assets, for an item to meet the definition of a liability and be recognised on the balance sheet, it must satisfy the recognition criteria. It must be probable that settlement of the liability will be required, and the amount must be capable of being measured reliably.

From the definition given, we can see that, in economic terms, a present obligation has to exist and this obligation must result in an outflow of economic benefits from the entity at a future date. Further, these obligations must have arisen because of past events.

As is the case with assets, liabilities are divided into two classes: current and non-current.

CURRENT LIABILITIES

8 **LEARNING OBJECTIVE**

Explain the distinction between current and non-current liabilities

The definition of current liabilities is similar to that of current assets. That is, these liabilities become due either in the operating cycle or within an accounting period normally defined as one year. As we did with assets, we will follow the realisation concept and use the definition given in AASB 101 *Presentation of financial statements*.

5.9   **KEY CONCEPT**

CURRENT LIABILITY

A current liability is a liability that satisfies any of the following criteria:

» it is expected to be settled in the normal course of the entity's operating cycle

» it is primarily held for trading

» it is due to be settled within 12 months of the balance sheet date

» the entity does not have an unconditional right to defer settlement of the liability for at least 12 months after the reporting date.

(AASB 101, para. 69)

Some examples of current liabilities are: amounts owed to suppliers (entities from whom we have purchased items on credit); short-term loans such as bank overdrafts, which are normally repayable on demand; and other short-term loans, such as promissory notes which have a life of 90 to 180 days.

NON-CURRENT LIABILITIES

Clearly there are other types of liabilities that do not have to be repaid in full in one year, for example, a mortgage on a house. In the case of a business, this type of liability may take a number of forms, such as a bank loan repayable in, say, three years or five years. These longer-term liabilities are normally put under the heading of non-current liabilities. Some texts refer to non-current liabilities as long-term liabilities, though this term is being used less and less in Australia.

When an item that has been classified as a non-current liability becomes due for settlement within 12 months it should be reclassified as a current liability. This is important information for users. The reclassification of the item may reveal that the entity has a possible liquidity and solvency problem, and may fail the going concern test if it doesn't have the capacity to meet the repayment. Imagine that an entity has a 10-year bank loan that was issued nine years ago. The entity may expect the bank to renew the loan and, therefore, it may continue to classify the loan as a non-current liability. Accounting standards require that such a loan be reclassified as a current liability unless firm arrangements in writing have been completed for the loan to be extended beyond 12 months (i.e. before the end of the accounting period). It is important for users to be fully informed of the amount and timing of an entity's obligations so that they can properly assess the entity's capacity to continue as a going concern. There are examples where entities have wrongly classified liabilities, such as Allco Finance Group in 2007, which admitted to wrongly classifying $1.9 billion of current liabilities as non-current liabilities. ABC Learning is another company which had an issue over the classification of current/non-current liabilities. (See www.youtube .com/watch?v=sMZExHXNlJQ for a YouTube clip on ABC Learning prepared by CPA Australia.) Non-current liabilities, like non-current assets, are not defined in the *Corporations Act,* although the term is used.

Denisenko Shutterstock.com

5.10

KEY CONCEPT

NON-CURRENT LIABILITIES

A non-current liability means a liability which is not a current liability.

(AASB 101, para. 69)

STOP AND THINK 5

List two current liabilities and two non-current liabilities, other than those mentioned in the text.

ASSETS AND LIABILITIES

There is a common thread to both assets and liabilities: both are concerned with the accounting period (current) and a time span greater than the accounting period (non-current). In general terms, the difference between the definitions of assets and liabilities centres on who controls the economic resources. Assets are resources controlled by the entity, and liabilities are economic resources owed to another entity; that is, claims against those resources. If the claims against an entity exceed the resources controlled, then the entity will no longer be a going concern. Conversely, if assets exceed liabilities the excess will accrue to the owners of the entity.

OWNERS' EQUITY

The owners' equity, or share of the capital of a business, can be viewed in a number of ways. In one sense it is a liability of the business in so far as it is a claim on the assets. However, it differs from other liabilities which have definite dates by which they are to be paid and are fixed in amount. The owners' equity is normally left in the business as long as it is required. Another way of viewing the owners' equity is as a residual claim on the assets of the business after all other liabilities have been settled.

9 LEARNING OBJECTIVE

Explain the meaning of 'equity'

The owners' equity is normally shown under two headings: that which is put into the business and that which is earned by and left in the business. The latter category is referred to as 'retained profits' or earnings. The total of the figures under these two headings, in the case of an individual, is analogous with wealth, whereas when the owner is in a business it is often referred to as capital. As shown in Chapter 4, the amount of this wealth or capital is dependent upon the measure used; that is, replacement cost, net realisable value, and so on. It is therefore better to view owners' equity as a residual claim rather than as capital or wealth because those expressions imply that an absolute measure of owners' equity is possible. Equity is not defined in the *Corporations Act,* although an acceptable definition is given in paragraph 4.4c of the IASB *Conceptual Framework* and was stated as Key concept 2.12 in Chapter 2, and revisited here.

5.11

KEY CONCEPT

EQUITY

Equity is the residual interest in the assets of the entity after deducting all its liabilities.

Equity can be seen as the residual interest due to the owners of the entity, hence the often-used term 'owners' equity' which is for a sole proprietor. In Chapter 2 we described the term as partner equity for a partnership; for a company it is called shareholder's equity.

5.1

CASE STUDY

BALANCE SHEETS ARE NOT INFALLIBLE

IT'S ALL A MATTER OF JUDGEMENT
BY JOE ROCK, KPMG, THAILAND

The balance sheet is supposed to present a snapshot of a company's financial position at a given date. If accurate, it should provide valuable information to readers about the company's assets and liabilities, its liquidity and its leverage.

There is, however, an inherent flaw in the balance sheet, one that is often misunderstood or underappreciated. The inherent flaw of the balance sheet is that it requires a considerable amount of management's judgement – and that could prove to be erroneous.

Preparing a balance sheet is not just an exercise of a company's accounting department lifting numbers from its accounting system's ledgers.

Management's judgement is required to determine the appropriate balances of numerous accounts. Working through some balance sheets, let's see where that judgement comes into play and what you, the financial statement reader, can do to get a feel for their assessment.

Receivables: The gross accounts receivable balance is most often a systems-generated figure, but generally accepted accounting principles require receivables to be reported at net realisable value.

❯

That means management has to estimate just how many current receivables will eventually turn 'bad' or be uncollectible. A reserve or provision is made for the uncollectibles and it is deducted from the gross receivables balance in order to present receivables at their estimated net realisable value.

For some industries, commercial banking being one example, this balance is perhaps the most important on the balance sheet. Management must spend a tremendous amount of time calculating the provision in line with local banking regulations and assessing how much of the current loan portfolio is expected to go bad. Their judgement is critical in determining the appropriate net receivable balance.

Inventory: The gross inventory balance is also a systems-calculated figure that may need to be adjusted to net realisable value in line with generally accepted accounting principles.

In the case of inventory, management will need to determine how much, if any, of its inventory is overvalued due to obsolescence. Once estimated, this obsolescence reserve is deducted from the gross inventory balance to present inventory at its estimated net realisable value.

In manufacturing and retail companies, inventory is often the largest current asset. Companies are constantly monitoring inventory levels in order to limit the costs of carrying large stocks.

Yet, as we are seeing in the United States, inventories can be extremely sensitive to economic fluctuations and even a slight dip in demand can lead to stockpiles and obsolescence. Management needs to exercise judgement on appropriate inventory levels in line with market demand in order to properly state inventory on the balance sheet.

Fixed assets: Fixed assets are generally based on historical cost, though in Thailand they can be revalued based on appraised values. Still, management must estimate the useful lives of its fixed assets for depreciation purposes and evaluate whether or not these assets are impaired and therefore need to be written down.

As a relatively new accounting standard in Thailand, the impairment standard has caused considerable pain in accounting departments and on balance sheets. Without appraisals, companies losing money need to prove that their operations will eventually make sufficient profit to justify the values of their fixed assets. This exercise demands a considerable amount of judgement as it relies on projected cash flows and discount rates.

Intangibles: Intangible assets, such as goodwill and franchise rights, are generally based on the price paid when one company acquires another.

Once acquired, the accounting treatment of intangibles is similar to that of fixed assets, so judgement is required on the points of estimating depreciable lives and determining if assets are impaired. Again, if the company isn't making any profits, how can it justify the values of such assets?

Liabilities: Contingent liabilities are obligations that are dependent on uncertain outcomes, such as litigation claims, tax audits and warranty or product guarantee liabilities.

It is management's responsibility to assess the likelihood of liabilities occurring from such contingencies in order to properly state the balance sheet.

What are some basic things that you, the financial statement reader, can do to be fairly sure that the balance sheet is a reasonable estimation of a company's financial position? First is to read the audit opinion. If the financial statements have been audited, an opinion should be attached. It should tell you whether or not the auditor has taken serious issue with any managerial judgements.

If the auditor believes that the balance sheet is materially misstated or for some reason cannot determine whether or not that is the case, the opinion should say so. Read the footnotes. They make up an integral part of the financial statements and should provide a wealth of information about a company's accounting policies and treatment of the areas mentioned.

Joe Rock, *Bangkok Post*, 27 June 2001

COMMENTARY

The article highlights the fact that the balance sheet contains many estimates, and needs to be used with this knowledge. It should be read in conjunction with all the notes that accompany financial statements. We say more about specific parts of the balance sheet in following chapters.

10 LEARNING OBJECTIVE

Explain and apply the balance sheet equation

THE BALANCE SHEET EQUATION

As we have already shown, the balance sheet of an entity is a statement of its assets and liabilities at a particular point in time. Because the business is an artificial entity, by definition all benefits arising from its assets belong to someone else. This is summed up in the balance sheet equation.

$$assets = liabilities$$

The equation describes the balance sheet in its simplest form; it must always hold true. However, it uses a very loose definition of liabilities. It can be refined to highlight the differences between pure liabilities and owners' equity, as follows:

$$assets = liabilities + owners' \ equity$$

This form of the equation will be used in our worksheet. The equation can be rewritten to highlight the fact that owners' equity is a residual claim on the assets.

$$assets - liabilities = owners' \ equity$$

The balance sheet equation underlies every balance sheet for every type of entity, large or small, private or public sector, manufacturing or retail, and is a fundamental principle of accounting.

A SIMPLE BALANCE SHEET

To illustrate the equation, a simple balance sheet can be constructed, as shown in the following worked example.

5.2

WORKED EXAMPLE

KEELSAFE

Susan Keel had been made redundant and decided to start up a small business making safety harnesses, which she called Keelsafe Safety Harnesses. For this purpose she purchased:

	$
One industrial sewing machine	1 100
A quantity of heavy-duty webbing material	600
A quantity of sewing materials	200
One second-hand computer	100
A supply of office stationery and letterheads	100
One cutting machine	800

The remaining $100 of her redundancy money was put into a business bank account.

At this stage we could draw up a list of assets of the business as follows:

ASSETS	$
Sewing machine	1 100
Webbing	600
Sewing materials	200
Computer	100
Stationery	100
Cutting machine	800
Cash at bank	100
	3 000

We could also identify the owners' equity in the business as being $3000; that is, the amount Susan Keel put in. Thus, the other side of the balance sheet – and of the equation – would be:

Owners' equity	3 000
	$3 000

Before moving on, it is worth thinking about how we obtained the figure for the owners' equity. All we did was list the economic resources Susan Keel's business controlled and then, as there were no outside claims against the business, we balanced the balance sheet by recording the amount of residual interest in the assets to the owners' equity.

Let us take this example further.

Because she was just starting out, Susan decided that, until the business got off the ground, she would operate from home by using the garage to manufacture the safety harnesses and the front room of her house as an office. The house had cost her $20 000 in 1979.

This additional information presents us with a problem: we do not know how much of the $20 000 relates to the garage and how much to the front room. We know that the business uses some of the house and that the house is an asset. But is it an asset of Susan's or of the business? If it is the latter, how should we record it and at what amount? To answer these questions we need to go back to our definition of an asset:

> An asset is a resource controlled by the entity as a result of past events and from which future economic benefits are expected to flow to the entity.
>
> (IASB *Conceptual Framework*, para. 4.4a). Copyright © IFRS Foundation. All rights reserved. Reproduced by Cengage Learning Australia with the permission of the IFRS Foundation ®. No permission granted to third parties to reproduce or distribute.

Bearing in mind the business entity principle, we can see from the definition that the garage is not an asset of the business — where the business is viewed as a separate entity from the owner. It is Susan Keel herself who owns both the house and the garage, and she also retains the legal right to enjoy the benefits from their use. The garage is not an asset of the business because the business has no legal right to use the garage, and has no control over it. Therefore, it does not need to be included in the balance sheet of the business. A similar argument can be applied to the front room, which is being used as an office.

However, suppose Susan entered into a long-term lease of the garage, whereby the business rented the garage from her, and this lease was secure, even if Susan sold the business to another person. In this case the lease would be an asset of the business because the use of the garage would now come under the control of the business and not Susan. If you are unsure of the argument, return to the discussion on the business entity and the definition of an asset.

When Susan starts to make the harnesses, she realises that she needs to buy some fasteners. She approaches her bank which agrees to give her a loan of $1000. She pays this sum into the business bank account and then buys the fasteners with a cheque for $600 drawn on that account.

We will look at this transaction and then draw up a new balance sheet. A new one is needed because we are now at a different point in time (remember: a balance sheet shows the position at one point in time only). The actual transaction on its own can be looked at in two stages:

Stage 1

The first stage occurred when Susan borrowed the money from the bank. This had two effects: it increased the business's assets, because the business will get a future benefit from the use of that money; and it also increased the business's liabilities, because the business now owes the bank $1000. Viewed on its own, this can be depicted as:

$$\text{assets} = \text{liabilities} + \text{owners' equity}$$
$$\text{in bank (\$1000)} = \text{loan (\$1000)}$$

Stage 2

In the second stage, $600 of the money in the bank is used to buy the fasteners. We can now extend Stage 1 and depict this as follows:

$$\text{assets} = \text{liabilities} + \text{owners' equity}$$
$$\text{cash in bank (\$1000)} = \text{loan (\$1000)}$$
$$\text{fasteners} + \$600 - \$600 \text{ cash in bank} = 0$$

All that has happened is that we have exchanged one asset for another, and the totals on either side of the equation remain the same.

Before going on to draw up a new balance sheet, you should note the important principle that we have just illustrated: there are two sides to every transaction. In Stage 1, the two sides of the transaction were an increase in assets with a corresponding increase in liabilities. In Stage 2, there was a decrease in one asset with a corresponding increase in another asset. This is often referred to as the principle of duality, which is simply a grand-sounding title for the rule that all transactions have two sides.

5.12

KEY CONCEPT

THE PRINCIPLE OF DUALITY

The **principle of duality** is the basis of the double-entry transaction-recording system on which accounting is based. It states that every transaction has two opposite and equal components.

Having established this principle, we can now draw up the new balance sheet of Keelsafe Safety Harnesses. We use the following balance sheet format:

$$\text{assets} - \text{liabilities} = \text{owners' equity}$$

The previous balance sheet was a very simple one. This time we will classify the assets into current and non-current, and group them together to make the statement more informative.

Another way to make the balance sheet more informative is to list the assets in order of liquidity. Liquid assets are those that can readily be converted into cash: the more difficult an item is to turn into cash, the less liquid it is. (The liquidity concept was stated in Key concept 5.3.) The sewing machine, as a non-current asset, is less liquid than the stocks of fasteners. Similarly, these are shown as less liquid than the cash at the bank.

You will also note that each group of assets is subtotalled and the subtotal is shown separately. The total of all assets is then shown. It is conventional to use single underlining for subtotals and double underlining to denote final totals.

Having classified and listed the assets of Keelsafe, we then show the claims against the business, subclassified into current and non-current liabilities. Total liabilities are deducted from total assets to give a figure for the residual assets. The residual assets amount is called the net assets. This is the value of the business after all external liabilities have been met. It has double underlining to show that it is a final total. The amount of the owners' equity, which comprises capital put into the business as well as residual profits, should balance against the net assets figure.

This is shown by our balance sheet equation:

$$\text{assets} - \text{liabilities} = \text{owners' equity}$$

KEELSAFE SAFETY HARNESSES
BALANCE SHEET AT 31 MAY 20X2

	$	$	$	$
Assets				
Current assets				
Cash at bank	500			
Fasteners	600			
Sewing material	200			
Webbing material	600			
Office stationery	100			
Total current assets		2000		

	$	$	$	$
Non-current assets				
Computer	100			
One cutting machine	800			
One sewing machine	1100			
Total non-current assets		2000		
Total assets			4000	
Liabilities				
Current liabilities				
Bank loan	1000			
Total liabilities			1000	
Net assets				3000
Owners' equity				3000

The balance sheet has been rearranged to emphasise the differences between the types of assets and Susan Keel's residual claim on the assets after any liabilities have been paid. Note that the statement is headed with the name of the business and the date on which it was drawn up.

Before you proceed any further, re-examine the definitions of current and non-current assets and ensure that you understand why the items in this balance sheet have been classified as they have.

It is worth examining the balance sheet for Woolworths (Appendix 1). Note the classification of assets and liabilities into current and non-current categories.

After studying the balance sheet for Woolworths you should be aware that it is not possible to obtain a complete understanding of all elements on the statement as they represent an aggregated statement of all assets, liabilities and equity for Woolworths. The annual financial statements of Woolworths contain detailed notes which are like the table of contents in a book. You will see references to notes in the balance sheet. Without reading the book, you cannot know the full story; similarly, without reading the notes accompanying the financial statements, it is not possible to fully understand an entity's position.

Finally we can now prepare a balance sheet for Beetle from the worksheet in Worked Example 5.1 at the beginning of the chapter.

BEETLE
BALANCE SHEET AT THE END OF THE PERIOD

	$	$	$	$
Assets				
Current assets				
Cash	4000			
Inventory	6000			
Total current assets		10000		
Non-current assets				
Van	4000			
Equipment	8000			
Total non-current assets		12000		
Total assets			22000	
Liabilities				

	$	$	$	$
Current liabilities				
Loan	12 000			
Total current liabilities		12 000		
Total liabilities			12 000	
Net assets				10 000
Owners' equity				
Capital	10 000			
Total owners' equity				10 000

A careful study of the figures in the balance sheet and a comparison with the last line of the worksheet on page 109 makes it clear that the balance sheet is in fact the bottom line of the worksheet after appropriate classifications have been made.

SOME BALANCE SHEET RATIOS

11 LEARNING OBJECTIVE

Explain and apply some common balance sheet ratios

In this section, we briefly examine a few balance sheet ratios that are extracted from the balance sheet. Chapter 10 discusses these and other ratios in more detail. Balance sheet ratios that are commonly used to assess short-term solvency are the relationship between current assets and current liabilities, and the relationship between current monetary assets (such as debtors and cash) and current liabilities.

The current ratio, for example, is calculated by dividing the current assets figure by the current liabilities figure.

$$\text{current ratio} = \frac{\text{current assets}}{\text{current liabilities}}$$

$$\text{Current ratio for Beetle} = \frac{10\ 000}{12\ 000} = 0.83$$

A current ratio of 0.83 means that for every one dollar of current liabilities there is 83 cents of current assets. The current ratio for Keelsafe is 2000/1000 or 2, which means for every $1 of current liabilities there is $2 of current assets. If we were comparing Beetle with Keelsafe we would conclude that Keelsafe is better placed to meet its current liabilities. A second commonly used ratio is the quick ratio, which normally excludes the inventory from the current assets and compares the remaining current assets with the current liabilities. The reasoning behind the exclusion of inventory is that it will take time to turn it into cash: it first has to be sold and then the customers have to pay before we can use the cash to pay our suppliers.

This ratio – the ratio of current assets, excluding inventory, to current liabilities – is often referred to as the acid test or quick ratio and is defined as follows:

$$\text{acid test or quick ratio} = \frac{\text{current assets} - \text{inventory}}{\text{current liabilities}}$$

A modification of this ratio is to deduct prepayments from the current assets, because prepayments are not normally available to pay debts.

Calculating this ratio for Beetle we obtain:

$$\frac{10\ 000 - 6\ 000}{12\ 000} = 0.33$$

For Keelsafe the ratio is:

$$\frac{2\,000 - 1\,400}{1\,000} = 0.6$$

A quick ratio of 0.33 means that for every $1 of current liabilities there is 33 cents of quick assets. The quick ratio for Keelsafe shows that for every $1 of current liabilities there is 60 cents of quick assets.

The final ratio we discuss in this section is the debt to equity ratio, which measures the amount of debt which may be total interest-bearing debt or total liabilities to total equity. These ratios provide information about long-term solvency and are calculated as:

$$\frac{\text{Total liabilities}}{\text{Total equity}}$$

$$\frac{\text{Total interesting-bearing liabilities}}{\text{Total equity}}$$

For Beetle the ratio is:

$$\frac{12\,000}{10\,000} = 1.2$$

For Keelsafe the ratio is:

$$\frac{1\,000}{3\,000} = 0.33$$

The ratios show that for every $1 of equity there is $1.20 of total liabilities for Beetle but only 33 cents for Keelsafe. The quick ratio for Keelsafe shows that for every $1 of current liabilities there is 60 cents of quick assets. If we were comparing Beetle with Keelsafe we would conclude that Keelsafe is less risky the bank that provided the loan and the equity providers.

12 LEARNING OBJECTIVE

Identify the limitations of a balance sheet

LIMITATIONS OF THE BALANCE SHEET

The fact that a balance sheet represents the position of an entity at one point in time is a limitation, because it is relevant only at that point in time. At any other time, as we have seen in the case of Keelsafe, a new balance sheet has to be prepared. For a statement to be useful, it should be as up-to-date as possible; its utility diminishes as time passes. Similarly, if the balance sheet is to provide a relevant measure of the assets and liabilities of an entity, the values assigned to those assets and liabilities should be as recent as possible, and herein lies another limitation.

As we saw in Chapter 4, assets can be valued in a number of ways, some of which are more subjective than others. The right value to choose depends on the purpose for which the balance sheet is being used. For example, if we want to know how much each item costs, then the historic cost would be appropriate. If, on the other hand, we wanted to know how much each item could be sold for, then the fair value or net realisable value would be appropriate. If we wanted to know how much the business as a whole was worth, it is likely that neither of these would be appropriate. This is partly due to difficulties involved in choosing an appropriate valuation method, and partly to accountants traditionally using historic cost as the basis for valuing assets in the balance sheet.

Clearly, this can lead to assets being stated at a figure that bears little, if any, relation to their current value. AASB 116 *Property, plant and equipment* allows entities to measure assets on either a cost or fair value basis. If an entity chooses fair value, then any changes in the fair value are reported as an asset revaluation reserve and form part of the equity in the balance sheet. In addition, if an entity uses fair value then it must ensure that the fair value on the balance sheet is not materially different to its fair value at that point in time. If, as a result of this requirement in AASB 116, an entity is forced to revalue land and buildings on an annual basis, the entity could incur significant costs associated with obtaining valuations of property every year.

Allied to the problem of fluctuations in the prices of specific assets is the fact that the unit of measurement (the dollar or other unit of currency) does not itself represent a constant value over time. You cannot buy as many goods with a dollar today as you could 10 years ago. Once again, this limits the usefulness of the information contained in the balance sheet.

We illustrated with the example of a gold mine that something that is a worthless asset for one business can be a valuable asset for another business undertaking a different activity. This case is reasonably clear-cut, but consider the problem of a football club trying to account for star players, or of a high-technology business trying to decide whether the cost of the patent on a new product is going to yield any future benefit when technology is changing so rapidly.

There are also issues relating to the ways in which a business is perceived and the ways in which management wishes the business to be perceived. Research has shown that managers, especially the managers of smaller entities, believe bankers are interested in the amount of assets available as security for a loan or overdraft. There is therefore a temptation to try to enhance the value of assets, perhaps by revaluing land and buildings, before applying for a loan. Similarly, in a number of cases where a business is in trouble, assets have been revalued in order to bolster the image of the business and to promote the impression of a sound asset base.

In Australia there are severe penalties for directors of public companies or other entities who attempt fraudulently to inflate assets or decrease liabilities. In Chapter 1 we discussed contacts, agency costs and incentives for managers to select certain accounting policies but this does not include fraudulent behaviour. In Chapter 3 we discussed the concept of ethics and the costs of unethical and fraudulent behaviour.

STOP AND THINK 6

What are the main limitations of a balance sheet? Does this mean a balance sheet is of no use?

We now examine the various influences on the balance sheet and then look at the needs of users. No discussion of financial statements would be complete without some reference to their needs.

INFLUENCES ON THE FORMAT OF THE BALANCE SHEET

Types of business

13 LEARNING OBJECTIVE

Discuss the factors that influence the format of a balance sheet

One of the prime determinants of the content and format of the balance sheet is the structure of the entity. For example, an incorporated business (a company) is subject to certain rules and regulations imposed by the state, whereas a partnership or sole proprietorship has no such restrictions. A company has to produce annual accounts as laid out in the *Corporations Act,* and file a copy with the Australian Securities and Investments Commission (ASIC). There is no such requirement of a partnership. A business that is part of a larger entity, however, may have to comply with the rules and form of accounts that suit that entity as a whole.

The need to comply with organisational requirements may also be affected by who owns the business. For example, a US-owned company operating in Australia would have to comply with Australian regulations, but would also report to the US parent company in a form that complies with US regulations. In contrast, there are no restrictions or rules imposed on a business that is owned by two partners, other than the *Partnership Act 1891*; the partners can decide for themselves what form the balance sheet takes. However, other bodies can affect the frequency and format of the balance sheet. For example, the tax office needs to know how much income the partners have earned, and if the accounts are drawn up by a professional accountant they must follow the accounting standards and rules of the profession.

Another factor affecting the format of the balance sheet is the size of the entity. In the case of a larger, more complex entity, assets need to be summarised under broad headings, otherwise the amount of detail would be so great that statement users would find it impossible to get an overall picture.

Finally, we should mention the influence of organisational goals. Consider, for example, an entity set up for charitable purposes (which may or may not be incorporated): of what relevance to that entity is a classification such as owners' equity? Similarly, if you looked at the accounts of your municipal council you would not expect to see a heading for owners' equity or retained profits.

5.3 WORKED EXAMPLE

BALANCE SHEETS

Personal balance sheet

JOE SMITH
BALANCE SHEET AT JUNE 30 20X9

	$
Assets	
Cash at bank	10 000
Car	8 000
Furniture	15 000
Home unit	300 000
Superannuation	35 000
Total assets	368 000
Liabilities	
Visa credit card	6 000
Mortgage loan: NAB	250 000
Loan from parents	25 000
Total liabilities	281 000
Equity	
Personal equity	87 000
Total equity	87 000
Total liabilities and equity	368 000

Partnership balance sheet

HANSMITREE PARTNERSHIP
BALANCE SHEET AT 30 JUNE 20X9

	$	$	$	$
Assets				
Current assets				
Cash at bank	40			
Finished goods inventory	1 220			
Raw materials inventory	1 400			
Total current assets		2 660		
Non-current assets				
Motor vehicles	10 100			
Machinery	5 000			
Land and buildings	100 000			
Total non-current assets		115 100		
Total assets			117 760	
Liabilities				
Current liabilities				
Bank overdraft	2 000			
Total current liabilities		2 000		
Non-current liabilities				
Bank loan, due 1 January 20X1	50 000			
Total non-current liabilities		50 000		
Total liabilities			52 000	
Net assets				65 760
Partners' equity				
Toni Milne current account	10 000			
Kellee Hancock current account	15 760			
Toni Milne capital account	15 000			
Kellee Hancock capital account	25 000			
Total partners' equity				65 760

Company balance sheet

SIMPLE LTD
BALANCE SHEET AT 31 DECEMBER 20X9

	$	$	$	$
Assets				
Current assets				
Cash at bank	40			
Finished goods inventory	1 220			
Raw materials inventory	1 400			
Total current assets		2 660		
Non-current assets				
Motor vehicles	10 100			
Machinery	5 000			
Land and buildings	100 000			
Total non-current assets		115 100		
Total assets			117 760	
Liabilities				
Current liabilities				
Bank overdraft	2 000			
Total current liabilities		2 000		
Non-current liabilities				
Bank loan, due 1 January 20X1	50 000			
Total non-current liabilities		50 000		
Total liabilities			52 000	
Net assets				65 760
Owners' equity				
Capital	50 000			
Retained earnings	15 760			
Total owners' equity				65 760

Users of accounts

As discussed in Chapter 1, different users may have conflicting needs for information. To some extent, the rules and regulations laid down by the state encompass some of these needs. However, these rules give only a minimum requirement. For example, while the *Corporations Act* requires loans and overdrafts to be shown, research shows that bankers would like to see details of loan repayment dates in accounts. On the other hand, company owners may not wish to have that information made public. A similar conflict arises between the needs of managers, who want to know what it will cost to replace an asset (rather than what the asset cost when they bought it) and the needs of owners, who want to know what management has spent their money on and how much each item cost.

FORMAT USED IN THE BOOK

In this chapter we have defined the nature, purpose and content of balance sheets and highlighted some of the problems with such statements. We have also introduced the wider context in which accounting reports can be viewed. Before proceeding, it is important to make sure you understand the definitions involved and can apply them to real problems. As you have seen, a balance sheet can take many forms and in a book of this nature there is no need to cover all of them. For simplicity, therefore, we use one format throughout the book – the one shown for Simple Ltd in worked example 5.3 on the previous page.

The needs of an entity determine the format of the balance sheet. We have chosen a format appropriate to an introductory text. Before following a different format, ensure that you understand the reasons behind it and consider whether the information is presented as clearly as it is in the Simple Ltd balance sheet. This format is the one previously required under the *Corporations Act* and many companies in Australia are still using it. Turn to Appendix 1 and study the balance sheet of Woolworths Limited and note its format.

The balance sheet is headed with the name of the entity and the date to which the statement relates. As explained previously, a balance sheet relates to one point in time and that date needs to be clearly stated in the heading.

Finally, we emphasise again that a balance sheet's format may differ according to the requirements of the users or the owners (as illustrated in the previous section by examples for an individual and a partnership). Other formats are also possible. For example, it is unlikely that a corner store would be part of a public company. A more appropriate format in this case may be to list the current assets less the current liabilities. If current assets are more than current liabilities, this would indicate that the business should be able to meet its short-term commitments when they become due.

SUMMARY

LEARNING OBJECTIVE 1

APPRECIATE THAT FINANCIAL STATEMENTS ARE A SUMMARY OF TRANSACTIONS, EXPLAIN THE FORMAT AND PURPOSE OF THE WORKSHEET

The worksheet is a method of recording and collecting data. It is a simple vehicle for recording and checking transactions and extracting a balance sheet and a statement of comprehensive income.

LEARNING OBJECTIVE 2

ANALYSE AND CLASSIFY BALANCE-SHEET-ONLY TRANSACTIONS ONTO A WORKSHEET

Beetle was used to demonstrate that the worksheet is a simple vehicle for recording, checking and extracting a balance sheet. We showed how the basis of accounting is very simple if you follow the basic principles. Furthermore, for those times when mistakes are made, the system used on the worksheet provides a simple and effective way of checking for errors.

LEARNING OBJECTIVE 3

EXPLAIN COMMON ERRORS IN SINGLE- AND DOUBLE-ENTRY RECORDING OF TRANSACTIONS

A single-entry error occurs when only one side of a transaction is recorded in the worksheet. It is detected by the amount of the transaction equalling the difference in the balances between the two sides of the worksheet. A double-entry error occurs when a transaction is recorded twice on the same side of the worksheet. It is detected by the amount of the transaction equalling one-half of the difference in the balances between the two sides of the worksheet. A transposition error can be detected when the difference in balances between both sides of the worksheet is exactly divisible by 9.

LEARNING OBJECTIVE 4

EXPLAIN THE MEANING AND PURPOSE OF THE BALANCE SHEET

The balance sheet is the financial statement that reports all the assets, liabilities and equity of an entity at one point in time. It is an important statement for assessing the financial position of an entity, and enables its user to answer various questions such as: does the entity have sufficient assets to meet its liabilities and therefore pass the going concern test?

LEARNING OBJECTIVE 5

IDENTIFY THE REQUIREMENTS AN ITEM MUST SATISFY TO BE RECOGNISED AS AN ASSET ON A BALANCE SHEET

To be recognised as an asset on the balance sheet, an item must satisfy the definition of an asset. This includes the following criteria:

» inflow of future economic benefits

» control by the entity

» resulting from a past event or transaction.

In addition, the asset must meet the following two recognition criteria:

» It is probable that benefits will flow into the entity

» A cost or other value can be reliably measured.

LEARNING OBJECTIVE 6

EXPLAIN THE DISTINCTION BETWEEN CURRENT AND NON-CURRENT ASSETS

Current assets include cash and assets that are to be consumed or converted into cash within 12 months of the reporting date (or by the end of the operating cycle if this is greater than 12 months). Non-current assets are all other assets.

LEARNING OBJECTIVE 7

IDENTIFY THE REQUIREMENTS AN ITEM MUST SATISFY TO BE RECOGNISED AS A LIABILITY ON A BALANCE SHEET

To be recognised as a liability on the balance sheet, an item must satisfy the definition of a liability. This includes the following criteria:

» outflow of future economic benefits
» present obligation for the entity
» arising as a result of a past event or transaction.
  In addition, the liability must meet the following two recognition criteria:
» It is probable that benefits will flow from the entity
» A cost or other value can be reliably measured.

LEARNING OBJECTIVE 8

EXPLAIN THE DISTINCTION BETWEEN CURRENT AND NON-CURRENT LIABILITIES

Current liabilities include all liabilities that are expected to be settled or expire within 12 months of the reporting date (or by the end of the operating cycle where this is greater than 12 months). Also included are those liabilities where the entity does not have an unconditional right to defer settlement of the liability for at least 12 months after the reporting date. Non-current liabilities are all other liabilities.

LEARNING OBJECTIVE 9

EXPLAIN THE MEANING OF 'EQUITY'

Equity is the residual interest in the assets of an entity, and is measured as assets less all liabilities.

LEARNING OBJECTIVE 10

EXPLAIN AND APPLY THE BALANCE SHEET EQUATION

The balance sheet equation is assets = liabilities + equity. It can also be expressed as assets − liabilities = equity. The balance sheet equation can be used to analyse all accounting transactions for recording into the accounting records.

LEARNING OBJECTIVE 11

EXPLAIN AND APPLY SOME COMMON BALANCE SHEET RATIOS

The ratios were the current, quick and debt to equity ratios. The current and quick ratios are measures of short-term solvency while the debt to equity ratio looks at long-term solvency.

LEARNING OBJECTIVE 12

IDENTIFY THE LIMITATIONS OF A BALANCE SHEET

Limitations of a balance sheet include those in the following list.

» It only relates to one point in time

» It only provides past information
» Some items, like research and development, may not be recognised as an asset because they fail the definition or recognition criteria
» If the cost method of asset measurement is used, some asset values may be reliable but less relevant.

LEARNING OBJECTIVE 13

DISCUSS THE FACTORS THAT INFLUENCE THE FORMAT OF A BALANCE SHEET

The format of balance sheets is not mandated by accounting standards. Factors that influence the format include:

» type of business (e.g. partnership or company)
» size of the entity
» goals of the entity
» needs of users.

REVIEW QUESTIONS

1 What is the purpose of a balance sheet and what information does it contain?

2 What are the essential elements of a useful definition of an asset?

3 Explain, in your own words, what a liability is and the differences between liabilities and owners' equity.

4 List three current assets and three non-current assets other than those mentioned in the text.

5 Describe, in your own words, what is meant by the concept of duality.

6 How would you identify a transposition error?

7 In each of the following cases, describe the two entries required on the worksheet.

   a The owner withdraws $200.

   b The business buys a vehicle for $27 500.

   c The business begins negotiations with a real estate agent for the purchase of shop premises for $156 500.

   d Salaries of $1760 are paid.

   e The business hires a consultant for $1000. This amount is paid on hiring.

   f The business receives an electricity account for $100, payable within 14 days.

   g The firm receives an order of $200 for merchandise.

8 In situations where doubt exists as to whether a transaction has resulted in an asset or expense, what questions should be posed?

9 If some doubt still remains, how should a choice be made? Explain any principles involved.

PROBLEMS FOR DISCUSSION AND ANALYSIS

1 Refer to the Woolworths 2013 financial report in Appendix 1.

   a What is the amount of (i) total assets, (ii) current assets and (iii) non-current assets?

   b Which class of non-current assets has the greatest value?

   c   What is the amount of (i) total liabilities, (ii) current liabilities and (iii) non-current liabilities?

   d   Which class of non-current liabilities has the greatest value?

2   In 20X6, XYZ Ltd had total assets of $200 000 and total liabilities of $250 000. Non-current assets and non-current liabilities were $50 000 and $25 000 respectively. What were the current assets, current liabilities and owners' equity for 20X6?

3   In 20X6, ABC Ltd had total assets of $100 000 and owners' equity of $50 000. In 20X7, total liabilities were $50 000 more than in 20X6, and the owners' equity was $60 000. Calculate:

   a   the total assets figure for 20X7

   b   the total liabilities figure for 20X6.

4   Given the following information, supply the missing figures. *Note:* Total assets were $10 000 less in 20X8 than in 20X9.

	PQR LTD 20X8	PQR LTD 20X9
Current assets	74 000	?
Non-current assets	112 000	86 000
Total assets	?	?
Current liabilities	23 000	?
Non-current liabilities	?	100 000
Total liabilities	?	100 000
Owners' equity	60 000	?

5   In each of the following situations, discuss the potential effect on the business and suggest possible ways in which those effects could be reflected on the worksheet.

   a   The owner starts up a new business and pays $2000 into the business bank account. In addition, it is decided that the owner's car will be used exclusively for the business. The car was purchased last year at a cost of $10 000 but a similar one-year-old car could be bought for $9000.

   b   Goods previously bought by the business for $1000 were sold to a customer who then changed his mind and decided that he did not want the goods after all.

   c   Another batch of goods, bought for $800 and sold for $1200, was subsequently found to be faulty. The options available are as follows:

     •   Give the customer a rebate on the purchase price of $200.

     •   Refund the full selling price to the customer and reclaim the goods. If this course of action is followed, a further $280 will need to be spent to rectify the faults.

6   In each of the following cases, describe the two entries required on the worksheet.

   a   The owner pays $769 cash for a desk and chair.

   b   The insurance premium of $549 for one year is paid by cash.

   c   The business checks the price of widgets from a supplier and is told the price is $650 per tonne.

   d   A computer is purchased for $4999 and payment is made by cash. The computer is subsequently found to be faulty and is returned to the supplier for a full refund. (Treat this as two separate transactions.)

   e   An owner withdraws $100 from the business for his personal use.

f   The owner offers to pay $599 for a new computer.

g   The purchase price of a Mazda De-Luxe is $48 999. A buyer offers $48 000 cash. The offer is accepted.

7   Prepare a balance sheet from the following information and comment on the financial position of the business. *Note*: The business had been experiencing a downturn in sales over the past three months due to the economic recession.

	$
Owners' equity	?
Cash	1 700
Accounts payable	42 250
Inventory	30 125
Motor vehicles	17 200
Bank overdraft	32 500
Accounts receivable	1 250
Office equipment	3 600
Low-interest loan to director	21 000

8   Prepare a balance sheet from the following information and comment on the position of the business as shown by the balance sheet.

	$
Stock of goods held for resale	13 000
Freehold land and building	64 000
Mortgage on land and building	58 000
Cash	1 000
Fixtures and fittings	15 200
Office furniture	4 600
Bank overdraft	20 700
Delivery van	3 200
Owners' equity	?

9   Prepare a balance sheet from the following information and comment on the financial position of the business.

	$
Cash	3 000
Inventory	8 000
Accounts payable	12 000

	$
Salaries payable	?
Accounts receivable	16 000
Land and buildings	20 000
Plant and equipment	7 000
Furnishings and fittings	2 500
Owners' equity	13 900
Bank loan	30 000

10 The final account balances (after all adjustments) of Debbie Ltd for the year ending 30 June 20X1 are listed below. From the information given, prepare a balance sheet, in good form, and list the accounts that would not be included in the balance sheet.

	$
Bank overdraft	11 900
Salaries payable	1000
Salaries expense	1000
Sales	137 250
Inventory	13 100
Accounts receivable	17 300
Owners' equity	?
Interest expense	330
Land and buildings (net)	110 000
Long-term loan (due 19 December 20X9)	100 000
Accounts payable	45 600
Plant and equipment (net)	22 000
Cost of goods sold	110 000

11 Below are the final account balances (after all adjustments) of ABC Ltd for the year ending 30 June 20X1. From these balances prepare a balance sheet, in good form, and list the accounts that would not be included in the balance sheet.

	$
Cash	126 000
Sales discount	5 000
Accounts receivable	50 000
Inventory	88 000

	$
Land	364 000
Plant and equipment	234 000
Accounts payable	26 000
Ninety-day bank bill payable	80 000
Long-term loan payable	45 000
Tax payable	10 000
Vehicle expenses	10 000
Cost of goods sold	40 000
Owners' equity	701 000
Tax expense	10 000

12 In each of the following situations, identify whether the item should be included in the balance sheet of Transom Trading as at 31 December 20X1, and, if so, at what amount and under which heading. Transom Trading is a retailer of motor parts and accessories. In all cases, reasons for your decision must be given.

a A freehold shop was bought in August 20X1 for $176 000. A mortgage of $60 000 was taken out to buy the shop in August 20X1 and the balance paid in cash.

b Goods on the shelves at the end of the day on 31 December 20X1 have a resale value of $24 000 and were purchased by Transom Trading for $16 000 cash.

c A delivery van, costing $12 000, which Transom Trading ordered on 20 December 20X1 was finally delivered and paid for by cash on 12 January 20X2.

d Shop fittings worth $6000 were bought at an auction by Transom Trading for only $3000 cash prior to opening the shop in August 20X1.

e A Ford Falcon costing $7000 was bought by the owner of Transom Trading through the business in November 20X1 for his wife's use. He did this because the Ford Escort he had bought privately second-hand in September for $8000 was being used exclusively for collecting and delivering goods for Transom Trading and not as a family car, as originally intended.

f One cash register was rented from Equipment Supplies at an annual rental of $400.

g One cash register was bought by Transom Trading in November 20X1 for $1200 cash.

h A bank overdraft was drawn down to $13 000 on 31 December 20X1.

i Seat belts which the owner of Transom Trading bought for $12 000 in September from a market trader in good faith were subsequently found to be defective and worthless.

13 Record the information in Problem 12 onto a worksheet and calculate the owners' equity and draw up the balance sheet of Transom Trading as at 31 December 20X1. Assume balances as at 1 January 20X1 were cash $192 000, seat belts $8000 and Capital $200 000.

14 Fred owns a garage and has tried to get everything together ready for the preparation of business accounts. He has drawn up the list of items below. You are required to identify, with reasons, the balance sheet heading under which each item should be classified, and the amount that should be included.

  a A motor car was bought for resale at a cost of $7000. The retail price was $10 000.

  b Various loose tools for car repairs cost $1400.

  c Two hydraulic jacks were bought for $240 each.

  d Freehold premises cost $80 000.

  e $1200 was spent on digging and finishing a pit for repairs.

  f The original cost of spare parts held as general stock was $1580.

  g Spare parts were bought from the previous owner at the time of purchasing the garage. A value of $12 000 was agreed upon. Subsequently it became apparent that only $400 of these spares was of any use.

  h The breakdown truck cost $6000 and $1200 was spent on fitting the crane.

  i A customer's car worth $3000 was being held because the customer had not paid an outstanding bill of $600.

  j Fred's own car cost $8000. This is used mainly for business but Fred also uses it in the evenings and at weekends for the family.

  k Fred believes he has built up customer goodwill worth at least $14 000 if he sold the garage tomorrow.

  l A bank loan for $48 000 is repayable within three months.

  m A 20-year mortgage on the property of $48 000 has not been fully repaid. The amount still outstanding is $36 000.

15 Month-end balance sheet amounts (for three consecutive months) for the dental practice of Dr Fang, a local dentist, are presented below. The information is complete except for the balance in the owners' equity account.

  a Determine the balance in Dr Fang's equity account at the end of each month.

  b Assuming that Dr Fang made no additional investments, determine his drawings for the months of November and December.

  c Prepare a balance sheet for the business at the end of December.

	31 OCT	30 NOV	31 DEC
	$	$	$
Cash	9 100	3 900	3 000
Accounts receivable	16 100	16 500	8 050
Prepaid insurance	700	800	600
Surgery equipment	29 800	29 700	38 300
Building	81 000	80 800	80 600
Land	33 000	33 000	33 000

	31 OCT	30 NOV	31 DEC
	$	$	$
Accounts payable	10 100	3 100	3 000
Wages payable	5 100	4 100	4 800
Mortgage payable	34 700	34 300	33 900
Owners' equity	?	?	?

16 The ledger accounts of Mickey Ltd as at 30 June 20X1 are listed below. Prepare a balance sheet in good form and insert the missing amounts.

	$		$
Total owners' equity	?	Other current assets	?
Total non-current assets	?	Total assets	?
Tax payable	?	Loan payable (31/12/20X3)	?
Total liabilities	?	Net assets	27 400
Bank	10 000	Loan receivable (30/6/20X3)	100 000
Accounts receivable	15 700	Total non-current assets	?
Accounts payable	10 300	Debentures payable (30/6/20X9)	137 000
Inventory	27 200	Loan receivable (1/7/20X1)	10 000
Fixtures/fittings (net)	7 200	Plant and equipment (net)	3 600
Salaries payable	6 200	Other current liabilities	1 200
Land and buildings	120 000	Total current assets	63 600
Total current liabilities	30 000		

17 The accounting department of ABC Co. Ltd was struck by lightning and some accounting records were destroyed. The senior accountant managed to salvage some records and has asked you to prepare a balance sheet, in good form, from the following information.

Accounts receivable $10 000, bank overdraft $12 000, motor vehicles $20 000, net assets $115 000, total assets $217 000, inventory $20 000, land $50 000, capital $80 000, total non-current assets $185 000, plant and equipment $15 000, prepaid rent ? (*note*: the rent is paid monthly in advance), total current assets ?, buildings ?, accounts payable ?, total current liabilities ?, retained earnings ?, total owners' equity ?.

18 A fire partially destroyed the offices of the Firesafe Company on 30 May 20X1. Some accounting records were retrieved. From the following information, prepare a balance sheet in good form. *Note:* One account does not belong in the balance sheet.

	$
Cash	200
Plant	30 000
Incendiary chemicals	17 500
Salary expenses	2 300
Accounts payable	?
Incendiary plastic containers	?
Total current assets	?
Equipment	7 000
Loan payable 29 May 20X2	17 000
Motor vehicles	?
Accounts receivable	17 800
Land	50 000
Buildings	12 500
Owners' equity	?
Total non-current assets	118 000
Total assets	156 000
Total current liabilities	47 300
Loan payable 30 June 20X0	?
Bank overdraft	7 300
Total non-current liabilities	50 000

Note to instructors: The following problems are considered more suitable for use in MBA courses. However, undergraduate courses may also find them useful.

19 At 30 June 2012, the non-current asset section of the balance sheet of Qantas included aircraft and engines owned $12 047 million at cost and aircraft and engines finance leased and hire-purchase $5079 million at cost. Explain the difference between the two and how the definition and recognition criteria of assets would be met for each class of asset in order for Qantas to report the aircraft as assets in the balance sheet?

20 X Ltd sold 2000 computers in June 20X0. The terms of a sale included a 12-month warranty. The warranty provides that X Ltd will meet the cost of repairs that are associated with faulty parts attributable to manufacture. Past experience indicates that 10 per cent of computer sales lead to warranty claims at an average cost of $70 for parts and $100 for labour, per computer. Discuss whether the warranty commitment would meet the definition and recognition criteria of a liability to the firm at 30 June 20X0.

21 In June 2002 WorldCom, a US telecommunications firm, announced that it had misreported financial information in previous accounting periods – to the sum of USD $3.9 billion – by recording routine operating expenses as capital expenditure.

Discuss

    a   The impact of the treatment on the financial statements.

    b   The possible reasons for management's accounting policy choice.

    c   Whether any party is likely to suffer from the misrepresentation.

22 ABC Company and XYZ Company conduct the same type of business. Both are recently formed entities; thus the balance sheet figures for assets can be assumed to be at fair values. The balance sheets of the two companies as at 30 June 20X0 are as follows:

ABC COMPANY
BALANCE SHEET AT 30 JUNE 20X0

	$	$	$	$
Assets				
Current assets				
Cash at bank	2 400			
Accounts receivable	4 800			
Total current assets		7 200		
Non-current assets				
Office equipment	6 000			
Land	18 000			
Building	30 000			
Total non-current assets		54 000		
Total assets			61 200	
Liabilities				
Current liabilities				
Accounts payable	21 600			
Unsecured loan payable, due 30 September 20X0	31 200			
Total current liabilities		52 800		
Total liabilities			52 800	
Net assets				8 400
Owners' equity				
T. Edwards capital	8 400			
Total owners' equity				8 400

XYZ COMPANY
BALANCE SHEET AT 30 JUNE 20X0

	$	$	$	$
Assets				
Current assets				
Cash at bank	2 000			
Accounts receivable	24 000			
Total current assets		26 000		
Non-current assets				
Office equipment	600			
Land	13 600			
Building	6 000			
Total non-current assets		20 200		
Total assets			46 200	
Liabilities				
Current liabilities				
Accounts payable	4 800			
Unsecured loan payable, due 30 September 20X0	7 200			
Total current liabilities		12 000		
Total liabilities			12 000	
Net assets				34 200
Owners' equity				
S. Allen capital	34 200			
Total owners' equity				34 200

Required

a   Assuming that you are a banker and that the owner of each business has applied for a short-term loan of $6000 (repayable in six months), which application would you select as being the more favourable? Why?

b   Assuming that you are a businessperson interested in buying one or both companies, and both owners have indicated their intentions to sell, for which business would you be willing to pay the higher price, assuming you will be taking over the existing liabilities of the company? Explain.

c   If the existing owners agreed to be accountable for all existing liabilities, how would this change your decision in (b), if at all?

(Adapted from B. Colditz and R. Gibbins, *Australian Accounting*, 3rd edn, McGraw-Hill, 1976, p. 45, business decision problem 2.)

23 For a number of years, the Remote Shire Council controlled a very large rubbish site in the southern area of Western Australia. Unfortunately, the site was nearly full and the council had to search for a new location. One of the preferred locations was an area that had previously been an open-cut coal mine. It was owned and controlled by the No More Coal Mining Venture, and the Remote Shire Council offered $4 per cubic metre to lease the quarry for a period of 10 years. This amounted to a total lease payment of $8.8 million. After this, the local paper reported the following:

> This has the appearance of something for nothing but, to some experts in private enterprise, it appeared more like nothing for something. One private company, Environmental Disposals, had previously tendered $5.00 per cubic metre for the same mine site for disposal purposes, a total of $11 million.

Using the above information, explain how an asset can consist of 'nothing', and, taking into account the amounts mentioned above, illustrate your understanding of the concept of asset valuation.

Using this information, discuss whether the No More Coal Mining Venture should recognise an asset for the abandoned coal mine.

24 Read the article 'The SEC: no more hiding games' and answer the following questions:

a   What do you believe is meant by the term 'off balance sheet'?

b   Why do companies want items 'off balance sheet'?

c   Discuss the damage that is done to the credibility of the balance sheet and the accounting profession from events such as the collapse of Enron.

THE SEC: NO MORE HIDING GAMES

EDITED BY ROBIN AJELLO

Enron made famous the corporate tactic of hiding debt in off-balance-sheet partnerships. Now, the Securities & Exchange Commission aims to put a stop to such practices. On October 30, the SEC proposed rules requiring public companies to disclose most such arrangements in their financial reports.

The proposed rules would lower the threshold for disclosure, requiring companies to reveal off-balance-sheet transactions if there is more than a remote chance they'll have a material effect on the company. The SEC will issue final rules by January 26.

25 Jill Wright, head of the Green Trees Playgroup, wanted to know how well the business was performing after six months of activity. To do this she needed to know the company's position at 30 June 20X1 and what the future outlook for the business was.

The Green Trees Playgroup was founded by Mrs Wright in January 20X1 to provide children of working parents with a specially supervised preschool education. Capital for the playgroup was raised by Mrs Wright, who took out a personal loan for $26 250 of which she invested $22 500 in ordinary shares of the company. A further $11 250 in cash was invested by local business, and a one-year loan of $7455 was made to the company by the local shire council.

With this capital, Mrs Wright purchased, on behalf of the playgroup, premises for $42 000, of which $8400 was for land and $33 600 for a building on the land. This was financed, in part, by a $28 350 mortgage, the remainder being paid in cash. Interest on the mortgage was to be paid in instalments every three months – though no repayment of the principal was required until the business had become established. Furniture and equipment were also purchased for $14 625 in cash.

During the first six months of operations, which ended June 20X1, the business paid in cash the additional amounts listed in the table.

	$
Salary to Mrs Wright	8 250
Salaries of part-time employees	5 526
Insurance (one-year policy)	1650
Electricity	1070
Food and supplies	4 590
Interest and miscellaneous	3 594
Total paid out	24 680

Other events that took place include those listed below.

a   Student fees of $17 724 were received in cash. A further $690 for fees was owed to the playgroup by parents. This amount was to be received in the period ending 31 December 20X1.

b   Mrs Wright estimated that $412 worth of supplies were still on hand at 30 June 20X1, and estimated that the same amount would be on hand at 31 December 20X1. The playgroup owed $712 to food suppliers at 30 June 20X1. This amount was to be paid in the period ending 31 December 20X1.

c   Mrs Wright estimated that for the next six months, to 31 December 20X1, student fees received would total $26 880.

d   She estimated that, for the next six months to 31 December 20X1, the following expenditures would occur:

- salaries of $13 768
- $1344 for the electricity bill
- $5880 for additional food and supplies
- $2850 for interest and miscellaneous items.

The loan from the council was also expected to be paid in this period.

e   No depreciation was recorded on the company's assets (buildings, furniture or equipment) as Mrs Wright has been offered $58 875 in cash for these assets from someone wanting to buy the business and she had thought it would not be appropriate to record any.

Required

a   Prepare a balance sheet for the Green Trees Playgroup as at 30 June 20X1. To minimise errors, treat each event separately. For events affecting owners' equity, other than the initial investment, record the transaction in the retained profits account. Show negative amounts in parentheses. Show non-current assets at their original cost.

b   Prepare an estimated balance sheet as at 31 December 20X1.

c   Should the non-current assets be reported on the 30 June 20X1 balance sheets at their cost, at $58 875, or at some other amount? (This amount need not be calculated.) If they were reported at an amount other than cost, how would the balance sheet prepared in (a) change?

d   Does it appear likely that the Green Trees Playgroup will become a viable business, assuming that Mrs Wright's estimations prove correct?

ETHICS CASE STUDY

The manager of Centura Ltd has asked you to classify a $500 000 loan due for repayment in nine months as a non-current liability in the balance sheet. The company's total assets are $2 million.

Discuss

a   the impact of this classification

b   possible reasons for the request

c   whether any party is likely to suffer from this treatment

d   what you would do.

SUGGESTED ANSWERS TO STOP AND THINK EXERCISES IN THE CHAPTER

1   The worksheet is a working paper which facilitates the recording and gathering of information about transactions without the need for debits and credits. The information from the worksheet can then be used to prepare the statement of comprehensive income and the balance sheet.

2 a   Decrease the inventory column by $100 and decrease the owners' capital column by $100.

   b   Reduce the bank column by $30 and charge an expense of $30 in the profit and loss column.

   c   No entry is required.

   d   Increase the cash at bank column by $400 and decrease the accounts receivable column by $400.

   e   Increase the plant and machinery column by $10 000 and decrease the cash at bank column by $10 000.

   f   No entry is required.

3   The following could be labelled as deficiencies: there is no mention of future benefits. This means an obsolete item of equipment would be classified as an asset. In addition, the concept of legal ownership is in itself too narrow because the IASB *Conceptual Framework* defines assets in terms of an entity's capacity to control them.

4   Current assets are cash or other assets that are consumed or converted into cash within 12 months, whereas non-current assets are used or consumed over periods greater than 12 months. The essential difference is therefore the length of the realisation period, which is important to the liquidity of the business.

5   Current: unearned income, tax payable, dividends payable, wages payable, and so on.

 Non-current: long-term loans, employee benefits for long-service leave, deferred taxes, and so on.

6   The following are some of the limitations of a balance sheet:

   a   It only documents one point in time

   b   It provides past information

   c   Items like research and development may not be recognised as an asset because they fail the definition or recognition criteria

   d   If the cost method of asset measurement is used, some asset values are reliable but less relevant.

 These limitations do not render the balance sheet useless; rather, they reinforce the notion that users need to be aware of a balance sheet's limitations. They should not, for example, use a balance sheet that is two years old. The most recent balance sheet should always be the one used for decision-making purposes. Furthermore, users should not ignore items such as contingent liabilities just because they are not recognised on the balance sheet.

CENGAGENOW

Go to http:\\login.cengagebrain.com to link to CengageNOW, your online study tool. First take the Pre-Test for this chapter to get your Personalised Study Plan, and then:

»   revise your understanding of the key terms related to the presentation of financial position and the worksheet by completing the online crossword

»   explore the concepts of the balance sheet, accounting equation, journal entries and transactions with animated examples

»   link to resource centre slides on the accounting equation.

 After you have completed the activities in your Personalised Study Plan take the Post-Test to determine what concepts you have mastered and what you still need work on.

PRESENTATION OF FINANCIAL PERFORMANCE AND THE WORKSHEET

Urfin/Shutterstock.com

LEARNING OBJECTIVES

At the end of this chapter, you should be able to:

1. discuss the importance of the measurement of financial performance and understand the options available for the presentation of financial performance
2. define and explain the terms 'income' and 'revenue'
3. explain and apply the principles involved in the recognition of revenue
4. give examples of revenue recognition
5. define and explain the term 'expense'
6. identify the recognition criteria for expenses
7. explain the process for deciding when business costs should be recognised as expenses
8. prepare a simplified income statement
9. analyse and classify balance sheet and income statement transactions onto a worksheet
10. identify the factors that influence the format of the income statement
11. explain the concept of earnings (or profit) management
12. explain the role of and prepare a simplified statement of comprehensive income
13. explain the role of and prepare a simplified statement of changes in equity.

INTRODUCTION

We have already seen that profit can be measured by comparing wealth at two points in time. We have also shown that the way wealth is measured in accounting terms can be roughly represented with balance sheets, and we have looked at some of the issues associated with choosing how to assign monetary values to wealth measurement.

In this chapter we consider an alternative way of measuring financial performance – using either a single statement of comprehensive income or an income statement and a statement of comprehensive income. We examine the importance of income statements, the reasons for producing them and what they contain. We also look at what is reported in statements of comprehensive income. We then consider how the content of income statements is determined and some of the issues that arise when preparing them.

Finally, while the determination of comprehensive income explains all non-owner changes in equity for a period, there may also be a number of owner changes in equity during a period, such as purchase of new shares and payment of dividends. All such changes are reported through a statement of changes in equity, which we discuss at the end of this chapter.

FINANCIAL PERFORMANCE MEASUREMENT

1 LEARNING OBJECTIVE

Discuss the importance of the measurement of financial performance and understand the options available for the presentation of financial performance

The objective of financial reporting as outlined in the *Conceptual Framework* is to 'provide financial information about the reporting entity that is useful to existing and potential investors, lenders and other creditors in making decisions about providing resources to the entity. Those decisions involve buying, selling or holding equity instruments and providing or settling loans and other forms of credit.' (IASB, 2010) The measurement and reporting of financial performance is part of the financial information that users require to assist them in making decisions about providing resources. The information may be used for purposes such as helping shareholders decide whether to buy or sell shares, helping lenders to assess the eligibility of borrowers for loans, and to price such loans.

What constitutes financial performance? For a small business or non-profit organisation this will often be measured as the excess or deficit of cash receipts over cash payments. However, in most businesses, performance is measured in an accrual accounting system and this involves the preparation of an income statement and/or a statement of comprehensive income so as to report (among other items) a profit or loss. The accruals process involves the allocation of costs and benefits to accounting periods based on receipt or delivery of goods and services, and not when cash is received or paid.

Unlike a balance sheet, which communicates information about a point in time, financial performance measurement relates to a period of time. From 1 January 2009 all entities reporting under the International Financial Reporting Standards (IFRSs) were required to provide information about financial performance in either a single statement of comprehensive income, or a statement of comprehensive income and a separate statement often called the income statement. We first discuss the information reported in a separate income statement should an entity choose to prepare both an income statement and a statement of comprehensive income. We then explain the statement of comprehensive income that is prepared when an entity elects to prepare two statements on financial performance. We conclude by illustrating the format of a single statement of comprehensive income. In the appendix you will see that Woolworths presents two separate statements. While there is no data on how many listed companies prepare one or two statements, it appears that the use of two statements is more common for large listed companies while it is common to use only one statement in the public sector.

In this chapter we illustrate both approaches but for all remaining chapters of this book we use a single statement of comprehensive income (SOCI) reporting on financial performance.

The income statement summarises certain transactions that take place during that period. In terms of published reports the period is normally one year, though most businesses of any size produce an income statement more regularly – usually quarterly and often monthly. The regular production of an income statement allows managers to compare performance against budget. This is important as it enables managers to identify problem areas and implement remedial action. For example, if advertising expenses are too high, management may reduce future advertising expenditure or change advertising agents.

These statements are normally for internal consumption only, although banks often request copies or make the production of such statements a condition of lending money. The reason that the banks require these statements on a regular basis is that they need to monitor the health of businesses they are lending to. They want to be confident that managers are aware of what is happening and are taking action to rectify losses.

For owners and managers, there is little point in finding out at the end of the year that the price at which goods or services were sold did not cover what it cost to buy goods or provide services. By that stage it is too late to do anything about it. However, if a problem is identified at the end of the first month, it can be dealt with immediately by raising prices, buying at a lower price, or whatever is appropriate to the particular business.

Clearly, the income statement is very important because it tells you whether a business is profitable or not. We have all heard the expression, 'What is the bottom line?' The bottom line is the amount of profit made by a project or business. By comparing that profit with how much wealth is needed to produce it, you can decide whether or not to invest in a business. Other factors that need to be taken into account are the risks involved and your own judgement of future prospects in order to decide whether the return (as measured by the income statement) is adequate. Therefore, it can be argued that the income statement provides some of the basic financial information for a rational decision to be made. Managers may receive a bonus based on profitability, as discussed in Chapter 1, and share markets generally reward companies that achieve profits above what is expected and penalise companies that underperform.

However, although most of us think of business as being primarily motivated by profits, this is not always the case. Many small businesses make profits which are unsatisfactory from the point of view of a rational economic assessment, but profit may not be the owner's sole motivation. They may simply hate working for a boss, or may value leisure more than additional profits. Then there are the many not-for-profit entities (NFP) operating in Australia that exist to primarily deliver services or achieve a particular outcome for society. These NFP entities require funds to operate, but their primary purpose is not the generation of a profit for a return to the owners of the entity.

Having considered why an income statement is important, let us now look at what it is and what it contains. We have said that it is a statement covering a period of time (normally one year) and that its purpose is to measure profit; that is, to measure the increase in wealth. It does this by summarising the income for that period and deducting the expenses incurred in earning that income. The process is simple, but to do it we need to look at the definitions of income and expenses.

2 LEARNING OBJECTIVE

Define and explain the terms 'income' and 'revenue'

INCOME

In Key concept 2.14, now repeated in Key concept 6.1, we use the definition of income found in the IASB *Conceptual Framework*.

This definition seems complex because it attempts to cover all possible outcomes. For our purposes we can substitute 'owners' equity' for 'equity participants'. As with the other elements, income is recognised in financial statements only when it is probable that the inflow, or other enhancement of assets (or decrease in liabilities), has occurred and can be reliably measured.

Key concept 6.1 shows that two main elements (apart from contributions by owners) can lead to increases in owners' equity. These are increases in assets and decreases in liabilities.

Increases in assets

In most cases, income recognition is fairly simple and needs no detailed discussion. For example, we would all agree that a greengrocer's income is the amount that the fruit and vegetables were sold for, and in most cases that amount is in cash, which we know is a current asset. However, if we suppose that our greengrocer supplies fruit and vegetables to a couple of local restaurants which settle their bills every month, we find that in order to define income we have to include not only cash sales but also other sales for which payment has not yet been received. The latter amounts are referred to as receivables or as debtors. Both these terms are used in Australia, although in large public companies trade debtors are often a subsection of receivables. (Other receivables, for example, are interest and short-term loans.) Accounts receivable are shown in our balance sheet as assets because they meet our definition of an asset (see Key concept 5.4). We discuss the treatment of accounts receivable in more detail in Chapter 8.

At this stage we should look at our balance sheet equation in the light of the two examples above. If the greengrocer has sold $100 worth of goods, either for cash or credit, and this we know has met our definition of an asset, then our balance sheet equation will be as follows:

$$\text{assets (\$100)} = \text{liabilities} + \text{owners' equity}$$

From our discussion of duality and the worksheet in Chapter 5, there must be another equal component to make the equation balance. (Please note that at this stage we are not discussing a reduction in an asset account through the goods being sold, but are only concerned with the cash received or the promise to pay.) It is obvious that another asset account has not decreased, nor has a liability increased; therefore, to balance the equation, the owners' equity account must have increased. This has intuitive appeal because with the receipt of cash for example, and with no other changes to the balance sheet, our wealth must have increased.

$$\text{assets (\$100)} = \text{income (\$100)}$$

At this stage we might believe we have a fair idea of what income is: it relates to goods and services sold. However, this view is not necessarily correct: income takes various forms, as our fairly broad definition of income shows. We need to ensure that we distinguish sales that are part of our normal business activity from other items of income.

To illustrate, let us assume that the greengrocer sells one of her two shops. Should this be seen as income or is it different from selling fruit and vegetables? Clearly it is different, because the selling of the fruit and vegetables relates to the business of the entity while business profit relies on the success of the

Baevskiy Dmitry/Shutterstock.com

trading venture. The sale of the shop should be treated differently and shown separately in financial statements from the income earned through greengrocery sales. If, for example, the business was trading at a loss but a gain was made on the sale of the shop, and the gain was greater than the trading loss, this information would be lost if the two items were merged.

For this reason, AASB 118 *Revenue* deals with that component of income that arises from the ordinary activities of the entity. It is more common to talk about an entity's revenue rather than income as it is the major source of income for nearly all entities in a normal operating year. In Chapter 2 we mentioned that income includes revenue, which arises from the entity's ordinary operations, and other gains. In Chapter 2 we provided a definition of revenue as Key concept 2.15 and it is repeated here as Key concept 6.2.

The IASB and FASB have issued a proposed new definition of revenue that adopts a more principles-based approach, but as it has not yet been adopted, we use the current definition in this 9th edition. We return to the concept of revenue a little later in the chapter.

6.2 KEY CONCEPT

REVENUE

Revenue is the gross inflows of economic benefits during the period arising in the course of the *ordinary activities* of an entity when those inflows result in increases in equity, other than those relating to contributions from equity participants. (AASB 118, para. 7)

Remember:

» income = revenue + gains
» revenue = inflows from ordinary activities
» gains = all other inflows

Finally, before leaving the greengrocer illustration let us assume that, having sold one of the shops, the greengrocer decides to invest the money in shares or in a building society until such time as a new shop can be found. In this situation the money invested, which is effectively surplus to immediate requirements, will generate additional income in the form of interest or dividends. This is a form of income that is different from our main source of income – which we report as revenue. It would, in this case, be shown separately but included in the total income for the period. In certain cases, however, the interest may be the major source of income. If, for example, the main activity of a business is lending money, then interest may be the major source of income and, in this instance, this is disclosed as revenue. Similarly, dividends may be the main source of income for an investment trust.

This discussion shows that, although revenue is often synonymous with sales, the actual revenue of a business depends on the type of business and the particular activity giving rise to the revenue. In the example we used, we saw that in its simplest form revenue is equal to cash sales. However, for some business activities the distinctions are not so clear and this leads to problems in deciding what revenue relates to a particular period. This, of course, would not be a problem if accounting periods were the same as the period of a business cycle. For example, if a builder takes 18 months to build and sell a house there is no problem in finding the revenue for the 18 months. Unfortunately, the normal accounting period is 12 months and, as we pointed out earlier, management and other users need information more frequently than that. What then is the revenue of the house builder for the first six months, or for the first year?

The definition of revenue requires an increase in equity. The borrowing of money therefore increases an asset (cash) but the transaction also creates a liability of an equivalent amount (loan payable). As we would expect, an entity does not create revenue by borrowing money.

Decreases in liabilities

Using the example of the greengrocer again, let us assume that she holds a staff party at one of the restaurants supplied by the greengrocer, and that the cost of staff parties is met by the business. After the function the restaurant sends an account for payment to the greengrocer. This account represents a liability incurred by the business. If it is agreed between the two parties that the greengrocer will supply vegetables up to the value of the debt, in settlement of the liability, then the extinguishment of the debt, in effect, represents an increase in owners' equity (remember our balance sheet equation). This increase in equity represents income (revenue). Note that we have not yet addressed the cost of the transaction to the greengrocer; that is, the cost of the goods supplied.

We discuss this transaction in more detail later in the chapter in the section 'Increases in liabilities'.

Excluding contributions by owners

Certain increases in owners' equity do not qualify as income. For example, the owners of a business may invest more capital in the entity. This transaction does not meet our definition of income because the definition precludes contributions by owners that result in an increase of equity during the reporting period. This contribution of additional capital by the owners is an investment decision, possibly with a view to generating future income.

STOP AND THINK 1

In your own words, define 'income' and 'revenue'.

Revenue recognition

3 LEARNING OBJECTIVE

Explain and apply the principles involved in the recognition of revenue

In the following sections about income, we deal specifically with the component of income described as revenue, that is, inflows from ordinary activities.

When does revenue arise and when should it be recognised? To help us answer this question we follow what is known as the recognition principle.

THE RECOGNITION PRINCIPLE

The recognition principle is defined in Key concept 6.3. Notice that, unlike our other definitions which are precise and all-inclusive, this simplified principle is carefully worded to avoid too much precision. It provides some basic criteria that can be applied to particular circumstances. The final decision on whether revenue is recognised is often a matter of judgement rather than fact. Before considering an example, look at the wording used in the simplified version of Key concept 6.3. First, you will see that it mentions the word 'process', which implies a period rather than a point in time. It also uses the term 'substantially complete', which raises the question of what is 'substantial' (is it two-thirds or 90 per cent or another amount?). The principle also says that payment should be 'reasonably certain'. Once again this leaves room for judgement and raises the question of what is reasonable certainty in an uncertain world. For instance, if we sell goods to a reputable customer of long standing we are still only reasonably certain that we will be paid.

6.3 KEY CONCEPT

THE RECOGNITION PRINCIPLE

Following on from the definition of 'revenue', the recognition principle states that revenue should be recognised only:

» when the increases in assets or reduction of liabilities have probably resulted from inflows of economic benefits and these movements can be reliably measured.

This can be simplified to:

» when the earning process is substantially complete and measurable and when the receipt of payment for the goods and services is reasonably certain.

(*Note*: Where something is simplified its meaning is often broadened and precision is lost.)

FIGURE 6.1 POSSIBLE POINTS IN THE BUSINESS CYCLE WHERE REVENUE COULD BE RECOGNISED

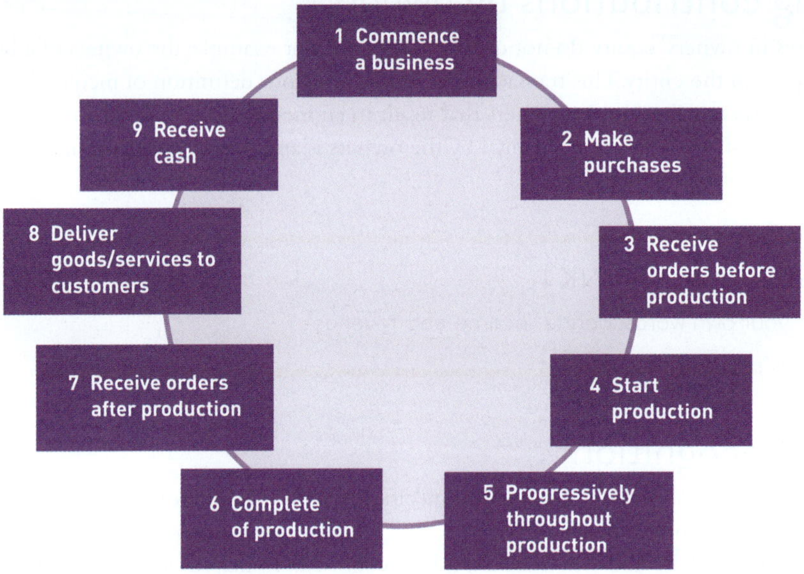

Let us continue by looking in general terms at the possible points at which we could recognise revenue in accordance with the recognition principle. Figure 6.1 shows a number of possible points in the business cycle where we could consider the recognition of revenue.

Figure 6.1 is relevant to a manufacturing-type business. It can be modified to apply to other types of businesses. For example, a retailer like Woolworths does not produce goods, so points 3 to 7 would not normally be relevant. For a mining company points 2 and 3 would be replaced with exploration and evaluation activities that precede production. Clearly, it is unlikely that revenue would ever be recognised at points 1 to 4 but, as we will see, most other points could be appropriate in different circumstances. The end of the process (point 9) seems to be a safe place to recognise revenue, because the earnings process is likely to be complete. Goods have been delivered and payment is certain because cash has been received. In many cases point 9 is the appropriate one – as in the case of our greengrocer or indeed for Woolworths, where delivery and cash collection occur simultaneously. However, our greengrocer also had other sales which were paid for monthly in arrears, so those may have to be recognised at point 8, as at that point the earning process is complete and payment is reasonably certain. On the other hand, if we take the example of the builder and use either of these points, we would have a situation where there was no revenue for the first 17 months but a lot in the 18th month. Of course, in the case of the builder, if there was a contract to build a house for someone, some cash would have been paid in advance and then progressively through the construction period. The point we are making is that points 8 and 9 are not appropriate in all cases.

One could argue that for a shipbuilder, points 8 and 9 are inappropriate because cash is received throughout a contract. In this case, because a ship takes a number of years to build, it is also inappropriate to choose point 6 as this would lead to all the revenue arising in one year. Therefore, it may be that point 5 is appropriate as this allows for revenue and hence profits to be recognised as the ship is constructed. Given that there is a contract with a customer to build the ship, it is likely that the receipt of cash is reasonably certain. Indeed there is an accounting standard, AASB 111 *Construction contracts*, which allows entities under certain conditions to use a percentage-of-completion method to recognise revenue throughout a construction period. A similar argument applies to the case of a building subcontractor and any long-term construction activity.

Recall from Chapter 2 that for accounting information to be useful it needs to be timely. Therefore, while waiting for the receipt of cash provides more certainty it may mean less-timely information for users. Conversely, if revenue is recognised too early it may result in overstatement of revenue and hence profits. For many businesses the delivery of goods or services is likely to be the point at which revenue is recognised.

Examples of revenue recognition

The discussion above shows that each case needs to be judged on its merits. Consider, then, the appropriate time for revenue recognition for the following businesses:

- a local newsagent
- a supplier of components to Ford Motors
- a gold mine where all output is bought by the government at a fixed price
- an aircraft manufacturer
- an airline company.

4 LEARNING OBJECTIVE

Give examples of revenue recognition

Applying the recognition principle, the first example is straightforward. The others are more complex.

A LOCAL NEWSAGENT

The business is likely to be mainly cash, so point 9 is probably most appropriate, although this will depend, for example, on how many customers buy their newspapers on account. Where customers buy on account, point 8 is the more appropriate point at which to recognise revenue, provided payment of the account is probable.

SUPPLIER OF COMPONENTS

Clearly point 9 is too late, because at point 6 the earnings process is complete and payment may be reasonably certain, especially if the component supplier has a fixed contract with Ford. Therefore, point 6 would be used if there was a contract and such contract could not be cancelled without significant penalties. Where there is no contract, point 8 is likely to be more appropriate.

A GOLD MINE

An argument similar to that for the component supplier could be applied here because the earnings process is substantially complete at the point of production and payment is certain because gold companies normally have forward contracts for the sale of all gold produced.

AN AIRCRAFT MANUFACTURER

The answer here will depend on assumptions you have made. For example, your judgement of certainty of payment would be different whether you assumed that the aircraft manufacturer was making to order or that it produced aircraft and then tried to sell them. Similarly, if you thought of an aircraft producer which made Boeing 747s, you might have seen the production process as spreading over a number of years, in which case point 5 might have been your choice. If, on the other hand, you thought of the manufacture of light aircraft such as Piper Cubs, you would have assumed a shorter production cycle, in which case point 5 would not be appropriate.

AN AIRLINE COMPANY

An airline is in the business of flying passengers so the earnings process is not completed until passengers arrive at their destination (and retrieve their luggage!). Of course, unlike a retailer, passengers pay cash before they take a flight. Therefore, the airline receives cash before providing the service. It is not appropriate to recognise revenue at this time because the earnings process is not completed. The receipt of cash creates a present obligation for the airline and so it must initially recognise a liability. When the flight takes place the liability is extinguished and revenue is recognised. You may want to inspect the annual report for Qantas to see how much the airline reports for this liability.

William West/AFP/Getty Images

The problem of when to recognise revenue is very important because the income statement is based upon the revenue, and other gains, for a period and the expenses for that period. The earlier revenue is recognised, the earlier profits are recognised.

6.1

CASE STUDY

CAPITALAND PROFIT FALLS 83% DUE TO ACCOUNTING CHANGES

ESTHER TEO

CapitaLand's third-quarter net profit sank 82.6 per cent to $80.2 million after the developer adopted a new accounting policy and also due to higher finance costs. Revenue for the three months ended Sept 30 plunged 58 per cent to $609 million, partly due to lower revenue recognition from development projects in China and Australia.

The slide was partly offset by revenue recognition from a development project in Vietnam, higher rental from its shopping malls and higher fee-based income, the firm said. Without the effect of the new accounting policy, quarterly profit would have fallen 50 per cent while revenue would have dipped 11 per cent. For the nine months to Sept 30, revenue fell 21 per cent to $1.96 billion, while profit decreased by 30 per cent to $581 million.

Under the new accounting rules, revenue is reflected only when control of the property is transferred to the buyers. Previously, developers smoothed their revenue streams from projects, by progressively recognising income over the contract period as certain milestones were met.

Esther Teo, *Straits Times*, 22 October 2011.

Straits Times © Singapore Press Holdings Limited. Permission required for reproduction.

❯

COMMENTARY

As mentioned earlier in this chapter, the IASB and the FASB have issued a proposed new standard in which revenue is to be recognised when control of the goods/services passes from seller to buyer. CapitaLand appears to have adopted a similar policy with its change in revenue recognition for development properties. The article highlights a concern expressed by some commentators with the proposed standard – that the recognition of revenue may become 'lumpy' and not 'smooth'. Volatility in revenue and profit numbers is normally interpreted as more risky by share markets.

STOP AND THINK 2

When should revenue be recognised? Why not recognise revenue only when cash is received?

EXPENSES

The definition of expenses in Key concept 2.13 is taken from paragraph 4.25b of the IASB *Conceptual Framework* and is restated in Key concept 6.4. The definition is straightforward and similar to that for income in that it relates to changes in assets, liabilities and owners' equity. In this case assets are reduced or liabilities increased, with a resulting reduction in equity. Note that the reduction in equity does not include dividends paid to, or withdrawals by, the business owners. Further, it must be probable that decreases in economic benefits have occurred and that the amount can be reliably measured. Put simply, an expense means a money sacrifice or the incurring of a liability in pursuit of business objectives.

For our purposes we can substitute 'owners' equity' for 'equity participants'. As with income, we discuss each aspect of the definition in turn: assets, liabilities and owners' equity.

5 LEARNING OBJECTIVE

Define and explain the term 'expense'

6.4

KEY CONCEPT

EXPENSES

Expenses are decreases in economic benefits during the accounting period, in the form of outflows or depletions of assets or incurrences of liabilities, which result in decreases in equity other than those relating to distributions to equity participants.

(IASB *Conceptual Framework*, para. 4.25b). Copyright © IFRS Foundation. All rights reserved. Reproduced by Cengage Learning Australia with the permission of the IFRS Foundation ®. No permission granted to third parties to reproduce or distribute.

Reductions in assets

The definition notes that expenses are 'decreases in future economic benefits … in the form of outflows or depletions of assets'. Using this part of the definition and applying it to the greengrocer mentioned earlier, we can see that when she sells goods for cash or credit, the cost of those goods is an expense. This expense results in a reduction of the asset account covering the greengrocery stock and a corresponding reduction in the equity account.

The stock of the greengrocer meets our asset definition: title to the goods passes to the purchaser, which results in an economic loss; the cost can be reliably measured; it is probable that the loss has occurred; the loss of this asset results in a reduction in wealth which reduces the equity balance. Note that the same reasoning applies whether the transaction is for cash or to a reliable debtor.

In the second scenario the greengrocer sells one of her shops. Whatever value is placed on the shop, and is disclosed in our balance sheet, would meet the definition of an expense. For example, if the net value of the shop in the balance sheet is $30 000 and the shop sells for $40 000 (assuming no transactions costs) then there would be a net addition to equity of $10 000. If the reverse is true – shop value $40 000 and sale price $30 000 – there would be a net reduction in equity of $10 000. As noted in the discussion on income, this information needs to be disclosed separately.

Increases in liabilities

From our definition we can see that an increase in a liability due to a decrease in economic benefits qualifies as an expense. Borrowing money creates a liability and an asset, but not an expense as there has been no consumption of economic benefit at this stage.

Using the example of the greengrocer's staff party on page 155, the same as we used for income, the cost of goods supplied to the restaurant owner as settlement of the liability is an expense. To explain this in greater detail: the original transaction, the staff party, gives rise to an expense; that is, the increase of the liability results in the reduction of the wealth of the greengrocer. If the greengrocer paid cash to settle this liability we would have a reduction in an asset and liability account. The restaurant owner exchanges the debt for goods which reduces the liability and increases the wealth of the greengrocer. This meets our income definition. The final part of the transaction, the supply of goods, results in a decrease in the asset account and a corresponding decrease in the equity account. Put simply, the cost of the goods supplied to the restaurant in settlement is the cost of the staff party. There were three parts to this transaction, two of which were expenses and one of which was income (a revenue):

- expenses of the staff party
- expenses of the cost of goods supplied to the restaurant
- income (revenue) of the goods supplied to the restaurant.

Excluding distributions to owners

When an owner withdraws goods, services or cash from the business, this is not a business expense but a withdrawal of capital by the owner. These withdrawals are often referred to in accounting literature as *drawings*. We could provide numerous examples of these, some of which are less obvious than others. For example, is the tax and insurance on the car a business expense if the car is also used for family transportation? The guiding principle in making a judgement is whether or not the cost has been incurred in pursuit of the objectives of the business.

Owners who believe that they are entitled to be remunerated for the work they do should pay themselves a wage or salary that equates to the effort expended. This is a legitimate business expense.

6 LEARNING OBJECTIVE

Identify the recognition criteria for expenses

The recognition principle

The criteria for the recognition of expenses are the same as for revenue. Therefore, an expense should be recognised in the current period when:

- it is probable that the decrease in economic benefits has occurred
- the amount can be reliably measured.

The application of the recognition criteria should help preparers of financial statements to decide when to recognise a cost incurred as an expense. However, while some costs such as rent payments are straightforward, others such as research and development expenditure, present difficulties. The following examples illustrate some of the different types of costs incurred by organisations.

Examples of expenses

It is worthwhile looking at examples of expenses, such as:

* the payment of wages, which normally involves a monetary sacrifice
* the use of electricity, which normally involves incurring a liability to pay at the end of a quarter
* the purchase of a machine, which normally incurs a money sacrifice or a liability
* the purchase of goods for resale, which normally incurs a money sacrifice or a liability.

Although all examples fit our definition of expenses, they are not necessarily expenses of the period. For example, the machinery is likely to last more than one period so it cannot be seen as an expired cost. Similarly, the goods bought for resale may not be sold during the period and cannot therefore be seen as an expense of the period. The benefit has not expired because those goods can be sold at some time in the future. There are other situations where the point at which a cost is incurred, and the point at which the benefit arises, do *not* coincide. We discuss this in more detail shortly.

Before we do that, it is worth emphasising once again that we are dealing with a separate business entity and only costs relating to the business objectives can ever become expenses. This is very important as in many small businesses the owner and the business are essentially the same; however, we are preparing accounts for the business only. Thus, if we find that a bill has been paid to buy a new lounge suite for the owner of a newsagency, this cost is not an expense of the business because it relates to the owner personally, not the business. Such items often go through a business bank account but need to be separated and shown as withdrawals of the owner's capital rather than business expenses.

We will return to the discussion of drawings later, but let us now consider some possible situations in which we have to decide whether a cost, which is clearly a business cost, is an expense of the period. There are three possible situations that we need to discuss. These are where:

* costs of this year are expenses of this year
* costs of earlier years are expenses of this year
* costs of this year are expenses of subsequent years.

COSTS OF THIS YEAR ARE EXPENSES OF THIS YEAR

This is the usual situation and is also the simplest to deal with. It occurs when an item or service is acquired during a year and consumed during that same year. That is, costs of this accounting period are expenses of this accounting period. Where the accounting period is less than one year – for example, one month – then the discussion applies to this shorter accounting period.

The question of the timing of payment is not relevant to the process of recognising an expense. An item may have been acquired and used, but not paid for. Telephone calls, which are paid for at the end of the quarter, are a good example of this.

COSTS OF EARLIER YEARS ARE EXPENSES OF THIS YEAR

These can be divided into costs that are wholly used up in the current period and those that are partly used up in the current period.

WHOLLY EXPENSES OF THIS YEAR

The most obvious example of this is the stock of goods in a shop at the end of a year. The cost of buying those goods was incurred in the year just ended, but the economic benefit has not expired. They are

7 LEARNING OBJECTIVE

Explain the process for deciding when business costs should be recognised as expenses therefore assets at the year's end. However, in the next year when they are sold, they become expenses of the next year. The process can be illustrated as follows.

We buy goods in June 20X7 but do not sell them until July. If our accounting period ends on 30 June, then the goods are an asset at that date – 30 June 20X7 – because the economic benefit is not used up. The cost, however, has been incurred in that year. In July, the goods are sold; therefore, the benefit is used up and there is an expense for the year ended 30 June 20X8, although the cost was incurred in the previous year. This can be seen in Figure 6.2.

A similar situation arises when services are paid for in advance and are not fully used up at the end of the accounting period. For example, if the rent is payable quarterly in advance on 31 March, 30 June, 30 September and 31 December, and the entity ends its year on 30 June, then the rent will be paid on 30 June in year 1 for the quarter to 30 September, year 2. However, the economic benefit will be used up in the first quarter of year 2 and, thus, the expense belongs to year 2.

FIGURE 6.2 COSTS INCURRED LAST YEAR, WHICH ARE EXPENSES OF THIS YEAR

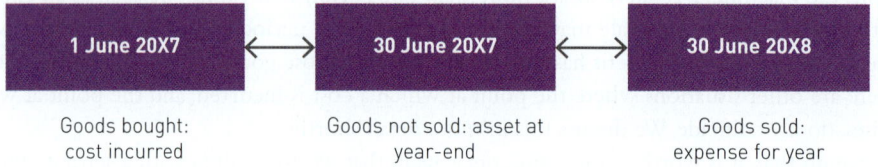

These expenses are normally referred to as prepaid expenses and frequently arise in respect of rent and water rates. For an individual, obvious examples of this type of expense are annual subscriptions to clubs and societies, car insurance, driver's licence fees, and so on. For a business, other situations where a cost may relate to more than one period arise frequently. For example, if the car insurance of the business was payable on 1 January 20X7, then half of that cost would be used up and become an expense for year ending 30 June 20X7, and half would be used up and be an expense for year ending 30 June 20X8. The crucial test is whether the economic benefit has been used up at the year-end. If not, there is a future economic benefit and we therefore have an asset.

PART EXPENSES OF CURRENT YEAR

An everyday example is any consumer durable such as a car, a washing machine or a TV set. In all these cases the costs are incurred at a point in time but the economic benefits are expected to accrue over a number of years. In a business entity, the equivalents of our consumer durables are non-current assets such as machinery and office equipment. The allocation of the cost of these items to subsequent accounting periods is called depreciation, and will be dealt with in more detail in Chapter 8.

COSTS INCURRED THIS YEAR THAT ARE EXPENSES OF LATER YEARS

Just as some costs incurred in previous years are expenses of the current accounting period, costs incurred in the current period may be expenses of future periods.

Examples include car registration, insurance, rates, and so on. The due date for payment of these is not likely to coincide with the end of the accounting period, nor would we want it to because this would lead to an uneven cash flow. Other examples are goods held in stock at the year-end and non-current assets bought during the year.

Using the example of annual car insurance, we can see that, if we pay for it in the current year 20X7 on 1 January, then half of that cost will relate to the current year ending 30 June 20X7 and the other half to next year ending 30 June 20X8.

The following decision tree (Figure 6.3) is also useful in the classification of costs to expenses.

FIGURE 6.3 DECISION TREE FOR CLASSIFYING ASSETS AND EXPENSES

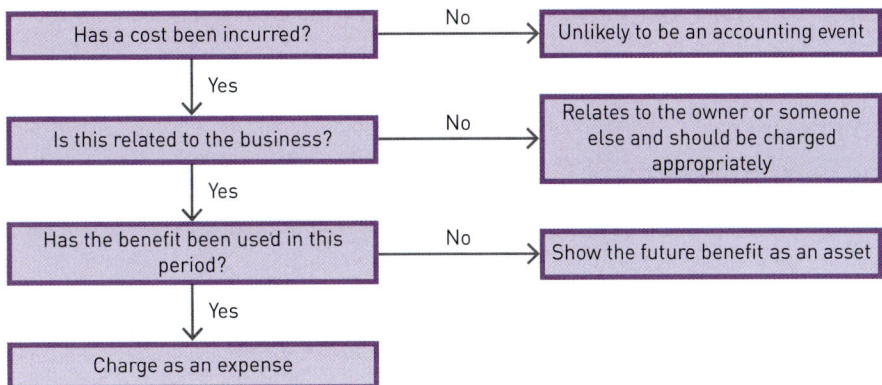

STOP AND THINK 3

Describe the difference between an expense and an asset.

THE INCOME STATEMENT

8 LEARNING OBJECTIVE

Prepare a simplified income statement

Having looked at income and expenses, we now examine how these fit together in the income statement, before looking at a simple numerical example. The purpose of this statement is to measure the profit or loss for the period. It does this by summarising the income for the period, and subtracting the expenses from the income to arrive at the profit or loss. This could be depicted as:

$$\text{income} - \text{expenses} = \text{profit}$$

Let us see how this fits with the measurement of wealth described in Chapter 4. We said that profit is the difference between wealth at the start of the year and the end of the year:

$$\text{wealth at } T_1 - \text{wealth at } T_0 - \text{profit at } T_1$$

The alternative way of measuring profit was to subtract expenses from income. We also said in Chapter 4 that wealth in accounting terms was measured by assets minus liabilities. The resultant figure, the residual, was referred to as the owners' equity. Thus, we said that at time T_0, the owners' equity is:

$$\text{assets at } T_0 - \text{liabilities at } T_0 = \text{owners' equity at } T_0$$

If we add the profit for the period T_0 to T_1 to the owners' equity at T_0, the resultant figure is our wealth at T_1. This equals our assets minus liabilities at T_1 (provided we have not changed our valuation method from one period to another). In other words:

$$\text{assets at } T_1 - \text{liabilities at } T_1 = \text{owners' equity at } T_0 + \text{profit at } T_1$$
$$= \text{owners' equity at } T_0 \pm (\text{income} - \text{expenses}) \text{ at } T_1$$

This shows us there is a relationship between the income statement and the balance sheet, which we illustrate with the worksheet after Example 6.1. Let us now look at an example of an income statement and then consider what it is used for, its format and its limitations. In Example 6.1 we use the transactions of Blake's Enterprises, a paint shop, and see what should go into the income statement for the year to 31 December 20X1.

WORKED EXAMPLE

BLAKE'S ENTERPRISES

Blake's Enterprises is a new retail paint outlet set up at the start of the year. Its transactions for 20X1, its first year, are summarised as follows:

DATE	DESCRIPTION	$
1 January	Purchase of freehold shop	120 000
1 January	Rates for the year	4 000
1 April	Purchase of van	16 000
1 April	Van registration and insurance for a year	1 200
1 July	Purchase of washing machine	600
Various	Wages to shop assistant for year	12 000
Various	Goods bought and resold	36 000
Various	Goods bought but unsold	8 000
Various	Motor expenses and petrol	2 400
Various	Cash from sales	90 000
Various	Money withdrawn by Blake	12 000

PURCHASE OF FREEHOLD SHOP

The economic benefit arising from this cost did not expire during the period, although some part of the economic benefit may have been used up. At this stage we will not try to measure the part that has been used up, but should keep in mind that at a later stage we will need to make such allocations.

RATES FOR THE YEAR

This is clearly a cost and expense of the year in question and should be included in the income statement.

PURCHASE OF VAN

As with the freehold shop, the economic benefit from the van is likely to be available over many periods and we should, theoretically, allocate the amount of the benefit used up to the income statement for the year. The allocation is made by means of a depreciation charge, which we discuss in Chapter 8. At this stage we simply note that an allocation should be made.

VAN REGISTRATION AND INSURANCE

This was paid for in advance on 1 April for a full year. At the end of our accounting period (31 December) we have used nine months' insurance and registration; that is, nine-twelfths of the total. The expense for the period, therefore, is 9/12 × $1200; that is, $900. The remaining $300 relates to the next year (next accounting period) and is an asset at the end of the year as the business will receive some future economic benefit.

PURCHASE OF WASHING MACHINE

We know that Blake's Enterprises is a retail shop selling paint. It is not likely that the washing machine was bought for use by the business, although it has been paid for out of the business bank account. Therefore, this is not an expense of the business nor is it an asset of the business as the business will not get any future economic benefit from it. It is, in effect, a withdrawal of capital by the owner and should be treated as drawings.

WAGES FOR YEAR

This is clearly a business expense as the wages are paid to the shop assistant and the economic benefit has been used up. From the information we have, the whole $12 000 relates to the accounting period, and therefore the expense charged to the income statement should be $12 000.

GOODS BOUGHT AND RESOLD

These goods have been sold to customers. The business no longer owns them and is not entitled to any future economic benefit. The whole of the $36 000 is an expired economic benefit and, as such, should be charged as an expense in the current year's income statement.

GOODS BOUGHT BUT UNSOLD

These goods are still held by the business at the end of the year. The economic benefit from the goods is still to come, in the form of cash or credit, when they are sold. Thus, goods held in stock are an asset rather than an expense of the period we are dealing with.

MOTOR EXPENSES AND PETROL

Once again, the economic benefit from these has expired. The whole of the $2400 should therefore be charged as an expense in this accounting period.

CASH FROM SALES

This is the revenue of the business for the year and, as far as we can tell, it is the only revenue. The full amount of $90 000 should be shown as sales revenue in the income statement.

MONEY WITHDRAWN BY BLAKE

Given the present information, we cannot categorically say whether this is a business expense or not. If it is, in effect, wages for Blake's work, then it could be argued that it is a genuine business expense. If, on the other hand, it has simply been withdrawn for personal use it is clearly drawings, and for the purposes of this example this is how we will classify it.

PREPARING THE INCOME STATEMENT

We can now draw up the income statement of Blake's Enterprises for the year ended 31 December 20X1.

BLAKE'S ENTERPRISES
INCOME STATEMENT FOR THE YEAR ENDED 31 DECEMBER 20X1

	$	$
Sales revenue		90 000
Less cost of goods sold		36 000
Gross profit		54 000
Rates	4 000	
Van registration and insurance	900	
Wages	12 000	
Motor expenses	2 400	
		19 300
Profit for the year		34 700

Notice that we have shown a gross profit and a net profit. Gross profit can be defined as sales less cost of goods sold. Net profit can be broadly defined as gross profit less operating and administrative expenses and other charges.

The reason for showing the gross profit is to enable Blake to see whether the business is doing as well as it should. Most retail businesses know the percentage of selling price that is profit, and the percentage of which is cost. Blake, for example, has costs of 40 per cent of the selling price and would expect a gross profit margin of 60 per cent of the selling price. If these figures alter, Blake would need to know why, particularly if the gross profit figure was less than expected. This information would allow Blake to take corrective action, particularly if the accounting period was, for example, one month.

The net profit figure can be affected by numerous expenses. It is the figure often referred to as the bottom line. Depending on the size of the business (and usually for an owner–manager) you may deduct the drawings from this net profit figure to arrive at a figure of profit retained in the business. If the drawings were subtracted in the expense section of the income statement, this would distort the ratio of net profit to sales (because the drawings figure may bear no relationship to the sales of the business). As with the gross profit percentages, managers often try to keep costs within certain percentage points.

STOP AND THINK 4

'As long as we are making profits, however small, we can always pay our debts as they fall due.' Discuss the truth (or otherwise) of this statement.

9 LEARNING OBJECTIVE

Analyse and classify balance sheet and income statement transactions onto a worksheet

THE WORKSHEET

In Chapter 5 we introduced the worksheet and illustrated how it can assist in recording transactions that facilitate the gathering of data for the preparation of a balance sheet. We now illustrate how the worksheet can be used to record transactions to facilitate the preparation of an income statement. We can illustrate this by reference to the example based on Mary's business, which is set out below.

WORKED EXAMPLE

MARY'S SECOND-HAND CARS

Mary decided to start a business selling second-hand cars. She had saved up some money of her own but this was not enough to get started so she obtained an interest-free loan for the business from her parents. The transactions of the business for the first month were as follows. All transactions were cash.

→ Day 1   Opened a business bank account and paid in $1000 of her own money.

→ Day 2   Paid into the bank $4000 she had borrowed from her parents for use by the business. (*Note*: As she will repay some of this loan within this trading month we treat the loan as a current liability.)

→ Day 3   Found a suitable showroom and paid a fortnight's rent of $200.

→ Day 4   Went to a car auction and bought the following cars for cash:

         2005 Ford Fiesta for $2000

         2003 Ford Escort for $1000

         2000 Volkswagen Beetle for $600.

→ Day 5   Bought some office furniture for $240.

→ Day 6   Employed a teenager (who was on social security benefits) to clean cars at the rate of $20 per car. Paid out $60.

→ Day 8   Placed advertisements for all three cars in the local paper. The cost of advertising was $40 per day for each car. She decided that all three should be advertised for two days, so the total cost was $240.

→ Day 9   Sold the Ford Fiesta for $3000 cash.

→ Day 10   Sold the Ford Escort for $1400 cash.

→ Day 11   Returned to the car auction and bought a Gemini for $3000.

→ Day 12   Employed her teenage friend to clean the Gemini for $20.

→ Day 15   Readvertised the Volkswagen for three days at $40 per day, total cost $120.

→ Day 17   Advertised the Gemini using a special block advertisement that cost $150 in total.

→ Day 18   Paid rent for showroom for the next fortnight, amounting to $200.

→ Day 19   Was offered $800 for the Volkswagen.

→ Day 20   Accepted the offer for the Volkswagen and was paid $800.

→ Day 22   Sold the Gemini for $3600.

→ Day 23   Went to the car auction and bought a Datsun 270 for $4600.

→ Day 24   Had the Datsun professionally cleaned at a cost of $80.

→ Day 25   Advertised the Datsun using the special block advertisement at a cost of $150.

→ Day 26   Decided that as things were going so well she would repay her parents $400.

→ Day 27   Took the Datsun on a test-drive with a customer, during which the engine seized.

→ Day 29   Had the Datsun repaired at a cost of $600.

→ Day 30   Sold the Datsun for $5400.

→ Day 31   Paid an electricity bill of $80 for the month.

It is possible for some of these transactions to be recorded in different ways. To illustrate the different treatments that are possible, let us consider the transaction on day 3 where Mary paid a fortnight's rent in advance. The question arises whether this is an expense or an asset. Let us consider the alternatives.

On day 3 it is reasonably clear that we have an asset, in that we will get a future benefit in the form of the use of the showroom for two weeks. On the other hand, if we are recording the transaction for the first time at the end of the month, we can then argue that the transaction is an expense because by then the benefit has expired. Thus we could record, on day 3, the payment as an asset and then re-evaluate all assets at the end of the month – as we have done on our worksheet. Conversely, we could wait until the end of the month and just record an expense. We would recommend at this stage that you adopt the former treatment for two reasons: first it ensures that you re-evaluate all your assets at the end of the month, and second, shortcuts often cause more problems than they are worth if you are unfamiliar with the territory.

Another transaction that should be mentioned is the advertising on days 8, 15, 17 and 25. Here we have a similar dilemma to that of the rent. However, there is an added problem: with the rent we knew there would be a future benefit; with the advertising a future benefit is far from certain. In other words, we do not know when we place the advertisement whether anyone will reply to it and, even if they do, whether they will buy the car. To answer this point we can look at our asset definition, which includes the words 'probable that the future economic benefits will eventuate'. In this case, as we are not certain that the advertisement will attract a buyer, we cannot classify this cost as an asset.

You are probably beginning to recognise that accounting is not just about recording; it is also about exercising judgement within a framework of broad and often very general principles. The important factor to remember as you work through the example is that you are making judgements and applying the definitions set out in the previous two chapters, and that you are aware of what you are doing and why you are doing it.

If your worksheet is correct, the balances on the bottom line of your worksheet should be those in the balance sheet set out below. The income statement follows the balance sheet and is merely a summary of the profit and loss column on the worksheet.

Even if you find that your answer is correct, before proceeding to the next chapter you should read the explanations for the treatment of the transactions on days 3, 6, 18, 19, 26, 27 and 29 as these are of particular interest and will assist you in the future. If your answer disagrees with ours, check the full worksheet and the explanations that follow.

Prepare your own worksheet before you read on.

TRANSACTION SUMMARY

The transactions that took place and their treatment have been set out on the worksheet, as have, where appropriate, explanations of that treatment and acceptable alternatives. If any items are still unclear, examine them in terms of the basic definitions referred to in Chapter 2 and earlier in this chapter.

➡   Day 1.   Opened a business bank account and paid in $1000 of her own money.

Here we created a business asset in the form of cash and opened an account to show the owner's stake in the business under the heading of owners' equity.

➡   Day 2.   Paid into the bank $4000 that she had borrowed from her parents for use by the business.

Once again, the business acquired an asset because it will get a future benefit from the cash. It also acquired an obligation to pay somebody some money and, therefore, has a liability for the amount borrowed.

MARY'S SECOND-HAND CARS
WORKSHEET

| | ASSETS | | | | = LIABILITIES + EQUITY | | |
DAY	CASH	CARS	PREPAID RENT	FURNITURE	LOANS	CAPITAL	PROFIT AND LOSS
1	1000					1000	
2	4000				4000		
3	−200		200				
4	−3600	3600					
5	−240			240			
6	−60						−60
8	−240						−240
9	3000						3000
9*		−2000					−2000
10	1400						1400
10*		−1000					−1000
11	−3000	3000					
12	−20						−20
15	−120						−120
17	−150						−150
18	−200		200				
20	800						800
20*		−600					−600
22	3600						3600
22*		−3000					−3000
23	−4600	4600					
24	−80						−80
25	−150						−150
26	−400				−400		
29	−600						−600
30	5400						5400
30*		−4600					−4600
31	−80						−80
Balance	+5460	+0	+400	+240	=3600	+1000	+1500
31†			−400				−400
Balance	5460	+0	+0	+240	=3600	+1000	+1100

* Notice that every time we sold a car (on days 9, 10, 20, 22 and 30) we immediately transferred the cost of that car from our cars column to the profit and loss column as an expense. This transfer was carried out because, having sold the car, we no longer expected a future benefit and, therefore, we no longer had an asset. An alternative treatment would be to do this exercise at the end of the month.

† When the worksheet is complete, it is important to review our assets and ask ourselves: are these still assets? If (as in this case) the answer is no, then we need to transfer their cost to the income statement as an expense of the period.

➡   Day 3.   Found a suitable showroom and paid a fortnight's rent of $200.

We discussed this transaction on page 168. Our treatment involved reducing our asset cash in the bank and recording an asset of the prepaid rent from which the business will derive a benefit in the future.

➡   Day 4.   Went to a car auction and bought the following cars for cash:

2005 Ford Fiesta for $2000

2003 Ford Escort for $1000

2000 Volkswagen Beetle for $600.

Clearly, by paying out $3600 Mary reduced cash at the bank, so this is one side of the entry. The other side is to record the cars as an asset because Mary will get a future benefit from them.

➡   Day 5.   Bought office furniture for $240.

This is exactly the same as the previous transaction. Mary has merely exchanged one asset, cash, for another, furniture.

➡   Day 6.   Employed a teenager (who was on social security benefits) to clean cars at the rate of $20 per car. Paid out $60.

In this case, one side of the transaction is clear – cash has been reduced by $60. The question that then arises is whether there is an asset or an expense. We have shown the cost of the car-cleaning as an expense because we are uncertain that any future benefit will arise from this particular expenditure. The fact that a car is cleaned does not add any intrinsic value and, in fact, it is probably necessary to clean all cars in the showroom regularly because customers expect to buy clean cars.

➡   Day 8.   Placed advertisements for all three cars in the local paper. The cost of advertising was $40 per day for each car. She decided that all three should be advertised for two days, and so the total cost was $240.

Refer back to page 168 for a detailed discussion of the reasons for our treatment of this item. We assumed there would be no future benefit and treated the item as an expense, charging the item to the income statement at the same time as we reduced our cash by $240.

➡   Day 9.   Sold the Ford Fiesta for $3000 cash.

Clearly, the business has another $3000 in the bank, so we increased the amount in the cash column. The sale accords with our definition of revenue, so we bring that revenue into the profit and loss column.

➡   Day 9*.

Here, Mary has reduced her assets by the cost of the car she sold; we charged that cost (the cost of the expired benefit) to the profit and loss column.

➡   Day 10.   Sold the Ford Escort for $1400.

See the explanations for day 9 above. If you have these wrong make sure you understand why, and then correct your worksheet for all similar items before reading on.

➡   Day 11.   Returned to the car auction and bought a Gemini for $3000.

This is, in essence, the same as the transaction on day 4. If you made an error, read that explanation again and check that your treatment of the transaction on day 11 is correct before moving on.

➡   Day 12.   Employed her teenage friend to clean the Gemini for $20.

This is, in essence, the same as the transaction on day 6. If you made an error, read that explanation again and check that your treatment of the transaction on day 12 is correct before moving on.

❯

→   Day 15.   Readvertised the Volkswagen for three days at $40 per day, total cost $120.

See the explanation for day 8 above.

→   Day 17.   Advertised the Gemini using a special block advertisement that cost $150 in total.

See the explanation for day 8 above.

→   Day 18.   Paid rent of showroom for the next fortnight amounting to $200.

This is, in essence, the same situation as day 3. The entry should therefore be the same. At this stage you could also reduce the amount in the rent column by the rent for the first two weeks and charge this to the profit and loss column because the benefit has now expired. We have not done this because we wished to illustrate the importance of the final review before a balance sheet and an income statement are finally drawn up.

→   Day 19.   Was offered $800 for the Volkswagen.

Although an economic event has happened, we cannot account for it because, at this stage, the effect of that event cannot be adequately expressed in monetary terms.

→   Day 20.   Was paid $800 for the Volkswagen.

Now we have a sale, and revenue can be recognised (as for day 9).

→   Day 22.   Sold the Gemini for $3600.

Once again, we have a sale and revenue can be recognised.

→   Day 23.   Went to the car auction and bought a Datsun 270 for $4600.

See day 14 for explanation of the treatment applying to this transaction.

→   Day 24.   Had the Datsun professionally cleaned at a cost of $80.

This is the same as the cleaning for day 6. The fact that it was done professionally does not alter the argument set out there.

→   Day 25.   Advertised the Datsun using the special block advertisement at a cost of $150.

This should be treated in the same way as previous advertisements – for the same reasons.

→   Day 26.   Decided that, as things were going so well, she would repay her parents $400.

This is a different transaction from any of those we have dealt with so far. Those transactions dealt with the expenditure of cash for either a past or a future benefit. In this case we have reduced our cash in order to pay back an amount that the business owes; that is, we have used cash to reduce our liability. Thus, we reduce the amount shown as owing in the loan column by the $400 and we reduce the amount of cash by $400.

→   Day 27.   Took the Datsun on a test-drive with a customer, during which the engine seized.

Although an economic event has happened, we cannot account for it because, at this stage, the effect of that event cannot be adequately expressed in monetary terms.

→   Day 29.   Had the Datsun repaired at a cost of $600.

We are now in a position to account for the event because we know its effect in monetary terms. However, we are left with the question of whether the expenditure is going to provide a future benefit or whether it is an expense. We need to decide whether the expenditure has increased the value of the asset. If it has, there is no problem in recognising the transaction as one that creates an asset. If, however, the expenditure has merely restored the asset to the state that it was in previously, then it is doubtful that it relates to an asset. We would be safer to charge it to the profit and loss column as an expense, which is what we have done.

In essence, this is a shorthand way of recording two events. The first is that the engine seized, reducing the future benefit we could expect from the asset. If we knew the extent of this reduction relating to this future benefit, we could have charged that as a past benefit. If we had done that, then the repairs could legitimately be viewed as enhancing the future benefit to be obtained in respect of the reduced asset. This whole process is, in fact, a shortcut because we do not know what the loss in value of future benefits was; we are therefore, in effect, using the cost of repairs as a surrogate for that loss in value.

→   Day 30.   Sold the Datsun for $5400.

See previous transactions of this type on, for example, days 9 and 10.

→   Day 31.   Paid electricity bill of $80 for the month.

Here we have a reduction of the cash with respect to the use of electricity over the past month. The benefit has clearly expired and we therefore have an expense.

→   Day 31†.   The prepaid rent has been consumed; therefore, the asset is reduced and an expense is recorded.

We can now prepare the balance sheet and income statement for Mary's business.

MARY'S SECOND-HAND CARS
BALANCE SHEET

	$	$	$	$
Assets				
Current assets				
Cash	5460			
Total current assets		5460		
Non-current assets				
Furniture	240			
Total non-current assets		240		
Total assets			5700	
Liabilities				
Current liabilities				
Loan	3600			
Total current liabilities		3600		
Total liabilities			3600	
Net assets				2100
Owners' equity				
Capital	1000			
Profit	1100			
Total owners' equity				2100

MARY'S SECOND-HAND CARS
INCOME STATEMENT

	$	$
Sales revenue		14200
Less cost of cars sold		11200

	$	$
Gross profit		3 000
Expenses		
Rent	400	
Cleaning	160	
Advertising	660	
Repairs	600	
Electricity	80	
		1900
Profit for the year		1100

STOP AND THINK 5

In each of the following cases, describe the two entries that are required on the worksheet.

a   The owner pays $1000 into the business bank account.

b   A desk is bought for $200 for the business and paid from the bank account.

c   The business buys goods for $400.

d   The rent of the premises ($100) is paid for the first week.

e   A potential customer makes an offer for the goods of $500.

f   The wages of the employee, amounting to $120, are paid.

g   The firm receives another offer of $700 for the goods, accepts this offer and is paid immediately.

FACTORS AFFECTING THE FORMAT OF THE INCOME STATEMENT

10 LEARNING OBJECTIVE

Identify the factors that influence the format of the income statement

As with balance sheets, a number of factors influence the format of income statements. These include the organisation's size and structure, as well as the type of people who will be using the statements. Indeed, given the changes made to accounting standards, an entity may even choose only to prepare a statement of comprehensive income as discussed in the next section. However, the issues discussed in this section are equally relevant to the format of both statements.

Types of business

To some degree the type of business activity determines the presentation of and context for the income statement. In the case of a retail business, such as Blake's Enterprises or Mary's Second-hand Cars, a gross profit figure may be useful, but in a service business such as a hotel, which is labour-intensive, the revenue earned may have very little to do with the inputs of physical goods. Therefore, the type of activity has an effect on what is being reported and how it should be reported.

As with the balance sheet, another prime determinant of the content and format of an income statement is the type of organisational structure. The content of an income statement for a company is influenced by regulations imposed by professional accounting bodies. The latter regulations are contained in Australian Accounting Standards, which are based on the IFRSs. While companies must report on certain items in income statements, accounting standards do not prescribe a particular format.

Another important determinant is ownership. For example, a company may have to produce statements that comply with both Australian and US regulations if it is owned by a US parent.

Refer now to the Woolworths income statement in Appendix 1 and study its format. Note that the income statement shows gross profit and net profit. The expenses are reported in large groupings such as branch expenses and you need to refer to the notes for more detail. The company also reports a statement of comprehensive income which is considered later in this chapter.

For organisational structures such as sole proprietorships and partnerships, there are virtually no regulations covering format. Because income statements are being prepared for owners who are also managers, the amount of detail in their income statements is normally greater. The reason for this is that the annual report, as well as being a report on performance, acts as a basis for management decisions about the organisation.

The size and complexity of an organisation determines the level of detail contained in statements prepared for external consumption. As we have said, regular income statements are normally prepared for internal use by managers and these internal reports are generally more detailed than those produced for external users.

Finally, it is important to remind ourselves that the type of organisation and its goals can make an income statement less relevant (and irrelevant in some cases). Should charitable organisations make profits, or are people more interested in knowing how any surplus monies have been used to further the charity's aims? Clearly, different statements are appropriate to the needs and aims of different organisations.

Users of accounts

The requirements of account users often differ. As we have said, owner–managers normally require detailed information, while tax authorities often require specific information to decide whether a particular expense is allowable for tax purposes. Apart from these influences, there is also confidentiality: a business does not necessarily want its competitors, or indeed its customers, to know how much profit it is making.

11 **LEARNING OBJECTIVE**

Explain the concept of earnings (or profit) management

EARNINGS (OR PROFIT) MANAGEMENT

Earnings management occurs when managerial judgement in relation to financial reporting and structuring transactions is used to achieve particular financial outcomes. The objective may be to influence the perceptions of stakeholders about the underlying economic performance of a company and/or to influence outcomes that depend on reported accounting numbers, as we discussed in Chapter 1.

It may be done so that a company reports a smooth profit stream rather than a volatile number stream, because share markets generally do not like volatile earnings (profits). However, if the accounts are being prepared for tax purposes, the owner may wish to reduce profit, or defer it to the next year if at all possible. Conversely, if the accounts are to be used to borrow money, the owner may want to portray a healthy profit. While we should not give the impression that profit can be manipulated at will, it is clear from our discussion that there are areas of judgement that allow slightly different results to be obtained from the same basic data.

The practice of earnings management can affect the reality of a client's financial performance or position to such an extent that decisions with respect to the allocation of resources may alter in the absence of the practice (i.e. if earnings management wasn't undertaken and the economic reality of an entity was clearer, decisions about the allocation of resources may be different/unfavourable). Earnings management may also be practised so that companies can meet earnings estimates that would otherwise be missed because the stock market penalises companies that fail to meet earnings estimates.

The extent to which the 'management' of profit is done within the scope of accounting standards, rather than as a fraudulent abuse of the rules, is often limited by the fact that there are several conflicting requirements, meaning that manipulation of profit for one purpose can prove detrimental to others. Also keep in mind that an income statement is only as good as the information on which it is based. Therefore, if a fish and chip shop owner only records every second sale through the till, the accounts will record only those transactions.

In their 2013 paper *Earnings Quality: Evidence from the Field*, Dichev, Graham, Harvey and Rajgopal estimate one in five companies in the USA manage earnings to misrepresent economic performance. These are not fraudulent actions like those taken by Enron and WorldCom, but use the choices available within accounting standards, which we will refer to where relevant in this book. Their results are based on interviews with the CFOs of 169 listed companies in the USA where the pressure to meet earnings estimates is often the reason cited. It is likely that earnings management occurs in other jurisdictions including Australia.

STATEMENT OF COMPREHENSIVE INCOME

12 **LEARNING OBJECTIVE**

Explain the role of and prepare a simplified statement of comprehensive income

Entities can choose to either:

* prepare an income statement and a statement of comprehensive income
* prepare only a statement of comprehensive income (SOCI).

The information presented is the same, irrespective of the approach chosen. Where an entity chooses to produce two statements, the opening line in the SOCI is the (ending line) profit from the income statement. Additional items that relate to other non-owner changes to equity, apart from those already reported in the income statement, are added or subtracted to arrive at comprehensive income. Such items are described as other comprehensive income. In this section we provide some examples of other comprehensive income. Where an entity chooses to prepare only a SOCI then the statement includes all the information that would be included in an income statement plus the items of other comprehensive income.

Other comprehensive income items that may be added (or subtracted) from net profit to arrive at total comprehensive income include the following.

* Any increase or decrease in the fair value of property, plant and equipment during the period where an entity chooses to revalue such assets subsequent to acquisition rather than leave the amount at cost.
* Any gain or loss in the value of a liability during the period for a defined benefit superannuation plan when the entity has elected to report such gains or losses directly in equity.
* Any increase or decrease in the fair value of financial instruments that qualify as effective cash flow hedges in accordance with AASB 139 *Financial instruments: recognition and measurement*.
* The gains and losses from the translation of a foreign subsidiary's accounts into Australian dollars.

WORKED EXAMPLE

6.3

WORKED EXAMPLE

ABC LTD

The following example illustrates a statement of comprehensive income for a company that also prepares a separate income statement. This is not like the statements in Worked examples 6.1 and 6.2 where we were dealing with sole proprietorship-type businesses.

ABC LTD
STATEMENT OF COMPREHENSIVE INCOME FOR THE YEAR ENDED 30 JUNE 20X9

	20X9 $MILLION	20X8 $MILLION
Profit for the year	36	27
Other comprehensive income		
Unrealised gain (loss) on revaluation of properties, net of tax	4	6
Unrealised gain (loss) on cash flow hedges, net of tax	10	20
Gains (losses) on foreign currency translation of investments in foreign operations, net of tax	(8)*	5
Other comprehensive income total for the year, net of tax	6	31
Total comprehensive income for the year	42	58

* Brackets are commonly used in published accounts to denote negatives.

The total comprehensive income in 20X8 is much higher than net profit, while in 20X9 the amount of comprehensive income is slightly less than profit for the year.

Refer to the consolidated statement of comprehensive income in the Woolworths 2013 financial report (Appendix 1). We explained the meaning of 'consolidated' in Chapter 2 as a group of entities comprising Woolworths Limited and other entities it controls (see Note 28 of the Woolworths 2013 annual report at www.woolworthslimited.com.au). Note the total of other comprehensive income (OCI) for 2013 from continuing operations was ($231.4m) and total comprehensive income was $2496.6m

STOP AND THINK 6

Using the 2013 Woolworths consolidated statement of comprehensive income, determine the following:

a amount of gain/loss on fair value hedges from continuing operations for 2013

b amount of cash flow hedge gain/loss from continuing operations transferred to the income statement in 2013.

6.4

WORKED EXAMPLE

ABC LTD

Entities that choose to produce only a single statement of comprehensive income simply combine the contents of the income statement and statement of comprehensive income, as illustrated below.

ABC LTD
STATEMENT OF COMPREHENSIVE INCOME FOR THE YEAR ENDED 30 JUNE 20X9

	20X9 $MILLION			20X8 $MILLION
Sales revenue		100		95
Less cost of sales		<u>30</u>		<u>35</u>
Gross profit		70		60
Expenses				
Rent	2		2	
Employee entitlements	8		8	
Advertising	3		5	
Other	<u>11</u>		10	
Total expenses		<u>24</u>		<u>25</u>
Profit before tax		46		35
Income tax expense		<u>10</u>		<u>8</u>
Profit for the year		<u>36</u>		<u>27</u>
Other comprehensive income				
Unrealised gain (loss) on revaluation of properties, net of tax	4		6	
Unrealised gain (loss) on cash flow hedges, net of tax	10		20	
Gains (losses) on foreign currency translation of investments in foreign operations, net of tax	(8)		5	
Other comprehensive income total for the year, net of tax		<u>6</u>		<u>31</u>
Total comprehensive income for the year		<u>42</u>		<u>58</u>

NOTE:

Irrespective of whether an entity elects to provide one or two statements about its financial performance, the profit for the year will always represent the result of the entity's operations. Other comprehensive income will report on asset/liability remeasurements that are initially recognised direct to equity in the balance sheet. As such, when assessing the success of an entity's operations the focus is on the revenues and expenses that result from operations. Other comprehensive income can then be separately compared between entities, provided the entities are comparable and use similar accounting policies. Users are then able to assess managers' decisions to hedge, to invest offshore, and so on. For many smaller entities, other comprehensive income will often be zero.

We use a single statement of comprehensive income in the remaining chapters of this book.

THE STATEMENT OF CHANGES IN EQUITY

All reporting entities must present a statement of changes in equity (SOCE). In this section we outline the content and elements of the SOCE, as set out in AASB 101 *Presentation of financial statements* (2007).

The statement of comprehensive income reports all non-owner changes in equity and the SOCE reports all owner changes to equity that are taken directly to the equity section of the balance sheet.

13 LEARNING OBJECTIVE

Explain the role of and prepare a simplified statement of changes in equity

Owner changes in equity consist of selling or buying shares from the owners (shareholders) and the payment of dividends. It enables users to observe the overall change in equity during a period as a result of transactions with the owners.

Paragraph 106 of AASB 101 specifies that a SOCE must show the following items on the face of the statement:

a. total comprehensive income for the period [*from the statement of comprehensive income*]

b. for each component of equity, the effects of retrospective application or retrospective restatement recognised in accordance with AASB 108 [*e.g. a change in depreciation policy, which we discuss in Chapter 8*]

c. the amounts of transactions with owners in their capacity as owners, showing separately contributions by and distributions [*e.g. dividends*] to owners

d. for each component of equity a reconciliation between the carrying amount and the end of the period, separately disclosing each change.

6.5 KEY CONCEPT

STATEMENT OF CHANGES IN EQUITY

The purpose of the statement of changes in equity is to report all owner changes to equity that are taken directly to the equity section of the balance sheet, together with the comprehensive income for the period. This, therefore, shows the total changes to the equity for the period. It enables users to observe the overall change in equity during a period.

6.5 WORKED EXAMPLE

ABC LTD

The following example illustrates a statement of changes in equity for ABC Ltd.

ABC LTD
STATEMENT OF CHANGES IN EQUITY FOR THE YEAR ENDED 30 JUNE 20X9

	SHARE CAPITAL $M	REVALUATION SURPLUS $M	CASH FLOW HEDGE $M	TRANSLATION OF FOREIGN OPERATIONS $M	RETAINED EARNINGS $M	TOTAL $M
Balance at 1 July 20X7	200	nil	nil	nil	265	465
Total comprehensive income for the year		6	20	5	27	58
Dividends					(10)	(10)
Issue of share capital	100					100

	SHARE CAPITAL $M	REVALUATION SURPLUS $M		CASH FLOW HEDGE $M	TRANSLATION OF FOREIGN OPERATIONS $M	RETAINED EARNINGS $M	TOTAL $M
Balance at 30 June 20X8	300	6		20	5	282	613
Total comprehensive income for the year		4		10	(8)	36	42
Dividends						(10)	(10)
Balance at 30 June 20X9	300	10		30	(3)	308	645

We will now discuss three of the columns as examples.

 *Share capital.* In this column the opening balance at 1 July 20X7 is $200m. During the year ending 30 June 20X8, $100m of new shares are issued. There is no change in the following year.

 *Retained earnings.* This column shows the opening balance at 1 July 20X7 of $265m. The profit of $27m for the year ending 30 June 20X8 is added. The dividends of $10m paid to shareholders are deducted to give an ending balance of $282m at 30 June 20X8. For the year ended 30 June 20X9, the profit for the year of $36m is added. The dividends of $10m paid to shareholders are deducted to give an ending balance of $308m at 30 June 20X9.

 *Total column.* This column shows the total of all columns.

STOP AND THINK 7

Explain the difference between profit and total comprehensive income.

SUMMARY

LEARNING OBJECTIVE 1

DISCUSS THE IMPORTANCE OF THE MEASUREMENT OF FINANCIAL PERFORMANCE AND UNDERSTAND THE OPTIONS AVAILABLE FOR THE PRESENTATION OF FINANCIAL PERFORMANCE

Financial performance measurement is important as the information may be used for many purposes including determining bonuses for managers, determining dividends, assisting in the valuation of an entity, helping lenders to assess the eligibility of borrowers for loans, and to price such loans. Entities can choose to prepare a single statement of comprehensive income, or an income statement and a statement of comprehensive income.

LEARNING OBJECTIVE 2

DEFINE AND EXPLAIN THE TERMS 'INCOME' AND 'REVENUE'

Income is defined as the increases in economic benefits during the accounting period in the form of inflows or enhancements of assets or decreases of liabilities that result in increases in equity (other than those relating to contributions from equity participants).

Revenue is similar except that it only includes inflows from the ordinary operations of the entity.

LEARNING OBJECTIVE 3

EXPLAIN AND APPLY THE PRINCIPLES INVOLVED IN THE RECOGNITION OF REVENUE

Revenue is only recognised when:

» the increase in assets or reduction of liabilities has probably resulted from inflows of economic benefits

» these movements can be reliably measured.

LEARNING OBJECTIVE 4

GIVE EXAMPLES OF REVENUE RECOGNITION

We looked at the revenue recognition for a local newsagent, a supplier of component parts to Ford Motors, a gold mine, an airline and an aircraft manufacturer.

LEARNING OBJECTIVE 5

DEFINE AND EXPLAIN THE TERM 'EXPENSE'

Expenses are decreases in economic benefits during the accounting period that result in decreases in equity, other than those relating to distributions to equity participants. Expenses take the form of outflows or depletions of assets or the incurrence of liabilities.

LEARNING OBJECTIVE 6

IDENTIFY THE RECOGNITION CRITERIA FOR EXPENSES

Expenses should be recognised in the period in which:

» it is probable that economic benefits have been consumed

» the amount can be reliably measured.

LEARNING OBJECTIVE 7

EXPLAIN THE PROCESS FOR DECIDING WHEN BUSINESS COSTS SHOULD BE RECOGNISED AS EXPENSES

The process involves deciding when the recognition criteria for expenses are satisfied. The following situations were used to illustrate this process:

» costs of this year are expenses of this year
» costs of earlier years are expenses of this year
» costs of this year are expenses of subsequent years.

LEARNING OBJECTIVE 8

PREPARE A SIMPLIFIED INCOME STATEMENT

A simple income statement for one year was prepared for Blake's Enterprises, a new retail paint outlet.

LEARNING OBJECTIVE 9

ANALYSE AND CLASSIFY BALANCE SHEET AND INCOME STATEMENT TRANSACTIONS ONTO A WORKSHEET

Mary's second-hand car business was used to demonstrate that the worksheet is a simple vehicle for recording, checking and extracting a balance sheet and an income statement. We have shown that the basis of accounting is simple if you follow the basic principles. Furthermore, when you lapse, the system used on the worksheet provides a simple and effective check.

LEARNING OBJECTIVE 10

IDENTIFY THE FACTORS THAT INFLUENCE THE FORMAT OF THE INCOME STATEMENT

The format of an income statement is not mandated by accounting standards. Therefore, there are various factors that influence its format. These factors include:

» the type of business (e.g. company or unincorporated association, for-profit versus not-for-profit)
» the size of the entity
» organisational goals
» the needs of users.

LEARNING OBJECTIVE 11

EXPLAIN THE CONCEPT OF EARNINGS (OR PROFIT) MANAGEMENT

Earnings management occurs when people use their judgement in relation to financial reporting and the structuring of transactions to achieve particular financial outcomes. The objective may be to influence the perceptions of stakeholders about the underlying economic performance of the company and/or to influence outcomes that depend on reported accounting numbers.

LEARNING OBJECTIVE 12

EXPLAIN THE ROLE OF AND PREPARE A SIMPLIFIED STATEMENT OF COMPREHENSIVE INCOME

Entities must report all items of income and expense recognised during a period either in an income statement and a statement of comprehensive income (SOCI), or they may elect to produce a single statement that must be called a SOCI. Where two statements are prepared the ending item in the income statement is the profit that is the opening line in the SOCI. Other comprehensive income

when added to profit (loss) allows users to assess all the non-owner changes in assets and liabilities that have occurred between two balance dates.

LEARNING OBJECTIVE 13

EXPLAIN THE ROLE OF AND PREPARE A SIMPLIFIED STATEMENT OF CHANGES IN EQUITY

The purpose of the SOCE is to report all owner changes to equity that are taken directly to equity, together with the comprehensive income for the period, showing the total changes to equity for the period. It enables users to observe the overall change in equity during a period represented by both owner and non-owner transactions and events.

REVIEW QUESTIONS

1   In your own words, define an expense.

2   How does an expense differ from a cost?

3   'Expenses for a period are always the same as costs.' Discuss the truth of this statement, using examples to illustrate your argument.

4   What is the purpose of a statement of comprehensive income, and who would use it?

5   Explain in your own words the concept of comprehensive income.

6   In what circumstances would it be inappropriate to recognise a cost as either an expense or an asset?

7   Which is more important – the balance sheet or the statement of comprehensive income?

8   Which accounts would you expect to be changed by the following transactions?

   a   cash invested in the business

   b   cash received from a cash sale

   c   supplies purchased on credit

   d   electricity account paid

   e   land purchased for $100 000 and paid for by $40 000 in cash and a $60 000 mortgage from the bank.

PROBLEMS FOR DISCUSSION AND ANALYSIS

1   Refer to the Woolworths financial report in Appendix 1 and answer the following questions.

   a   What is the revenue from operations for the year to 30 June 2013?

   b   What is the gross profit from ordinary activities before tax for the year ended 30 June 2013, and for 2012? By how much did this increase in the year?

   c   What is the profit from ordinary activities before tax for the year ended 30 June 2013, and for 2012? By how much did this decrease in the year? Why?

   d   What would be the total comprehensive income for 2013 and 2012?

2   From the information in the table below calculate:

   a   owners' equity at 1 January 20X0

   b   owners' equity at 31 December 20X0

   c   profit earned for the 12 months ending 31 December, assuming there were no inputs or withdrawals of equity by the owner.

	TOTAL ASSETS ($)	TOTAL LIABILITIES ($)
At 1 January 20X0	132 400	68 300
At 31 December 20X0	333 000	128 300

3 Calculate the missing amounts for each independent case in the following table. Assume in case (d) that the assets are twice the amount of the liabilities and the expenses are 80 per cent of revenue.

CASE	TOTAL ASSETS ($)	TOTAL LIABILITIES ($)	OWNERS' EQUITY ($)	TOTAL REVENUE ($)	TOTAL EXPENSES ($)	NET PROFIT (LOSS) ($)
a	100 000	?	50 000	32 000	?	6 000
b	?	27 000	(100)	7 000	8 000	?
c	32 000	16 000	?	?	10 000	3 000
d	50 000	?	?	?	?	3 000

4 Study the figures below. Calculate the missing amounts for each independent case. Assume in case (f) that net profit is 25 per cent of revenue.

CASE	CURRENT ASSETS ($)	NON-CURRENT ASSETS ($)	TOTAL ASSETS ($)	CURRENT LIABILITIES ($)	NON-CURRENT LIABILITIES ($)	TOTAL LIABILITIES ($)	OWNERS' EQUITY ($)	TOTAL REVENUE ($)	TOTAL EXPENSES ($)	NET PROFIT (LOSS) ($)
a	20 000	?	140 000	30 000	?	?	20 000	112 500	?	200
b	18 200	?	?	?	110 000	132 000	33 300	86 200	?	(7 300)
c	?	86 300	103 700	12 800	?	?	?	17 350	17 300	?
d	21 270	?	86 350	3 200	?	43 580	?	158 600	?	3 200
e	?	110 200	?	?	98 300	110 260	23 400	?	33 000	7 800
f	?	36 400	?	10 400	NIL	?	27 300	133 800	?	?

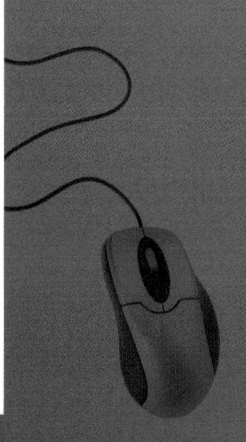

5   There are two partners in XY & Co., an electrical retailer. They have each withdrawn $10 000 in cash from the business during the year. X has also taken from the business, for personal use, a washing machine that cost $400 and had a selling price of $560. Y has been paid wages of $24 000 and X has been paid wages of $12 000.

Discuss how each of the above should be dealt with in the accounts, giving reasons for your decisions.

6   J. Blemish's financial year ends on 30 June. However, he pays his annual insurance premium in advance on 1 January each year. How should he record the unused premium in the balance sheet on 30 June?

7   J. Blemish's balance sheet at 30 June 20X0 showed net assets of $134 645. During the year ending 30 June 20X1 an additional $5000 of capital was put into the business and the owner withdrew $56 737. The statement of comprehensive income for the 12 months showed a surplus of $34 692. What was the figure for owners' equity for the year ending 30 June 20X1?

8   J. Blemish's statement of comprehensive income for the month ending 31 March 20X1 showed a surplus of $2231. During the same month, the owner withdrew $2500 from the business. Would it be correct to say that the business incurred a loss of $269 during the month? Discuss.

9   Your friend James Smith, knowing that you are a 'top gun' accounting student, has asked you to prepare a balance sheet and a statement of comprehensive income from the following information. He does not know the owners' equity figure as he has not been able to calculate the profit for the period. Provide the statements that James has requested.

	$
Salaries expense	1 236
Cash sales	132 000
Insurance expense	932
Cost of supplies used to make cash sales	32 400
Equipment	3 200
Electricity and telephone expense	9 560
Accounts payable	14 020
Bank overdraft	2 300
Wages expense	38 900
Land and buildings	125 000
Vehicles	23 230
Mortgage on land	23 000

10 Jimmy Jones receives a $200 000 legacy from his great-aunt. As he has some knowledge of the textile industry he decides to go into business manufacturing garments. He commences trading on 1 July 20X1 and uses all of the $200 000 as capital. Unfortunately, because he does not have an accounting background, he does not keep adequate records. At the end of the financial year, he

realises that he will have to prepare financial accounts so he can ascertain whether or not he has made a profit, and whether he is liable for tax on any such profit. From the information given below, prepare, in good form, a statement of comprehensive income for the year and a balance sheet at 30 June 20X2. Note that all figures given are for a full year and the owner, Jimmy Jones, withdraws amounts periodically from the business to cover his expenses.

Accounts receivable $50 000, inventory $100 000, bank loan (due 1 January 20X6) $80 000, machinery $80 000, total current assets $160 000, sales $127 800, rent $5000, motor vehicles $40 000, wages $42 100, motor vehicle expenses $8230, total non-current assets $132 500, electricity expense $2500, council rates $2500, total liabilities $117 600, advertising expense $2022, cost of goods sold $84 070, cash at bank?, office equipment?, selling expense?, total assets?, net assets?, accounts payable?, gross profit?, capital?, retained earnings?, total owner's equity?

11 In each of the following situations, discuss whether the item would be included in the statement of comprehensive income for the year to 31 December 20X8 and at what amount. The business is that of a builder and builder's trader.

a   Sales of general building materials by the builder's trader to third parties amounted to $52 000, of which $48 000 was received in cash by 31 December 20X1 and the remainder was received in January 20X9.

b   Three house conversions were started and completed during the year at a price of $48 000 each. These amounts were received in full by 31 December 20X8.

c   One office conversion, which was 60 per cent complete at the end of 20X7, was completed in 20X8 at a price of $80 000. Invoices on account amounting to $48 000 had been sent out in 20X7.

d   Building materials bought from third parties during the year cost $28 000, of which all but $2000 had been paid by December 20X8.

e   Building materials used on the three houses referred to in item (b) cost $36 000 and had all been paid for by December 20X8.

f   Wages paid in respect of the houses mentioned in item (b) amounted to $40 000 for the year.

g   The costs relating to the office mentioned in item (c) were as follows:

	$
Wages paid in 20X7	16 000
Wages paid in 20X8	12 000
Materials used in 20X7	16 000
Materials used in 20X8	14 000

h   The storeworkers' wages in the yard amounted to $16 000 for the year.

i   The owner, who worked full-time in the business, paid himself a salary of $18 000 and also withdrew $2000 cash from the business to pay a pressing personal debt.

j   The motor expenses paid in the year were broken down as follows (assume the owner uses his car 80 per cent for business).

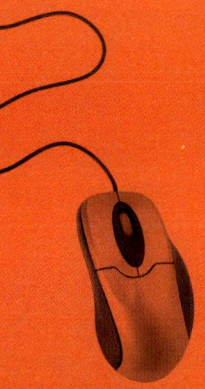

		$
Annual registration on three vans paid	1 April 20X8	600*
Annual insurance on vans paid	1 April 20X8	960*
Repairs and petrol for vans		1200
Annual registration on owner's car paid	1 June 20X8	200*
Annual registration on owner's wife's car paid	1 June 20X8	200*
Annual insurance on owner's car paid	1 June 20X8	240*
Annual insurance on owner's wife's car paid	1 June 20X8	240*
Repairs and petrol for the two cars (50 per cent for each car)		1600*

* The charge for registration went up by $40 per vehicle and insurance premiums rose by 20 per cent. All these charges are paid annually in advance.

k   The following bills were also paid during the year:

		$
Electricity (payable at end of each quarter)	1 February	108
	1 May	90
	1 August	90
	1 November	120
Rent for one year to 1 April 20X9	1 April 20X8	800*
TV rental to 1 April 20X9	1 April 20X8	120*

* The rent remained the same but the TV rental went up from $100 to $120 from the previous year.

12   l. Cover decided to open Re-cover Upholstery Repairs on 1 January 20X4. She contributed office equipment valued at $20 000 and a van valued at $24 000. She also opened a new business account with a bank and deposited $10 000 cash. Transactions during January are summarised in the table below.

January 4	Signed a three-year lease on a shop and paid first month's rent of $350
January 4	Purchased office supplies worth $850 – paid $100 with a cheque and the balance on credit
January 6	$500 cash was received for small repairs to chairs
January 6	$1000 revenue earned on credit for repair work for Shipshape Ltd
January 7	Purchased a special machine for sewing upholstery for $5000, paying $1000 cash with the balance payable in 90 days
January 8	Cash revenue earned $600
January 11	Engaged an upholsterer at an agreed wage of $550 per week.
January 12	Paid cash for petrol $60, postage $10 and electricity $130

January 13	Cash of $700 received for immediate repairs
January 13	Revenue of $1200 earned from credit sales to Jon Abbott
January 14	Paid for office supplies purchased on credit on 4 March
January 15	Withdrew $300 for personal use
January 16	Purchased office supplies for $300 on credit
January 17	Cash received for minor restoration work $700
January 18	Paid weekly wages to the upholsterer
January 21	Revenue earned for repairs: cash $400, on account $1200
January 23	Shipshape Ltd paid the amount owing from 6 January services
January 24	Petrol expenses paid $70
January 25	Paid weekly wages to the upholsterer
January 28	Revenue earned for repair work $600, receiving $100 in cash and the remainder on credit
January 31	Office supplies used $850

Required

Complete a worksheet for the month of January using the above data. Also, prepare a statement of comprehensive income for the period and a balance sheet at 31 January.

13 Joe decided to start a business selling second-hand boats. He had some money of his own, but this was not enough so he borrowed money (on interest-free terms) from a rich uncle. The transactions of the business during March were all cash transactions as summarised in the table.

March 1	Opened a bank account for the business and deposited $10 000 of his own money
March 2	Deposited $20 000 (borrowed from his rich uncle) into the business bank account
March 3	Paid a fortnight's rent ($500) on a yard suitable for use as a boat saleyard
March 4	Went to an auction and was able to purchase the following boats (including trailers) for cash: Thunderbird $4000 Chivers $2500 Swiftcraft $900
March 5	Furnished the yard office with second-hand furniture costing $2900
March 6	Employed a young nephew to clean the boats
March 8	Advertising for all three boats in the local paper over two days cost $300, which included photos of the boats
March 9	Sold the Thunderbird for $5500 cash
March 10	Sold the Chivers for $3200 cash

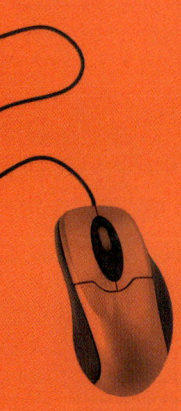

March 11	Attended another auction and bought a Bertram for $15 000
March 12	Paid his nephew $20 to clean the new boat
March 15	Readvertised the Swiftcraft for three days at a total cost of $300
March 17	Advertised the Bertram in a boating magazine at a cost of $800
March 18	Paid rent for the yard for the next fortnight ($500)
March 19	Was offered $1200 for the Swiftcraft
March 20	Accepted the offer for the Swiftcraft and was paid $1200
March 22	Sold the Bertram for $19 000
March 23	Went to another auction and bought a Sports Fisherman for $8000
March 24	Had the Sports Fisherman professionally cleaned at a cost of $180
March 25	Advertised the Sports Fisherman in a fishing feature in the newspaper at a cost of $300
March 26	Decided things were going so well he would repay his rich uncle $3000
March 27	Took the Sports Fisherman on a test-run with a customer and damaged the hull on a submerged reef
March 29	Had the Sports Fisherman repaired at a cost of $900
March 30	Sold the Sports Fisherman for $9300
March 31	Paid the electricity bill of $180 for the month

Required

a Complete a worksheet for the month using the provided data.

b Prepare a statement of comprehensive income for the accounting period from the worksheet.

c Prepare a balance sheet at the end of the accounting period.

14 K. Kitten was made redundant from his job as a senior civil servant and was paid a $15 000 redundancy fee. With this money, he invested in a toy business. Transactions during June are summarised in the following table.

| June 1 | Deposited $150 000 into a business account and signed a seven-year lease on premises, paying one month's rent in advance of $600. |
| June 2 | Purchased shop fittings for $27 000 on 30-day credit. Purchased stock from Whoopee Doo wholesalers for $58 000, paying $30 000 cash with the balance to be paid in 14 days. |

June 3	Employed Jill Smith on a casual basis for three days to help with stocking the shop. Payment was $100 per day paid at the end of the three days.
June 4	Paid for installation of phone, fax and internet services from Telstra. As he was a new business customer, with no business credit history, Telstra required immediate payment of the connection fees of $750 and a deposit of $500 against future charges.
June 5	Purchased office equipment from Charge It for $5600, payment due in seven days.
June 6	Hired caterers for an opening party, paying $3100 cash, and advertised in the local newspaper for the next three weeks, on seven days' credit, for $500.
June 7	Hired two salespersons at a weekly wage, including outgoings, of $500 each per week. Paid Jill Smith $300.
June 7–12	Took $3456 in cash sales.
June 12	A bicycle sold to R. Wobbly on 8 June for $375 was returned due to a faulty frame. The customer was told that it would be repaired at the shop's expense or he could have a refund. R. Wobbly said he would give a decision on the following Monday, 14 June, after discussing it with his wife.
June 12	Paid Charge It, paid local newspaper, paid wages $1000.
June 14	R. Wobbly decided to have a refund for the faulty bike.
June 14–19	Took $6320 in cash sales.
June 15	One salesperson resigned and two days' wages were paid.
June 16	Paid Whoopee Doo.
June 21–26	Took $5321 in cash sales.
June 21	Hired new salesperson at $450 per week. Paid the other salesperson $500 plus an additional $275 overtime.
June 23	Purchased additional stock of $23 000 from Whoopee Doo on 14 days' credit.
June 28–30	Took $1289 in cash sales.
June 28	Realised that the property and stock were not insured and took out a year's contract at an annual cost of $14 400. The first month was paid in advance.
June 28	Paid wages of $950.
June 30	Counted stock and found that $16 300 wholesale value must have been sold.

Required

a   Complete a worksheet for the month of June using the data provided.

b   Prepare a statement of comprehensive income for the month of June and a balance sheet as at 30 June.

15 Mandy Plover recently completed her professional accounting qualification and has registered as a tax agent. During the three years in which she was fulfilling the work requirement for her professional status she managed to save $30 000. As she had always wanted to run her own

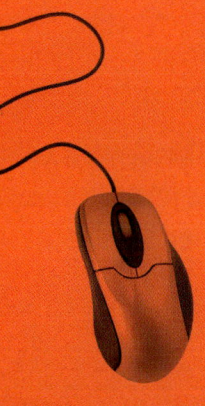

practice, she rented premises and opened for business. She decided the best time of year to commence her business was on 1 July, as this coincided with the beginning of the tax year.

During the month of July the following transactions took place.

July 1	Deposited $30 000 into a business bank account.
July 1	Paid three months' rent in advance on premises of $3000.
July 1	Placed an order with Quick Printers for stationery, business cards and letterheads. The stationery is expected to last for one year.
July 1	Paid Telstra a connection fee of $275 for the telephone and fax.
July 1	Paid the electricity company a meter rental fee of $50.
July 1	Signed a three-year lease with Office Supplies Pty Ltd at a rent of $475 per month, payable in advance, for office equipment, telephones and fax.
July 2	Paid Super Signs $1000 for a sign advertising her accounting services, to be placed outside the premises.
July 3	Purchased a computer from Wizard Computers for $7500, with payment due in 15 days.
July 4	Received the order from Quick Printers – payment of $1380 due on receipt of goods.
July 4–15	Completed a number of tax returns for clients with a total billing of $2750. Clients given 30 days' credit.
July 15	Signed a contract with the Widget company for bookkeeping services. The terms of the contract were that Mandy would spend one day a week at the Widget factory and be paid a weekly fee of $300.
July 15	Paid herself a fortnightly salary of $750.
July 16	Received payment from one of the tax clients (listed above: 4–15 July) of $225.
July 16	Signed a three-year lease on a BMW at $2000 per month, payable in advance.
July 18	Paid for the computer.
July 22	Received $300 weekly fee from the Widget company.
July 23	The liquidator of Jimmy Jones Holdings informed Mandy that one of her clients who took tax advice (period: 4–15 July) has no assets and will be unable to pay the credit account of $780.
July 29	Paid herself a fortnightly salary of $750.
July 29	Received $300 weekly fee from the Widget company.
July 16–31	Completed work for additional clients amounting to $3450. One of these clients paid $340 in cash; the rest were given 30 days' credit.

Required

a Prepare a worksheet for the month of July.

b From your worksheet prepare a statement of comprehensive income and a balance sheet.

c Comment on the financial position of the business.

16 Jill has recently gone into business selling office chairs. Details of her transactions for the first month are given below.

Day 1	Opened a bank account and paid in $10 000 of her own money. Transferred the ownership of her car to the business at an agreed price of $4000. Rented an office–showroom at a rental of $240 per month and paid one month's rent. Bought a desk, a typewriter, an answering machine and sundry office equipment at a cost of $1600.
Day 2	Bought 100 chairs at $70 per chair and paid for them immediately.
Day 3	Received delivery of the chairs.

Day 5	Placed an advertisement in a trade paper offering the chairs for sale on the following terms:
	  Single chairs, $100 per chair including delivery
	  10 or more chairs, $90 per chair including delivery.
	The advertisement cost $400 and was paid for immediately.

Day 8	Received separate orders for 12 chairs at $100 each, together with accompanying cheques.
Day 9	Paid the cheques into the bank and despatched the chairs. The delivery costs were $144 in total and were paid straight away.
Day 11	Received six orders for 10 chairs each at a price of $90 per chair, together with six cheques for $900. Banked the cheques and despatched the orders. The delivery charges were $100 for each order, making a total of $600 which was paid immediately.
Day 14	Jill paid herself two weeks' wages from the business, amounting to $300 in total.
Day 16	Bought another 20 chairs for $70 each and paid for them immediately.
Day 21	Paid $300 for car repairs.
Day 23	Received an order for 20 chairs at $90 each; banked the cheque and arranged delivery for $80 which was paid immediately.
Day 24	Placed a further advertisement in the trade paper at a cost of $400, which was paid immediately.
Day 27	Received one order for 15 chairs at a price of $90 each (this order totalled $1350) and another order for seven chairs at a price of $100 each (a total of $700). The cheques were banked and the chairs were despatched at a total cost of $200, which was paid immediately.
Day 28	Drew another $300 from the bank for her own wages. Sold the remaining six chairs at a price of $500 for all six to a customer who walked into the showroom. The customer paid the $500 in cash and this money was banked. No delivery costs were incurred because the customer took the chairs away. Paid the telephone bill of $60 and the electricity bill, $80.

a In each situation where there are two possible treatments, discuss the arguments for and against each alternative.

b Based on the outcome of your discussions, draw up a worksheet and enter the transactions for the month.

c Extract a balance sheet at the end of the month and an income statement for the month.

d Discuss the performance of the business for the period as revealed by the accounts you have prepared, paying particular attention to its cash position and its profitability.

17 Using the following information, prepare statements of comprehensive income and changes in equity for Waterloo Ltd for the year ended 30 June 20X5. Assume all amounts are net of tax where appropriate.

a Net profit from the income statement for the period is $130m.

b Dividends of $50m were paid.

c Available-for-sale investments acquired at the start of the year for $160m had a fair value of $152m at the end of the year.

d The fair value of the cash flow hedges declined by $15m during the year.

e Land was revalued by $25m.

f The translation of foreign operations resulted in a foreign currency translation gain of $24m.

g A foreign subsidiary was sold during the month. There was an accumulated foreign currency translation loss of $15m in relation to this subsidiary.

h The company issued shares during the year for a total of $50m.

i The opening balances of accounts were share capital $500m; retained profits $200m.

18 The core business of Greenmango Ltd involves the sale of anti virus software. The following took place during the financial year ended 30 June 20X0. The company earned $25 000 000 from the sale of software; $3 000 000 from update downloads; and $50 000 in interest from investing on the short-term money market. The company also received a $2000 discount arising out of the early settlement of a liability; and issued shares in exchange for $500 000 cash during the year.

a Discuss whether the foregoing five financial items would meet the definition of income to the company during the year. Given reasons for your answer.

b Which, if any, of the items would meet the definition of revenue to the company for the year? Given reasons for your answer.

19 When a CitiPower customer uses electricity, the commission earns revenue. It is impossible, however, to read the meters of all customers on the last day of its financial year. How does CitiPower determine its revenue for a given year?

20 The R & I Bank charges a 5 per cent service fee when issuing traveller's cheques to customers. Recently, a customer bought $1000 Diners Club International traveller's cheques, for which the bank received a fee of $50. How would the bank record this transaction, and how would the Diners Club International balance sheet be affected?

21 During November 20X0, DEF Ltd sold goods for $50 000 to XYZ Ltd, which used them as security for a hire-purchase agreement and sent the $50 000 to DEF Ltd. DEF Ltd agreed to repurchase the merchandise on or before 30 June 20X1 for $52 000, the difference being interest on the hire-purchase agreement and payment for XYZ Ltd's services. Will DEF Ltd have revenue in 20X0?

22 Swallow Ltd is a statewide real estate brokerage company that is well known for selling small businesses through local real estate brokers. A local broker joining the group pays Swallow Ltd an initial contract fee of $8000 plus 5 per cent of all future revenue as a service fee. In return, Swallow Ltd allows use of its well-known name, arranges various seminars throughout the year and provides a statewide referral system for the brokers. The initial contract fee currently accounts for 30 per cent of Swallow Ltd's revenues, but it anticipates that the WA market will become flooded with competitors over the next two years, from which time the company will have to rely on the service fees and any new sources of revenue. Should each $8000 be recorded as revenue by Swallow Ltd in the year in which the contract agreement is signed? If so, what will be the effect on its profits after the market has become flooded with competitors?

23 In an article titled 'Money to be made from forensic accounting', published in the *Australian Financial Review* on 2 July 2013, John Authers states: 'Big discrepancies between revenue recognised and the flows recorded on the cash flow statement inmply a company is, in effect, borrowing sales from the future to make quarterly targets.' Explain what Authers means and how this impacts current and future profits.

Note to instructors: the following problems are considered more suitable for use in postgraduate courses. However, undergraduate courses may also find them useful.

24 You are the chief accountant of Elphick & Company, a firm of chartered accountants. Paul Cruit and his wife, Debbie, have asked for your advice regarding the following business proposition.

At present, Paul earns $30 000 per annum and Debbie has a part-time job in which she earns $7000 per annum. Their eldest son is a third-year apprentice and gives his mother $50 a week towards household expenses.

Paul has been left a legacy of $250 000 by his great-aunt. This money can be invested in a bank deposit, earning 6 per cent per annum. However, Paul and Debbie favour buying a newsagency costing $370 000 (including stock, plant, equipment, a vehicle and goodwill).

The business broker selling the business states that Bankeast would be prepared to grant them a loan of $200 000 at 10 per cent per annum, repayable over 20 years.

At present, the business is operated by a husband and wife, plus one other staff member who earns $550 per week. This figure includes all employee outgoings such as payroll tax, insurance, superannuation, and so on.

Additional information

The following table provides sales information for the past 12 months.

	$
Newspapers and periodicals	780 000
Books	60 000
Stationery	87 500
Confectionery	27 600
Sundry sales	10 000

Gross profit details are as follows.

	%
Newspapers and periodicals	15
Books	40
Confectionery	50
Stationery	40
Sundry sales	30

The previous year's expenses are as follows.

	$			$
Telephone	3 000		Wages and associated costs	28 820
Rent of premises	4 000		Rates	15 000
Insurance	12 750		Electricity and gas	7 300
Security	2 700		Advertising	3 450
Accountant's fees	3 620		Trade subscriptions	1 500
Vehicle expenses	2 300		Depreciation expense	3 820

Required

a What would your advice be?

b It was suggested by the business broker that the son work in the business, at a reduced wage, instead of the present employee. This would increase profits. What points need to be considered if this course of action is to taken?

c What other factors should the Cruits consider before making a decision?

25 The Northshore Sailing Association (NSA) is a not-for-profit association with 1875 members. The association represents the interests of its members through a management committee, which organises the publication of a quarterly newsletter, and holds an annual meeting. It has subcommittees that create competitions and outings for members, as well as getting involved in community-care programs.

Every June, the newly appointed management committee meets with the old committee to discuss whether the general policy of the NSA has been adhered to over the pervious 12 months. The financial policy of the association for each year focuses on matching expenses with revenues; in other words, the expenses of the year should approximately equal the income of the year.

At the annual meeting on 30 June 20X2, the executive secretary presented an estimated income statement for the past financial year to the new management committee (as it is a not-for-profit organisation, the use of a statement of comprehensive income was deemed unnecessary). Even though some of the June transactions had been estimated, the executive secretary assured the committee that these figures were carefully prepared and approximated actual totals for the month.

NSA
ESTIMATED INCOME STATEMENT FOR THE PERIOD 1 JULY 20X1 30 JUNE 20X2

	$
Revenues	
Membership fees	76 680
Newsletter subscriptions	8668
Publication sales	3168
Government grant	14 400
Annual national sailing championship, 20X1 profit	908
Total revenues	103 824
Expenses	
Printing and mailing publications	24 640
Committee meeting expense	13 120
Annual national sailing championship advance	2880
IBM publishing system	7200
Administrative salaries and expenses	45 724
Miscellaneous	6680
Total expenses	100 244
Excess of revenues over expenses	3580

One new committee member asked whether a grant of $14 400 from the government should be included as income. If it was not, a deficit would show. This would mean that the association's reserves had been touched and, therefore, that the 20X1–X2 board had not adhered to the general financial policy of the NSA.

This resulted in further questions about other items on the income statement, and led to the disclosure of the following information by the executive secretary.

– In March 20X2, the NSA received a $14 400 grant from the government to finance a clean-up and erosion prevention operation along the Swanlee River, to commence in August of the same year. Up to 30 June 20X2, $720 had been spent in preparations for the operation and was included in committee meeting expenses. When asked to explain why the $14 400 had been recorded in the 20X1–X2 financial year instead of 20X2–X3, the executive secretary explained that the grant had been obtained as a result of the persuasiveness of the 20X1–X2 committee and, therefore, it should receive the credit for securing the grant. The grant period was two years, at the end of which any unspent funds had to be returned to the government.

– In late June 20X2 the association had fully installed and paid for an IBM publishing system which cost $7200. This system would dramatically reduce the hours involved in preparing membership lists, correspondence and manuscripts for publication. All of the other equipment in the association office was old.

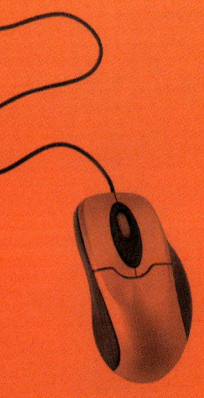

- Members normally paid their fees during the first two months of the financial year. Due to the need to raise finance for the new IBM system, the association announced to members in April 20X2 that anyone paying their fees before 20 June 20X2 would receive a free T-shirt which would be on sale when the Swanlee River clean-up and erosion prevention operation commenced later in the year. The approximate cost of producing this T-shirt was expected to be $7.20, and it was expected to sell for $15. As a result, $8640 of fees for 20X2–X3 was received by 20 June 20X2.

- In May 20X2, the association sent a membership directory to each member; such a directory was published and sent out to members once every two years. The preparation and printing costs totalled $5760. Of the 2000 copies printed, 1875 were posted to members while the remaining 125 were held until new members joined the NSA, at which time a directory would be sent to them free of charge.

- One of the entitlements of NSA membership was the receipt of the association newsletter free of charge. The $8668 reported as subscription revenue was the cash received from non-members, such as libraries and interest groups, in the 20X1–X2 financial period, of which $2160 was for newsletters that would be delivered during the next financial period, 20X2–X3. Offsetting this was $1440 of subscription revenue received in 20X0–X1 for newsletters delivered in 20X1–X2.

- The association had advanced $2880 for preliminary expenses to the committee responsible for planning the 20X2 annual national sailing championship, held in late May. Entrance fees at the competition were set at a price to cover all of the championship costs, so it was expected that the $2880, plus any profit, would be returned to the NSA after the committee had paid the championship bill. The 20X1 championship led to a $908 profit; the 20X2 results were not known, although the anticipated attendance was about the same.

Required

Prepare a revised income statement for 20X1–20X2 for the Northshore Sailing Association assuming it had used appropriate accrual accounting principles for all transactions.

ETHICS CASE STUDY

1   The sales staff at Ellenmere are paid a bonus each year provided they sell a certain number of cars. One of your best friends, James, works as a salesperson, and you work in the accounting department. In reviewing the sales records for James, you discover that his last sale for the period was large enough for him to qualify for the bonus. All that remained was for you to approve the sale. You tell James the good news and he is elated as he will now be able to pay for his daughter to receive special medical treatment for a rare disease she suffers from.

Before the bonus can be paid, it is your job to check that the customer meets the company's credit rating requirements so that the sale can be approved. As it happens, you know the customer and you notice that his profits, as stated on the company form, are about 30 per cent overstated. If you adjust the profits, the customer does not meet the company's requirements and James will lose the sale and the bonus.

Discuss what you would do in this situation.

2   Sam is an employee in the accounting department and his boss has asked him to copy the worksheet he prepared for a meeting that afternoon in order to finalise the company's financial statements

for the period. As Sam is copying the worksheet, he notices that a sale on account has not been correctly recorded. The amount has been transposed from the ledger – it was recorded as $54 000 instead of $45 000. Sam remembers the transaction as the sale was to one of his friends. If Sam says nothing, he will receive a higher bonus because the company pays a bonus to all its employees according to their total sales. The bonus will be very useful as Sam is leaving the company at the end of next week to go on an extended working holiday in Europe.

Discuss what you would do if you were Sam.

SUGGESTED ANSWERS TO STOP AND THINK EXERCISES IN THE CHAPTER

1   Income includes gross inflows to an entity while revenue only includes inflows to an entity that result from its ordinary activities. Therefore, for a company like Woolworths, revenue arises from sales of food and groceries. If the company sells some plant and equipment, any gain would be regarded as income but not revenue.

2   In essence, the recognition principle allows for revenue to be recognised when it is probable that the inflow, or other enhancement or saving in the outflow of future economic benefits, has occurred and can be reliably measured. If revenue was only recognised when cash was received, this would be called cash accounting and not accrual accounting. The framework states that, in order for relevant information to be provided to assist users, the accrual basis of accounting should be used.

3   An asset provides a future benefit, whereas with an expense the benefit has already been consumed. However, in some cases, there are activities (like research and development, exploration and evaluation activities) which will provide future economic benefits. However, the likelihood of such benefits flowing to the entity may be too vague to pass the probable test, or it may be too difficult to reliably measure them.

4   Profits are based on accrual accounting; therefore, it is possible to have a profit and yet have no cash. Profit means that the assets have increased by more than the liabilities – but the assets don't have to be in the form of cash.

5   a   Increase the bank column by $1000 and increase the owners' equity column by $1000.

   b   Reduce the bank column by $200 and open up a new asset column for the new asset, a desk, and put $200 in that column.

   c   Here we have to assume that the goods have been paid for. In this case, we decrease cash by $400 and open a new asset column for the goods bought and put $400 in there.

   d   If we assume the rent is paid in arrears then the entries would be to reduce cash and charge an expense of $100 in the profit and loss column. If the assumption is that the rent is paid in advance, then the entry would be to reduce cash and open an asset account for a prepayment. As students have not been introduced to prepayment in any detail at this stage it is better if the former assumption is made.

   e   No entry is required as the earning process is not substantially complete.

   f   Reduce the bank column by $120 and charge $120 as an expense in the profit and loss column.

   g   Increase the bank column by $700 and increase the profit and loss column by $700 for sales as, in this case, the earnings process is complete and receipt of money is certain.

6   a $256.4m

     b $231.9m.

7   The profit is determined after all revenues, other income and expenses for the period have been recognised, in accordance with accounting standards. Total comprehensive income is the sum of profit and items of other comprehensive income that are either never recognised in profit or loss or are initially recognised directly to equity and later recycled to the profit or loss.

CENGAGENOW

Go to http:\\login.cengagebrain.com to link to CengageNOW, your online study tool. First take the Pre-Test for this chapter to get your Personalised Study Plan, and then:

»   revise your understanding of the key terms related to presentation of financial performance and the worksheet by completing the online crossword

»   watch animated examples of income statements and sales transactions

»   follow links to relevant sections of the Corporations Act.

    After you have completed the activities in your Personalised Study Plan take the Post-Test to determine what concepts you have mastered and what you still need work on.

7

PRESENTATION OF CASH FLOWS

At the end of this chapter, you should be able to:

1 explain what is included in the terms 'cash' and 'cash equivalents'

2 explain internal control procedures for cash, and why they are important

3 explain the main purpose of a statement of cash flows

4 discuss what is meant by the concept of cash flows of operating, investing and financing activities

5 identify cash flows from operating activities, and explain the difference between operating cash flows and profit

6 identify cash flows from investing and financing activities.

Tatuasha/Shutterstock.com

INTRODUCTION

In chapters 5 and 6 we considered the three accrual-based financial statements. While accrual accounting provides valuable information it does not provide information about movements in cash. Hence, in this chapter we consider the statement of cash flows which provides information on the inflows and outflows of cash, as it is cash that is used to pay the bills! To be successful a business must make profits and have adequate cash flows. Cash is an important asset and one that is most susceptible to being misappropriated and so we first examine the internal control of cash and then examine in some detail the content and use of the statement of cash flows.

CASH AND CASH EQUIVALENTS

1 LEARNING OBJECTIVE

Explain what is included in the terms 'cash' and 'cash equivalents'

What is cash? The statement of cash flows shows the net increase or decrease in cash during the accounting period. AASB 107 *Statement of cash flows* defines cash as 'cash on hand and cash equivalents'. Cash equivalents are highly liquid investments such as money-market accounts and government Treasury bills. They can be readily converted to cash on hand by the entity, and their use is part of a cash management function. Cash equivalents also include borrowings, such as bank overdrafts; again, these are used by the entity as part of its cash management function. Cash equivalents must also be subject to an insignificant risk of changes in value.

7.1

KEY CONCEPT

CASH

Cash includes cash on hand and cash equivalents, which include highly liquid investments and borrowings used as part of an entity's cash management function.

Many businesses, especially retailers, receive large amounts of cash and credit card receipts each day. Cash is the most difficult asset to control as anyone can spend cash. It is therefore important to establish effective management procedures not only to protect the cash of the business but also to:

- enable accurate reporting of cash and cash flows in the financial statements
- ensure that adequate cash is available to meet commitments as they are due
- allow idle cash to be invested so as to maximise the return to the business.

Cash budgeting is an important tool in the management of cash. We discuss the preparation of cash budgets in Chapter 15.

Internal control of cash

2 LEARNING OBJECTIVE

Explain internal control procedures for cash, and why they are important

Given the ease with which cash can be misappropriated, it is important for a business to establish effective internal control procedures to protect the cash of the business. Internal controls refer to the procedures and processes in place within a business to safeguard all assets including cash. The processes should be part of written policies within the business and, for larger businesses, an internal auditor may be employed to ensure that such processes are adequate and are being followed.

An overriding principle in internal control is to separate duties so that the same person is not responsible for receiving and recording cash. At a sports stadium we will buy a ticket at one counter and then pass the ticket to a different person as we enter the ground. This is an internal control procedure to minimise the opportunities for employees to steal cash. One of the main reasons Barings Bank failed in the 1990s, resulting in losses of billions of dollars, was failure to observe this basic internal control rule. Nick Leeson, the 'rogue trader' responsible for the large trading losses which ultimately led to the bank's failure, was in charge of trading transactions on the floor of the stock exchange and of recording such trades in the accounting records. He was therefore able to cover up the large trading losses he was incurring by falsifying the accounting records. In this way, he was able to escape detection for a much longer period of time than would have been the case if the duties of trading and recording had been carried out by different individuals.

Internal control procedures will vary across companies depending on their size and particular needs. However, effective internal control over cash should ideally include separation of:

- the duties of receiving and paying cash
- the duties of recording cash receipts from cash payments
- handling cash and recording cash movements in the accounting records.

In very small businesses, it may not always be possible to establish such procedures, so other security measures may be employed.

For example, a proprietor of a small corner shop employed a number of part-time staff. It came to his attention that, a few weeks after employing a new person, the cash receipts of the store were somewhat lower than normal. While there were always two or more staff working at any time, there were times when one person was alone behind the counter. The proprietor therefore called in a security company and had a security camera installed in the roof of the store, over the cash register. The camera revealed the new employee taking money from the register and placing it in his pocket.

Effective internal control over cash should also provide for individual responsibilities that require:

- all cash receipts to be deposited with a financial institution on a daily basis.
- different individuals to approve a requisition to order goods and services from the individual who approves payment for the goods and services. There have been instances where a person orders goods to be delivered to his home address and then arranges for payment of the goods from the business bank account.
- approval to make a cash payment and the actual signing of the cheque or electronic funds transfer are by different individuals.
- regular reconciliation of the bank statement (which is the bank's record of the business's cash position) with the accounting records of the business. This reconciliation should result in both balances being the same (after allowing for outstanding deposits and cheques not recorded on the bank statement but recorded in the accounting records of the business, and for various bank charges and fees recorded on the bank statement but not in the accounting records of the business). If this is not the case, it may signal that misappropriation of cash has occurred. Once again, the bank reconciliation should not be done by the same individual responsible for collecting and disbursing cash in the business. To do so would allow the individual to misappropriate cash and cover up his or her theft.

KEY CONCEPT

INTERNAL CONTROL

An important principle of internal control is to have separation of duties so that it requires collusion between two or more employees to misappropriate the assets of a business.

The internal control principles outlined in this section, while particularly relevant for cash, also apply to other assets such as accounts receivable. Having briefly reviewed what we mean by cash and the importance of establishing effective internal control procedures over cash, we now examine the reporting of cash flows to external users through a statement of cash flows.

3 LEARNING OBJECTIVE

Explain the main purpose of a statement of cash flows

THE STATEMENT OF CASH FLOWS

In addition to the balance sheet and the statement of comprehensive income, reporting entities are required to prepare a statement of cash flows following the release of AASB 107 *Statement of cash flows*. In this part of the chapter, we examine the objective of a statement of cash flows and the relationship between the statement of cash flows and the statement of comprehensive income. We then look at an example of a statement of cash flows and how it is interpreted.

Purpose

The main purpose of the statement of cash flows is to provide information about the cash receipts and cash payments of an entity during its accounting period. It is cash and not profits that an entity must use to pay its bills. It is possible for a profitable business to have insufficient cash to meet its debts and be insolvent.

The balance sheet shows the assets an entity has at a particular point in time and how these assets are financed. The statement of comprehensive income shows how much profit the entity has earned during the accounting period. Both these statements are based on accrual accounting and not cash accounting. These statements cannot be used to answer the following types of questions:

- Did the entity's operations produce sufficient cash to meet dividend payments?
- Did the entity issue shares or increase liabilities during the year and, if so, what happened to the proceeds?
- Did the entity purchase any new assets during the year? How did the entity pay for these new assets?

The statement of cash flows is intended to provide answers to these and other questions.

4 LEARNING OBJECTIVE

Discuss what is meant by the concept of cash flows of operating, investing and financing activities

What does a statement of cash flows show?

Having established the need for a statement of cash flows, we need to look in more detail at what the statement shows. In broad terms it tells us where we got money from and how it was used. For the purposes of the statement of cash flows, any transfers of cash between cash equivalents and cash on hand do not need to be reported as cash receipts or payments. The money coming in is referred to as cash inflows, while money going out is referred to as cash outflows. The difference between the cash inflows and the cash outflows is known as the net cash flow, which can be either a net cash inflow or a net cash outflow, depending on the comparative amounts of the two components. Typical cash inflows would be monies generated from trading (commonly referred to as cash flows from operations), monies from new share issues or other forms of long-term finance, and any monies received from the sale of assets. Typical outflows would be monies used to buy new non-current assets, to pay tax and dividends, and to repay debenture holders or other providers of long-term capital. As we shall see, the statement of cash flows separates these cash flows into various categories. The format we shall follow is the one recommended in the accounting standard. We shall use the example of a statement of cash flows shown in Worked example 7.1.

STOP AND THINK 1

What are the reasons for requiring a statement of cash flows?

WORKED EXAMPLE 7.1

SAMPLE STATEMENT OF CASH FLOWS

	THIS YEAR		LAST YEAR
	$000s	$000s	$000s
Cash flow from operating activities		1060	1400
Cash flow from investing activities			
Payments to acquire non-current assets	(900)		(200)
Payments to acquire investments			(100)
Receipts from disposal of non-current assets	50	(850)	
Cash flow from financing activities			
Dividends paid	(2500)		(1200)
Issue of ordinary share capital	300		
Repayment of loan	(150)	(2350)	
Increase/(decrease) in cash in period		(2140)	(100)

Worked example 7.1 shows that the statement of cash flows not only provides the detail of the change in cash as the last figure ($2.14 million this year and $100 000 last year) but also divides the cash flows into the business and out of the business under a number of separate headings. These headings or subdivisions are intended to provide information about the source and nature of the cash flow. For example, Cash flow from operating activities tells us that the cash comes from the normal continuing operations of the business, and these operations and their related cash flows are likely to continue each year. The cash flows under Cash flow from investing activities, on the other hand, are not likely to recur each year.

You can equate these differences with the cash flows related to running a car, where expenditure on such items as petrol and insurance will recur throughout each year and are classed as operating cash flows. The capital investment of buying another car does not occur each year and is, therefore, an investing cash flow. Finally, if you had to borrow money from the bank to finance the purchase of the new car, this would be a financing cash flow. Before we move on to looking at the subheadings and what they mean in more detail, we first need to define cash flows.

KEY CONCEPT 7.3

CASH FLOWS

» Cash inflows are increases in cash.

» Cash outflows are decreases in cash.

» Net cash flow consists of the net effect of cash inflows and cash outflows.

STOP AND THINK 2

Explain what is meant by the cash flows of operating, investing and financing activities.

Cash flow from operating activities

The first subheading in the statement of cash flows is Cash flow from operating activities. If our business was the simple cash-based model, the cash flow from operating activities would be the same as profit. However, as stated in Chapter 2, accrual accounting is the accounting used in general-purpose financial statements. These statements do not report the cash flows because some of the spending relates to future years and some to past years, among other factors. This presents us with a problem because what we have done is to adjust the cash figure to arrive at a figure for profit based upon the principles of accrual accounting. Therefore, if we start with the profit figure, we have to reverse all those adjustments in order to arrive at the cash flow from operations.

Adrian Matthiassen/Shutterstock.com

It is very important for your understanding of the statement of cash flows, and its relationship with the statement of comprehensive income and the balance sheet, that you understand this process and the reasons for it.

7.2 WORKED EXAMPLE

VALERIE'S BUSINESS

VALERIE'S BUSINESS HAD THE FOLLOWING BALANCES AT THE START OF THE YEAR

Accounts receivable	350
Accounts payable	760
Bank and cash	580

At the end of the year the balances were:

Accounts receivable	210
Accounts payable	530
Bank and cash	1 640

If we look first at the accounts payable, we can see that we have used our cash to reduce the amount we owe from $760 to $530. As a result, we would expect our cash balance to be reduced by $230, but, in fact, it has increased by $1 060, so clearly there are other factors involved. One of these is that we sell goods for more than we buy them so we get more cash in than we pay out. Some of that cash is used to buy more stock, some is put in the bank and some is used to finance accounts receivable.

In order to proceed we need more information:

Sales for the period	3 000
Purchases for the period	1 850
Cash received from accounts receivable	3 140
Cash paid for accounts payable	2 080

From the information we have we could produce the statement of cash flows very easily because we have the cash flows in (from our customers) of $3 140 and the cash flows out (to our suppliers) of $2 080, so we have a net cash flow of $1 060 ($3 140 − $2 080) which is the difference between the opening and closing bank balances. However, as pointed out in Chapter 1, users also want to know how much profit has been made. Once again, from the information, we could produce a statement of comprehensive income as follows:

STATEMENT OF COMPREHENSIVE INCOME FOR VALERIE'S BUSINESS: VERSION 1

	$	$
Sales		3 000
Opening inventory	0	
Purchases	1850	
Closing inventory	0	
Cost of sales		1850
Profit for the year		1150
Other comprehensive income		0
Total comprehensive income for the year		1150

The worksheet for Valerie's transactions is shown below:

VALERIE'S WORKSHEET: VERSION 1

DESCRIPTION	ASSETS			LIABILITIES	EQUITY	
	BANK	INVENTORY	ACCOUNTS RECEIVABLE	ACCOUNTS PAYABLE	CAPITAL	PROFIT AND LOSS
Balances	580	0	350	760	170	
Sales			3000			3000
Purchases		1850		1850		
Cash received	3 140		−3 140			
Cash paid	−2 080			−2 080		

❯

DESCRIPTION	ASSETS			LIABILITIES	EQUITY	
	BANK	INVENTORY	ACCOUNTS RECEIVABLE	ACCOUNTS PAYABLE	CAPITAL	PROFIT AND LOSS
Cost of goods sold		−1 850				−1 850
Balances	1 640	+0	+210	=530	+170	+1 150

The difficulty we have now is that we have told the users that the cash that came in was $1060 ($3 140 – $2 080) more than the cash going out, and we have also told them that we have made a profit of $1150. Given this information, they might justifiably ask, why are these figures different?

Of course, by now we know that the answer is because one system is based on cash measures and the other is based on accrual accounting, which takes into account sales made that we have not yet received money for, purchases that are not yet paid for, changes in the levels of inventory held, and so on.

So how can we reconcile the two figures? We can start by thinking about the effect that changes in the level of accounts receivable would have on the cash figure. If we decrease the level of accounts receivable, we get more cash in than is shown by our sales figure. Conversely, if we increase the level of accounts receivable, we will get less cash in than is shown by the sales figure. In the case of Valerie's business, the cash coming in was $3140 and the sales for the period were $3000. The difference between the cash received and the sales of $140 was due to the fact that at the start of the year we had $350 due to be received from our accounts receivable and at the end of the year we only had $210 due from our accounts receivable, a difference of $140. The general rule we have just derived is given as Key concept 7.4.

KEY CONCEPT

7.4

SALES, ACCOUNTS RECEIVABLE AND CASH RECEIVED

An *increase* in the accounts receivable due over the period must be *subtracted* from the sales to arrive at the cash received.

A *decrease* in accounts receivable due over the period must be *added* to sales to arrive at the cash received.

This is useful to help us on our way but is not the whole story, because our starting point is profit, not sales, and what we are trying to reconcile is net cash flow from operating activities, not cash received.

Profit is derived by subtracting the cost of goods sold figure from the sales figure, so it is also a net figure like the cash flow from operating activities. Thus, we are dealing with two net figures. This is a useful starting point. We now need to look at the effect that an increase in the gross figures – sales and cash received – has upon the net figures we are dealing with. In the case of goods sold there is a direct relationship between sales and profit; that is, an increase in sales leads to an increase in profit and a decrease in sales leads to a decrease in profit.

Similarly, in the case of cash received, an increase in cash received leads to an increase in the net cash flow from operating activities and a decrease in cash received leads to a decrease in net cash flow. Thus, the gross figures and net figures follow the same pattern as a result of increases or decreases: the effect on the net figures is the same as the effect on the gross figures. Consequently, we can simply restate Key concept 7.4 in terms of profit rather than sales, as shown in Key concept 7.5.

KEY CONCEPT

PROFIT, ACCOUNTS RECEIVABLE AND NET CASH FLOW FROM OPERATING ACTIVITY

An *increase* in the accounts receivable due over the period must be *subtracted* from the profit to arrive at the net cash flow from operating activity.

A *decrease* in accounts receivable due over the period must be *added* to profit to arrive at the net cash flow from operating activity.

If we now think about accounts payable, we have a similar situation to that for accounts receivable. If we increase the amount that we owe at the end of the year it means that our cash payments will be less than our purchases. If we reduce the amount that we owe, then our cash payments will be more than our purchases. In the case of Valerie's business, the cash paid and the purchases were $2080 and $1850 respectively, a difference of $230. This difference was due to the fact that, at the start of the year, we had $760 owing to our accounts payable and, at the end of the year, we only had $530 owing, a reduction of $230. The general rule we have just derived is given as Key concept 7.6.

KEY CONCEPT

PURCHASES, ACCOUNTS PAYABLE AND CASH PAID

An *increase* in the accounts payable over the period must be *subtracted* from the purchases to arrive at the cash paid.

A *decrease* in accounts payable over this period must be *added* to purchases to arrive at the cash paid.

At this point, we need to acknowledge an important distinction between differences in accounts receivable and their effect on sales and profits, and differences in accounts payable and their effect on profits. The important point here is that the relationship between an increase in sales and an increase in cash received on the net figures is the same; that is, an increase in sales results in an increase in profit and an increase in cash received results in an increase in the net cash flow from operating activity. Therefore, the relationships are direct and in the same direction.

In the case of cash paid, the relationship between increases in cash paid and the net cash flow is an inverse relationship; that is, an increase in cash paid will have the effect of decreasing the net cash flow. Conversely, a decrease in cash paid will increase the net cash flow. Similarly, the relationship between an increase or decrease in purchases and the effect on profit is an inverse relationship. If we leave aside the effect of holding inventory for the moment, as Valerie has no opening or closing inventory, we can see that an increase in purchases would have the effect of increasing the costs and therefore reducing the profit. A decrease in purchases, on the other hand, would reduce costs and increase profits.

So, in order to adjust profit to take account of the differences between purchases and cash payments in respect of those purchases, we need to reverse the effects set out in Key concept 7.6. Key concept 7.7 sets out the relationship between profits, increases and decreases in accounts payable, and profits and net cash flows from operating activities.

KEY CONCEPT

PROFIT, ACCOUNTS PAYABLE AND NET CASH FLOW FROM OPERATING ACTIVITY

An *increase* in the accounts payable over the period must be *added* to the profit to arrive at the net cash flow from operating activity.

A *decrease* in accounts payable over the period must be *subtracted* from the profit to arrive at the net cash flow from operating activity.

So far, so good, hopefully! Let us see how what we have done to date works:

RECONCILIATION OF OPERATING PROFIT AND CASH FLOW FROM OPERATING ACTIVITY: VERSION 1

Profit for the year	1150
Less Decrease in accounts payable	(230)
Add Decrease in accounts receivable	140
Increase in cash	1060

Note: Brackets are commonly used in published accounts to denote negatives.

As you can see, we have been successful in reconciling the profit to the cash flow from operating activity. Unfortunately, the accounts receivable and accounts payable are only one part of the adjustments we make when using accrual accounting. The most common of these relate to the effect of holding inventories and the effects of having non-current assets. In general terms, these have an effect on the statement of comprehensive income but not on the cash flows arising out of the operating activity. In the case of non-current assets, as we discussed in relation to Worked example 7.1 using the example of a car, there may be an effect on cash flows in respect of capital expenditure but no effect on operating cash flows.

To understand the effects of inventory and depreciation, let us extend our Valerie example a little further by adding some inventory figures and some figures for non-current assets and depreciation.

	$
Opening inventory	420
Closing inventory	480
Non-current asset – cost	1000
Accumulated depreciation at start of year	400
Depreciation for year	200
Accumulated depreciation at end of year	600

The new worksheet for Valerie would be as shown below:

VALERIE'S WORKSHEET: VERSION 2

| | | | ASSETS | | | LIABILITIES | EQUITY | |
DESCRIPTION	BANK	NON-CURRENT ASSETS	ACCUMULATED DEPRECIATION	INVENTORY	ACCOUNTS RECEIVABLE	ACCOUNTS PAYABLE	CAPITAL	PROFIT AND LOSS
Balances	580	+1000	−400	+420	+350	=760	+1190	
Sales					3000			3000
Purchases				1850		1850		
Cash in	3140				−3140			
Cash paid	−2080					−2080		
Cost of sales			−	−1790				−1790
Depreciation			−200					−200
Balances	1640	+1000	−600	+480	+210	=530	+1190	+1010

If we look at the difference between the profit under version 1 and version 2 of the statement of comprehensive income, we can see that there are two reasons for the difference. The first is that the cost of goods sold figure has changed, due to the presence of opening and closing inventory. The second is that the resultant profit has also been reduced by the depreciation charge for the year. However, it is obvious from a quick glance at the cash column of version 2 of the worksheet that there has been no change in the cash received or paid. The double entry for both these items is between the statement of comprehensive income and the item concerned, and the cash column is not affected.

STATEMENT OF COMPREHENSIVE INCOME FOR VALERIE'S BUSINESS: VERSION 2

	$	$
Sales		3000
Opening inventory	420	
Purchases	1850	
Closing inventory	2270	
	480	
Cost of goods sold		1790
Gross profit for the year		1210
Depreciation		200
Profit for the year		1010
Other comprehensive income		0
Total comprehensive income for the year		1010

Looking first at the depreciation, we can see that if we charge depreciation we reduce the profit but do not affect the net cash flow. Therefore, we need to add back the depreciation charge for the year to the operating profit to arrive at the cash flow. We state this as a general rule in Key concept 7.8.

7.8 KEY CONCEPT

PROFIT, DEPRECIATION AND NET CASH FLOW FROM OPERATING ACTIVITY

Charges for depreciation and amortisation of non-current assets charged to the statement of comprehensive income for the period must be added back to the operating profit to arrive at the net cash flow from operating activities.

If we now turn to decreases and increases in the inventory held over the period, we can see from the Valerie example that because we held more inventory at the end than at the start, this led to a decrease in cost of goods sold and an increase in profit. Similarly, a decrease in inventory would lead to an increase in cost of goods sold and a decrease in profit. Thus, we can state a general rule for inventory as shown in Key concept 7.9.

7.9 KEY CONCEPT

PROFIT, INVENTORY AND NET CASH FLOW FROM OPERATING ACTIVITY

An *increase* in the inventory held over the period must be *subtracted* from the profit to arrive at the net cash flow from operating activity.

A *decrease* in the inventory held over the period must be *added* to the profit to arrive at the net cash flow from operating activity.

It is important to note that, although the effects of an increase in inventory are the same as an increase in accounts receivable, the relationship is different. In the case of accounts receivable, the relationship is direct. In the case of inventory, it is indirect and can be thought of as two inversions that cancel each other out.

Let us now see if we can reconcile the new profit from version 2 of Valerie's statement of comprehensive income with the net cash flow from operating activity.

We already have some of the figures in respect of accounts receivable and accounts payable, and now need to deal with inventory and depreciation. For inventory we have an increase of $60: as this is an increase it has to be taken off the profit to arrive at cash flow from operations. In the case of depreciation, we need to add back the charge for the year, $200, to profit.

RECONCILIATION OF OPERATING PROFIT AND CASH FLOW FROM OPERATING ACTIVITY: VERSION 2

	$
Profit for the year	1 010
Less Decrease in accounts payable	(230)
Add Decrease in accounts receivable	140
Less Increase in inventory	(60)
Add Depreciation charge	200
Cash flow from operating activitiess	1060

As a by-product of the explanation of how the figure for net cash flow from operating activity is arrived at and reconciled with the operating profit, we have produced a reconciliation statement. Under AASB 107, this reconciliation statement is specifically required to be disclosed in financial reports if an entity elects to use the indirect method to determine cash flows from operating activities (although it is not required in IAS 7). The direct method occurs when the gross receipts from customers and the gross payments to employees and suppliers are reported. The indirect method shows operating profit and then adds or subtracts items (as we have just done in the reconciliation) to yield operating cash flows. Users are not told the gross receipts and payments in the indirect method. We now show the cash flow from operating activities for Valerie's business using the direct method as the cash flow information is provided.

CASH FLOW FROM OPERATING ACTIVITIES

	$
Cash receipts from customers	3140
Less Cash paid to suppliers	(2080)
Cash flow from operating activities	1060

The statement of cash flows in the Woolworths 2013 financial statements has been prepared using the direct method.

Having completed a reconciliation statement, let us now return to our example of a sample statement of cash flows and look at the other headings. To remind ourselves of the format of the statement of cash flows, the sample is reproduced below.

SAMPLE STATEMENT OF CASH FLOWS

	20X4		20X3	
	$000s	$000s	$000s	$000s
Cash flow from operating activities		1060		1400
Cash flow from investing activities				
Payments to acquire non-current assets	(900)		(200)	
Payments to acquire investments	0		(100)	
Receipts from disposal of non-current assets	50		0	
		(850)		(300)
Cash flow from financing activities				
Dividends paid	(2500)		(1200)	
Issue of ordinary share capital	300		0	
Repayment of loan	(150)		0	
		(2350)		(1200)
Increase/(decrease) in cash in period		(2140)		(100)

STOP AND THINK 3

Explain the difference between cash flow and profit.

7.1

CASE STUDY

THE ART OF TURNING PROFITS INTO A LOSS

MAX NEWNHAM

Managing the cash flow of a business is also vital if you want it to grow.

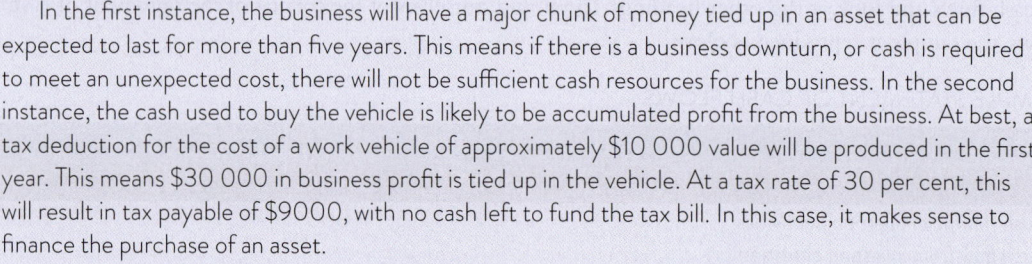

Managing cash flow is all about anticipating the peaks and troughs of a business and making the right decisions when it comes to spending generated cash. One area in which many small-business owners can get into trouble is not understanding the tax effect of the cash they spend, particularly when it comes to large asset purchases.

The viability of a business can be adversely affected when cash is used to fund asset purchases rather than using finance. For example, if a business has $40 000 in accumulated cash and the owner needs to buy a new work vehicle, it does not make sense, either for cash-flow or tax purposes, to pay cash for the vehicle.

In the first instance, the business will have a major chunk of money tied up in an asset that can be expected to last for more than five years. This means if there is a business downturn, or cash is required to meet an unexpected cost, there will not be sufficient cash resources for the business. In the second instance, the cash used to buy the vehicle is likely to be accumulated profit from the business. At best, a tax deduction for the cost of a work vehicle of approximately $10 000 value will be produced in the first year. This means $30 000 in business profit is tied up in the vehicle. At a tax rate of 30 per cent, this will result in tax payable of $9000, with no cash left to fund the tax bill. In this case, it makes sense to finance the purchase of an asset.

Max Newnham, *The Age*, 6 July 2011. This work has been licensed by Copyright Agency Limited (CAL). Except as permitted by the *Copyright Act*, you must not re-use this work without the permission of the copyright owner or CAL.

COMMENTARY

The article identifies cash flow problems that arise when small business owners use cash to acquire assets with long lives, like a motor vehicle, instead of considering using debt. The writer argues that there are better tax deductions when using debt and the cash remains in the business and is available to pay the bills. However, while the cost of using debt is tax deductible, a business needs to have the capacity to borrow and must consider the risks of borrowing.

6 LEARNING OBJECTIVE

Identify cash flows from investing and financing activities

Cash flow from investing activities

There are broadly two types of cash flow from investing activities: the first relates to non-current assets like property, plant and equipment; the second to shares in other companies and similar investments. As far as non-current assets are concerned, this would involve cash outflows in relation to the purchase of non-current assets and cash inflows from the sale of non-current assets (see Figure 7.1). Clearly, such cash flows are different from those we have discussed so far. They tend to be non-recurrent, as an individual non-current asset or investment can only be replaced or sold once. The second type is when a business purchases shares in another business or acquires a total business, and this results in cash outflows. Cash inflows arise when an entity sells some of the shares or the business that has been acquired. The intention here is to differentiate the cash flows that relate to these one-off activities from the recurring cash flows.

Cash flow from financing activities

The final heading involves the cash flows relating to the financing of the business. These include amounts received from share issues, new loans or debentures – in other words, from long-term financing. It would also show amounts paid out in respect of loans or debentures that have been repaid during the year, and in respect of any shares redeemed and dividends paid. Figure 7.1 summarises the classification of cash flows.

Increase or decrease in cash in the period

The final figure shown on the statement of cash flows is the increase or decrease in cash. This can be reconciled fairly easily with the information in the balance sheet.

Interest, dividends and income tax

The accounting standards require amounts paid for interest and dividends to be separately disclosed – normally as either operating or financing activities. Amounts received for interest and dividends need to be separately disclosed – normally as either operating or investing activities. As Figure 7.1 shows, the most common classification for interest paid and received and dividends received is operating cash flows. Dividends paid are normally shown as a financing cash flow. It is important when comparing entities that you check on the classification of interest and dividends, otherwise you may not be comparing like items. For example, if Qantas

FIGURE 7.1 CLASSIFICATION OF CASH INFLOWS AND CASH OUTFLOWS

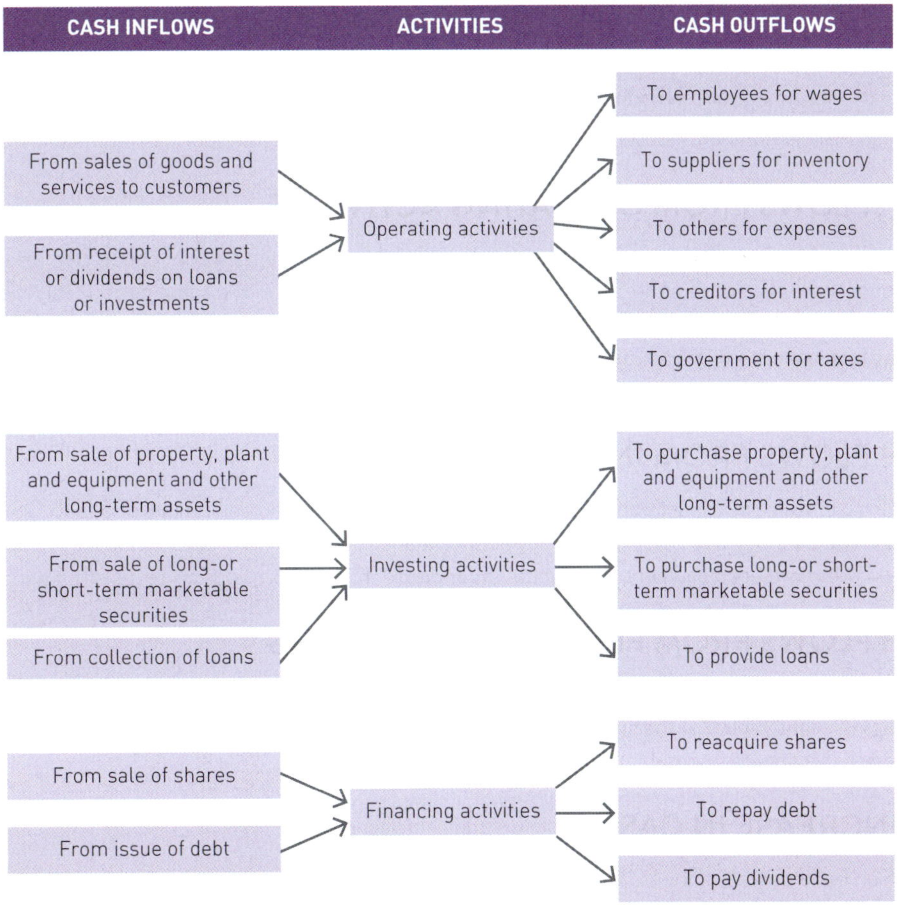

Adapted from T.D. Wise et al., *Accounting in Australia*, Houghton Mifflin, 1990, p. 714.

classifies interest received as an operating cash flow and Singapore Airlines classifies it as an investing cash flow then you would need to adjust for this before comparing the operating cash flows of both companies. Income taxes paid must also be separately disclosed and are normally included as an operating cash flow.

Non-cash investing and financing activities

Sometimes an entity is involved in transactions such as acquiring land and buildings by issuing shares that do not involve cash. Such transactions, where significant, must be disclosed in a note to the statement of cash flows, so that the user has a complete picture of the entity's investing and financing activities.

STOP AND THINK 4

A company issued 200 000 $1 shares, fully paid, in exchange for land with a fair market value of $200 000. How would this transaction be reported on a statement of cash flows?

7.3

WORKED EXAMPLE

WOOLWORTHS STATEMENT OF CASH FLOWS

You should now study Woolworths' statement of cash flows in Appendix 1. Note that the company has presented the cash flows from operating, investing and financing activities, as required by AASB 107. It also reports a reconciliation of net cash flows from operations and operating profit after income tax following the statement of cash flows.

We can make a number of observations based on Woolworths' statement of cash flows.

CASH FLOWS FROM OPERATING ACTIVITIES

Net cash flows from operating activities were $2 719 900 000 for the 53 weeks ended 30 June 2013. This amount more than covers the $1 396 700 000 paid in dividends in the same period. This is a positive position for the company. The cash receipts from customers were $63 789 800 000 while payments to suppliers and employees were $58 695 100 000 – a very healthy result for the company. The company has a very healthy cash balance as at 30 June 2013 of $849 200 000.

CASH FLOWS FROM INVESTING ACTIVITIES

The three major items in this section are payment for property, plant and equipment of $1 136 000 000, the $767 400 000 payment for property development and the $802 800 000 inflow from the sale of property. There have been payments for capital expenditure from the previous corresponding period.

CASH FLOWS FROM FINANCING ACTIVITIES

This section shows that the company borrowed $5 974 500 000 during the current period and repaid borrowings of slightly more in the sum of $6 501 800 000, which is a slight increase in net borrowings compared to the previous period.

NET INCREASE IN CASH

The cash on hand decreased by $2 200 000 for the period. The effects of exchange rate adjustments relates to the translation of the cash held by foreign subsidiaries.

SUMMARY

EXPLAIN WHAT IS INCLUDED IN THE TERMS 'CASH' AND 'CASH EQUIVALENTS'

Cash includes cash on hand and cash equivalents such as highly liquid investments and borrowings used as part of an entity's cash management function.

EXPLAIN INTERNAL CONTROL PROCEDURES FOR CASH, AND WHY THEY ARE IMPORTANT

Effective internal control over cash is important, as cash is the most liquid asset and the one that is most easily misappropriated. The internal controls should ideally include separation of:

» the duties of receiving and paying cash
» the duties of recording cash receipts from cash payments
» handling cash and recording cash movements in the accounting records.

EXPLAIN THE MAIN PURPOSE OF A STATEMENT OF CASH FLOWS

Both the balance sheet and the statement of comprehensive income are based on accrual accounting and not cash accounting. These statements cannot be used to answer the following types of questions:

» Did the entity's operations produce sufficient cash to meet dividend payments?
» Did the entity issue shares or increase liabilities during the year and, if so, what happened to the proceeds?
» Did the entity purchase any new assets during the year? How did the entity pay for these new assets?

The statement of cash flows is intended to provide answers to these and other questions by reporting cash flows from operating, investing and financing activities.

DISCUSS WHAT IS MEANT BY THE CONCEPT OF CASH FLOWS OF OPERATING, INVESTING AND FINANCING ACTIVITIES

Cash flow from operating activities reports cash flows from the normal continuing operations of the business. These operations, and their related cash flows, are likely to continue each year. Cash flows from investing activities are different in that they are not likely to recur each year and are related to the purchase and sale of non-current assets. Cash flows from financing activities report the cash flows associated with equity and debt providers. Financing cash flows reveal how a company has funded any large cash outflows in the operating and/or investing activities.

IDENTIFY CASH FLOWS FROM OPERATING ACTIVITIES, AND EXPLAIN THE DIFFERENCE BETWEEN OPERATING CASH FLOWS AND PROFIT

Cash flow from operating activities includes:

» cash receipts from customers
» cash payments to suppliers
» cash payments to employees

» interest paid and received
» dividends received.

The cash flows from operating activities are not the same as profit (which is determined using accrual accounting). To reconcile the profit figure to operating cash flows, adjustments have to be made for various items arising from the accruals process. This includes adding non-cash expenses (like depreciation and amortisation) back to profit. It is also necessary to adjust for changes in the balances of accounts such as accounts receivable, accounts payable, accrued expenses and prepaid assets.

LEARNING OBJECTIVE 6

IDENTIFY CASH FLOWS FROM INVESTING AND FINANCING ACTIVITIES

There are broadly two types of cash flow arising from investing activities. The first type relates to non-current assets like property, plant and equipment. As far as non-current assets are concerned, this involves cash outflows for their purchase and cash inflows from their sale.

The second type of cash flow arising from investing activities relates to shares in other companies and similar investments. When a business purchases shares in another business or acquires a total business, this results in cash outflows. Cash inflows arise when an entity sells some of the shares or the business that has been acquired.

The cash flows from financing activities include amounts received from share issues, new loans or debentures – in other words, from long-term financing. Cash outflows for financing activities would include amounts paid out for loans, amounts for debentures that have been repaid during the year, and shares redeemed and dividends paid.

REVIEW QUESTIONS

1   What are the main principles of the internal control of cash?

2   What information can be obtained from a statement of cash flows?

3   Give three examples of operating cash inflows and outflows.

4   Bill Smith owns and runs a supermarket. He is certain that one of the check-out staff is stealing money but, on every occasion, her till balances. If Bill is correct, how is the theft being committed and what steps can he take to overcome the problem?

5   When a business provides a service to another business, it normally does so 'on account' rather than as a cash transaction. This results in an account receivable for the business providing the service and an account payable for the business receiving the service. At some later date, the account will be paid. In contrast, when individuals conduct transactions it is usually a cash transaction.

Why is it unusual for businesses to engage in cash transactions, while for individuals it is more common?

PROBLEMS FOR DISCUSSION AND ANALYSIS

1   Refer to the Woolworths 2013 financial report in Appendix 1.

a   Did cash increase or decrease over the 53 weeks ended 30 June 2013? If so, by how much?

b   Why did operating cash flows decline in 2013?

2   Explain how it is that a business that is making profits can have difficulties in meeting its debts. Perhaps you can bring to class some examples of businesses in this situation.

3   You have been appointed treasurer of your cricket club. The cricket club runs a bar and members are rostered to work on the bar. All the transactions across the bar are cash and the club uses a drawer to store the cash. After reviewing the bar records, you notice a significant decline in the profits. You are concerned about the lack of control of the cash and believe that this is the cause of the decrease in profits. What procedures would you recommend to improve the control of cash in the bar?

4   Explain how the following transactions would be recorded on a statement of cash flows:

   a   Salaries payable were $50 000 at the beginning of the year and $45 000 at year-end.

   b   Fully depreciated equipment with a cost value of $20 000 was discarded as follows:

      i   sold to a scrap merchant for $1000

      ii   given to an employee.

   c   A toy store had accounts payable of $23 000 at the beginning of the year and $27 000 at year-end.

   d   A company issued, for cash, 200 000 $1 shares for $1.20 per share.

   e   Bigboy Ltd reported in its annual report that it had issued 1 000 000 $1 shares, fully paid, for a company that had a net worth of $900 000.

5   Discuss the impact of each of the items below on the balance sheet, the statement of comprehensive income and the statement of cash flows, giving reasons for your answer where appropriate.

   a   During the year the company sold a non-current asset with a carrying value of $5000 for $3000.

   b   The company also revalued its land from its original cost of $130 000 to $200 000.

   c   The building, which had cost $90 000, and on which depreciation of $30 000 had been provided, was revalued to $100 000.

   d   The company has also made an issue of 100 000 8 per cent $1 preference shares at a price of $1.20 per share.

   e   The company had paid back a long-term loan of $80 000 to the bank.

6   Identify the type of cash flow activity for each of the following events (investing, operating, financing or non-cash transaction):

   a   received cash from customers

   b   paid employees for wages

   c   signed a four-year lease agreement for a motor vehicle

   d   paid interest

   e   issued debentures

   f   issued ordinary shares

   g   sold long-term investments

   h   paid cash dividends

   i   redeemed debentures

   j   issued preference shares

   k   sold equipment for a gain

   l   purchased buildings

   m   purchased patents

   n   loss on disposal of a non-current asset

   o   increase in inventory.

7   Each of the transactions listed below will affect one of the four categories on the statement of cash
     flows: cash flows from operating activities, cash flows from investing activities, cash flows from
     financing activities, or non-cash investing and financing activities. Analyse each transaction and state
     which category will be affected.

   a Machinery to the value of $80 000 was acquired for cash.

   b A patent that was sold for $30 000 had a carrying value of $20 000.

   c Office supplies on hand, valued at $2000, were exchanged for a second-hand car.

   d Used machinery having a carrying value of $50 000 was traded for 500 shares of another
      company. The shares are intended to be a long-term investment.

   e Dividends to the amount of $5000 were paid.

   f Long-term debenture notes payable for the amount of $20 000 were paid in cash.

   g Interest of $5000 was paid.

8   Classify the following transactions according to whether they relate to operating, investing or
     financing activities or none of those categories for the purposes of preparing a statement of cash
     flows.

   a Received cash of $14 000 from the sale of equipment previously used in carrying out the
      entity's operations.

   b Paid cash of $10 000 to accounts payable for inventory previously purchased on credit.

   c Received $45 000 cash from accounts receivable.

   d Paid cash dividends to shareholders of $54 000.

   e Issued shares in exchange for land for $105 000.

   f Paid insurance in advance for $9000 cash.

   g Purchased vehicles for use in the business for $48 000 cash.

   h Deposited $12 000 into a short-term deposit, redeemable at call.

   i Issued $85 000 in shares in exchange for cash.

   j Borrowed $40 000 in cash repayable in five years.

9   From the following information, determine the cash flows from operating activities.

	END OF YEAR	BEGINNING OF YEAR
	$	$
Cash	27 579	32 333
Receivables	17 632	10 849
Accounts payable	23 581	33 134
Salaries payable	6 373	5 687
Wages payable	11 045	11 044
Inventory	123 879	114 453
Prepaid expenses	499	1006

10 The following information about Thompson Corp. applies to the entity for the year ended 30 June 20X7.

Payment to suppliers	$ 150 000
Receipts from owners	405 000
Receipts from long-term borrowing	250 000
Payment of rates	130 000
Payment of wages	125 000
Purchase of other companies' shares	80 000
Retirement of long-term borrowing	165 000
Receipts from customers	500 000
Payment for equipment	190 000
Depreciation on equipment	90 000
Average total assets	1 200 000

a What was Thompson Corp.'s cash flow from operating activities?

b What was Thompson Corp.'s cash flow from investing activities?

c What was Thompson Corp's cash flow from financing?

11 The Royal Park Company statement of comprehensive income for 20X1 appears below:

ROYAL PARK COMPANY
STATEMENT OF COMPREHENSIVE INCOME FOR THE YEAR ENDED 31 DECEMBER 20X1

	$000
Sales	160 000
Cost of goods sold	96 000
Gross profit on sales	64 000
Operating expenses:	
Rent expense	20 000
Depreciation expense	15 000
Other operating expenses	18 000
Total operating expenses	53 000
Profit	11 000
Other comprehensive income	0
Total comprehensive income for the year	11 000

The following information from Royal Park's balance sheet is available:

ACCOUNT TITLE	BALANCE 1 JANUARY $	BALANCE 31 DECEMBER $
Accounts receivable	10 000	12 000
Inventory	3 000	10 000
Prepaid rent	5 000	8 000
Accounts payable	26 000	28 000

Required

Determine the cash flow from operating activities for Royal Park.

12 Stephanie Flight has recently been hired as the manager of Tender Chickens. Tender Chickens is a national chain of franchised gourmet chicken retailers. During her first month as store manager, Stephanie encountered the following internal control situations:

  a The store has only one cash register. Prior to Stephanie joining Tender Chickens, each employee working on a shift would take a customer order, accept payment and then prepare the order. Stephanie made one employee on each shift responsible for taking orders and accepting the customer's payment. Other employees prepared the orders.

  b Since only one employee uses the cash register, that employee is responsible for counting the cash at the end of the shift and verifying that the cash in the drawer matches the amount of cash sales recorded by the cash register. Stephanie expects each cashier to balance the drawer to the cent every time with no exceptions.

  c Stephanie caught an employee putting a box of chicken steaks in his car. Not wanting to create a scene, Stephanie smiled and said, 'I don't think you're putting those steaks on the right tray. Don't they belong inside the shop?' The employee returned the chicken steaks to the cooler shelf.

Required

State whether you agree or disagree with Stephanie's method of handling each situation and explain your answer.

13 Read the extract from the article 'Former bookkeeper charged with 170 counts of theft'. What procedures would have helped prevent Inaba from being able to steal successfully for eight years?

FORMER BOOKKEEPER CHARGED WITH 170 COUNTS OF THEFT
BY TRACY JOHNSON, P-I REPORTER

A woman who kept the books for a Bellevue produce company was charged yesterday with 170 counts of theft, accused of stealing $4.6 million in the largest embezzlement case King County has ever prosecuted.

Police say Denise A. Inaba took tens of thousands of dollars each month while working part time at Jaspo Inc., a business that buys local produce and sells it in Asia. She allegedly wrote herself more than 1200 checks over a period of eight years, signing them with the owner's name. Deputy prosecutor Scott Peterson said she made fake entries in the business's books to hide what she was doing. 'She was the sole bookkeeper and had complete and total control,' he said.

Tracy Johnson/Seattlepi.com, 31 December 2002

14 List the errors you find in the following statement of cash flows. The cash balance at the beginning of the year was $70 700. All other figures are correct, except the cash balance at the end of the year.

THE FUTURE ZONE INC.
STATEMENT OF CASH FLOWS FOR THE YEAR ENDED 31 DECEMBER 20X3

	$	$	$
Cash flows from operating activities			
Profit		100 500	
Add: Depreciation	49 000		
Increase in accounts receivable	11 500		
Gain on sale of investments	7 000	67 500	
		168 000	
Deduct: Increase in accounts payable	4 400		
Increase in inventories	18 300		
Decrease in accrued expenses	1 600	24 300	
Net cash flow from operating activities			143 700
Cash flows from investing activities			
Cash received from sale of investments		85 000	
Less: Cash paid for purchase of land	90 000		
Cash paid for purchase of equipment	150 100	240 100	
Net cash flow used for investing activities			(155 100)
Cash flows from financing activities			
Cash received from sale of $1 ordinary shares		107 000	
Cash paid for dividends		36 800	
Net cash flow provided by financing activities			143 800
Increase in cash			132 400
Cash at the end of the year			105 300
Cash at the beginning of the year			237 700

15 The following statement of cash flows is available for the Bee Pee Company:

	20X0	20X1
	$M	$M
Cash flows from operating activities		
Receipts from customers	3 000	3 000
Payments to suppliers and employees	(2 500)	(2 600)
Interest received	60	35
Interest paid	(75)	(150)
Taxation paid	(17)	(13)
Net cash from operating activities	468	272
Cash flows from investing activities		
Acquisition of property, plant and equipment	(250)	(1 800)
Proceeds from sale of non-current assets	50	200
Net cash from investing activities	(200)	(1 600)
Cash flows from financing activities		
Short-term borrowing – increase (decrease)		1 450
Long-term borrowing – increase (decrease)	40	
Dividends paid	(200)	(200)
Net cash from financing activities	(160)	1 250
Net increase (decrease) in cash held	108	(78)
Add opening cash brought forward	(50)	58
Closing cash carried forward	58	(20)

Required

Analyse the statement of cash flows for Bee Pee. What changes to the cash management policies would you recommend to the company? Should the company continue to pay a dividend?

16 The directors of Kowloon Enterprises Ltd are concerned about the results of trading activities reported for the year ended 30 June 20X6, and failure to keep within the limit of the bank overdraft ($12 000).

KOWLOON ENTERPRISES LTD
STATEMENTS OF COMPREHENSIVE INCOME FOR THE YEARS ENDED 30 JUNE

	20X4		20X5		20X6	
	$	$	$	$	$	$
Sales		200 000		180 000		165 000
Less Cost of sales						
Opening inventory	36 000		41 000		44 000	
Purchases	95 000		87 000		80 000	
	131 000		128 000		124 000	
Less Closing inventory	41 000	90 000	44 000	84 000	49 000	75 000
Gross profit		110 000		96 000		90 000
Less:						
Selling and distribution expenses	40 000		40 000		46 000	
General and administrative expenses	20 000		20 000		18 000	
Financial expenses	15 000	75 000	16 000	76 000	20 000	84 000
Net operating profit before tax		35 000		20 000		6 000
Less Taxation expense		15 000		9 000		2 500
Net operating profit after tax		20 000		11 000		3 500
Less Loss on sale of investment		-----		---		1 000
Profit for year		20 000		11 000		2 500
Other comprehensive income						
Gain (loss) on revaluation of land		0		10 000		0
Total comprehensive income for the year		20 000		21 000		2 500

KOWLOON ENTERPRISES LTD
BALANCE SHEETS AT 30 JUNE

	20X4		20X5		20X6	
	$	$	$	$	$	$
Assets						
Current assets						
Bank	1000					
Inventory	41000		44000		49000	
Accounts receivable	26000		31000		37000	
Less Allowance						
For doubtful debts	(1000)		(1000)		(2000)	
Prepayments	2000		3000		3000	
Total current assets		69000		77000		87000
Non-current assets						
Plant and equipment	10000		10000		21000	
Less Depreciation (1000 in X3)	(2000)		(4000)		(7000)	
Vehicles	80000		80000		114000	
Less Depreciation (4000 in X3)	(16000)		(32000)		(54000)	
Land (at valuation)	60000		70000		70000	
Buildings (at cost)	40000		56000		56000	
Investments (at cost)	25000		25000			
Total non-current assets		197000		205000		200000
Total assets		266000		282000		287000
Liabilities						
Current liabilities						
Bank overdraft			8500		12500	
Accounts payable	12000		8000		14000	
Accrued wages and interest	1000		1500		2000	
Provision for taxation	15000		9000		2500	
Provision for dividend	13000		15000		3000	

	20X4		20X5		20X6	
	$	$	$	$	$	$
Total current liabilities		41 000		42 000		34 000
Non-current liabilities						
Mortgage on land (due 30 June 20X9)			21 000		34 500	
Term loan (due 20Y2)	75 000		75 000		75 000	
Total non-current liabilities		75 000		96 000		109 500
Total liabilities		116 000		138 000		143 500
Net assets		150 000		144 000		143 500
Shareholders' equity						
50 000 6% $1 preference shares		50 000		50 000		50 000
75 000 $1 ordinary shares		75 000		75 000		75 000
Asset revaluation reserve				10 000		10 000
General reserve		18 000		8 000		8 000
Retained earnings		7 000		1 000		500
Total shareholders' equity		150 000		144 000		143 500

KOWLOON ENTERPRISES LTD
STATEMENTS OF CHANGES IN EQUITY

	SHARE CAPITAL	RESERVES	RETAINED EARNINGS	TOTAL
	$M	$M	$M	$M
Balance at 1 July 20X3	125 000	18 000	10 000	153 000
Total comprehensive income for the period			20 000	20 000
Dividends – Preference			(3 000)	(3 000)
Dividends – Ordinary			(20 000)	(20 000)
Balance at 30 June 20X4	125 000	18 000	7 000	150 000
Transfer to retained earnings		(10 000)	10 000	

	SHARE CAPITAL	RESERVES	RETAINED EARNINGS	TOTAL
	$M	$M	$M	$M
Total comprehensive income for the period		10 000	11 000	21 000
Dividends – Preference			(3 000)	(3 000)
Dividends – Ordinary			(24 000)	(24 000)
Balance at 30 June 20X5	125 000	18 000	1 000	144 000
Total comprehensive income for the period			2 500	2 500
Dividends – Preference			(3 000)	(3 000)
Balance at 30 June 20X6	125 000	18 000	500	143 500

Required

a What factors have contributed to this cash problem?

b What steps would you recommend for Kowloon Enterprises Ltd to overcome the current cash problem?

ETHICS CASE STUDY

Jane Golly is the chief financial officer for Woppet Enterprises Ltd. She has decided to add a new ratio to the financial statements based on cash flow per share. The ratio will be reported on the statement of cash flows and she believes it will provide useful information to readers of the financial statements. The cash flow per share this year will show a 25 per cent increase from last year. This will contrast with the 5 per cent decline in earnings per share.

Discuss whether there is anything unethical about Jane Golly's decision.

SUGGESTED ANSWERS TO STOP AND THINK EXERCISES IN THE CHAPTER

1   The statement of cash flows is included in financial statements because it is cash, and not profits, that the entity requires in order to meet its debts. Profitability alone does not ensure that an entity has sufficient cash to be solvent.

2   The cash flow of operating activities shows the cash that is received from customers and the cash that is paid to suppliers, employees, and so on. It is the cash flow associated with the entity's operations. The cash flow related to investing activities is the cash flow from the acquisition and disposal of non-current assets such as property, plant and equipment. The cash flow of financing activities shows the cash inflows from accounts payable and shareholders, which are used to finance the investing and operating activities. Repayments to creditors and shareholders are shown as cash outflows.

3   The statement of cash flows is based on movements in cash while profit is based on accrual accounting principles (i.e. revenues and expenses are recognised when they are earned or incurred, not when the cash is received or paid).

4   This transaction would not appear in the statement of cash flows as there is no cash involved. However, it would be reported as a non-cash investing transaction after the statement of cash flows.

CENGAGENOW

Go to http:\\login.cengagebrain.com to link to CengageNOW, your online study tool. First take the Pre-Test for this chapter to get your Personalised Study Plan, and then:

»   revise your understanding of the key terms related to internal control of cash and the statement of cash flows by completing the online crossword

»   explore the purpose of the statement of cash flows with the animated examples

»   follow links to preparing cash flow statement guides.

After you have completed the activities in your Personalised Study Plan take the Post-Test to determine what concepts you have mastered and what you still need work on.

ACCOUNTING FOR SELECTED ASSETS

LEARNING OBJECTIVES

At the end of this chapter, you should be able to:

1. explain what is meant by the terms 'accounts receivable'
2. explain and apply the direct write-off and allowance methods for handling bad and doubtful debts
3. identify the accounting policy implications of the accounting for bad and doubtful debts
4. explain what is meant by the term ' inventory'
5. identify and apply the valuation rule for inventory
6. explain and apply the principles used to determine the cost of inventory
7. identify the implications of the accounting policy choice used for determining inventory costing methods
8. explain the concept of depreciation
9. explain why non-current assets are depreciated
10. appreciate that the process of depreciation does not involve the setting aside of cash funds for asset replacement
11. summarise and apply the straight-line, reducing-balance and units-of-production methods of depreciation
12. identify the implications of depreciation accounting policy choices for financial reporting
13. explain what is meant by the term 'intangible assets' and identify the difference between identifiable and unidentifiable intangible assets
14. explain the accounting treatment for identifiable and unidentifiable intangible assets.

INTRODUCTION

In this chapter we discuss how entities account for four major categories of assets: accounts receivable, inventories property, plant and equipment and intangible assets. In the case of Woolworths, its largest current asset is inventory, and property, plant and equipment is the largest non-current asset. Woolworths sells inventories effectively on a cash basis with few customers purchasing on credit. Other retailing entities, such as Harvey Norman, have over a billion dollars owing by its customers, known as trade and other receivables.

Each of these assets poses a particular financial reporting issue and requires entities to make choices about how it ought to be accounted for. Decisions as to how a firm will account for assets such as receivables, inventories, property, plant and equipment and intangibles are accounted for will be guided by accounting standards. However, as there is some flexibility in how some accounting standards are to be applied in practice, the accounting treatment selected by the firm is known as an accounting policy choice and must be disclosed in the accounting policy notes to the accounts prepared by the firm.

ACCOUNTS RECEIVABLE

Accounts receivable are sometimes known as debtors, trade receivables or just receivables. Since the term often used to describe amounts owing to a firm's suppliers is often referred to as being 'accounts payable', you may find it easier to use the term 'accounts receivable' as it more clearly indicates the flow of future benefits and how they would be presented in the balance sheet: receivables imply a receipt of future economic benefits and are an asset, whereas payables imply a sacrifice of future economic benefits and are a liability

1 LEARNING OBJECTIVE

Explain what is meant by the terms 'accounts receivable'

KEY CONCEPT

8.1

ACCOUNTS RECEIVABLE

Accounts receivable occur when a business sells goods or services to a customer on credit; that is, when goods or services are sold to the customer on the understanding that the amount owing will be received at a later date.

Receivables, referred to in Key concept 8.1, are created when a sale is made by the business during the year for which amount owing by the customer is not received at the point of sale. On an accrual basis of accounting, we need to recognise the revenue from the sale even though cash has yet to be received. We discussed the recognition of revenue in Chapter 6. Since an economic transaction has occurred, it must be accounted for. As a sale transaction has occurred, revenue being an increase in equity would need to be recognised. If payment was received from the customer at the point of sale, such as a cash sale for Woolworths, we would record an increase in the asset cash at bank. However, with the sale occurring on credit, no cash has been received and in its place we have an undertaking that the customer will pay the outstanding amount within some agreed time frame. Because this undertaking represents a right to receive cash in the future (i.e. an economic benefit), and at the time of sale it is probable the amount will be received and it can be reliably measured, it is recognised as an asset. Thus, the increase in asset relating to a sale made on credit is to accounts receivable. Normally, the terms of a sale made on credit require a customer to settle his or her outstanding account within a short period (e.g. 30 days in many industries). Thus, as amounts to be received from accounts receivable are to be collected relatively quickly, they are generally classified as being current assets.

STOP AND THINK 1

Why are accounts receivable classified as a current asset?

Accounts receivable represent a significant part of working capital, which are the current assets minus the current liabilities of a business. The management of accounts receivable is extremely important for most firms. Not allowing customers to purchase goods on credit may result in a loss of potentially profitable sales. However, if a firm allows all customers to purchase goods on credit, as some customers may not be able to settle the amount owing either in full or part, it will suffer a loss. Therefore, a business must develop a policy on credit sales that balances the benefit it provides in attracting customers who would not otherwise purchase from the firm with the costs of providing credit. Costs not only include the losses relating to receivables that prove to be irrecoverable but also to the opportunity cost of providing credit (i.e. interest forgone on funds that could be invested elsewhere) as well as the out-of-pocket costs incurred in managing the credit approval and collection function.

BAD AND DOUBTFUL DEBTS

If a business eventually collects all the amounts owing from accounts receivable then the revenue recognised from selling goods on credit is earned. However, it is unlikely that a business will collect all monies owing because some customers will not settle the amount they owe. When amounts owing from accounts receivable are not collected, the business has incurred a **bad debt**. The firm's inability to collect from a customer could be for a variety of reasons including the debtor's bankruptcy, death, disappearance, and so on. As bad debts result in a loss, it needs to be accounted for. There are two ways in which we can account for this loss and are discussed next.

STOP AND THINK 2

Explain what a bad debt is and give examples.

2 LEARNING OBJECTIVE

Explain and apply the direct write-off and allowance methods for handling bad and doubtful debts

Direct write-off

With this approach, the amount owing by a debtor is eliminated when it becomes apparent the debt is not going to be recovered. We reduce the accounts receivable balance, and the other side of the transaction is the recognition of an expense: the loss of future economic benefits (i.e. cash that will no longer be received) which results in a reduction in equity.

Allowance for doubtful debts

A business might not discover that a customer is unable to pay until the period following the credit sale. Therefore, if we use the **direct write-off method** the revenue (and the related profit) and assets will be overstated in the year of sale. However, in the subsequent year when the debt is written off (and accounts receivable decrease), the loss results in an expense that decreases equity. To overcome this problem, a common method for accounting for bad debts is to create an allowance at balance date for the amount expected to be irrecoverable. How is this amount calculated? Accountants have techniques for estimating the amount of expected uncollectable accounts, even though it might be too difficult to exactly determine which outstanding accounts will be irrecoverable. For example, an accountant might determine that, of the outstanding accounts receivable of $100 000 at balance date, an amount of $8 000 should be allowed for expected uncollectable debts. While at balance date we do not know which customers will default on payment, we might be able to estimate the dollar amount we do not expect to receive.

Where do we get the estimates from? Accountants use a number of methods to estimate the amount expected for bad debts. These include:

- taking a percentage of credit sales based on previous years
- analysing all outstanding accounts receivable at balance date according to the length of time amounts have been owing. The assumption is that the longer a debt has been outstanding, the greater the likelihood (or probability) that the amount owing will prove to be irrecoverable. This estimation method is known as an ageing of accounts receivable.

To illustrate the application of an ageing analysis we use Pamjen, a small partnership business, and provide the following analysis of receivables.

AGED ANALYSIS OF ACCOUNTS RECEIVABLE

DETAILS	NOT YET DUE (I.E. N < 30 DAYS	1–30 DAYS PAST DUE	31–60 DAYS PAST DUE	36–90 DAYS PAST DUE	OVER 90 DAYS PAST DUE	TOTAL
Balance owing	$500	$100	$50	$100	$250	$1 000
% expected to be irrecoverable	0%	2%	6%	10%	20%	
Amount to allow for	$0	$2	$3	$10	$50	$65

From this age analysis we determined that $65 of accounts receivable outstanding at balance date will be uncollectable. As we do not know the identity of customers who are likely to default in settling their account, we cannot reduce individual customer's balances as would be the case with the direct write-off method. To overcome this problem, accountants create an allowance for doubtful debts as a means by which the anticipated future loss can be accounted for. The word 'doubtful' is more appropriate than 'bad' because, at balance date, no formal assessment as to whether a particular customer's debt is in default had been made. As the allowance for doubtful debts is intended to recognise the potential non-collection of an outstanding account receivable, it is an adjustment to the value of the asset accounts receivable. Thus, the allowance for doubtful debts does not represent a liability: it is not a future disposition of economic benefits the business is obliged to make. As the amount of the allowance for doubtful debts is deducted from accounts receivable (just as we did in the direct write-off method), in effect it becomes a negative or contra asset. The deduction of this contra asset from the asset allows for the net amount of future economic benefits expected to be collected to be recognised.

8.2 KEY CONCEPT

ALLOWANCE FOR DOUBTFUL DEBTS

The allowance for doubtful debts is a contra asset account that shows the estimated total of receivables that are anticipated to be irrecoverable.

STOP AND THINK 3

Why does an entity, where all sales are made for cash, not need to make an allowance for doubtful debts?

In the following worksheet for Pamjen, the allowance for doubtful debts has a negative balance because it is a contra asset. The asset accounts receivable effectively has a positive balance. Thus, if the allowance for doubtful debts is to be deducted from accounts receivable it must have a negative balance. The accounts receivable and the allowance for doubtful debts would be reported in the balance sheet as follows:

Accounts receivable (gross)	$1000
Less allowance for doubtful debts	–$65
Balance	$935

The allowance for doubtful debts allows us to record our assets and profit in the period in which the related credit sale occurred. Thus, assuming that the estimate of irrecoverable debts is accurate, neither the net book value of accounts receivable (i.e. gross receivables – allowance for doubtful debts) or the calculated profit would be overstated. While the estimation of the allowance for doubtful debts involves some uncertainty, most estimates are reliable.

8.1

WORKED EXAMPLE

PAMJEN WORKSHEET

The following transactions occurred for Pamjen:

1. Inventory was sold for $6000 cash
2. Inventory was sold for $4000 on credit
3. $3000 cash was collected from the sales made on credit
4. Based on an age analysis of outstanding accounts receivable, an allowance of $200 will be created for debts that are anticipated to be irrecoverable.

   Assume that the cost of inventory sold is currently not accounted for.

PAMJEN WORKSHEET

	ASSETS			+ LIABILITIES	= EQUITY
	CASH	ACCOUNTS RECEIVABLE	ALLOWANCE FOR DOUBTFUL DEBTS		PROFIT AND LOSS
Transaction 1	6000				6000
Transaction 2		4000			4000
Transaction 3	3000	–3000			
Balance	9000	+1000	0	≡	10000
Transaction 4			–200		–200
Balance	9000	+1000	–200	≡	9800

Note that the above worksheet would effectively reveal the net accounts receivable at the end of the period to be $800, being the gross accounts receivable of $1000 minus the allowance for doubtful debts of $200. In the following accounting period, when we discover amounts owing from the prior period's credit sales are uncollectable, we reduce both the allowance for doubtful debts and accounts receivable by the same amount. Remember we recorded the expense for anticipated bad debts in the previous year and this resulted in a more accurate estimate of profit in that year, together with a more reliable measure of the amount expected to be collected from accounts receivable.

For example, let us now assume that in the following period, Pamjen determines that Bill Bear is not likely to pay the $100 he owes because he has been declared bankrupt. If this write-off is to be recorded as Transaction 5, then the allowance for doubtful debts would be decreased by recording +$100 and the decrease in the outstanding accounts receivable balance would be shown as a −$100. Since the total accounts receivable and allowance for doubtful debts change by the same amount, the net book value of accounts receivable remains the same, as shown in version 2 of the worksheet.

PAMJEN WORKSHEET VERSION 2

	CASH	ACCOUNTS RECEIVABLE	ALLOWANCE FOR DOUBTFUL DEBTS	+ LIABILITIES	PROFIT AND LOSS
Cash sales	6000				6000
Credit sales		4000			4000
Cash from sales	3000	−3000			
Balance	9000	+1000		≡	10000
Doubtful debts expense			−200		−200
Balance	9000	+1000	−200	≡	9800
Transaction 5		−100	+100		
Balance	9000	+900	−100	≡	9800

Note that after recording Transaction 5 in the above worksheet, the net accounts receivable is still $800, being the adjusted gross accounts receivable of $900 minus the revised allowance for doubtful debts of $100.

ACCOUNTING POLICIES FOR BAD AND DOUBTFUL DEBTS AND IMPLICATIONS FOR USERS

3 LEARNING OBJECTIVE

Identify the accounting policy implications of the accounting for bad and doubtful debts.

It is important when comparing the financial statements of two firms to take into account policies relating to the provision for bad and doubtful debts. If two firms are in the same industry, operate in similar locations and with similar credit-granting policies, you would expect similar levels of bad and doubtful debts for both firms. If this is not the case, and unless there is an explanation for the difference, it is possible that the difference could just be due to the use of different accounting policies with one company using the direct write-off method and the other the allowance method. If this is the case, then some adjustment for the difference may be required before a proper comparison can be made between the two sets of financial statements. In Chapter 5, the practice of earnings management was discussed. The allowance for doubtful debts is an example of one of many choices a firm can make to manage its earnings by using different estimates of the allowance. For example, in highly profitable reporting periods, adding more to the allowance for doubtful debts than is really required effectively defers profits in that period to subsequent periods. In a period where profits are less than considered desirable, as the allowance for doubtful debts has been over-provided for in prior periods, the expense to record for debts expected to be irrecoverable in future periods can be less than what is required. Thus, the doubtful debts expense would be lower than otherwise might be expected and profits are correspondingly higher. Many reasons might explain why a firm would be inclined to use the allowance for debts as a mechanism for managing earnings. For example, some firms may have an earnings number that is used in various contracts (e.g. interest coverage ratio in debt contracts or earnings before interest and tax as a metric used to determine the amount of bonuses payable to managers) and the accounting treatment for bad and doubtful debts allows the firm to remain within the terms of those contracts. Alternatively, some firms might wish to report a history of improving profitability that is not characterised by significant positive and negative changes in the firm's earning stream. Previously, banks and other financial institutions judiciously used allowances for doubtful debts as a way of smoothing their year-to-year earnings.

We now turn from receivables to a second major current asset for many organisations: inventories.

4 LEARNING OBJECTIVE

Explain what is meant by the term 'inventory'

INVENTORY

In this section we consider what we mean by the terms 'inventory', 'work in progress' and 'finished goods'. We look at examples of inventory, work in progress and finished goods, as this will lead to a better understanding of what these terms mean in practice.

Inventory can be said to comprise:

- goods purchased for resale. For example, fruit and vegetables are purchased by a supermarket to sell to its customers; second-hand vehicles are purchased by a dealer in second-hand commercial vehicles to sell to his or her customers
- raw materials purchased for incorporation into the product or products being manufactured or assembled for sale. Examples are wood purchased by a furniture manufacturer or aluminum purchased by a car manufacturer
- consumables, which are bought solely for use within the business. Consumables consist of such things as supplies of grease for machine maintenance, stationery and cleaning materials.

You might have noticed from the examples above that the inventories relate to the type of business they are associated with. For example, delivery vehicles owned by a furniture manufacturer are not classified as inventory because they are held for use in the business and not for resale. Thus, the same type of asset (i.e. a delivery vehicle) would be treated as being a current asset 'inventory' by the dealer in second-hand commercial vehicles whereas the furniture manufacturer would classify such a vehicle as being the non-current asset vehicle. For the last category, consumables, while they are not held for resale, they typically have a short useful life. Thus, consumables are another form of inventory and are classified as being a current asset. The term 'inventory' is used to describe consumables as there is no other suitable term that describes them.

8.3

KEY CONCEPT

INVENTORIES

Inventories are assets:

» held for sale in the ordinary course of business

» in the process of production for such sale

» in the form of materials or supplies to be consumed in the production process or in the rendering of services.

(AASB 102, para. 6)

Having looked at some examples of inventory, our attention turns to work in progress and finished goods. Again these are both different types of inventory – the difference lies in the fact that they have normally gone through some manufacturing process.

In general, all these forms of inventory and work in progress fall within the definition of current assets which we defined as Key concept 5.6 (you may wish to refer back to this key concept).

You will notice from these examples that it is expected inventories will be disposed of within the year, as in the case of a supermarket's fruit and vegetables and a commercial dealer's stock of second-hand delivery vehicles.

8.4

KEY CONCEPT

WORK IN PROGRESS AND FINISHED GOODS

'Work in progress' is the term applied to products and services that are at an intermediate stage of completion. For example, on an assembly line for personal computers, at any point in time there will be some partly assembled machines and, at balance date, a computer manufacturer's financial statements will need to include the value of such work in progress. Other examples include partially completed buildings which would be the work in progress of a building contractor, or the time spent to date on a half-finished drawing by an architect.

Finished goods are goods that have been through the complete manufacturing process and are ready for resale to the customer. Examples are cars assembled by General Motors Holden, computers manufactured by Lenovo, or iPhones and iPads assembled by Foxtron for Apple.

Valuing inventory

In theory, if the prices of inventory items stayed constant over time, tastes did not change and there were no changes in technology, inventory valuation would be a relatively straight forward task. However, as the real world is characterised by continual innovation that is driven by rapid changes in technology and consumer preferences, the task of accounting for inventory is not so easy to carry out.

The question of how changes in prices affects the valuation of inventory is a wide-ranging one, and will, as discussed below, address the question of how the value of inventory is to be determined. Initially, we will consider the effects of changes in taste and technology before then examining how this affects the value to be attached to inventory. We will then look at how changes in price affect the valuation of inventory.

5 LEARNING OBJECTIVE

Identify and apply the valuation rule for inventory

Scout Kozakiewicz

Technology and taste have been grouped together because, although the causes are different, the effects on inventory valuation are the same. Consider the effect of changes in technology, of which there are many everyday examples, and how this change might impact on the value of inventory. A good example is the use of electronic data processing devices which have progressed over time from large main frame machines to desktop personal computers, laptop computers to tablets and palm-held devices. When IBM introduced the personal computer in 1981 it transformed the market for business-related information-processing machines to the extent that manufacturers of main frame computers were no longer as competitive as before in terms of both operational performance and price. In turn, after other computer manufacturers had invested in research and development of information technology they were in a position to offer personal computers that surpassed the performance of machines manufactured by IBM. Thus, IBM personal computers were overpriced and for IBM to remain competitive, it had to significantly reduce retail prices of its machines. For the purposes of illustration, assume that ABC Limited, a computer retailer, has an inventory of 10 personal computers bought at a cost of $3 000 each which it plans to sell at a mark-up on cost of 25%. While the expected selling price is $3 750 per machine (i.e. $3 750 = $3 000 + ($3 000 × 25%)), the retailer would initially value the inventory of 10 personal computers at the total cost of $30 000.

Due to competition, the manufacturer of these personal computers has had to decrease the price it charges its resellers to $2 000. How does this price reduction affect ABC Limited? Since an asset is defined as being the right to receive a future economic benefit, the 'value' of the inventory is now unlikely to be $30 000. For ABC Limited, the future economic benefit that can be obtained is likely to be significantly less than the previously anticipated selling price of $3 750 per machine. Given that rival retailers can purchase the same personal computers for only $2 000 per machine, the retail price charged by these competitors could be much less than the cost of $3 000 per machine incurred by ABC Limited. In this case cost no longer reflects the future economic benefit that ABC Limited is likely to receive. A fairer reflection would be the amount that the computers could now be sold for. If retailers of this brand of personal computer have a uniform 25% mark-up on cost, the market price would now be set at $2 500 (i.e. $2 500 = $2 000 + ($2 000 × 25%). However, even the revised market price of $2 500 per machine probably overstates the economic benefit to be received as undoubtedly there will be some costs incurred in selling the personal computers. If these costs were estimated to be $100 per machine, then the amount of the future economic benefit would in fact be a net $2 400. The $2 400 can be referred to as being the net realisable value of the inventory of personal computers.

KEY CONCEPT

8.5

NET REALISABLE VALUE

Net realisable value is defined as the estimated selling price in the ordinary course of business less the estimated costs of completion and the estimated costs necessary to make the sale.

(AASB 102, para. 6)

A similar effect would have arisen if the goods could be sold only at a reduced price or for scrap because of changes in consumer preferences. In each of these cases, the cost paid for the goods is not relevant to the future benefit: a better valuation would be the net realisable value. This leads us to the idea that we should compare the cost of an item with what we can get for it and, if the latter figure is lower, use that figure to value our inventory. Expressed in more formal terms, this is the valuation rule.

You might well wonder why, if the net realisable value is higher than the cost, that higher value is not used. The reason for this, it is argued, is that the attainment of the higher value is uncertain as consumer preferences, for example, might change.

In certain situations (e.g. the inventories held by a not-for-profit entity for distribution at zero or minimal cost), the valuation rule is the lower of cost or current replacement cost.

Having established the general rule for inventory valuation and seen the reasons for the rule, the next question is how to establish the cost referred to in the rule.

> **8.6**
>
> **KEY CONCEPT**
>
> ## THE VALUATION RULE
>
> The valuation rule states that inventory should be valued at the lower of cost and net realisable value.
>
> (AASB 102, para. 9)

In July 2013, the spun-off Southcorp, now known as Treasury Wine Estates, had an unexpected write down of inventory by $160 million. This write down triggered a class action against the company on the grounds that the company had failed to properly inform the market as to the extent of over valued inventory.

Establishing the cost of inventories

6 LEARNING OBJECTIVE

Explain and apply the principles used to determine the cost of inventory

The more complex the process by which inventory is acquired, the more difficult it is to establish the cost of the inventory. The problem is in deciding what costs are to be included and what to exclude. In the manufacturing sector, the determination of product cost is a matter of ongoing debate and will be examined in Chapter 15. Fortunately, for financial reporting purposes we need only be aware in general terms of the alternative methods because the choice between them has been made for us, to some extent, through custom, practice and the rules laid down for entities in AASB 102 *Inventories*. This standard deals with the question of inventories and work in progress.

AASB 102 *INVENTORIES*

Paragraph 10 of AASB 102 states that cost consists of:
- the cost of purchase
- the cost of conversion
- other costs incurred in bringing the inventories to their present location and condition.

In the manufacturing sector, the costs of conversion include direct labour and other production costs (such as the salary of a production supervisor or other costs incidental to the manufacturing process) ascertained in accordance with the absorption costing method. An example of conversion costs would be the expense incurred by Toyota in moving engines from its production plant to the company's assembly facility. In the retail sector, a grocer might purchase fruit and vegetables in bulk but sell this produce to customers in small prepacked shrink-wrapped packs. While the costs associated with breaking down the bulk fruit and vegetables and the shrink-wrapping of this produce is an example of a conversion cost, the expense may be immaterial in amount so as to not warrant being included in the cost of inventory.

To summarise, we can say that costs will normally include:
- the cost of purchase
- the cost to transport goods to a location for sale or conversion
- the cost of import duty or other taxes incurred prior to sale
- the cost of conversion or repackaging to make goods ready for sale.

WORKED EXAMPLE

WASHING MACHINES

A Perth appliance dealer orders 10 washing machines from a manufacturer in Adelaide. The washing machines have a list price of $2000. The retailer buys on terms 2/10, net/30. This means that the dealer can deduct 2 per cent off the list price (i.e. $40) and pay only $1960 if he or she pays within 10 days. If he/she pays after 10 days, the dealer should pay $2000 within 30 days. Transport charges paid by the retailer are $50 per machine. Goods and services tax (GST) of 10 per cent is levied on the supplier's list price. The retailer incurs handling charges of $20 per unit to get the machines onto the showroom floor. It is assumed that no GST is payable on freight or for the handling of the washing machines. Sales staff who sell the machines are paid a bonus of $50 per machine. What is the cost per machine, assuming that the retailer pays in eight days?

	$
List price	2000
Less Discount (2% x $2000)	40
	1960
Plus	
GST	0
Transport	50
Handling	20
	2030

Two costs are excluded. Firstly, on completion of the retailer's Business Activity Statement (BAS), the GST paid to the washing machine manufacturer of $300 per machine will be refunded by the Australian Taxation Office. Thus, the GST is not included in the cost of each washing machine. As the bonus to be paid to sales staff is a selling expense, it is not part of cost. More complex examples of cost determination will be covered in Chapter 15. We now consider the effects of price changes on the valuation of inventory.

Effects of price changes

It is a reality of life that prices for goods and services do not remain static through time. Many prices increase through time – although some items, such as consumer electrical products, have actually declined in price over time. As previously noted, there would be no problem if all sales could be identified with the actual goods sold. In practice, where inventory comprises multiple heterogeneous items that are indistinguishable from each other, this is not so readily achieved. For example, a builder's merchant has stacks of loose second-hand bricks which are sold in any order and for the convenience of customers (e.g. ease of access). Therefore, we cannot know whether a given quantity of bricks sold was purchased by the builder's merchant when the price of second-hand bricks was 30 cents each or whether it was bought after the price had risen to 33 cents each. From the builder's merchant's perspective, it is not cost-effective to trace each brick through from initial acquisition to eventual sale. We have to find some system that will give a reasonable approximation of the cost of the goods we have sold and the cost of the inventory that is remaining. There are many possible methods with various levels of complexity. The two methods allowed in AASB 102 are weighted average cost or first in, first out. In some jurisdictions (e.g. the United States), a third alternative to FIFO and weighted average can be used for financial reporting purposes provided it is also used for tax purposes. This alternative is the last-in, first-out method (LIFO) where costs are attached to units sold in terms of last-in prices, first out. While this cannot be used for external reporting purposes in Australasia, a reporting entity may still use LIFO purely for internal management purposes.

In order to illustrate the differences between these three methods, let us take some simple data.

8.3

WORKED EXAMPLE

JACKIE

Jackie started the year with some goods in inventory and bought additional goods as required during the year. The price of the goods she bought rose steadily during the year. The summarised data for her transactions are as follows:

	UNITS	COST PER UNIT	TOTAL COST
Goods in stock at the start of the year	400	$1.10	$440
Purchases, quarter 1	500	$1.20	$600
Purchases, quarter 2	400	$1.25	$500
Purchases, quarter 3	400	$1.35	$540
Purchases, quarter 4	300	$1.40	$420
Total inventory available for sale	2000		$2500
Inventory sold during the year	1800 units sold for a total of $2700.		

Using this data, we illustrate how the adoption of different valuation rules not only affects the inventory value at the end of the year, but also affects the cost of sales and the profit. We start by considering the **first in, first out (FIFO)** method.

FIRST IN, FIRST OUT

The FIFO method is based on the assumption that the first goods bought are the first sold. In effect, the inventory held at the end of the period is assumed to be that purchased most recently. There are many situations when this is a logical assumption: for those industries dealing in perishable consumables such as fruit and vegetables, dairy and meat. However, the choice of method for arriving at the cost of inventory generally has little, if anything, to do with actual physical flow of inventory and is simply a means by which costs are attached to the goods that have been sold and those that remain on hand.

With this method, as the unsold inventory is estimated to be only 200 units (i.e. 200 = 2000 units available for sale – 1800 units sold during the year) it is assumed to have been from the fourth quarter's purchases and would be valued at a unit cost of $1.40 each. Thus, it is assumed that the 1800 units sold were drawn from the opening inventory, together with all inventories purchased in the first three quarters and 100 units bought in the fourth quarter.

		$	$		$
Sales	1800	1.50			2700
Less cost of sales					
Opening inventory	400	1.10	440		
Quarter 1	500	1.20	600		
Quarter 2	400	1.25	500		
Quarter 3	400	1.35	540		
Quarter 4	100	1.40	140		
Cost of sales			2220		2220
Gross profit					480
Ending inventory	200	1.40	280		

The LIFO method would value the closing inventory using the prices of the opening inventory, which would be 200 units at $1.10 or $220. The cost of sales would be total cost of goods available for sale of $2500 less $220 or $2280 and gross profit would therefore be $2700 less $2280 or $420.

WEIGHTED AVERAGE COST

The weighted average cost method is a compromise between the FIFO and LIFO methods discussed above. Like FIFO and LIFO, the weighted average method makes no assumptions about the way in which goods flow through the business.

For the purposes of arriving at the cost of sales expense, all that is needed is to work out the weighted average cost per unit of inventory and multiply that by the number of units sold. Similarly, the closing inventory is arrived at by taking the estimated units of inventory still on hand and multiplying this number by the weighted average cost per unit.

	$	$		$
Sales	1800	1.50		2700
Less cost of sales				
Opening inventory	400	1.10	440	
Quarter 1	500	1.20	600	
Quarter 2	400	1.25	500	
Quarter 3	400	1.35	540	
Quarter 4	100	1.40	140	
	2000	$1.25	2500	
Cost of sales	1800	$1.25		2250
Gross profit				450
Closing inventory	200	1.25	250	

STOP AND THINK 4

If the price of goods in inventory was falling over the year, which of the two methods, FIFO or average cost, would give:

a   the highest cost at year-end?

b   the lowest cost a year-end?

c   the highest gross profit at year-end?

d   the lowest gross profit at year-end?

Accounting policies for inventories and implications for users

AASB 102 permits the use of either FIFO or average cost. It is important when comparing the financial statements of two or more entities to know how the financial statements were prepared. Did the companies use average cost or FIFO? For example, Woolworths uses average cost to determine the cost of its inventory. If we were to compare Woolworths' financial statements with those of Tesco, and the UK-based retailer uses FIFO, then this must be allowed for when comparing the results of both companies. In times of rising prices, Tesco's profits would generally be higher than Woolworths', based on the use of FIFO. Thus, the difference in profits between the two companies is partly due to each company's choice of accounting policy for the valuation of inventory. This difference should be distinguished from differences in profits due to higher sales or lower operating costs. Also remember that earnings management and meeting contractually pre-specified targets or financial numbers may explain differences in the accounting policy choices of managers.

7 **LEARNING OBJECTIVE**

Identify the implications of the accounting policy choice used for determining inventory costing methods

PROPERTY, PLANT AND EQUIPMENT, AND DEPRECIATION

An examination of the balance sheet of Woolworths shows that the largest asset representing about 40 per cent of total assets is property, plant and equipment (P, P & E). P, P & E are non-current assets with an expected useful life of longer than one year, which could extend beyond 40-50 years. This poses an issue under accrual accounting since unlike inventory the benefits of P, P & E are not fully consumed in one year, and the cost of P, P & E must be spread over periods beyond one year. The process used to spread the cost over future periods is called depreciation. The definition of depreciation is given in AASB 116, as reported in Key Concept 8.7.

8 **LEARNING OBJECTIVE**

Explain the concept of depreciation

KEY CONCEPT

8.7

DEPRECIATION

Depreciation is the systematic allocation of the depreciable amount of an asset over its useful life.

(AASB 116, para. 6)

The definition refers to a 'systematic allocation', which means that it is not an ad hoc process but should be done on a consistent and economically plausible basis each year. It is also clear from the definition that depreciation is a process of allocation, not valuation. In other words, the depreciation amount is not meant to represent the decline in the value of the asset. It is meant to represent the allocation of the depreciable cost of the asset over its useful life. Therefore, the depreciable amount of the asset less the depreciation represents the unallocated amount, and not necessarily the asset's value at any one point in time. We could spend some time analysing the definition, but it is more important to consider the question of why we depreciate assets and what depreciation can and cannot achieve.

Why depreciate?

9 LEARNING OBJECTIVE

Explain why non-current assets are depreciated

A **depreciable asset** is one that has a finite life extending over several accounting periods. Thus, machinery is a depreciable asset, where as freehold land is not. Depreciation is intended to show the consumption of economic benefits during an accounting period. The economic benefits associated with all depreciable assets and that are to be realised by the entity need to be accounted for, and depreciation shows the consumption of these benefits as as an expense in the statement of comprehensive income as they occur in each period.

A second and more contentious argument that is sometimes given for providing for depreciation is that it will allow a business to maintain its capacity to continue to operate. Clearly, if a machine comes to the end of its useful life, the business will need a new machine if it is to carry on manufacturing the products it sells. This, of course, assumes that the business wishes to replace the machine, that the product is still to be produced, that the production technology processes remain the same, and so on. These issues directly relate to our original problem of measuring wealth in Chapter 4. Such a measure depends on how you define wealth, and whether that changes. For example, a car might be seen as an asset until such time as the world either runs out of oil or the price of petrol rises to levels that make the continued use of the vehicle economically unviable. At that stage we might not want to include a car in our measurement of wealth. Therefore, to have retained profits in order to ensure that we always had a car would not be appropriate.

A third reason for providing for depreciation to maintain productive capacity is also contentious because, in fact, all depreciation does is to spread the original cost and potentially only maintain the original capital. In fact, operating capacity is not maintained through depreciation, as no account is taken of changes in prices, in technology, or in consumer demand. Neither are the changes that may occur in the size of the business taken into account. There could be further implications in terms of the economies of scale that might accrue from replacing a machine with a bigger one. We cannot guarantee, should we wish to, that the process of depreciation will have accumulated sufficient funds retained in the business to replace an existing machine with one of equal capacity.

10 LEARNING OBJECTIVE

Appreciate that the process of depreciation does not involve the setting aside of cash funds for asset replacement

STOP AND THINK 5

What is the purpose of depreciation?

We begin with Worked example 8.3 to show that depreciation does not involve the setting aside of cash in order to be able to replace the asset in the future.

8.3

WORKED EXAMPLE

TONI'S BUSINESS

Toni buys a van for $40 000 and sets up a business as an ice-cream seller. In addition to the van, she puts $10 000 cash into the business, which is subsequently used to buy inventories of ice-cream.

At the end of the first year, sales have amounted to $60 000 and the total expenses, including the cost of ice-creams, van repairs and running costs, are $30 000. As all the inventory has been sold, the only asset on hand is cash. Thus, the business has $40 000 in cash: being the sum of the original $10 000 invested plus the money from sales of $60 000, less the expenses paid of $30 000.

Toni decides that she will withdraw $30 000 cash on the assumption that the business is still as well off as it was at its inception. That is, at the start of the year the business had a van plus $10 000 in cash; and it still has the van, so there needs to be only $10 000 left in for the status quo to be maintained. Let us assume that the situation is repeated for the next three years.

Under these assumptions, the statement of comprehensive income and the balance sheet of the business are as follows:

TONI'S BUSINESS
STATEMENT OF COMPREHENSIVE INCOME

	YEAR 1 $	YEAR 2 $	YEAR 3 $	YEAR 4 $
Sales revenue	60 000	60 000	60 000	60 000
Cost of sales	30 000	30 000	30 000	30 000
Profit for the year	30 000	30 000	30 000	30 000
Other comprehensive income	0	0	0	0
Total comprehensive income for the year	30 000	30 000	30 000	30 000
Withdrawal	30 000	30 000	30 000	30 000
Retained profit	0	0	0	0

TONI'S BUSINESS
BALANCE SHEET

	YEAR 1 $	YEAR 2 $	YEAR 3 $	YEAR 4 $
Current assets				
Cash	10 000	10 000	10 000	10 000

	YEAR 1 $	YEAR 2 $	YEAR 3 $	YEAR 4 $
Non-current assets				
Van	40 000	40 000	40 000	40 000
Total assets	50 000	50 000	50 000	50 000
Owners' equity	50 000	50 000	50 000	50 000

If we assume that the van will last for four years and have no further useful life, we can see that, in fact, the balance sheet at the end of year 4, assuming it reflects the value of future economic benefits, should be as follows:

TONI'S BUSINESS
BALANCE SHEET AT THE END OF YEAR 4

	$
Current assets	
Cash	10 000
Non-current assets	
Van	–
Total assets	10 000
Owners' equity	10 000

As we can see, there is insufficient cash left in the business to replace the van, and in this situation, the business cannot continue at its previous level of operating capability. If we compare the results with our definition of profit in Chapter 4, it is clear that our profit measure must have been wrong, because Toni is not as well-off at the end of year 4 as at the finite beginning of year 1.

The problem is that the profit has been overstated because no allowance has been made for the fact that the van has a useful life, which is progressively being consumed each year. If we assume that the cost should be spread evenly over the four years and call this expense depreciation, then the statement of comprehensive income would appear as follows:

TONI'S BUSINESS
REVISED STATEMENT OF COMPREHENSIVE INCOME

	YEAR 1 $	YEAR 2 $	YEAR 3 $	YEAR 4 $
Sales revenue	60 000	60 000	60 000	60 000
Cost of sales	30 000	30 000	30 000	30 000
Gross profit	30 000	30 000	30 000	30 000
Depreciation expense	10 000	10 000	10 000	10 000
Profit for the year	20 000	20 000	20 000	20 000
Other comprehensive income	0	0	0	0
Total comprehensive income for the year	20 000	20 000	20 000	20 000
Withdrawal	20 000	20 000	20 000	20 000
Retained profit	0	0	0	0

Thus, the net profit has reduced by $10 000 for the annual depreciation expense each year and Toni has only be able to withdraw $20 000 each year. Toni's balance sheet would now show as follows:

TONI'S BUSINESS
REVISED BALANCE SHEET

	YEAR 1 $	YEAR 2 $	YEAR 3 $	YEAR 4 $
Current assets				
Cash	20 000	30 000	40 000	50 000
Non-current assets				
Van	40 000	40 000	40 000	40 000
Less Accumulated depreciation	(10 000)	(20 000)	(30 000)	(40 000)
	30 000	20 000	10 000	0
Total assets	50 000	50 000	50 000	50 000
Owners' equity	50 000	50 000	50 000	50 000

As we have seen, the effect of charging an expense for depreciation in the statement of comprehensive income is to reduce the net profit, which in turn has led to a reduction in the amount that Toni has been able to withdraw each year. The reduced level of withdrawals has led to the cash balance increasing by $10 000 each year until, at the end of year 4, there is $50 000 in the bank and Toni is potentially in a position to replace the van, assuming of course that the price of vans has not changed. If you compare the two sets of balance sheets there is another change: the non-current asset reduces each year by the amount of the depreciation charge. The accumulated depreciation is a contra or negative asset account. It is similar, in a way, to the allowance for doubtful debts account that we discussed earlier in this chapter. On the worksheet, it is shown as part of the assets with a negative balance as it is a negative asset; that is, the accumulated depreciation is deducted from the asset in the balance sheet. These two effects should not be mixed up. The increase in cash is a result of Toni withdrawing less cash, and not a result of providing for depreciation. The latter does not affect the cash balance. This is obvious if we work through year 1 of this example on a worksheet.

WORKSHEET SHOWING YEAR 1 OF TONI'S BUSINESS

	ASSETS			= LIABILITIES	+ EQUITY	
	CASH	VAN	(ACCUMULATED DEPRECIATION)		CAPITAL	PROFIT AND LOSS
Balance	10 000	40 000			=50 000	
Sales	60 000					60 000
Expenses	–30 000					–30 000
Depreciation			–10 000			–10 000
Withdrawal	–20 000				–20 000	
Balance	20 000	+40 000	–10 000	=	30 000	+20 000

Accumulated depreciation does not represent cash. The only cash in the business is shown in the cash column.

KEY CONCEPT

WRITTEN-DOWN VALUE (CARRYING VALUE OR BOOK VALUE)

The written-down or carrying value is normally the **cost of the non-current asset** less the total depreciation to date. In certain cases, usually with freehold buildings, the asset might be revalued. In these cases the written-down value is the valuation less total depreciation to date.

STOP AND THINK 6

Why is it unlikely that depreciation will provide for the replacement of a non-current asset?

11 LEARNING OBJECTIVE

Summarise and apply the straight-line, reducing-balance and units-of-production methods of depreciation

Methods of depreciation

As we have said, there are several alternative methods of depreciation. Theoretically, the choice of the appropriate method depends on the nature of the asset being depreciated. In practice the two most common methods in use are the **straight-line method** and the **reducing-balance method**. A third method called the units-of-output or **units-of-production method** is used by some entities, especially those in the resources industry. The straight-line method is used by most businesses because it is simple to calculate. In this regard, it is useful to look at the accounting policies statement in published accounts to ascertain the reasons underlying the choice of depreciation method. As we will see in the discussion below, a case can be made for using different methods for different assets or classes of assets.

THE STRAIGHT-LINE METHOD

We have already seen that this is a simple method, which explains why so many companies use it. The assumption concerning asset life underlying this method is that the asset is equally useful over its entire life. The depreciation charge is calculated by taking the cost of the asset, subtracting the estimate of any **residual value** at the end of its life, and dividing the resulting amount by the useful life of the asset. Therefore, a machine which costs $100 000 has an estimated life of four years and an estimated residual value of $20 000, is depreciated by $20 000 per year. This was arrived at by using the following formula:

$$\frac{\text{cost} - \text{residual value}}{\text{useful life}}$$

In our case this works out as follows:

$$\frac{100\,000 - 20\,000}{4} = \$20\,000 \text{ per annum}$$

THE REDUCING-BALANCE METHOD

The reducing-balance method assumes that the future benefits associated with the asset declines more rapidly in the earlier years of the asset's life than in the latter years. In fact, in most cases, the cost of repairs and maintenance increase as the asset grows older. Thus, when the cost of repairs is added to the annual depreciation expense the reducing-balance method potentially yields a more uniform cost for using the asset over its total life. It is less frequently used than the straight-line method because it is slightly more difficult to calculate, although with the increasing use of computerised accounting systems and spreadsheets this should be a less onerous task. To ascertain the charge for the year, the reducing-balance method applies a pre-calculated percentage to the written-down value, or carrying value. In order to arrive at the percentage the following formula could be used and would yield a rate of approximately 33.13 per cent per annum:

$$\text{Rate of depreciation} = 1 - \text{useful life}\sqrt{\frac{\text{residual value}}{\text{cost of asset}}}$$

Using the figures from the above example:

$$\text{Rate of depreciation} = 1 - \sqrt[4]{\frac{20\,000}{100\,000}}$$
$$= 1 - \sqrt[4]{0.2}$$
$$= 1 - 0.6688$$
$$= 0.33 \text{ (approximately)}$$
$$= 0.33\%$$

In practice, a simpler approach to determining the percentage rate under the reducing-balance method is used. An often-used rate for the reducing-balance method is a rate of 1.5 times or double the straight-line rate. We determine the straight-line rate by dividing the expected life of the asset into 100. Hence, an asset with an expected life of 10 years and a straight-line depreciation rate of 10 per cent would have a rate of say 15 per cent for the reducing balance method. In our example, as the life expectancy of the machine is four years, the straight-line rate is 25 per cent and the rate for the reducing-balance method would be 37.5 per cent if set at 1.5 times the straight-line rate. (i.e. 37.5% = 25% × 1.5 times). For our example, we will use both the 33.13 per cent (as determined by application of the formula) and the simpler calculated rate of 37.5 per cent.

Using the following table for 33.1 per cent:

YEAR	OPENING BALANCE	DEPRECIATION (@ 33.13%)	CLOSING BALANCE
1	$100 000	− $33 126 [A]	$66 874
2	$66 874	− $22 153 [B]	$44 721
3	$44 721	− $14 814 [C]	$29 907
4	$29 907	− $9 907 [D]	$20 000
Totals	$100 000	$80 000	$20 000

[A] Depreciation in Year 1 = 33.13% of $100 000
[B] Depreciation in Year 2 = 33.13% of $66 874
[C] Depreciation in Year 3 = 33.13% of $44 721
[D] Depreciation in Year 4 = 33.13% of $29 907

Using the following table for 37.5 per cent:

YEAR	OPENING BALANCE	DEPRECIATION (@ 37.5%)	CLOSING BALANCE
1	$100 000	− $37 500 [E]	$62 500
2	$62 500	− $23 438 [F]	$39 062
3	$39 062	− $14 648 [G]	$24 414
4	$24 414	− $9 155 [H]	$15 259
Totals	$100 000	$84 741	$15 259

[E] Depreciation in Year 1 = 37.50% of $100 000
[F] Depreciation in Year 2 = 37.50% of $62 500
[G] Depreciation in Year 3 = 37.50% of $39 062
[H] Depreciation in Year 4 = 37.50% of $24 414

COMPARISON OF THE TWO METHODS FOR CALCULATING THE REDUCING-BALANCE ANNUAL DEPRECATION RATE

While the use of the 33.13% rate calculated by formula results in a more accurate determination of the depreciation expense, many firms will simply choose to use the reducing-balance method rate based on 1.5 times the straight-line method rate. As indicated with the above example, the 37.5 per cent rate is over 4 per cent greater than the true reducing-balance rate and too much depreciation expense is charged each year, yielding an accumulated excess amount of $4741 and a lower net book value of $15259 by the end of Year 4. Thus, if the machine is disposed of at the estimated residual value of $20000, a gain on disposal (the difference between the proceeds of sale and the carrying value) equal to $4741 will result in Year 4. The gain recognised on the disposal of the machine corrects the excess depreciation expense that has been charged in each of the asset's four years of useful life. It is important to understand that the calculation of depreciation is only an estimate, irrespective of which method is used.

COMPARISON OF TWO METHODS OF DEPRECIATION: STRAIGHT-LINE METHOD VERSUS THE REDUCING-BALANCE METHOD USING 37.5 PER CENT

As can be seen in the table below, the charge to the statement of comprehensive income in each year and the accumulated depreciation in the balance sheet are quite different when comparing the two methods. The difference in the total depreciation over the life of the asset is reflected in the difference of $4741

STRAIGHT-LINE METHOD USING 20 PER CENT PER ANNUM

DEPRECIATION EXPENSE IN STATEMENT OF COMPREHENSIVE INCOME FOR				
INCOME STATEMENT ITEM	YEAR 1	YEAR 2	YEAR 3	YEAR 4
Depreciation expense	− $20000	− $20000	− $20000	− $20000

NET BOOK VALUE OF MACHINE IN THE BALANCE SHEET AS AT END OF				
BALANCE SHEET ITEM	YEAR 1	YEAR 2	YEAR 3	YEAR 4
Machine at cost	$100000	$100000	$100000	$100000
Accumulated depreciation	− $20000	− $40000	− $60000	− $80000
Net book value	$80000	$60000	$40000	$20000

REDUCING-BALANCE METHOD USING 37.5 PER CENT PER ANNUM

DEPRECIATION EXPENSE IN STATEMENT OF COMPREHENSIVE INCOME FOR				
INCOME STATEMENT ITEM	YEAR 1	YEAR 2	YEAR 3	YEAR 4
Depreciation expense	− $37500	− $23438	− $14648	− $9155

NET BOOK VALUE OF MACHINE IN THE BALANCE SHEET AS AT END OF				
BALANCE SHEET ITEM	YEAR 1	YEAR 2	YEAR 3	YEAR 4
Machine at cost	$100000	$100000	$100000	$100000
Accumulated depreciation	− $37500	− $60938	− $75586	− $84741
Net book value	$62500	$39062	$24414	$15259

between the carrying value at the end of year 4 under both methods. This will result in a different gain or loss on the sale of the asset.

The differences between the two methods can be summarised as follows:
- Under the straight-line method, the charge to the statement of comprehensive income is $20 000 each year, so the accumulated depreciation rises at a rate of $20 000 a year.
- Under the reducing-balance method, the charge to the statement of comprehensive income is based on 37.5 per cent of the carrying value at the end of the previous year.
- While both methods result in approximately the same amount of depreciation in total, it is the incidence of the charge to the statement of comprehensive income which varies, not the total charged over the useful life of the machine.

In theory, the choice of depreciation method should be governed by the nature of the asset and the way in which the benefit is used up. In practice, little if any attention is paid to this. However, it is worth spending some time understanding when each method might be the more appropriate.

We have said that the straight-line method implies that the benefit from the use of the non-current asset is used up in an even pattern over its useful life. This suggests that it is time which is the determining factor governing the life of the asset, rather than the amount of use. In the case of a building, it is unlikely that the amount of use it gets will materially affect its life span, thus the straight-line method of depreciation is more economically plausible. On the other hand, the way in which a car engine wears out is likely to relate to usage; that is, the greater the distance travelled by the car, the more wear and tear on the engine. In such a case, the straight-line method is unlikely to be the appropriate method. In these cases it is possible to use the units-of-production method, as outlined in the following section. This involves calculating the depreciation charge based on the kilometres travelled in each accounting period as a percentage of the total kilometres the car is expected to travel during its useful life, multiplied by the depreciable value of the car (i.e. cost less residual value).

However, the reducing-balance method has characteristics that make it a plausible alternative to a measure directly related to usage: it charges the most benefit used to the early years, as would be the case if the asset were used up, for example, by the kilometres alone or by the number of hours a machine was used. It is, of course, only an approximation. However, from a cost-benefit point of view, it may not be worthwhile measuring the number of hours a machine is run and calculating a precise figure, because the total life of the machine is subject to estimation errors. Therefore we can argue that where the life of the asset relates to time, the straight-line method is likely to be appropriate, but where the asset is used up through hours of use, or kilometres, or any other measure relating to usage, the reducing-balance method will provide a better approximation of the benefit used up in a period.

Refer now to the financial report of Woolworths in Appendix 1. Note 1 (G) reveals that the company uses the straight-line method for all plant and equipment.

UNITS-OF-PRODUCTION METHOD

A third method determines the amount of depreciation each year based on the depletion of the resource. This method is often used in the resources sector. For example, a company has a gold mine with a capitalised cost of $10 million and it is expected to produce 100 000 ounces of gold and have zero residual value. If, at the end of the first year of production, the company had extracted 10 000 ounces of gold then the depreciation would be:

$$\text{Cost} - \text{residual value} \times \frac{\text{number of units produced in period}}{\text{expected total number of units}}$$

$$= 10\,000\,000 - 0 \times \frac{10\,000}{100\,000}$$

$$= 10\,000\,000 \times 10\%$$

$$= \$1\,000\,000$$

The method can easily be applied to a motor car by basing depreciation on the kilometres the car travels in a period as a percentage of the total number of kilometres it is expected to travel. However, as stated earlier, this method is used more by firms operating in the resources sector. In the mining sector the rate of depreciation of assets integral to the mine is often based on the rate of depletion of the mine rather than a time-based approach such as the straight-line method.

Jason Benz Bennee/Shutterstock.com

STOP AND THINK 7

What are the assumptions underlying the two main methods of depreciation?

12 LEARNING OBJECTIVE

Identify the implications of depreciation accounting policy choices for financial reporting

ACCOUNTING POLICIES FOR DEPRECIATION AND IMPLICATIONS FOR USERS

When comparing the financial statements of two or more entities, it is important to be aware of how the financial statements were prepared. Did both companies use straight-line or reducing-balance methods of depreciation? For example, Woolworths uses the straight-line method for all non-current assets. Tesco uses a reducing-balance method of depreciation. In comparing the two, we should note that Tesco will record higher levels of depreciation when assets are new. Users of financial statements must adjust for this when comparing the results of both retailers. Thus, as with accounting for inventories and bad and doubtful debts, a component of the difference in profits between the two companies could simply be due to differences in the accounting policies adopted. This difference should be distinguished from differences in profits due to higher sales revenue or lower operating costs.

Another complication for users is the impact of different accounting policies on cash flows. If a company records a higher depreciation expense than another company, then, all other things being equal, the company with the higher depreciation expense will initially report a lower profit. However, we know depreciation is a non-cash-flow adjustment and that, over time, the differences between the two companies will not be materially different as a result of the different depreciation methods being applied. Therefore, differences in profit due only to different depreciation policies should not result in a different valuation of either company.

However, what if the companies use the same depreciation method for both the report to shareholders and the calculation of taxable income? The company with the higher initial amount of depreciation will have greater tax deductions in earlier years than the other company. Due to the time value of money (i.e. the value of $1 today is greater than $1 in one year's time) the company with the higher initial amount of depreciation should have a higher value than the other company because it pays less tax in the earlier years of the life of the asset.

INTANGIBLE ASSETS

13 LEARNING OBJECTIVE

Explain what is meant by the term 'intangible assets' and identify the difference between identifiable and unidentifiable intangible assets

Many firms have non-current assets which lack a physical substance and are not held for investment purposes. Yet these items still provide future economic benefits similar to plant, machinery and buildings. Such assets are described as intangible assets. Examples of intangible assets include trademarks, patents, intellectual property, franchises and goodwill. Assets such as accounts receivable and prepaid expenses also lack a physical substance and are not investments. However, such assets are classified as current assets and not intangible assets since they are expected to be converted to cash or consumed within one year.

Intangible assets are either identifiable or unidentifiable. Identifiable intangible assets include those intangibles that have a separate existence, such as patents, trademarks, franchises and brand names. Unidentifiable intangible assets are the economic benefits that flow to the business from such things as a good location, a high reputation (e.g. brand) or excellent customer relations. Goodwill is the name used to describe the future economic benefits that flow from the collection of such unidentifiable assets.

The cost of intangible assets

Determining the cost of intangible assets is relatively straightforward for those assets purchased externally, but far more complicated for those developed internally. For example, if Delta Company pays $200 million to acquire the patent for a new product, then the acquisition cost of the patent in Delta's accounts is $200 million. The cost of an identifiable intangible asset is the purchase price paid as this was the result of an arm's-length transaction between a fully informed buyer and seller. Goodwill is normally purchased when one firm acquires all or a significant portion of the net assets of another business. Goodwill is the excess of the amount paid for the fair value of the net assets acquired. For example, Company A pays $100 million to acquire all the assets and liabilities of Company B. The fair value of all the assets less the liabilities, once recorded in the balance sheet of company A, is $95 million. The $5 million difference is recognised as goodwill.

Many companies develop their own intangible assets, and establishing a cost for these assets is far more difficult. In the case of identifiable intangibles, the cost could include items such as the legal fees to develop the documents (e.g. patents and copyrights), the registration costs of such documents and, possibly, any legal costs incurred in successfully defending the ownership of the asset. Accounting Standard AASB 138 *Intangible assets* prohibits the recognition of internally developed goodwill, brands, mastheads, publishing titles and customer lists.

Companies that develop intangible assets internally have been keen to recognise such assets on their balance sheets. In being able to recognise the value of internally developed intangible assets, when the external users of financial statements compare their company to another which has purchased similar types of intangible assets, they are not at a disadvantage. However, it is important that only those expenditures which provide future economic benefits beyond the current period are recorded as an asset. Those expenditures where all the benefits are consumed in the current period should be recorded as an expense. Expenditures wrongly recorded as assets will overstate the current periods profit and understate the profits to be reported in future periods as such assets are expensed.

Research and development

Many companies spend large sums of money in the area of research and development (R&D). They may be hoping to discover a new product or process, or to improve an existing product or process.

The financial reporting question is whether such expenditures should be recorded as assets or expenses. In theory, the answer should be determined by applying the definition and recognition criteria for assets and expenses. Is it probable that future economic benefits will arise from the R&D expenditures? Does the company control such benefits? Can the benefits be reliably measured?

AASB 138 requires that all research in relation to intangible assets be expensed. On the other hand, as developmental costs occur when initial research evolves into a product or process that has potential commercial viability, such expenditure is more than likely to result in the generation of future economic benefits. Such costs may be carried forward as an asset, but only when they satisfy certain criteria such as probable future economic benefits and reliable measurement.

Because all research costs are expensed, does this mean that no future economic benefits will flow to the firm? Of course the answer is no, but in theory the expensing of all research expenditures could be interpreted as conveying this message to the external users of financial statements.

Patents

A patent is a legal right granted to one person or company for the exclusive use of a certain product or manufacturing process. When a company develops a new product, say through research and development, it will register a patent. The legal life of a patent is 16 years, but typically the useful life may be shorter as new products are often developed to compete against it. Furthermore, a company holding a patent can sell to other firms the right to manufacture and sell the product. Thus, the patent can be a valuable asset whether used by the firm or from having assigned the rights attached to the patent to others. How would you like to have been the owner of the patent on products like television, digital cameras or even the electric shaver?

Copyright

Copyright provides protection to the creators of original work, which could be a book like this text, a film, a song, a piece of music or a computer game. For a small fee, a copyright can be registered. Other parties are then not permitted to copy such original work without paying a royalty to the creator. For example, the estates of John Lennon and Elvis Presley continue to earn millions of dollars in royalties for their music, despite both musicians having been dead for over 30 years.

Trademarks or brand names

The costs of creating a trademark or brand name may be relatively small and may include costs paid to an artist or advertising agency, and a small registration cost. However, the values of trademarks and brand names can be huge. For example, the Coca-Cola brand name and logo would be very valuable intangible assets to have control over.

Franchises

A franchise provides the franchisee with the right to sell or distribute a certain product. For example, McDonald's and Hungry Jack's are conducted through both company-owned stores and franchise arrangements. In the latter case, the owner of a McDonald's franchise store pays a fee to McDonald's. This is recognised on the balance sheet as an intangible asset and is measured using the amount paid.

STOP AND THINK 8
What is the difference between identifiable and unidentifiable intangible assets? Give examples.

Accounting for intangible assets

The treatment of intangible assets once they are recognised on the balance sheet has been a very controversial issue over many decades. Some argue that intangible assets are no different from tangible assets in that they have a finite life during which the economic benefits are assumed to have been consumed. This consumption of economic benefits should be recognised as an expense in a similar fashion to the depreciation of tangible non-current assets. On the other hand, others argue that the life of some intangible assets, such as brand names, is extremely long and the amortisation (write-off) of such assets is not appropriate.

Traditionally, accounting standards in Australia required that purchased goodwill be amortised over a period not exceeding 20 years. However, AASB 138 now requires that the carrying value of purchased goodwill, and other intangible assets deemed to have an indefinite life, be assessed at least once a year. Only where this value has declined will the difference be recognised as an impairment of the asset. This essentially means that the value of the intangible asset on the balance sheet will be reduced and an expense of the same amount recognised in the statement of comprehensive income.

There have been some large goodwill write-downs in Australia, like Noni B in 2011 and Foster's Group Limited's 2010 report of a $1.16 billion impairment of its wine assets, which included Southcorp. As a result of this large impairment, Foster's recorded a loss of $464 million in that year. The write-down of goodwill reflected poor investments by Foster's and contributed to the sacking of its then chief executive officer. For those intangible assets deemed to have a finite life, such as copyright and patents, a process similar to depreciation is required to amortise the cost over the life of the intangible asset. The methods available to amortise intangible assets are the same as those used for tangible non-current assets such as property, plant and equipment. The term 'amortisation' has essentially the same meaning as depreciation; that is, the systematic allocation of the cost of the intangible asset over its expected useful life. The straight-line method of amortisation is the one normally used and the formula is:

$$\text{amortisation amount} = \frac{\text{cost of intangible asset} - \text{residual value}}{\text{useful life in years}}$$

The amortisation amount is recorded as an expense in the statement of comprehensive income and as an increase in accumulated amortisation (similar to accumulated depreciation). These assets are generally not replaced at the end of their useful life, and information about the estimated useful lives of intangibles is included in the notes to the accounts.

14 LEARNING OBJECTIVE

Explain the accounting treatment for identifiable and unidentifiable intangible assets

SUMMARY

LEARNING OBJECTIVE 1

EXPLAIN WHAT IS MEANT BY THE TERMS 'ACCOUNTS RECEIVABLE'.

Accounts receivable (or debtors) occur when a business sells goods or services to a customer on credit terms; that is, when the goods or services are sold on the understanding that payment will be received at a later date.

LEARNING OBJECTIVE 2

EXPLAIN AND APPLY THE DIRECT WRITE-OFF AND ALLOWANCE METHODS FOR HANDLING BAD AND DOUBTFUL DEBTS

Under the direct write-off approach, the amount owing by the customer is eliminated when it becomes apparent the customer is not going to pay. We reduce the accounts receivable balance for that customer while also recognising an expense (this is the other side of the transaction). The loss of future economic benefits has caused a reduction in equity.

The allowance method involves an entity estimating the amount of doubtful debts it expects to incur as a result of the amount owing for accounts receivabe at balance date. This estimate is recognised as an expense prior to an accounts receivable being classified as a bad debt. Then, when the amount owing by a customer is classified as being irrecoverable, the receivables amount is reduced, as is the allowance for doubtful debts. The allowance is a negative or contra asset as the amount of the allowance for doubtful debts is deducted from the gross amount of outstanding accounts receivable so as to determine the net amount of future economic benefits an entity expects to obtain from accounts receivable.

LEARNING OBJECTIVE 3

IDENTIFY THE IMPLICATIONS OF THE ACCOUNTING FOR BAD AND DOUBTFUL DEBTS.

It is important when comparing the financial statements of two entities to evaluate the allowance for doubtful debts. If two entities are in the same industry, operate in similar locations and use the same credit-granting policies, you would expect similar allowances for doubtful debts. If this is not the case, and unless there is an explanation for the difference, an adjustment for this difference is necessary before a proper comparison can be made of the financial statements of the two entities.

LEARNING OBJECTIVE 4

EXPLAIN WHAT IS MEANT BY THE TERM 'INVENTORY'

Inventory includes raw materials which are the inputs into a productive process, work in progress which are goods in the productive process that have yet to be completed, and finished goods which are items that have fully passed through the productive process and are ready for immediate sale.

LEARNING OBJECTIVE 5

IDENTIFY AND APPLY THE VALUATION RULE FOR INVENTORY

AASB 102 requires that inventory be measured at the lower of cost and net realisable value. Not-for-profit entities which hold inventory for distribution at no cost to the recipients of those goods measure inventory at the lower of cost and current replacement cost.

LEARNING OBJECTIVE 6

EXPLAIN AND APPLY THE PRINCIPLES USED TO DETERMINE THE COST OF INVENTORY

This was illustrated with the example of washing machines. The principle is that the term 'cost' includes all reasonable and necessary costs incurred to get the inventory ready for sale and to the location where it will be sold.

IDENTIFY THE IMPLICATIONS OF THE ACCOUNTING POLICY CHOICE USED FOR DETERMINING INVENTORY COSTING METHODS

AASB 102 allows entities to use either weighted average or FIFO to assign costs to inventory. In times of rising prices, FIFO profits will generally be higher than profits determined using the weighted average method. Therefore, the difference in profits between two companies may be due, partly at least, to the choice of inventory costing method used by each company. This difference should be distinguished from differences in profits due to higher selling prices or lower operating costs.

EXPLAIN THE CONCEPT OF DEPRECIATION

Depreciation is the systematic allocation of the cost or revalued amount of an asset over its useful life.

EXPLAIN WHY NON-CURRENT ASSETS ARE DEPRECIATED

The future economic benefits of a non-current asset with a finite life are consumed over time, and depreciation is meant to represent the consumption of the economic benefits of a non-current asset.

APPRECIATE THAT THE PROCESS OF DEPRECIATION DOES NOT INVOLVE THE SETTING ASIDE OF CASH FUNDS FOR ASSET REPLACEMENT

Depreciation is a non-cash expense, and accumulated depreciation is the sum of all the depreciation expenses since the asset was first put into use. The only cash in a business is in the cash at bank account in current assets. By depreciating an asset, the entity reports lower profits. Therefore, less is available for dividends, but there is no cash as such in the accumulated depreciation account.

SUMMARISE AND APPLY THE STRAIGHT-LINE, REDUCING-BALANCE AND UNITS-OF-PRODUCTION METHODS OF DEPRECIATION

1   The straight-line method allocates an even amount to depreciation expense each year and the formula is:

$$\frac{\text{cost} - \text{residual value}}{\text{useful life}}$$

2   The reducing-balance method allocates more depreciation expense to the earlier years of an asset's life and the formula is:

$$\text{Rate of depreciation} = 1 - \sqrt[\text{useful life}]{\frac{\text{residual value}}{\text{cost of asset}}}$$

The units-of-output method involves calculating the depreciation charge based on the units extracted each year as a percentage of the total units the asset is expected to yield, multiplied by the cost less residual value:

$$\text{Cost} - \text{residual value} \times \frac{\text{number of units in period}}{\text{total expected number of units}}$$

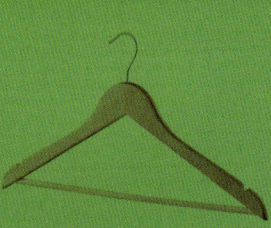

IDENTIFY THE IMPLICATIONS OF DEPRECIATION ACCOUNTING POLICY CHOICES FOR FINANCIAL REPORTING

The reported profit of an entity can vary based on its choice of depreciation policy. Moreover, even when two entities use the same policy, the depreciation expense can still vary based on the choice of variables, such as the useful life or the residual value. Users need to be aware of these potential effects on reported profits.

EXPLAIN WHAT IS MEANT BY THE TERM 'INTANGIBLE ASSETS' AND IDENTIFY THE DIFFERENCE BETWEEN IDENTIFIABLE AND UNIDENTIFIABLE INTANGIBLE ASSETS

Intangible assets are those items that meet the definition of an asset but lack any physical substance. Identifiable intangible assets include intangibles that have a separate existence, such as patents, trademarks, franchises and brand names. Unidentifiable intangible assets are the benefits that flow to an organisation from such things as a good location, an outstanding image in the marketplace or excellent customer relations. Goodwill is the name used to describe the future economic benefits that flow from the collection of these unidentifiable assets.

EXPLAIN THE ACCOUNTING TREATMENT FOR IDENTIFIABLE AND UNIDENTIFIABLE INTANGIBLE ASSETS

The accounting treatment is specified by AASB 138. Goodwill is not amortised, but is assessed annually for impairment. Any impairment in the value of goodwill is recognised as an expense. An impairment loss on goodwill can never be reversed. Identifiable intangibles with an indefinite life are accounted for in the same manner as goodwill. Identifiable intangibles with a finite life are amortised over their expected life.

REVIEW QUESTIONS

1 Why is it necessary to identify accounts receivable?

2 Discuss the difference between the direct write-off method and the allowance method for writing off bad and doubtful debts.

3 How do accounts receivable affect the statement of comprehensive income?

4 An expense has been described as a past or expired benefit. In what way does depreciation differ from other expenses?

5 Explain what is meant by the term 'intangible asset' and give examples.

6 Why is it necessary to value inventory at the lower of cost and net realisable value?

7 Explain what is included in inventory.

8 What main categories of inventory are likely to be held by a manufacturing business?

PROBLEMS FOR DISCUSSION AND ANALYSIS

1 Refer to the Woolworths 2013 financial report in Appendix 1.

   a What is the value of trade and other receivables?

   b What is the value of inventory?

   c What is the value of property, plant and equipment? What is the value of property only?

2   XYZ Ltd makes all its sales on credit. For customers who pay within 10 days of purchase, XYZ gives a discount of 5 per cent. (Assume all sales are made evenly over the month and there are 30 working days in every month.) XYZ knows that, on average, 50 per cent of its customers pay within the discount period, 40 per cent pay within 30 days and 8 per cent within 60 days. The remaining 2 per cent are uncollectable.

Sales figures are shown below.

How much cash did XYZ collect in months 4 and 5?

MONTH 1	MONTH 2	MONTH 3	MONTH 4	MONTH 5
$1 200 000	$1 300 000	$880 000	$1 000 000	$1 250 000

3   Toyshop Ltd makes approximately 50 per cent of its sales on credit. Credit sales for six months are as follows. (Assume credit sales are made evenly over each month.)

Toyshop gives a 2 per cent discount for those debtors that pay within 15 days. On average, 45 per cent of Toyshop customers pay within the discount period, 35 per cent within one month, 16 per cent within two months and 4 per cent prove to be uncollectable.

JANUARY	FEBRUARY	MARCH	APRIL	MAY	JUNE
$170 000	$132 000	$167 000	$149 000	$156 000	$112 000

Required

Calculate the monies collected each month, January to June inclusive. Assume each month has 30 days.

4   In each of the following situations, describe the way that the transaction would be dealt with in the accounts of the business and identify, where appropriate, the effect on the balance sheet and the statement of comprehensive income:

a   purchase of inventory of raw materials on credit terms

b   purchase of production machines for cash

c   receipts from customers in respect of credit sales

d   repayment of a loan

e   payment in respect of research expenditure

f   sale of goods on credit

g   payment of wages to clerical workers

h   payment of wages to production workers

i   payment of loan interest

j   receipt of cash from the owner

k   withdrawal of inventory for personal use by the owner

l   a customer going into liquidation owing money.

5   One of the items sold by Bodybuild, a sporting goods company, is cricket bats. One such bat, 'the Humdinger', sells well. Beginning inventory, purchases and sales for this item for the month of December were as follows:

December 1	Beginning inventory 4 bats @ $56 each
3	Purchased 6 bats @ $58 each
6	Sales of 3 bats
8	Purchased 6 bats @ $44 each
10	Sales of 5 bats
13	Sales of 6 bats
18	Purchased 12 bats @ $50 each
20	Sales 3 bats
24	Sales 5 bats
25–31	Closed

Calculate, using FIFO, periodic method, the total cost of sales for each sale day and the inventory balance after each sale day.

6   On 1 June 20X0 Billy Bond paid $6 000 into a business bank account as capital for his new business. The business bought and sold artwork from impoverished artists. Billy marked all merchandise up by 100 per cent on cost. During June, the following transactions were made.

June 1	Bought shop equipment for $1750 on 30-day credit.
June 2	Bought three paintings for $150 each, paying cash.
June 4	Bought a set of pottery vases for $100, paying cash.
June 6	Allowed J. Simpson to take one painting home to see if it fitted in with his lounge decor.
June 9	Bought, for cash, a statue of David, paying $300.
June 12	J. Simpson returned the painting as being unsuitable. However, he was taken with the vases and bought these on a 30-day credit arrangement.
June 15	Sold a painting for cash.
June 17	Paid phone bill of $123 and electricity account of $86.
June 18	J. Simpson returned the vases saying his wife did not like them and asked for a full refund. He was told that there was a no-refund policy but Billy would buy them back for $150 cash. Billy put the vases back into stock.
June 20	Sold a painting on a 30-day credit arrangement.
June 23	Sold the statue for cash.
June 25	Bought two wall hangings for $500 each on 30-day credit.
June 26	Sold one wall hanging for cash and the other on 10-day credit with a 2 per cent discount if paid within three days.

June 27	Bought six paintings for $150 each, paying cash.
June 29	Buyer of wall hanging paid account and took discount.
June 30	Paid assistant monthly salary of $600.

Required

a Discuss how each transaction should be treated.

b Draw up a worksheet, a balance sheet and a statement of comprehensive income.

7 A machine priced at $220 000 is acquired by trading in a similar machine and paying cash for the difference between the trade-in allowance and the price of the new machine.

  a Assuming that the trade-in allowance is $35 000, what is the amount of cash given?

  b Assuming that the carrying value of the machine that is traded in is $18 750, what is the cost of the new machine for financial reporting purposes?

8 A vehicle was purchased on 1 Jan 20X0 for $23 000. The vehicle was estimated to have a useful life of six years, after which time it could be traded in for $2000.

  a What was the amount in accumulated depreciation at 31 December 20X5 using the straight-line method?

  b If the vehicle was traded in for a new one after three years for $11 500, was there a gain or loss on trade-in?

  c If the reducing-balance method had been used in (b) above, at a rate of one-and-a-half times the straight-line method, would your answer be different from (b) above and, if so, what would that answer be?

9 The Philjet company makes all its sales on 30-days credit. For the year ending 31 December 20X9, cash collections from customers amounted to $1 078 333. Net credit sales in 20X9 totalled $1 022 111 and the balance of accounts receivable on 31 December 20X9 was $187 000. What was the balance of accounts receivable on 31 December 20X8?

10 A lawyer received $20 000 from a client on 1 August 20X0 as a retainer. In return, the lawyer agreed to give legal advice whenever required by the client for a year. Neither the lawyer nor the client knew at this stage when such advice would be sought, if indeed it would be sought at all. Of the $20 000, how much should be recorded in 20X0? Assume the financial year ends on 31 December 20X0.

11 Using a worksheet, draw up the balance sheet and statement of comprehensive income for the business whose transactions are set out below:

  • Month 1 Bert put in $9000 of his own money and transferred his own car into the name of the business. At the time of the transfer, it would have cost $6000 to buy a new model of the same car, but as the car was one year old its second-hand value was only $4000. The business then bought a machine for $4000 paying cash, and, at the same time, bought a second machine on credit terms. The credit terms were a deposit of $1000 which was paid in cash and two equal instalments of $900 payable at the start of months 4 and 7 respectively. The cash price of the machine was $2500.

  • Month 2 Bought raw materials for $3000 cash, and made cash sales of $3000.

  • Month 3 Paid rent in arrears for the three months, amounting to $600 in cash. Paid wages of $1500 for the three months to date. Made cash sales of $4000 and purchased more raw materials, again for cash, amounting to $8000.

  • Month 4 Paid instalment on machine of $900 in cash and made cash sales of $4000.

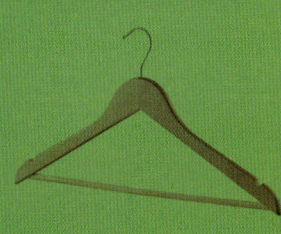

- Months 5–7 Bought raw materials for cash for $2000 and made cash sales of $5000, paid wages for three months of $1500, the rent for three months ($600) and the second and final instalment on the machine of $900.

- Months 8–12 Made cash sales of $14 000, bought raw materials for cash for $6000, paid wages for six months of $3000, and paid rent for three months of $600.

- At the end of the year Bert has raw materials in inventory which cost $2000. He calculates that the car will last two more years, after which he will be able to sell it for $400. The machines have useful lives estimated at three years and will then be sold for $100 each. Since Bert is not very good with figures, he opts for straight-line depreciation on all the non-current assets.

12 In each of the following situations, discuss the most appropriate method of depreciation, giving reasons for your choice:

  a land and buildings. The land was purchased for $300 000, and $400 000 was spent on the erection of the factory and office accommodation.

  b motor vehicles. The business owns a fleet of cars and delivery vans, all of which were bought new. The owners have decided to trade in the vehicles for new models after four years or 60 000 kilometres, whichever is sooner. The anticipated kilometre figures are 12 000 kilometres per annum for the cars and 20 000 kilometres per annum for the vans.

  c plant and machinery. The plant and machinery owned by the business can be broadly classified into three types, as follows:

   type 1. Highly specialised machinery used for supplying roller bearings to Manicmotors Ltd. The contract for supply is for five years, after which it might be renewed at the option of Manicmotors. The renewal would be on an annual basis. The machinery is so specialised that it cannot be used for any other purpose. It has an expected useful life of 10 years and the residual value is likely to be negligible.

   type 2. Semi-specialised machinery which is expected to be productive for 10 years and have a residual value of 10 per cent of its original cost. However, other businesses operating similar machines have found that, after the first three years, it becomes increasingly costly in terms of repairs and maintenance to keep them productive.

   type 3. General-purpose machinery which has an estimated useful life of 80 000 running hours. At present levels of production the usage is 6000 hours a year, but as from next year this is expected to rise to 8000 hours a year if the sales forecasts are correct.

Note to instructors: the following problems are considered more suitable for use in MBA courses. However, undergraduate courses may also find them useful.

13 Fun Travel Agency chartered an aeroplane to tour the Kimberley region for the week commencing 14 February 20X1, at a cost of $150 000. The plane's owner agreed to finance the fuel and staffing costs of the tour. During December 20X0, the travel agency sold all of the seats on the plane to passengers for $180 000 in cash. As an advance payment, the Fun Travel Agency paid $30 000 to the plane's owner. Of the $180 000 received by the travel agency, how much, if any, should be recorded as revenue by the firm in 20X0? Would your answer change if passengers were entitled to a refund in 20X1 if they cancelled their reservations?

14 Examine the data on loans and delinquent loans (bad debts) as a percentage of total loans for credit unions and answer the questions below:

ASSET QUALITY

	DELINQUENT LOANS/TOTAL LOANS					
CREDIT UNION SIZE	20X1	20X2	20X3	20X4	20X5	20X6
Less than $5m	4.79%	3.97%	3.73%	3.76%	3.58%	3.74%
$5m to < $10m	3.27%	3.01%	3.70%	3.45%	3.29%	2.80%
$10m to < $50m	2.36%	2.15%	2.16%	2.12%	2.07%	2.32%
$50m to < $100m	2.14%	2.24%	2.63%	2.26%	2.32%	2.26%
$100m to < $200m	1.81%	1.91%	1.94%	2.12%	2.04%	2.04%
Over $200m	1.31%	1.42%	1.44%	1.48%	1.56%	1.34%
All credit unions	1.75%	1.79%	1.89%	1.88%	1.89%	1.80%

a   Which category of credit unions performs best in terms of loan delinquency rates?
b   What reasons do you think may explain this performance?
c   Is information on doubtful debts more important for financial institutions than other types of commercial entities? Explain your answer.

15 Ultra Conservative Ltd is a small credit union with total assets of $50 million, most of which is made up of loans to members, amounting to $46 million. The following selected data relates to the credit union's first three years.

SELECTED ACCOUNTS

	31 DECEMBER 20X1	31 DECEMBER 20X2	31 DECEMBER 20X3
	$	$	$
Loans to members	40 000 000	43 000 000	46 000 000
Allowance for doubtful debts	400 000	430 000	460 000
Doubtful debts expense	400 000	110 000	116 000

The credit union commenced operations on 1 November 20X1, and by 31 December 20X1 had established loans worth $40 million and incurred no bad debts. However, the board of directors wanted to be conservative and, based on other credit unions' experiences with delinquent loans, decided to establish an allowance amount of 1 per cent of loans outstanding as at each balance date (hence the figure of $400 000 at 31 December 20X1). All loans regarded as uncollectable were written off against the allowance for doubtful debts account. Since Ultra Conservative Ltd commenced operations there have been no cases of a loan previously written-off having to be reinstated.

Required

a   Determine the amount of loans written off against the allowance account in 20X2 and 20X3.
b   Given your answer to (a), evaluate the directors' policy of providing for doubtful debts at 1 per cent of loans outstanding at balance date. Evaluate the impact of this policy on the balance sheet and the statement of comprehensive income.

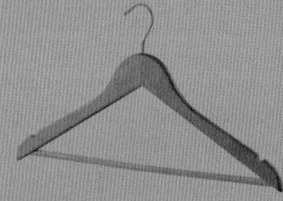

c   Would you recommend any changes to the policy? If so, would adjustments be required to the allowance for doubtful debts account? What would the worksheet entries be?

16 Joan Robbins, the owner of Joan's Fishing Tackle Shop, marks up the goods in her shop by 30 per cent. Figures for the past financial year, 20X0, are outlined below:

	$	$
Sales		1 550 000
Less Cost of goods sold		
Opening inventory	168 000	
Purchases	1 218 000	
	1 386 000	
Closing inventory	178 500	1 207 500
Gross profit		342 500
Less Operating expenses		340 000
Net profit		2 500

Joan has given no discounts during the 20X0 period and has kept turnover constant so her inventories have moved quickly. Nevertheless, she is unhappy with the year's results and asks you for your advice on the following:

a   Is it possible to determine from the figures whether there has been any theft by staff and/or customers?

b   On the assumption that theft has occurred, can it be determined from the figures whether it was cash or inventory that was taken?

c   A perpetual inventory control system could be established at a cost of $21 000 per year to monitor the more expensive goods in the shop. Would you recommend such a measure?

d   On the assumption that Joan is able to deter future theft, would you advise her to embark on a $21 000 advertising campaign if sales would rise by $210 000, leaving all other expenses unchanged?

Adapted from B. Colditz and R. Gibbins, *Australian Accounting*, 3rd edition, McGraw-Hill, 1976.

17 Elvin Company began operations in 20X2 by selling a single product. Data on purchases and sales for the year are as follows:

PURCHASES			
DATE	UNITS PURCHASED	UNIT COST	TOTAL COST
		($)	($)
April 8	3 875	12.20	47 275
May 10	4 125	13.00	53 625
June 4	5 000	13.20	66 000
July 10	5 000	14.00	70 000
August 3	3 400	14.25	48 450

PURCHASES			
DATE	UNITS PURCHASED	UNIT COST	TOTAL COST
		($)	($)
October 5	1 600	14.50	23 200
November 1	1 000	14.95	14 950
December 10	1 000	16.00	16 000
	25 000		$339 500

SALES	
	UNITS SOLD
April	2 000
May	2 000
June	2 500
July	3 000
August	3 500
September	3 500
October	2 250
November	1 250
December	1 000
Total units	21 000
Total sales	$552 000

On 3 January 20X3 the president of the company, Robert Bilbo, asks for your advice on costing the 4000-unit physical inventory that was taken on 31 December 20X2. Moreover, since the business plans to expand its product line, he has asked for your advice on the use of a perpetual inventory system in the future.

a Determine the cost of the 31 December 20X2 inventory under the periodic system, using:

i first in, first out method

ii last in, first out method

iii average cost method.

b Determine the gross profit for the year under each of the three methods in (a).

c i What argument can be used to justify why each of the three inventory costing methods may best reflect the results of operations for 20X2?

ii Which of the three inventory costing methods may best reflect the replacement cost of the inventory on the balance sheet as of 31 December 20X2?

iii Discuss the advantages and disadvantages of using a perpetual inventory system. From the data presented in this case, is there any indication of the adequacy of inventory levels during the year?

Adapted from C.S. Warren, J. M. Reeve and P.E. Fess, Accounting, 20th edition, South-Western, Mason, OH, 2002, Chapter 9, activity 9.5.

18 Multiplex Ltd used its own construction crew to extend its existing factories. What would be the most appropriate accounting treatment for the following?

  a   Architects' fees.

  b   Cost of debris removed during construction, following a storm.

  c   Cash discounts received for payment of materials purchased for construction before the invoiced due date.

  d   Cost of building a workshop (to assist with construction) that will be demolished once the extensions have been completed.

  e   Interest on money borrowed to finance construction.

  f   Government land taxes on the portion of land to be occupied by the new extensions for the period of construction.

  g   The cost of major errors made during construction.

  h   Overhead costs of the construction department, including supervision, depreciation on buildings and equipment of construction department, electricity, water, and allocation costs for the cafeteria, medical office and personnel department.

  i   Cost of workers' compensation insurance during construction and the cost of damages on any injuries not covered by insurance.

19 Kent Pty Ltd purchased a new machine for its manufacturing plant. While it was clear that both the invoice price of the machine and the transport costs of bringing the machine to the manufacturing plant should be brought to account, there was some uncertainty surrounding the treatment of the following items:

  a   Installation costs of reinforced steel to support the new machine, which is heavier than the machine it is replacing. Should this cost be charged to the building, added to the cost of the machine, or treated as an expense?

  b   An outside fitter was called in to assist with the installation of the machine because the regular maintenance crew were unable to do it. Costs of the fitter included his fee, transport, accommodation and meals. The supervisor of the maintenance crew and a senior engineer both spent a considerable amount of time assisting the fitter. Before the new machine was working properly, a large quantity of materials had been ruined during trial runs. How should all of these costs be treated?

  c   A state sales tax was paid when the machine was purchased. Should this be included in the machine's cost?

  d   Part of the finance agreement between Kent Pty Ltd and the machine manufacturer was a trade-in on the old machine as part payment. The amount given for the trade-in exceeded the depreciated value of the old machine in the books of Kent Pty Ltd. Should the difference be treated as a reduction in the cost of the new machine or a gain on disposal of the old one?

20 A business which manufactured office equipment sold approximately 30 per cent of its products (in dollar volume) and leased the rest. On average, the equipment was leased for five years. The initial cost of the leased equipment was recorded as an asset and was depreciated over the five years. The company assisted its customers in installing the office equipment and provided a regular maintenance service. Both these services were provided free of charge and recorded as a service expense. Service costs averaged about 7 per cent of the sales value of a piece of office equipment, but about 25 per cent of the first-year rental revenue of a leased piece of equipment.

    Over the past year, the company's installation of office equipment grew rapidly, but because the service cost was such a high percentage of lease revenue, reported income showed no increase at all. Research and development costs were treated as expenses as they were incurred. Should the same principle apply to service costs, or could these costs be added to the asset value of leased office equipment and amortised over the lease period? If so, should other service costs relating to leased office equipment be treated in the same manner?

Problems 14-16 adapted from R. Anthony and J. Reece, *Accounting: text and cases*, 8th edn, Richard D. Irwin Inc., 1988, Chapter 7, Case 7-2.

21 Two brothers are planning to start a bakery with a store in Melbourne and one in Sydney. They are contemplating the purchase of two stores currently owned by the same company and used as retail outlets for shoes. For this reason, the buildings and fixtures for both shops have the same cost, residual value and useful lives. They also plan to purchase the same type of equipment.

   The following schedule provides details of the assets:

	COST OF EACH $	RESIDUAL VALUE $	USEFUL LIFE OF EACH
Building	408 000	8 000	40 years
Fixtures	40 000	5 000	5 years
Equipment	34 000	2 000	8 years

   In addition, each building will need to be renovated at a cost of $40 000. The estimated statements of comprehensive income for the first year for the two shops have been separately determined by each brother and are shown in the schedule below.

PROJECTED STATEMENT OF COMPREHENSIVE INCOME FOR YEAR ENDED 31 DECEMBER 20X1	$	$
Sales		380 000
Cost of goods sold		200 000
Gross profit on sales		180 000
Operating expenses:		
Salaries expense	60 000	
Building renovation	40 000	
Other expenses	8 000	
Depreciation expenses:		
Building	20 400	
Fixtures	16 000	
Equipment	8 500	
Total expenses		152 900
Profit for the year		27 100
Other comprehensive income		0
Total comprehensive income for the year		27 100

PROJECTED STATEMENT OF COMPREHENSIVE INCOME FOR YEAR ENDED 31 DECEMBER 20X1	$	$
Sales		380 000
Cost of goods sold		200 000
Gross profit on sales		180 000
Operating expenses:		
Salaries expenses	60 000	
Other expenses	8 000	
Depreciation expenses:		
Building	11 000	
Fixtures	7 000	
Equipment	4 000	
Total expenses		90 000
Profit for the year		90 000
Other comprehensive income		0
Total comprehensive income for the year		90 000

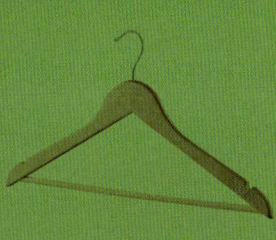

The brother who plans to open a store in Sydney does not understand how his projected profits can be so much lower than his brother's when they are projected to make the same sales, employ the same number of people, and spend about the same amount for other necessary operating items.

Required

a   Which depreciation method has each elected to use for their buildings, fixtures and equipment? Show the calculation of depreciation for each of the assets.

b   How did each brother account for the $40 000 cost of renovation? Which is correct?

c   Based on the projected statements of comprehensive income, which shop would you invest in? Lend money to?

ETHICS CASE STUDY

John Jerkins is the chief executive officer of a chain of retail stores which trade as Bains Ltd in Australia and New Zealand. The company has been operating for 50 years and has been very successful, except for the past three years. The entry of new competition from overseas, plus a downturn in the economy, has made trading difficult.

In reviewing the year's performance to date, John is concerned that the company's profit is down again from last year. If current trends continue, the predicted result will bring added pressure on the company from its bankers and the financial press.

To alleviate the problem John develops the following plan.

1   He instructs all stores to reduce the level of income required for customers to qualify for credit. This, he reasons, will allow more families to purchase appliances such as television sets and video recorders.

2   He proposes to amend the method of providing for doubtful debts according to the following schedule:

AGE CATEGORY	TOTAL AMOUNT OWING IN EACH AGE CATEGORY	ORIGINAL PERCENTAGE EXPECTED TO BE UNCOLLECTABLE	PROPOSED PERCENTAGE FOR EXPECTED UNCOLLECTABLE
	$	%	%
Not yet due	10 000 000	2	1.5
1–30 days past due	5 000 000	6	4
31–60 days past due	2 500 000	20	18
61–90 days past due	1 000 000	35	30
Over 90 days past due	600 000	80	60
Totals	19 100 000		

Required

a   Determine the amount of increase in profit as a result of the revised schedule for determining doubtful debts expense.

b   Discuss the effects of the revised credit policy on the company's profitability.

c   Discuss the ethical issues associated with John's plan.

SUGGESTED ANSWERS TO STOP AND THINK EXERCISES IN THE CHAPTER

1 Accounts receivable are classified as a current asset because they change form in the next accounting period to cash. Hence, they meet the definition of a current asset as defined in Chapter 2.

2 A bad debt occurs when a debtor who owes you money is not expected to pay. An example would be when a debtor dies, goes bankrupt or disappears.

3 An entity that is entirely a cash business makes no allowance for bad debts because, as a cash business, there are no credit sales and, hence, no accounts receivable.

4 a Average cost
   b FIFO
   c Avearge cost
   d FIFO

5 Depreciation is an accounting process by which the consumption or loss of the service potential of depreciable assets is progressively brought to account by means of periodic charges against revenue.

6 Because of the effects of changes in other factors, such as the price of the asset, it is unlikely that depreciation will provide for the replacement of a non-current asset. This will mean that the cost of replacement is greater than the original cost. However, it should be borne in mind that the effects of technological advances may mitigate or even reverse this effect. The discussion should also emphasise that depreciation does not provide cash for replacement.

7 Straight-line method: asset usage and the rate at which the asset is worn out is governed by time and is equal over the asset's life.

   Reducing-balance method: asset usage and the rate at which the asset is worn out is greater in the earlier years than the later years.

8 Identifiable intangible assets relate to special items like patents, copyright, brand names or trademarks. Unidentifiable assets relate to factors referred to as goodwill, such as a good reputation, good management and a good location.

CENGAGENOW

Go to http:\\login.cengagebrain.com to link to CengageNOW, your online study tool. First take the Pre-Test for this chapter to get your Personalised Study Plan, and then:

» revise your understanding of the key terms related to accounts receivable, accounts payable, accruals and prepayments

» follow animated examples on processes for different adjustments

» review the key concepts with online flashcards.

   After you have completed the activities in your Personalised Study Plan take the Post-Test to determine what concepts you have mastered and what you still need work on.

9

LIABILITIES AND SOURCES OF FINANCING

SUGGESTED ANSWERS TO STOP AND THINK
EXERCISES IN THE CHAPTER

LEARNING OBJECTIVES

At the end of this chapter, you should be able to:

1. identify and explain accounts payable, provisions and accruals
2. explain the meaning of deferred tax liabilities
3. discuss the concept of matching the type of finance with the purpose for which it is to be used
4. explain what is meant by short-term sources of finance such as bank overdrafts, trade credit and factoring
5. explain what is meant by medium-term sources of finance such as loans, hire-purchase and leases
6. explain what is meant by long-term sources of debt finance such as long-term loans and debentures
7. explain what is meant by equity finance and how it varies according to the type of business organisation
8. explain the criteria for classifying securities as either debt or equity, and apply this to different types of preference shares
9. explain what is meant by gearing, and the effect this can have on returns to shareholders in a company.

INTRODUCTION

The previous chapter deals with accounting issues in relation to different types of assets. In this chapter we turn our attention to different types of liabilities including the debt and equity instruments organisations use to fund the acquisition of assets. The most common liabilities of accounts payable, provisions and accrued liabilities are discussed. We then examine the various types of finance available to different types of organisations, which are another major category of liabilities. We then examine the different types of equity instruments that can be used to fund the organisation's investment in assets.

We also consider an organisation's financing structure and its effect on financial risk. For these purposes, it is necessary to differentiate between business risk and financial risk. Broadly speaking, business risk applies equally to all entities in an industry, with some variations according to size and diversity – that is, it is industry-specific rather than entity-specific. For example, changing economic regulations affecting the retail industry. Financial risk is more entity-specific: it relates to the financial structure of a business; that is, the way in which a firm finances its assets.

1 LEARNING OBJECTIVE

Identify and explain accounts payable, provisions and accruals

ACCOUNTS PAYABLE, PROVISIONS AND ACCRUALS

KEY CONCEPT

ACCOUNTS PAYABLE OR CREDITORS

Accounts payable (creditors) are sums owing at a point in time, the amounts of which are known.

Normally, a supplier allows its customers a period of time after goods and services have been supplied before requiring payment. The period of time and the amount of credit a business gets from its suppliers are dependent on a number of factors. These include the standard terms of trade for that industry, the creditworthiness of the business and its importance to the supplier. Thus, a small clothing retailer is likely to receive less favourable terms than a major group such as Woolworths. Accounts payable or creditors are one source of funds for a business, and this is generally called trade credit, which we discuss in the next section of this chapter.

KEY CONCEPT

PROVISIONS

A provision is a liability of uncertain timing or amount.

For example, where a manufacturer sells goods with a warranty it is necessary at the time of sale to make a provision for the expected future costs of providing remedies to customers under the warranty. These costs will include labour costs and any parts that need to be replaced.

Accruals are in some ways similar to accounts payable in that they relate to amounts due for goods or services already supplied to the entity. They differ not because of the nature of the transaction, but because, at the time of preparing the balance sheet, the amounts involved are not known with certainty.

KEY CONCEPT

ACCRUALS

Accruals are liabilities to pay for goods or services that have been received or supplied but have not been paid, invoiced or formally agreed with the supplier, including amounts due to employees (e.g. amounts relating to accrued leave pay).

This is usually because the invoice for the goods has not yet been received. Telephone accounts, which are always issued in arrears, are a common example, as are other utilities such as electricity and gas. In these situations, we can only estimate what we think is owed for the service that the business has used during the accounting period. This estimate is based on the last quarter of the previous year or on some other basis that the business considers more accurate (e.g. a self-reading of a meter). While accruals require an estimate there is much less uncertainty than what is associated with provisions. Worked example 9.1 clarifies the treatment of accounts payable, accruals and provisions.

STOP AND THINK 1

Explain the difference between accounts payable, accruals and provisions.

9.1

WORKED EXAMPLE

MIKE & CO.

For the year up to 31 December Mike & Co. made the following transactions.

1. Paid $75 000 of Mike's own money into a business bank account, together with $25 000 borrowed from a friend of the business.
2. Bought 100 tablet computers on credit from a supplier at $500 each.
3. Sold 20 tablet computers for $1000 cash.
4. Each tablet computer has a 12-month warranty. Mike estimated warranty work would amount to 5 per cent of retail sales value.
5. Paid a supplier $50 000 for items purchased.
6. Paid the electricity accounts for lighting and heating for three quarters, amounting to $1500.

If we enter these transactions on a worksheet and explain how they have been dealt with, we can then move on to Mike's other business transactions.

Let us examine each of the transactions in turn.

Transaction 1

By now we are familiar with transactions of this type, which create an asset and an equity balance for the owner. The second part of the transaction also creates an asset but in this case a corresponding liability in the form of money owing to the friend.

MIKE & CO. WORKSHEET VERSION 1 IN YEAR 1

	ASSETS		= LIABILITIES			+ EQUITY	
TRANSACTION	BANK	INVENTORY	LOAN PAYABLE	ACCOUNTS PAYABLE	PROVISION FOR WARRANTY CLAIMS	PROFIT AND LOSS	CAPITAL
1	75 000						75 000
1	25 000		25 000				
2		50 000		50 000			
3	20 000					20 000	
4					1 000	–1 000	
5	–50 000			–50 000			
6	–1 500					–1 500	
Balance	68 500	+50 000	=25 000	0	+1 000	+17 500	+75 000

Transaction 2

Up until now, we have assumed that the inventory was paid for when we received it. In this case, however, we are only told that during the year Mike bought 100 tablet computers for $50 000. We have no idea, at present, how much was actually paid out in respect of these items or how much he still owes. Therefore, we show that Mike owes money for all the items: we open a column for accounts payable and show $50 000 in that column.

Transaction 3

This records cash sales.

Transaction 4

This is slightly different from previous transactions that we have dealt with and is based on an estimate of the costs of repairing tablet computers under warranty. It is important to recognise the expense and liability at the time of sale as it is the sale that creates the warranty obligation.

Transaction 5

This shows the payment of the amount owing to suppliers.

Transaction 6

Once again, this is a familiar item because we received an account that was paid for in cash. However, we have in fact paid for only three-quarters, while we have consumed a year's supply of electricity. We therefore need to make some allowance for the other quarter. A reasonable estimate is that the fourth quarter's account will be the same as the other quarters; that is, approximately $500. It might, of course, turn out to be more or less. We are not attempting 100 per cent accuracy; we just need to give a reasonable picture of the situation.

TREATMENT OF ACCRUAL AMOUNT

Let us now return to the electricity account. We said we needed to make an accrual, which we estimated to be $500. Version 2 of the worksheet, which uses the balances from version 1, still balances and now gives a more accurate picture of the goods Mike controls and the amounts he owes.

The accrual of $500 for the electricity account is carried forward to the next period as being a current liability. When the next electricity bill is received the accrued liability is reversed and the balance recorded as an expense for the period. For example, if Mike

MIKE & CO. WORKSHEET: VERSION 2 IN YEAR 1

	ASSETS		= LIABILITIES				+ EQUITY	
TRANSACTION	BANK	INVENTORY	LOAN PAYABLE	ACCOUNTS PAYABLE	ACCRUALS	PROVISION FOR WARRANTY CLAIMS	PROFIT AND LOSS	CAPITAL
1	75 000							75 000
1	25 000		25 000					
2		50 000		50 000				
3	20 000						20 000	
4						1 000	–1 000	
5	–50 000			–50 000				
6	–1 500						–1 500	
Balance	68 500	+50 000	=25 000	0	0		+17 500	+75 000
Accrual					+500		–500	
Balance	68 500	+50 000	=25 000	0	+500	+1 000	+17 000	+75 000

receives the yearly electricity bill for $2 200 three months into the next year the entry to record the payment of the bill would be as shown in the Mike & Co. version 3 worksheet.

MIKE & CO. WORKSHEET: VERSION 3 IN YEAR 2

	ASSETS		= LIABILITIES				+ EQUITY	
TRANSACTION	BANK	INVENTORY	LOAN PAYABLE	ACCOUNTS PAYABLE	ACCRUALS	PROVISION FOR WARRANTY CLAIMS	PROFIT AND LOSS	CAPITAL
Balance	68 500	+50 000	=25 000	0	+500	+1 000	0	+92 000
Pay electricity	–2 200				–500		–1 700	

TAXATION

A company's tax liability is determined by the taxable income of the company in Australia as calculated in an income tax return, but the tax expense is based on accounting profit reported in the statement of comprehensive income. In Chapter 1 we mentioned that accounting profit and taxable income are not necessarily the same. This is because the accounting rules that are used to determine accounting profit sometimes differ from the tax rules used to determine taxable income. The example used in Chapter 1 was income that is exempt from tax but is still included as income in the determination of accounting profit. Another example is the differences that arise from the different depreciation rates used for accounting and tax purposes. These differences between taxable income and accounting profit result in the recognition of a current liability for taxes payable based on taxable income and tax expense based on accounting profit. For example, if the taxable income for a company is $100 000 it will have tax payable of $30 000. If accounting profit is $110 000 it will record a tax expense of $33 000. Hence the entry to record these two items would be:

$$\text{Assets} = \text{liabilities} + \text{equity}$$
$$0 = 30\,000 - 33\,000$$

The entry does not balance and we need to recognise $3000 to balance the entry as shown below:

$$0 = 30\,000 + 3000 - 33\,000$$

The $3000 to balance the equation is called deferred taxes payable and is a non-current liability which means the company will pay more tax in future periods, which meets the definition of a liability. It is also possible for companies to have deferred tax assets, which means a company will pay less taxes in the future. In this section, we explain deferred tax liabilities. The approach is based on that required by AASB 112 *Income taxes*.

Temporary differences

The use of different rules for tax and accounting leads to temporary differences between the carrying value of an asset or liability in the balance sheet in a company's books, and the balances for the same asset and liability for taxation. This is best explained with an example.

9.2

WORKED EXAMPLE

RENT RECEIVABLE

Assume Company A recognises revenue of $10 000 at 30 June for rent it is owed but has not yet received in cash. This results in the recognition of an asset, rent receivable, of $10 000. For accounting purposes, the rent revenue increases the accounting profit by $10 000. However, as the company uses the cash basis for tax purposes, it is not required to pay tax until the rent is received in cash. When the rent is received, the company will then pay tax. This means the company will pay more tax in future periods, which meets the definition of a liability.

The future tax consequence for the company of receiving the rent and reducing the asset rent receivable to a zero balance is a tax liability of $10 000 × the tax rate. If we assume a tax rate of 30 per cent, this results in future tax of $3000. This will be recognised in the current year as a deferred tax liability. If we assume that the accounting profit is $100 000 for the year ending 30 June and taxable income is $90 000, the worksheet entries involved in the current period are as follows:

WORKSHEET: COMPANY A, CURRENT YEAR

ASSETS	LIABILITIES		EQUITY
	TAX PAYABLE	DEFERRED TAX PAYABLE	TAX EXPENSE (PROFIT AND LOSS)
	27 000	3 000	−30 000
	(30% × $90 000)	(30% × $10 000)	(30% × $100 000)

Tax expense is determined by taking the tax payable and adding (or subtracting) increases (or decreases) in the deferred tax payable.

In the following year, if we assume that the rent was paid to Company A and the taxable income is $100 000 and the accounting profit $90 000, the worksheet would be as follows:

The tax payable the following year is $3000 higher than the previous year and this, in effect, represents settlement of the deferred tax amount from the previous period.

The deferred tax payable arises because of the temporary difference in the balance of the asset rent receivable in the books of Company A ($10 000) and the value of the asset for tax purposes (zero).

❯

WORKSHEET: COMPANY A, NEXT YEAR

ASSETS	LIABILITIES		EQUITY
	TAX PAYABLE	DEFERRED TAX PAYABLE	TAX EXPENSE (PROFIT AND LOSS)
	30 000	−3 000	−27 000
	(30% × $100 000)	(30% × $10 000)	(30% × $90 000)

STOP AND THINK 2
What are deferred tax liabilities?

9.4 **KEY CONCEPT**

ACCOUNTING FOR INCOME TAX

The approach adopted in accounting for income tax gives rise to deferred tax assets and liabilities which occur because of temporary differences between the tax value and the carrying value (for accounting purposes) of assets and liabilities, and tax losses.

3 LEARNING OBJECTIVE

Discuss the concept of matching the type of finance with the purpose for which it is to be used

9.5 **KEY CONCEPT**

TYPE OF FINANCE

The finance used, and the period of that finance, should be matched to the period for which it is required and the purpose for which it is to be used.

SOURCES OF FINANCE

Ideally, the type of finance should match the purpose for which it is to be used. For example, using short-term finance for the purchase of a building merely creates problems when the lender has to be repaid. The building is still needed, and so replacement finance has to be found. Similarly, taking out a loan repayable over 20 years to buy an asset that is only going to be needed for a few years would leave the business in the position of having to pay interest on money it no longer needs. These are extreme examples, but they serve to illustrate the point that the finance must be matched with the purpose for which it is to be used. Although any attempt to classify different types of finance is problematic, it is useful to look at some broad categories. In this book we have chosen to use a division based on the period of finance. In considering the various forms of finance, we shall endeavour to follow a pattern that provides a general description of the source of finance as well as a discussion of its uses, limitations, costs and availability.

Pali Rao/Shutterstock.com

> ### STOP AND THINK 3
> Why is it important to match the type of finance with the purpose of raising that finance?

SHORT-TERM FINANCE

4 **LEARNING OBJECTIVE**

Explain what is meant by short–term sources of finance such as bank overdrafts, trade credit and factoring

In this section we discuss sources of short-term finance. Conventionally, this is seen as finance for a period of less than one year. This means that the funds provided are repayable within 12 months from the date of accessing the finance and should be reported as current liabilities. Therefore, according to the principle stated in Key concept 9.5, it is important that short-term finance is only used for short-term investments such as inventories and accounts receivable. A number of sources of short-term finance are available, the most common being accounts payable (or trade credit), factoring and bank overdrafts.

Working capital

Working capital is represented by the current assets of a business minus its current liabilities. The management and funding of working capital is an important issue for all businesses. A business that fails to properly plan its working capital requirements is likely to experience financial difficulties, and may ultimately fail. As discussed in Chapter 8, organisations need to hold certain levels of inventories and accounts receivable. Having the right level of inventories and accounts receivable is an important business issue. In order to hold inventories and accounts receivable, organisations must be able to finance such assets. A major way to help fund the investment in accounts receivable and inventories is to use the short-term sources of finance discussed in this section.

Accounts payable (or trade credit)

We have already dealt with trade credit in the early part of this chapter.

In general, trade credit, which is widely used as a source of finance, provides short-term finance. This is normally used to finance, or partially finance, accounts receivable and inventory. As such, its importance varies from industry to industry. Manufacturing industries, where there is greater investment in inventory and work in progress, are more likely to rely on trade credit than are service-providing industries, which have minimal inventories such as stationery supplies. There may also be variations within an industry. A restaurant is less likely to rely on trade credit than is a hotel, where inventories can be very significant. In fact, within the licensed trade many hoteliers quite heavily rely on trade credit and this reliance makes them vulnerable if that credit is not managed effectively. Effective management in a small-business setting requires a balance to be struck between taking advantage of trade credit and not being perceived as a slow payer. If too long a period is taken to pay, the supplier may subsequently offer less favourable terms of trade. The temptation to extend the repayment date can lead to the withdrawal of credit, which means supplies have either to be paid for in advance or on a cash-on-delivery basis. Ultimately, too much reliance on trade credit can leave a business vulnerable to suppliers petitioning for bankruptcy or liquidation. Although suppliers are generally reluctant to take such steps, they will do so if they believe that they are more likely to recover the funds owed through such a course of action.

Trade credit is often thought of as cost-free credit. This is not strictly true, as quite often suppliers allow a small discount for early payment. Therefore, using the full period to pay an outstanding trade payable has an opportunity cost in the form of the discount forgone. This cost can be significant. For example, assume a supplier offers terms of 2/10, net/30. This means that a 2 per cent discount is given if payment is received within 10 days of receipt of the invoice; otherwise, the net amount due is payable in 30 days. To forgo the discount means a cost of 2 per cent is paid for a further 20 days' use of the money.

This equates to an approximate cost of 36 per cent per annum, which is a very expensive source of funds. This opportunity cost has to be weighed against the availability of funds within the business, or the cost of raising additional funds. Unlike other forms of short-term finance, there is generally no requirement for security. In 2013, Woolworths trade and other payables provided $5.39 billion in short-term finance, of which $4.08 billion were for trade credit. Whereas inventories amounted to $4.21 billion and accounts receivable were only $0.23 billion. In the past, Woolworths usually owed more in trade credit than the value of inventory it had on hand.

9.6 KEY CONCEPT

TRADE CREDIT

Trade credit is a form of short-term finance provided to a business by suppliers. It has few costs and security is not required.

Factoring

If a business makes sales on credit, it will have to collect payment from its accounts receivable at some stage. Until that point, it will have to finance the amounts it is owed, either through trade credit, an overdraft, or its own capital. The costs of this finance can be very high and many small businesses might find the amount, period of credit and overdraft constraints becoming increasingly challenging.

In Chapter 8 we discussed the importance of the management of accounts receivable. Entities offer discounts for early payment as one strategy to manage the amounts owing by customers. Another strategy used by some entities to reduce the money tied up in accounts receivable is to approach a factoring company. Factoring is a service provided by a finance company for collecting monies owing from accounts receivable.

Essentially, the factoring finance company assesses the firm's accounts receivable in terms of risk and collectability. It then agrees to collect the money owing on behalf of the firm. Once an agreement has been reached, the factoring company pays the firm for each month's invoices virtually immediately. It then becomes the factoring company's responsibility to collect the amounts owing from the firm's customers within the credit terms agreed at the time of sale. In this form of finance, the security provided by the business is in the form of the debt to be collected. For providing the firm with almost immediate access to the amounts owed by its customers, the factoring company charges for the service in the form of interest on the finance provided and a fee for managing the collection of factored accounts receivable. Therefore, this form of finance is more expensive than trade credit, but can be useful as it allows the firm to concentrate on production and sales, and it improves business cash flows. However, factoring is not available to all industries. In some cases (e.g. most retailing operations) this is because it is inappropriate, while in others factoring companies are reluctant to be involved because of a lack of clear legal definitions. In many cases, factoring occurs with recourse where, if a factored debt owing from a firm's customer cannot be collected, the firm may have to compensate the factoring company for the loss suffered.

9.7 KEY CONCEPT

FACTORING

Factoring provides short-term finance. Costs include an interest charge and a receivables management charge. Finance is secured on the accounts receivable and is provided by a finance company specialising in factoring. The finance company collects payment from the customers.

Bank overdrafts

Banks and other types of financial institutions provide short-term finance for working capital, either in the form of short-term loans or, more commonly, in the form of an overdraft. The difference is that a loan is for a fixed period of time and interest is charged on the full amount of the loan, less any agreed repayments, for that period. By contrast, an overdraft can be used as required and interest is only charged when it is used. Thus, if a business knows that it needs money for a known period of time, then a bank loan may be appropriate. On the other hand, if the finance is only required to meet occasional short-term cash flow needs, then an overdraft could be more suitable. We discuss loans in more detail under the heading of medium-term finance.

Although many businesses use overdrafts as a semi permanent source of finance, this is not how the banks would like to see them used. Bank managers like to see a business bank account, on which an overdraft facility has been provided, 'swinging' between having money in the bank account and using the overdraft. They do not see an overdraft as a form of permanent working capital.

A bank overdraft carries with it a charge in the form of interest and a fee for setting up the facility. The bank may also charge an annual fee for having provided the firm with an overdraft facility. As far as the interest is concerned, the rate charged is related to the risk involved and market rates of interest for the size of business. In general, the more risk involved, higher rates of interest would be charged. Because they operate in a volatile market, small businesses tend to be charged higher rates of interest than large firms.

In addition, banks normally require security, which can take various forms. In the case of a small business, the security could be a charge on the assets of the business. However, in many cases the property is already subject to a charge as it is mortgaged. In these situations, a bank may take a second charge on the property or on the personal assets of the owners of the business (e.g. residential properties). Alternatively, or in addition, the bank may require personal guarantees from the owner or, in the case of a limited company, its directors.

For large companies, the security may be a fixed charge on certain assets, or a floating charge on all of the firm's assets. In the case of very large companies, the risk involved is lower and the level of competition between potential providers of finance is greater. Because of this competition, overdrafts tend to be cheaper and more accessible for large companies, and security is less of a factor.

9.8 **KEY CONCEPT**

BANK OVERDRAFT

Bank overdrafts provide finance when it is needed to meet short-term cash flow needs. Costs include interest and, often, a set-up charge. In general, some form of security will be required – usually a fixed charge on certain assets or a floating charge on all assets.

STOP AND THINK 4

What are the forms of short-term finance discussed in this chapter?

5 **LEARNING OBJECTIVE**

Explain what is meant by medium-term sources of finance such as loans, hire-purchase and leases

MEDIUM-TERM FINANCE

Short-term sources of finance impose certain restrictions on borrowers because the funds must be repaid reasonably quickly, otherwise the borrower risks being forced into liquidation by disgruntled creditors. Because of this, there usually is a need to access sources of finance through medium- or long-term, permanent arrangements. While there is no strict definition, medium-term finance can be thought of as being for periods from one to 10 years. Hence, these forms of finance are reported as non-current liabilities except for any portion of the debt due to be repaid in the next 12 months. Medium-term finance can be used for plant and equipment, and other asset classes with useful lives of 10 years or less. There are a number of sources of medium-term finance for a business: we limit our discussion to medium-term loans, leases and hire-purchase.

Loans payable

As we pointed out, bank loans are an alternative to overdraft finance for short-term finance requirements. In general, loans should only be used when finance is required for a known period of time. Ideally, that period should relate to the life of the asset or the purpose for which the finance is to be used. Loans can be obtained for short-term, medium-term or long-term finance. Compared to an overdraft facility, which can be used when needed, a loan is more structured and fixed. Repayment of the loan is negotiated at the time the loan is taken out, and is generally at fixed intervals (e.g. monthly, quarterly, half-yearly and so on). Loans are often secured in the same way as overdrafts and, if the repayment conditions are not met, the lender may take action to recover outstanding amounts.

Bank loans are often granted for a specified purpose and limitations may be imposed as to the use of the loan and the raising of other finance while the loan is outstanding. Unlike an overdraft, the cost of this form of finance is known in advance as interest accrues from the time the business borrows the money – irrespective of the fact that it may not use it straight away. As with the other forms of finance discussed so far, the rate of interest charged and the availability of this source of finance is dependent upon the size of the business and the lender's assessment of the lending risk involved. Thus, in general, the larger and more diversified a business, the easier it will be for it to access this form of finance at a lower cost than smaller firms.

9.6

KEY CONCEPT

LOANS

Loans are generally made for a fixed purpose and a fixed period of time. They have set repayment dates, and costs include interest and set-up fees. They are normally secured on assets.

Hire-purchase

An alternative way of financing the acquisition of an asset is through the use of hire-purchase. Under a hire-purchase agreement, a finance company buys the asset and hires it to the business. Thus, a business can acquire the asset and use it, even though it has not yet paid for it in full. The finance company owns the asset during the period of the hire-purchase agreement.

The hirer has the right to use the asset and carries all the risks associated with using that asset. So, for example, if a car is purchased on hire-purchase, the hirer would be responsible for all the repairs and costs associated with the use of the car in the same way as if they had directly bought the car. The ownership of the asset is transferred to the hirer at the end of the period of the hire-purchase agreement. A normal hire-purchase agreement consists of a deposit and a set number of payments over a number of years.

This type of finance can only be used when a specific asset is purchased; that is, the finance is for a specified asset purchase and the amount borrowed is limited by the price of the asset. Therefore, hire-purchase finance cannot be used for directly financing working capital requirements

AaresTT / Shutterstock.com

or for any other purpose. A hire-purchase company directly pays the supplier for the asset and the asset belongs to the hire-purchase company. If repayments are not made in accordance with the hire-purchase agreement, the hire-purchase company has the right to repossess the asset. The money borrowed is repaid by instalments that include both a repayment of the capital borrowed and a charge for interest. The rate of interest charged will be dependent upon the market rate of interest, but is likely to be higher than the interest on a bank loan.

9.10

KEY CONCEPT

HIRE-PURCHASE

Hire-purchase is for a fixed period of time. Costs are in the form of interest charges. Ownership of the asset remains with the provider of the finance until all instalments are paid.

Hire-purchase is available to all businesses and individuals, subject, of course, to the hire-purchase company being satisfied as to the creditworthiness of the person or business.

Leasing

A lease is an agreement between a lessor (who owns the asset) and a lessee (who uses the asset). It conveys the right to use that asset for a stated period of time in exchange for payment, but does not normally transfer ownership at the end of the lease period. Leases can vary from very short periods to very long periods. Leasing companies often provide leases tailored to the needs of an industry. For example, in the hospitality industry it is possible to obtain lease finance for the internal telephone system or even the complete furnishing of a hotel.

In general, the cost of leasing is similar to that of hire-purchase. The major difference between the two types of finance is that, in general, leases tend to be for longer periods of time and are frequently used as sources of finance for specialised assets. In essence, there are two distinct types of leases – operating leases and finance leases. An operating lease is the same, in reality, as renting the equipment, and usually applies to items such as photocopiers, computers and cars.

9.11 **KEY CONCEPT**

LEASING

Leases are for a fixed period of time; the costs are in the form of interest charges. Security is related to the asset in question.

The underlying economic substance of a finance lease, on the other hand, is equivalent to borrowing money from a finance company and using that money to buy an asset. These differences are reflected in the definitions given in Key concept 9.12.

9.12 **KEY CONCEPT**

TYPES OF LEASE

» the underlying substance of an operating lease is a rental agreement.
» the underlying substance of a finance lease is a financing arrangement.

The reason for emphasising the difference between the two types of lease is that they are accorded different treatment in the accounts.

Operating leases present few accounting problems. The lessee records a lease payment as a decrease in cash and an increase in expenses. Apart from any accrual (as discussed earlier in the chapter) owing at year's end for the amount of the yearly lease payments to balance date, no asset or liability is recorded.

The most contentious issue has been whether certain leases, which are non-cancellable, should result in the recognition of an asset and a liability on the balance sheet of the lessee. This is illustrated in Case study 9.1.

Case study 9.1 demonstrates that the absence of information about the lease arrangements in the case of Company B could lead to an incorrect assessment of the relative risk positions of both companies A and B. The fact that lease arrangements were traditionally not reported on the lessee's balance sheet was aggressively used by leasing companies to market leasing as a form of finance. This advantage is normally referred to as off-balance-sheet financing. As the name implies, it refers to a method whereby an organisation obtains funds but the method used does not result in the recognition of a liability on the balance sheet. Prior to the release of accounting standards on leases, a firm could acquire the use of an asset via a finance lease, but it was not required to recognise the liability owing to the lessor.

In response to the problem of the non-disclosure of leases, the accounting profession issued accounting standards that required the reporting of leases that met certain criteria. In Australia, AASB 1008 *Accounting for Leases* was the initial standard and, with the adoption of IFRSs, this was replaced with AASB 117 *Leases*. AASB 117 requires a lessee to record a finance lease as an asset and a liability at the fair value of the

9.1 CASE STUDY

	COMPANY A	COMPANY B
	$	$
Assets		
Current assets	100 000	100 000
Non-current assets	1 900 000	1 400 000
Total assets	2 000 000	1 500 000
Liabilities		
Current liabilities	500 000	500 000
Non-current liabilities	500 000	–
Total liabilities	1 000 000	500 000
Net assets	1 000 000	1 000 000
Shareholders' equity		
Paid up capital	500 000	500 000
Retained profits	500 000	500 000
	1 000 000	1 000 000

COMMENTARY

The only difference between the balance sheets of Company A and Company B is $500 000 in non-current assets and $500 000 in non-current liabilities. Company A has just borrowed $500 000 from the bank over a period of 10 years. It has purchased a machine that has an estimated life of 10 years with zero residual value. B has just signed a lease agreement to acquire the use of an identical machine to that purchased by A. The lease agreement is for 10 years and cannot be cancelled by either party unless B fails to make a lease payment. Given these facts, should the balance sheets of A and B be any different? In Company A's balance sheet, total liabilities to shareholders' equity is 100 per cent. However, for Company B this ratio is only 50 per cent. This suggests that the lease arranged by Company B is less risky than that arranged by Company A. Is this a fair conclusion?

leased property or, if lower, the present value of the minimum lease payments. The present value of the lease payments, when the residual value is guaranteed by the lessee, equates with the fair value of the asset at the inception of the lease. A finance lease is defined (in paragraph 4 of AASB 117) as one which:

> transfers substantially all the risks and rewards incidental to ownership of an asset. Title may or may not eventually be transferred.

AASB 117 also provides criteria to assist in deciding whether substantially all the risks and rewards have been transferred from lessor to lessee. A lease will normally be a finance lease when the lease is non-cancellable and:

1. the term of the lease is for a major portion of the expected useful life of the asset being leased

    or

2. the present value of the minimum lease payments amounts to at least substantially all of the fair value of the lease asset at inception of the lease

    or

3. the lease transfers ownership to the lessee at the end of the lease, or the lessee can purchase the asset for a bargain price.

The asset recorded in the lessee's accounts is then amortised or depreciated to the statement of comprehensive income over a period equal to either the lease period or the asset's useful life. The finance lease liability is reported as a non-current liability except the portion payable in the next 12 months which is reported as a current liability. In Woolworths' 2013 financial statements, finance leases were reported as being only $1.3 million in current liabilities and $5.3 million in non-current liabilities. Woolworths do have significant operating leases reported in the notes.

Each lease payment incorporates principal and interest components; the interest component is treated as an expense. The liability is systematically reduced in each period by the principal component of each lease payment. Therefore, each lease payment is similar to the loan repayment that Company A would be required to make in Case study 9.1. In 2010 the IASB signalled further changes to accounting for leases with an exposure draft proposing that all non-cancellable leases should give rise to the recognition of assets and liabilities for the duration of the period in which the lease cannot be cancelled. The proposed accounting treatment is to require an asset to be recognised for the period the lessee has a 'right of use'. This would also normally result in the recognition of an associated liability. The proposal would have a major impact on organisations that make significant use of operating leases as a way of 'financing' their investment in assets. The exposure draft was subsequently revised and reissued in 2013 but will still have the same impact if it were to be issued as an accounting standard.

STOP AND THINK 5
What are the differences between an operating lease and a finance lease?

6 LEARNING OBJECTIVE

Explain what is meant by long-term sources of debt finance such as long-term loans and debentures

LONG-TERM FINANCE

In the previous two sections, we discussed short- and medium-term sources of finance. We noted that short-term sources of finance are suitable for financing investments in accounts receivable, inventories and other types of current assets. Medium-term finance is for periods from one to 10 years, and is suitable for financing investments in plant and equipment, and other asset classes with useful lives of 10 years or less. When an entity wants to invest in long-term assets (e.g. land and buildings) or to permanently finance the excess of current assets over current liabilities, it should use long-term sources of finance.

Long-term sources of finance are generally those with maturity periods of more than one year, and normally more than 10 years and are reported as non-current liabilities. The number of alternative sources of long-term finance available is, to some extent, dependent on the type of organisation involved. We start our discussion with debt finance, such as long-term loans, which are more generally available, and then discuss equity finance. The latter discussion will be subdivided in terms of organisation types as these affect the type and amount of equity funding available.

Working capital

Trade credit is one of the major sources of finance for current assets (i.e. it is a short-term source of finance). However, in many entities, the amount of current assets exceeds the current liabilities, and this excess is referred to as working capital. The working capital must be financed by either medium- or long-term finance. Where it is likely that the entity will always have positive working capital, it should consider using long-term finance to fund this investment.

Debt finance

This is the term given to any source of long-term finance that is not equity finance. Often, debt finance is seen exclusively as long-term interest-bearing finance. This is a misconception as all the finance we have discussed so far has been debt finance. We look at two broad categories of long-term debt finance: long-term loans, which are available to all organisations, and debentures, which tend to be used by incorporated businesses.

Long-term loans

Loans can be used for short-, medium- or long-term finance. Interest rates are likely to be different for different loan periods as these will need to be adjusted to take into account the higher risk associated with lending money for longer periods of time. Long-term loans are often for a specific purpose, such as the purchase of property, and the time period is affected by the life of the asset, the repayments required and the willingness of the lender to provide the loan. For many small businesses, these loans often take the form of a commercial mortgage on property. As with the other types of finance we have discussed, the availability of this source of finance is also heavily dependent upon the lender's assessment of the creditworthiness of the prospective borrower.

In the case of large companies, international groups and, in particular, multinationals, there is also the opportunity to raise funds from global financial markets.

DEBENTURES

Debentures refer to particular types of long-term loans that are limited to companies. Debentures are essentially long-term loan finance. The main difference between debentures and long-term loans is that debenture interest tends to be at a fixed (or coupon) rate and the repayment of the debenture principal tends to be at a fixed point in time, rather than periodically as would be the case during the term of a commercial mortgage or other long-term loan payable. Debentures are issued by the company raising the finance and can usually be traded on what are known as secondary markets. A secondary market is not an official market such as a securities exchange (e.g. the Australian Securities Exchange). The market for second-hand cars is a secondary market where we know that cars sell at prices well below the initial purchase price. Similarly, prices in the secondary market for the debentures being sold and bought will not be the same as the price at which they were first issued by the borrower. This variation is related to changes in interest rates over time. For example, if a debenture has a coupon rate of 8 per cent and the market rate for equivalent debt has fallen to 6 per cent, the price of this debenture in a secondary market will rise to a level where the effective interest rate becomes the prevailing market rate for debt of that type (i.e. 6 per cent). In virtually all debenture deeds, there is a right to repayment or appointment of a receiver if interest is not paid when due. The cost of this type of finance is similar to that for long–term loans and is affected by the market rate of interest, the security available and the risk involved. For this reason, they are more commonly seen in the financial statements of larger companies. For example, as at 30 June 2013 Woolworths had a form of debentures known as notes payable of $3.59 billion in long-term securities and $0.69 billion in Woolworths Notes.

STOP AND THINK 6

Why is it important to properly fund working capital?

Equity finance

The other major source of long-term finance is equity finance. Here we will look at organisational types, as this can have a major effect on both the type and amount of equity finance available.

7 **LEARNING OBJECTIVE**

Explain what is meant by equity finance and how it varies according to the type of business organisation

KEY CONCEPT

DEBT FINANCE – LONG TERM

Long-term debt finance is generally for a fixed period of time and interest rates can be higher than for short- or medium-term finance.

SOLE PROPRIETORSHIPS

In the case of a sole proprietorship the only sources of equity finance are those supplied by the owner and retained profits. In many small businesses, the amount of funds that the owner has available to invest is limited. This means that the only source of equity finance is retained profits. In a fast-growing business, it is unlikely that there will be sufficient retained profits to finance the firm's expansion. As such, sole proprietorships and many small businesses can become overly reliant on debt finance and, as we will see, this exposes them to more risk, as a downturn in the market or an increase in interest rates could dramatically impact their ability to service the debt. Unlike debt finance, equity finance has no limitations in terms of the use to which can be put.

PARTNERSHIPS

Partnerships, as the name implies, are organisations owned, and often managed, by a number of individuals. Partnerships are commonly used in the professions (e.g. doctors, dentists, lawyers, architects and, of course, accountants often work in partnership with one another). In essence, the sources of equity finance for partnerships are the same as for sole proprietorships; that is, money contributed by the owners and retained profits. As there are more people involved, more equity can be raised by a partnership from the contributions made by its owners.

NotarYES/Shutterstock.com

Partnerships are governed by a *Partnership Act*, and by case law. In general, the main difference between partnerships and sole proprietorships is that, in a partnership, the partners are jointly and severally liable. This means that if a partner cannot pay his or her share of partnership debts, the other partners will be required to cover any remaining debt owing. The other important difference is related to the division of profits; these must be divided among the partners in accordance with the partnership agreement.

We looked at the subject of partnerships in more detail in Chapter 2. For our purposes here, we can view partnerships as having the same sources of equity finance as sole proprietorships. The only difference is that they are likely to have access to a wider source of funds. In addition, there may be differences in relation to the availability of retained profits as some partners may leave more profits in the business than others. This will, of course, depend upon the individual partner's own personal financial requirements.

LIMITED COMPANIES

Limited companies have the advantage, from an investor's point of view, that the liability of the owners is limited to the amount they have invested in the company. As with partnerships and sole proprietorships, the major source of equity comes from the owners. However, in the case of limited companies, this is through the issue of ordinary shares.

ORDINARY SHARES

In the case of a company, the amounts in shareholders' equity represent the shareholders' interest in the company. Some amounts have been directly contributed by the shareholders when they initially subscribed to shares issued by the company. This is described as issued capital. The other amounts represent retained or undistributed profits and various reserves. Reserves can be created in a number of ways. However, one element common to all reserves is that there is *no cash* actually in them (i.e. reserves are not treasure chests filled with cash, precious metals and stones). While reserves are on one side of the balance sheet equation, cash appears as an asset on the other side of the equation. Thus, reserves are matched against unspecified assets that could include cash at bank and other assets such as property, plant and equipment.

You should now study the Woolworths financial statements in Appendix 1. The balance shows issued capital is $4522.7 million. Note 17 in the annual report discloses that the company has issued 1250 million shares. This is the book value of the share capital and does not represent the market value of a Woolworths shares. The market value is obtained from the price of the shares on a stock exchange such as the ASX. You might like to see what the current price of Woolworths' share and determine how much greater the total market value of those shares are in comparison to the book value as at 30 June 2013. The Woolworths financial statements show retained earnings as at 30 June 2013 of $4661.1 million.

As with any form of business, the other main source of equity capital is retained earnings or profits. Unlike a sole proprietorship or partnership, a company distributes its profits by way of dividends. The directors decide on the amount and timing of dividend payments, and until such time as a dividend is declared by directors, shareholders have no prima facie right to receive a dividend. Dividends can be paid during the year and/or at the end of the year. Interim dividends are paid during the year and final dividends are paid at the end of the year. Dividends are treated differently from drawings, which, as we have seen, are normally deducted from the owners' equity.

As discussed in Chapter 2, a company has the advantage over a sole proprietorship or a partnership in that it can, subject to any securities exchange guidelines in terms of secondary capital raisings and corporate governance principles, issue shares to whomever it wishes in whatever proportions it wishes. The shareholders do not have to take part in the management of the company, and in most large companies such as Woolworths, the vast majority of shareholders play virtually no part in the management of the company. They merely invest their money and take the risk that they will get better returns, in the form of their share of the profits, than they would by investing in fixed-interest investments. Ultimately, all the profits belong to the shareholders. Where profits are retained in the company and are not distributed to shareholders in the form of dividends, shareholders will still benefit from the returns, in the form of the future profits, and the higher share price that more than likely results from the company's reinvestment in itself.

PREFERENCE SHARES

8 LEARNING OBJECTIVE

Explain the criteria for classifying securities as either debt or equity, and apply this to different types of preference shares

Apart from ordinary shares, a company can also issue preference shares. Unlike an ordinary share, a preference share normally has a fixed dividend: even if more profits are made, the preference dividend remains the same. In addition, it normally carries a right to preference in the order of payment in the event of the company going into liquidation. Therefore, preference shares are less risky than ordinary shares and appeal to different types of investors.

The decision as to whether preference shares should be classified as equity or debt depends on the particular type of preference shares issued, and the rights attached to them. Remember that the definition of a liability includes a present obligation to sacrifice future economic benefits, so the existence of a present obligation is critical. The distinction between debt and equity can be clarified further by referring to the principle of substance-over-form approach, identified in the AASB *Framework* as essential. It means that a financial instrument is not classified as an equity instrument merely because it is called a preference share or a subordinated share or, indeed, any type of share! It is the substance of the financial instrument that determines whether it should be classified as debt or equity. This is important given the increased number of hybrid securities that are now being issued into financial markets.

To illustrate the application of the substance-over-form principle, we examine three types of redeemable preference shares with differing characteristics:

*   *Redeemable preference shares with a fixed redemption date*

    This imposes a contractual obligation on the issuer to redeem the preference share at the maturity date. Such an obligation is no different to that which exists with a loan. Therefore, these preference shares meet the definition of a financial liability and their balance sheet presentation would be as a liability.

*   *Redeemable preference shares that are redeemable on request by the holder*

    In this case, the redemption of these shares is dependent on the holder and AASB 132 *Financial instruments: presentation* requires such a share to be classified as a financial liability.

*   *Redeemable preference shares that are redeemable at the discretion of the issuer*

    These shares would not meet the definition of a financial liability because there is no present obligation for the issuer to redeem them. The issuer controls when, and indeed if, redemption will occur. However, where the issuer has formally informed the holders of such shares of its intention to redeem, the shares should be classified as debt and included with other financial liabilities.

Preference shares may also carry a right to dividends on a cumulative basis, meaning that, if the directors do not pay any dividends in any particular year, the preference shareholders will have a right to be paid that year's dividend and any others yet to be paid, before the ordinary shareholders receive any dividends. Some preference shares are participating preference shares, whereby they also receive a share of profits if the profit is over a specified amount.

The adoption of IFRSs in Australia meant that there was a need for some reclassification of securities due to the strict definition of financial liabilities under IFRS. If there is any termination or end date in a security contract then, under IFRS, it is generally classified as a liability. Many Australian reporting entities were concerned by this requirement when IFRS-compliant domestic accounting standards were first adopted. For example, many companies in Australia had issued resetting preference shares that often provided the holder with the right to convert such preference shares into ordinary shares of the issuer. Prior to 2005, most companies classified such shares as equity but, with the adoption of IFRSs, these shares had to be reclassified as debt until such time as they were converted to equity in the form of ordinary shares.

9.14 KEY CONCEPT

EQUITY FINANCE

This is long-term permanent finance and comes from three main sources: contributed capital, reserves and retained profits.

STOP AND THINK 7

Preference shares, rather than ordinary shares, are often favoured by retired people. Why do you think this is?

FINANCING STRUCTURES AND FINANCIAL RISK

The mix of debt finance and equity finance is known as gearing, or leverage, and it affects the financial risk of an entity. Basically, the more reliant a business is on debt finance – that is, the more highly geared it is – the greater the risk. The risk we are referring to here is that if interest rates go up or the profit margin comes down, the entity will not be able to pay interest or make the repayments due on its debt. There are, of course, advantages to being highly geared as well as disadvantages, as Example 9.3 illustrates.

9 LEARNING OBJECTIVE

Explain what is meant by gearing, and the effect this can have on returns to shareholders in a company

9.3 WORKED EXAMPLE

TWO COMPANIES

Ellenmere has equity capital consisting of 20 000 ordinary shares of $1 each. It has retained profits of $10 000 and $40 000 in loans on which interest at 3 per cent above bank base rate (which currently stands at 12 per cent) is due.

Roseview has equity capital consisting of 40 000 ordinary shares of $1 each. It has retained profits of $10 000 and $20 000 in loans on which interest at 3 per cent above bank base rate, that is, 15 per cent, is due.

Situation 1

Both companies make sales of $100 000, and their net profit before interest and tax is 10 per cent on sales.

The extracts from the statements of comprehensive income for the two companies are shown below:

	ELLENMERE	ROSEVIEW
	$	$
Sales	100 000	100 000
Less Costs	90 000	90 000
Net profit	10 000	10 000
Less Interest expense	6 000	3 000
Available for equity shares	4 000	7 000
Profit per share	0.20	0.17

The profit per share, which is normally referred to as the earnings per share, is arrived at by dividing the profit by the number of shares on issue. Thus, for Ellenmere, the profit of $4000 is divided by 20 000 shares to arrive at the profit per share of 20 cents. The ordinary shareholders of Ellenmere are getting a better return (20 cents per share) than the shareholders of Roseview (17 cents per share). This is despite the fact that both companies have the same sales, costs and net profit. The differences arise as a result of the financing structure, its effect on the interest charges and the remaining profit after interest.

Situation 2 – increased costs

In this situation, instead of making a net profit before interest of 10 per cent of sales, the companies find that they can only make 8 per cent.

In this case, the extracts from the statements of comprehensive income of the two companies are as follows.

	ELLENMERE	ROSEVIEW
	$	$
Sales	100 000	100 000
Costs	92 000	92 000
Net profit	8 000	8 000
Interest	6 000	3 000
Available for equity shares	2 000	5 000
Profit per share	0.10	0.13

The profit margin of both businesses has fallen by the same amount. As a result, the profit available for the equity shares has dropped in both cases. However, the effect on the profit per share is more dramatic in the case of Ellenmere than it is in the case of Roseview, due, once again, to the financing structure. Although in Situation 1 it looked as though Ellenmere had the better financing structure, we find from a shareholder's point of view that it is more vulnerable to a reduction in the profit margin than Roseview.

Situation 3 – increased interest rates

In this situation, the facts are the same as in Situation 2 above; that is, the net profit before interest is 8 per cent on the sales. However, in addition, the bank base rate moves to 13 per cent and the interest on the loans increases to 16 per cent.

In this case, the extracts from the statements of comprehensive income of the two companies would be as follows.

	ELLENMERE	ROSEVIEW
	$	$
Sales	100 000	100 000
Costs	92 000	92 000
Net profit	8 000	8 000
Interest	6 400	3 200
Available for equity shares	1 600	4 800
Profit per share	0.08	0.12

Once again, both businesses are affected by the change in circumstances. However, the effect of the rise in interest rates is greater, in terms of the return to the shareholders, in Ellenmere than it is in Roseview.

Effects of high gearing

Worked example 9.3 illustrates the effects of high gearing, which are to increase the returns to shareholders but, at the same time, make them more vulnerable to decreases in the profit margin. In addition, the returns of a highly geared company are also affected more by increases in interest rates than are those of a low-geared company.

On the other hand, a fall in interest rates is more beneficial to the shareholders of a highly geared company. Therefore, there is a trade-off between risk and return.

It is worth mentioning that the lower the share of the business that is financed by equity, the more difficult it is to raise debt as a source of finance. Banks will often include clauses in debt contracts which impose restrictive covenants on borrowers if the proportion of debt to equity increases beyond a specified level (e.g. the early repayment of borrowed funds). Such clauses mean that decisions on how much profit to retain, whether to revalue land and buildings, and so on, can have a significant effect on a company's ability to raise finance.

STOP AND THINK 8
What are the advantages and disadvantages of being highly geared?

SUMMARY

LEARNING OBJECTIVE 1

IDENTIFY AND EXPLAIN ACCOUNTS PAYABLE, PROVISIONS AND ACCRUALS

Accounts payable (or trade creditors) are sums owing at a point in time, the amounts of which are known. A provision is a liability of uncertain timing or amount. Accruals are liabilities to pay for goods or services that have been supplied but have not been paid, invoiced or payment formally agreed to with the supplier, including amounts due to employees (for example, amounts relating to accrued leave entitlements). While many accruals involve estimates, provisions are subject to a higher level of uncertainty.

LEARNING OBJECTIVE 2

EXPLAIN THE MEANING OF DEFERRED TAX LIABILITIES

Accounting for income tax required by AASB112 *Income taxes* gives rise to deferred tax liabilities which occur because of temporary differences between the tax value and the carrying value (for accounting purposes) of assets and liabilities, and tax losses.

LEARNING OBJECTIVE 3

DISCUSS THE CONCEPT OF MATCHING THE TYPE OF FINANCE WITH THE PURPOSE FOR WHICH IT IS TO BE USED

The finance that is used, and the period of that finance, should be matched to the period and purpose for which it is required.

LEARNING OBJECTIVE 4

EXPLAIN WHAT IS MEANT BY SHORT-TERM SOURCES OF FINANCE SUCH AS BANK OVERDRAFTS, TRADE CREDIT AND FACTORING

Conventionally, short-term finance is seen as finance for a period of less than one year. It should be used to finance short-term capital requirements, such as working capital requirements.

Trade credit

Trade credit is a form of short-term finance provided to a business by its suppliers. It has few costs and security is not required.

Factoring

Factoring provides short-term finance. Costs include an interest charge and a debt management charge. Finance is secured on the debtors and provided by a finance company specialising in factoring. The finance company collects payment from the debtors.

Bank overdrafts

A bank overdraft provides finance when it is needed to meet short-term cash flow needs. Costs include interest and, often, a set-up charge. In general, some form of security will be required – usually a fixed charge on certain assets or a floating charge on all assets.

LEARNING OBJECTIVE 5

EXPLAIN WHAT IS MEANT BY MEDIUM-TERM SOURCES OF FINANCE SUCH AS LOANS, HIRE-PURCHASE AND LEASES

Medium-term finance usually refers to finance for periods between one and 10 years.

Loans

Loans are generally made for a fixed purpose and a fixed period of time. They have set repayment dates, and costs include interest and set-up fees. They are normally secured on assets.

Hire-purchase

Hire-purchase is for a fixed period of time. Costs are in the form of interest charges. Ownership of the asset remains with the provider of the finance until all instalments are paid.

Leases

Leases are for a fixed period of time; the costs are in the form of interest charges. Security is related to the asset in question.

Types of leases

An operating lease: A lease where the underlying substance of the transaction is a rental agreement.

A finance lease: A lease where the underlying substance of the transaction is a financing arrangement.

LEARNING OBJECTIVE 6

EXPLAIN WHAT IS MEANT BY LONG-TERM SOURCES OF DEBT FINANCE SUCH AS LONG-TERM LOANS AND DEBENTURES

Long-term finance is generally for periods of 10 years or more.

Debentures are financial securities issued to raise funds for the borrower. The holder is entitled to receive periodic interest payments and repayment of the face value of the debenture at maturity.

Long-term loans are generally for a fixed period of time and interest rates can be higher than for short- or medium-term finance.

LEARNING OBJECTIVE 7

EXPLAIN WHAT IS MEANT BY EQUITY FINANCE AND HOW IT VARIES ACCORDING TO THE TYPE OF BUSINESS ORGANISATION

The main source of equity finance is from ordinary shareholders. Equity finance is long-term permanent finance and comes from three main sources: contributed capital, reserves and retained profits.

Equity providers earn a return from dividends and the appreciation in the price of the company's shares.

LEARNING OBJECTIVE 8

EXPLAIN THE CRITERIA FOR CLASSIFYING SECURITIES AS EITHER DEBT OR EQUITY, AND APPLY THIS TO DIFFERENT TYPES OF PREFERENCE SHARES

As the definition of a liability includes a present obligation to sacrifice future economic benefits, the existence of a present obligation is critical to deciding if a security is debt or equity. The distinction between debt and equity is also assisted by reference to the principle of substance over form. This approach is used in the AASB *Framework* where:

» Redeemable preference shares with a fixed redemption date are classified as debt
» Redeemable preference shares which are redeemable on request of the holder are classified as debt
» Redeemable preference shares which are redeemable at the discretion of the issuer are classified as equity.

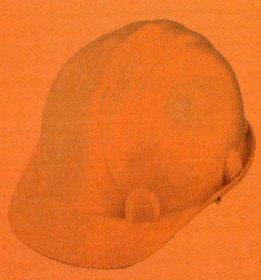

LEARNING OBJECTIVE 9

EXPLAIN WHAT IS MEANT BY GEARING, AND THE EFFECT THIS CAN HAVE ON RETURNS TO SHAREHOLDERS IN A COMPANY

'Gearing' is the term used to describe the use of debt. Worked example 9.3 illustrates the effects of high gearing, which include increasing the returns to shareholders while, at the same time, making them more vulnerable to decreases in the profit margin. In addition, increases in interest rates also affect the returns of shareholders in a highly geared company to a greater extent than returns of a low-geared company. In contrast, a fall in interest rates is more beneficial to the shareholders of highly geared companies. Therefore, there is a trade-off between risk and return.

REVIEW QUESTIONS

1   In your own words, describe what accounts payable (e.g. trade creditors) are and when they occur.

2   Why might accounting profit and taxable income differ?

3   What are the main differences between equity and debt finance?

4   What are the differences between drawings and dividends?

5   What does the term 'highly geared' refer to?

6   Which types of short-term finance require a business to provide some form of security?

7   What form of security is required for each of the forms of short-term finance discussed in this chapter?

8   What is a lease? Give an example.

9   Explain what is meant by equity finance and how it varies according to the type of business organisation using it.

10 Explain what is meant by the term 'factoring'.

11 What information is a bank likely to require before granting an overdraft to a business?

12 How does a hire-purchase agreement differ from a lease?

13 What is a debenture?

PROBLEMS FOR DISCUSSION AND ANALYSIS

1   Refer to the Woolworths 2013 financial report in Appendix 1 and answer the following in relation to the consolidated amounts.

    a   What is the value of trade and other payables?

    b   Calculate what percentage of total liabilities is made up by trade and other payables.

    c   What are the total liabilities in 2013?

    d   What is the level of liabilities to equity in 2013? In 2012?

    e   What is the level of interest-bearing debt to equity in 2013? In 2012?

2   Accruals are sums owing at a point of time, the amounts of which are not known with certainty. How would you estimate the liability for the following, and what points need to be considered?

    a   electricity

    b   council rates

    c   telephone

    d   water rates

    e   income taxes.

3 In each of the following situations, describe the way the transactions would be dealt with in the sole proprietor's financial statements and identify, where appropriate, the effect on the statement of comprehensive income and the balance sheet.

    a   Applied for a bank overdraft.

    b   Granted a bank overdraft of $10 000.

    c   Used the overdraft to pay a creditor; the bank was overdrawn by $4563.

    d   Paid annual insurance premium.

    e   Paid telephone rental.

    f   Advised by bank that the interest on the overdraft for the month was $100 and this amount had been deducted from the firm's bank account.

    g   Purchased land and settled with a cash payment and the balance by taking out a mortgage.

    h   Paid salaries.

    i   Bought equipment on credit.

    j   Made sales for the day of $300 cash and $400 credit.

    k   The sole proprietor withdrew cash for personal use.

    l   The sole proprietor contributed a truck to the business which had been previously purchased for personal use. This truck was bought before the sole proprietor commenced business.

    m   Paid accounts payable.

    n   Looked at new shop premises and made an offer to purchase them.

4 Big Bikes makes all bike purchases on credit. For the year ending 31 December accounts payable paid amounted to $3 000 124. Net bike purchases for the year amounted to $2 975 345 and the balance of accounts payable on 31 December was $200 376. What was the balance of accounts payable as at the beginning of the year on 1 January?

5 ABC Company depreciates its equipment at 20 per cent per annum, straight-line. The company is allowed, for tax purposes, to depreciate at 25 per cent per annum. Assume the company purchases an item of machinery for $100 000 on 1 July 20X3.

    Assume a tax rate of 30 per cent and an accounting profit of $100 000 each year.

    Required

    Prepare a statement for this machinery for the five years under the headings of:

    »   Tax payable

    »   Deferred tax payable

    »   Tax expense.

6 On 1 January 20X4 the Widget Company acquires a piece of equipment which costs $40 000 and has an estimated life of four years with no residual value. The equipment is to be written off at 25 per cent per annum, straight-line. Assume the operating profit for the next four years is $100 000 per annum (before the deduction of depreciation and tax). For tax purposes, the company is allowed to write off the asset over two years at 50 per cent per annum, straight-line. The tax rate is 50 per cent.

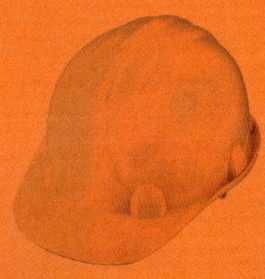

Set up a table with the following headings and fill in the blank spaces:

YEAR ENDING 31 DECEMBER	PROFIT BEFORE DEPRECIATION AND TAX	TAXABLE PROFIT AFTER TAX DEPRECIATION	TAX PAYABLE	TAXABLE PROFIT AFTER ACCOUNTING DEPRECIATION	TAX EXPENSE	DIFFERENCES BETWEEN TAX PAYABLE AND TAX EXPENSE
20X4						
20X5						
20X6						
20X7						
Total						

7   XYZ Ltd wishes to acquire a new widget machine. The machine costs $30 000 and is expected to have a useful life of five years and no residual value. As it is short of liquid funds, the company has approached a finance broker for help. It is offered two alternatives:

a   a loan of $30 000 with an annual reducing-interest component of 20 per cent, the principal of the loan to be paid in equal annual instalments over five years at the same time the annual interest payments are made

b   a hire-purchase agreement that requires the company to pay a monthly instalment of $799 over five years.

Given there are no other options available to the company, which proposition should it accept? Give reasons for your decision.

8   Winjet Ltd is a small coastal aircraft operator normally taking on charter work. In a bid to expand its business it wishes to purchase a second-hand Gulfstream jet for $10 million. Winjet does not have the funds to make a cash purchase and has approached a business broker to find the funds for the aircraft.

The broker submits two alternatives:

a   a loan of $10 million to be repaid over 10 equal annual repayments at the same time as the annual interest payments of 6 per cent are made on the capital sum

b   a hire-purchase agreement that requires Winjet to pay $398 000 per quarter over 10 years.

Assuming that Winjet's only option is to use the broker, which of the two choices should the company favour? Give reasons for your decision.

9   Bettause Ltd, maker of plastic mouldings, wishes to expand its business and will need additional capital to do so. A bank has offered the following options:

a   an overdraft with an interest rate set at 4 per cent above bank rate (the present bank rate is 8 per cent)

b   a term loan with an annual interest rate of 12 per cent

c   a 50 per cent holding by the bank in the company, achieved through the company issuing shares to the bank in exchange for cash.

Discuss the merits, or otherwise, of the three proposals.

10 The sub-prime lending crisis caused a meltdown in financial markets around the world and credit markets closed down as banks became increasingly reluctant to lend to other banks. Consequently, debt and equity funds became more difficult to access. Explain the meaning of this statement and include examples of companies that experienced difficulties as a result of the sub-prime lending crisis. What other sources of funds could be accessed if bank loans and equity financing are difficult to arrange?

11 Below is a brief balance sheet for ABC Ltd. You are a bank manager and ABC Ltd has approached you for a loan to expand its business. ABC Ltd makes chocolate products and has sales of approximately $300 000 per annum. What questions need to be asked before the loan is given or refused?

ABC LTD   BALANCE SHEET AS AT 31 DECEMBER 20X0

	$	$	$	$
Current assets				
Receivables		98 000		
Inventory		112 000		
Loan to supplier		50 000		
Total current assets			260 000	
Non-current assets				
Equipment	30 000			
Less Accumulated depreciation	(17 000)	13 000		
Vehicles	12 000			
Accumulated depreciation	(8 000)	4 000		
Total non-current assets			17 000	
Total assets				277 000
Current liabilities				
Accounts payable		33 000		
Taxation		5 000		
Bank overdraft		12 000		
Total current liabilities			50 000	
Total liabilities				50 000
Shareholders' equity				
Ordinary shares (88 000 shares @ $2.50)			220 000	
Retained profits			7 000	
Total shareholders' equity				227 000
Total liabilities and shareholders' equity				277 000

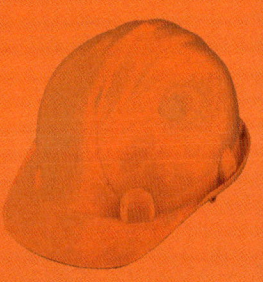

12 A friend has been to see the bank manager about borrowing some money to finance the acquisition of a new van and a new machine. The bank manager has said that, in view of the current financial structure of the company, the bank would not be prepared to provide funds unsecured. The latest balance sheet of the company is given below.

BALANCE SHEET

	$	$	$	$
Current assets				
Cash		15 000		
Inventory		36 000		
Total current assets			51 000	
Non-current assets				
Equipment	60 000			
Less Accumulated depreciation	(15 000)	45 000		
Vehicles	36 000			
Less Accumulated depreciation	(12 000)	24 000		
Total non-current assets			69 000	
Total assets				120 000
Current liabilities				
Accounts payable		7 500		
Taxation		10 800		
Bank overdraft		12 900		
Total current liabilities			31 200	
Non-current liabilities				
Bank loan		25 000		
Total non-current liabilities			25 000	
Total liabilities				56 200
Shareholders' equity				
Ordinary shares		60 900		
Retained profits		2 900		
Total shareholders' equity				63 800
Total liabilities and shareholders' equity				120 000

a   Advise your friend what alternative sources of finance are available and which would be appropriate for the purpose of buying a van and a new machine.

b   Explain why, in your opinion, the bank manager was not prepared to lend on an unsecured basis.

13 Read the then Australian Stock Exchange (ASX) company announcement 'New listing statement in relation to working capital'. Discuss why the company would be requested by the ASX to give such a report. Why is working capital so important?

NEW LISTING STATEMENT IN RELATION TO WORKING CAPITAL

In accordance with the requirements of the Australian Stock Exchange (ASX), we have been requested to provide a statement that ABB Grain Limited and its controlled entities (ABB Grain) have enough working capital to carry out its stated objectives. We have been engaged to provide an Investigating Accountant's Report for the Prospectus for ABB Grain in respect to its proposed listing on the Australian Stock Exchange. On the basis of the work we have completed as Investigating Accountant, we have not become aware of any matter that makes us believe that ABB Grain does not have enough working capital (or access to existing finance facilities to obtain further working capital) to carry out its stated objectives.

14 In each of the cases below, decide whether the leases described are finance or operating leases for a lessee. For cases (a) to (d) the lease is non-cancellable. Give your reasons.

a

Motor vehicle leased for	3 years
Fair value (cost)	$10 000
Lease rental	$230 per month
Total lease payments	$8 280
Estimated residual value	$6 000 (60%)
Implicit interest rate	18%
Present value of minimum lease payments (no guaranteed residual)	$6 500
Useful life in years	6 years
Lease term as a percentage of useful life	50%
Present value of minimum lease payments	65%

b Same particulars as in (a), except that this is the first time a motor vehicle has been leased. All previous vehicles have been purchased and sold three years later. (There is a workplace agreement that motor vehicles operated by employees must be no older than three years.)

Lease term as a percentage of useful life	50% or 100%
Present value of minimum lease payments	65%

c   Same particulars as in (a), but there is a guaranteed residual value of $6000. The present value of minimum lease payments, therefore, is $10 000.

Lease term as a percentage of useful life	50%
Present value of minimum lease payments	100%

d   Same particulars as in (a), but the lessee guarantees the lessor that he will make up any deficiency of the residual amount between $4000 and $6000. The maximum present value of minimum lease payments is $7700.

Lease term as a percentage of useful life	50%
Present value of minimum lease payments	77%

e   As in (d), except that there is no guaranteed residual and the lessee can cancel (subject to conditions) at any time.

Lease term as a percentage of useful life	50%
Present value of minimum lease payments	65%

Note to instructors: The following problems are considered more suitable for use in MBA courses. However, undergraduate courses may also find them useful.

15   Study the latest Woolworths' annual report in Appendix 1 and available at www.woolworths.com.au, and locate the note on operating leases and answer the following questions:

a   What would be the impact on the balance sheet if the proposed new standard on accounting for leases is adopted?

b   Will this have an impact on the borrowing capacity of Woolworths?

c   Think about which types of companies are likely to have large operating leases and identify three companies where the proposed new standard will have a significant impact on their financial statements.

16   Ben was planning to open a fish and chip shop. He has produced the following projections for the first year, based on his experience of this type of business and some careful research:

Sales	36 000
Cost of 10-year lease	30 000
Refurbishment	3 000
Equipment	20 000
Rent	2 000
Electricity	900
Wages	8 000
Personal drawings	5 000

Ben estimates that the costs of fish and other purchases required to make the sales target of $36 000 will be $12 000. He says that the equipment will last for five years and have no residual value. He has $40 000 in savings but is reluctant to invest all of that in the business. He has been offered a loan of $20 000 to help buy the lease, at an interest rate of 10 per cent per annum for the first year, with no repayments required during that year. After the first year, the rate will be 4 per cent above base rate. Base rate currently stands at 12 per cent. Alternatively, he can borrow money, using a bank overdraft at a rate of 17 per cent per annum.

a   Calculate what Ben's profit would be in the first year if he were to put in all his own money and use the bank overdraft to borrow anything else he needs.

   Hint: The receipts and payments have to be looked at in terms of their regularity and their timing.

b   Calculate what Ben's profit would be in the first year, assuming he takes the loan.

c   Calculate what Ben's profit would be in the second year, assuming he does not take the loan and sales and costs are the same as the first year.

d   Calculate Ben's profit in the second year, assuming he takes the loan.

e   Ben has asked you to advise him on the choice between the two financing alternatives. How would you advise him, and what reasons would you give?

ETHICS CASE STUDY

Jack is finance director for the New Horizons Company. The company has had declining profits for the past two years, and is in serious trouble in the current year. With just two weeks before year-end, the company is set to report a loss. If this occurs, it will be in default of a loan contract with its major bank, which will result in the bank appointing an official manager to begin winding up the company. At the end of the previous year the bank had been persuaded to allow the company another year to trade out of its difficulties after reporting a small loss. This is not likely to happen this year if the company reports a larger loss.

Jack has developed the following plan: New Horizons will sell $1 million worth of goods for $2 million to Close Encounters Ltd, which is a company run by his brother-in-law. The $1 million profit on the sale will allow New Horizons to report a modest profit for the year. At the same time, a put option will be given to Close Encounters, giving that company the right to sell the goods back to New Horizons in three months for $2 100 000. The goods will actually remain hidden from the company's external auditors in New Horizons' warehouse for the three months that they were 'sold' for.

Discuss

a   how the transaction with Close Encounters should be recorded

b   whether the bank would still be able to appoint an official manager if New Horizons records the transaction as a sale and reports a profit

c   whether Jack's plan is ethical.

SUGGESTED ANSWERS TO STOP AND THINK EXERCISES IN THE CHAPTER

1   Accounts payable (creditors) are sums owing at a point in time, the amounts of which are known. A provision is a liability of uncertain timing or amount. Accruals are liabilities to pay for goods or services that have been received or supplied but have not been paid, invoiced or payment formally agreed to with the supplier, including amounts due to employees (for example, amounts relating to accrued leave entitlements). While accruals involve estimates, provisions are subject to a higher levels of uncertainty.

2   Deferred tax liabilities arise because of temporary differences between the tax value and carrying value (for accounting purposes) of assets and liabilities, and tax losses. It represents the amount of future tax payable.

3   It is important to match the type of finance with the purpose of raising that finance because this will provide the greatest benefit to the business, and the least risk. Companies should borrow short-term finance for short-term investments and long-term finance for long-term investments. For example, borrowing over the short term for the purchase of land and buildings can be a mistake because the benefits from the land and buildings will flow to the business over the long term. Therefore, a short-term loan would need to be renegotiated well before the firm might contemplate disposing of the asset acquired with the loan.

4   The forms of short-term finance discussed in this chapter are as follows:

   Trade credit – where the company benefits from buying goods on credit.

   Factoring – selling receivables to another company and obtaining cash immediately.

   Bank overdraft – short-term borrowing from a bank or other financial institution.

5   The essential differences between an operating lease and a finance lease are as follows: (i) for an operating lease, the risks and rewards associated with ownership of the property remain with the lessor; (ii) with a finance lease, the risks and rewards of ownership transfer from the lessor to the lessee.

6   Working capital is the amount that is left when current liabilities are subtracted from current assets. In order to effectively operate a business, it is important to have adequate working capital. Many new businesses fail to properly plan for the working capital required to pay bills, offer credit to customers and allow inventories to be held. It is important for a firm to have sufficient funding (whether it is equity or long-term debt) to ensure that it can maintain its working capital at the required levels without getting into difficulties. Insufficient working capital can result in an inability to pay wages or accounts payable and can lead to unintended business failure.

7   Preference shares normally offer a fixed rate of dividend and generally meet the stable income needs of retirees. Ordinary shares do not provide for a dividend payment that is fixed each year. However, most companies endeavour to maintain a predictable level of dividend payments to shareholders.

8   The advantages of high gearing occur when the cost of interest is below the return on assets. Shareholders benefit when this is the case. Interest on debt is tax-deductible while dividends are not.

   Disadvantages relate to the risk of highly geared companies going bankrupt when interest rates increase. This happened to the formerly ASX-listed Bond Corporation in the late 1980s.

FINANCIAL STATEMENT ANALYSIS

LEARNING OBJECTIVES

At the end of this chapter, you should be able to:

1. discuss the information needs of the various users in relation to the analysis of financial statements
2. identify possible sources of external and internal information
3. explain the significance of profitability and risk in the analysis of financial statements
4. identify and apply trend analysis
5. identify and use common-size statements
6. identify the issues to be considered when choosing a benchmark for ratio analysis
7. identify and apply various ratios that can be used to assess profitability
8. identify and apply various ratios that can be used to assess efficiency
9. identify and apply various ratios that can be used to assess short-term solvency
10. identify and apply various ratios that can be used to assess long-term solvency
11. discuss the implications of the efficient markets hypothesis for financial statement analysis
12. explain the limitations involved in financial statement analysis.

INTRODUCTION

In previous chapters we considered the way in which accounting information is produced and what the components of financial statements mean. In this chapter we consider the statements themselves and, more specifically, the ways in which the financial statements can be analysed. This chapter is not intended to be comprehensive in its approach to financial analysis, but will offer some guidelines on the subject and provide you with some basic tools of analysis.

USERS' INFORMATION NEEDS

It is important to consider the needs of the person for whom the analysis is being undertaken or, in other words, the user group. By using this approach, it is possible to establish the form of analysis that is most appropriate to these needs. The user groups were discussed in Chapter 1.

The investor group

Among the resource providers are the investors, who were discussed previously as if they were a homogeneous group with similar needs. There are, however, different types of investors. For sole traders and partnerships, the investor is the owner or partner. The equivalent of this type of investor in a company is the ordinary shareholder. All these investors will be referred to from now on as equity investors. We need to establish what this group has in common, and what distinguishes the equity investor in a large company from his or her equivalent in a sole trader.

In general, equity investors take on all the risks associated with ownership and are entitled to any rewards after other prior claims have been met. For a sole trader the equity investor (the owner) is also likely to be heavily involved in the management and day-to-day running of the business. Where there is direct involvement, the owner's information needs are the same as those of managers. In the case of larger organisations, such as large private companies and all public companies, there is likely to be a separation of ownership and management as discussed in Chapter 1. For large businesses, the final accounts meet the information needs of the shareholders, who are, in the main, properly characterised by the term 'absentee owners'. In general, the smaller the organisation and the greater the direct involvement of the owners in the day-to-day running of the business, the less detail that is required in the accounts. However, the information required to meet the needs of equity investors is broadly the same, irrespective of the type of ownership involved. The needs of this group of users can be met with information about the following:

- profitability, especially future profitability
- management efficiency; for example, are assets being utilised efficiently?
- return on their investment
  - within the entity
  - compared with alternatives
- risk being taken
  - financial risk
  - business risk
- returns to owners
  - dividends
  - drawings, and so on.

Preference shareholders

Investors in some companies are able to purchase shares known as preference shares. These shares are generally seen as less risky than ordinary shares and, therefore, normally earn a smaller return. Although it is difficult to generalise the differences between these shares and ordinary shares (this varies from share to share), normally preference shareholders are entitled to a fixed rate of dividend and to repayment before ordinary shareholders in the event of the business being wound up. Because of the nature of these shares, these users are likely to be interested in:

- profitability, mainly future profitability
- the net realisable value of the assets
- the extent to which their dividends are covered by profit.

If we compare the needs of these two groups of investors, we see that preference shareholders are more likely to be interested in the extent to which profit is safe, rather than in the growth of the business. This is because, in most cases, only ordinary shareholders benefit from such growth. The preference shareholders' return is in the form of a dividend at a fixed rate, irrespective of the profits that are made.

Preference shares can either be in the form of equity or debt depending on their characteristics, as discussed in Chapter 9. Redeemable preference shares, which have a fixed redemption date, are regarded as debt, and dividends paid on such shares are classified as interest. Therefore, this type of preference share is similar to a long-term loan. Non-redeemable preference shares are repaid only if the business ceases to exist and sufficient funds are available. Therefore, such shares are similar to ordinary shares and are classified as equity.

We can now move on to look at other resource providers who are also users of accounting information.

Lenders

Lenders can be conveniently subdivided into three subgroups: short-term creditors, medium-term lenders and long-term lenders. These types of debt finance were discussed in Chapter 9.

Short-term creditors are normally trade creditors; that is, creditors which supply the business with goods on credit. Their areas of interest are:

- short-term liquidity or solvency
- net realisable value of the assets
- profitability and future growth
- risk (financial and business).

Medium-term lenders are usually banks and other financial institutions. Their areas of interest are:

- profitability (future profits providing cash for repayment of loans)
- security, and the nature of the security
- financial stability.

Long-term lenders have the same needs as medium-term lenders, unless they are secured lenders. A secured lender is one that has a legal charge over the assets of the business and can claim those assets if the business does not repay or service the loan in accordance with the lending agreement. The charge may be a fixed charge over a specific asset, such as land, or it may be a floating charge over all the assets in general but none specifically. A fixed charge gives the holder the right to seize that asset if the business defaults on its loan payments. The lender can then sell the asset to recoup the amount owed. A floating charge gives the holder a higher priority in liquidation than an unsecured creditor, but not the right to seize any specific asset. In the case of secured lenders, the areas of interest are as follows:

- risk, especially financial risk
- security: net realisable value of specific assets
- interest cover: how well their interest is covered by the profits being made.

These different types of lenders have broadly the same needs for information. It is the emphasis that changes, depending on whether the loan is short-term or long-term.

Employees

Employees are interested in judging their job security and assessing whether their wages are relatively fair. The collapse of Centro Properties Group in 2007 also highlighted the status of other employee entitlements, such as long service leave, if an entity goes into liquidation. This is another reason why employees have a vital interest in the financial health of their employer. Their areas of interest are:

- profitability: average profits per employee for the purposes of productivity bargaining
- liquidity: future trends in profit.

There has been considerable debate over the extent to which these needs are met by conventional accounts and whether a value-added statement would meet these needs better.

Analysts

Many investors rely upon the advice of analysts. Analysts may be employed in a number of different types of organisations such as superannuation funds, investment banks, stockbroking firms, large companies and many others. The analysts have a wide-ranging interest in all types of information about an entity – in a similar way to the investor/ ownership group.

Pincasso/Shutterstock.com

Auditors

Auditors are not normally seen as users of accounting information. However, in order to carry out an audit efficiently, they frequently carry out an analysis of accounts. The audit function was discussed in Chapter 2. For the purposes of planning and carrying out their audit, the auditors are interested in:

- trends in sales, profit, costs, and so on
- variations from the norm
- accounting policies.

Management

It is difficult to describe the needs of managers because they vary greatly from situation to situation. They require all of the above information, because they are likely to be judged on their performance by outside investors or lenders. In addition, they require detailed information on the performance of the business as a whole, and on its parts, to enable them to manage the business on a day-to-day basis. This information includes such items as profitability by major product, costs per product, changes in sales or component mix.

COMMON INFORMATION NEEDS

The lists of users needs in the previous section are not intended to be comprehensive. We have tried to give the reader a flavour of the differing types of information required by the various groups, and to indicate that some of this will not be provided by the annual accounts. At this stage we need to establish any common information needs and what other factors need to be considered.

Some common information needs that can be readily identified are profitability, liquidity and risk. The problem is how these are measured and how to judge good or bad performance. Before going on to discuss these specific issues in detail, let us first examine more closely the common information needs and look at the context in which the financial analysis is to be carried out.

The most obvious information that all these groups want is information about the profitability of the business. This can be divided into two components: past profitability and future profitability. One factor common to many groups is the requirement for information about financial risk and liquidity. Another theme that emerges is the return on the investment in the business. This has associated measures such as the riskiness of the return (dividend cover or interest cover). There are also information needs that are specific to particular user groups. A good example of these is the security measures used by lenders.

We will examine how the common needs can be analysed in some detail after we have established the context in which the analysis should take place.

> ### STOP AND THINK 1
> How do the needs of long-term lenders differ from those of equity investors?

The context for financial statement analysis

In analysis, you must take a wide view; it is not merely a mechanical exercise using various techniques. Below, we outline some of the factors that are directly relevant to analysis of business performance.

SIZE OF THE BUSINESS

The fact that a business is the size of Woolworths makes it less vulnerable to the decisions of people outside the organisation. For example, a banker might lend money to a small business at a rate of 3 or 4 per cent above base rate, whereas for Woolworths or BHP Billiton the rate would be much lower. Similarly, the banker is likely to ask for security from the small business whereas, with Woolworths, the name itself is enough security for the banker.

> **10.1**
> **KEY CONCEPT**
> ## FINANCIAL ANALYSIS
> Good financial analysis requires that the person for whom the analysis is being done is clearly identified, together with the purpose of the analysis. It is unlikely to be useful if it does not take into account as many relevant factors as possible.

RISKINESS OF THE BUSINESS

Besides size, the nature of the business needs to be taken into account. For example, a gold prospecting entity has a level of risk (and return) that is different from a bank's. Other factors that affect the risk, known as business risk, are reliance on a small number of products, degree of technological innovation, and vulnerability to competition.

ECONOMIC, SOCIAL AND POLITICAL ENVIRONMENT

Examples of the way in which the economic, social and political environment affects industry can be found in virtually any daily newspaper. For example, if the Australian dollar declines relative to the US dollar, imports and exports will be affected and businesses will gain or suffer accordingly. Changes in interest rates often have sharp effects on businesses that are financed by a large amount of borrowing (loans or overdrafts).

The effects of social and environmental issues have, in the past, been more subtle. However, in Chapter 1 we discussed the role of environmental and social issues, and the expanding practice of triple bottom line reporting. The impact of social and environmental issues on entities is reflected in a growing acceptance that profit is not the sole motivation for business, and must be balanced with a regard for the natural environment or ensuring full employment. Furthermore, when there is a price placed on carbon emissions either through a trading scheme or some type of tax, companies must allow for this cost. A carbon tax was introduced in Australia in July 2012. These social and environmental changes frequently coincide with political changes, although the natural environment is a good example of a social concern that is likely to transcend political changes. As mentioned in Chapter 1, investors can now choose to invest in 'green' companies, and many superannuation funds now offer members this choice.

INDUSTRY TRENDS AND THE EFFECTS OF CHANGES IN TECHNOLOGY

In order to make any judgements about the performance of a business, and more especially about the future, it is vital to understand which way the industry is headed. For example, the sub-prime lending crisis caused significant problems for financial institutions and a number failed from the fallout.

EFFECT OF PRICE CHANGES

Inflation indicators like the Consumer Price Index report movements in the general level of prices for a basket of goods and services – but the effect of price changes may be more specific. For example, the price of property in the early 2000s rose faster than the general change in prices. Over the last 50 or more years, several methods have been proposed for taking account of price changes in corporate reports, none of which has gained general acceptance. Although the perfect solution has not been found, the problem cannot be ignored. Even with a low rate of inflation of 5 per cent, what appears to be a gentle growth in sales is, in fact, a decline. It should be pointed out that, although we normally think of price changes in terms of increases, there are many examples where the effects of new technology, competition and economies of scale have led to reductions in price. The most obvious examples are in the electronics industries and the computer industry. For example, the most basic model of calculator cost approximately $25 at the start of the 1970s; an equivalent today costs less than $5.

2 **LEARNING OBJECTIVE**

Identify possible sources of external and internal information

PROJECTIONS AND PREDICTIONS

While we can all take a guess at the future, clearly there is a case for taking into account the opinions of those closely involved in the business and those who have expertise in the industry and in analysing likely economic trends. Financial analysis must, after all, relate not only to what has happened but also to what is going to happen.

Having looked at some of the factors that need to be considered, it should be clear that, although a set of accounts contains some of the required information, a lot more information will have to be obtained from other sources. These other sources of information can be conveniently divided into sources external to the business and those that are internal. Some examples are discussed below.

Sources external to the business

Sources of information external to the business include:

- *Government statistics.* These are available from the Australian Bureau of Statistics.
- *Trade journals.* These include journals specific to the trade, and more general professional or business journals such as *Business Review Weekly*.
- *Financial press.* A lot of information can be gleaned from the financial pages of quality newspapers (e.g. the *Australian Financial Review*) and from specialist publications (e.g. *The Professional Administrator*).
- *Databases.* There are now a number of on-line databases, which contain information about companies, industry statistics and economic indicators.

Bloomberg via/Getty Images

- *Specialist agencies.* These can provide an industry-wide analysis, general financial reports, credit-scoring services and many other services. Moody's Rating Agency is an example.

Most of these sources are now readily accessible in good libraries and through the use of various search engines on the Internet. However, some of the more specialist sources are more difficult to access, and much more expensive.

Sources internal to the business

CHAIRMAN'S STATEMENT

In the case of public companies, a chairman's statement is included with the annual accounts. It contains summarised information for the year, as well as some predictions for the future. The information should not be taken at face value because it is likely to reflect one point of view – which may be biased. The statement often highlights the positive side of the company's operations. As a leading banker commented, 'It is as important to ascertain what is left out as it is to ascertain what has been included'.

DIRECTORS' REPORT

This is a statutory requirement for all companies, and the information that is to be contained in it is laid down in the *Corporations Act*. The statutes, however, only lay down the *minimum* requirement, the result being that the minimum is normally all that is given.

BALANCE SHEET

This gives information about the company's financial position at a point in time and is only valid at that point in time. Given that the median time for publication by large companies is over three months after the balance sheet date (and thought to be at least 10 months for small companies) the information might have little bearing on the current position. The question of how timely the information is has a major bearing on what can be concluded from an analysis of the accounting information contained in the published accounts.

STATEMENT OF COMPREHENSIVE INCOME

As with the balance sheet, the information in the statement of comprehensive income is quite old by the time it is published. A further problem is that the information is summarised: this may disguise the weak performance of parts of the business because it is offset by the strong performance of others.

STATEMENT OF CHANGES IN EQUITY

The purpose of the statement of changes in equity is to report all owner changes to equity arising from distributions to equity holders and any sale or repurchase of shares from the equity holders.

STATEMENT OF CASH FLOWS

As discussed in Chapter 7, the requirements for the cash flow statement are set out in AASB 107 *Cash flow statements.* The statement of cash flows shows the gross cash inflows and outflows of a business. It normally shows the cash flows associated with the business's operating, financing and investing activities.

It has been argued that this statement will allow users to assess an organisation's ability to meet its obligations and continue to operate as a going concern. Chapter 7 gave some further information on cash flow statements and we studied the cash flow statement for Woolworths.

STATEMENT OF ACCOUNTING POLICIES

As we have seen, there are a number of different ways of dealing with items such as inventory. Is FIFO or average cost being used? For depreciation, is reducing-balance or straight-line being used? Many other items are subject to similar preconditions, so it is vital to understand the basis which has been adopted. This is included in the statement of accounting policies. Unfortunately, these statements are often so generalised that they mean little. It is not uncommon to find a statement on depreciation which says, 'depreciation is charged on the straight-line method over the useful life of the assets'. The problem with such a statement is that different assets have different lives and residual values. In fact, it is quite likely that similar businesses have different estimates for the *same* asset. This makes it difficult to compare one company with another, because the basis adopted affects the profits, balance sheet values, and so on. The problem of comparability is explained in Key concept 10.2.

KEY CONCEPT

COMPARABILITY

It is not sufficient that financial information is relevant and reliable at a particular time, in a particular circumstance or for a particular reporting entity. The users of general-purpose financial statements need to be able to compare aspects of an entity at one time and over time, and compare entities at one time and over time.

An important implication of this concept of comparability is that users need to be informed of the policies employed in the preparation of the general-purpose financial statements, changes in those policies and the effects of those changes.

Within the one business, the problem of comparability is to some extent alleviated by the requirement to follow the basic accounting concept of consistency, defined in Key concept 10.3.

KEY CONCEPT

CONSISTENCY

Consistency implies that the measurement and display of transactions and events need to be carried out in a consistent manner throughout an entity, and over time for that entity, and that there is consistency between entities in this regard.

NOTES TO THE ACCOUNTS

These are vital to any financial analysis because they contain the detailed information. Without this information, the level of analysis is likely to be superficial, especially in complex business organisations. Looking at financial statements without studying the notes would be like only reading the table of contents of a novel. You don't get the full story until you read the novel. The same is true for the notes that accompany the annual financial statements. However, users often find that the level of detail in the notes, their complexity and their technical language make it difficult to understand the treatment of various items in the accounts. The first note to the accounts is the statement of accounting policies discussed above.

AUDITOR'S REPORT

Every company that prepares a general-purpose financial report is subject to an annual audit of its accounts. Included in the accounts is a report from the auditors stating whether, in their opinion, the accounts show a 'true and fair' view. As far as financial analysis is concerned, this report is best treated as an exception report: that is, unless it is qualified in some way, no account needs to be taken of it.

It is worth mentioning that, for most bankers, an auditor's report does add credibility to the figures. It does not, however, mean that the accounts are correct in their details. Quite often, the report contains a number of disclaimers in relation to certain figures. The auditor's report was discussed in Chapter 2.

STOP AND THINK 2

What sources of information outside the business are available to you and how would you use this information in your analysis?

THE COMMON NEEDS EXPLAINED

We have identified common needs for information about profitability, liquidity, financial risk and so on, but before we can carry out any analysis we need to know what is meant by these terms. We will therefore discuss what each term means and identify what we are trying to highlight in our analysis. For this purpose we will use the example of Jack Pty Ltd, which was introduced in Chapter 2, and is reproduced in Worked example 10.1.

3 LEARNING OBJECTIVE

Explain the significance of profitability and risk in the analysis of financial statements

WORKED EXAMPLE 10.1

JACK PTY LTD

STATEMENT OF COMPREHENSIVE INCOME FOR THE YEAR ENDED 30 JUNE 20X4

	NOTES	THIS YEAR		LAST YEAR	
		$	$	$	$
Sales	1		60 000		45 000
Cost of sales			40 000		30 000
Gross profit			20 000		15 000
Distribution costs	2	3 000		2 500	

	NOTES	THIS YEAR		LAST YEAR	
		$	$	$	$
Administration costs	2	11000	14000	9000	11500
Profit before taxation			6000		3500
Taxation	3		2600		1400
Profit after taxation			3400		2100
Other comprehensive income					
Gain on property revaluation			15000		nil
Total comprehensive income for the year			18400		2100

Profitability

To assess profitability, it is obvious that the starting point is the statement of comprehensive income. Where a company elects to prepare an income statement and a statement of comprehensive income, it is important to look at both statements in order to understand the changes during the period from all sources including the remeasurement of assets and liabilities. Before looking at the information provided by the statement of comprehensive income, we need to establish what information is required.

We need some sort of comparison. Is the business more profitable from its operations (i.e. revenues less expenses from operations) than it was last year? Is it more profitable than a similar business, or even a dissimilar business? Each of these questions requires us to measure the profit relative to something else. The last question cannot be answered by looking at one set of statements. We need to compare a number of different businesses, and to do this we have to make sure that the accounts are comparable. Are assets being depreciated over the same time period? The shorter the life of the asset, the greater the charge, and the smaller the final profit figure. It is for these comparisons that the accounting policies statement is required.

We will look at comparisons over time within Jack Pty Ltd. The business made more profits this year, when it earned $6000 profit before taxation, as compared to last year when the figure was only $3500. It is the profit from operations (whether it is reported in a single statement of comprehensive income or in a separate income statement) that we focus on and not the total comprehensive income. This is because we are assessing the performance of Jack's operations and not the impact of asset/liability remeasurements on the overall position of Jack Pty Ltd. The question is whether it is more profitable because it is selling more – $60000 this year compared with $45000 last year – or whether it is more efficient, or whether it is a combination of the two.

We can go some way to answering this by working out what the increase in sales was and what the increase in profit was. In this case, the sales increased by 33 per cent, as follows:

$$\text{sales increase} = \$60\,000 - \$45\,000$$

$$\text{percentage increase} = \frac{\$15000}{\$45000} \times 100 = 33\%$$

The profit, however, increased by over 70 per cent:

$$\text{profit increase} = \$6000 - \$3500$$

$$\text{percentage increase} = \frac{\$2500}{\$3500} \times 100 = 71\%$$

Thus, we have discovered that not only is Jack making more profit by selling more items but it is also making a greater profit on each sale. However, we do not know whether this seemingly favourable change is because this year was a good year or last year was a bad year, nor do we know whether Jack has had to invest a lot of money in order to increase the profitability. The former question can only be satisfactorily answered by comparisons over a longer period than two years, and then comparing Jack Pty Ltd with a similar business in the same industry. In the case of a small company, the question about investment can, perhaps, be answered by determining the return on investment, as represented by the profit. This then requires us to ask: what is the amount invested? Often in a small business the major investment made by the owner is the time spent in the business. However, for a public company, there is normally very little relationship between the amount of equity shown in the accounts and the amount you would have to pay to buy the company.

While not ignoring those problems, we can, for the present, look at the statement of changes in equity and the balance sheet, reproduced below, as a rough guide in the absence of any other information. We can see that, in this case, the investment in the form of capital and reserves has changed from $74 500 last year to $96 300 this year. These changes consist of the profit for the period, $3400, less dividends of $2600, the issue of $6000 of new share capital, and an increase of $15 000 to the valuation of land – as reported in the statement of comprehensive income. The change to the valuation of the land is a remeasurement of an asset rather than a profit from the operations of the business and is not relevant when assessing the operations of the business. However, the revaluation is included in total comprehensive income and would be relevant when comparing total comprehensive income across different entities. However, as revaluing property is optional under AASB 116 *Property, plant and equipment* one would need to be careful about such comparisons. We use the profit figure in most of the ratios in this chapter.

JACK PTY LTD
STATEMENT OF CHANGES IN EQUITY AS AT 30 JUNE 20X4

	SHARE CAPITAL	REVALUATION SURPLUS	RETAINED EARNINGS	TOTAL
	$000	$000	$000	$000
Balance at 1 July 20X3	64 000	6000	4500	74 500
Dividends			(2600)	(2600)
Issue of share capital	6000			6000
Total comprehensive income for the year		15 000	3400	18 400
Balance at 30 June 20X4	70 000	21 000	5300	96 300

JACK PTY LTD
BALANCE SHEET AT 30 JUNE 20X4

	NOTES	THIS YEAR		LAST YEAR
		$	$	$
Assets				
Current assets				
Cash at bank		3 500		2 000
Accounts receivable		11 000		4 000
Inventory	7	10 000		7 000
Total current assets			24 500	13 000
Non-current assets				
Equipment	5	10 000		11 000
Land and buildings	6	70 000		56 000
Total non-current assets			80 000	67 000
Total assets			104 500	80 000
Liabilities				
Current liabilities				
Accounts payable		4 000		3 000
Taxation	3	2 600		1 400
Dividends	4	1 600		1 100
Total current liabilities			8 200	5 500
Non-current liabilities			–	–
Total liabilities			8 200	5 500
Net assets			96 300	74 500
Capital and reserves				
Share capital	8	70 000		64 000
Retained profits	9	5 300		4 500
Reserves	10	21 000		6 000
Total capital and reserves			96 300	74 500

Before leaving the question of profitability, we need to discuss the future profitability of the business because this was identified as a common need for many users. The fact that a company has been profitable is comforting, but if you want to make a decision about whether to buy or sell a business you need information about the future, not the past. This information is not contained in the statement of comprehensive income, although it could be argued that information about the past is the best guide to the future. In practical terms, the only way you can form an opinion about the future is by using a combination of information, including past profits, knowledge of the industry, predictions about the economy and many other factors. When estimating future profits, the revaluation of land is not relevant because, as stated above, it is a remeasurement of an asset and not profit arising from the company's operations.

SUMMARY OF PROFITABILITY INFORMATION NEEDS

Profitability requires comparisons:

- over time
- with other businesses.

Profitability relates to:

- the past, for evaluation
- the future, for prediction.

Financial and business risk

Business risk relates to the type of business and is impacted by many factors including prices, costs, competition and so on. It is generally riskier to be in the mining industry than, say, banking. Financial risk refers to the amount of debt and equity on a balance sheet. The area of financial risk (or solvency) was discussed in Chapter 9. It is of vital importance: there are many cases where a business has gone bankrupt because of cash flow problems, even though it was profitable. There are also cases where two companies in the same line of business produce dramatically different results purely because of the way they are financed. For example, if a business makes a return of 15 per cent on every dollar invested and it can borrow money at 10 per cent, it is worthwhile for the business to borrow money because the excess return goes to the owners. However, there is some risk involved in such a course of action because the business will lose if the interest rate rises to, say, 17 per cent and it is still making only 15 per cent. This caused problems for many businesses in the late 1980s and early 1990s. A way of measuring the financial risk is to look at the balance sheet of a business and identify the amount of debt finance (loans, debentures, bank overdrafts and other borrowings) and compare this with the amount of equity finance (owners' capital, retained profits and reserves). The term 'leverage' is used to describe the amount of debt in a balance sheet.

In Australia, debt finance does not normally exceed equity finance, although the extent to which this generalisation holds true depends on the size and nature of the business. This is largely as a result of the banks' policy of lending on a dollar-for-dollar basis; that is, for each dollar of your money that you invest in the business the bank lends a dollar. While this is not a hard-and-fast rule, it is used as the benchmark by bank managers in Australia. It is interesting that other countries adopt different benchmarks. For example, banks in Germany and Japan tend to lend well above the one-for-one norm.

In the case of Jack Pty Ltd there is no long-term borrowing; there isn't even a bank overdraft. This might be a good thing as the company is making only $6000 on the shareholders' equity of $96 300 capital invested of over $75 000. This is less than 10 per cent, but it should be compared with the rate at which money could be borrowed.

Turning now to short-term solvency: a company has to maintain sufficient assets to meet its commitments as they fall due. The major area for concern is the short term, which is generally taken to be one year. This is convenient as it fits the definition used for current assets and current liabilities; therefore, we have a suitable measure which is apparent in the balance sheet. For example, Jack Pty Ltd has current assets of $24 500 and current liabilities of only $8200. It has to reserve enough funds in the next year to meet its commitments in that year.

One of the problems that arises with this measure is that 'current' can mean due tomorrow or due in 12 months. In the case of some current assets (e.g. inventory), the asset first has to be sold and then the money has to be collected. Another problem is the question of what is the correct level of current assets for the business. If, for example, there is a lot of cash, this is hardly an efficient use of resources. In the case of Jack, the amount of $3500 in the bank may be far in excess of real needs. There is also the question of whether $11 000 tied up in accounts receivable is excessive on sales of $60 000 – especially if we compare this to last year where the accounts receivable were $4000 on sales of $45 000.

Other problems with interpreting the information about short-term solvency arise if we try to compare different businesses. For example, an aircraft manufacturer has different requirements from a food wholesaler. Even within the same industrial sector, the needs differ. For example, a whisky distiller has different needs from a brewer: whisky has to be matured over years, whereas beer is produced in a few months and has a limited shelf life.

SUMMARY OF FINANCIAL RISK INFORMATION NEEDS

- Financial risk involves long-term and short-term solvency.
- Requirements and norms differ widely from industry to industry.

The general conclusion to be drawn is: analysis of the financial statements is only a small part of the story; that analysis needs to be put into a wider context of knowledge of the industry and the environment. The maxim that a little learning is a dangerous thing applies as much to business analysis as it does elsewhere. With this point in mind, we can now look at some of the techniques that are used to analyse financial information.

STOP AND THINK 3

Explain, briefly, the difference between financial risk and business or commercial risk.

TECHNIQUES OF ANALYSIS

Many techniques are used in financial analysis: they range from simple techniques, such as studying the financial statements (as we have just done) and forming a rough opinion of what is happening, to sophisticated statistical techniques. It should be pointed out that this rough analysis, based on 'eyeballing' the accounts, is vital: it forms the base on which the more sophisticated techniques are built. If, for example, we fail to notice that a business has made a loss for the past few years, the application of the most sophisticated techniques will not help, because we have failed to grasp an essential point.

We will examine some of the simpler techniques. The choice of technique is, once again, a function of what you are trying to do and the purpose of your analysis. For example, managers and auditors might be interested in establishing any variations from past norms and explaining these and, where necessary, taking appropriate action. For a shareholder in a large company, such an analysis, even if it were possible, would be inappropriate as no action could be taken and the level of detail is too specific.

Comparison of financial statements over time

A simple comparison of the rate and direction of change over time can be very useful. This can be done both in terms of absolute amount and in percentage terms. Both are normally required in order to reach any conclusions. For example, a 50 per cent change on $1000 is less significant than a 50 per cent change on $50 000. If you have only $1000 to start with, a change of $500 is significant. It is not only the absolute amount, but also the amount relative to other figures, that is important.

The period of time chosen is also worth considering. Too short a period will not be informative. This was the case with Jack where we could only say that the profit had increased but had no idea whether that was part of a trend or whether it was because last year was a particularly bad year. Consider the results of companies in the late 1990s and early 2000s compared to the period starting in 2007–08 with the sub-prime lending fiasco; the economy in Australia changed dramatically in this period from strong growth to recession. Finally, it must be borne in mind that other changes might have affected the figures; for example, the business might have decided to depreciate its vehicles over three years instead of four. Having taken account of these warnings, let us now look at how we can make the comparisons.

Trend analysis

Trend analysis is normally used for periods of more than two or three years in order to make the results easier to understand and interpret. It involves choosing a base year and then plotting the trend in sales, profits, or whatever from then on. We will illustrate the use of trend statements with statements of comprehensive income, but it can apply to other statements too.

4 LEARNING OBJECTIVE

Identify and apply trend analysis

10.4 KEY CONCEPT
TREND ANALYSIS

In trend analysis, the choice of an appropriate base year is vital. If the base year chosen is not typical the resultant analysis will be, at best, extremely difficult and, at worst, actually misleading.

10.2 WORKED EXAMPLE
XYZ LTD

We will use the financial statements for XYZ Ltd to illustrate the trend analysis technique.

XYZ LTD
STATEMENTS OF COMPREHENSIVE INCOME

	20X1 $000	20X2 $000	20X3 $000	20X4 $000	20X5 $000
Sales	12 371	13 209	16 843	14 441	13 226
Cost of sales	11 276	11 896	14 818	12 595	13 017
Operating profit	1 095	1 313	2 025	1 846	209
Interest charges	215	252	460	768	676
Pre-tax profit	880	1 061	1 565	1 078	–467
Taxation	464	529	875	579	–2
Net profit after tax	416	532	690	499	–465
Other comprehensive income	nil	nil	nil	nil	nil
Total comprehensive income for the year	416	532	690	499	–465

If we take the cost of sales, it is clear from a casual examination of the figures that it rises in 20X1 and 20X2 to a peak in 20X3, after which it falls in 20X4. This is shown as a graph in Figure 10.1. As you can see, the information in the graph is limited; it reflects what we have already found. To make any sensible comment, we need to see how these costs are behaving in relation to other factors. This could be in relation to another item in the statement of comprehensive income such as sales, or in relation to the costs in a comparable company. To make the latter comparison, however, we first have to find some common means of expression because the companies being compared are unlikely to be exactly the same size. One way of doing this is to use index numbers to express the figures we are looking at and the way in which they change from year to year.

FIGURE 10.1 COST OF SALES FOR XYZ LTD, 20X1–X5

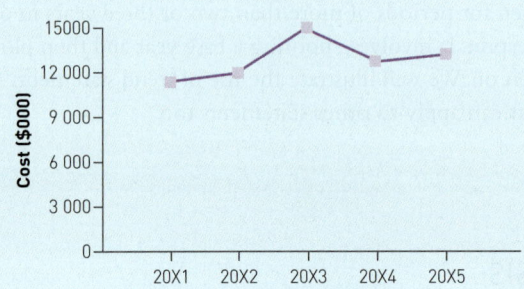

Adapted from Berry A. & Jarvis R., *Accounting in a business context*, Thomson, 1997, pp. 249, 252, 253 & 254

XYZ LTD
STATEMENTS OF CHANGES IN EQUITY

	SHARE CAPITAL $000	RETAINED PROFITS $000	TOTAL $000
Balance at 1 July 20X0	1584	1281	2865
Dividends		(164)	(164)
Total comprehensive income for the year		416	416
Balance at 30 June 20X1	1584	1533	3117
Dividends		(185)	(185)
Issued shares	152		152
Total comprehensive income for the year		532	532
Balance at 30 June 20X2	1736	1880	3616
Dividends		(336)	(336)
Share buyback	(243)		(243)
Total comprehensive income for the year		690	690
Balance at 30 June 20X3	1493	2234	3727
Dividends		(387)	(387)
Shares issued	485		485
Total comprehensive income for the year		499	499
Balance at 30 June 20X4	1978	2346	4324
Dividends		(123)	(123)
Total comprehensive income for the year		(465)	(465)
Balance at 30 June 20X5	1978	1758	3736

INDEX NUMBER TRENDS

As with other forms of trend analysis, this technique is normally used for periods of more than two or three years. It is intended to make the results easier to understand and interpret. An index number is determined by choosing a base year, setting that base year at 100 and expressing figures for all other years in terms of that index.

Using the example of the sales of XYZ Ltd, if we took 20X1 as the base year and set that at 100, we would calculate the index for 20X2 as follows:

$$\frac{20X2 \text{ sales}}{20X1 \text{ sales}} \times 100 = \frac{13209}{12371} \times 100 = 107$$

For 20X3 the calculation would be:

$$\frac{20X3 \text{ sales}}{20X1 \text{ sales}} \times 100 = \frac{16843}{12371} \times 100 = 136$$

Using the same formula, we can find the index for each of the other years and then study the sales trend. In this case the figures are:

20X1, 100; 20X2, 107; 20X3, 136; 20X4, 117; 20X5, 107

We can do the same with the figures for the cost of sales and the profit and then analyse these trends. In the case of sales, we can see that they peaked in 20X3 and then declined in 20X4 and 20X5. This can be seen more easily in the following table, which reports the trend numbers for the statement of comprehensive income for XYZ for the five years. Other numbers which are significant are the decline in sales in 20X5 by more than the decline in cost of sales; this is the main reason for the loss in 20X5. The interest charges have also risen substantially over the period.

XYZ LTD
STATEMENTS OF COMPREHENSIVE INCOME

	20X1 %	20X2 %	20X3 %	20X4 %	20X5 %
Sales	100	107	136	117	107
Cost of sales	100	105	131	112	115
Operating profit	100	120	185	169	19
Interest charges	100	117	214	357	314
Pre-tax profit	100	121	178	122	−53
Taxation	100	114	189	125	0
Profit after tax	100	128	166	120	−118
Other comprehensive income	0	0	0	0	0
Total comprehensive income for the year	100	128	166	120	−118

PERCENTAGE CHANGES

Another technique used in trend analysis is to identify the percentage change from year to year and then examine the trends in it. For example, if we look at the sales we find that the change from

20X1 to 20X2 was 7 per cent, while that from 20X2 to 20X3 was 29 per cent. These figures are calculated as follows:

$$\frac{\text{this year's sales}}{\text{last year's sales}} \times 100 = \frac{13209}{12371} \times 100 = 107$$

that is, an increase of 7 per cent.

Once again, it should be pointed out that these trends are of most use if they are compared with other trends, either in the business itself or in the industry. You should also bear in mind that percentage increases are often illusory because they could merely be reflecting the increase that would be expected as a result of the prevailing rate of inflation.

Common-size statements

In examining accounts, we often encounter large numbers; these are more digestible if they are presented as **common-size statements**. This technique, as the name implies, deals with the problem of comparing companies of different sizes. It involves expressing the items in the balance sheet, for example, as percentages of the balance sheet total.

This is illustrated by looking again at XYZ Ltd, the balance sheets of which are reproduced below. We can derive some information by examining the balance sheets, but it is not easy to identify exactly what is happening. For example, why has the land and building account gone up in 20X3 by a greater amount than the other non-current assets? Where did the intangibles come from, and what are they? These questions can often be answered, in part at least, by using the detailed information contained in the notes to the accounts.

5 LEARNING OBJECTIVE

Identify and use common-size statements

XYZ LTD
SUMMARY BALANCE SHEETS

	20X1 $000	20X2 $000	20X3 $000	20X4 $000	20X5 $000
Assets					
Current assets					
Cash	400	464	183	15	41
Accounts receivable	2 259	2 389	3 012	2 776	2 508
Inventory	3 645	3 952	3 903	3 289	3 255
Total current assets	6 304	6 805	7 098	6 080	5 804
Non-current assets					
Plant and equipment	875	849	959	863	767
Land and buildings	639	660	682	1070	1103
Other non-current assets	450	554	486	663	683
Intangibles	0	0	470	451	460
Total non-current assets	1964	2 063	2 597	3 047	3 013
Total assets	8 268	8 868	9 695	9 127	8 817
Liabilities					
Current liabilities					
Bank overdraft	0	3	86	427	663

	20X1 $000	20X2 $000	20X3 $000	20X4 $000	20X5 $000
Accounts payable	3701	3706	4842	3311	4277
Taxation	110	415	196	44	48
Dividends	121	137	224	225	1
Total current liabilities	3932	4261	5348	4007	4989
Non-current liabilities					
Deferred tax	922	843	320	400	0
Loans	297	148	300	396	92
Total non-current liabilities	1219	991	620	796	92
Total liabilities	5151	5252	5968	4803	5081
Net assets	3117	3616	3727	4324	3736
Shareholders' equity					
Share capital ($1 ordinary shares)	1584	1736	1493	1978	1978
Retained profits	1533	1880	2234	2346	1758
Total shareholders' equity	3117	3616	3727	4324	3736

The problem when looking at standard balance sheets is that the figures often disguise what is really happening. If we convert the statements to some common measure, the underlying trends become clearer. We could take, for example, the share capital for 20X1 and express it as a percentage of the total assets. We find that it is 19 per cent in that year compared with 20 per cent in 20X2. To calculate this we divided the share capital figure by the total assets and then multiplied the result by 100. Thus, for 20X3 we have:

$$\frac{\text{share capital}}{\text{total assets}} \times 100 = \frac{1493}{9695} \times 100 = 15\%$$

Following this procedure for all items in the balance sheets produces common-size statements as follows:

XYZ LTD
COMMON-SIZE BALANCE SHEETS

	20X1 %	20X2 %	20X3 %	20X4 %	20X5 %
Assets					
Current assets					
Cash	5	5	2	0	0
Accounts receivable	27	27	31	31	29
Inventory	44	45	40	36	37
Total current assets	76	77	73	67	66
Non-current assets					
Plant and equipment	11	10	10	9	9

	20X1 %	20X2 %	20X3 %	20X4 %	20X5 %
Land and buildings	8	7	7	12	12
Other non-current assets	5	6	5	7	8
Intangibles	0	0	5	5	5
Total non-current assets	24	23	27	33	34
Total assets	100	100	100	100	100
Liabilities					
Current liabilities					
Bank overdraft	0	0	1	5	8
Accounts Payable	45	42	50	36	49
Taxation	1	5	2	0	0
Dividends	1	1	2	2	0
Total current liabilities	47	48	55	45	57
Non-current liabilities					
Deferred tax payable	11	9	3	4	0
Loans	4	2	3	4	1
Total non-current liabilities	15	11	6	8	1
Total liabilities	62	59	62	53	58
Net assets	38	41	38	47	42
Shareholders' equity					
Share capital ($1 ordinary shares)	19	20	15	21	22
Retained profits	19	21	23	26	20
Total shareholders' equity	38	41	38	47	42

One of the many things that we can see from an analysis of these statements is that the current assets declined over the period, from 76 per cent of total assets in 20X1 to only 66 per cent in 20X5. At the same time, the current liabilities increased from 47 per cent to 57 per cent. By 20X5 the bank overdraft had risen to its highest level ever and the business had little cash. It should be noted that, with this technique, the choice of the base amount is just as important as it was with trend analysis.

Common-size statements can be applied as easily to the statement of comprehensive income as to the balance sheet. In the case of the statement of comprehensive income, it is usual to express all items as a percentage of sales, as illustrated below:

XYZ LTD
COMMON-SIZE STATEMENTS OF COMPREHENSIVE INCOME

	20X1 %	20X2 %	20X3 %	20X4 %	20X5 %
Sales	100	100	100	100	100
Cost of sales	91	90	88	87	98

	20X1 %	20X2 %	20X3 %	20X4 %	20X5 %
Operating profit	9	10	12	13	2
Interest charges	2	2	3	6	5
Pre-tax profit	7	8	9	7	−3
Taxation	4	4	5	4	0
After-tax profit	30	40	40	30	−30
Other comprehensive income	0	0	0	0	0
Total comprehensive income	3	4	4	3	−3

This statement is self-explanatory. Note the obvious rounding errors which occur when working in whole numbers. An item that is worth highlighting is that the cost of sales in 20X5 squeezed the operating profit down to only 2 per cent return on sales in a year when the interest charges were in excess of 5 per cent of sales. This illustrates the risk of high levels of debt, referred to earlier in the chapter when discussing financial risk. There could be several reasons why the cost of sales as a percentage of sales has increased. Recessionary conditions in the economy could have squeezed margins; new competitors or a price-cutting war could have reduced selling prices. Consider the impact on the price of computers caused by the development of the Apple Macintosh computer. Again, we need to consider the results for XYZ Ltd together with other information.

10.5 KEY CONCEPT

COMMON-SIZE STATEMENTS

Common-size statements express all items in the financial statement as a percentage of one significant item in the relevant financial statement (such as total assets for the balance sheet). It allows for a fast review of the financial statements and fast detection of any significant changes.

We have not prepared common-size statements for the statement of changes in equity or the cash flow statement but they would be prepared using the same principles.

Common-size statements and the other techniques that we have examined so far have largely ignored the relationship between any two components of the financial statements of a business. Other techniques of analysis are available which look at the relationship between items in the balance sheet, the statement of comprehensive income, the statement of changes in equity, and the cash flow statement. The most common of these techniques is known as ratio analysis and this is explored more fully in the following section.

Ratio analysis

Ratio analysis is explained in virtually every introductory accounting textbook, and most students have little difficulty in calculating ratios. However, many students find that they have extreme difficulty with understanding what the ratios mean once they have been calculated. Because of this, we will not deal extensively with all the possible ratios that can be calculated; instead we will concentrate on the relationships that the ratios express. This approach will increase your understanding of the reasons for calculating these ratios and enable you to interpret results.

Table 10.1 (page 325) gives a list of ratios often used in analysis, together with an indication of their significance. We compute the ratios for XYZ Ltd to illustrate the calculations involved. We have used 20X4 figures from XYZ Ltd to illustrate the calculations involved, as 20X5 results show a loss. However, we also report the ratios for 20X5 and will comment on the comparison of 20X4 with 20X5. We assume a tax rate of 40 per cent for the calculations. You should refer to the formulas used in this book (as reported in Table 10.1) as you work your way through this section of the chapter.

Some ratios only express relationships between items in the balance sheets, while some ratios are only based upon items in the statements of comprehensive income. Finally, some ratios combine information from both these statements, the statement of changes in equity and the statement of cash flows – which is presented below for XYZ Ltd for the years 20X4 and 20X5:

XYZ LTD
CASH FLOW STATEMENTS

	20X4 $000S	20X4 $000S	20X5 $000S	20X5 $000S
Cash flow from operating activities		226		423
Cash flow from investing activities				
Payments to acquire non-current assets	(800)		(85)	
Payments to acquire investments	0		(10)	
Receipts from disposal of non-current assets	50		10	
		(750)		(85)
Cash flow from financing activities				
Dividends paid	(225)		(1)	
Issue of ordinary share capital	485		(11)	
Loans	96		(300)	
		356		(312)
Increase (decrease) in cash in period		(168)		26

First, we need to understand exactly what a ratio is. A ratio compares two quantities. The common mathematical notation used is A:B. For example, the ratio 3:2 ('three to two') means that for every 3 units of A, there are 2 units of B. Ratios can be expressed in a number of ways including a percentage (10 per cent), as a decimal (0.1) or in a ratio form (0.1:1). Ratios are often written as simply as possible, for example, 10:4 is written as 5:2. It is convenient if one of the numbers in the ratio is a 1. For example, if A:B = 10:4, dividing by B gives A:B = 2.5:1.

The concept of ratios, as used in accounting, is defined in Key concept 10.6.

10.6

KEY CONCEPT

RATIO

In accounting, when comparing quantity A with quantity B, the ratio R is defined by R = A ÷ B. This means that A is R times B, and may be written R:1. In essence, a ratio is merely a shorthand notation for the relationship between two or more things. It is the relationship which must be understood. Without that understanding, the ratio, no matter how precisely calculated or sophisticated, is meaningless.

For example, if we want to know how many police are needed to maintain order at a football match, we could work out a ratio of police officers to spectators. If we found that we needed 200 police for a crowd of 40 000 spectators, the ratio would be 1 to 200 or 1:200.

As well as understanding the relationship expressed by the ratio, we also need to examine ratios in a wider context. The above ratio is meaningless on its own: it does not give us any idea whether we are using the right number of police. To decide this we would need to establish whether there were problems of violence or, if not, whether we could achieve the same result with fewer police. To answer the first question we require additional information while the latter could be answered, in part at least, by looking at other football clubs and what ratio of police to spectators they use. This simple example serves to illustrate the fact that the ratio on its own cannot tell us very much. It needs to be looked at in the context of other information and experience.

Benchmarks

6 LEARNING OBJECTIVE

Identify the issues to be considered when choosing a benchmark for ratio analysis

As we have already said, the important point to bear in mind is what the ratio is attempting to illustrate. For example, we could look at the balance sheet of XYZ Ltd and calculate the ratio of plant and equipment to other non-current assets, but this would be of little use unless we knew what the relationship meant and what we expected. The calculation of ratios is not an end in itself. We could do a comparison of ratios for the same entity through time (times-series). We could also do a comparison of one entity with another entity across time (cross-sectional) or, indeed, we could do both. Therefore, it is important to choose an appropriate benchmark against which to compare the ratios of the entity you wish to analyse (i.e. the subject/entity). A number of factors are relevant in the selection of appropriate benchmarks, and these include:

- *Relative size of the entities.* While the benchmark and the subject don't need to be of identical size, it would not make a lot of sense to compare Woolworths with the local corner store.
- *Industry.* It is important to match the benchmark and the subject as closely as possible in terms of their operations.
- *Geographical location.* To minimise problems that may be specific to certain locations, it is preferable to match the location of the benchmark and the subject.
- *Similar accounting policies and periods.* It is easier to compare benchmarks and entities that have similar accounting policies. Also, while it is not essential to have the same year-end dates (such as 30 June), it is preferable.

Scout Kozakiewicz

We will now discuss some of the ratios presented in Table 10.1 in the following categories:
- profitability
- efficiency
- short-term solvency
- long-term solvency
- market-based ratios.

To demonstrate the application of ratio analysis, we will compare the ratios for Coles Group (based on figures reported as a separate entity before it was acquired by Wesfarmers Limited) and Woolworths for the period ending 30 June 20X7. If numbers appear in brackets next to a ratio they relate to the numbers in Table 10.1 – to allow you to check the formula for that ratio. Coles and Woolworths tables are found on pages 328.

Scout Kozakiewicz

TABLE 10.1 ANALYSIS RATIOS

PROFITABILITY RATIOS

RATIO	COMPONENTS	XYZ LTD (20X4)	20X5	USE
1 Net profit margin before after-tax cost of interest	$\dfrac{\text{net profit}^* + \text{after} - \text{tax interest cost}}{\text{sales}}$	$\dfrac{499 + 768(1 - 0.4)}{14\,441} = \dfrac{960}{14\,441} = 6.6\%$	–0.5%	Profit produced by each dollar of sales before any payment to equity or debt providers.
2 Net profit margin	$\dfrac{\text{net profit}}{\text{sales}}$	$\dfrac{499}{14\,441} = 3.5\%$	–3.2%	Profit produced by each dollar of sales after payment of interest.
3 Gross profit margin	$\dfrac{\text{net sales} - \text{cost of goods sold}}{\text{net sales}}$	$\dfrac{14\,441 - 12\,595}{14\,441} = 12.8\%$	1.6%	Indicates the efficiency of management in turning over the company's goods at a profit.
4 Interest cost as a percentage of sales	$\dfrac{\text{interest expense}}{\text{sales}}$	$\dfrac{768}{14\,441} = 5\%$	5%	Shows the cost of interest as a percentage of sales.
5 Asset turnover	$\dfrac{\text{sales}}{\text{average total assets}}$	$\dfrac{14\,441}{(9695 + 9127) \div 2} = \dfrac{14\,441}{9411} = 1.53$	1.47	Shows how efficiently assets are used to generate sales.
6 Return on assets**	$\dfrac{\text{net profit} + \text{after} - \text{tax interest cost}}{\text{average total assets}}$	$\dfrac{499 + 768 \times (1 - 0.4)}{9411} = \dfrac{960}{9411} = 10.2\%$	–0.7%	Shows the overall earning power of total assets before any payments to equity or debt providers.
7 Return of ordinary shareholders' equity	$\dfrac{\text{net profit} - \text{preference dividend}}{\text{average ordinary shareholder's equity}}$	$\dfrac{499 - 0}{(3727 + 4324) \div 2} = \dfrac{499}{4026} = 12.4\%$	–11.5%	Shows the profitability of ordinary shareholder's equity.

RATIO	COMPONENTS	XYZ LTD (20X4)	20X5	USE
8 Earnings per share	$\dfrac{\text{net profit} - \text{preference dividend}}{\text{weighted average number of ordinary share issued}}$	$\dfrac{499}{1978} = 25.2$ cents (assume shares are \$1)	−23.6 cents	To facilitate comparisons of earnings between companies.
EFFICIENCY RATIOS				
9 Accounts receivable turnover	$\dfrac{\text{net sales}}{\text{average accounts receivable}}$	$\dfrac{14\,441}{(3012 + 2776) \div 2} = \dfrac{14\,441}{2894} = 5$	5	Shows the effectiveness of the collection of customers' accounts.
10 Average days sales uncollected	$\dfrac{\text{days in year}}{\text{accounts receivable turnover}}$	$\dfrac{365}{5} = 73$ days	73 days	Shows the time taken to collect customers' accounts.
11 Inventory turnover	$\dfrac{\text{cost of goods sold}}{\text{average inventory}}$	$\dfrac{12\,595}{(3903 + 3289) \div 2} = \dfrac{12\,595}{3596} = 3.5$	4	Shows the effectiveness of investment in inventories.
12 Inventory turnover in days	$\dfrac{\text{days in year}}{\text{inventory turnover}}$	$\dfrac{365}{3.5} = 104.3$ days	91 days	Shows the number of days to convert inventory into sales.
SHORT-TERM SOLVENCY RATIOS				
13 Current ratio	$\dfrac{\text{current assets}}{\text{current liabilities}}$	$\dfrac{6080}{4007} = 1.52$	1.2	Shows short-term debt-paying ability.
14 Quick ratio	$\dfrac{\text{quick assets}}{\text{current liabilities}}$	$\dfrac{2791}{4007} = 0.70$	0.5	Shows immediate ability to meet current debts.
15 Cash flow from operations to current liabilities	$\dfrac{\text{operating cash flows}}{\text{current liabilities}}$	$\dfrac{226}{4007} = 5.6$ cents	8.5 cents	Shows short-term debt-paying ability based on operating cash flows.
LONG-TERM SOLVENCY RATIOS				
16 Debt to equity	$\dfrac{\text{total liabilities}}{\text{total shareholders' equity}}$	$\dfrac{4803}{4324} = 1.11$	1.36	Shows the relationship between debt financing and equity financing.
17 Debt to total assets	$\dfrac{\text{total liabilities}}{\text{total assets}}$	$\dfrac{4803}{9127} = 0.53$	0.58	Shows the proportion of total assets financed by debt.

RATIO	COMPONENTS	XYZ LTD (20X4)	20X5	USE
18 Leverage ratio	$\dfrac{\text{total assets}}{\text{total shareholders' equity}}$	$\dfrac{9127}{4324} = 2.13$	2.38	Shows the use of leverage. The higher the number the greater the use of debt.
19 Interest coverage	$\dfrac{\text{net profit + income + interest}}{\text{interest expense}}$	$\dfrac{499 + 579 + 768}{768} = \dfrac{1846}{768} = 2.40$	0.3	Shows the protection of lenders from a default on interest payments.
20 Cash flow from operations to total liabilities	$\dfrac{\text{operating cash flow}}{\text{total liabilities}}$	$\dfrac{226}{4903} = 4.7\text{c}$	8.3c	Shows ability to pay total debt from operating cash flows.

MARKET-BASED RATIOS

RATIO	COMPONENTS	XYZ LTD (20X4)	20X5	USE
21 Price/Earnings (P/E)	$\dfrac{\text{market price per ordinary share}}{\text{earnings per share}}$	$\dfrac{\$3.30^{***}}{0.252} = 13.09$		Shows the amount the market will pay for \$1 of profit.
22 Earnings yield	$\dfrac{\text{earnings per share}}{\text{market price per ordinary share}}$	$\dfrac{0.252}{\$3.30} = 7.6\%$		Shows the earnings yield based on the current market price.
23 Dividend yield	$\dfrac{\text{dividend per ordinary share}}{\text{market price per ordinary share}}$	$\dfrac{337 \div 1978}{\$3.30} = \dfrac{0.1703}{3.30} = 5.1\%$		Shows current yield on dividends.

OTHER RATIOS

RATIO	COMPONENTS	XYZ LTD (20X4)	20X5	USE
24 Net tangible asset backing	$\dfrac{\text{net tangible assets}}{\text{number of ordinary shares issued}}$	$\dfrac{4324 - 451}{1978} = \$1.96$	\$1.85	Shows the value per ordinary share based on net tangible assets at carrying values.

* See page ?? for issues about which net profit to use.

** The numerator in the ratio for return on assets in some books is net profit + interest + tax.   Either formula is acceptable, the important requirement is to be consistent in the way you measure ratios across different firms.

*** Assume market price is \$3.30 at end of 20X4.

Adapted from Berry A. & Jarvis R., *Accounting in a business context*, Thomson, 1997, pp. 249, 252, 253 & 254.

> **10.7 KEY CONCEPT**
>
> ## RATIO ANALYSIS
>
> The analysis of ratios involves comparison with appropriate benchmarks through time (time-series) for the same entity and across time (cross-sectional) for two or more entities.

Profitability ratios

7 LEARNING OBJECTIVE

Identify and apply various ratios that can be used to assess profitability

Most ratios that relate solely to the statement of comprehensive income are expressions of costs as a percentage of sales; for example, the gross profit or net profit expressed as a percentage of sales. These relationships are also made apparent with common-size statements, which we have already examined. We have also shown the various profitability ratios in Table 10.1.

Before commenting on the profitability ratios in Table 10.1, we need to consider which profit figure is used. When analysts assess the profitability of a company and attempt to predict future profitability, they generally focus on profit from *ordinary activities*. Any unusual events which have been included in the determination of profit are generally excluded by analysts when attempting to predict future maintainable profits. AASB 108 *Accounting policies, changes in accounting estimates and errors* requires entities to disclose the following items, if relevant, in the statement of comprehensive income:

- revenue or expense items which are due to a revision of an accounting estimate, such as a revision of depreciation expense
- revenue or expense items arising from an error in a prior reporting period
- impact on reported profits from a change in accounting policy.

In assessing future profitability, analysts normally use the profit figure (excluding the effects of the above items if such items do not influence the entity's future profitability). They are concerned with future maintainable profits, and any change to current profits due to irregular items (e.g. an error) are discounted.

From Table 10.1 we see that both the gross profit and net profit margin ratios have declined from 20X4 to 20X5. The gross profit margin decreased from 12.8 per cent to 1.6 per cent and is the major reason for the decline in profitability in 20X5. Therefore, the cost of sales in 20X5 has squeezed the operating profit down to only 1.6 per cent return on sales in a year when the interest charges were in excess of 5 per cent of sales. As stated earlier, there could be several reasons why the cost of sales as a percentage of sales has increased. Recessionary conditions in the economy could have squeezed margins; new competitors, or a price-cutting war, could have reduced selling prices.

As mentioned, the ratio of interest cost to sales has increased in 20X5 to 5 per cent. Other ratios we could calculate are the various other expenses that a business incurs as a percentage of sales, to see if these have significantly affected the change in profits. In the case of XYZ Ltd, there are no other categories of expenses other than the interest costs. Therefore, the decline in the gross profit margin is the major cause of the lower profits in 20X5.

RETURN ON ASSETS

The return on assets declined from 10.2 per cent to −0.7 per cent. It is possible to break down or disaggregate the return on assets into its component parts to assess what is driving the change in the ratio. This is illustrated in the following equation:

Rate of return on assets (6) = net profit margin ratio (before interest expense net of tax) (1)

× total assets turnover ratio (5)

The formulas for each of these ratios can be extracted from Table 10.1 and we now insert them into the equation:

$$\frac{\text{net profit} + \text{after} - \text{tax interest cost (NPBATIC)}}{\text{average total assets (ATA)}} = \frac{\text{NPBATIC}}{\text{sales}} \times \frac{\text{sales}}{\text{ATA}}$$

We can now insert the relevant numbers for XYZ for the years 20X4 and 20X5:

XYZ Ltd, 20X4	XYZ Ltd, 20X5
$6.66 \times 1.53 = 10.2\%$	$-0.5 \times 1.47 = 0.7\%$

The breakdown of the return on assets ratio for XYZ Ltd shows that the net profit margin before the after-tax cost of interest declined significantly while the asset turnover figure remained reasonably constant. Therefore, it was the decline in the profit margin and not a lower turnover of assets which caused the loss for XYZ Ltd in 20X5.

Let us now look at these ratios for Woolworths and Coles Group for 20X7:

WOOLWORTHS (WOW) AND COLES GROUP (CGJ) FOR 20X7

	RETURN ON ASSETS	PROFIT MARGIN	ASSET TURNOVER
WOW	10.42%	3.45%	3.02
CGJ	8.83%	2.45%	3.6

Woolworths has a higher return on assets than the Coles Group. This must be due to the higher profit margin, because the Coles Group has a higher asset turnover. Even though the profit margin differential is only 1 per cent, this, in effect, means that Woolworths' margin is 40 per cent higher than Coles. This was attributed in part to a major cost-cutting exercise at Woolworths called Project Refresh as mentioned in Chapter 1. Project Refresh resulted in a more efficient system for managing inventories – a very large item for the big retailers. Coles has also embarked on a similar cost-reduction exercise since being acquired by Wesfarmers and has significantly improved its performance. The asset turnover is higher for Coles which means that it generates more sales dollars from its assets.

RETURN ON ORDINARY SHAREHOLDERS' EQUITY

The return on assets ratio looks at the total return from assets before any payments of dividends or interest to equity and debt providers. The return on equity (ROE) ratio examines the return for the providers of the equity to the business. It is ratio number 7 under the Profitability ratios heading in Table 10.1. The results for Woolworths and Coles for 20X7 are reported here:

	ROE
WOW	24.53%
CGJ	19.53%

Why did Woolworths outperform Coles? To help us answer this question, we can dissect the ROE figure in the same way as we did for the return on assets, as indicated in the following equation:

Rate of return on ordinary shareholders' equity (7) = profit margin ratio (after interest expense and preferred dividends) (2) × total assets turnover ratio (5) × leverage ratio (18)

WOOLWORTHS (WOW) AND COLES (CGJ) FOR 20X7

	NET PROFIT MARGIN	ASSET TURNOVER	FINANCIAL LEVERAGE
WOW	3.04%	3.02	261.4%
CGJ	2.19%	3.6	248.8%

You can verify the relationship with the ROE by performing the following calculation for Coles:

$$ROE = 2.19 \times 3.6 \times 2.488$$

$$= 19.6\%$$

This is the same as the ROE of 19.53 per cent in the results table (subject to rounding differences). So, the ROE for WOW is higher than CGJ due to the higher profit margin, as is the case with the return on assets. However, the higher leverage figure for CGJ has benefited shareholders in 20X7. This will be the case when an entity generates a higher return on assets than the cost it incurs to borrow funds. However, this may result in an unacceptable level of financial risk, which we discuss below.

The above relationship between the three ratios might seem to suggest that an easy way to improve ROE is to increase leverage by borrowing more money. However, by borrowing more money, the entity's cost of interest may rise, thereby causing a decline in the profit margin. Also, if the entity has no use for the funds, the asset turnover figure will decline. Both of these outcomes will negatively impact the ROE.

STOP AND THINK 4

XYZ Ltd reported an increase in net profit of 20 per cent over the preceding year. Does this show an improved operating performance? Discuss.

Efficiency ratios

Suppose we have an increase in sales: we would expect our accounts receivable to increase; we would probably have to buy more goods to sell, and so our creditors might rise; and in all probability our level of inventories would have to rise to cope with the increased demand. In the case of XYZ Ltd, the sales have risen, as have the accounts receivable. At this stage, we are not sure whether the increase in accounts receivable is solely due to the increase in sales or is, in part, caused by the customers taking longer to pay. The use of a ratio that compares sales and accounts receivable would provide the answers. The efficiency ratios show how effective an entity is in collecting monies owing and converting inventories into sales. Most businesses operate with inventories and receivables and, as stated in Chapter 8, it is important to closely monitor the amount invested in such assets. When calculating ratios that relate 'balance sheet' items to 'statement of comprehensive income' items we have to bear in mind that, if prices are changing, the relationship can be distorted. This is because the balance sheet represents prices at one point in time, whereas the statement of comprehensive income represents the results of operations for a period. This can be shown diagrammatically:

$$\underset{\text{opening balance sheet}}{T_0} \overline{\underset{}{\text{statement of comprehensive income}}} \underset{\text{closing balance sheet}}{T_1}$$

Thus, the opening inventory figure or accounts receivable figure is expressed in beginning-of-the-year prices, the profit and loss figures in average prices, and the closing figures in end-of-year prices. In addition to changing price levels there is the problem that the volume will also change. For example, as sales increase we need to hold more units of inventory in order to provide the same service. So, we have two problems: changes in prices and changes in volumes. One way to compensate for this is to use the average of the opening and closing balance sheet figures and compare that average figure for inventories, accounts receivable, and so on, with the figure from the statement of comprehensive income which is already expressed in average prices. Thus, to calculate the relationship between sales for 20X5 and the accounts receivable, we take the accounts receivable at 20X4 and 20X5 and average the two figures. This gives us a better approximation of the true level of accounts receivable required to sustain that

8 **LEARNING OBJECTIVE**

Identify and apply various ratios that can be used to assess efficiency volume of sales. In fact, an average based on monthly balances of accounts receivable might be even more appropriate. However, this information is not available in annual reports.

The relationship thus calculated can be expressed either as the turnover of the balance sheet figure, that is, accounts receivable turnover, or as the number of days customers take to repay. We use the latter for purposes of illustration, because experience shows it is more readily understood.

To calculate this ratio the formula we require is:

$$\text{accounts receivable collection period (days)} = 365 \div \frac{\text{net sales}}{\text{average accounts receivable}}$$

So, for 20X5 for XYZ Ltd the accounts receivable collection period is:

$$365 \div \frac{13\,226}{1/2\,(2776 + 2508)} = 73 \text{ days}$$

Once again, we cannot comment on whether this is good or bad without some reference point and some more information. For example, if the sales mix had changed and XYZ Ltd had moved into overseas markets, the business might need longer to collect money due to it. Knowledge about how long XYZ Ltd gives its customers to pay their accounts would enable a comparison with this figure. For example, if XYZ Ltd allows 60 days for customers to pay, then 73 days is reasonable. However, if XYZ Ltd only allows 30 days then the current position is much worse. From Table 10.1 we can see that the ratio is the same in 20X4 for XYZ Ltd. A comparison of XYZ Ltd's ratios with a competitor's figures would enable further assessment of XYZ Ltd's position.

Several other ratios of this type can be calculated, such as the number of days inventories are held. Table 10.1 shows this as 104 days in 20X4 and 91 days (an improvement) in 20X5. This means that XYZ Ltd was able to convert its inventories into sales at a faster pace in 20X5 when compared to 20X4. This is one of the few positive signs for XYZ Ltd in 20X5. It is also possible to calculate other ratios like the period taken to pay creditors, using cost of sales and purchases respectively. We will not deal with these other ratios in depth; instead we encourage you to identify the relationships which will aid your understanding, and derive your own ratios. Table 10.1 provides some for you to consider.

WOOLWORTHS (WOW) AND COLES (CGJ) FOR 20X7

	DAYS INVENTORY	DAYS RECEIVABLES
WOW	23.5	0.82
CGJ	30.9	2.54

From the table, we see that Woolworths performs better than Coles on both ratios because it takes less time to collect accounts receivable and less time to sell inventory. However, as the nature of a supermarket business is mainly cash, the days receivables is not a critical issue for the two companies. You can verify this by checking the amount of receivables on the balance sheet for Woolworths. The days of inventory reinforces the advantage Woolworths had over Coles in managing this very important asset for supermarkets.

9 LEARNING OBJECTIVE

Identify and apply various ratios that can be used to assess short-term solvency

Short-term solvency ratios

Having assessed the profitability and efficiency ratios, we now turn to risk assessment to answer such questions as:

- Does the entity have enough cash to repay the loan tomorrow?
- Will the entity have enough cash to repay the loan if it is due in six months?
- Will the entity have enough cash to repay the loan if it is due in five years?

In this section, we examine ratios that assist with short-term decisions; in the next section we examine ratios concerning long-term decisions. The balance sheet ratios that are commonly used are the relationship between current assets and current liabilities, and the relationship between current monetary assets (such as accounts receivable and cash) and current liabilities. The current ratio, for example, is calculated by dividing the current assets figure by the current liabilities figure. Once again, on its own, the result of this calculation does not necessarily tell us very much. We need to look at trends and take into account the nature of the business. For example, we expect a greengrocer's optimum level of inventory to be different to that of, say, a car manufacturer. This is because the greengrocer's inventory, being perishable goods, has a limited shelf life. Besides the nature of the business, we also need to take into account industry norms and the size of the business.

Turning now to the trends in XYZ Ltd's short-term solvency ratios, we can see whether they give us any idea of what is happening.

$$\text{current ratio} = \frac{\text{current assets}}{\text{current liabilities}}$$

$$\text{current ratio for 20X1} = \frac{\$6\,304\,000}{\$3\,932\,000} = 1.6 \text{ or } 1.6\!:\!1$$

The ratios for the other years are as follows:

20X2, 1.6:1; 20X3, 1.3:1; 20X4, 1.5:1; 20X5, 1.2:1

These show that the ratio is declining, but what does this mean? To answer that, we need to think about the relationship being expressed; that is, the relationship between those assets that will be converted into cash in the short term and the amounts we potentially have to pay out in the short term. If the ratio is going down, it means that we have less cover and, therefore, there is more risk.

STOP AND THINK 5

Taking the following ratios in isolation, list their weaknesses, if any:

a   current ratio

b   inventory turnover.

With more risk, we might wish to use a more sensitive measure. One such measure simply excludes the inventory from the current assets and compares the remaining current assets with the current liabilities. The reasoning behind the exclusion of inventory is that it will take time to turn it into cash: it first has to be sold and then the debtors have to pay before we can use the cash to pay our creditors.

This ratio – the ratio of current assets, excluding inventory, to current liabilities – is often referred to as the acid test or quick ratio and is defined as follows:

$$\text{acid test or quick ratio} = \frac{\text{current assets} - \text{inventory}}{\text{current liabilities}}$$

A modification of this ratio is to deduct prepayments from the current assets, because prepayments are not normally available to pay debts.

Calculating this ratio for XYZ Ltd for 20X1 we obtain:

$$\frac{\$6\,304\,000 - \$3\,645\,000}{\$3\,932\,000} = 0.67 \text{ or } 0.67\!:\!1$$

The fact that the ratio is less than 1:1 tells us that we could not pay our current debts if we were called upon to do so. To put it another way, the ratio tells us that we have 67 cents to pay each \$1 of current liabilities.

The question is: does this matter? XYZ Ltd did, after all, stay in business well after 20X1. In reality, the business on which XYZ Ltd is based carried on for a further five years.

The interpretation of the information obtained from calculating this ratio, as with all the other ratios, can make sense only if it is compared to a set of industry norms. This is not as straightforward as it sounds: there are often different norms within an industry, depending on the size and relative power of the businesses in that sector. Moreover, any norm based on a number of businesses will be the average rather than the best, and so care has to be exercised when applying it to a particular business. This all seems to imply that comparisons with norms are not informative. This is certainly true if the comparison is made without adequate attention to what the norms really represent.

The question of the usefulness or otherwise of an industry norm does not apply in the case of XYZ Ltd as we do not have that information. However, we do have the information to calculate trends, and the trend in the quick ratio for XYZ Ltd is as follows:

20X2, 0.67:1; 20X3, 0.6:1; 20X4, 0.7:1; 20X5, 0.5:1

Once again, the trend shows an overall decline, with 20X4 being the odd year out. As before, we can conclude that the risk is increasing but cannot say whether this is in line with what is happening generally because we are looking at the company in isolation. In reality, our knowledge of what was happening in the economy generally would tell us whether credit was getting tight or easing off, and this information would help us in our interpretation of the trend shown above.

As it is ultimately cash that pays debts, another ratio used to assess short-term debt-paying capacity is to examine the ratio of cash flows from operating activities to current liabilities. This ratio also has the advantage of using a figure in the numerator which is not based on year-end figures – as is the case with the current and quick ratios. Hence, it may be regarded as more representative of an entity's capacity to pay its current liabilities.

For XYZ Ltd, the ratio is 0.14 in 20X4 and 0.10 in 20X5. This tells us that the operations generated cash flows in 20X4 sufficient to pay 14 per cent of the current liabilities. In 20X5 it had declined to 10 per cent. This decline in 20X5 is of concern, but we still need to compare this to other companies in the industry.

In summary, we can say that the short-term solvency of XYZ Ltd has deteriorated in 20X5 and is a cause for concern. However, we still need to compare the position of XYZ Ltd with some of its competitors.

To demonstrate the application of ratio analysis, we will compare the ratios for Coles Group (based on figures reported as a separate entity before it was acquired by Wesfarmers Limited) and Woolworths for the period ending 30 June 20X7. The numbers that appear in brackets next to a ratio relate to the numbers in Table 10.1 – to allow you to check the formula for that ratio.

WOOLWORTHS (WOW) AND COLES (CGJ) FOR 20X7

	WOW	CGJ
Current ratio (13)	0.76	0.99
Quick ratio (14)	0.26	0.25
Cash flow from operations to current liabilities ratio (15)	$0.42	$0.23

The current ratio is slightly higher for Coles compared to Woolworths. However, given the size of the two companies, there is little risk of either company not meeting its short-term liabilities. The quick ratio for both companies is much lower than the current ratio which tells us that both companies have very large amounts of inventory (as it is deducted from current assets in the calculation of the quick ratio). Given the nature of the inventories held in supermarkets, the assumption that these could not be easily and quickly converted into cash is not appropriate and not relevant. This would be different for a construction company where the inventory may be a half-finished building that would not be readily and easily convertible into cash.

STOP AND THINK 6

Based on the following information for Jaybond Corporation, we can see that working capital at the end of the current year is $5000 greater than the working capital at the end of the preceding year. Has the current position improved? Explain.

	CURRENT YEAR $	PRECEDING YEAR $
Current assets		
Cash	4000	5000
Accounts receivable	30000	25000
Inventories	51000	32500
Total current assets	85000	62500
Current liabilities	42500	25000
Working capital	$42500	$37500

Long-term solvency ratios

10 **LEARNING OBJECTIVE**

Identify and apply various ratios that can be used to assess long-term solvency

In this section, we look at ratios that assist in answering the last of the three questions posed at the start of the previous section: will the entity have enough cash to repay a loan if it is due in five years? Therefore, will the entity be able to survive and remain a going concern? There are some relationships that are significant in answering this question. For example, earlier in this chapter we discussed the need to find out about short-term solvency and financial risk. We said that financial risk was related to the amount of debt finance compared with equity finance.

To express this as a ratio using XYZ Ltd as an example, we could take the total liabilities and compare them with the equity in that same year. This ratio is referred to as the debt to equity ratio. In 20X1, the ratio was $5151 ÷ $3117 or 1.65, in 20X5 it was $5081 ÷ $3736 or 1.36. This shows that the amount of total liabilities to equity has decreased from the start of the period. However, from Table 10.1 we see that the ratio of total debt to equity was 1.11 in 20X4 and this means that XYZ Ltd has increased its reliance on total debt in 20X5 compared with 20X4 – but it is still less than what it was in 20X1.

We could also look at the total liabilities to total assets ratio – which is another way of observing the amount of leverage for an entity. In order to form an opinion about whether this amount of debt is too high, one must compare the levels of debt with other benchmark entities in the same industry.

Another way to measure leverage is to measure the relationship between total assets and shareholders, funds. We refer to this as the leverage ratio, as listed in Table 10.1. It shows how many dollars of assets for every $1 of shareholders' funds. This must mean that there is $10 – $1, or $9, of total liabilities because we know that the sum of liabilities and shareholders' funds must equal total assets. For XYZ, the leverage ratio in 20X1 was $8268 ÷ $3117 or 2.77 and in 20X5 it was $8817 ÷ $3736 or 2.36.

It is important to note that all the ratios represent different ways of measuring the amount of leverage or gearing for an entity. The ratios do not reveal different outcomes because, if an entity is highly geared, this will be disclosed by all of the above ratios. They simply represent a different way to view an entity's use of debt. Both the debt to equity and leverage ratios report that XYZ Ltd had less leverage in 20X5 when compared to 20X1.

It is also possible to look at other ratios to highlight any relationship the analyst deems important. For example, the size of the interest-bearing debt or long-term loans may be of particular interest when assessing long-term solvency. For XYZ Ltd, the figure for loans for 20X4 was $396 000 and the equity figure was $4 324 000. The ratio is calculated by dividing the equity figure by the loans figure as follows: $4 324 000 \div 396 000 = 10.91$

This tells us that for every $1 of long-term loan finance there is $10.91 of equity finance, or that there is 10.91 times more equity than loans. If we compare this with 20X5 we find that the ratio in that year was $3736 \div 92$ or 40.6. This tells us that XYZ was in a much stronger position in terms of its long-term solvency in 20X5 as there were more dollars of equity to the loan compared with 20X4.

However, with the debt to equity ratios discussed above, we noted that the debt to equity ratio increased from 20X4 to 20X5. If the relationship between total debt to equity has increased but the ratio for long-term debt or non-current liabilities has decreased, then we know that current liabilities must have increased. In fact, we determined this in the previous section on short-term solvency ratios. The short-term debt, in the form of the bank overdraft for XYZ Ltd, has increased from nil in 20X1 to $663 000 in 20X5.

Calculation of the total liabilities to equity ratio and the total non-current liabilities to equity ratio will highlight any changes in leverage, and the use of current versus non-current liabilities. Of course, the common-size statements will also reveal this information at a glance.

We have calculated the long-term loans ratio by dividing the equity figure by the loans figure but we could easily have calculated the ratio of loans to equity and the results would show the amount of loans XYZ Ltd has for every $1 of shareholders' funds. Remember, the essential requirement with ratios is that the same formula is used when you are calculating a ratio for different years or different entities – otherwise the ratios cannot be compared.

WOOLWORTHS (WOW) AND COLES (CGJ) FOR 20X7

	DEBT TO EQUITY (16)	NET INTEREST COVER (19)	CASH FLOW FROM OPERATIONS TO TOTAL DEBT (20)
WOW	1.61	8.9	$0.26
CGJ	1.49	11	$0.16

Woolworths had a debt to equity ratio of 1.61 in 20X7. This means that there were $1.61 worth of liabilities for every $1 of shareholders' equity. Coles is similar with about $1.50 of liabilities for every $1 of shareholders' equity. Does this mean that both companies have too much debt? A closer analysis of the Woolworths balance sheet reveals that accounts payable represents 47 per cent of total liabilities. Long-term interest-bearing liabilities only account for 29 per cent of total liabilities. While Woolworths must pay interest on the interest-bearing liabilities, this is not the case with accounts payable. In Chapter 1 we discussed the concept of the economic consequences of accounting information, and debt contracts were mentioned. It is common in Australia for debt contracts to contain covenants placing limits on a borrower's debt to equity and interest coverage ratios. Where this is the case, managers must ensure that they do not default on such covenants and risk having the debt recalled by the lender.

11 **LEARNING OBJECTIVE**

Discuss the implications of the efficient markets hypothesis for financial statement analysis

Market-based ratios

There is a substantial amount of evidence supporting the notion that share prices adjust very quickly to the release of accounting information. This body of knowledge is called the **efficient markets hypothesis** (EMH). The semi-strong form of the EMH states that share prices, on average, reflect all publicly available information. As a consequence, it is not possible to consistently use publicly available information to generate above-average profits from trading.

If one subscribes to the EMH (and following the GFC and the financial problems experienced in Europe there are some who challenged this) then there are some interesting implications for managers and investors.

For managers, the EMH would mean that any attempt to influence share prices by choosing accounting policies which increase reported net profit will not succeed. The share market will see through the cosmetic change in reported profit and, thus, share prices will not change. Of course, if managers do not subscribe to the EMH, or if they are concerned about compensation plans and debt contracts as discussed in Chapter 1, then incentives still exist for the selection of profit-increasing accounting policies.

For investors, the EMH would suggest there is little point in spending time analysing publicly available information. Instead, they would be better served in investing in a diversified portfolio. In fact, it might seem that the annual reports and financial statements have very little information for investors. However, without financial statements and published annual reports, the share market would be less efficient. Financial statements are used by analysts who diligently analyse the information as soon as it is publicly available. This ensures that share prices are efficient and enhances the efficiency of the allocation of resources. Furthermore, the EMH applies on average; therefore, it is possible that at any time there will be individual inventories which are under- or overpriced. Some investors may see this as a worthwhile challenge.

Another important implication of the EMH for investors concerns the role of market-based ratios. Market-based ratios that are shown in Table 10.1 include the price/earnings ratio (P/E) and the earnings yield. In an efficient market, the price of any shares should represent the intrinsic value of the shares; that is, what they are worth. Therefore, a company's price/earnings ratio can be compared to other businesses in the industry. A higher than normal P/E ratio could mean that either the price is too high or, as is more likely in an efficient market, the market is expecting an increase in earnings per share (EPS) in the future and is adjusting the share price to reflect this. For example, XYZ Ltd has a P/E ratio of 13.09. If we assume that the average in the industry is 10, then, if the EMH is valid, the price on average will not be too high because this would mean that the share is overpriced. However, this may happen in some instances for individual shares.

In our example, the price of $3.30 for XYZ Ltd is what the shares are worth. Therefore, the share market believes the current EPS of 25.2 cents is lower than what it expects the future level of EPS to be. In our example, we assumed a P/E ratio of 10 was appropriate for XYZ Ltd. Therefore, the market is expecting the future EPS of XYZ Ltd to be around 33 cents.

The other explanation for the difference in P/E ratios between companies could relate to the use of different accounting policies. For example, a company that uses reducing-balance depreciation methods should, other things being equal, report a lower P/E ratio than a comparable company that uses straight-line depreciation. Therefore, before comparing P/E ratios between different companies, adjustments should be made to the EPS to compensate for differences in accounting policies.

10.1 CASE STUDY

DECODING THE MUMBO JUMBO – SECRETS OF READING COMPANY REPORTS
BY JOANNA TOVIA

The rows of numbers in an annual report may look daunting to anyone without an economics degree. A quick look, however, at key figures is all you really need to get a good idea of how your shares are likely to perform over the coming year. Lonsdale Securities head of equity research John Watson says you do not have to be a financial whiz or carry out complex analysis to find out how things are going within a company or pick up on brewing problems.

'Many mum and dad investors feel understandably daunted by annual reports, especially if they don't have much knowledge of accounting practices,' Mr Watson says. 'But that's no excuse for filing it away unread.' Annual reports will tell you what the company does, what it owns and what it owes. It will reveal what the company has earned and how those earnings have been distributed. But it can be difficult judging the company from information released at the annual meeting, where the best spin is often put on results.

There are three main parts to an annual report: the statement of financial performance [income statement], the statement of financial position [balance sheet] and the statement of cash flows. 'These financial reports provide the nitty-gritty of a company's financial performance ... it's worth becoming familiar with them all,' says *Share Investing for Dummies* author James Dunn.

Mr Watson recommends time-poor investors leave the financial analysis side of things well alone. He recommends this three-step approach to speed-reading an annual report:

» Step one: Read the chairman's report. This usually includes a review of the company's operating conditions and performance, details of any management changes, and expectations for future business conditions and earnings growth.

» A careful reading of the report can reveal other useful information, such as the company's business strategy and capital management (including future capital raisings, dividend policy and share-buybacks, etc.).

» Step two: Look for warning signs in the auditor's report. This is usually located towards the end of the annual report and may also be called an 'independent audit report'. Mr Watson says the thing to watch out for is any mention of a company's accounts being qualified in some way. Likewise, make sure the auditors state the accounts fairly represent the financial position of the company as at year-end. The auditor's report should disclose any concerns regarding the company's cash position, ability to service debt, or capacity to remain as a going concern.

» Step three: Do some basic analysis of the financial statements. Unless you've studied financial analysis, Mr Watson says you probably won't have much joy interpreting the consolidated statement of financial position (balance sheet) and the consolidated statement of financial performance (income statement), as the reported numbers often need to be adjusted to make them meaningful. Mr Watson says investors should focus their attention on the consolidated statement of cash flows.

But ASIC recommends starting with the statement of financial performance [income statement], taking note of the following:

» Did the company make a profit or a loss?

» Was it better or worse than last year?

» Look for a trend, and see if any major event caused the change. Then look at the dividend:

» What is the dividend going to be and how does it compare with last year? How does it compare with the profit? ASIC says if the company is paying out nearly all or even more than its profit as dividends, then trouble could lie ahead.

Mr Dunn says the key figure in a profit and loss statement is the operating profit after tax. This is the amount left over after all wages, operating costs, overheads, interest, taxes, and allowances for depreciation and the like have been subtracted from sales revenue.

ASIC suggests looking at the statement of cash flows which tells you about cash the company has already received and spent. The company's cash is provided from, and employed in, three areas: operations, investing and financing.

'A company doesn't have to rely on operations to generate overall positive cash flow, it can bring in cash through investing or borrowing,' Mr Dunn says. Eventually, however, a company must make a living from selling products or services. 'If operating cash flow doesn't provide enough cash, the other two wells will run dry.' If the company reports profits much higher than the cash flows from operations, then

ASIC says it may be having trouble collecting its debts. Next comes the balance sheet, or statement of financial position. A quick look at this will tell you what your company owns or owes.

Compare current assets (what it owns) and current liabilities (what it owes) from this year to last year. Does the company look as though it might have trouble meeting its commitments? Check its assets for large amounts in 'intangibles', such as brands or licences.

ASIC says it is very difficult to value intangible assets accurately, and changing conditions can slash the value of even blue chip brands.

Joanna Tovia, *The Courier-Mail*, 'Decoding the mumbo jumbo – secrets of reading company reports', 7 December 2002. This work has been licensed by Copyright Agency Limited (CAL). Except as permitted by the *Copyright Act*, you must not re-use this work without the permission of the copyright owner or CAL.

COMMENTARY

The article provides some interesting comments and advice about analysing a company's financial statements. It is important to seek advice if you are unable to devote the time and don't have the necessary skills to read and understand financial statements. The article has some suggestions to enable you to look for important signals about the company like a qualified audit report, or a consistently poor record of cash flow from operations.

KEY LIMITATIONS OF FINANCIAL STATEMENT ANALYSIS

12 LEARNING OBJECTIVE

Explain the limitations involved in financial statement analysis.

Unfortunately, there are some limitations that have to be borne in mind when discussing financial analysis. These limitations can be usefully summarised under three headings, as follows.

Information problems

- The base information is often out-of-date; that is, timeliness of information leads to problems of interpretation.
- Historic cost information might not be the most appropriate information on which to base the decision for which the analysis is being undertaken.
- Information in published accounts is generally summarised; detailed information might be needed.
- Analysis of accounting information identifies only symptoms, not causes, and thus is of limited use.

Comparison problems over time

- Effects of price changes make comparisons difficult unless adjustments are made.
- Changes in technology affect the price of assets, the likely return, and the future markets.
- A changing commercial environment affects the results and this is reflected in the accounting information. The Global Financial Crisis had an impact on the financial results of many companies.
- Changes in accounting policies may affect the reported results.
- There are problems in establishing a normal base year with which other years can be compared.

Comparison problems between entities

The selection of industry norms and the usefulness of norms based on averages are problematic. It is difficult to compare the distribution of ratios for each entity without industry averages or some other appropriate benchmark, such as another business in the same industry.

- The financial risks and business risks of entities differ, and this affects the analysis.
- Entities use different accounting policies.
- The size of the business and its comparators affects risk, structure and returns.
- Environments affect results; for example, different countries, or home-based versus multinational businesses.

These are the issues that you need to bear in mind when carrying out your analysis, and interpreting and reporting the results. They should not, however, be used as a reason not to attempt the analysis.

SUMMARY

DISCUSS THE INFORMATION NEEDS OF THE VARIOUS USERS IN RELATION TO THE ANALYSIS OF FINANCIAL STATEMENTS

» Investor groups: Groups will be interested in the return on their investment and will look at all aspects of the entity, including current and future profitability, management performance, solvency and financial risk, and future prospects.

» Lenders: Interests will vary depending on whether they are short-term or long-term lenders. Both want to have their funds repaid but long-term lenders will be concerned with the long-term viability of the borrower; this will be of less interest to short-term lenders.

» Employees: Employees are interested in judging their job security and assessing whether their wages are relatively fair. Their areas of interest are profitability (average profits per employee for the purposes of productivity bargaining) and liquidity (future trends in profits).

» Auditors: For the purposes of planning and carrying out their audit, auditors are interested in trends in sales, profit, costs and so on, variations from the norm and accounting policies.

» Analysts: Because they earn a living from making good decisions, analysts are, like investors, interested in all aspects of an entity including current and future profitability, management performance, solvency and financial risk, and future prospects.

» Management: Managers need all the above information because they are likely to be judged on their performance by outside investors or lenders. In addition, they require detailed information on the performance of the business as a whole and on its parts to enable them to manage the business on a day-to-day basis. This information includes such items as profitability by major product, costs per product, and changes in sales or component mix.

IDENTIFY POSSIBLE SOURCES OF EXTERNAL AND INTERNAL INFORMATION

The following is a summary of some external sources of information:

» Government statistics available from the ABS

» Trade journals, as published by broking firms for example

» Financial press such as the *Australian Financial Review*

» Databases like Bloomberg Data Stream

» Specialist agencies like Standard and Poor's.

The following are some internal sources of information:

» Chairman's statement

» Directors' report

» Balance sheet

» Statement of comprehensive income

» Statement of changes in equity

» Statement of cash flows

» Accounting policies

» Notes to the accounts

» Auditor's report.

LEARNING OBJECTIVE 3

EXPLAIN THE SIGNIFICANCE OF PROFITABILITY AND RISK IN THE ANALYSIS OF FINANCIAL STATEMENTS

Investors invest in order to earn a return on their investment. The return will, in part, be dependent on the risk the investor is willing to take. Any analysis of potential investments must assess the expected profitability, but the expected profitability must be assessed in terms of the risk involved. Investors who take a higher risk only do so on the basis that they expect a higher rate of return.

LEARNING OBJECTIVE 4

IDENTIFY AND APPLY TREND ANALYSIS

Trend analysis involves choosing a base year and assigning the number 100 to all items in the base year. In periods after the base year, items are calculated on the basis of their relationship with the corresponding item in the base year. If they are above the base year figure, the number will be above 100, and if they are below the base year figure, the number is less than 100.

In trend analysis, the choice of an appropriate base year is vital. If the base year that is chosen is not typical, the resultant analysis will be, at best, extremely difficult and, at worst, actually misleading. Trend analysis allows identification of declining or increasing amounts of items.

LEARNING OBJECTIVE 5

IDENTIFY AND USE COMMON-SIZE STATEMENTS

Common-size statements express all the items in a financial statement as a percentage of one significant item in the relevant financial statement – such as total assets for the balance sheet. It allows for a fast review of the financial statements and fast detection of any significant changes.

LEARNING OBJECTIVE 6

IDENTIFY THE ISSUES TO BE CONSIDERED WHEN CHOOSING A BENCHMARK FOR RATIO ANALYSIS

The following are some of the items to be considered when selecting an appropriate benchmark:

» Relative size of the entities: While the benchmark(s) and subject don't need to be of an identical size, it would make little sense to compare Woolworths with the local corner store

» Industry: It is important to match the benchmark(s) and subject as closely as possible in terms of their operations

» Geographical location: To minimise problems that are specific to certain locations, it is preferable to have similar areas of location for both the benchmark and the subject

» Similar accounting policies and periods: The more closely aligned the accounting policies, the easier is the comparison. Also, while it is not essential to have the same year-end dates (such as 30 June), it is preferable.

LEARNING OBJECTIVE 7

IDENTIFY AND APPLY VARIOUS RATIOS THAT CAN BE USED TO ASSESS PROFITABILITY

There are many ratios that can be used to assess profitability. In this chapter we illustrated return on assets, return on ordinary shareholders' equity, net and gross profit margins, asset turnover, and earnings per share.

LEARNING OBJECTIVE 8

IDENTIFY AND APPLY VARIOUS RATIOS THAT CAN BE USED TO ASSESS EFFICIENCY

There are many ratios that can be used to assess efficiency. In this chapter we illustrated inventory and accounts receivable turnover ratios. We also expressed them in days. The total asset turnover is also a measure of the efficiency with which the entity generates sales from the asset base.

LEARNING OBJECTIVE 9

IDENTIFY AND APPLY VARIOUS RATIOS THAT CAN BE USED TO ASSESS SHORT-TERM SOLVENCY

There are many ratios that can be used to assess short-term solvency. In this chapter we illustrated the current and quick ratios. We also looked at the cash flow from operating activities as a percentage of current liabilities.

LEARNING OBJECTIVE 10

IDENTIFY AND APPLY VARIOUS RATIOS THAT CAN BE USED TO ASSESS LONG-TERM SOLVENCY

There are many ratios that can be used to assess long-term solvency. In this chapter we illustrated debt to equity, debt to total assets, leverage and the interest coverage ratio. We also looked at the cash flow from operating activities as a percentage of total liabilities.

LEARNING OBJECTIVE 11

DISCUSS THE IMPLICATIONS OF THE EFFICIENT MARKETS HYPOTHESIS FOR FINANCIAL STATEMENT ANALYSIS

The efficient markets hypothesis would suggest that for investors there is little point in spending time analysing publicly available information. Instead, investors would be better served by investing in a diversified portfolio. In fact, it might seem that the annual reports and financial statements have very little information for investors. However, without financial statements and published annual reports, the share market would be less efficient. Financial statements are used by analysts who diligently analyse the information as soon as it is publicly available. This ensures that share prices are efficient and this enhances the efficiency of the allocation of resources.

LEARNING OBJECTIVE 12

EXPLAIN THE LIMITATIONS INVOLVED IN FINANCIAL STATEMENT ANALYSIS

A range of limitations were covered and include the problems of historical information, the choice of an appropriate benchmark, changes in structures over time, changes in accounting policies, the different sizes of businesses, problems with exchange rates and the role of other factors like the entity's social and environmental policies.

REVIEW QUESTIONS

1   Identify the main user groups and their common needs in terms of financial analysis.
2   What factors do we need to take into account in order to put a financial analysis in context?
3   What information would you derive from reading the chairman's statement?
4   What other parts of the annual report would you use in your analysis?
5   How would you measure financial risk in the short and long term?

6   What are the limitations to analysis that are inherent in the accounting data we are using?

7   When comparing similar entities, what steps need to be taken to make the comparisons meaningful?

8   Explain the relevance of sources external and internal to the business in the analysis of financial statements.

PROBLEMS FOR DISCUSSION AND ANALYSIS

1   Refer to the Woolworths annual financial report for 2013 in Appendix 1.

   a   What were the two major liabilities as at 30 June 2013?

   b   Calculate the following ratios for Woolworths (consolidated accounts):

      i   current ratio

      ii   quick ratio

      iii gross profit margin

      iv   debt to equity.

2   The following information is available concerning Wuffalot Pet Foods Ltd:

Current ratio	1.5:1
Non-current liabilities to equity ratio	0.5:1
Issued capital	$150 000
Retained profits	$50 000
Total assets	$400 000

   a   What is the value of Wuffalot's current assets?

   b   What is the value of the non-current assets?

3   DEF Ltd has provided its bank with the following information. The bank manager did ask for a statement showing the current liabilities and assets. What are the current liabilities and assets?

Debt to total assets	0.3:1
Total assets	$300 000
Current ratio	2:1
Non-current liabilities	$40 000

4   Skippy Ltd reported the following current assets and current liabilities at the end of 20X1 and 20X2:

	20X2 $	20X1 $
Cash	311	1928
Marketable securities	83	955
Accounts receivable	2453	2150
Inventories	1016	732

	20X2 $	20X1 $
Prepaid expenses	499	486
Short-term borrowings	3 921	–
Creditors	3 870	3 617
Income taxes payable	123	640

a Determine, for both years (rounding to two decimal points):

  i the current ratio

  ii the quick ratio.

b What conclusions can you draw from this data?

5 Phantom Ltd reported the following information:

	20X2 $	20X1 $
Sales	3 600 000	3 900 000
Beginning inventories	310 000	290 000
Cost of goods sold	2 010 000	2 400 000
Ending inventories	360 000	310 000

a Determine, for each year (rounding to two decimal points):

  i the inventory turnover

  ii the inventory turnover in days.

b What conclusions can be drawn from this data concerning inventories?

6 Homer and Bart Ltd reported the following information for a five-year period. From the data, prepare a trend analysis and comment on the results.

	20X1 $	20X2 $	20X3 $	20X4 $	20X5 $
Sales	400 000	425 000	450 000	525 000	650 000
Gross profit	200 000	220 000	230 000	265 000	330 000
Net profit	40 000	41 000	42 000	38 000	45 000

7 Bazz Co. has provided the following information. Prepare a trend analysis and comment on the results.

	20X2 $	20X3 $	20X4 $	20X5 $	20X6 $
Sales	129 000	130 000	131 000	129 000	130 000
Gross profit	83 000	87 000	88 000	89 000	73 000
Net profit	13 500	12 900	12 500	11 875	8 800

8 Following is a simplified balance sheet for XYZ Ltd.

XYZ LTD
BALANCE SHEET AT 30 JUNE 20X1

	$
Current assets	
Bank	12 000
Inventory	7 500
Accounts receivable	5 000
Total current assets	24 500
Non-current assets	
Land and buildings	100 000
Total non-current assets	100 000
Total assets	124 500
Liabilities	
Current liabilities	
Accounts payable	20 000
Total liabilities	20 000
Net assets	104 500
Equity	
Share capital	100 000
Retained profits	4 500
Total equity	104 500

» The present current ratio is: 1.225:1.

» The company has been told by its bank to increase its current ratio to 1.5:1. Given the balance sheet, what simple step does the company have to take to achieve the required current ratio?

9 As an analyst, you have extracted the following information from the accounts of Romeo Construction Co. Ltd:

ROMEO CONSTRUCTION CO. LTD
STATEMENTS OF COMPREHENSIVE INCOME FOR THE YEARS ENDED 30 JUNE

	20X4 $	20X5 $	20X6 $
Sales	60 000	54 000	75 000
Less Expenses			
Material	22 500	21 000	35 813

	20X4 $	20X5 $	20X6 $
Labour	15 000	13 500	18 000
Production expenses	7 500	6 000	6 750
Administrative expenses	7 500	7 500	8 250
Finance expenses	500	1 500	1 500
	54 000	49 500	70 313
Profit for the year	6 000	4 500	4 687
Other comprehensive income	0	0	0
Total comprehensive income	6 000	4 500	4 687

ROMEO CONSTRUCTION CO. LTD
BALANCE SHEETS AS AT 30 JUNE

	20X4 $	20X5 $	20X6 $
Work in progress	60 000	52 500	67 500
Non-current assets	30 000	37 500	37 500
	90 000	90 000	105 000
Bank overdraft	15 000	18 000	12 000
Other current liabilities	15 000	12 000	18 000
Shareholder funds	60 000	60 000	75 000
	90 000	90 000	105 000

Other information

All profits have been distributed as dividends each year.

The company issued $15 000 of shares in 20X6.

Required

a   Comment on the profitability of the business.

b   Comment on the financial situation of the business.

c   What action do you suggest for the coming year?

10 You have been given the following financial information for Bigboy Catering Ltd:

BIGBOY CATERING LTD
STATEMENTS OF COMPREHENSIVE INCOME FOR YEARS ENDING 31 DECEMBER

	20X1 $	20X2 $	20X3 $	20X4 $
Sales (net)	87000	78000	85000	90000
Food and beverage expenses	50000	51000	49000	51000
Wages	22000	21000	23000	23500
Finance expenses	1000	2000	1500	1000
Other operating expenses	10000	12000	13500	9500
Profit before tax	4000	(8000)	(2000)	5000
Tax	500	0	0	2000
Profit after tax	3500	(8000)	(2000)	3000
Other comprehensive income	0	0	0	0
Total comprehensive income	3500	(8000)	(2000)	3000

BIGBOY CATERING LTD
BALANCE SHEETS AS AT 31 DECEMBER

	20X1 $	20X2 $	20X3 $	20X4 $
Cash at bank	500	0	0	3000
Inventory	19500	19000	16500	21000
Non-current assets	125000	123000	121000	119000
Bank overdraft	0	1000	13500	0
Accounts payable	28000	32000	17000	13000
Issued shares	100000	100000	100000	120000
Retained profits	17000	9000	7000	10000

Other information

The company issued $20000 of shares in 20X4.

Required

a Comment on the profitability of the business.

b Comment on the financial situation of the business.

c What would be your advice to the company after viewing the figures for 20X4?

11 The balance sheets and selected information are given below for Katrina Ltd and Catherine Ltd for the year ended 30 June 20X2.

KATRINA LTD AND CATHERINE LTD
BALANCE SHEETS FOR YEAR ENDED 30 JUNE 20X2

	KATRINA		CATHERINE	
	$	$	$	$
Assets				
Current assets				
Cash at bank	80 000		220 000	
Marketable securities	8 000		190 000	
Accounts receivable (net)	100 000		130 000	
Merchandise inventory	560 000		300 000	
Total current assets		748 000		840 000
Non-current assets				
Property, plant and equipment (net)	1 200 000		1 280 000	
Intangibles	6 000			
Total non-current assets		1 206 000		1 280 000
Total assets		1 954 000		2 120 000
Liabilities and shareholders' equity				
Current liabilities		180 000		310 000
Non-current liabilities		340 000		330 000
Paid-up capital ($10 value)		1 300 000		1 300 000
Retained profits		134 000		180 000
Total liabilities and shareholders' equity		1 954 000		2 120 000
Other information				
Accounts receivable, 1 July 20X1	130 000		110 000	
Merchandise inventory, 1 July 20X1	520 000		420 000	
20X1–X2 Sales:				
Cash	852 000		400 000	
Credit	1 100 000		1 500 000	
20X1–X2 Cost of goods sold	1 200 000		1 100 000	
20X1–X2 Net profit	310 000		400 000	
20X1–X2 Interest expense	60 000		40 000	
Total shareholders' equity, 1 July 20X1	1 334 000		1 380 000	
Total assets, 1 July 20X1	1 854 000		2 020 000	
Tax rate: 30%				

Required

    a Calculate the current ratio, quick ratio, inventory turnover, accounts receivable turnover and average days sales uncollected for each company.

    b Which company do you think has a better liquid position? Why?

    c Calculate, for each company, the rate of return on total assets (ROA), asset turnover and net profit margin before after-tax cost of interest. Which company has the higher ROA? Why?

    d Calculate, for each company, the rate of return on ordinary shareholders' equity (ROE), asset turnover, net profit margin and financial leverage ratios. Which company has the higher ROE? Why?

    e Which company is using leverage more effectively to increase the rate of return to ordinary shareholders? Explain.

    f What do accountants mean by 'window dressing'? Show how Katrina Ltd and Catherine Ltd could improve their liquid ratios by window dressing.

12 Following are the summarised accounts of Apple Ltd for the past five years. These accounts form the basis for the questions that follow.

APPLE LTD
SUMMARISED BALANCE SHEETS OF APPLE LTD

	20X1 $000	20X2 $000	20X3 $000	20X4 $000	20X5 $000
Non-current assets					
Intangible non-current assets	5 247	5 220	7 305	9 969	10 674
Tangible assets	20 175	23 130	43 920	43 740	69 225
	25 422	28 350	51 225	53 709	79 929
Current assets					
Inventory	20 031	23 034	53 091	74 823	99 606
Accounts receivable	17 589	24 693	60 270	48 987	66 768
Bank and cash	4 698	6 801	7 839	3 273	9 747
	42 318	54 528	121 200	127 083	176 121
Current liabilities					
Accounts payable	16 197	24 588	55 659	41 130	72 831
Taxation	459	768	4 302	2 712	3 444
Dividends	801	1 812	3 339	3 738	3 672
Bank loans and overdraft	10 581	4 026	18 180	29 316	37 638
	28 038	31 194	81 480	76 896	117 585
Net current assets	14 280	23 334	39 720	50 187	58 536
Total assets *less* Current liabilities	39 702	51 684	90 945	103 896	138 465

	20X1 $000	20X2 $000	20X3 $000	20X4 $000	20X5 $000
Non-current liabilities					
Loans	<u>14 793</u>	<u>15 477</u>	<u>35 241</u>	<u>35 430</u>	<u>67 844</u>
Net assets	<u>24 909</u>	<u>36 207</u>	<u>55 704</u>	<u>68 466</u>	<u>70 621</u>
Represented by					
Ordinary share capital	5 160	10 359	17 994	18 039	19 464
Retained profits	19 749	25 848	30 975	43 692	41 734
Revaluation reserve			6 735	6 735	9 423
Total equity	<u>24 909</u>	<u>36 207</u>	<u>55 704</u>	<u>68 466</u>	<u>70 621</u>

i During 20X3 and 20X5 some of the freehold properties were revalued.

ii Loans amounting to $22 million were repaid during 20X5.

iii No non-current assets were disposed of during the year.

SUMMARISED STATEMENTS OF COMPREHENSIVE INCOME OF APPLE LTD

	20X1 $000	20X2 $000	20X3 $000	20X4 $000	20X5 $000
Sales	93 930	116 232	259 470	278 340	372 753
Cost of goods sold	<u>65 751</u>	<u>82 525</u>	<u>197 197</u>	<u>208 775</u>	<u>294 475</u>
Gross profit	<u>28 179</u>	<u>33 707</u>	<u>62 273</u>	<u>69 585</u>	<u>78 278</u>
Operating expenses	<u>17 022</u>	<u>21 398</u>	<u>36 830</u>	<u>35 130</u>	<u>59 881</u>
Profit before interest and tax	11 157	12 309	25 443	34 455	18 397
Interest	<u>2 727</u>	<u>2 652</u>	<u>7 707</u>	<u>10 167</u>	<u>14 082</u>
Profit after interest and before tax	8 430	9 657	17 736	24 288	4 315
Taxation	<u>2 517</u>	<u>1 746</u>	<u>9 270</u>	<u>7 833</u>	<u>2 601</u>
Profit after tax	5 913	7 911	8 466	16 455	1 714
Other comprehensive income	0	0	6 735	0	2 688
Total comprehensive income	<u>5 913</u>	<u>7 911</u>	<u>15 201</u>	<u>16 455</u>	<u>4 402</u>

STATEMENTS OF CHANGES IN EQUITY FOR APPLE LTD

	SHARE CAPITAL $000	RETAINED EARNINGS $000	REVALUATION SURPLUS $000	TOTAL $000
Balance at 1 July 20X0	5160	14637	0	19797
Total comprehensive income for the year		5913		5913
Dividends		(801)		(801)
Balance at 30 June 20X1	5160	19749		24909
Total comprehensive income for the year		7911		7911
Dividends		(1812)		(1812)
Issued shares	5199			5199
Balance at 30 June 20X2	10359	25848		36207
Total comprehensive income for the year		8466	6735	15201
Dividends		(3339)		(3339)
Issued shares	7635			7635
Balance at 30 June 20X3	17994	30975	6735	55704
Total comprehensive income for the year		16455		16455
Dividends		(3738)		(3738)
Issued shares	45			45
Balance at 30 June 20X4	18039	43692		68466
Total comprehensive income for the year		1714	2688	4402
Dividends		(3672)		(3672)
Issued shares	1425			1425
Balance at 30 June 20X5	19464	41734	9423	70621

Required

a Complete the common-size statements of comprehensive income (see table on next page) for the five years and analyse these statements with particular reference to the profitability of Apple Ltd.

b Using whatever form of analysis you consider appropriate, analyse and comment on the financial performance and financial position of Apple Ltd.

c What are the limitations of your analysis?

COMMON-SIZE STATEMENTS OF COMPREHENSIVE INCOME OF APPLE LTD

	20X1 $000	20X2 $000	20X3 $000	20X4 $000	20X5 $000
Sales	100	100	100	100	100
Cost of goods sold	70	71	76		
Gross profit	30	29	24		
Operating expenses	18	18	14		
Profit before interest and tax	12	11	10		
Interest	3	2	3		
Profit after interest and before tax	9	8	7		
Taxation	3	2	4		
Profit after tax	6	7	3		
Other comprehensive income	0	0	3		
Total comprehensive income for the year	6	6	6		

13 The balance sheets and additional information follow for Jayco Ltd:

JAYCO LTD
BALANCE SHEETS AT 30 JUNE

	20X4 $	20X5 $	20X6 $
Assets			
Current assets			
Cash	364 700	292 720	123 790
Inventories			
Finished products	600 000	700 000	800 000
Work in progress	245 500	258 000	342 000
Raw materials and supplies	483 050	450 000	550 000
Accounts receivable	521 000	669 280	1 184 210
Total current assets	2 214 250	2 370 000	3 000 000
Non-current assets			
Land (at cost)	600 000	816 300	1 334 104
Buildings (at cost)	1 215 500	1 323 000	2 400 000

	20X4 $	20X5 $	20X6 $
Machinery (at cost)	1538980	1500370	3505640
Goodwill (at cost)	2000000	2000000	2000000
Total non-current assets	5354480	5639670	9239744
Total assets	7568730	8009670	12239744
Liabilities			
Current liabilities			
Accounts payable	355700	360000	544620
Current tax payable	500000	500000	800000
Provision for dividend	130000	430000	672000
Total current liabilities	985700	1290000	2016620
Non-current liabilities			
Debentures	683030	903370	2999020
Mortgages	500000	400000	1000000
Total non-current liabilities	1183030	1303370	3999020
Total liabilities	2168730	2593370	6015640
Net assets	5400000	5416300	6224104
Owners' equity			
8% preference shares	500000	500000	1200000
Ordinary shares ($1)	4000000	4000000	4000000
Retained profits	900000	916300	1024104
Total owners' equity	5400000	5416300	6224104

ADDITIONAL INFORMATION FROM JAYCO LTD'S FINANCIAL STATEMENTS

		20X4 $	20X5 $	20X6 $
i	Annual sales			
	Credit (terms 2/10 net 45)	2605000	3011760	4500000
	Cash	120000	142600	1500000
ii	Cost of goods sold	1662250	1861070	3720000
iii	Net profit (after tax at 50%)	463250	473150	789902
iv	Interest expense	94642	104269	399902

		20X4 $	20X5 $	20X6 $
v	Share price	$1.50	$1.52	$2.08
vi	Balances as at 30 June 20X3			
	Accounts receivable			450 000
	Total tangible assets			5 000 000
	Inventory			1 441 870
vii	Selected financial ratios			Industry
				20X6
	Current ratio			2.25
	Quick ratio			1.10
	Accounts receivable turnover			6 x
	Inventory turnover			4 x
	Debt/Total assets			33%
	Debt/Net tangible assets			0.6
	Equity ratio			72%
	Rate of return on ordinary shareholders' funds			16%
	Gross profit margin			40%
	Net profit margin			16%
	Net operating profit rate of return			26%
	Overall interest coverage			11 x
	Return on assets			14%

Required

Evaluate the position of Jayco Ltd. Cite specific ratio levels and trends as evidence.

14 The directors of Efficient Distributors Ltd are concerned at the results of trading activities reported for the year ended 30 June 20X6, and failure to keep within the limit of the bank overdraft ($12 000).

They request that a comprehensive survey be made of the financial state of the company, and provide the following information:

STATEMENTS OF COMPREHENSIVE INCOME FOR THE YEARS ENDED 30 JUNE

		20X4		20X5		20X6
	$	$	$	$	$	$
Sales		200 000		180 000		165 000
Less Cost of sales						
Opening inventory		36 000		41 000		44 000
Purchases		95 000		87 000		80 000
		131 000		128 000		124 000
Less Closing inventory	41 000	90 000	44 000	84 000	49 000	75 000
Gross profit		110 000		96 000		90 000
Less:						
Selling and distribution expenses	40 000		40 000		46 000	
General and administration expenses	20 000		20 000		18 000	
Financial expenses	15 000	75 000	16 000	76 000	20 000	84 000
Net operating profit before tax		35 000		20 000		6 000
Less Income tax expense		15 000		9000		2500
Net operating profit after tax		20 000		11 000		3500
Less Loss on sale of investment			–	–		1000
Profit for year		20 000		11 000		2500
Other comprehensive income		0		10 000		0
Total comprehensive income for the year		20 000		11 000		2500

STATEMENTS OF CHANGES IN EQUITY

	ORDINARY SHARE CAPITAL $	PREFERENCE SHARE CAPITAL $	RETAINED EARNINGS $	REVALUATION SURPLUS $	TOTAL $
Balance at 1 July 20X3	75 000	50 000	28 000		153 000
Total comprehensive income for the year			20 000		20 000
Dividends			(23 000)		(23 000)
Balance at 30 June 20X4	75 000	50 000	25 000		150 000
Total comprehensive income for the year			11 000	10 000	21 000
Dividends			(27 000)		(27 000)
Balance at 30 June 20X5	75 000	50 000	9 000	10 000	144 000
Total comprehensive income for the year			2 500		2 500
Dividends			(3 000)		(3 000)
Balance at 30 June 20X6	75 000	50 000	8 500	10 000	143 500

BALANCE SHEETS AS AT 30 JUNE

	20X4		20X5		20X6	
	$	$	$	$	$	$
Assets						
Current assets						
Bank	1000					
Inventory	41 000		44 000		49 000	
Accounts receivable	26 000		31 000		37 000	
Less Allowance for doubt-ful debts	(1000)		(1000)		(2 000)	
Prepayments	2 000		3 000		3 000	
Total current assets		69 000		77 000		87 000
Non-current assets						
Plant and equipment	10 000		10 000		21 000	
Less Depreciation (1000 in X3)	(2 000)		(4 000)		(7 000)	

	20X4		20X5		20X6	
	$	$	$	$	$	$
Vehicles	80 000		80 000		114 000	
Less Depreciation (4000 in X3)	(16 000)		(32 000)		(54 000)	
Land (at valuation)	60 000		70 000		70 000	
Buildings (at cost)	40 000		56 000		56 000	
Investments (at cost)	25 000		25 000		–	
Total non-current assets		197 000		205 000		200 000
Total assets		266 000		282 000		287 000
Liabilities						
Current liabilities						
Bank overdraft			8 500		12 500	
Accounts payable	12 000		8 000		14 000	
Accrued wages and interest	1 000		1 500		2 000	
Current tax payable	15 000		9 000		2 500	
Provision for dividend	13 000		15 000		3 000	
Total current liabilities		41 000		42 000		34 000
Non-current liabilities						
Mortgage on land (due 30 June 20X9)			21 000		34 500	
Term loan (due 20X10)	75 000		75 000		75 000	
Total non-current liabilities		75 000		96 000		109 500
Total liabilities		116 000		138 000		143 500
Net assets		150 000		144 000		143 500
Owners' equity						
50 000 6% $1 preference shares	50 000		50 000		50 000	
75 000 ordinary shares	75 000		75 000		75 000	
Revaluation surplus			10 000		10 000	
Retained earnings		25 000		9 000		8 500
Total owners' equity		150 000		144 000		143 500

Required

a   Analyse the company's financial position, indicating the causes of the present situation and recommending future policy. What are the implications of continuation of the company's present practices?

b   Indicate any limitations of your analysis.

c   What additional information (if any) would you like to assist you with your analysis?

ETHICS CASE STUDY

Allandale Ltd is a company that builds small luxury boats and employs 500 people. The company has been operating for 10 years. Two years ago the company underwent a major expansion of its boat-building facilities because of increased demand for its boats from overseas buyers. To do this it borrowed $20 million through a mortgage loan with a major bank.

The loan agreement contains the following clauses:

i   Allendale is to maintain a current ratio of at least 2:1

ii   the after-tax return on assets must be at least 10 per cent.

If the company fails to meet either ratio in any year, the $20 million is immediately repayable.

Last year the government removed a 10 per cent tariff on small luxury boats and the company has had difficulty competing in overseas markets. Consequently, the company has had to reduce its profit margin in order to compete against suppliers from other countries.

Tom Lyons is the accountant of Allandale Ltd, and he has completed the preliminary financial results for the current year. Based on these results, the current ratio is 2.1:1 and the return on assets is 11 per cent. However, Tom has some concerns about the following items:

1   One boat that was still unsold at year-end is recorded in the balance sheet at $500 000. However, Tom is certain that the most it could be sold for is $350 000.

2   An overseas customer who owes the company $1 million has recently informed Allandale Ltd that they are in severe financial trouble and will only be able to pay half the amount owing. The balance in the provision for doubtful debts is only $300 000.

If Tom recognises the decline in the net realisable value of $150 000 and the $200 000 uncollectable account in excess of the provision, the company's current ratio will fall to 1.6:1 and the return on assets to 2 per cent. This would result in a call for immediate repayment of the $20 million loan. In turn, this would force the company into bankruptcy and Tom and his best friends will lose their jobs.

Discuss

a   the ethical problems faced by Tom

b   what Tom should do.

SUGGESTED ANSWERS TO STOP AND THINK EXERCISES IN THE CHAPTER

1   Long-term lenders and equity investors have many common needs, but they differ in that long-term lenders look at interest cover rather than dividend cover or earnings per share. They are also interested in measures of security.

2   Sources are given below. Students should be encouraged to identify, for themselves, how this information would be used and what they could get out of it. External sources include government statistics, trade journals, the financial press, databases and specialist agencies. Internal sources include the chairman's statement, the directors' report, balance sheets, statements of comprehensive income, statements of changes in equity, cash flow statements, the accounting policies statement, notes to the accounts and the auditor's report.

3   Financial risk relates to the mix of owners' equity and debt financing, whereas business risk refers to the type of business or trade in which the enterprise is engaged.

4   A 20 per cent increase in net profit is, on the surface, an improvement. However, we need to consider how the company's competitors have performed so that we have a benchmark for comparison. If the average increase of other companies' net profit was 30 per cent, then the company has fallen behind. It may also be that last year's net profit was low, so achieving a 20 per cent increase may not mean much in terms of dollars.

5   a   The current ratio can be manipulated by using cash to pay creditors at year-end.

    b   The inventory turnover ratio can be manipulated by running down inventories at year-end.

6   The amount of working capital and the change in working capital are just two indicators of the strength of the current position. A comparison of the current ratio and the quick ratio, along with the amount of working capital, gives a better analysis of the current position. Such a comparison shows:

	CURRENT YEAR	PRECEDING YEAR
Working capital	$42 500	$37 500
Current ratio	2.0	2.5
Quick ratio	0.8	1.2

It is apparent that, although working capital has increased, the current ratio has fallen from 2.5 to 2.0, and the quick ratio has fallen from 1.2 to 0.8.

CENGAGENOW

Go to http:\\login.cengagebrain.com to link to CengageNOW, your online study tool. First take the Pre-Test for this chapter to get your Personalised Study Plan, and then:

» revise your understanding of the key terms related to financial statement analysis by completing the online crossword

» explore the accounting standards framework

» follow the animated example to identify and use common-size statements.

After you have completed the activities in your Personalised Study Plan take the Post-Test to determine what concepts you have mastered and what you still need work on.

11

WORKSHEET TO DEBITS AND CREDITS

LEARNING OBJECTIVES

At the end of this chapter, you should be able to:

1. explain the use of debits and credits, and identify the relationship between the worksheet approach and the use of debits and credits

2. explain the role of journals, ledgers and a trial balance

3. explain end-of-period adjustments and prepare a trial balance and an extended trial balance

4. prepare final accounts from an extended trial balance.

INTRODUCTION

This chapter has been included to assist readers who wish to continue with their studies using other textbooks, as these are likely to use a more traditional approach for explaining accounting and its mechanics. It will also be helpful to readers who are familiar with the traditional approach as an aid to understanding how the exposition in this book relates to that of other texts. In the next part of the chapter we move on to look at the **trial balance** and the final adjustments that are required before final accounts are extracted from the worksheet.

1 LEARNING OBJECTIVE

Explain the use of debits and credits, and identify the relationship between the worksheet approach and the use of debits and credits

THE TRADITIONAL APPROACH

In the traditional approach, instead of using columns to portray the individual accounts in an organisation's accounting system, these accounts are represented by **T accounts**. In many basic bookkeeping courses, these T accounts form a major part of the course and students are required to spend a lot of time practising entries to these accounts. Often this is done on the basis of rote learning. It is further complicated by the terminology used: 'debits' and 'credits'.

For people studying accounting for the first time, the worksheet approach has been shown to be superior. Moreover, it is more in line with the use of electronic spreadsheets. However, experience has shown that those who already know something of accounting often have initial problems in converting from one representation of an accounting system to another. In this chapter, we work through a simple example to illustrate that the difference between the two methods is superficial and does not in any way change the principles involved.

11.1 WORKED EXAMPLE

PHIL'S BUSINESS

Phil started a business, and during the first year the following transactions took place:

1　Opened a business account and paid in $10 000 of his own money.

2　Bought a van for $5000 and paid cash.

3　Bought goods for $35 000 on credit, of which $33 000 was paid for at year-end.

4　Sold goods for $45 000, all for cash.

5　Had goods in inventory at the end of the year that cost $4000.

6　Paid expenses on the van of $1000.

7　Paid rent on his premises of $1500.

This is what the worksheet looks like for Phil's business.

Fotimages/Shutterstock.com

PHIL'S BUSINESS WORKSHEET: VERSION 1

	ASSETS				LIABILITIES	EQUITY	
TRANSACTION	CASH	PREPAIDS	VAN	INVENTORY	ACCOUNTS PAYABLE	PROFIT AND LOSS	CAPITAL
1	10000						10000
2	−5000		5000				
3				35000	35000		
	−33000				−33000		
4	45000					45000	
5				−31000		−31000	
6	−1000					−1000	
7	−1500	1500					
Balance	14500	+1500	+5000	+4000	=2000	+13000	+10000

You should make sure that you understand the entries on the worksheet before moving on. If you do have problems, refer back to the appropriate chapters.

Now we will show the same transactions using the traditional T accounts.

PHIL'S BUSINESS T ACCOUNTS

CASH

Transaction 1	10000	Transaction 2	5000
Transaction 4	45000	Transaction 3	33000
		Transaction 6	1000
		Transaction 7	1500
		Balance c/d*	14500
	55000		55000
Balance b/d**	14500		

INVENTORY

Transaction 3	35000	Transaction 5	31000
		Balance c/d	4000
	35000		35000
Balance b/d	4000		

PREPAIDS

Transaction 7	1500		

VAN

Transaction 2	5000		

CAPITAL

		Transaction 1	10000

ACCOUNTS PAYABLE

Transaction 3	33000	Transaction 3	35000
Balance c/d	2000		
	35000		35000
		Balance b/d	2000

PROFIT AND LOSS				
Transaction 5		31 000	Transaction 4	45 000
Transaction 6		1 000		
Balance c/d		13 000		
		45 000		45 000
			Balance b/d	13 000

* The term 'balance c/d' means the balance of the account at the end of the period carried down.

** The term 'balance b/d' means the balance of the account at the end of the period brought down.

If we examine the two systems carefully, we can see that they have recorded the same transactions. All that has changed is the way in which the recording is shown. This will be clearer if we explain some of the transactions and the ways in which they have been treated.

In the worksheet, to deal with transaction 1 where Phil puts some money into the business, we opened columns headed Cash and Capital. We then entered the amount involved, $10 000, in each of these columns. By contrast, under the traditional approach we opened two T accounts: one for cash and the other for capital. We then entered the amount involved, $10 000, in these two accounts. All that is happening is that, in contrast with the use of T accounts to represent accounts, the worksheet uses columns.

Using T accounts, it is perhaps less clear which side of the account the entry should go on. However, we can apply some simple rules to make the transposition of entries from the worksheet to debits and credits relatively straightforward. All pluses on the left side of the worksheet are recorded as debits and all minuses are recorded as credits. A debit is placed on the left-hand side of the T account and a credit on the right-hand side. The reverse situation applies on the right side of the worksheet, where all pluses are recorded as credits and all minuses as debits. Therefore, transaction 1 is a debit for cash and a credit for capital.

KEY CONCEPT

DEBITS AND CREDITS

Under the traditional approach, assets are shown as debit balances and liabilities and equities are shown as credit balances.

We now consider the way in which transaction 2, the purchase of the non-current asset, is dealt with. In the worksheet, a new column is opened for the asset and the cash column is reduced by the amount paid for the new asset, that is, $5000. The traditional approach starts in the same way by opening a new account for the new asset, and puts the cost of $5000 on the left side because it is an asset. So far, the methods are essentially similar. The other half of the transaction is perhaps slightly more difficult to follow because we have to reduce the cash balance. This is done by putting the $5000 on the right-hand side of the cash account. This is called crediting an account – in this case we are crediting a cash account.

Even at this stage it is obvious that the worksheet is easier to follow because it relies less on jargon and rote learning than the traditional approach. Another advantage of the worksheet is that we know at the end of the exercise that the accounts are balanced; if they do not balance, the error can be found by working back through the worksheet (as described in Chapter 5). In the case of the traditional approach, we do not yet know if our accounts balance, so we have to extract what is commonly known as a trial balance. If, having extracted this trial balance, we found that it did not balance we would have to check through the entries in our accounts to find the error. It is to be hoped that that will not be the case with the trial balance for Phil's business, which is as follows:

PHIL'S BUSINESS TRIAL BALANCE

	DEBIT	CREDIT
	$	$
Cash	14 500	
Prepaids	1 500	
Capital		10 000
Accounts payable		2 000
Van	5 000	
Inventory	4 000	
Profit and loss		13 000
	25 000	25 000

We can see that the accounts do balance. You may have noticed that the columns are headed Debit and Credit. All the accounts from the left side of our worksheet (the asset accounts) are in the debit column. All the accounts from the right side of the worksheet, those that relate to what the business owes, are in the credit column. The accounts with a negative balance would have the opposite title to the one they would have if they had a positive balance. For example, an asset account with a negative balance would be a credit. The negative asset accounts, like allowance for doubtful debts and accumulated depreciation, have a credit balance. An entity overdrawing on its bank account would have a negative (credit) balance. If an entity pays more than the amount owing to suppliers, the accounts payable will have a negative (debit) balance. In this case, we assume that we have not made an error in our double entries because the trial balance balances. However, as was pointed out in Chapter 5, a trial balance can balance and still be incorrect; for example, $1000 may be recorded as $10 000 on both sides of the worksheet as a debit and a credit.

KEY CONCEPT

RULES FOR DEBITS AND CREDITS

For asset accounts, increases are recorded as debits and decreases as credits. For liability and equity accounts, increases are recorded as credits and decreases as debits.

STOP AND THINK 1

In accountancy, what are debits and credits, and how do they relate to liabilities and equity?

Ledgers

Up until now we have used T accounts to demonstrate the traditional approach to accounting. In practice, the T accounts are called ledger accounts and are a means for a business to accumulate information to assist with decision making. A typical ledger account is shown below.

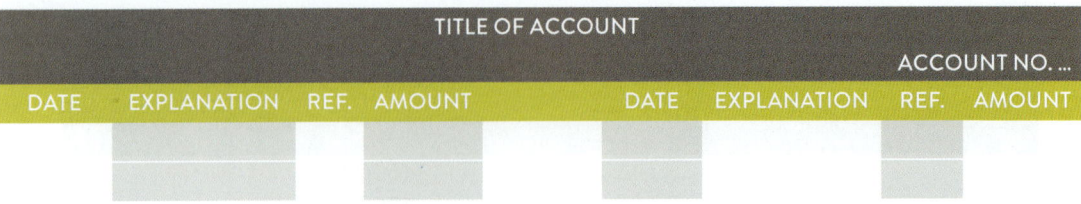

TITLE OF ACCOUNT							ACCOUNT NO. ...
DATE	EXPLANATION	REF.	AMOUNT	DATE	EXPLANATION	REF.	AMOUNT

As you can see there are two sides to this ledger: the left-hand side for debit entries and the right-hand side for credit entries. These sides are separated by the middle space between the amount and the date.

The columns show the following data:

- Date: the date of the transaction
- Explanation: only recorded for unusual items, so seldom used
- Ref.: the page or folio number of the journal where the transaction is recorded
- Amount: the amount of the entry.

The journal

Transactions are normally not entered directly into a ledger account. Under the traditional approach, most businesses use a journal to initially enter a transaction into the accounting records. The journal is often called the book of original entry. It is a chronological record showing the debits and credits from transactions. At convenient intervals these transactions are transferred (or posted) from the journal to the relevant ledger accounts.

11.1

WORKED EXAMPLE

PHIL'S BUSINESS (CONTINUED)

We will now record the transactions from Worked example 11.1 into a journal. The journal we use is called a general journal. Many businesses use a number of journals for different items. Some examples are the cash receipts journal, the cash payments journal and the purchases journal. We record all the transactions in the general journal.

GENERAL JOURNAL PAGE ...

DATE (TRANSACTION)	ACCOUNT TITLES AND EXPLANATION	LP	DEBIT	CREDIT
1	Cash		10 000	
	Capital			10 000
	Invested cash in the business			
2	Van		5 000	
	Cash			5 000
	Bought a van for cash			
3	Inventory (or purchases)		35 000	
	Accounts payable			35 000
	Bought goods on credit			
	Accounts payable		33 000	
	Cash			33 000
	Paid suppliers (in practice these occur throughout the year)			
4	Cash		45 000	
	Profit and loss (or sales)			45 000
	Sold goods for cash			
5	Profit and loss (or cost of goods sold)		31 000	
	Inventory			31 000
	Cost of goods sold for the period			
6	Profit and loss (or van expenses)		1 000	
	Cash			1 000
	Paid van expenses			
7	Prepaids		1 500	
	Cash			1 500
	Paid rent for the period			

The column LP is used to record the ledger account number when the entry is posted from the journal to the ledger. Until the entry is posted, no number is entered into the LP column. The number assists cross-referencing, and can help to locate errors.

All transactions that involve entries to the profit and loss account have an alternative account name in brackets. What happens in practice is that information is accumulated in various income (revenue) and expense accounts throughout the period. At the end of the period a closing entry is recorded in the journal, and these closing entries transfer the totals of the income (revenue) and expense accounts, to the profit and loss account. We have recorded these amounts directly to the profit and loss account in this example.

We will now move on to the next stage, where final adjustments are made for accruals, depreciation, and so on. These adjustments are often referred to as end-of-period or end of year adjustments.

3 LEARNING OBJECTIVE

Explain end-of-period adjustments and prepare a trial balance and an extended trial balance

End-of-period adjustments

End-of-period adjustments are required to provide for inventories, depreciation, bad debts, accruals, prepayments, and so on. These have all been covered in chapters 8 and 9 and you should be familiar with the way in which they are dealt with in the worksheet. For the purposes of comparison, we will show again how they are dealt with in the worksheet and then look at how they are dealt with in the traditional approach.

11.1 WORKED EXAMPLE

PHIL'S BUSINESS (CONTINUED)

We continue with the example of Phil's business. At the end of the year Phil decides that the van will have no scrap value and should be depreciated at $1000 a year for five years. He also tells you that the rent is payable quarterly in advance, so that only $1200 relates to this year.

Entering these adjustments on the worksheet results in version 2 of the worksheet. You will notice that we have had to open two new accounts or columns to deal with the changes and then arrive at a new balance.

PHIL'S BUSINESS WORKSHEET: VERSION 2

| TRANSACTION | ASSETS | | | | LIABILITIES | | EQUITY | |
	CASH	VAN	(ACCUM. DEP.)	INVENTORY	PREPAIDS	ACCOUNTS PAYABLE	PROFIT AND LOSS	CAPITAL
1	10 000							10 000
2	–5000	5000						
3				35 000		35 000		
	–33 000					–33 000		
4	45 000						45 000	
5				–31 000			–31 000	
6	–1000						–1000	
7	–1500					1500		
Balance	14 500	+ 5000	±	4000	+ 1500	= 2000	+ 13 000	+ 10 000
Adjustment			–1000				–1000	
Adjustment					–1200		–1200	
Balance	14 500	+ 5000	–1000	+ 4000	+ 300	= 2000	+ 10 800	+ 10 000

In the traditional approach, we also have to create the new accounts and then extract another trial balance. However, there is a shortcut that is often shown in textbooks, which involves making adjustments on what is effectively a type of worksheet. The difference between that worksheet and the one we use is that the rows become columns and vice versa. This worksheet is shown below and, as you can see, it merely extends our earlier trial balance to the new trial balance.

This type of worksheet is often referred to as the extended trial balance. The main difference between the two approaches in this respect is that, when using our worksheet approach, the final adjustments are automatically part of the double-entry system. Under the traditional approach they can be, and often are, outside the double-entry system. This can, of course, lead to errors and omissions that might be difficult to trace. Let us look at the extended trial balance of Phil's business.

PHIL'S BUSINESS EXTENDED TRIAL BALANCE

	UNADJUSTED TRIAL BALANCE		ADJUSTMENTS		ADJUSTED TRIAL BALANCE	
	DEBIT $	CREDIT $	DEBIT $	CREDIT $	DEBIT $	CREDIT $
Cash	14 500				14 500	
Capital		10 000				10 000
Accounts payable		2 000				2 000
Van	5 000				5 000	
Inventory	4 000				4 000	
Profit and loss		13 000	2 200			10 800
Accum. dep.				1 000		1 000
Prepaids	1 500			1 200	300	
	25 000	25 000	2 200	2 200	23 800	23 800

As can be seen, the extended trial balance has also resulted in the need to open a new account for accumulated depreciation and to make some adjustments to our existing profit and loss account. If these adjustments were done through double-entry in the journal and T accounts they would be shown as follows:

GENERAL JOURNAL

DATE	ACCOUNT TITLE AND EXPLANATION	LP	DEBIT	CREDIT
Adjustment	Profit and loss (depreciation expense)		1000	
	Accumulated depreciation			1000
	To record depreciation for the period			
Adjustment	Profit and loss (rent expense)		1200	
	Prepaids			1200
	To recognise rent expense for the year			

These entries are called adjusting journal entries. Like all journal entries they are posted to the relevant ledger accounts as shown below.

PREPAIDS			
Transaction 7	1500	Adjustment	1200
		Balance c/d	300
	1500		1500
Balance b/d	300		
PROFIT AND LOSS			
Transaction 5	31 000	Transaction 4	45 000
Transaction 6	1000		
Balance c/d	13 000		

				45 000
	45 000			
Adjust	1 000	Balance b/d		13 000
Adjust	1 200			
Balance c/d	10 800			
	13 000			13 000
		Balance b/d		10 800
ACCUMULATED DEPRECIATION				
		Adjustment		1 000

4 LEARNING OBJECTIVE

Prepare final accounts from an extended trial balance.

Comparison with the worksheet approach

We have seen that the differences between the two approaches are not differences of principle. Rather, the two methods are alternative ways of depicting the same entries in an entity's accounting books. In the authors' opinion, the advantages of the worksheet outweigh those of the traditional approach and make it easier for those coming to the subject for the first time to assimilate the main principles of double-entry bookkeeping. We now consider the way in which final accounts are produced, and the rules and regulations governing their format.

FINAL ACCOUNTS

The final step in the process is the preparation of the financial statements; how the balance sheet and the income statement are derived from the worksheet. (As Phil's business is a sole proprietorship it does not prepare general-purpose financial reports and hence does not need to use the statement of comprehensive income.) This is readily understood if we consider the example of Phil's business. We will extract the final accounts from version 2 of Phil's business worksheet (see page 394).

11.1

WORKED EXAMPLE

PHIL'S BUSINESS (CONTINUED)

PHIL'S BUSINESS

INCOME STATEMENT FOR THE YEAR ENDING 30 JUNE 20X9

	$	$
Sales		45 000
Cost of goods sold		31 000
Gross profit		14 000
Rent	1 200	
Van expenses	1 000	
Van depreciation	1 000	3 200
Profit for the year		10 800

You will notice that the formal income statement merely summarises what is contained in the profit and loss column of the worksheet. You will also notice that it is called the income statement for the period ended on a certain date. This emphasises that the income statement is a period statement. If we contrast its heading with the heading of the following balance sheet, we can see that the latter refers to a particular point in time; it is a snapshot of one moment in time.

PHIL'S BUSINESS

BALANCE SHEET AS AT 30 JUNE 20X9

	$		$		$		$
Assets							
Current assets							
Cash	14 500						
Prepaids	300						
Inventory	4 000						
Total current assets			18 800				
Non-current assets							
Van (at cost)	5 000						
Less Accumulated depreciation	(1 000)						
Total non-current assets			4 000				
Total assets					22 800		
Liabilities							
Current liabilities							
Accounts payable	2 000						
Total current liabilities			2 000				
Non-current liabilities	NIL		NIL				
Total liabilities					2 000		
Net assets							20 800
Equity							
Capital	10 000						
Profit and loss	10 800						
Total equity							20 800

Notice that the balance sheet merely takes the final line of the worksheet and classifies it under appropriate headings to enable the reader to interpret the information more readily, as covered in Chapter 10.

Figure 11.1 summarises the various steps involved in the recording of financial information and the preparation of financial statements.

COMPUTERISED ACCOUNTING SYSTEMS

These days most business organisations use a computerised accounting system to prepare financial statements. There are a large number of computerised systems (e.g. Quicken, MYOB, AcPac, Quick Books Attaché and Microsoft Money) and the software an entity chooses depends on the size, type and complexity of its business. In all cases, however, the bookkeeping process is simplified using a computerised system.

FIGURE 11.1 THE FINANCIAL RECORDING PROCESS

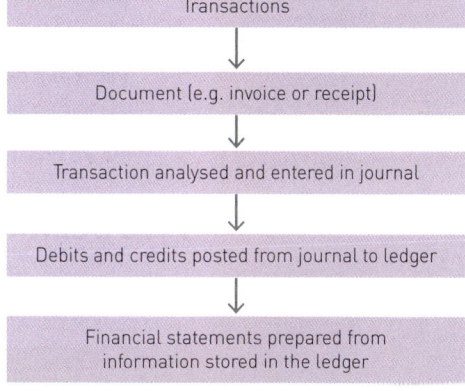

Transactions

↓

Document (e.g. invoice or receipt)

↓

Transaction analysed and entered in journal

↓

Debits and credits posted from journal to ledger

↓

Financial statements prepared from information stored in the ledger

SUMMARY

LEARNING OBJECTIVE 1

EXPLAIN THE USE OF DEBITS AND CREDITS AND IDENTIFY THE RELATIONSHIP BETWEEN THE WORKSHEET APPROACH AND THE USE OF DEBITS AND CREDITS

Under the traditional approach, assets are shown as debit balances and liabilities and equities are shown as credit balances.

For asset accounts, increases are recorded as debits and decreases as credits. For liability and equity accounts, increases are recorded as credits and decreases as debits.

LEARNING OBJECTIVE 2

EXPLAIN THE ROLE OF JOURNALS, LEDGERS AND A TRIAL BALANCE

Transactions are normally not entered directly into a ledger account. Under the traditional approach, most businesses use a journal to initially enter a transaction into the accounting records. The journal is often called the book of original entry. It is a chronological record showing the debits and credits from transactions. At convenient intervals these transactions are transferred (posted) from the journal to the relevant ledger accounts. At the end of accounting periods, a trial balance (a listing of all ledger balances) is prepared.

LEARNING OBJECTIVE 3

EXPLAIN END-OF-PERIOD ADJUSTMENTS AND PREPARE A TRIAL BALANCE AND AN EXTENDED TRIAL BALANCE

End-of-period adjusting journal entries are prepared for items like allowance for doubtful debts and depreciation expense. Once all the entries are recorded they are posted to the ledger accounts and an extended trial balance is prepared.

LEARNING OBJECTIVE 4

PREPARE FINAL ACCOUNTS FROM AN EXTENDED TRIAL BALANCE.

The final step in the process is to prepare journal entries that record any losses. The extended trial balance can be prepared from the financial statements.

REVIEW QUESTIONS

1   Explain the role of journals and ledger accounts.
2   Explain why it is important to prepare journal entries instead of simply posting transactions directly to the ledger accounts.
3   Explain the differences between a trial balance prepared under a traditional approach and one prepared from a worksheet.
4   Explain, in your own words, the meaning of the terms 'trial balance' and 'extended trial balance'.
5   Explain the meaning of the term 'final adjustments'.
6   Why are final adjustments not required in the cash basis of accounting?

PROBLEMS FOR DISCUSSION AND ANALYSIS

1   Identify the affected accounts from the following list of transactions and the effect of the transactions on the accounts as illustrated in the first transaction.

TRANSACTION	ACCOUNT	EFFECT	ACCOUNT
Purchased office furniture on credit	Office furniture Accounts payable	Increasing Increasing	Debit Credit
A vehicle is donated to the business by the owner			
A building is purchased with 50% paid in cash and the remaining 50% from a short-term loan			
Goods that had been sold on credit were returned (ignore the cost of the goods sold)			
Received payment for an outstanding account receivable			
Sold goods for cash			
Recorded the cost of goods sold for cash			
Purchased goods on credit			
Paid 6 months insurance in advance			
Paid land rates in arrears			
Recorded interest income due to be received at the end of the period			
Collected bill receivable plus interest			

2   Amber Ltd. had the following transactions during June:

» 3 Paid electricity bill, $480

» 5 Purchased inventory on credit, $2500

» 7 Sold goods on credit, $12 000

» 9 Prepaid insurance for June to October, $6000

» 12 Paid salary expense, $2500

» 15 Paid account payable from June 5

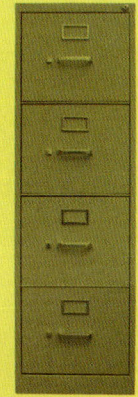

» 22 Purchased furniture for cash, $8500

» 26 Purchased inventory on credit, $3400

» 31 Recorded adjusting entry for June insurance

» 31 Accrued June salary of $1800.

Explain how each transaction would be handled under the cash basis and the accrual basis of accounting.

3 At the end June the following trial balance was prepared:

From the additional information provided in the list below prepare the adjusting journal entries and an extended trial balance.

a $6500 sales revenue has not yet been earned.

b June salaries of $4300 will be paid in July

c June interest due on loan of $1500 not yet paid.

	DEBIT $	CREDIT $
Cash	49680	
Accounts receivable	33700	
Inventory	27840	
Land and buildings	188000	
Accounts payable		22000
Loan		28000
Capital		80000
Sales		275420
Cost of goods sold	45000	
Advertising expense	16000	
Electricity account	7700	
Rent expense	12000	
Salaries expense	25500	
	405420	405420

4 Prepare a balance sheet from the following information:

	$
Accounts payable	7500
Accounts receivable	10000

	$
Equipment	137 000
Land and buildings	270 000
Inventory	7 300
Dividends	6 000
Debentures payable	250 000
Cash	6 500
Taxation	10 000
Retained profits	24 500
Paid-up capital	?

5 Prepare a balance sheet from the following information:

	$
Bank overdraft	10 000
Land and buildings	120 000
Accounts receivables	13 450
Accounts payable	29 600
Inventory	63 230
Short-term loan payable	15 000
Vehicles	27 300
Equipment	7 600
Taxation	10 000
General reserve	27 000
Dividends payable	13 500
50 000 $1 preference shares fully paid	50 000
Prepaid insurance	750
50 000 $1 ordinary shares fully paid	50 000
Retained earnings	?

6 Refer to Problem 16 in Chapter 6 of this textbook. Prepare a trial balance from your worksheet.

7 Refer to Problem 15 in Chapter 6 of this textbook. Record the transactions as debits and credits, and show them in the form of T accounts. Prepare a trial balance.

8 Record the following transactions, using a worksheet, and then translate each transaction into debits and credits and show them in the form of T accounts.

		$
Jan. 2	J. Smith paid capital into bank account	20 000
2	Bought goods from Hall; paid cash	3 400
3	Purchased shop fittings, on credit, from Alco	1 450
3	Returned faulty shop fittings to Alco	450
3	Sold goods to Jones on credit	200
5	Paid account due to Alco	1 000
6	Received payment from Jones, less the allowed discount	190
8	Paid wages	200
9	Paid a fee to have the telephone connected	50
10	Paid the rent for January	100

9 Record the following transactions using a worksheet, and then post each transaction into T accounts. Prepare a trial balance.

		$
June 1	B. Bloggs deposited money in a business bank account	25 000
2	Negotiated overdraft from bank as additional capital	10 000
3	Bought inventory from A. Fiddle on credit	16 500
3	Bought equipment from T. Xerox on credit	3 000
4	Paid one month's rent in advance on shop premises	1 000
5	Sold goods on credit to I. Dunno	2 000
8	Cash sales for the week ending June 8	9 750
10	I. Dunno returned faulty goods, gave full credit	630
11	Purchased stock from B. Fawlty for cash	13 560
15	Cash sales for the week ending June 15	6 760
17	Paid A. Fiddle	16 500
18	Bought vehicle on 14 days credit	27 600
19	Paid T. Xerox	3 000
19	Paid telephone account	175
19	Paid electricity account	150

		$
20	Bought insurance and prepaid three months	1800
24	I. Dunno paid his account	2000
26	Sold goods on account to M. Mouse	13750
27	Paid bank $2000 plus interest to reduce overdraft	2100
29	Cash sales, week ending 29 June	5330

10 Philjen balances its books on 31 December each year. As the accountant, you are required to make adjustments to balances in the business's accounts. Journalise, in general journal form, the following items. Each adjustment is independent of the others.

   a   The next electricity account is due on 31 January the following year. Over the past three years the January quarterly account has averaged $7500.

   b   The annual insurance premium was paid on 15 December and amounted to $2880.

   c   Debentures to the value of $100 000 were issued on 1 August with a coupon rate of 10 per cent paid quarterly.

   d   An order worth $40 000 was received by phone from Pamik to be delivered next January. Confirmation of the order was to be sent by post but had not been received by balance date.

   e   In December, Philjen ran an advertising campaign stating that cash received 28 days in advance of goods being delivered would receive a cash discount of 20 per cent. At balance date, the cash discount account had a balance of $23 000.

11 Prepare the trial balance at the end of the period, after recording the following opening balances and transactions in the appropriate accounts:

	DEBIT	CREDIT
	$	$
Cash at bank		4000
Accounts payable		5600
Mortgage		10000
Capital		20000
Accounts receivable	9600	
Inventory	13200	
Delivery vehicles	2400	
Premises	14400	
	39600	39600

    The transactions were:

   a   Purchases (on credit) amount to $2800.

   b   Sales bring in $1600 cash, $800 credit.

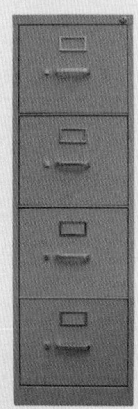

c   Capital is increased by $8000.

d   A $2000 bill for rates and taxes is received, not yet paid.

e   Suppliers are paid $2800.

f   Wages are paid $800.

12 Prepare general journal entries to record the following transactions:

a   A building worth $100 000 is acquired and financed by paying $20 000 in cash and negotiating a mortgage for the remaining $80 000.

b   Depreciation on factory machines is estimated to be $2000.

c   A total of 100 shares in Ravan Publishing are acquired as a long-term investment for $1350 cash.

d   A partner introduces a new truck valued at $3000 as part of his partnership capital.

e   Henry Smith opens a business bank account with his own personal cheque for $4000.

f   Provided $1000 for depreciation on the factory building for this period.

g   A 10-year $100 000 debenture secured by the company's real estate is issued at a discount of 5 per cent with the balance of $95 000 received in cash.

h   A 2-hectare vacant block at Welshpool is acquired for a cash payment of $50 000, to provide for future expansion.

i   Faulty goods which had cost a business $25 are returned to the supplier for a credit to the business's account.

j   Harold Black, a partner in Black, Brown, Green and White, withdraws $200 cash to meet his own personal expenses.

k   A cheque for $6000 is received for six months' interest to 30 June, on debentures held as an investment.

Note to instructors: The following problems are considered more suitable for use in MBA courses. However, undergraduate courses may also find them useful.

13 Prepare general journal entries for the following independent transactions. You can also prepare a worksheet for the same data. *Note:* Some of the terms that are used will need to be looked up in the Glossary or an accounting dictionary.

a   Issued 5000 fully paid $1 shares for cash.

b   Exchanged a piece of equipment with a fair value of $10 000 for 5000 fully paid $2 shares in DEF Ltd.

c   The profit for the year was $12 500. The directors decided to pay a total dividend of $5000 on issued shares, the balance transferred to retained profits.

d   Transferred $6000 from retained profits to general reserve.

e   Repaid $100 000 of debentures, together with accumulated interest of $4000 from cash.

14 Prepare general journal entries for the following independent transactions. *Note:* Some of the terms that are used will need to be looked up in the Glossary or an accounting dictionary.

a   Issued 25 000 $1 ordinary shares paid to 80 cents for cash.

b   Issued 200 $2 ordinary shares to a solicitor in exchange for legal advice.

c   Profit for the year was $123 000. Directors paid the 5 per cent dividend on 100 000 $1 preference shares, and on $60 000 to ordinary shareholders, and the balance was transferred to retained profits.

d   Issued $1 000 000 of 5 per cent debentures at par and for cash.

e   Exchanged 10 000 $2 fully paid ordinary shares for equipment with a fair market value of $19 500.

15 The following trial balance and extended trial balance has been prepared. Record the adjustments on the table provided and journalise the adjusting entries.

ACCOUNT TITLE	TRIAL BALANCE DEBIT	TRIAL BALANCE CREDIT	ADJUSTMENT	ADJUSTMENT	EXTENDED TRIAL BALANCE DEBIT	EXTENDED TRIAL BALANCE CREDIT
Cash at bank	7 100				7 100	
Accounts receivable	4 800				4 800	
Interest receivable					100	
Bill receivable	3 500				3 500	
Supplies	4 000				3 400	
Prepaid rent	2 800				1 900	
Equipment	50 000				50 000	
Accounts payable		5 400				5 400
Salary payable						1 000
Unearned revenue		6 000				2 000
Capital		49 900				49 900
Sales revenue		15 100				19 100
Interest income						100
Salary expense	3 100				4 100	
Rent expense					900	
Insurance expense	700				700	
Supplies expense					600	
Telephone expense	400				400	
	76 400	76 400			77 500	77 500

16 The trial balance of the Hourglass Organisation (presented overleaf) does not balance. On examining the records, you discover the following information:

a   The purchase of supplies using $500 cash was incorrectly recorded as a purchase on credit.

b   The debits and credits of accounts payable totalled $10 000 and $14 000 respectively.

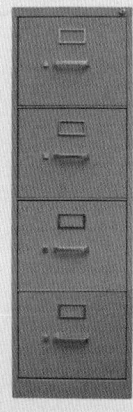

c C. Hourglass's capital balance is $8500.

d A $1000 payment for supplies was not posted to the cash at bank account.

e A payment of $500 for rent was not recorded in the cash at bank account.

Required

Prepare a corrected trial balance.

THE HOURGLASS ORGANISATION
TRIAL BALANCE AT 30 JUNE 20X3

ACCOUNT TITLE	DEBIT	CREDIT
	$	$
Cash at bank	7 620	
Accounts receivable	3 000	
Supplies inventory	480	
Plant and equipment	10 600	
Accounts payable	4 000	
Loan payable		6 000
G. Hourglass capital		5 800
G. Hourglass drawings	3 800	
Repairs revenues		18 000
Salary expense	6 000	
Rent expense	4 000	
Other expenses	2 500	
Totals	42 000	29 800

17 The following trial balance has been extracted from the books of the Tiger Partnership:

THE TIGER PARTNERSHIP
TRIAL BALANCE AT 30 JUNE 20X7

	DEBIT	CREDIT
	$	$
J. Lion Capital (1 July 20X6)		25 000
K. Jaguar Capital (1 July 20X6)		31 000
Commission received		2 500
Cash at bank	22 680	
J. Lion drawings	3 700	
K. Jaguar drawings	2 100	

	DEBIT	CREDIT
	$	$
Rent expense	6 000	
General office expenses	3 000	
Motor vehicle expenses	4 600	
Accounts payable		23 000
Purchases	126 000	
Allowance for doubtful debts		1 800
Inventories (1 July 20X6)	24 000	
Sales		165 000
Insurance expense	1 200	
Bad debt expense	1 100	
Gain on sale of van		1 200
Accounts receivable	25 000	
Motor vehicles (cost)	20 000	
Accumulated depreciation: motor vehicles		4 500
Furniture (cost)	6 000	
Accumulated depreciation: furniture		880
Salaries expense	9 500	
Totals	254 880	254 880

The following additional information is available.

a Inventories at 30 June 20X7 are $15 000.

b Depreciation is to be charged at the following rates:

  i   motor vehicles: four years straight-line with 10 per cent residual value

  ii furniture: 10 years straight-line with zero residual value.

c Rent for June 20X7 ($600) is unpaid.

d The allowance for doubtful debts is to be increased to $2000.

Required

a Record the adjusting journal entries

b Prepare an extended trial balance

c Prepare an income statement for the partnership for the year ended 30 June 20X7, and a balance sheet at that date.

ETHICS CASE STUDY

Carl Killjoy has been employed by Phil's Perfect Printers for three years as a junior sales representative. Recently, Carl undertook an online accounting computer packages course and has been rewarded with a more senior position in the accounting department. After examining the trial balance at the end of the month, Phil noticed that accounts receivable had an extremely high balance and that the cash at bank account was less than expected. Carl was asked to examine the accounts to see if he could find any anomalies. Carl had only ever entered transactions into a computerised system and was unsure how to go about checking for any anomalies. He reported to Phil that all the balances were correct. Phil decided to examine the accounts himself. After looking at the ledger accounts and tracing several transactions back to the journal entries, Phil found that four sales transactions totalling $34 000 had been recorded under accounts receivable when they should have been posted to the cash at bank, as all four sales were paid for in cash. Carl had not prepared the initial transactions but had merely processed the information he had been given. I.M. Devious, the person responsible, had left the company and Phil discovered that the names of the accounts receivable that had been created were fictional.

Required

1 Look at the journal entries I.M. Devious had recorded and explain what he had done. What should the entries have been?

2 If Phil had not been concerned with the accounts receivable balances, when would the fraud have been discovered?

3 Discuss what you would do, in relation to Carl and I.M. Devious, if you were Phil.

SUGGESTED ANSWERS TO STOP AND THINK EXERCISES IN THE CHAPTER

1 Debits and credits are rules concerning the recording of transactions into asset, liability, income, revenue, expense and equity accounts.

2 Ledgers and journals are part of the recording process. Transactions are initially recorded in journals and then the journal entries are transferred to the relevant ledger accounts for individual accounts such as cash, accounts receivable, and so on.

AN INTRODUCTION TO MANAGEMENT ACCOUNTING: A STRATEGIC PERSPECTIVE

LEARNING OBJECTIVES

At the end of this chapter, you should be able to:

1. identify the range of decisions made by managers and explain the differences between strategic and operating decisions
2. explain why management's decision making needs cannot be met solely by the information supplied in the general-purpose financial reports (GPFR)
3. explain why external stakeholders generally desire access to accounting information beyond that disclosed in GPFR and why some are successful in gaining access
4. explain the value chain concept and how it is used to describe the creation of value
5. explain how information technology has influenced the structure and performance of value chains
6. explain what is meant by strategic management
7. explain the concept of strategic choice and Porter's generic competitive strategies
8. explain how accounting information contributes to strategic management
9. explain how organisational size and structure, the technology employed and environmental factors influence the design of accounting information systems and the information supplied to managers.

INTRODUCTION

As discussed in prior chapters, accounting is an important source of information for various parties when making resource allocation decisions. Until now, our focus has been on the users of accounting information who are external to the entity (e.g. shareholders, creditors and providers of debt capital). We saw how transactions and other economic events were accounted for and financial accounting information reported to external users in the form of the general-purpose financial reports (GPFR). It was noted that the decisions made by external users about the allocation of scarce economic resources could be guided, in part, by the insight provided by financial statement analysis.

As discussed in Chapter 10, external users also use other sources of information to make resource allocation decisions. For example, when existing shareholders in Woolworths review their equity investment, apart from the company's GPFR, other disclosures made by the firm itself (e.g. announcements relating to the opening of new Masters Home Improvement outlets or disposal of business segments) would be examined. Beyond company-sourced disclosures, shareholders would also look at information about the state of the Australian economy; changing regulations in the form of industrial relations and wage rates; and trading hours and levels of competition as they impact on the financial performance and position of Woolworths. Furthermore, information about the activities and performance of Woolworths' competitors (e.g. Coles, Metcash and ALDI) would be reviewed by shareholders when making decisions about maintaining, increasing or decreasing their shareholdings.

Our attention now turns to the information produced for the benefit of an entity's management. As managers also make decisions about the allocation of scarce economic resources, they require access to relevant and reliable information. However, given the many different types of resource allocation decisions made by a firm's managers, the information they require is provided in more detail, tailored to particular decision-making needs, produced more frequently, presented in both financial and non-financial forms and with varying time perspectives (i.e. past, present and future).

1 LEARNING OBJECTIVE

Identify the range of decisions made by managers and explain the differences between strategic and operating decisions

MANAGERIAL DECISION MAKING AND ACCOUNTING INFORMATION

Due to the complexity and scale of operations undertaken by many firms, it would be difficult for any one manager to plan and control all activities. Complete knowledge of inputs, the nature of the business transformation process and the marketability of products or services is rarely held by one manager. Thus, responsibilities for carrying out business activities are distributed within a hierarchical chain of command where managers perform different types of tasks (e.g. research and development, production, marketing, human resource management, treasury and cost management) at differing levels of complexity (e.g. strategic, tactical and operational).

The primary responsibility of a firm's managers is to make decisions and these are usually partitioned into three levels of decision making.

TABLE 12.1 DECISION MAKING: STRATEGIC, TACTICAL AND OPERATIONAL

DECISION MAKING LEVELS	MANAGERIAL LEVEL	DECISION ACTIVITY	NATURE OF DECISION OUTPUTS
Strategic	Top	Strategic planning	Goals, objectives, strategies and policies.
Tactical	Middle	Management control	Implementation of strategies and administration of policies.
Operational	Lower	Task control	Performance of tasks efficiently and effectively.

As indicated by Table 12.1, each management level may relate to a similar type of decision task (e.g. developing a new product) but markedly differ in scope. While top management may set a firm's strategic goals, it delegates to middle-level managers the making of decisions about how plans to achieve strategic goals are implemented. Middle-level managers, in turn, delegate the day-to-day decision making over the implementation activities to lower level managers. In a sense, middle-level managers act as 'agents' to top-level management and lower-level managers serve as the agents of middle-level managers.

12.1 KEY CONCEPT

STRATEGIC DECISIONS

Strategic decisions determine the long-term goals of the organisation and identify and allocate the economic and other resources required to achieve these goals. Given the long-term time horizon and the scale of resources required to implement strategic decisions, they are typically very difficult to change or reverse.

12.2 KEY CONCEPT

OPERATIONAL DECISIONS

Operational decisions focus on the short-term efficient use of resources currently made available to the organisation. Given the time horizon and limited resources required for the implementation of operational decisions, they can be quickly modified or reversed.

Table 12.2 provides specific examples of the different scope of decision-making tasks performed at the three levels of management activity.

TABLE 12.2 STRATEGIC PLANNING, MANAGEMENT AND OPERATIONAL CONTROL

STRATEGIC PLANNING	MANAGEMENT CONTROL	TASK CONTROL
Determine direction and funding of research and development.	Administer research and development department.	Engage in individual or group research and development project.
Add a new product line.	Expand production capacity.	Production scheduling.
Acquire a business that is in an unrelated industry.	Establish new products (or brand name) within the existing product line.	Process customer orders.
Alter marketing focus to social media channels.	Administer advertising budget.	Book and monitor promotions on social media websites.
Adopt equal employment opportunity policy.	Implement equal employment opportunity policy.	Maintain equal employment opportunity records.
Alter weighted average cost of capital by restructuring capital.	Issue new debt.	Prepare cash flow forecasts and monitor actual cash flows.
Adopt just-in-time inventory management policy.	Determine inventory levels.	Reorder inventory when reorder point triggered.
Implement total quality management system.	Identify and implement supplier quality assurance performance metrics.	Monitor and report on supplier performance.

2 LEARNING
OBJECTIVE

Explain why
management's decision
making needs cannot
be met solely by the
information supplied in
the GPFR

As a starting point, we examine an existing business where management has already decided upon a course of action to follow. In this situation, management is interested in the outcomes of past decisions. Managers can obtain some information from GPFR, but often this is insufficient as they contain highly aggregated and simplified information. While this information might alert management to the fact that profits are lower than anticipated, it is unlikely to identify the cause of this shortfall.

Managers almost always need more detailed information about the results of past decisions and actions than provided in the annual GPFR. As the name implies, annual GPFR are drawn up once a year. Thus, they are unlikely to be sufficient to meet the needs of managers, who require more regular and up-to-date information. The fact that annual GPFR are produced only at the year's end means, even if explanations for results varying from those anticipated are provided, means that it might be too late for corrective action. For example, with a June 30 year-end for accounting purposes, a firm's GPFR may not be released until the end of September. Although management has access to the year's results before they are published, there still might be a considerable delay, with the effect that corrective action is correspondingly delayed. Furthermore, as annual GPFR are for a year, matters requiring managerial attention may have occurred more than 12 months previously and corrective action is no longer feasible.

Managers require the more frequent provision of information so they can promptly monitor the results of their actions and decisions and finetune the business as required. This is not to imply that the needs of managers cannot be met by the accounting information system on which the annual GPFR are based. For example, although the annual GPFR show only one figure for accounts receivable, the underlying accounting records provide information about the individual debts making up total receivables. This includes information about when credit sales occurred and the customer's past payment record. This detailed information allows management to more quickly collect moneys owing and to follow-up receivables where collection is slow. By doing this, management will ensure that the business does not face the problems that could be avoided if cash flows has been properly managed.

There are other examples of information contained within the accounting information system which, if presented and used in different ways from those required for drawing up annual GPFR, would better meet management's needs. For example, the basic information required for both variable and absorption costing is available from the accounting information system (AIS). Accounting Standard AASB 102 on absorption and variable costing for reporting purposes only permits the use absorption costing for external reporting purposes. However, for internal decision-making purposes, a manager may find variable costing provides a more useful way of valuing inventories. Chapter 14 provides a fuller explanation of absorption and variable costing systems and the problems associated with their use in practice. This discussion provides the basis for understanding the relative merits and limitations of these alternatives from the point of view of management.

Thus, depending on the decision faced, management might need information presented in different ways. For example, in deciding if to continue making a particular product, managers will require forward-looking information such as sales forecasts. Managers will need to know the point at which revenue equals cost (i.e. the break-even point) and how likely it is that this point will be reached. While sales and marketing will be the source of information about future sales, information about product costs at different levels of output will be sourced from the accounting information system.

If good decisions are to be made by managers, a sound understanding of these principles is required. For example, in the airline industry you might need to know several break-even positions: one that covers operating costs, a second that covers costs plus the finance charges incurred in buying aircraft, and a third at which the airline is profitable. In this case, the break-even positions could be expressed in terms of seat occupancy (i.e. passenger load carried). Of course, the break-even point is only part of the information required by an airline's managers.

Although management needs other information, possibly in different forms, it is important to understand that the base information used for the annual GPFR can be used for many different reports provided to managers. As for the other users referred to in Chapter 1, financial information is only one of a number of types of information required by managers to make decisions about the future direction and actions of a business. While a discussion of other types of information is beyond the scope of this text, they include marketing information, employment legislation, and so on. Our discussion of meeting the decision-making needs of management will be within the narrow confines of management accounting information.

12.3 KEY CONCEPT

INFORMATION AND THE DECISION-MAKING NEEDS OF MANAGERS

Managers generally need to have access to frequently supplied, detailed and up-to-date information tailored to the decisions they are required to make.

Managers do require frequent and detailed information in formats different to the annual GPFR. This information is used to monitor progress and take appropriate actions to finetune the business. Implicit in this monitoring process is that the results are judged against some expectations. As discussed below, these expectations might be the rough plans committed to memory by the owner-operator of a small business or, in the case of a larger entity, highly detailed and documented plans and budgets.

The process of strategic planning, and the ways in which the accounting information is derived and used to support this process, are discussed later in this chapter. Chapter 13 examines how accounting information is used to measure and evaluate business performance and Chapter 15 discusses the budgeting process and provides a detailed analysis of the ways in which budgets can be used to facilitate organisational control. Budgets secure organisational control through their feed-forward or planning role and their feedback or performance reporting role. The impact of performance measures and budgets on managers is briefly discussed in this chapter, with a more detailed discussion to follow in chapters 13 and 15.

As noted, most, if not all, of this information is also useful to users other than the organisation's managers. We now consider what the external users' needs might be, who they are, and the factors (e.g. relative power, competition and confidentiality) that determine the level of access such users can have to internal information.

STOP AND THINK 1

What are the main reasons management requires more information than is given in the GPFR?

EXTERNAL STAKEHOLDERS AND ACCESS TO MANAGEMENT AND OTHER ACCOUNTING INFORMATION

3 LEARNING OBJECTIVE

Explain why external stakeholders generally desire access to accounting information beyond that disclosed in the GPFR and why some are successful in gaining access

We commenced with a brief review of the financial accounting information provided to external stakeholders such as shareholders and lenders. Would external users also find the accounting information provided to managers to be beneficial? Given the level of detail, timeliness and forward-looking properties of the accounting information provided to management, external stakeholders would most certainly appreciate having access to this information. However, some of it is commercially sensitive, and the achievement of organisational goals might be dependent on the company's plans being kept secret from competitors. For example, if a competitor was aware of the costs and profit margins of a rival firm's products, this knowledge could be used by the competitor to develop strategies for attacking the rival's market share. Thus, few incentives exist for firms to provide access to information beyond their statutory obligations (e.g. the annual GPFR).

While there are important reasons for a business restricting access to management accounting information, some external users have the power to command access to information beyond that reported in the GPFR. As to who can gain access to internal information: it depends not only on who they are, but also upon their relationship with the organisation.

By virtue of statutory requirements, a firm can be obliged to disclose more detailed information than is reported in the annual GPFR. For example, taxation authorities, which include the Australian Taxation Office (ATO) and the Australian Customs and Border Protection Service, have the power to demand access to accounting information so that they can assess the taxes or tariffs that are due. Other statutory authorities, such as the Australian Bureau of Statistics (ABS), also have the power to command a firm provides information in the form of responses to a survey. For example, firms selected to complete the ABS Economic Activity Survey are required to provide information about employment numbers, income, expenses, inventories and capital expenditure and asset disposals. Other external users who may gain access to information beyond GPFR include a firm's bankers. Bankers would not be dependent users, which is part of the definition of a reporting entity as discussed in Chapter 2. The information they access depends on the circumstances involved. For example, when a company is seeking to borrow, a bank might require the applicant to supplement the loan application with not only its GPFR and income tax returns but also to provide more detailed information about the planned use of the borrowed funds. A firm may be required to submit a business case in support of its loan application, which documents the background to the loan (i.e. what the borrowed funds are to be used for), expected economic benefits and costs of the investment, analysis of rival firms (competitor analysis) and expected changes in the firm's market share, incremental income and costs, anticipated risks and strategies to mitigate these risks, and so on.

Once a loan has been approved, a bank's decision changes from accepting or rejecting the loan application to monitoring the ongoing creditworthiness of the borrower. Depending on the bank's exposure to loss in terms of both the amount lent and the risk of the debt being partially or fully irrecoverable, monitoring of the borrower's financial health would vary in its level of intensity. For example, if a borrower is trading profitably with positive operating cash flows, the information required would be different to that required if the firm was in financial difficulty.

4 LEARNING OBJECTIVE

Explain the value chain concept and how it is used to describe the creation of value

THE ORGANISATION AS A VALUE CHAIN

Porter (1985) describes the sequence of activities engaged in by an organisation as being a value chain. All organisations acquire and transform inputs into outputs (e.g. products or services) that are supplied to customers or clients. Successful organisations create the greatest value from the way they acquire and transform inputs into products or services valued by their customers.

Activities are the means by which value is created in products or services. An activity is any task or unit of work engaged in with the intention of achieving a specified goal. As activities use resources, they incur costs and, in combination with other activities, provide a product or service that earns revenue. There are two points to note about the relationship between a business and its customers:

- Customers purchase value, which they measure by comparing the firm's products and services with similar offerings made by rivals.
- A business creates value by carrying out its activities either more efficiently than its rivals, or by combining activities in such a way as to provide a product or service for its customers superior to that of its rivals. As discussed below, the first approach to value creation can enable a business to pursue a

cost-leadership strategy while the second approach may allow a business to follow a differentiation strategy.

Figure 12.1 provides a very simple example of a generic value chain where a business procures inputs from suppliers (e.g. raw materials, components and finished products), transforms those inputs into a product (or service) and distributes those products (or provides services) to customers (or clients).

FIGURE 12.1 A GENERIC VALUE

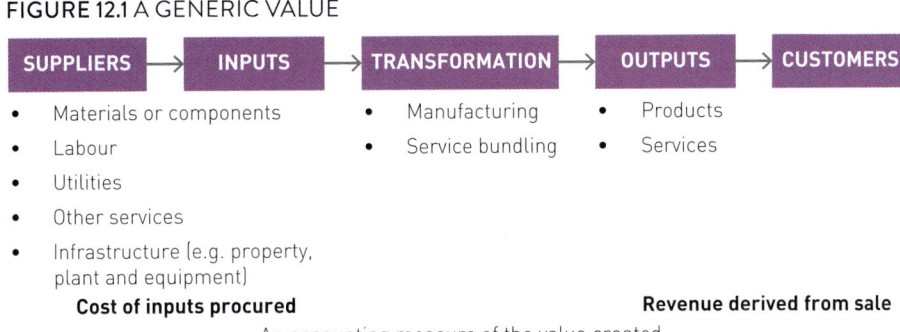

As indicated by Figure 12.1, given costs are incurred in procuring and transforming inputs, these might be more correctly identified as being expenses. Where customers pay for the products or services supplied to them, this constitutes income in the form of sales or fee revenue. From our coverage of financial accounting, we know the difference between income and expenses is profit and this number can be one measure of the value created by a business.

KEY CONCEPT

VALUE CHAIN

The value chain comprises the sequence of activities that transforms acquired inputs into products or services valued by customers

Porter (1985) analysed the activities of organisations and developed models of their value chains. Porter categorised value chain activities as being either primary or support activities.

- Primary activities comprise those product- and market-related activities that create value.
- Product-related primary activities include:
  - inbound logistics (e.g. transportation and receipt of materials from suppliers, management of raw materials inventories and in-house movement of raw materials to production)
  - operational activities that transform inputs into finished products (e.g. development, testing, processing, packaging and maintenance)
  - after-sales service (e.g. customer support and training, installation, warranties, spare-parts management and repair services).
- Market-related primary activities include:
  - marketing and sales (e.g. advertising, channel selection, product promotion, selling, product pricing and customer relationship management)
  - outbound logistics (e.g. warehousing of finished products prior to sale, order fulfilment, transportation and distribution management).

- Support activities do not create value by themselves but are essential if primary activities are to function efficiently and effectively. Support activities include:
  - procurement (e.g. sourcing of goods or services delivered at the best price, in the right quantity, to the right place, at the right time and to the required quality specifications)
  - technology management (e.g. value engineering through product and process design and automation)
  - human resource management (e.g. design and definition of occupational roles, recruitment and retention of employees, appraisal and reward, development and training, maintenance of organisational culture and values, and change management)
  - corporate-provided services (e.g. strategic planning, quality management, accounting and finance, public relations, information and communications technology, legal services, general management and corporate governance).

Figure 12.2 illustrates how a manufacturing firm identifies market opportunities that can be met through the development of a new product, determines how that product is to be manufactured through process design, procures the required inputs, adds value to the inputs by processing them, and generates outputs of value to its customers through distribution and after-sales service.

FIGURE 12.2 THE VALUE CHAIN OF A MANUFACTURING ORGANISATION

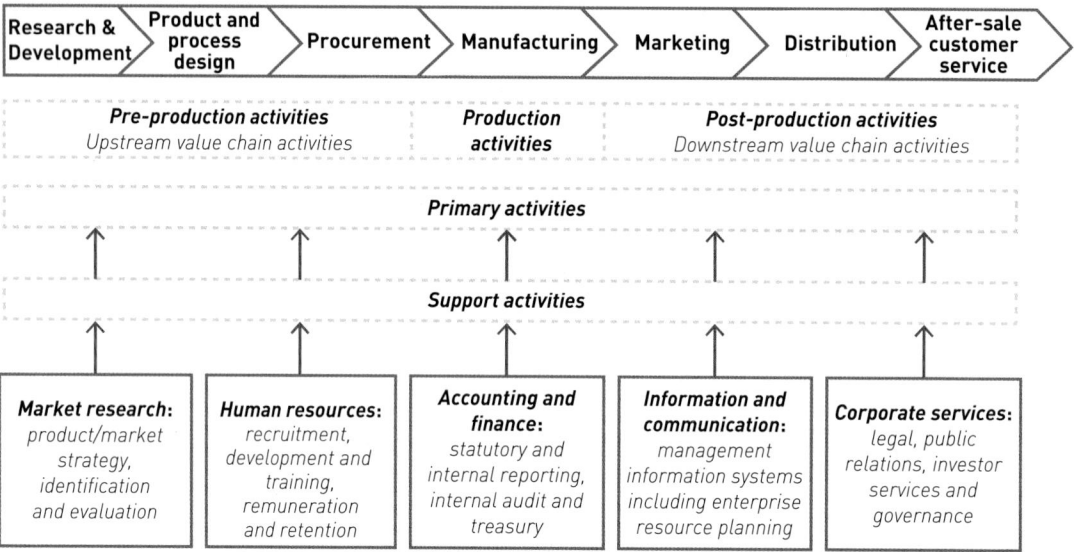

Adapted from: Porter, M. E. (1985), *Competitive Advantage: Creating and Sustaining Superior Performance*, The Free Press, New York, p. 37.

The industry value chain

The value chain concept is not limited to just the organisation and it can be used to analyse an industry. Figure 12.3 provides an illustration of the industry value chain for a manufactured product. Six discrete roles are identified in this industry. It begins with the production of raw materials and ends with the retail distribution of products and services. In order to better understand Figure 12.3, consider the automobile industry. Role 1 relates to the production of raw materials. An important material in the automotive industry is steel. A mining company that extracts iron ore from a mineral deposit could fill role 1. Role 2 relates to primary-level manufacturing where the iron ore is processed into steel. Role 3 is the fabrication of automotive parts, such as car body panels, from the steel. Role 4 is the assembly of cars. Role 5 is the distribution of the cars to dealers and Role 6 is retail sales. A seventh automotive industry role might include after-sales service, where extended warranties are provided by other businesses.

FIGURE 12.3 AN INDUSTRY VALUE CHAIN

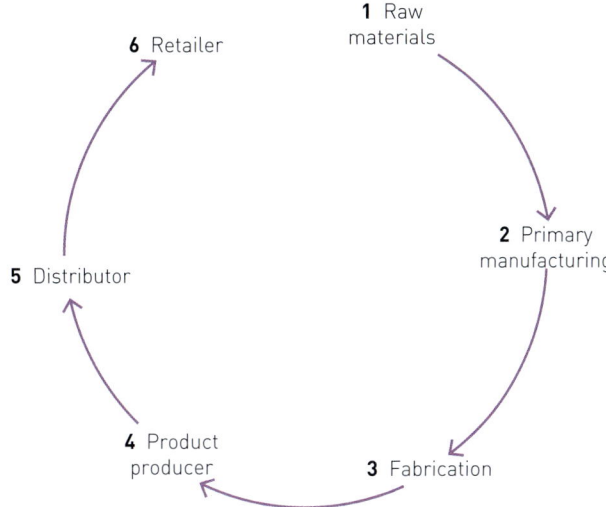

Vertical integration occurs within an industry value chain where one firm takes on multiple industry roles. This often occurs because a firm has determined that it is more efficient to perform a number of industry roles itself rather than relying on the marketplace. Such a vertical consolidation of roles is intended to reduce the transactional costs resulting from inter-organisational exchanges. Vertical integration within an industry value chain flows upstream or downstream. Upstream integration is movement towards the raw-materials end of the industry value chain. Downstream integration is movement closer to the end-use customer. In Chapter 2 we discussed consolidated financial statements that report the financial performance and position of firms that control other firms.

Information technology and the value chain

Information technology has had a dramatic effect on many value chains. For example, Australia's Big Four banks have made significant investments in information technology (IT) and automation while simultaneously rationalising the use of branch networks. As a result of these investments, the value chain of the Australian banking industry has moved from one based on face-to-face personal service at a bank branch to online self-service. Arguably, the banking industry's use of IT has improved the accessibility and quality of banking services (i.e. 24/7 from nearly anywhere in the world) beyond that which can be supplied through a physical branch network. From the customer's perspective, as online banking delivers lower operating costs to a bank, it potentially provides customers with a more attractive offer in terms of convenience and cost (i.e. lower fees and charges for online banking transactions). Larger banks will be the best positioned to exploit their IT investments and so achieve the lowest unit costs.

IT has also been used as a tool for extracting greater value out of the transactions that business has with suppliers and customers. Since 1999, IT has enabled Woolworths to extract significant cost savings from its supply chain with cumulative savings of some $8 billion. In more recent years, Woolworths has used IT to generate data about the buying behaviours of customers which it uses to develop tailored customer offers: attractive to customers and profitable for the retailer. Finally, the use of IT in place of labour continues to accelerate and is not limited to computer-controlled manufacturing equipment or production lines. For example, Rio is well progressed with its 'mine of the future' concept where mining roles across various functions and processes have been automated. The automated activities range from automated drilling and blasting through to the use of driverless trucks and trains for moving extracted ore from mine site to shipment port.

5 LEARNING OBJECTIVE

Explain how information technology has influenced the structure and performance of value chains

6 LEARNING
OBJECTIVE

Explain what is
meant by strategic
management

STRATEGIC MANAGEMENT

The environment for many firms is dynamic and for any particular business to succeed it must be able to respond to rapidly changing circumstances. For example, emerging competitive forces (e.g. in the form of new competitors or substitute products) can challenge the commercial viability of a firm's existing product range and marketing strategies. If a firm chooses to ignore the arrival of new competitors or substitute products and continues to focus solely on its current products and marketing strategies, its existing market share and profitability will be put at risk. To remain competitive, a firm may need to reinvent itself in terms of the products offered and the business model it employs. This process of responding to market change is called strategic management. The print media is currently facing such a strategic challenge from online news sources. Strategic management must be distinguished from the primarily short-term focus and internal orientation of tactical or operational management. Where tactical management is intended to ensure the continued efficient deployment of resources in pursuit of an agreed strategy, strategic management is about the development and implementation of new strategies for dealing with change in a firm's market.

Competitive advantage is anything that gives a firm an edge over its rivals in the products it sells or the services it offers. Ideally, a firm will aim to find a 'sustainable competitive advantage' (Porter 1985). Unless advantage can be sustained, profitability will be eroded as competitors seek to share in the benefits created by the firm. Therefore, strategic management is about trying to establish a competitive position that rival firms are not able to readily challenge. A firm that obtains a dominant position in a market (e.g. as a monopolist or even as a duopolist or oligopolist) can expect to earn above-average profits in the period in which its market power is not diminished.

KEY CONCEPT

COMPETITIVE ADVANTAGE

Competitive advantage is the advantage that a business has over its rivals in the products or services supplied to customers. By definition, this advantage cannot be readily replicated by business rivals.

Strategic management can be viewed as a cycle of planning and control undertaken at the strategic level. Strategic management occurs when an organisation's governing board and senior executives undertake the following tasks:

- development and communication of organisational goals and objectives. Given the purposeful nature of organisations it is essential that an understanding of organisational goals is shared by senior managers.
- identification and development of strategies that are consistent with the organisation's environment and facilitate the achievement of the organisation's goals and objectives. Completion of this leads to the documentation of a strategic plan, providing management with a long-term plan of action for how the organisation will be structured and its resources deployed.
- manage risks, evaluate strategies and implement strategies.
- integration of implemented strategies so that they are compatible with and reinforce one another.

12.6

KEY CONCEPT

STRATEGIC MANAGEMENT

Strategic management is the cycle of planning and control that determines the long-term policies of the organisation and identifies the tasks that must be carried out by managers if the company is to achieve its goals.

As will be evident in subsequent chapters, accounting information systems (AIS) support strategic management in many ways. For example, through the development of key financial and non-financial indicators, goals become measurable, strategies become capable of formal and quantifiable evaluation, and implementation becomes controllable through the identification and analysis of variances.

While varying views exist about the critical functions of strategic management, generally it includes:

- strategic analysis
- strategic planning
- strategy choice
- strategy implementation.

Strategy choice

Strategy choice follows from strategic analysis (see corporate analysis), which is commonly done using a SWOT (strengths, weaknesses, opportunities and threats) analysis or value chain analysis, and the formulation of clearly articulated mission statements, goals and objectives. In order to select a strategy, managers must develop and evaluate alternative strategies before a choice of strategy is made. Thus, strategy choice will involve:

- *Strategic option generation*

Strategic options generation entails the development of feasible options for creating organisational value consistent with a firm's mission and goals. Strategic options for a business could include: increasing market share through the introduction of new or improved products or services; achieving greater economies of scale through the development of new markets; focusing on activities that generate the greatest value by disposing of or outsourcing non-core or lower value-adding activities and the acquisition of other value-creating activities through horizontal or vertical integration.

- *Strategic options evaluation*

Feasible strategic options are evaluated by examining how well existing strengths are made use of, existing weaknesses are remedied or avoided, current and future opportunities are taken advantage of, and weaknesses are overcome. It is important to note that a strategic option that ticks all of the SWOT boxes may not progress beyond this point if it is unacceptable to the organisation's stakeholders.

- *Strategy selection*

The strategy-selection process is influenced by the values of the organisation's governing board and senior management. Strategy selection involves deciding: how a business will compete (e.g. with price or product quality); the product and market strategies the firm intends to pursue; and institutional strategies (linkages with other organisations) that determine the method of growth (e.g. horizontal or vertical integration).

7 LEARNING OBJECTIVE

Explain the concept of strategic choice and Porter's generic competitive strategies

PORTER'S GENERIC COMPETITIVE STRATEGIES

According to Porter (1980), to be successful, a firm must develop and implement strategies that deliver a competitive advantage. While Porter acknowledges that there are many different approaches for securing a competitive advantage – and the best strategy for a firm is ultimately determined by its own particular circumstances – he suggests that competitive strategies can be classified in terms of their source and scope.

As shown in Figure 12.4, a business may be able to deliver products or services at the lowest cost which allows it to set prices lower than its rivals (i.e. it will pursue a cost-leadership strategy). Alternatively, a firm might have products or services that, for reasons of quality or branding, provide such greater value to customers that it is able to set prices higher than its competitors. This latter strategy is termed as being a differentiation strategy. In terms of scope, a firm could be seeking to compete in the market as a whole or within a segment of the market. Thus, a firm may pursue either cost leadership or differentiation as an industry-wide strategy or alternatively seek to focus its activities on a segment of the market where again it will be pursuing, within that segment, a strategy of cost leadership (cost-focus strategy) or differentiation.

FIGURE 12.4 PORTER'S GENERIC COMPETITIVE STRATEGIES

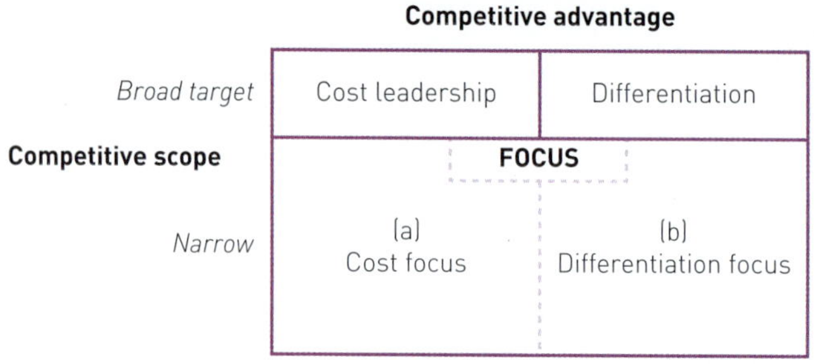

The competitive strategy a business adopts will be influenced by the competitive strategies pursued by its rivals. However, while a firm might pursue a particular strategy in an industry or segment, this does not preclude other rival firms from seeking to follow the same strategy. For example, in the Australasian grocery industry, the major national retailers have aggressively pursued cost-leadership strategies. However, at any one point in time, only one retailer can truthfully lay claim to being the industry's cost leader. As to whether or not such a cost leadership strategy is successful in the long run depends upon the retailer's ability to generate profit margins, providing an adequate return on investment. In some industries (e.g. tobacco and commercial aviation), the pursuit of cost leadership through price wars has eroded profit margins to such an extent that some industry members are no longer as profitable as they once were.

Table 12.3 highlights the advantages that each industry-wide strategy has in minimising threats from the industry's competitive forces, and their respective drawbacks.

TABLE 12.3 ADVANTAGES AND DISADVANTAGES OF COST LEADERSHIP AND DIFFERENTIATION COMPETITIVE STRATEGIES

ADVANTAGES	COST LEADERSHIP	DIFFERENTIATION
New entrants	Economies of scale raise barriers to entry.	Brand loyalty and perceived uniqueness are barriers to entry.
Substitutes	The firm is less vulnerable than less cost-effective competitors to the threat of substitutes.	Customer loyalty is a weapon against substitutes.

ADVANTAGES	COST LEADERSHIP	DIFFERENTIATION
Customers	Customers cannot drive down prices any further than the next most efficient competitor.	Customers have no comparable alternative.
Suppliers	Flexibility to deal with cost increases.	Higher margins can offset vulnerability to supplier price rises.
Industry rivalry	Firm remains profitable when rivals go under through excessive price competition.	Brand loyalty should lower price sensitivity.

DISADVANTAGES	COST LEADERSHIP	DIFFERENTIATION
Technology	Technological change requires capital investment as production will eventually become cheaper for competitors.	Where technology is a critical differentiating factor, a sustained investment in research and development is required.
Imitation	Competitors can learn via imitation.	Imitation narrows differentiation.
Product	Cost concerns ignore product design or marketing issues.	Customers may no longer require the differentiating factor.
Price	Increases in input costs can reduce any price advantage.	Eventually customers become price sensitive.

KEY CONCEPT

12.7

COST LEADERSHIP

Cost leadership is when a business competes by setting the selling prices of products or services lower than its competitors do.

KEY CONCEPT

12.8

DIFFERENTIATION

Differentiation is when a business competes by offering customers products or services that have non-price-related factors different to those of its competitors (e.g. superior product quality).

STOP AND THINK 2

Various stages in strategic management have been identified. Briefly describe the nature and contribution of:

- value analysis, SWOT analysis and Porter's **five forces model** to strategic analysis
- the identification of mission, goals and objectives for strategic planning
- Porter's generic competitive strategies to the choice of strategies.

Strategy implementation

Finally, chosen strategies need to be implemented. As discussed in Chapter 18, most strategies entail a significant change in business activities and models, and require a significant commitment of financial and other organisational resources. Thus, a more detailed discussion of the implementation of strategies will be deferred to Chapter 18 where the techniques for making capital investment decisions will be examined. However, aspects of strategy implementation will also be canvassed in our consideration of product costing systems in Chapter 14, budgeting in Chapter 15 and short-term decision making with and without resource constraints in Chapters 16 and 17.

Once a strategy is implemented, actual performance needs to be monitored and controlled. Monitoring is the measurement of actual against planned or budgeted performance and from this comparison, differences (commonly known as variances) are identified. It is highly unlikely that a firm's actual performance will be exactly the same as planned, the reason being that the strategic and operating decisions embodied in a budget are normally determined well in advance of actual performance, and great uncertainty surrounds the process of forecasting costs and revenues in a dynamic economic environment.

12.9 KEY CONCEPT

MONITORING AND CORRECTIVE ACTION

Monitoring is the process of comparing actual performance with a predetermined target (plan). It provides the basis from which corrective action can be planned and undertaken.

Ridofranz/iStockphoto

As discussed above, decision-making responsibility is distributed throughout a business, with managers at different hierarchical levels being responsible for different types of decisions. As most decisions involving the allocation of scarce economic resources have financial consequences, they can typically be measured in terms of cost, revenues and the use of capital in the form of property, plant and equipment. To effectively monitor performance, managers who incur expenses, generate revenues and/or use assets are identified and made responsible for these costs, revenues and/or capital. This approach is known as responsibility accounting. It recognises various decision centres throughout a business and traces the financial consequences of making resource-allocation decisions to the managers who made those decisions. As will be discussed in Chapter 13, responsibility centres are normally identified as departments, branches or divisions.

A manager's more detailed knowledge and participation in the preparation of his or her own budgets can be important in terms of the quality of decisions made and enhance the probability for effective planning and control. However, this more detailed knowledge coupled with opportunity of participating in setting budgets also places managers in a privileged position within the firm. The behavioural consequences of allowing managers to identify what resources are actually required to ensure targets are achieved by their responsibility centre and to explain why actual performance differs from planned performance will be addressed in Chapter 15.

12.10 KEY CONCEPT

RESPONSIBILITY ACCOUNTING

Responsibility accounting occurs when a firm's structure is divided into strategic business units and the performance of these units is evaluated with accounting numbers and other relevant non-financial measures.

To support a system of responsibility accounting, the AIS must communicate relevant information. The reports should show actual against planned performance and the deviations (variances) from what was planned. How budgeted and actual costs and revenues are collected and reported (e.g. by product, labour or material input costs) will be determined by management. The major factors influencing the extent and sophistication of performance reporting systems are the costs of installing and operating such systems compared with the benefits generated from the quality of information supplied for decision-making purposes.

When variances have been identified, it is necessary to determine the reason for them in order for corrective action to be taken. Where a budget reflects realistic targets, if deviations from a budget are not corrected, it could be harmful to the business in the long run. For example, the use of materials in a production process might exceed budget in a particular control period due to the use of poorly skilled personnel. The failure to ensure production employees have the required skills will result in the problem of unnecessary material losses continuing and the future profitability of the business being put at risk.

While the methods for the identification of variances and their causes are outside the scope of this text, you should have some insight into the general causes of variances. Traditionally, textbooks have tended to concentrate on variances that are caused by operating problems. For example, the prices of raw materials might be greater than anticipated by the budget as the firm's procurement practices are inefficient. Other potential causes of variances include the following:

- Operating variances related to human or mechanical factors (e.g. human error in the setting of the operational parameters of a machine).
- Random variances caused by divergences between actual and planned costs that arise without any pattern (i.e. they occur by chance and it is not possible to control them). For example, in some chemical processes, the ratio of actual output per unit of input can differ from expected because of variations that are inherent in the process itself (e.g. evaporation of heated liquids).
- Planning variances occur if plans are not realistic at the time of actual performance, even if operations have been efficiently carried out. For example, during the planning stage, oil costs might have been set with due care. However, global political instability can affect the oil industry's supply chain and the price of oil may rise. Thus, planned costs may no longer represent realistic budget targets simply because of the changes that have subsequently occurred and were unknown at the time the plan was formulated.

Although the analysis of operating, random and planning variances is theoretically sound, there are a number of problems that limit its use in practice. For a realistic budget that reflects recent operating conditions to be established, the budget must be flexed to these actual conditions, which, by their nature, can only be determined after the event. While such flexed budgets, known as performance reports, are useful for variance analysis purposes, they do not provide management with targets to work towards during the actual production period. This is a major deficiency in the use of these types of budgets. Another effective limitation is the cost of investigating the causes of variances. The task of investigating variances can be costly. It might not be worth the time and money to carry out an investigation for the benefits derived, particularly for variances that might be classified as being insignificant.

In Chapter 13 we will discuss issues relating to the assessment of performance at the levels of the individual and responsibility centres.

8 **LEARNING OBJECTIVE**

Explain how accounting information contributes to strategic management

STRATEGIC MANAGEMENT AND MANAGEMENT ACCOUNTING INFORMATION

A primary focus for this text is to build an understanding of how accounting information is developed and used strategically. For an appreciation of how management accounting information can be used strategically, consider Table 12.4:

TABLE 12.4 STRATEGIC MANAGEMENT AND MANAGEMENT ACCOUNTING INFORMATION

STRATEGIC MANAGEMENT TASK	CONTRIBUTION OF MANAGEMENT ACCOUNTING INFORMATION TO STRATEGIC MANAGEMENT
Strategic thinking	Provides significant information that directs managerial attention to strategic issues. Prompts include reporting a reduction in profitability, the loss of a major contract, a failure in the implementation of a project of strategic significance or a major change to the balance of competitive forces in the industry.
External analysis	Provides estimates of competitor costs and capital investment projects. Conduct industry life-cycle growth and profitability analysis and identifies the bargaining power of suppliers and customers through the gathering of market intelligence.
Internal analysis	Provides a full mapping of the business including product life-cycle costing, market share, product profitability, process or activity evaluation and costing, developing and reporting on performance using balanced scorecard-type financial and non-financial measures (e.g. quality, time, innovation and customer satisfaction) and customer profitability analysis.
Strategic choice	Provides information that enables the sound evaluation and ranking of the feasibility and profitability of strategies, considering both capital investment criteria (e.g. discounted cash-flow measures) for the quantifiable variables (e.g. cash flows) and strategic cost-benefit analysis of those factors that are more qualitative in nature (e.g. potential environmental impacts and level of community concerns).
Strategic implementation	Provides accurate and timely product costing as well as financial and non-financial performance measures that can be used to manage the implementation process.
Strategic review	Provides accurate KPIs for measuring the success of implemented strategies. Reviews the effectiveness of the strategic planning process in terms of the development of accurate estimates (e.g. prices and product costs) and the appropriate use of performance measures and incentives.

9 **LEARNING OBJECTIVE**

Explain how organisational size and structure, the technology employed and environmental factors influence the design of accounting information systems and the information supplied to managers

Factors influencing the form and types of management accounting information

Traditionally, textbooks have suggested that there is one best way in which a particular task can be carried out, regardless of the environment within which a firm operates. As illustrated in many textbooks, accounting information systems have thus have adopted this approach and rarely differentiate among the accounting needs of different organisations. This typical approach follows classical management and scientific management theories in which contextual factors are ignored. However, for different types of organisation to function effectively, contingency theory recognises that differing types of accounting information is required.

Emmanuel, Otley and Merchant (1990) identify three major classes of contingent factors:
- structural: for example, the size and type of organisation.
- technological: for example, whether the manufacturing process is labour-intensive or automated
- environmental: for example, the degree of competition and the degree of predictability in the organisation's industry

We have discussed the needs of managers in terms of the information they require for making decisions about the future, to plan future actions and to control the business on a day-to-day basis. However, not all firms provide their managers with exactly the same information. For example, the more complex and sophisticated the business, the more likely that its managers will require information beyond what might be required for a simple and less sophisticated business. Similarly, the managers of larger firms would expect to have access to more detailed and comprehensive information than provided to their counterparts in a small business.

ORGANISATIONAL SIZE AS A DETERMINANT OF MANAGEMENT ACCOUNTING SYSTEM DESIGN

Until now, little reference has been made to the use of management accounting information in the small business sector. The managers of small businesses (e.g. typically owner-operators) are confronted by the need to make decisions similar to the operational and strategic decisions of larger firms. Thus, as for large firms, the making of good decisions will be influenced by the quality of the accounting information that is made available to small business managers and how well they use it. However, unlike larger firms, a small business is constrained by the level of economic and human resources that can be committed to acquiring accounting information and the financial literacy skills that can be applied to analysing and evaluating that information.

As the size of the business increases, more formal systems are needed. The nature of the business also has an effect on information needs: a multi-product business requires more sophisticated information systems than a single-product business. Consider the information required to run a restaurant, where the only product is food, compared with the information required to run a hotel. In the latter case, not only do you need information about the food services component of the hotel, but information is required on bed occupancy rates, beverage profitability, and so on.

In discussing the information needs of managers, it must be remembered that the information to be supplied is not free. In general, the more sophisticated the AIS, the more it will cost to set up and run. Thus, the need for better and more up-to-date information always has to be balanced against the costs and benefits of obtaining that information. While there is a considerable literature on cost-benefit analysis, the practical implementation of such an approach is fraught with difficulty. We should also remember that more up-to-date information is not, in itself, better: it also must be relevant. A fuller discussion of what constitutes relevant information in relation to costs and benefits and how these relate to short-term decisions is provided in Chapter 16.

The need to obtain relevant information at a reasonable cost partly explains why many small firms produce little in the way of a formal management information system. In many cases, the information, if it exists at all, is held in a form that is not readily accessible to others (e.g. the memory or knowledge base of the owner-operator). In these situations, not only does the manager have limited access to formal management information, so do external parties. Thus, providers of loans, such as a bank, which might be expected to be able to exert sufficient pressure on the loan applicant to be supplied with more detailed information, fail to do so simply because that information does not exist in the form they require. Typically, the only form of financial accounting information that exists for a smaller business is the annual GPFR and other related information (e.g. income tax return).

Nonetheless, as the failure of many small firms is often attributed to a lack of planning and control over cash flows, some level of investment in accounting information is essential. At an elementary level, a small business should prepare periodic budgets and regularly monitor actual against planned performance. Where cost effective, other forms of accounting information, such as more complete product cost data, may also be supplied.

ORGANISATIONAL STRUCTURE AS A DETERMINANT OF MANAGEMENT ACCOUNTING SYSTEM DESIGN

It is clear that different organisations have different structures and this means that their information needs also will differ. If we consider the Australasian retailing industry, Woolworths engages in a wide range of retailing activities in differing locations (i.e. in Australia and New Zealand) and in different product categories (e.g. fresh produce and groceries, liquor, petrol, consumer products and apparel, hardware and home improvements). AISs need to be designed in a way that permits the performance of the whole business to be disaggregated into meaningful and relevant units of analysis. As will be discussed in Chapter 13, a typical unit of analysis is a business unit where the manager is held accountable for and rewarded for the performance of their unit. Thus, apart from taking into account the effect of different currencies, the AIS used by a company, such as Woolworths, will need to collect and report information about the revenue earned and costs incurred by different business units (e.g. for each of the Australian-based Woolworths and New Zealand's Countdown supermarket divisions). In such circumstances, the AIS meets the structural requirements of the business by producing reports tailored to the firm's distribution of managerial responsibility and accountability.

These and similar matters are examined in the discussion of performance measurement and evaluation in Chapter 13 and the impact and uses of budgets in Chapter 15. Note that there are many more examples of different structures apart from those above. Other structures depend on, and to some extent are determined by, the product, the market in which the business operates, and the competitive environment, as well as more mundane factors such as geography and the location of branches or outlets. In general terms, the more decentralised a firm is, the more complex its information requirements will be.

TECHNOLOGY AS A DETERMINANT OF MANAGEMENT ACCOUNTING SYSTEM DESIGN

The scale and complexity of the manufacturing processes will also influence a firm's need for information. For example, the decision-making needs of managers in high-technology industries or for those firms that employ flexible manufacturing systems and management techniques such as just-in-time or total quality management will require different forms of information than would be supplied to the managers of firms using less advanced production technologies or techniques.

ENVIRONMENTAL FACTORS AS A DETERMINANT OF MANAGEMENT ACCOUNTING SYSTEM DESIGN

In the context of strategic planning, businesses based in relatively risky markets tend to invest more in planning in an attempt to reduce their risk through better predicting outcomes and undertaking a more complete analysis of alternative opportunities. Thus, information required for meeting the decision-making needs of managers of firms competing in a more risky or turbulent market will be more comprehensive and forward-looking than would be required if the firm's markets were more stable and less risky.

12.11

KEY CONCEPT

CONTEXTUAL FACTORS AND ACCOUNTING INFORMATION SYSTEM DESIGN

Businesses are affected by and dependent on the commercial environment. For example, the survival of a business is often dependent on its ability to adapt to changing circumstances. Therefore, the design of an AIS must be carefully tailored to match the environment and the organisational context in which it will be employed. These contingent factors affect not only the design of an AIS but also how it is to be deployed.

In subsequent chapters we will look at different industries in both the manufacturing and service sectors. However, at this point it is important to acknowledge that the design of an AIS should take account of these wider issues if a business is to survive.

Management accounting information and other organisational settings

Just as for their for-profit counterparts, not-for-profit and public sector organisations are defined by the scope of their value chains, their key stakeholder groups and the strategies they employ to fulfil their missions or organisational purpose. While subsequent discussions about the development and use of accounting information will focus on the for-profit business sector, all of the concepts to be examined are broadly applicable to organisations located in the not-for-profit and public sectors.

For example, national and state or provincial governments deliver services to vulnerable individuals and families in areas such as housing, mental health, disability, alcohol and drug misuse, child protection and family violence. Over the past decade, governments have questioned how and by whom services ought to be delivered to those in need. Typically, the choice of service delivery has been between retaining the public sector as the provider of services or outsourcing the task to the not-for-profit sector. As a specific illustration of the scale of this type of decision, in 2013 the Victorian Government budgeted over $5 billion to the task of attending to the needs of vulnerable and disadvantaged Victorians. Given the level of spending involved, the Victorian Government commissioned a whole-of-government review in May 2013 with the intent of identifying how improved outcomes could be realised through the delivery of services in more effective, efficient and innovative ways. The final report (*Service Sector Reform: A roadmap for community and human services reform*, July 2013), publically released in November 2013, indicated that although the demand for services is ever-growing and providers are confronted by both budgetary and supply-side constraints, a solution could be found in making greater use of partnerships between government and non-government providers. Apart from addressing issues about the quality of the services provided by each source of supply (i.e. government or non-government providers), costs will be a key factor in determining the amount that government is prepared to pay for the services it wants provided, and whether or not it can be sustainably supplied by the provider at that level of funding. Thus, accounting information can help government to identify which service delivery option delivers the greatest value for its money.

ACCOUNTING INFORMATION SYSTEMS AND ORGANISATIONAL CONTROL: A BEHAVIOURAL PERSPECTIVE

The role of an AIS in securing organisational control (e.g. through planning and control) is often compared to that of engineering, where the analogy of a central heating system is used. Figure 12.5 is a diagram of a central heating system. In this system the desired temperature is set and a comparator compares this with actual room temperature. If there is any deviation, action is automatically taken by the system to fuel the boiler to enable it to adjust to the desired temperature. This system involves the process of monitoring actual output against a desired output, and when a variance is identified, automatically taking corrective action.

Earlier, when examining the planning and control process, we identified and described similar stages. However, there are several differences between the two systems that provide greater insight into the limitations of the planning and control process.

FIGURE 12.5 A CENTRAL HEATING SYSTEM DEMONSTRATES AUTOMATIC MONITORING AND CONTROLS

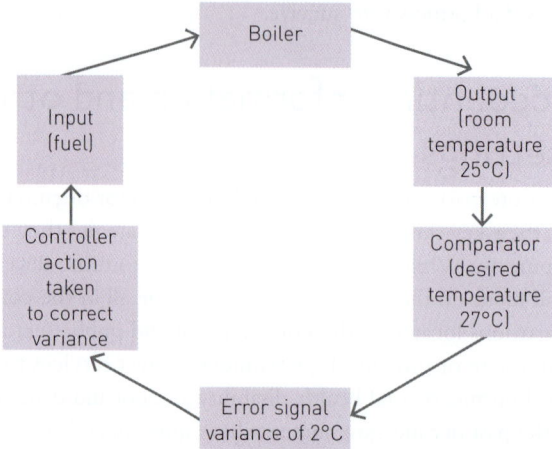

An important difference is that the central heating model is a physical system where there are automatic responses to outputs; that is, corrective action is taken to obtain the desired temperature without any human intervention. In contrast, the control model within the planning and control process of a business normally depends on humans; that is, the response to deviations from the budget is not automatic. Time lags are experienced by most AIS and people have to be motivated to respond to variances and take corrective action if and when it is perceived to be necessary.

The extent of these time lags in reporting depends on the sophistication of the AIS. Some large companies monitor performance every week and, with computerised information systems helping to speed up the reporting process, corrective action can be taken relatively quickly. However, in most firms, control reports are produced on a four-weekly basis. As before, the restriction on implementing a more timely information system is the relationship between the installation and running costs of the system relative to the benefits generated from the system. As past mistakes cannot be remedied, the variances reported by the AIS can only be used as a guide for future operations.

It is only in recent decades that accounting and its interaction with human behaviour have been brought to the forefront of research. It is now recognised that the effectiveness of an AIS is very much dependent upon the personal and collective attitudes of organisational members. While attention is now correctly given to the influence of individuals on AISs, there is still considerable scope for further research into how human behaviour distorts the effectiveness of accounting systems.

In the context of control systems, the process of setting targets is influenced and affected by the behaviour of individuals. A sales manager might respond negatively if set a target that, in his or her opinion, is impossible. Another example is the action required to correct further undesirable variances. This action very much depends upon the motivation of the responsible manager and his or her subordinates. A manager who perceives targets to be unrealistic is unlikely to be motivated to take corrective action to ensure they are met in the future. Thus, the control function of an AIS is constrained by the motives of individuals when setting budgets and in determining what action is to be taken in respect to identified variances.

STOP AND THINK 3

Define responsibility accounting with reference to the planning and control process.

SUMMARY

LEARNING OBJECTIVE 1

IDENTIFY THE RANGE OF DECISIONS MADE BY MANAGERS AND EXPLAIN THE DIFFERENCES BETWEEN STRATEGIC AND OPERATING DECISIONS

Decisions are made by managers at different hierarchical levels of an organisation, and the type of decision made varies with the level of responsibility held by a manager. Strategic decisions are the decisions made by senior managers about what the long-term policies of a business will be, and these decisions identify the strategies that are expected to help the organisation to achieve its goals. Operating decisions are generally made by lower-level managers and focus on ensuring the efficient use of short-term resources. Where strategic decisions are reflected in the strategic plan, and capital investment budgets document how economic resources will be used, operating decisions are linked to the annual budget, which provides a plan of how economic and other resources are to be used in the short term. Collectively, strategic and operating decisions are directed at assisting the organisation to achieve its goals.

LEARNING OBJECTIVE 2

EXPLAIN WHY MANAGEMENT'S DECISION MAKING NEEDS CANNOT BE MET SOLELY BY THE INFORMATION SUPPLIED IN THE GENERAL-PURPOSE FINANCIAL REPORTS (GPFR)

The decision-making needs of managers require information about macro-economic factors, legal and other regulatory requirements, environmental and social issues, marketing, production, and distribution. The GPFR alone cannot meet these needs. While annual GPFRs provide an overview of the organisation's financial performance for the past year, they only become available after the end of the year and are of little value to management if corrective action is required during the year. Managers need frequent, up-to-date information tailored to their needs so that corrective decisions can be made.

LEARNING OBJECTIVE 3

EXPLAIN WHY EXTERNAL STAKEHOLDERS GENERALLY DESIRE ACCESS TO ACCOUNTING INFORMATION BEYOND THAT DISCLOSED IN GPFR AND WHY SOME ARE SUCCESSFUL IN GAINING ACCESS

Just as managers have needs for information beyond the GPFR, so to do external users. External users will also draw upon a variety of other sources of information when making their resource allocation decisions including macro-economic data, other disclosures made by a business and competitors, and the reports of financial analysts. While external users would also like to have access to the more organisation-specific information that managers receive, few incentives exist for a business to voluntarily provide this access. However, some external users are in a position to obtain additional information because:

1 they have a statutory right (e.g. the Australian Taxation Office or New Zealand's Inland Revenue)

2 the business requires the support of an external user (e.g. a lender or bank) who will not provide this support without first being given the information it requires.

LEARNING OBJECTIVE 4

EXPLAIN THE VALUE CHAIN CONCEPT AND HOW IT IS USED TO DESCRIBE THE CREATION OF VALUE

The value chain is the sequence of activities that transforms procured inputs into products or services valued by a firm's customers. Each value chain activity is undertaken with the intention of contributing to the creation of value. Primary value chain activities are more directly associated with the creation of value whereas other value chain activities support primary activities. Knowledge of value chain activities allows managers to identify non-value-adding activities and to target them for elimination.

LEARNING OBJECTIVE 5

EXPLAIN HOW INFORMATION TECHNOLOGY HAS INFLUENCED THE STRUCTURE AND PERFORMANCE OF VALUE CHAINS

Across a wide range of industries, including manufacturing, financial services and retailing, IT has become a critical resource to many organisational value chains. IT contributes to improved value chain performance through its ability to automate previously labour-intensive activities; its facilitation and support of process redesign and innovation, leading to a transformation of the value chain itself; and through the enhanced capability for collecting, processing, storing, analysing and reporting information that positively influences the quality of decisions made by managers. The appropriate deployment of IT can lead to greater operational efficiency and effectiveness and thereby strengthen a firm's competitive advantage.

LEARNING OBJECTIVE 6

EXPLAIN WHAT IS MEANT BY STRATEGIC MANAGEMENT

Strategic management is the cycle of planning and control that determines the long-term policies of a business and identifies the tasks that must be carried out by managers if the firm is to achieve its goals.

LEARNING OBJECTIVE 7

EXPLAIN THE CONCEPT OF STRATEGIC CHOICE AND PORTER'S GENERIC COMPETITIVE STRATEGIES

Most firms have a range of strategic options that could feasibly be implemented. Where strategic options are mutually exclusive, a choice must be made with the selection guided by the nature of a firm's competitive advantage. For example, if the firm is able to deliver products or services at low cost and it can set its prices below those of its rivals, it would make sense to choose strategic options consistent with a cost-leadership strategy. Alternatively, a firm might have products or services that provide, for reasons of quality or branding, such greater value to customers that it can set prices above its rivals. Thus, where strategic options promote the selection of non-price-related factors, such as superior product quality, a firm is pursuing a differentiation strategy.

LEARNING OBJECTIVE 8

EXPLAIN HOW ACCOUNTING INFORMATION CONTRIBUTES TO STRATEGIC MANAGEMENT

Management accounting information is used by managers to make decisions about how improvements in the performance of the firm's value chain can be secured in the broader context of having to deal with the five competitive forces in the firm's industry. For example, an unexpected reduction in profitability, the loss of a major contract or a project implementation failure (e.g. a significant cost overrun) will indicate that the organisation is unlikely to realise its strategic ambitions. The recognition of a potential gap between desired and likely strategic outcomes will trigger investigations in terms of organisational resources and capabilities (e.g. requiring management accounting information about process productivity, product costs, market share and product profitability) and environmental factors (e.g. requiring management accounting information about competitor costs and pricing and the terms of trade with suppliers and customers), leading to the development, evaluation and selection of strategies (requiring management accounting information about relevant costs and revenues and cash flows, discounted cash flows and net present values).

LEARNING OBJECTIVE 9

EXPLAIN HOW ORGANISATIONAL SIZE AND STRUCTURE, THE TECHNOLOGY EMPLOYED AND ENVIRONMENTAL FACTORS INFLUENCE THE DESIGN OF ACCOUNTING INFORMATION SYSTEMS AND THE INFORMATION SUPPLIED TO MANAGERS

A small business with few employees and a restricted product or service is unlikely to want additional information because this information is likely to be already known by the owner or manager. On the other hand, a large company such as Woolworths, which has diverse business activities (e.g. in grocery, liquor and petrol retailing, hotels, and home improvements and hardware) with many points of sale, would require a detailed breakdown of relevant information for each type of business activity and for each area of operations. Similarly, the extent to which a firm is subject to market, environmental or technological change also impacts on the information required by managers and the design of the AIS that will provide this information. The economic benefits of implementing any particular AIS must be borne in mind. Thus, not only might a small business be unable to afford costly monitoring systems, but it may not have a need for them, as the size of the business means that there are fewer critical variables to contend with.

REVIEW QUESTIONS

1 One of the major improvements that bankers wish to see in respect of financial information is more timely information. Explain what this means and why it is so important to bankers. How might this not be the case for the managers of a firm that wants to borrow from a bank?

2 What is likely to be the major impact of organisational size on the information needs of managers?

3 What useful management information is available from the accounting records from which annual reports are prepared?

4 Explain why some external users are able to access internal company information beyond that published in the annual GPFR.

5 What additional information would bankers wish to have and for what purposes would they use this?

6 In recent years, more external users of accounting information have required access to accounting information that is normally reserved for internal management. Explain why such information is useful to these decision makers.

7   How might the competitive strategy of cost leadership or differentiation influence the accounting information provided to a firm's managers? Would the management accounting information vary according to the operational responsibilities (e.g. product development, process improvement, production, marketing and distribution, and customer service) and position within the organisational hierarchy (e.g. senior, middle- and lower-level managers)?

8   Similar types of healthcare services are provided by for-profit (e.g. the Australian Securities Exchange–listed Ramsay Health), not-for-profit (e.g. St John of God Health Care) and public sector organisations (e.g. state government health departments).

   i   How might the sector within which a healthcare service provider is located influence the organisation's mission statement and its corporate goals and objectives?

   ii Would you expect the type of financial and non-financial information to be reported to senior organisational managers on a regular basis (e.g. weekly, monthly or quarterly) to be different across the for-profit, not-for-profit and public sectors?

   iii Briefly explain if the need for strategic planning would vary across healthcare providers located in different sectors (i.e. organisations in the for-profit, not-for-profit and public sectors).

9   Briefly explain how advances in information and communications technology have influenced the provision of accounting information to a firm's managers.

10 The strategic planning process entails four stages: strategic analysis, strategic planning, strategy choice and strategy implementation. Briefly explain what each stage of the strategic planning process entails. Providing a relevant example, explain how accounting information contributes to the decisions made by management at each stage of the strategic planning process.

11 In determining the design of a management accounting system (MAS) and the information to be provided to organisational managers, the cost-benefit test is said to be an influential factor. Briefly explain why costs and benefits need to be taken into account when determining the form and scale of a firm's MAS and the information to be reported to managers.

PROBLEMS FOR DISCUSSION AND ANALYSIS

1   Refer to the extract of the Woolworths Limited financial report for financial year ending 30 June 2013 located in Appendix 1.

   a   Do you think there is more information in the annual GPFR than is required by the average investor?

   b   Who do you consider would most likely benefit from reading the detailed GPFR?

2   With regard to the information that you identified in your answer to Problem 1 above: would a manager's use of this information differ from the way it is used by bankers, and if so, how would it differ?

3   In each of the situations below, identify what you believe your information needs would be.

   a   If you are the manager of a local branch of a national retailer. All buying is done centrally and prices are fixed. You are in charge of the day-to-day management, and hiring and firing of staff. Your annual remuneration is fixed.

   b   The situation is the same as in (a) except that, in addition to your annual salary, you receive a bonus of $2 for each $200 profit made above that expected by your employer.

    c The situation is the same as in (b) except that you are allowed to set the selling prices.

    d You have been so successful as a branch manager that the company has promoted you to the position of regional manager in charge of 20 shops. Each subordinate store-level manager works under the same conditions as those outlined in (c).

4 Discuss the meaning of and difference between strategic and operating decisions.

5 Discuss how the control models of accountants and engineers might differ. Through this comparison, provide details of any limits on the planning and control process that you can identify.

6 Give illustrations of ways in which the behaviour of individuals can affect the planning and control process.

7 'For plans to be effective, management should consider the wider environmental factors that relate to the organisation.' Discuss.

8 Describe why it is important to set objectives for a business and comment on the problems of setting objectives.

9 You work for a business primarily involved in health care, which runs a number of nursing homes for the elderly and has a head-office staff consisting of you and two owner-directors. Each of the nursing homes has a sister-in-charge who looks after the day-to-day running of the nursing home, but the advertising of the service and the overall administration are carried out by one of the directors, while the other director looks after the billing of the patients and the collection of monies due. The overall profitability of the firm has fallen drastically in the last year and you have been asked to investigate the situation.

    Identify what information you would need and what level of detail is required in order for you to start your investigation.

Note to instructors: The following problem is considered more suitable for use in MBA courses. However, undergraduate courses may also find the problem useful.

10 Giggling Brothers, wholesalers of fine wines, has been trading profitably for a number of years using a manual accounting system. However, the company has experienced, every six months or so, severe cash-flow problems caused by a number of factors including the excessive purchase of 'special price' stock from vineyards, inappropriate timing of stock purchases relative to sales, inadequate control of accounts receivable and mis-timed marketing drives. Giggling Brothers management believes that many of these problems are caused by inadequate and untimely feedback from the accounting department. For example, purchasing department staff maintain that they are given inadequate financial information by the accounting department, and that the sales department consistently misrepresents expected sales. Sales department staff consider that management has unrealistic expectations of their performance and that the accounting department does not keep them sufficiently informed about the collectability of outstanding accounts receivable. Additionally, accounting department staff maintain that they are not consulted with regard to expenditure on purchases or given sufficient information about the credit history of customers. Management believes that the implementation of a computerised accounting and reporting system would obviate most of these problems.

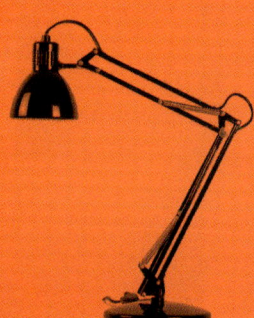

Required

a   What type of accounting and reporting information system should be designed for Giggling Brothers?

b   What benefits would such a system offer to the business and how might the information produced be incorporated into the planning process?

c   Suggest how Giggling Brothers might best evaluate the cost against the benefit of implementing a new system.

d   Who do you think should be involved in the design and development of operating specifications for the new system?

e   Do you think that an examination and evaluation of the approaches used by the firm's competitors would be of benefit to Giggling Brothers?

ETHICS CASE STUDY

John Kellog is the financial controller for Energisers Ltd. He is preparing a report for a proposed plant expansion at two possible locations in Western Australia: Mandurah or Rockingham. He is of the opinion that Mandurah is the better location for the new plant and he intentionally excludes any reference to the fact that land and other property taxes are 100 per cent higher in Mandurah than they are in Rockingham. Kellog owns some properties in Mandurah and if the plant is built there, a significant increase in property values is expected.

Discuss whether John is behaving in an ethical manner.

SUGGESTED ANSWERS TO STOP AND THINK EXERCISES IN THE CHAPTER

1   Annual GPFRs contain summarised information – more detail may be required by management. More frequent and more up-to-date information is also needed by managers to take action. The information in the annual GPFR may not be suitable for decision making in relation to planning, control or investment. There are a number of examples in the chapter but students should be encouraged to identify others.

2   Stage 1: Setting objectives. This involves detailing the objectives of the organisation in the short and long term. Organisations do not have objectives per se; the objectives will reflect the objectives of those people involved in the organisation. These objectives can be expressed in quantitative terms (e.g. statements about the organisation's responsibility to the public).

Stage 2: Making strategic decisions. Strategic decisions are those that determine the long-term policies of the business and are necessary if it is to meet its objectives (e.g. policy changes relating to the range of products that are sold).

Stage 3: Making operating decisions. Operating decisions are those that focus on the efficient use of the resources that are available to the business in the short term. These decisions are embodied in plans that are conventionally referred to as budgets.

Stage 4: Monitoring and taking possible corrective action. Monitoring is the process of comparing actual performance with a predetermined plan. It provides the basis from which corrective action can be planned and taken.

3   Responsibility accounting is a system that identifies decision centres and the managers responsible for those centres (e.g. departments). Costs and revenues are traced to these centres and compared with planned costs and revenues. Therefore, the performance of managers, and their centres, can be measured.

CENGAGENOW

Go to http:\\login.cengagebrain.com to link to CengageNOW, your online study tool. First take the Pre-Test for this chapter to get your Personalised Study Plan, and then:

* revise your understanding of the key terms related to internal users, internal information, and planning and control
* review the key concepts through the online flashcards
* follow online links to establishing and implementing control systems.

   After you have completed the activities in your Personalised Study Plan take the Post-Test to determine what concepts you have mastered and what you still need work on.

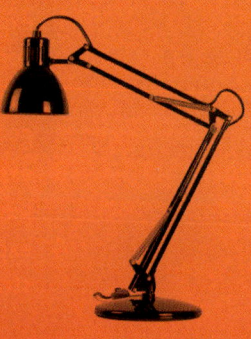

13

PERFORMANCE MEASUREMENT AND THE BALANCED SCORECARD

5   explain the concept of responsibility accounting

6   identify cost, profit and investment centres

7   explain how performance measures and executive compensation schemes are used to align managerial interests to organisational goals

8   explain why financial measures are used to assess organisational performance

9   explain and apply the return on investment (ROI) method of measuring investment centre performance

10 explain and apply the residual income (RI) method of measuring investment centre performance

11 explain how ROI and RI may provide conflicting outcomes for a proposed investment

12 explain the strengths and weaknesses of ROI and RI

13 explain and apply the Economic Value Added (EVA) method of measuring investment centre performance and its usefulness

14 explain and evaluate the use of non-financial measures of performance

15 explain what is meant by the term 'balanced scorecard'

16 explain and identify the difference between driver and outcome and lead and lag KPIs

17 explain the four perspectives of a balanced scorecard.

LEARNING OBJECTIVES

At the end of this chapter, you should be able to:

1   explain what is meant by the term 'goal congruence'

2   explain the relationship between organisational goals and performance measurement

3   explain the nature and qualities required of performance measures

4   explain the relationship between organisational strategies and performance measurement

INTRODUCTION

1 LEARNING OBJECTIVE

Explain what is meant by the term 'goal congruence'

Organisations themselves do not have goals; the goals of the organisation are those of the people involved in it. These individuals have their own personal goals, and it is likely that some will conflict with those of other organisational participants. For example, a sales manager's goal of being the industry's number one retailer might lead to the development of strategies intended to maximise sales volumes (i.e. grow market share) and which give little consideration to how actually profitable a bigger market share might be. This may conflict with the goals of the firm's senior management whose primary goal of profit maximisation might be achieved through the setting of higher prices and lower market share. This conflict between the goals of individual managers and the organisation as a whole is commonly referred to as a lack of goal congruence.

The problem of goal congruence is more acute in large organisations because of the greater number of participants and the wider range of vested interests held. For example, the employees of a listed company probably desire an increase in remuneration and this could be one of their primary personal goals. However, higher levels of remuneration paid to employees absent any offsetting productivity or performance improvements, will conflict with the interests of shareholders as increased employee remuneration erodes the level of profits available for the payment of dividends.

13.1 KEY CONCEPT

GOAL CONGRUENCE

Goal congruence is the alignment of organisational goals with the personal and collective goals of individuals within an organisation.

From a wider social perspective, there is a growing awareness of the need to recognise the interests of parties external to the organisation itself when setting goals. In particular, customers, government and the local community all have an interest in the survival and the activities of the organisation. For example, in recent years there has been a growing public concern about environmental issues. As a result of public pressure, a number of organisations have changed policies regarding their production activities. A good illustration of this is the change in policy of the petroleum industry to the production of unleaded and other less polluting fuels. Thus, it is highly likely that a firm will have multiple goals which may include:

* to generate a reasonable financial return for shareholders
* to maintain a high market share
* to deliver improved levels productivity each year
* to offer an up-to-date product range of high quality and proven reliability
* to be known as a responsible employer
* to acknowledge and be responsive to social responsibilities
* to grow and survive as an independent organisation.

If an organisation's goals are to be effective, there must be a congruence of goals. Thus, when an organisation sets its goals, the interests of all the participants need to be recognised and common goals identified. As will be discussed below, the development of a performance measurement system such as the balanced scorecard (BSC) can be a very powerful means for articulating and gaining consensus within the organisation as to what the organisation's goals are.

ORGANISATIONAL GOALS AND PERFORMANCE MEASUREMENT

Why do organisation need to measure and report upon their performance? From our coverage of financial accounting, we know legislative requirements (e.g. the *Corporations Act* and Australian Securities Exchange (ASX) listing rules) oblige listed companies to report their performance in the audited annual general-purpose financial statements (GPFR) supplied to external stakeholders, such as shareholders and lenders. Reporting the impact of organisational activity beyond the strictly economic considerations covered in the financial statements has also gained in importance with many companies now choosing to extend their accountability to include environmental and social matters. With increasing pressure on organisations to be more transparent and accountable in how they report their performance to external parties, it is not surprising that many have extended their performance reporting well beyond what is required by law (e.g. see Chapter 1's discussion of integrated reporting).

In Chapter 12, we noted that managers also require information about organisational performance when making and evaluating the consequences of resource allocation decisions. Apart from facilitating the planning and control of organisational activities, performance measurement also contributes to organisational learning in two ways:

- *Organisational learning as service improvement*

An oft-cited business adage is: 'What gets measured, gets done'. This statement suggests that the target-setting aspect of performance measurement along with the control aspect of performance reporting provide the baseline data required for organisational improvement. Knowing what is intended to be achieved and having actual performance assessed against those intentions, not only focuses the minds of managers upon securing improved process efficiency and productivity, it will also achieve better outcomes.

- *Organisational learning as management improvement*

Where the performance reported to managers goes beyond just the outcomes achieved and includes information that reveals why a particular result might have been achieved, managers are provided with the opportunity to learn about the effect of decisions they have taken. While information about a particular outcome (e.g. earnings before interest and tax were 5 per cent greater than budgeted) is useful, but information about how that improved performance was achieved (e.g. the $100000 investment in an enhanced web page increased market share by 20 per cent) is more than likely to lead to better-quality management decisions being made in the future. Hence, better decisions lead to improved business performance.

WHAT IS A PERFORMANCE MEASURE AND WHAT PROPERTIES SHOULD IT HAVE?

As noted above, performance measurement is an important topic given the many roles performance measures can occupy. In this chapter, we examine the development of financial and non-financial measures as used by an organisation's managers which are, in turn, used to evaluate and reward the performance of managers.

Hronec (1993, p. 6) defines a performance measure as being 'a *quantification* of how well the activities within a process or the outputs in a process achieve a specified goal' (emphasis added). As implied by Hronec, performance measures must be expressed quantitatively rather than qualitatively. If it is difficult to express the performance of the organisation in quantitative terms, then the task of measuring performance also becomes problematic. While we do not not intend to suggest that qualitative 'measures' are unimportant to organisational planning and control, such measurement systems lack the rigour of quantitative performance measurement systems. Moreover, given the apparent difficulty in quantifying qualitative measures, their use in evaluating the performance of managers, and of the responsibility centres they administer, is more implicit than explicit.

The development and use of performance measures require the careful consideration of the following questions:

- Are the performance measures consistent with the goals of the organisation? The performance measure should link to organisational goals and direct managerial attention and decision making to the attainment of those goals.
- Do the performance measures accurately reflect the performance of the manager and/or responsibility centre being evaluated? For a performance measure to be effective, it must be able to satisfy the manager undergoing evaluation that the measure is objective, free from bias and properly accounts for the controllable aspects of performance.
- Do the performance measures relate to a budget factor? As budgets and periodic performance reports are the primary means for planning and controlling organisational activity, performance measures should link to the financial (e.g. cost per unit) and non-financial (e.g. on-time order fulfilment) targets expressed in these documents.
- Do the performance measures encourage managers to provide realistic forecasts? As performance measures signify those aspects of the manager's performance that are considered to be critical to the organisation's success, a manager must be able to appreciate that reliable forecast data influences the quality of strategic decisions made.
- Do the performance measures discourage managers from making dysfunctional decisions? Performance measures must ensure that managers are aware of the organisational consequences of the decisions made and to appreciate that, at times, what appears to be the best for them may not be the best for the organisation as a whole.
- How frequently should performance measures be reported to managers? If performance measures are reported with a significant time lag, managers will not be able to implement corrective action as quickly as required. On the other hand, too frequent reporting of performance measures may distract managers from effectively carrying out their functions as they continually react to small deviations from desired short-term performance rather than focusing on longer-term trends that might be less troubling.

In summary, performance measures must be able to facilitate the communication of the organisation's goals, encourage managers to make decisions consistent with those goals and provide a timely measure of each manager's contribution towards the attainment of those goals.

THE STRATEGIC NATURE OF PERFORMANCE MEASURES

4 LEARNING OBJECTIVE

Explain the relationship between organisational strategies and performance measurement

Figure 13.1 illustrates the link between a manufacturing firm's strategy and measures used to monitor its performance. The firm's strategy is to produce products of the highest quality, where the attainment of that strategic goal is the achieving a product finish to a grade that superior to that of its competitors. The factors driving superior product finish could include the engineering department's specification of the raw materials to be used in manufacturing the product, the purchasing department's use of vendors that supply raw materials to purchase (and production) specifications, and the production department's ability to keep equipment operating within specified tolerances. Measures of each department's contribution to manufacturing products of the highest quality would be:

- quality costs incurred due to improper material specification (engineering department)
- percentage of raw material purchases sourced from non-certified vendors (purchasing department)
- defective parts per million (production department).

It is important to acknowledge that a downstream performance measure (e.g. the production department's defective parts per million) may be influenced by poor performance on an up stream measure (e.g. the engineering department's incorrect specification of the raw material to be used).

FIGURE 13.1 LINKING PERFORMANCE MEASURES TO STRATEGIC GOALS

Strategy	Leverage Point	Drivers	Performance Measures
Highest-quality product	Superior product finish	Engineering Raw material specifications Purchasing Raw material purchased Production Ability of equipment to operate within tolerance	Quality costs incurred due to improper material Certified/non-certified supplier ratio Rejected parts per million

The choice of quantitative measures will be influenced by their ability to unambiguously target the area of performance to be evaluated and the cost associated with the collection and analysis of data that measures performance. The benefit derived from calculating, reporting and acting upon a performance measure should be greater than the costs incurred in collecting and processing the performance data.

5 LEARNING OBJECTIVE

Explain the concept of responsibility accounting

ORGANISATIONAL STRUCTURE AND PERFORMANCE MEASUREMENT SYSTEMS

According to Coase (1937), the emergence of the firm is attributable to it being a lower-cost alternative than the market for undertaking particular types of economic transactions. Not surprisingly, a firm's structure (or organisational hierarchy) is influenced by the nature and magnitude of the costs incurred, and the allocation of managerial decision-making responsibilities should reflect that structure. For example, many large organisations find it more cost-effective to use a decentralised structure through the creation of departments, business units or divisions than having a centralised structure.

As discussed in Chapter 12, the creation of a decentralised organisational structure allows for the operation of a system of responsibility accounting (RA). RA describes a system of decentralised authority with performance being potentially measured in financial and non-financial terms. As suggested by the word 'accounting' in RA, many performance measures are accounting numbers, such as costs, revenues, assets and liabilities, where pertinent, and are traced to the manager primarily responsible for the financial consequences of the decision made.

RA facilitates organisational planning and control by placing the responsibility for the preparation and administration of budgets and accountability through performance reports with individual managers. However, as indicated in Chapter 12, the organisation exists as a set of interrelated value chain activities (e.g. procurement of inputs, transformation and delivery of outputs in the form of goods and services) and an individual manager may only have a limited span of control or influence over organisational activities. Thus, RA measures, in financial terms, particular parts of, or relationships, in the organisation's input, transformation and output process.

As will be discussed below, a manager's control over organisational activity and the financial consequences of decisions made can be measured in terms of revenue, cost, profit or return on investment. Thus, within a system of RA, there can be four types of responsibility centres.

- *Revenue centres*
  A revenue centre is where the manager of an organisational sub-unit only has control over revenue and has no costs to be held accountable for. An example of a revenue centre is an organisational sub-unit tasked with the sale of otherwise unsold non-inventoriable services such as hotel rooms, and theatre and aircraft seats. Since very few examples of 'pure' revenue centres exist, we will not give this type of responsibility centre any further consideration.

- *Cost centres*
  A cost centre is where the manager of an organisational sub-unit only has control over costs and has no revenue to be held accountable for. Cost centres are quite common and invariably relate to the functions (e.g. research and development, market research, human resources, accounting and finance, and information technology services) that support the primary value-adding activities of the organisation. Two types of cost centres are identified:
  - engineered cost centres. The elements of cost (e.g. materials, labour and other services) per unit of output can be estimated with a reasonable degree of certainty (e.g. the standard cost per unit processed by a manufacturing department).
  - discretionary cost centres. Costs cannot be reasonably estimated and the amount incurred is dependent upon the judgement of the cost centre manager (e.g. the costs for research and development).

- *Profit centres*
  A profit centre is where the manager of an organisational sub-unit has control over both revenues and costs. As will be discussed below, revenues might come from external sales of goods or services or from transfers made to other organisational sub-units.

- *Investment centres*
  An investment centre is where the manager of an organisational sub-unit also has some discretion over the amount of the investment they are entrusted with along with having control over revenues and costs.
  Table 13.1 indicates the different types of accounting measures employed for a cost centre, a profit centre or an investment centre.

6 LEARNING OBJECTIVE

Identify cost, profit and investment centres

TABLE 13.1 RESPONSIBILITY CENTRES, MANAGERIAL CONTROL AND PERFORMANCE MEASURES

RESPONSIBILITY CENTRE	MANAGER HAS CONTROL OVER	PRIMARY PERFORMANCE MEASURES
Cost centre	Costs (only controllable costs)	Product cost variances
	Output volumes	Efficiency/productivity measures
Profit centre	Costs (controllable costs)	Product cost variances and expense ratios
	Sales prices (including transfer prices)	Profit and analysis of financial ratios (e.g. profit margin and expense ratios)
	Output volumes	Efficiency/productivity measures
Investment centre	Costs (controllable costs)	Product cost variances
	Sales prices (including transfer prices)	Profit and analysis of financial ratios (e.g. profit margin and expense ratios)
	Output volumes	Efficiency/productivity measures
	Investment in current and non-current assets	Other financial ratios including return on investment (ROI), residual income (RI) and Economic Value Added (EVA)

STOP AND THINK 1

Explain the terms 'cost', 'profit' and 'investment centres'.

While the adoption of a decentralised organisational structure affords many benefits, it also brings with it the problem of the asymmetrical distribution of information (e.g. only lower-level managers are in a position to make particular decisions). Therefore, organisational success depends upon how well subordinate managers communicate to senior management the range of feasible actions, the resources required for the efficient performance of particular actions and the outputs (and outcomes) expected to be achieved from actual task performance.

While decentralisation notionally places the decision-making power in the area of least uncertainty, it still remains. This residual uncertainty may lead subordinate managers to intentionally bias planning information (e.g. restrict the range of possible actions to only those that are easily performed or to overstate budget estimates so as to provide financial slack) or to misreport outcomes (e.g. falsify the outcomes achieved or to manipulate cost classifications so as to keep total expenditure within the limits set for individual heads of expenditure). Management accounting systems (MAS) contribute to the resolution of these problems by encouraging the sharing of relevant information through:

- providing real and meaningful participation in planning
- linking managerial compensation to performance measures consistent with shareholder interests and awarded over a longer time horizon.

The contribution of MAS in terms of the provision of real and meaningful participation in planning will be discussed in Chapter 15 when the topic of budgets is addressed. The incentivising effect of MAS will now be discussed.

EXECUTIVE REMUNERATION AND BUSINESS PERFORMANCE

7 LEARNING OBJECTIVE

Explain how performance measures and executive compensation schemes are used to align managerial interests to organisational goals

Monetary compensation is often the primary mechanism by which a company seeks to align the interests of managers to those of shareholders and other key external stakeholders. As noted above, the development of performance measurement systems is intended to facilitate goal congruence. Previously it was stated: 'What gets measured, gets done'. Similarly it is has been stated that: 'You only get what you pay for'. Hence, the incentive contracting aspects of managerial remuneration and its linkage to the measures used for assessing organisational performance are important.

While all levels of the organisational hierarchy will be compensated for the work undertaken, the particular components of that compensation can markedly vary. For example, at lower levels of management, the compensation might be primarily a fixed monetary salary and any other bonuses constituting a relatively small proportion of the total remuneration received. With higher levels of managerial responsibility, not only does the absolute dollar value of a fixed salary increase but the range of performance-triggered bonuses change in both form and proportion of the total remuneration paid. For senior executives, sometimes described as being key management personnel (KMP), remuneration packages typically comprise three components (i.e. fixed salary, cash bonuses and equity-based remuneration) and are split into two time horizons (i.e. those intended to have a short-term incentivising impact, with the remainder being structured as long-term incentives).

The linking of management compensation to performance measures within the planning and control framework provided by responsibility accounting should:

- direct managerial attention to areas of operations under their control where they might be able to improve organisational performance
- reveal the consequences of decisions made in terms of 'measured' organisational performance. For example: Will withdrawing a product from market lead to a reduction in profits? Will a proposed investment in a new manufacturing facility decrease costs?

THE USE OF FINANCIAL MEASURES TO ASSESS ORGANISATIONAL PERFORMANCE

Before examining how performance measures might be used, we will briefly outline the benefits of financial measures. An obvious advantage of financial measures is their numerical property. Thus, as many financial measures are readily verified and understood, they can give the impression of being objective and reliable. They provide an easy standardised performance measure in a money-based economy. In addition, financial measures can be used:

- to identify trends over several time periods. For example, the comparison of profits over several years will reveal the trend in the firm's performance.
- for inter-organisational comparisons. For example, the comparison of the ROI of a firm with the ROI of another business allows for the performance of each to be evaluated.
- for evaluating the results of responsibility centres within the organisation. For example, the cost performance of a manufacturing facility in Queensland could be compared to one located in Victoria.
- to compare actual performance with planned performance. For example, comparing actual to budgeted costs reveals how successfully plans were implemented and provides feedback for control and future planning purposes.

From a financial accounting perspective, we saw how financial measures could be used to compare the performance of firms within an industry. For example, the performance of the ANZ Bank could be compared with the National Australia Bank, Westpac and the Commonwealth Bank using key profitability and return on investment ratios (e.g. interest rate spread, cost of doing business, the percentage of bad and doubtful loans to total loans, and return on assets). From a management accounting perspective, similar types of financial ratios can be used to evaluate the performance of responsibility centres within a bank (e.g. retail banking or a branch) to be compared.

When using financial measures to evaluate the performance of a responsibility centre, a centre's performance should be evaluated with reference to the objectives set and the degree of freedom its manager has to make decisions. As will be discussed below, for a financial responsibility centre performance measure to be acceptable:

- the measure (e.g. profit) must not be increased by decisions or actions that adversely impact on the performance of the organisation as a whole
- the measure should be as independent as possible of the consequences of the decisions and performance (e.g. efficiency) of other responsibility centres
- the measure should reflect all items subject to the control of the responsibility centre manager (or his or her subordinates).

Thus, effective financial performance measures recognise that what is good for a responsibility centre must also be good for the organisation as a whole: independence of action is necessary if managers are to be held accountable for the decisions taken, and managers can only be held responsible for the things they can control.

8 LEARNING OBJECTIVE

Explain why financial measures are used to assess organisational performance

As Chapter 14 provides a more detailed examination of costs, and the use of budgets for planning and control is covered in Chapter 15, consideration of how the performance of a cost centre could be evaluated using financial measures will be deferred until these chapters. Similarly, as the relationship between cost and revenues (i.e. profit) is covered at length in Chapters 16 and 17, further discussion on the use of profit as a performance measure will be delayed until then. Thus, the remaining part of this chapter will focus on investment centres. Furthermore, as investment centres by definition assume that a responsibility centre manager controls costs, revenue and the investment base, it incorporates many of the performance measurement and evaluation issues associated with the use of financial measures for cost and profit centres. Finally, as an investment centre constitutes a smaller representation of the organisation as a whole, its financial performance measures will be consistent with those used at an organisational level.

INVESTMENT CENTRES AND FINANCIAL PERFORMANCE MEASURES

In essence an investment centre is a profit centre whose performance can also be measured by the return it generates on the assets employed. Therefore, investment centre managers have responsibility and authority for costs, revenues and assets employed. For an investment centre to be established, the conditions necessary for a profit centre must also exist. Thus, it must be feasible for different incentive centres to be attributed with their own revenues and costs. Furthermore, the assets used by the investment centre in generating revenues must also be capable of being separately identified. The assets must be under the control of the responsibility centre manager and the composition of those assets must be affected by the manager's decisions about investing in new assets, replacing old assets or selling off assets surplus to need.

Managers of business segments (e.g. Woolworths' Australian and New Zealand supermarket, liquor, Big W and home improvement business units) are often treated as investment centre managers, as they are accountable for the profits generated and the capital employed. Within each segment, some business activities might be grouped into a profit centre, with a manager being assigned the authority to decide prices, costs and output volumes. Within a profit centre, there could be other lower-level managers who only have control over inputs (e.g. costs) and their responsibilities are more related to being a cost centre. All managers should receive regular, periodic performance reports for their own areas of responsibility that focus on the financial and non-financial variables under their control.

An investment centre's performance report in absolute money terms would be similar to a profit centre performance report. In addition, an investment centre's performance report would state the amount of capital employed in the investment centre. This should comprise only directly attributable non-current assets and working capital. As many large firms have a centralised treasury function with cash being under corporate control, directly attributable working capital is normally the sum of inventories, accounts receivable and prepayments less accounts payable and other related accruals. Thus, the responsibility of an investment centre manager for assets and liabilities should be only to the extent that they are controllable by the manager (e.g. has authority to increase or reduce them).

Where an investment centre is apportioned a share of corporate or head office non-current assets, the amount of capital employed in these assets should be separately recorded as it is not directly under the control of an investment centre manager and should not be attributed to the investment centre when evaluating the manager's performance.

Responsibility accounting attempts to associate costs, revenues, assets and liabilities with the managers most capable of controlling them. Therefore, as a system of accounting, it distinguishes between controllable and uncontrollable costs. While a more detailed discussion of costs will be given in Chapter 14, these points are pertinent:
* most variable costs within an investment centre would be controllable in the short term because managers can influence the efficiency with which resources are used, even if they cannot do anything to raise or lower price levels

- many fixed costs are uncontrollable (or committed) in the short term, although some fixed costs may be discretionary
- many fixed costs are directly attributable to an investment centre in that although they are fixed (in the short term) within the relevant range of output, a drastic reduction in output, or complete shutdown of the centre, would reduce or remove these costs. The existence of directly attributable fixed costs is an important factor for responsibility accounting.

A critical performance measurement issue for many organisations is where goods or services are first exchanged between different responsibility centres before one or more has an exchange with external parties, such as customers. Irrespective of whether a responsibility centre is designated a cost, profit or investment centre, assigning a value (or price) for such internal transfers is problematic. For example, the manager of a 'supplying' investment centre will be motivated to improve their 'revenues' by raising the price for goods or services transferred to another investment centre. Similarly, managers of the receiving investment centre will be inclined to reduce costs by disputing the cost of goods transferred in from another responsibility centre. Problems such as these are addressed through the development of transfer prices where the rules governing intra-organisational exchanges between responsibility centres are intended to ensure that managers take decisions not only in their own best interest but also for the organisation as a whole. Transfer prices between investment centres located in different tax jurisdictions can be used to transfer profits from a high to a lower tax jurisdiction as a way of lowering tax paid by the organisation. This has been a concern of taxing authorities in some countries including Australia. While a detailed coverage of transfer pricing is beyond the scope of this text, where appropriate, references will be made to this topic.

As will be illustrated below, three financial measures for evaluating the performance of an investment centre can be used:
- Return on investment (ROI)
- Residual income (RI)
- Economic Value Added (EVA)

As will be discussed, all three measures can be used for (i) planning purposes by serving as ex-ante targets to motivate investment centre managers and guide their decision-making and (ii) control purposes by serving as ex-post appraisal measures for evaluating investment centre managerial and financial performance.

STOP AND THINK 2

Give examples of financial measures of performance.

For the purposes of explaining and illustrating the calculation and use of each investment centre measure, an illustrative case based on a fictitious Aussie Fries is introduced.

13.1

CASE STUDY

AUSSIE FRIES

Aussie Fries is a well-established chain of fast-food outlets operating throughout Australia and has been listed on the Australian Securities Exchange since 1998. The company was first established in New South Wales in 1985 and its oldest stores are located in this state. Over the past five years, the company ❯

has expanded its operation from the eastern states to Western Australia where it has now established a strong market presence.

Aussie Fries sells a wide range of takeaway foods and it has a highly credible reputation for the quality of its barbecued chicken meals. As is well known, the Australian takeaway foods industry is highly competitive, with members of the industry having to compete on product quality, price and product innovation. Customers are demanding and they want the best meal provided to them at the lowest cost.

Aussie Fries appreciates that if it is to generate adequate returns for its shareholders, it must (a) devote sufficient resources to new product development, (b) be prepared to engage in suitable promotional activities and (c) monitor and readily respond to the intentions and actions of its competitors. The mission statement of Aussie Fries asserts that 'Aussie Fries commits itself to creating a business which is a compelling place to work, a compelling place to buy nutritious and affordable meals, a compelling place to invest and an environmentally and socially aware corporate citizen.' The mission statement is given high prominence in all fast-food outlets and other company premises and is discussed during the company's induction program for new employees.

Aussie Fries has 487 outlets throughout Australia and approximately 40 per cent of those are operated under franchising agreements. All other fast-food stores are owned by Aussie Fries with store managers being compensated on the basis of a base salary and a performance-based bonus. For the managers of company-owned stores, the performance-based at-risk bonus typically represents 35 per cent of the total annual compensation they receive. Store-level managerial bonuses are tied to an annual return on investment (ROI) measure generated by each store.

Aussie Fries has its corporate headquarters and dry goods warehouse located in Sydney. Sydney-based corporate staff provide product development, quality assurance, marketing and after-sales support for all Aussie Fries outlets. In order to ensure that all Aussie Fries outlets obtain the highest quality dry goods (e.g. herbs and spices, packaging, etc.) at the lowest prices, all buying is centralised through the Sydney dry goods warehouse. Weekly deliveries are made to Aussie Fries outlets and each outlet carries a minimum dry goods inventory of two weeks. All fresh food ingredients (e.g. chicken meat, salad products, desserts, and dairy-based beverages such as flavoured milk) are sourced by each outlet from local suppliers who are under long-term supply contracts negotiated and monitored by staff in the Sydney office.

9 LEARNING OBJECTIVE

Explain and apply the return on investment (ROI) method of measuring investment centre performance

Return on investment (ROI)

ROI shows how much profit has been made in relation to the amount of capital invested.

13.2 KEY CONCEPT

RETURN ON INVESTMENT (ROI)

ROI % = (net profit = investment) × 100%

13.1

WORKED EXAMPLE

AUSSIE FRIES: SYDNEY AND NEWCASTLE INVESTMENT CENTRES AND ROI

Aussie Fries has two investment centres based on the geographic region in which they operate and the financial results for the year are as follows.

DETAILS	SYDNEY	NEWCASTLE
Investment centre profit	$3 000 000	$600 000
Capital employed	$20 000 000	$3 000 000
ROI	$3 000 000 / $20 000 000	$600 000 / $3 000 000
	15%	20%

Aussie Fries' Sydney investment centre has made five times the profits of Newcastle and, in terms of profits alone it appears to have been more 'successful'. However, Newcastle has achieved its profits with a much lower capital investment base and has earned a higher ROI. Thus, the use of the ROI measure suggests that Aussie Fries' Newcastle investment centre is outperforming the Sydney centre.

While the notion of investment centre profit can be a matter of debate, most discussion focuses on the definition of the investment base. For example, the investment base could be measured as being the net book value (NBV) of assets employed; the gross book value (GBV) of assets employed; or the NBV of assets employed valued at replacement cost (RC). The most commonly used method for calculating ROI is to measure the return on the NBV of assets employed, although it does have some disadvantages. For example, if an investment centre maintains the same annual profit and keeps the same assets without a policy of regular replacement, its ROI will increase year by year as assets age and are depreciated. This can give a false impression of improved financial performance over time that is not reflected in the true future earning power or profitability of the investment centre's assets.

As will be discussed in Chapter 18, the manager of an investment centre can improve ROI year by year by simply allowing non-current assets to depreciate. Thus, any improvement in ROI could be a disincentive for investment centre managers to reinvest in new or replacement assets, because the centre's ROI would initially fall. However, such a strategy will eventually fail as other expense streams, such as repairs and maintenance (R&M) and revenues are adversely affected by the continued use of ageing and inefficient plant and equipment.

A further disadvantage of measuring ROI as profit divided by the NBV of assets employed is that, for similar reasons, it is not fair to compare the performance of one investment centre with another where the investments were made at different times.

Despite this problem, the arguments for using NBV for calculating ROI are as follows:
- It is the 'normally accepted' method of calculating ROI.
- Firms continually buy new non-current assets to replace old assets that wear out, and so the total NBV of all non-current assets will remain constant, assuming insignificant levels of inflation and market growth.
- Older non-current assets will usually cost more to repair and maintain in order to keep them running. Thus, an investment centre with older assets may have future profitability reduced by R&M costs and ROI will decline as its assets grow older and such costs increase.
- Inflation and technological change alter the cost of non-current assets. If an investment centre has non-current assets acquired 30 years ago with a gross cost of $24 million, and another investment

centre, in the same line of business operations, has non-current assets acquired very recently for $24 million, the capacity and operational performance of the non-current assets of the two investment centres is likely to be very different as the newer equipment delivers higher-quality products at lower cost.

10 LEARNING OBJECTIVE

Explain and apply the Residual Income (RI) method of measuring investment centre performance

Residual income (RI)

RI is an alternative to ROI for measuring the performance of an investment centre. RI is a dollar measure of the investment centre's profits after deducting a notional or imputed interest cost. It is defined as the investment centre's pre-tax profit less an imputed interest charge for the capital invested in that centre.

13.3

KEY CONCEPT

RESIDUAL INCOME (RI)

$RI = investment centre net profit − (investment x cost of capital)

13.2

WORKED EXAMPLE

AUSSIE FRIES: SYDNEY AND NEWCASTLE INVESTMENT CENTRES AND RI

Aussie Fries has two investment centres located in Sydney and Newcastle. The cost of capital used by Aussie Fries is 12 per cent per annum and the financial results for the year are as follows.

DETAILS	SYDNEY	NEWCASTLE
Investment centre profit	$3 000 000	$600 000
Capital employed	$20 000 000	$3 000 000
RI		
Investment centre profit	$3 000 000	$600 000
Less imputed interest charge		
Sydney: [$20 000 000 × 12%]	($2 400 000)	
Newcastle: [$3 000 000 × 12%]		($360 000)
RI	$600 000	$240 000
RI as a % return on investment		
Sydney: $600 000 ÷ $20 000 000	3.00%	
Newcastle: $240 000 ÷ $3 000 000		8.00%

While the RI number for the Sydney investment centre suggests that it is outperforming Newcastle, it has done so on the basis of an investment base that is over six times greater. As reflected in the residual income return on investment percentage (RI ÷ investment centre assets), the Newcastle investment centre has generated a residual income return per dollar of invested assets of 8 per cent compared to just 3 per cent for the Sydney investment centre. Residual income will increase whenever a proposed investment earns above the cost of capital (e.g. 12 per cent) and will decrease when a proposed investments earns below the cost of capital.

RI VERSUS ROI AND MARGINALLY PROFITABLE INVESTMENTS

RI will increase if a new investment is undertaken by an investment centre if it generates a profit in excess of the imputed interest charge on the value of the asset acquired. Thus, if the return on the proposed investment just exceeds the imputed interest rate, an investment centre manager will still be likely to undertake marginally profitable investments as RI will increase. In contrast, where a manager is evaluated using ROI, a marginally profitable investment would be less likely to be undertaken as it would reduce the average ROI earned by the centre as a whole. Worked example 13.3 illustrates this point.

11 LEARNING OBJECTIVE

Explain how ROI and RI may provide conflicting outcomes for a proposed investment

---

13.3

WORKED EXAMPLE

AUSSIE FRIES: MELBOURNE INVESTMENT CENTRE, ROI, RI AND A MARGINAL INVESTMENT

Aussie Fries' Melbourne investment centre currently earns an ROI of 30 per cent. The investment centre manager is considering a proposal to refurbish 20 older company-owned stores at a total cost of $4 million. The refurbishment is forecast to lead to an increase in average net profit $600 000 per annum over five years. Aussie Fries uses 12 per cent as the cost of capital.

DETAILS	BEFORE	REFURBISHMENT	AFTER
Investment centre profit	$2 400 000	$600 000	$3 000 000
Capital employed	$8 000 000	$4 000 000	$12 000 000
RI			
Investment centre profit	$2 400 000	$600 000	$3 000 000
Less imputed interest charge			
Before: [$8 000 000 × 12%]	($960 000)		
Refurbish: [$4 000 000 × 12%]		($480 000)	
After: [$12 000 000 × 12%]			($1 440 000)
RI	$1 440 000	$120 000	$1 560 000
RI as a % return on investment			
Before: $1 440 000 ÷ $8 000 000	18.00%		
Refurbish: $120 000 ÷ $4000 000		3.00%	
After: $1 560 000 ÷ $12 000 000			13.00%
ROI	$2 400 000	$600 000	$3 000 000
	$8 000 000	$4 000 000	$12 000 000
	30%	15%	25%

As shown by worked example 13.3, if ROI was to be used for internal performance evaluation purposes, the project to refurbish 20 stores only provides an incremental return of 15 per cent. Thus, the manager of the Melbourne investment centre would not recommend the project be accepted as the investment centre's before ROI would fall from 30 per cent to 25 per cent. However, if RI were used to measure the performance of the Melbourne investment centre, as the proposed refurbishment generates an incremental return of 15 per cent, this is greater than the cost of capital rate of 12 per cent and will yield an increase in residual income of $120 000 if accepted.

While most firms would choose to use the same percentage cost of capital across all investment centres, it is possible to adjust the cost of capital to allow for the risk characteristics of different investment centres with higher rates being applied to the higher-risk centres. Thus, RI is more flexible since a different cost of capital can be applied to investments with different risk characteristics. For example, the Melbourne investment centre could have a cost of capital rate higher or lower than the company-wide rate of 12 per cent based upon management's assessment of the risk Aussie Fries faces in the Victorian fast-food industry segment.

ROI AND RI STRENGTHS AND WEAKNESSES AS A FINANCIAL PERFORMANCE MEASURE

12 LEARNING OBJECTIVE

Explain the strengths and weaknesses of ROI and RI

The main reasons for the widespread use of ROI and, to a lesser extent, RI as measures of investment centre performance include:

- The calculation of ROI and RI directly ties to the accounting process, being based on numbers extracted from the statement of comprehensive income and the balance sheet. Therefore, managers easily understand where the numbers used in computing ROI and RI are derived from.
- As ROI and RI are financial measures of performance that examine the return on investment for an investment centre, they correspond to how external stakeholders evaluate whole-of-firm performance.
- As ROI is calculated as profit divided by the investment base and RI examines the incremental return on those assets above the cost of capital, they both encourage investment centre managers to pay closer attention to the relationship between the factors influencing profit (i.e. revenues and expenses) and the assets invested in the investment centre. Thus, it promotes greater cost efficiency and discourages excessive investments in operating assets (e.g. raw materials, finished goods inventories and accounts receivables).

The disadvantages commonly cited for ROI and RI include:

- ROI and RI are based upon numbers derived from accrual-based financial statements and this exposes the computation of both financial measures to creative accounting practices, some of which we discussed in earlier chapters.
- ROI and RI are not always appropriate for all types of firms. For example, service-providing firms may have few recorded assets (e.g. the intellectual capital and strategic knowledge held within human resources cannot be recognised as assets) and the calculation of ROI or RI can be meaningless.
- As ROI and RI may be calculated on a periodic basis (e.g. quarterly, semi-annually or annually), managers may become preoccupied with whichever financial measure is used to evaluate the performance of the investment centre and start making decisions that improve short-run results at the expense of long-run goals.

A further weakness of ROI is that it may discourage a manager from investing in a project that, while generating an acceptable return and one above the firm's cost of capital, yields a marginal return below the investment centre's historic ROI. Thus, as will be discussed in Chapter 18, the ex-post performance evaluation rule (i.e. ROI) does not conform to the ex-ante decision rule (i.e. discounted cash flow techniques such as net present value). A weakness of RI is that it does not facilitate comparisons between investment centres nor does it relate the size of a centre's income to the size of the investment. In this respect, ROI being a ratio is a better measure of performance.

13 LEARNING OBJECTIVE

Explain and apply the Economic Value Added (EVA) method of measuring investment centre performance and its usefulness

Economic value added (EVA): an alternative investment-related performance measure

In explaining ROI and RI, the notion of accounting profit as a measure of performance was accepted as if it were an exact measure. In reality, this is far from true. Firstly, it can be manipulated by increasing or decreasing deductible expenses, choosing to realise (or not realise) assets which have risen (or fallen) in value over time, or by implementing different accounting policies (e.g. provisioning for doubtful debts or the depreciation of non-current assets). Secondly, it is very questionable whether accounting profit can be judged as a relevant measure of performance when it does not reflect economic or true profit. In finance, true profit is defined as the amount added to the discounted value of a firm as a whole for the period being measured. While coverage of how true profit is calculated is beyond the scope of this text, the present value approach, upon which it is based, will be covered in Chapter 18.

While accrual-based accounting financial statements are widely used to measure of the performance of the firm, they are subject to the bias of accounting standards and fail to specifically focus on cash flows. For example, as many firms over time increase the amount of deferred tax liabilities under tax effect accounting, actual taxes paid will be less than the tax expense recognised for financial reporting purposes. Similarly, changes in allowances for doubtful debts and provisions for employee entitlements and warranty claims can have an accrual accounting effect greater than would be the case on a strictly cash flow basis.

Similarly, while depreciation is a measure of the value of non-current assets consumed during a period, it is not the cash opportunity cost that would need to be paid to replace the lost investment in existing non-current assets. Furthermore, an investment in research that may create valuable intangible assets is expensed in the period incurred. However, as these investments are made in expectation that they will generate future economic benefits, the immediate writing-off of such expenditures fails to appreciate their true economic life.

EVA is a financial performance measure that removes the distortions of accrual accounting by making various adjustments. The proponents of EVA note that some 165 adjustments in respect to American generally accepted accounting principles (GAAP) could be required to remove the distortions of accrual accounting so as to reveal actual cash flows. In practice, the firms that have adopted EVA find that no more than 20 GAAP adjustments are required to eliminate the most significant distortions of accrual accounting.

The format of accrual-based financial statements is not readily usable for calculating EVA. A separation between operating and financing decisions is required by EVA and this necessitates the deduction of financing expenditures (e.g. interest expense) from operating expenditures (e.g. the cost of sales, wages and salaries, and utilities such as telephone, power and water).

> **13.4**
> **KEY CONCEPT**
> ## ECONOMIC VALUE-ADDED (EVA)
> $EVA = NOPAT - (Investment \times WACC)$
> where:
> NOPAT = net operating profit after tax
> WACC = weighted average cost of capital

As with ROI and RI, EVA is a measure of return on capital and, conceptually, is similar to RI.

$$EVA = NOPAT - [(\text{weighted average cost of capital})(\text{capital employed})]$$

Similar to RI, a positive EVA occurs if an investment earns more than the WACC and negative measures result from investments earning less than the cost of capital. As for RI, better performance is reflected by increases in EVA.

Worked example 13.4 provides an illustration of the approach used to calculate EVA. It is important to note that EVA uses a company's weighted average cost of capital (WACC) as being the rate for calculating the capital charge. While the coverage of the calculation of WACC is deferred until Chapter 18, worked example 13.4 provides the data upon which it can be calculated for Aussie Fries.

13.4

WORKED EXAMPLE

AUSSIE FRIES: EVA AND AN INVESTMENT DECISION

Aussie Fries has 70 000 000 shares on issue which have a current market price of $2.00 per share. The firm is seeking to invest in new stores, which it plans to finance through a debenture issue. The investment will cost $20 000 000 and debentures will be issued with a coupon rate of 9.30 per cent which is line with the current rates set for equivalent debt and that of Aussie Fries' overall interest-bearing debt. Upon completing the planned debenture issue, the debt ratio of Aussie Fries will be 30 per cent. The risk-free rate for Australian Government Bonds with an equivalent maturity to Aussie Fries' debt capital is 4 per cent, the market return is 13 per cent and Aussie Fries has a beta (which is a measure of a listed entity's systematic risk) of 1.15. Aussie Fries has calculated its WACC to be 12 per cent per annum.

As a result of the investment in the new equipment, Aussie Fries anticipates that the annual cash operating profit before interest and tax will rise to a sustainable $4 500 000 for the calendar year commencing 1 January. The corporate tax rate is expected to remain at 30 per cent.

To calculate EVA for the proposed investment in new stores, three numbers are required:

1. NOPAT. As the incremental cash operating profit before interest and tax is $4 500 000 and the corporate tax rate is 30 per cent, NOPAT will be $3 150 000; that is, $3 150 000 = ($4 500 000 × (1.00 − 0.30).

2. WACC. The WACC is given as being 12 per cent per annum.

3. Investment. This is given as being $20 000 000.

With these three numbers now known, EVA can now be calculated:

$$
\begin{aligned}
EVA &= NOPAT - [\text{investment} \times WACC] \\
&= \$3\,150\,000 - (\$20\,000\,000 \times 12\%) \\
&= \$3\,150\,000 - \$2\,400\,000 \\
&= \$750\,000.
\end{aligned}
$$

As EVA from investing in new stores is a positive $750 000, it would be recommended as being a worthwhile investment.

Apart from being used to assess whether or not a proposed investment should be made, EVA can be used to evaluate the performance of an investment centre or the firm, provided applicable numbers for NOPAT, the investment base and WACC are known.

The drivers of EVA include:

- Revenue growth through increases in selling price or sales volume.
- Improved operating margins (EBIT %) by selling more-profitable products or lowering the cost of sales.
- Reductions in the investment in working capital or making better use of working capital.
- Reductions in cash taxes by appropriate investment decisions (e.g. acquiring non-current assets that attract investment allowances).
- Improvements in the efficiency of (or return from) non-current assets that generate higher revenue from the same net asset base. This could be achieved through (i) the investment in new non-current assets that generate higher revenue inflows, (ii) the sale of underperforming non-current assets and/or (iii) non-replacement of underperforming assets.
- Reductions in the WACC through adjusting the financial structure to a more optimal debt/equity mix.

EVA STRENGTHS AND WEAKNESSES

While EVA overcomes the distortions of accrual accounting and focuses managerial attention on a measure of earnings that is of interest to external users (i.e. a form of operating cash flows), it lacks the simplicity of ROI and RI. As with other accounting technique decisions, a firm will use EVA provided the benefits from the performance measure in terms of better decisions exceeds the cost of calculating and using the measure. Thus, given the greater complexity of EVA, it is not surprising that only the largest of multinational firms (e.g. Bausch & Lomb, Coca-Cola, Dun & Bradstreet and Siemens) have adopted EVA.

STOP AND THINK 3

What are the strengths and weaknesses of financial performance indicators?

Non-financial measures: an alternative view of organisational performance

14 LEARNING OBJECTIVE

Explain and evaluate the use of non-financial measures of performance

As discussed in Chapter 12, the MAS, in terms of planning and monitoring variables, is influenced by the organisation's structure and the assignment of particular decision tasks. Thus, key planning and control variables are likely to differ between different responsibility centres. While financial measures such as cost, profit and return on investment will individually or collectively figure prominently for most responsibility centres, they need to be supplemented with other measures of performance that serve as an early warning of gaps emerging between planned and actual outcomes. As will be discussed below, many of these measures will be non-financial in nature.

The shifting of focus beyond financial measures has occurred for many reasons including:
- the move towards a focus on quality and customer satisfaction, away from a traditional emphasis on increasing volume and reducing costs
- increasingly competitive world markets, requiring a 'world class' response
- recognition that the way to achieve improved quality and customer satisfaction and a 'world class' response is through the empowerment of those who have most direct control over the product or service
- the impact of advanced manufacturing, operational and information technology on the form of many value chain activities and the way in which they are undertaken
- the opportunity provided by activity-based approaches to management.

Rather than valuing items such as inputs, operational processes and outputs in financial terms, the MAS can also express these in the form of non-financial measures. Non-financial performance measures include quality, number of customer complaints and warranty claims, lead times, rework rates, delivery time, idle time, down time, market share and repeat business. Measures such as these can be provided very quickly, per shift or on a daily or even hourly basis as required. They are typically easy to calculate and easier for non-financially literate managers to understand and use. Many non-financial measures also report on key factors about the business and what drives it, which financial information ignores or can obscure.

STOP AND THINK 4

Give examples of non-financial measures of performance.

The main advantages of non-financial performance indicators include:

- non-financial performance indicators are more readily linked to organisational strategies
- non-financial performance indicators do not require measurement in monetary terms
- at an operational level, non-financial performance indicators are more easily understood and acted upon by lower-level management than financial indicators (e.g. unfavourable standard cost variances)
- non-financial performance indicators are made available on a more timely basis than many financial performance indicators.

The main disadvantages of non-financial performance indicators include:

- non-financial performance indicators may conflict with financial performance measures in the short term (e.g. an investment in new technology which reduces the defect rate in products produced may result in increased operating expenses such as depreciation and a lower ROI)
- as non-financial performance indicators are not measured in monetary terms, management finds it difficult to assess the monetary benefit obtained from improving performance (e.g. what is the impact on the bottom line flowing from a reduction in manufacturing cycle time?)
- non-financial performance indicators are not readily integrated within traditional accounting and financial reporting systems
- no overall theoretical framework explaining the emergence and application of non-financial performance indicators exists. Thus, the choice of measures may be made on an ad hoc basis, and conflicts and sub-optimal trade-offs may occur between different non-financial performance indicators (e.g. in order to reduce occupational stress levels, employees might be required to strictly conform to paid hours of work; however, the reduced hours of work mean customer complaints are not dealt with in a timely manner).

In many firms, performance measurement is a complex task and financial measures clearly cannot fully capture all strategic realities of business. Does this mean that financial measures should no longer be used? Some argue that financial measures are inevitably short term and if other aspects of the business are well run, the bottom line will 'take care of itself'. An extreme example of this approach is where the focus of monthly performance review meetings is on quality-related and operational measures to the exclusion of what is occurring in terms of business profitability. While the two are related, a firm that focuses on quality and process productivity without assessing the financial consequences of this inattention for business profitability might find that it is not as successful as it should be. Inevitably trade-offs are required between short-term gain and long-term investment returns, and, as argued above, management must ensure that enough attention is paid to the long-term competitive strategy in the context of immediate need (e.g. current period profits).

With the power of modern information technology, there is a danger that too many such measures could be reported, overloading managers with information that is not truly useful, or that sends conflicting signals. A framework that has been developed to integrate both financial and non-financial measures is the balanced scorecard (BSC).

THE BSC: A COMPREHENSIVE PERFORMANCE MANAGEMENT FRAMEWORK

Explain what is meant by the term 'balanced scorecard'

As a strategic management accounting framework, the BSC evolved over the past 20 years and, with the development of strategy maps, it has become of great value in not only determining the soundness of the firm's overall business strategy but also in facilitating the development and communication of strategy. As indicated, the BSC is a tool that focuses on more than just the financial measures of performance. First developed by Kaplan and Norton (1992, p. 71) the BSC is defined as a:

> set of measures that give top managers a fast but comprehensive view of the business. The balanced scorecard includes financial measures that tell the

> results of actions already taken. And it complements the financial measures with operational [non-financial] measures on customer satisfaction, internal processes, and the organization's innovation and improvement activities – operational measures that are the drivers of future financial performance.
>
> Kaplan, R. S., & Norton, D. P. (1992). The Balanced scorecard: Measures that drive performance. *Harvard Business Review*, January-February

By allowing managers and other key stakeholders to look at business performance from different perspectives and by the explicit linkage of performance measures to strategy, the BSC provides a comprehensive performance management framework. Although not suggesting that all organisations will have the same BSC, Kaplan and Norton (1992) proposed that a typical for-profit business would need to use four perspectives to capture performance:

- *Financial perspective*. From this perspective, the firm asks the question: 'How do we appear to our shareholders?' Key performance indicators (KPIs) such as return on assets and return on shareholders' equity are used as measures in this perspective. They are referred to as outcome measures.
- *Customer perspective*. Here the firm asks: 'How do we appear to our customers?' KPIs such as customer retention and customer satisfaction measures can be used and are also referred to as outcome measures.
- *Internal business process perspective*. Here the entity asks: 'What do we need to do within the core processes of our business in order to satisfy our shareholders and customers?' KPIs such as delivery time to customers and product quality can be used and are referred to as driver measures. Improvements in this perspective will drive improvements in the customer and financial perspectives.
- *Learning and growth perspective*. Here the entity asks: 'What do we need to do to develop our employees, work practices and technologies for the future?' KPIs such as employee satisfaction and employee training can be used, and are also known as driver measures.

Some organisations like Volkswagen add another perspective on social or environmental outcomes in recognition of the importance of this perspective to their business. An alternative is to embed KPIs in relation to social and environmental drivers and outcomes into the four perspectives.

As illustrated with Figure 13.2, the BSC incorporates various KPIs into a road map which identifies how a firm can improve outcome measures, such as the return on equity, by making improvements in the aspects of its business which drive those improvements.

FIGURE 13.2 A HIERARCHICAL STRUCTURE TO THE BSC

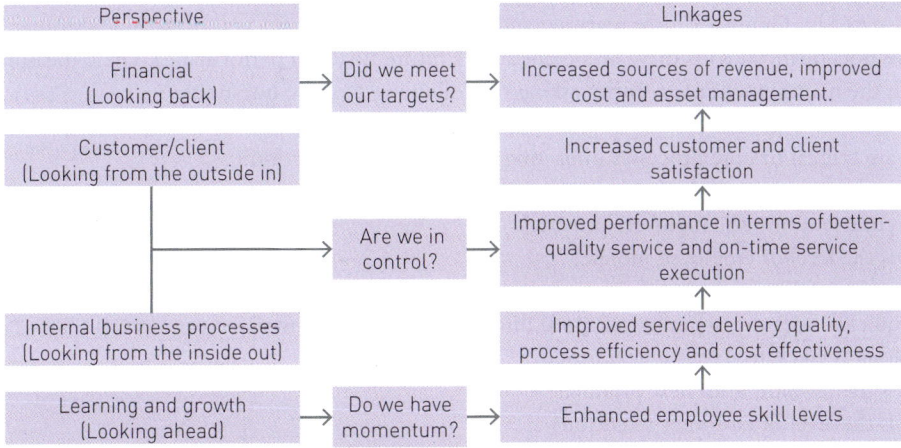

Note the use of two different labels for KPIs: outcomes and drivers. Outcome KPIs are the performance measures that could be used by parties external to management (e.g. customers and shareholders). The use of 'out' in outcome reminds us that outcomes are intended to benefit 'outsiders'. For Aussie Fries it would be in providing take-away meals that satisfy the needs of customers while at the same time maximising shareholder wealth. Customer-related outcome KPIs could be in the form of data gathered through mystery-shopper feedback and customer comments (and complaints), or in the proportion of repeat business. Shareholder-related outcome KPIs could be measured as increases in return on equity or the value of the company's shares. Outcome KPIs reveal how effectively a firm has achieved its strategy, the conceptual underpinning for the BSC.

As suggested, drivers influence outcomes and comprise those activities that initially create value for customers and subsequently for shareholders as well. Recognising that not all activities are undertaken as well as they might be, driver KPIs identify where opportunities for improvement might be taken. Where outcome and driver KPIs can include both financial and non-financial KPIs, as revenues relate to exchanges with customers, revenue-based measures can only be used for outcomes. Thus, where financial measures are used for driver KPIs, they can only be cost-based.

KPIs can also be classified according to their place in the monitoring of organisational activity. Some KPIs are defined as being leading measures of performance whereas others lag those early-warning measures. Lagging KPIs reflect what has been achieved to date whereas lead KPIs are more forward-looking and direct managerial attention to the matters that must be done well to execute the organisation's strategy.

The BSC reports a mixture of leading and lagging KPIs with lead indicators providing a sense of organisational direction or a road map of anticipated future performance, whereas the lag indicators are more results-oriented and answer questions such as 'are we there yet?'. Thus, lead KPIs report on the progress an organisation has made towards attaining strategic goals (e.g. financial sustainability). Being predictive in nature, where performance is not on track lead KPIs can drive early managerial action such as adjusting how a strategy is being implemented. On the other hand, lag KPIs focus on results and are the 'proof' of improved customer and financial outcomes.

Lag indicators are typically dominated by financial measures. Therefore, lag KPIs are easier to identify and capture in comparison to lead indicators, some of which are more qualitative in nature. However, given the historical perspective of many lag indicators, they lack the predictive intelligence of lead indicators. For example, reporting that net operating profit has declined by 10 per cent despite a 5 per cent growth in revenues tells managers what has happened, but not why. A well-developed BSC will provide an appropriate mix of lead and lag KPIs.

As illustrated by Figure 13.2, the learning and growth, internal business process and customer perspective non-financial KPIs drive an organisation's future financial performance. These measures depend on the management of an entity asking the following types of questions:

- What does the organisation need to excel at to achieve its goals?
- What are critical or core processes impacting on customer satisfaction?
- What are the organisation's core competencies?
- What contributions do employees provide?
- What is the level of employee morale?
- What is the effect of process efficiency training?
- How quickly does the organisation move through the learning curve?
- How long is taken to develop new products?
- What is the revenue from new products?
- What is the level of customer retention?

16 LEARNING OBJECTIVE

Explain and identify the difference between driver and outcome and lead and lag KPIs

When managers address these types of questions and develop target KPIs for critical driver areas, this will result in improved customer satisfaction and, ultimately, improved financial performance. Of course, the development of a BSC, particularly for large organisations, requires a significant amount of investment in both time and resources. Given the more detailed revelation of organisational performance provided by a BSC, it is important to involve as many stakeholders as possible so that they all buy in to the concept and are prepared give it their full support. The success or failure of a BSC implementation may have nothing to do with the intrinsic qualities of the KPIs that it reports but may simply be a consequence of how it was developed (e.g. top-down with minimal, if any, engagement from subordinate managers and employees).

It is important to appreciate linkages in performance revealed by a BSC. Again, this is shown in Figure 13.2, where the drivers in the learning and growth and internal business process perspectives, drive the outcomes in the customer and financial perspectives. The strategies, goals and objectives of the organisation drive the development of KPIs in each of the four perspectives. However, the achievement of one objective, such as a 5 per cent increase in productivity from having implemented better processes and recruiting a more skilled work force, means that production output will increase with the same number of employees may be ineffectual. For example, if improved productivity is not accompanied by increased sales, improved financial results (i.e. profits) will not occur. Ultimately, managers must translate improvements in the other three perspectives into better financial measures.

STOP AND THINK 5

What are the strengths and weaknesses of non-financial performance indicators?

Table 13.2 provides a simplified BSC framework of goals and leading and lagging KPIs for a financial institution. As such, this BSC would require the more precise definition of goals in the form of objectives and targets to be truly useful. For example:

Financial: Objective: Increase net operating profit before interest and tax. KPI: $12 million revenue stream and $5 million in direct costs from the marketing of new financial product in the calendar year ending 31 December.

Customer: Objective: Customers satisfied with purchase of new financial products. KPI: 90 per cent of customers surveyed in September rate financial product as very good or excellent and churn rate less than 5 per cent (i.e. a proxy for client retention) for calendar year ending 31 December.

Internal business process: Objective: Effective engagement with prospective clients. KPI: Conversion rate of prospective customer leads to sale of new financial products to be 65 per cent by 30 June.

Learning and growth: Objective: Enhanced knowledge of newly developed financial products that are to be marketed to prospective clients. KPI: 95 per cent of relevant staff will have successfully completed the in-house training program by 31 March.

17 LEARNING OBJECTIVE

Explain the four perspectives of a balanced scorecard

STOP AND THINK 6

Name two performance measures that are useful in evaluating investment centres.

TABLE 13.2 A BSC FOR A FINANCIAL INSTITUTION: PERSPECTIVES, GOALS AND KPIs

PERSPECTIVE AND STRATEGIC GOALS	STRATEGIC MEASURES	
	LEAD INDICATORS	LAG INDICATORS
Financial		
F-01 Improve returns.	• Strategic asset evaluation.	• Return on investment.
F-02 Broaden revenue mix.	• Change in revenue mix.	• Grow revenue in targeted product lines.
F-03 Reduce cost structure.	• Reduction in wastage rates.	• Reduced cost per unit.
Customer		
C-01 Increase point-of-sale satisfaction.	• Depth of relationship.	• Market share.
C-02 Increase after-sale satisfaction.	• Satisfaction survey.	• Customer retention.
Internal business processes		
I-01 Understand and know the customer.	• Hours with prospective customers.	• New customer acquisitions.
I-02 Create innovative products.	• New product development cycle time.	• Revenue from new products.
I-03 Cross-sell products.	• Number of new products developed.	• Increased number of products per customer.
I-04 Shift customers to cost-effective channels.	• Development of an alternative business channel (e.g. web-based marketing).	• Changes in channel use.
I-05 Minimise operational errors.		• Service error rate.
I-06 Responsive service.		• Request fulfilment time.
Learning and growth		
L-01 Develop strategic skills.	• Strategic job coverage ratio.	• Revenue per employee.
L-02 Provide strategic information.	• Strategic information availability ratio.	
L-03 Align personal goals.	• Personal goals alignment index.	• Employee satisfaction/culture assessment.

STOP AND THINK 7
What are outcome and driver and lead and lag key performance indicators?

SUMMARY

LEARNING OBJECTIVE 1

EXPLAIN WHAT IS MEANT BY THE TERM 'GOAL CONGRUENCE'

Goal congruence occurs when managers acknowledge that their own personal interests are advantaged by committing themselves to the achievement of organisational goals.

LEARNING OBJECTIVE 2

EXPLAIN THE RELATIONSHIP BETWEEN ORGANISATIONAL GOALS AND PERFORMANCE MEASUREMENT

Organisational goals help to define the organisation's purpose and, when expressed in the form of objectives, the time-bounded and quantitative targets provide a road map for organisational performance. Performance measurement entails the development of indicators that can be used for planning purposes (i.e. Where does the organisation want to go?) and managerial control (i.e. Did the organisation get there? If not, why not?).

LEARNING OBJECTIVE 3

EXPLAIN THE NATURE AND QUALITIES REQUIRED OF PERFORMANCE MEASURES

For a performance measure to be deemed acceptable, it must include these three key characteristics: relevance (i.e. provide information that aids performance assessment), appropriateness (i.e. relate to the performance assessment task to be completed); and reliable (i.e. quantifiable, neutral or free from bias and verifiable). In summary, the best key performance indicators are: relevant, quantifiable, verifiable, accountable, actionable and linked to the organisation's performance recognition and reward system.

LEARNING OBJECTIVE 4

EXPLAIN THE RELATIONSHIP BETWEEN ORGANISATIONAL STRATEGIES AND PERFORMANCE MEASUREMENT

Organisational strategies define the direction that an organisation intends to take in pursuit of its mission. Performance measurement supports the development, implementation and evaluation of executed strategies by providing measures for both planning and control purposes. For example, the introduction of a customer-facing IT application is expected to achieve a 25 per cent increase in customer acceptances by 30 June (i.e. a planning measure), actual take-up as at 31 March is 40 per cent behind schedule, and back on track as a result of managerial intervention by 30 April (i.e. both control measures).

LEARNING OBJECTIVE 5

EXPLAIN THE CONCEPT OF RESPONSIBILITY ACCOUNTING

Responsibility accounting occurs when an entity is structured into strategic business units and the performance of these units is measured in accounting results. This type of accounting is used to identify and monitor the decisions and actions of managers who incur expenditure and generate income and are ultimately responsible for these costs and earnings.

LEARNING OBJECTIVE 6

IDENTIFY COST, PROFIT AND INVESTMENT CENTRES

A cost centre is a business unit (which could be a function, an activity or even an item of equipment) that is liable for certain costs. A profit centre is a business unit that is accountable for both costs and revenue. An investment centre is a business unit where the manager not only has control over the profits of the unit but also has some discretion as to the amount of investment undertaken by that unit.

LEARNING OBJECTIVE 7

EXPLAIN HOW PERFORMANCE MEASURES AND EXECUTIVE COMPENSATION SCHEMES ARE USED TO ALIGN MANAGERIAL INTERESTS TO ORGANISATIONAL GOALS

By linking part of an executive's compensation, in the form of potentially at-risk remuneration, to the achievement of predefined performance hurdles, a firm hopes to align the interests of the manager to those of key external stakeholders such as shareholders. Where such a reward system is in place, a manager's performance will need to be assessed with regard to performance indicators. This assessment is usually based on budget outcomes or previously set goals. The achievement of the reward(s), which can be monetary or share-based, is determined by assessing whether organisational goals, as expressed in the form of objectives and targets, have been met or exceeded. However, the measures used to assess performance may be manipulated in a non-observable manner by the manager so as to increase his or her rewards above what is actually warranted.

LEARNING OBJECTIVE 8

EXPLAIN WHY FINANCIAL MEASURES ARE USED TO ASSESS ORGANISATIONAL PERFORMANCE

Financial measures are the traditional measures of performance and include net profit, return on assets and return on equity. As key external stakeholders (e.g. shareholders and lenders) focus on the economic performance of the firm, financial measures used for internal decision-making purposes remind managers that financial outcomes are important. Financial measures are easy to calculate, can be easily verified and provide a standardised monetary measure. However, numbers can be manipulated, inflation can increase a result without increasing performance and inappropriate targets can lead to inefficiencies.

LEARNING OBJECTIVE 9

EXPLAIN AND APPLY THE RETURN ON INVESTMENT (ROI) METHOD OF MEASURING INVESTMENT CENTRE PERFORMANCE

ROI is a commonly used measure of performance for investment centres where the profit of the centre is related to the book value of the centre's assets, giving a percentage return. An upward trend in an investment centre's ROI would be favourably viewed by senior managers.

LEARNING OBJECTIVE 10

EXPLAIN AND APPLY THE RESIDUAL INCOME (RI) METHOD OF MEASURING INVESTMENT CENTRE PERFORMANCE

RI is the residual profit after having charged notional interest to the investment centre, with interest calculated by applying a suitable percentage rate to the value of the centre's assets. Under the RI approach, a manager is evaluated on how well he or she maximises dollars of residual income.

EXPLAIN HOW ROI AND RI MAY PROVIDE CONFLICTING OUTCOMES FOR A PROPOSED INVESTMENT

It is in the long-term interest of any firm to make new investments. New investment proposals must be evaluated by discounting the expected cash flows of the investment over its expected useful life. However, profits from a new investment will typically be low in early years before eventually rising to higher levels over time. At the same time, the net book value of the assets will be falling. With such investments, ROI in early years will be low. However, if the rate used to discount expected cash flows is also the rate used for RI calculation purposes, RI will be positive. If ROI is the investment centre performance measure used, such a situation might deter management from making new investments that are really in the long-term interests of the firm. On the other hand, provided that the extra profit from a new investment exceeds the notional interest charge on the investment's asset value, RI would increase and the proposed investment would be implemented.

EXPLAIN THE STRENGTHS AND WEAKNESSES OF ROI AND RI

ROI and RI are commonly used measures of investment centre performance, with performance being assessed at regular intervals (e.g. six monthly or annually). Whichever measure is used, investment centre performance is judged by considering the profit achieved over a short span of time and relating this in some way to asset values. As an investment centre's assets increase in value, its short-term profits must increase too, otherwise ROI or RI will fall and the investment centre manager might be criticised for his or her perceived poor performance. In the long term as well as the short term, profits should rise if investment is increased, and so as a general principle, long- and short-term interests should not be in conflict. However, new investments do not usually provide a quick return, and there might have to be some short-term sacrifice of profits in pursuit of long-term profit maximisation. This is the nature of the short-term/long-term conflict and ROI would tend to count against the acceptance of investments that generate an incremental return lower than historical investment centre ROIs. A further weakness of RI is that it does not facilitate comparisons between investment centres, nor does it relate the size of a centre's income to the size of the investment. In this respect, ROI might be viewed as being a better measure of performance. Finally, while performance is measured in the short term, both long-term and short-term considerations should influence investment and operating decisions. Thus, financial measures will need to be buttressed by the use of non-financial measures that have some appreciation of the long-term implications of strategic investments.

EXPLAIN AND APPLY THE ECONOMIC VALUE ADDED (EVA) METHOD OF MEASURING INVESTMENT CENTRE PERFORMANCE AND ITS USEFULNESS

EVA is a method of measuring how effectively a firm achieves the objective of creating shareholder value. It is another performance measure which, some argue, is more closely aligned to a company's share price. It is a simple measure to apply once the required variables have been collected. A positive EVA means the firm is creating wealth for shareholders, while a negative EVA means the firm is destroying shareholder wealth. This measure is easy to understand and can easily be incorporated into

a firm's strategy. For example, it could be included as one of the financial measures in the balanced scorecard. To calculate EVA, we use the following equation:

$$EVA = \text{after tax profit} + \text{interest} - (\text{cost of capital} \times \text{total capital employed})$$

LEARNING OBJECTIVE 14

EXPLAIN AND EVALUATE THE USE OF NON-FINANCIAL MEASURES OF PERFORMANCE

Non-financial measures are a quantification of organisational performance in non-monetary form (e.g. 95 per cent of customers are satisfied or highly satisfied). Non-financial measures are more difficult to quantify and can be more subjective indicators of organisational performance (e.g. customer satisfaction, employee satisfaction, product/service quality or supplier reliability). Non-financial measures are useful for setting strategies and providing an overall goal. They are difficult to measure and, at times, can be at odds with the organisation's financial objectives of an entity.

LEARNING OBJECTIVE 15

EXPLAIN WHAT IS MEANT BY THE TERM 'BALANCED SCORECARD'

A balanced scorecard is a set of measures that give managers a comprehensive picture of a business. It includes financial and operational measures. These operational measures can be the drivers of future financial performance.

LEARNING OBJECTIVE 16

EXPLAIN AND IDENTIFY THE DIFFERENCE BETWEEN DRIVER AND OUTCOME AND LEAD AND LAG KPIs

The driver measures are those that lead to or cause a change in the outcome measures. Financial performance measures, such as profit margins, return on equity and others, are outcome measures. The drivers tend to alter these indicators (e.g. increased productivity as reflected in throughput rates). Therefore, an improvement in operational performance will lead to improved outcomes. Lag measures indicate the outcome achieved (e.g. increased profit margin) whereas lead measures typically measure driver performance (e.g. quality assurance program has resulted in a 20 per cent reduction in wastage rates).

LEARNING OBJECTIVE 17

EXPLAIN THE FOUR PERSPECTIVES OF A BALANCED SCORECARD

The four perspectives are as follows: financial, customer, internal business processes and learning and growth. The financial perspective measures outcomes for external parties such as shareholders (e.g. ROI). The customer perspective measures business performance from the customer viewpoint (e.g. customer satisfaction rates). The internal business perspective focuses on the operational or process drivers that lead to the satisfaction of customers and shareholders (e.g. productivity measures such as manufacturing cycle time). Finally, the learning and growth perspective focuses on employee and work-related practices (e.g. staff morale index) and the use of technology which drive improved business process performance and ultimately satisfy customers and shareholders.

REVIEW QUESTIONS

1 Explain what is meant by the term 'responsibility centre'.

2 For what decisions is the manager of a cost centre not responsible?

3 What are driver and outcome KPIs?

4 What is a BSC?

5 Explain the four perspectives of a BSC.

6 Why would an entity use a BSC in evaluating divisional performance?

7 Table 13.2 provides a basic BSC for a financial institution. For each of the four perspectives, provide two financial and/or non-financial measures performance measures in addition to those provided in the chapter.

PROBLEMS FOR DISCUSSION AND ANALYSIS

1 Visit the Woolworths Limited website (www.woolworths.com.au) and download the company's most recent annual report. Locate within the Director's Statutory Report the report of the Remuneration Committee which provides comprehensive disclosures about the remuneration paid to key management personnel (KMP).

   a What is Woolworths' remuneration strategy and what are the goals the strategy is designed to achieve?

   b What are the principles embodied in Woolworths' remuneration framework?

   c How will Woolworths apply these remuneration principles in terms of the use of external data, the setting of targets and the awarding of incentives to KMP?

   d What is the structure of the remuneration package offered to KMP?

   e Focusing on the at-risk short- and long-term rewards offered by Woolworths to KMP, identify, review and comment on the components of the incentives, the weightings allocated to each component and the performance measures (or hurdles) used to determine whether an incentive will be awarded.

   f Review the performance measures Woolworths uses for the awarding of short-term annual cash incentive for the KMP identified in the Remuneration Report.

      i What are those financial and non-financial measures?

      ii How would you assess the balance between financial and non-financial measures?

      iii Why would the financial and non-financial measures for individual KMP be different in terms of applicability and weighting?

2 Discuss the concept of responsibility accounting. What does it mean and why is it important in the assessment and rewarding of performance?

3 Indicate, for each of the following independent cases, whether they are best structured as cost, profit or investment centres:

   a Kellee is head of the marketing and public relations department at Satellite University. The department receives funding from the central administration for teaching and research. The department is allocated funds based on projected expenditures. Kellee is responsible for 10 academic staff and two general staff.

   b Leigh is head of the school of business located on the campus at Planet University. The school enrols only full-fee-paying students and is responsible for all operating costs and a share of

the university's overheads. The university provides a building and teaching venues. Leigh is responsible for 30 academic staff and 10 general staff.

c Troy is head of the division of business at Universe University. The division is located in its own building in the city as part of a strategic move by the university. The division enrols only full-fee-paying students and it also conducts short courses for businesses in the CBD. The division is responsible for all capital and operating costs.

4 Four different responsibility centres in Hancock Ltd are: (i) Human Resources, (ii) Repairs and Maintenance, (iii) Dairy Products and (iv) Frozen Goods. The Dairy Products and Frozen Goods responsibility centres manufacture packaged consumer food products that are sold into the Australian grocery market. Both, while not being responsible for the capital investment decisions in their respective areas, control the selling prices and costs incurred in manufacturing dairy products and frozen goods.

a What do you understand by the term 'decentralisation' as it might be applied to Hancock's ?

b Hancock's four responsibility centres could be designated as cost, profit or investment centres. On the basis of the information provided about each responsibility centre, identify and explain why Human Resources and Dairy Products should be designated as a cost, profit or investment centre.

c What are the likely behavioural consequences of corporate head office staff continually imposing their decisions on the managers of the Dairy Products and Frozen Goods responsibility centres?

5 You are a director of a credit union and you have been appointed to the remuneration subcommittee. One of your first tasks is to consider a bonus for the general manager. You believe that a bonus should be paid based on performance. The credit union has 10 000 members and total assets of $50 million, with $40 million in loans to members. It operates four branch locations and a head office and employs a total of 30 people. You are familiar with using KPIs such as return on assets as a measure of performance. However, the board of directors has a policy of not aiming to maximise profit as the credit union exists for the benefit of its members. Therefore, you consider it to be inappropriate to use return on assets as a measure of the performance of the general manager.

Required

What other financial and non-financial measures of performance could be used to assess the performance of the general manager?

6 List three performance measures that would be appropriate for the following centres:

a an academic department in a university established as a cost centre

b a branch of a bank established as a profit centre

c a division of a large steel company established as an investment centre.

7 Roy Rogers is the divisional manager for Trigger Enterprises and he is rewarded based on overall divisional return on investment (ROI). Currently, his division produces a 25 per cent ROI. Roy is investigating an opportunity to expand the plant of his division. The projected ROI for the expansion is 18 per cent and the company's cost of capital is 13 per cent.

Required

Do you think Roy will proceed with the expansion? Discuss the issues involved looking at it from Roy's position and from the shareholders' position.

8 Jack Thomson, the CEO of Thomo Ltd, has been reading about EVA. Because you have completed your MBA, he asks you to calculate the EVA amount for the company. You gather the following data:

Net profit for the last year	$40 000
Interest expense	$10 000
Accounts payable	$100 000
Long term loans (6%)	$200 000
Shareholders' equity	$300 000
Total liabilities and shareholders' funds	$500 000

You have found that the rate of return on government bonds is 6 per cent, and you estimate that shareholders expect a premium on the government bond rate of 6 per cent. The tax rate is 30 per cent.

Required

a Calculate the economic value added amount for Jack.

b Explain what your answer means for the company.

9 Jack Thomson approaches you at the end of the next year and asks you to determine whether the company has created value for its shareholders during the year. The details are the same as in the question above, except that net profit for the year was $30 000.

10 Determine the EVA amount for Woolworths Ltd for the year ended 30 June 2013 from the annual report in Appendix 1 (using the following assumptions):

a interest cost, 6 per cent

b equity cost, 12 per cent

c tax rate, 30 per cent.

State any other assumptions you need to make.

Comment on the economic value added result you obtain for Woolworths.

11 Explain the differences between strategic, operating, driver and outcome KPIs. Give examples of each of the four types for a financial institution (see Table 13.2).

12 Eggleton Limited provides a range of professional services to the Australasian business community. An indicator that would not be directly relevant to assessing the market profile and client acceptance of Eggleton Limited in the Australasian business community is:

a editorial comments in the Australasian financial and business press about Eggleton Limited and the industry in which it operates

b the ratio of new clients signed by Eggleton Limited (measured in number and dollar value of billings) to client terminations (measured in number and dollar value of fees lost)

c the annual budget allowance by Eggleton Limited for expenditure on corporate and service promotion

d the average number of complaints lodged by clients of Eggleton Limited per quarter.

Explain the reasons for your selection.

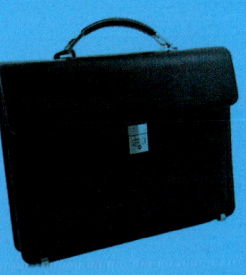

13 The following KPIs are calculated on a monthly basis for the loans department in a credit union. Classify each KPI as strategic or operating; driver or outcome:

a dollars spent on advertising

b time taken for loan approval

c dollar value of loans approved

d number of loan applications received via the internet

e number of loans referred to the credit department for non-payment after 60 days

f profitability of loans approved

g percentage of loans funded out of the total number approved.

14 The list below contains a variety of performance measures that could be used in a balanced scorecard. Classify each measure as financial, customer, internal business process, or learning and growth:

a market share

b net profit

c defect rate

d number of employees attending training programs

e lead time to delivery

f growth in sales

g employee morale

h number of repeat sales.

15 Recent articles have focused on summary information for running a business and a BSC style approach (using a suite of financial and non-financial performance measures).

Explain the following in relation to the sentence above:

a The arguments for using the profit measure as the all-encompassing measure of business performance.

b The limitations of the profit-measure approach, and of undue dependence on the profit measure.

c The problems of using a broad range of non-financial measures for the short- and long-term control of a business.

Note to instructors: The following problems are considered more suitable for use in MBA courses. However, undergraduate courses may also find the problem useful.

16 One of Kaplan's recommendations for improving management accounting was the increased use of non-financial performance indicators to control organisational performance. Explain and discuss the advantages and disadvantages of using non-financial performance indicators in controlling organisational performance.

17 The generic BSC, as conceived by Kaplan and Norton (1992), has four perspectives: financial, customer, internal process, and innovation and learning. In contrast, the triple bottom line envisages three forms of performance reporting: economic, social and environmental.

BestWest, the state government agency responsible for promoting the use of sustainable practices by the West Australian community, reports the following triple bottom line performance measures:

a Waste material produced by BestWest as a percentage of total materials used.

b BestWest operating surplus for the year ending 30 June.

c Number of people attending a BestWest workshop promoting the use of environmentally friendly packaging.

d Number of BestWest employees completing a fitness program intended to improve the physical and mental wellbeing of agency employees.

e Percentage of total BestWest revenue received from corporate philanthropists (e.g. Gill Bates the CEO of MacroHard Software) due to the sound environmental management policies promoted by the agency within the business community.

f Community satisfaction with BestWest that is attributable to the agency's reputation of being a good corporate citizen.

g Tonnes of waste paper recycled by BestWest in the year ending 30 June.

h Percentage reduction in BestWest energy consumption (as measured in gigajoules and cost per full-time employee) due to the agency's adherence to the targets set in the state government's Energy Smart policy.

i The total number of BestWest employees on occupational stress-related sick leave as at 30 June.

Required

Classify each of the TBL measures into one of the four perspectives of the BSC. Explain your reasons for each classification.

18 ElectroWizardry Enterprises (EWE) is a small electronics business that buys circuit boards from overseas suppliers, inserts various electronic devices into these boards, and then sells the modified boards on to local computer assemblers. The owner of EWE is concerned because the business's profits have been well below the budgeted targets for the past few years. For this reason, the services of a consultant have been engaged to identify the sources of the low profit levels. The consultant undertook a detailed study of the business's processes and as a result determined that 10 per cent of the modified boards were being returned to EWE because they were defective. Related to the high defective rate were low levels of customer satisfaction and a diminishing level of sales over the past few years. The consultant's discussions with EWE employees led to the conclusions that (i) many employees had had insufficient training in essential skills such as soldering; (ii) some of the electronic insertion diagrams provided to employees were inaccurate; and (iii) approximately 5 per cent of the overseas-supplied boards had defects of various sorts, which the employees were expected to correct (but without any extra time being allowed for such corrections).

Required

a Using the terminology of the BSC, determine some financial and non-financial KPIs that the business needs to improve in order to achieve its budgeted profit target.

b Illustrate your answer in (a) using a vertically structured balanced scorecard similar to the one shown in Table 13.2.

19 The senior executive team of Aussie Fries attended a presentation made by Robert Kaplan on the nature and use of the BSC. After the presentation, the senior executives decided that they should develop a BSC for Aussie Fries. As a first attempt they decide that they will use the four balanced scorecard perspectives proposed by Kaplan and Norton: customers, internal business

processes, learning and growth, and financial. You have been asked to assist the senior executives by completing the following tasks:

a Identify one strategic objective that Aussie Fries should establish for each BSC perspective. Each strategic objective must be consistent with the mission statement of Aussie Fries.

b For each BSC perspective, identify one critical success factor and provide two key performance indicators (KPIs) for measuring the performance of Aussie Foods on that factor. One KPI must be a financial measure and the other must be a non-financial measure. Where possible, identify if the performance measure is a lead or lag indicator.

c Identify one major advantage that the managers of Aussie Fries would expect to obtain from the implementation of the BSC as promoted by Kaplan and Norton.

20 Two years ago, Kanton Enterprises implemented a low-cost strategy to improve its competitive position. Its objective was to become the low-cost producer in its industry. To lower costs, Kanton undertook a number of improvement activities such as just-in-time production, total quality management and activity-based costing. Now, after two years of operation, the president of Kanton wants some assessment of the system's achievements. To help provide this assessment, the following information on one product has been gathered:

	TWO YEARS AGO	THIS YEAR
Theoretical annual capacity*	96 000	96 000
Actual production**	76 000	88 000
Production hours available (20 workers)	40 000	40 000
Scrap (kilograms)	5000	2000
Materials used (kilograms)	50 000	50 000
Actual cost per unit	$125	$100
Days of inventory	6	3
Number of defective units	5000	2000
Suggestions per employee	2	6
Hours of training	100	400
Selling price per unit	$150	$140
Number of new customers	2000	8000

* Amount that could be produced given the available production hours.
** Amount that was produced given the available production hours.

Required

a Compute the following measures for the two years of data:
  i theoretical operating cycle time per unit
  ii actual operating cycle time per unit
  iii labour productivity (output/hours)

    iv   scrap as a percentage of total material used

    v   percentage change in actual product cost (for this year only)

    vi   percentage change in days of inventory (for this year only)

    vii   defective units as a percentage of total units produced

    viii   new customers per unit of output

    ix   total hours of training

    x   selling price per unit (as given)

    xi   total employee suggestions.

b For the measures listed in (a), list likely strategic objectives, classified according to the four BSC perspectives. Next, classify each measure as a driver or outcome measure. Finally, evaluate the success of the strategy. Would you like any additional information to carry out this evaluation? Explain.

(Adapted from D. Hansen and M. Mowen, *Cost Management: Accounting and Control*, 4th edn, South-Western, Mason, OH, 2002, question 14–15, pp. 586–7.)

ETHICS CASE STUDY

This case is based upon a story by Ian Dunlop published in the *Australian Financial Review*, 11 October 2002.

In 2002, Ian Dunlop observed that senior executive remuneration was a matter of some concern and he questioned whether or not companies were appropriately compensating executives for their efforts. While Dunlop had no objection to there being 'reasonable reward for genuine performance and results', he was not sure as to what was reasonable and whether or not executives, who insisted on multi-million-dollar remuneration, were the right individuals to be running sustainable businesses.

Dunlop suggested that executive remuneration should not be a matter for legislative oversight, with such supervision being best left to the market. He also argued that executives had an obligation to show leadership as to the amount of executive compensation paid and to act 'ethically, not only in regard to business in general but also in regard to self-interest.' In particular he felt that senior executive compensation was already at levels that provided more than adequate 'financial independence'.

Beyond that, Dunlop observed that since business success was not exclusively the result of the efforts of a firm's CEO and a small cadre of senior executives because lower level managers and employees had also contributed to the outcomes obtained, corporate reward structures ought to reflect this reality. He then noted that the entire concept of executive remuneration needed to be rethought as 'sadly, business has demonstrated that performance-based incentives are not producing superior results or responsible outcomes.'

In noting how ethics provides the framework for the setting of executive remuneration, Dunlop quoted Dr Attracta Lagan, then head of KPMG's National Ethics & Sustainability practice, where she observed, 'Being ethical is essentially about accepting our interdependence with each other and taking the other's needs into consideration before acting. It sometimes boils down to an ability to manage the tension between self-interest and what is good for the group or community.'

While the financial fortunes of companies and shareholders have continued to wax and wane over the past 20 years, levels of executive remuneration have increased when economic times are good but appear to be relatively insulated from declines when economic conditions are less favourable. Since the onset of the Global Financial Crisis, executive remuneration continues to be a matter of considerable debate and coverage within the media, has fuelled community anger towards what are perceived to

be excessive levels of compensation awarded and, contrary to Dunlop's opinion, triggered legislative action directed at enhancing the level of shareholder oversight of executive compensation.

For many Australian listed companies, the total remuneration paid to individual senior executives and as a whole is initially determined by a board-level remuneration committee and then subsequently reported to shareholders at the company's annual general meeting (AGM). In the past, the reporting of senior executive remuneration to shareholders has typically been a matter of rubberstamping the recommendations of directors. However, with amendments to the *Corporations Act* that came into effect on 1 July 2011, the enactment of the two-strikes rule has increased the level of director accountability surrounding the determination and approval of executive remuneration. Where 25 per cent or more of shareholders vote no to the remuneration report submitted to a company's AGM, this is deemed to be a first strike. If the subsequent remuneration report also receives a no vote of more than 25 per cent of shareholders at the next AGM, it is deemed to be a second strike and shareholders will vote at this AGM whether or not board members, other than the managing director, need to stand for re-election. Where 50 per cent or more of shareholders vote in favour of the spill motion, a subsequent (or spill) meeting of shareholders must be held within 90 days where the directors serving at the time that the directors' report was voted upon will be required to stand for re-election.

In each of the financial years ending 30 June 2011 and 2012, over 100 ASX-listed companies have been subject to a first strike, with 21 having attracted subsequent second strikes. While the AGMs of only five companies with second strikes voted in favour of a spill of incumbent directors, three boards were subsequently re-elected with no change in directors and, in the two other cases, the composition of the board was changed subsequent to the AGM and did not really require the holding of a spill general meeting. Nevertheless, research evidence suggests the companies that experience the ire of shareholders at an AGM have not only become more sensitive to the amount of remuneration awarded to senior executives but have taken action to ensure remuneration policies and practices are consistent with the ASX's good corporate governance principles.

Discuss

a The article refers to the team effort that is involved in large organisations, and argues that successful organisations require good teams and good leaders. When a football team wins the premiership, is it due to the players, the coach or both? The CEO is like the coach of the team. How do we assess the performance of the CEOs of large organisations?

b Is it reasonable to expect CEOs to moderate their remuneration demands when they have achieved 'financial independence'? Is acting in self-interest unethical?

c Why should shareholders be afforded the right to vote against the executive compensation recommendations of the board of directors' remuneration committee? Should the two-strike rule have a threshold higher or lower than the current 25 per cent?

SUGGESTED ANSWERS TO STOP AND THINK EXERCISES IN THE CHAPTER

1 A cost centre is a business unit (which could be a function, an activity or even an item of equipment) whose costs may be attributed to it. A cost centre is appropriate when a manager only has control

over costs and not revenues. A profit centre is a business unit that is accountable for both costs and revenues. An investment centre is a business unit where the manager not only has control over the profits of the unit but also has some discretion as to the amount of investment undertaken by the unit.

2 Examples of financial measures are total income/revenue, return on assets, return on shareholders' equity and cost per unit.

3 Financial measures are easier to calculate than non-financial measures and are more well-known. Financial measures provide standards for comparison across entities. However, financial measures can be manipulated, and inflation causes problems with measures involving dollars. Non-financial measures can be more directly linked to strategy, may be more readily available than measures like profit and are less susceptible to manipulation. However, non-financial measures are often more difficult to measure, may conflict with financial measures in the short term and are not as easily understood as financial measures.

4 Examples of non-financial measures are customer satisfaction, supplier reliability, quality of production, customer complaints, the morale of employees and delivery time.

5 Strengths: non-financial performance indicators are more readily linked to organisational strategies, do not require measurement in monetary terms, are more easily understood and acted upon by lower-level management and are made available on a more timely basis. Weaknesses: non-financial performance indicators may conflict with financial performance measures in the short term, are not measured in monetary terms, are not readily integrated within traditional accounting and financial reporting systems, and lack an overall theoretical framework explaining their emergence and application.

6 Performance measures that would be useful in evaluating investment centres are the rate of return on investment, return on assets and net profit. Non-financial measures could include customer or employee satisfaction rates, throughput time, number of new products developed and so on.

7 Outcome KPIs report how the organisation has performed in terms of meeting organisational goals from the perspective of key external stakeholders (e.g. customers and shareholders) whereas driver KPIs report on the activities undertaken and resource use of the organisation in pursuit of the organisation's goals. Lag indicators, in having more of a historical perspective, indicate what has been achieved whereas the forward-looking characteristics of lead indicators provide an early warning of what is likely to occur.

CENGAGENOW

Go to http:\\login.cengagebrain.com to link to CengageNOW, your online study tool. First take the Pre-Test for this chapter to get your Personalised Study Plan, and then:

» revise your understanding of the key terms related to performance measurement and the balanced scorecard by completing the online crossword

» follow online links about assessing and rewarding performance

» review concepts of responsibility accounting, the -balanced scorecard and performance measurement through the online flashcards.

After you have completed the activities in your Personalised Study Plan take the Post-Test to determine what concepts you have mastered and what you still need work on.

COSTS AND COST BEHAVIOUR

LEARNING OBJECTIVES

At the end of this chapter, you should be able to:

1. identify reasons why management need reliable information about the costs of goods and services they provide to customers
2. explain the difference between variable and fixed costs
3. explain what is meant by a linear cost function
4. identify what is meant by the relevant range of activity
5. explain the cost assignment process
6. explain the difference between direct and indirect costs
7. identify what is meant by product and period costs
8. explain the absorption and variable costing methods
9. identify the stages that are involved in determining the allocation of overheads to products
10. explain what is meant by predetermined overhead absorption rates
11. explain the difference between traditional volume-based and activity-based costing methods
12. explain the terms 'activity', 'cost pool' and 'cost driver' as used in activity-based costing
13. explain how time-driven activity-based costing (TDABC) provides a simpler and less costly activity-based method of allocating indirect costs.

INTRODUCTION

Subsequent to the Global Financial Crisis (GFC) in September 2008, many businesses found that their previously profitable revenue streams were starting to dry up. For many firms, declining revenues also led to the fall in another financial metric: the revenue generated per employee. Despite some costs falling as revenues decreased, the problem of declining revenue per employee was addressed by cutting the employee headcount. Such workforce downsizing was undertaken in the hope that there would be no further erosion in revenues. If such hopes were well-founded, that meant that every dollar in cost savings immediately flowed straight to an equivalent increase in business profitability.

While such a focus on the cost component of the profit equation has been necessary in the short term, if a firm is to be successful in the future, profitable revenue streams are essential. Thus, it is essential that managers have a sound understanding of the long-run implications of decisions taken to reduce costs. Often many short-term cost-reducing initiatives, such as across-the-board cuts (i.e. efficiency dividends) or the deferral of expenditure, deliver short-term profitability at the cost of customer loyalty and heightened business risk. These, in turn, sabotage a firm's ability to take advantage of more favourable business conditions as they emerge and thereby limit future growth opportunities and profitability.

This is not to suggest that a firm should never transform its existing value chain activities. For example, Project Refresh was a very successful supply-chain initiative implemented in 1999 by Woolworths with the primary motivation of eliminating costs from the retailer's supply chain. Over the past decade, Project Refresh has delivered cumulative cost savings in the order of some $8 billion. These significant savings in supply-chain costs were redirected to not only improving the overall operating efficiency of retailing in terms of the procurement, holding and distribution of inventories but also in enhancing the 'offer' to customers in terms of lower prices and an aggressive approach to marketing the company's brand (as 'Australia's fresh food people'). Such was the strategic advantage created by Project Refresh that it ultimately delivered a competitive position to Woolworths that its major rivals, Coles and IGA, found initially difficult to emulate. From a shareholders' perspective, Woolworths' harvesting of cost savings in its supply chain and the 'investment' of these funds elsewhere in the business delivered a significant increase in shareholder wealth, as evidenced in the dividends paid and an increased share price.

Whereas the cost-reduction initiatives of many firms have been implemented as one-time or a finite exercise and had a relatively short-lived benefit, as indicated by Woolworths' Project Refresh, approaching cost management as a continuous process is more likely to deliver sustainable improvements in business performance. To ensure managers make decisions that make sense in the longer term, it is essential that they have a sound understanding of their business value chain and appreciate what activities directly or indirectly create value. In assessing whether or not such activities are value-adding, managers need to be fully informed of the costs incurred throughout the value chain. By being in possession of this cost information, managers should be able to take a more systematic approach to managing costs and ensure that the resources for creating long-term value are preserved.

Having established the importance of cost information to managerial decision making, Chapter 14 introduces costs as a theoretical and practical concept as well as the alternatives views about cost. As will be discussed, 'costs ain't costs' and what 'cost' is depends upon the decision to be made by a manager. On the basis of the understanding of cost established in this chapter, our attention will turn to how costs are planned and controlled through the preparation of budgets and performance reports in Chapter 15, and how they influence short- and long-term decision making in Chapters 16, 17 and 18.

1 LEARNING OBJECTIVE

Identify reasons why management need reliable information about the costs of goods and services they provide to customers

MANAGEMENT'S NEED FOR INFORMATION ABOUT COSTS

Management needs information about costs for many reasons, including the following.

- *To control costs*

Actual product costs are compared with planned costs. If the actual costs deviate from the plan, management may need to take corrective action so that their predetermined targets are met in the future. A business needs to know its costs in order to control them.

- *To aid planning*

Past product costs are a useful base for estimating future product costs in the planning process. But when using past costs for this purpose, management must be careful to take account of potential changes in the level of costs in the future, due to inflation, resource scarcity and so on.

- *To value inventories*

Product costs need to be determined so that the value of products which are complete (finished goods) and products which are partially complete (work in progress) can be established at the end of each accounting period for inclusion in the balance sheet and the statement of comprehensive income.

- *To aid the setting of selling prices*

For some firms, the cost of products influences the setting of prices. From a marketing viewpoint it can be argued that price is determined through market forces, that is, from consideration of what the market can bear. However, in a number of situations, particularly where there is little or no competition, prices are often set with reference to cost. Ultimately, for profit-making entities goods and services must be supplied at prices that exceed costs if they are to survive!

- *To ascertain the relative profitability of products*

In times of scarce resources, when a firm's level of output is constrained, it is likely that management will favour supporting only its most profitable products. In these circumstances, knowledge of product costs is essential. This enables an organisation to make more informed decisions about continuing or abandoning each of its products or services. Similarly, where a firm is a price taker rather than price maker, knowledge of cost is important in being able to determine whether a product generates an acceptable profit margin. Where an existing (or proposed) product appears to be less profitable than required, management can examine ways for increasing the profit margin by improving the value of the product to customers, targeting the cost of the product or a combination of both.

For managers to be able to choose among alternative business opportunities, they need information regarding future costs and revenues, and the ways in which these vary at different levels of activity. In order to use this information effectively, managers also need to understand how costs are determined. In Chapter 14 we initially examine some basic cost concepts, such as how costs behave, and direct and indirect costs. We then look a simple costing system for a one-product (or -service) firm. We will subsequently examine more complex costing systems where a firm manufactures (or supplies) multiple products (or services) and the problem of the allocation of indirect costs to products (or services) becomes a strategic issue.

2 LEARNING OBJECTIVE

Explain the difference between variable and fixed costs

FIXED AND VARIABLE COSTS

To understand how costs behave, it is first necessary to recognise the different types of costs. Some costs are essentially fixed in nature; for example, the service and equipment charge for a telephone service. Others vary with usage or activity; for example, the cost of calls made. The latter are known as variable costs. Unfortunately, as not all costs fall neatly within these categories, it is necessary to make some simplifying assumptions for the purpose of decision making. Before examining fixed and variable costs it is worthwhile to define them.

14.1 **KEY CONCEPT**

FIXED COSTS

A cost is fixed if it does not change in total in response to changes in the level of activity. The activity level may be measured in terms of either production or sales output in units or some other measure of activity (e.g. machine or labour hours). The choice will depend upon what is being measured. However, the fixed cost per unit of activity will increase or decrease with changes in the activity being measured. If the annual service and equipment charge for a telephone service is $12 000, the total fixed cost incurred will not change irrespective of the number of calls made. On the other hand, if 120 000 calls are made during the year, the average service and equipment cost would be 10 cents per call. Were only 100 000 calls made during the year the average service and equipment cost per call would be 12 cents.

14.2 **KEY CONCEPT**

VARIABLE COSTS

A cost is variable if it changes in total in response to changes in the level of activity. Again activity can be measured in terms of units, machine or labour hours or another relevant measure. For simplicity, it is assumed per-unit costs do not change with changes in activity. If the variable cost of a telephone call is 30 cents, then this cost per call is the same whether 100 000 or 120 000 calls are made so total variable costs will increase or decrease in direct proportion to activity level. The total variable call cost incurred would be $30 000 if 100 000 calls were made and $36 000 if 120 000 calls were made.

COST FUNCTIONS

3 **LEARNING OBJECTIVE**

A basic notion of science is the idea that one thing may depend on another according to some mathematical relation. It is likely that in your study of economics you have also come across mathematical relations. For example, to show that the total spending (c) of a nation depends on the total income (y) of all persons in the nation, economists use the following equation:

Explain what is meant by a linear cost function

$$c = f(y)$$

This states that consumption is a function of the level of income.

Mathematical formulas are also used in accounting to show relationships between costs and activity levels. There are two important variables involved in the construction of cost functions. We will use the example of the cost of travelling to illustrate the nature of these variables and their interrelationship.

- The dependent variable, expressed as variable y, is the cost to be predicted – the total cost for an activity; for example, the cost of petrol consumed in making a journey.
- The independent variable x is the level of activity; for example, the number of kilometres to be travelled on the journey.

The dependent variable is expressed as a function of the independent variable:

$$y = f(x)$$

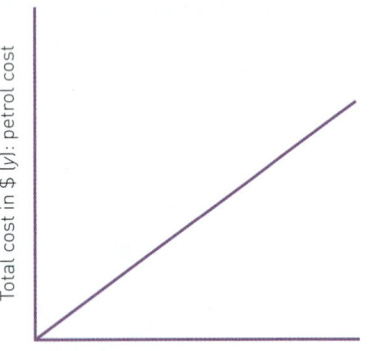

FIGURE 14.1 THE RELATIONSHIP BETWEEN A DIRECTLY DEPENDENT VARIABLE (PETROL COST) AND AN INDEPENDENT VARIABLE (KILOMETRES TRAVELLED)

In our example, this relationship can be expressed as: 'The total cost of petrol for a journey is a function of (or depends upon) the number of kilometres travelled'.

The relationship between the dependent and independent variables is illustrated in Figure 14.1, where the vertical axis shows the dependent variable – the total cost of petrol – and the horizontal axis shows the independent variable – the activity; that is, the kilometres travelled.

A cost function may be linear or non-linear. Traditionally, accountants assume cost functions to be linear, which is not necessarily a realistic assumption.

THE CHOICE OF THE INDEPENDENT VARIABLE

Often, there is more than one independent variable that affects the total cost of an activity. The amount of petrol consumed and the total cost of a journey are affected by the speed at which the vehicle travels, the weight carried and the distance travelled. However, as it is usually too complex to take account of all variables that affect total costs, typically the independent variable selected is the most influential variable in relation to the cost.

In some cases, the selection of the most influential variable is obvious. When it is not, past costs should be examined to establish which of the independent variables are most influential.

Scout Kozakiewicz

Variable costs

The cost of raw material is a good example of a cost that varies directly with the level of production output. For example, if one unit of output requires 2 kilograms of material that costs $3.00 per kilogram, then the material cost for 50 units of output will be:

2 kilograms × $3.00 per kilogram × 50 units = $300

Sales commission normally varies with sales output. For example, if a salesperson receives 10 per cent commission on every unit sold and the selling price per unit is $40, the commission received will be $4 per unit. If the salesperson sold 3000 units during the year, the total commission received would be:

$$4 \times 3000 \text{ units} = \$12\,000$$

Labour paid on an hourly basis is conventionally classified as a cost that varies with production output. However, in reality permanent employees are paid a fixed wage which bears no direct relationship to output levels. While there might be some output-linked incentive bonus included in the pay structure, most remuneration will be fixed for a set working week. Nevertheless, for decision-making purposes it is assumed that this category of labour is variable because, physically, production levels are a function of the labour input.

Figure 14.2 illustrates a cost which varies directly with activity levels. Note that the graph goes through the origin; that is, when the activity is zero, the costs are zero. As activity increases, the variable cost increases. This can be compared with Figure 14.6, where fixed costs are also included.

In reality, it is unlikely that costs which are traditionally classified as variable will behave in a strictly linear fashion. The variable cost function often tends to be curvilinear, or made up of several straight lines. The following examples illustrate why variable costs are not always strictly linear:

- Manufacturers are likely to benefit from bulk discounts for the purchase of raw materials.
- Prices of resources tend to increase as a scarcity arises, due to increased demand.
- Increased activity may lead to diminishing returns. For example, attempts to sell more units of a product may entail transporting the additional units sold over longer distances to more distant markets. Therefore, distribution costs may increase at a faster rate than activity. Assuming that selling prices are constant, higher distribution costs result in diminishing profit margins.

Figure 14.3 shows a variable cost function with diminishing returns.

Fixed costs

Examples of costs that are normally classified as fixed are rent, rates, salaries, and the service and equipment charge for utilities such as the telephone service referred to earlier. As discussed below, fixed costs of this type are normally also classified as being overhead (see Figure 14.4).

However, the concept that fixed costs are constant over all levels of activity is often unrealistic. In reality, a fixed cost

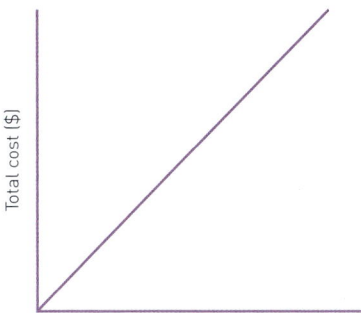

FIGURE 14.2 A LINEAR COST FUNCTION

Total cost ($)

Activity level: production or sales output

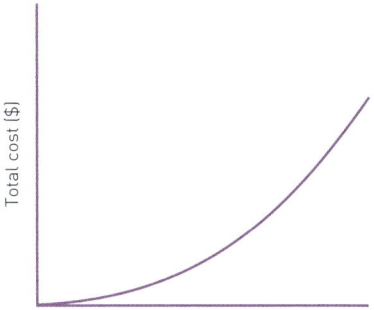

FIGURE 14.3 A CURVILINEAR COST FUNCTION

Total cost ($)

Activity level: production or sales ouptut

FIGURE 14.4 A FIXED COST IS NOT AFFECTED BY INCREASES IN ACTIVITY LEVELS

Total cost ($)

Activity level: production or sales output

FIGURE 14.5 A STEPPED COST FUNCTION: RENTING FACTORY SPACE

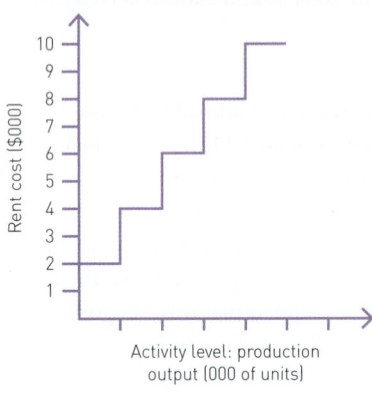

is fixed only for a limited range of output. For example, in the case of a telephone utility, theoretically the service and equipment charge is fixed. However, if the telephone service provider increases its charges, or if additional service capacity is required (e.g. more extension lines), the service and equipment charge will increase. Similarly, if a manufacturing facility has limited capacity and production was to exceed that capacity, another facility would be required and costs would increase. Therefore, these types of costs tend to behave in a stepped fashion. Figure 14.5 illustrates a stepped cost function in the case of renting a factory. The rent is $2000 for one factory, which has a capacity, in output terms, of 1000 units. Another factory will be required for output levels exceeding 1000 units, and the total rent will increase to $4000 (assuming that the rental and the capacity are the same). This cost will remain at $4000 up to 2000 units, when another factory will be required and costs will increase in the same stepwise fashion.

STOP AND THINK 1

Variable and fixed costs are traditionally assumed to be linear. Explain why this assumption is unrealistic.

STOP AND THINK 2

What is the difference between a linear fixed cost and a stepped fixed cost? Give examples, other than those given.

LINEAR COST FUNCTIONS

In reality, many cost functions are made up of two parts – a fixed cost and a variable cost.

KEY CONCEPT

LINEAR COST FUNCTIONS

In general, we can express a linear cost function as:

$$y = a + bx$$

where y is the total cost to be predicted; x is the level of activity measured in units of output; a is the fixed cost; and b is the variable cost.

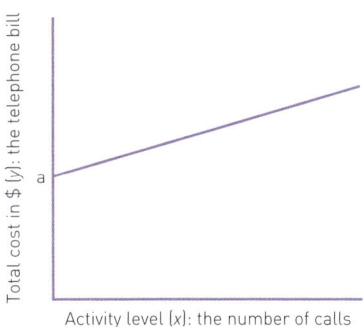

FIGURE 14.6 A LINEAR COST FUNCTION OF A TELEPHONE BILL

Total cost in $ (y): the telephone bill

a

Activity level (x): the number of calls

Let us again consider a telephone bill, since this is a good example of a linear cost function. Examine the graph in Figure 14.6. Point *a* represents the fixed costs – the service and equipment charge – which remain the same for any level of activity. The line illustrates the variable cost (the cost of calls) rising in proportion to increases in activity *x* (the number of call units).

We can determine the total telephone bill (*y*) using the equation in Key concept 14.3 if we know the monthly service and equipment charge (*a*), the cost per unit call (*b*) and the number of units registered (*x*). These are as shown below:

- Service and equipment charge, $a = \$50$
- Cost per unit call, $b = 20$ cents (or $\$0.20$)
- Number of unit calls made, $x = 1500$

The total cost of the bill, *y*, can be calculated thus:

$$y = \$50 + (\$0.20 \times 1500) = \$350$$

If the number of unit calls increased to 1800, the total cost of the bill would be:

$$y = \$50 + (\$0.20 \times 1800) = \$410$$

To help you to understand this equation and its use, examine a recent telephone bill for your household and calculate the total cost of the bill if the number of unit calls made increased by, say, 50 per cent. This exercise might also result in you making fewer telephone calls! The same principles also apply to mobile telephone calls where the service provider levies a base call connection fee plus a call time charge per block of actual call time.

THE RELEVANT RANGE OF ACTIVITY

Assuming that an entity's intention is to operate in the relevant range of activity, we can be reasonably confident about predicting the pattern of cost behaviour. This confidence is important to managers because the information regarding the way in which costs behave is the basis for many decisions. If costs do not behave as predicted, decisions could be taken that could jeopardise the organisation's future.

4 LEARNING OBJECTIVE

Identify what is meant by the relevant range of activity

KEY CONCEPT

14.4

THE RELEVANT RANGE OF ACTIVITY

The relevant range of activity relates to the levels of activity that the firm has experienced in past periods. It is assumed that, in this range, the relationship between the independent and dependent variables will be similar to previously experienced behaviours.

FIGURE 14.7 COST FUNCTIONS INSIDE AND OUTSIDE THE RELEVANT RANGE OF ACTIVITY

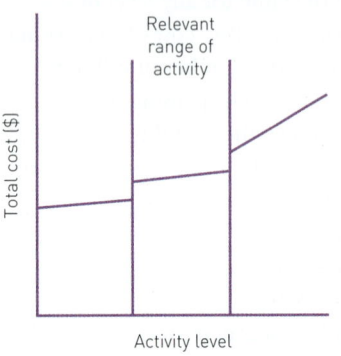

Outside the relevant range, we cannot be confident that the relationship between the variables will hold. Figure 14.7 shows a cost function in the relevant range of activity and other cost functions outside this range, which are not of a similar pattern.

If an organisation is intending to operate at an activity level not previously experienced, it must be extremely cautious in the prediction of future costs, and should rely more on forecasting methods than on predicting costs on the basis of past behaviour. While the examination of forecasting methods is outside the scope of this text, you can find references to the methods in advanced management accounting texts.

Conventionally, for convenience, graphical representations of the relations between costs and volumes show cost functions that are the same for all levels of activity; that is, the same pattern of costs is shown inside and outside the relevant range of activity. This is the case in all the graphical representations showing cost functions illustrated in Figures 14.1 to 14.6.

STOP AND THINK 3

Explain what is meant by the relevant range of activity.

COST BEHAVIOUR: ASSUMPTIONS AND LIMITATIONS

As we have already mentioned, accountants conventionally employ linear cost functions when providing the cost information that managers will use in making operating decisions. This practice is based on a number of assumptions and we have discussed most of them. For clarity, they are repeated here:

- All costs can be divided into either fixed or variable costs
- Fixed costs remain constant over different activity levels
- Variable costs vary with activity but are constant per unit of output
- Efficiency and productivity remain constant over all activity levels
- Cost behaviour can be explained sufficiently by one independent variable.

From our earlier analysis, it is obvious that these assumptions are simplistic and are approximations of reality. Therefore, the question arises: Are the cost functions used by accountants in providing information to management justified? The answer is often difficult to establish with confidence. Primarily, this is a cost–benefit question: are the net benefits greater when accountants' linear cost functions are used, compared with more sophisticated cost functions such as curvilinear functions? In the past, non-linear functions were more costly to establish. However, developments in information technology have tended to reduce the cost of constructing these more sophisticated models of cost behaviour.

FIGURE 14.8 A CURVILINEAR COST FUNCTION APPROXIMATES TO A LINEAR COST FUNCTION WITHIN THE RELEVANT RANGE OF ACTIVITY

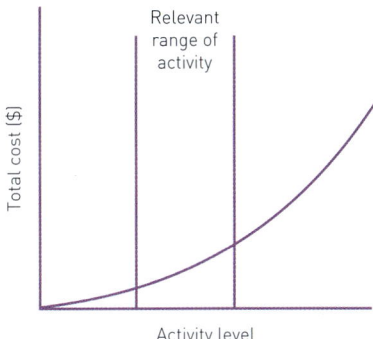

Figure 14.8 shows a curvilinear cost function. Look closely at the curve in the relevant range of activity. In fact, it is very close to a straight line. You might like to use a ruler to mark in such a line. Note that the curve on either side of the relevant range could be approximated with two different straight lines.

ESTIMATING COSTS

Managers need to understand the relationship between the costs incurred and the activities undertaken by the firm. This knowledge of how costs behave as activity changes enables management to plan the operations of the firm more effectively. Furthermore, an understanding of what the cost should have been at the achieved level of activity enables management to exercise control through comparing actual with planned costs.

FIGURE 14.9 OBSERVED COSTS

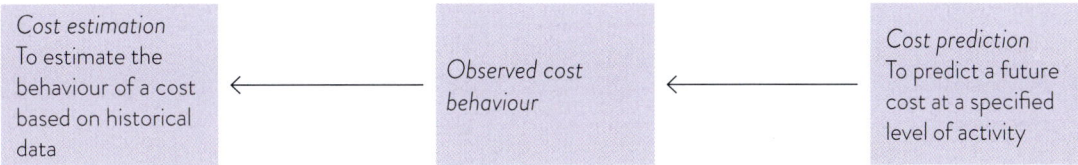

KEY CONCEPT

14.5

COST ESTIMATION

Cost estimation relates to methods used to measure past (historical) costs at varying activity levels. These costs are then employed as the basis for predictions of future costs that will be used in decision making.

There are many methods of cost estimation. Detailed knowledge of each of these methods is not necessary at this stage of your studies. However, it is important that you appreciate the basic principles and limitations of cost estimation.

Methods of cost estimation range from simple to mathematically complex. It is essential is to choose the estimation technique that generates the greatest benefit net of the costs of deriving the information. This, to a great extent, depends on the size of the organisation. The smaller the organisation, as the costs will be relatively high compared to the benefits generated from the use of mathematically complex methods, the less likely a sophisticated method will be employed.

Cost estimates are based on historical cost accounting data: the costs of past production, service and sales activity. One of the simplest methods is the account classification method, which involves simply observing how costs behaved in a previous period and classifying these costs as fixed or variable. For example, inspection of utility bills (e.g. telephone, power, gas and water) will readily separate a fixed supply charge and a variable cost per unit of consumption (e.g. per call or kilowatt). Where this method relies on subjective judgement, it will be limited in its ability to accurately predict the future behaviour of costs.

A variation on the account analysis approach is the High–Low method, where only two data points are used to estimate cost behaviour. A fundamental assumption of the High–Low method is that the two selected pairs of data points fall within a relevant range of activity where the fixed cost and the variable cost per unit of activity behave in a consistent manner. A simple illustration will be used to explain the High–Low method.

WORKED EXAMPLE

14.1

The following production activity and cost data has been collected for the past six months:

MONTH	ACTIVITY IN UNITS	TOTAL MONTHLY COST
July	81 000	$172 000
August	84 000	$178 000
September	83 000	$176 000
October	85 000	$180 000
November	79 000	$168 000
December	82 000	$174 000
Total	494 000	$1 048 000

Two data pairs of data points are selected: one high activity and its related total cost and one low activity and its related total cost. Inspection of the six months of data reveals a high activity level in October of 85 000 units (and $180 000 in total costs) and low activity of 79 000 units (and $168 000 in total costs) in November. The following table analyses the differences between each month's data points:

TOTAL COST AND ACTIVITY DATA POINTS	HIGH: OCTOBER	LOW: NOVEMBER	DIFFERENCE (Δ)
Total costs	$180 000	$168 000	$12 000
Monthly activity	85 000	79 000	6 000

Note that the additional 6000 units produced in October resulted in total costs to increase by $12 000. As the only cost that varies with changes in activity is variable cost, we can use a rearrangement of the formula:

$$y = a + bx$$

where y is the total cost to be predicted; x is the level of activity measured in units of output; a is the fixed cost; and b is the variable cost.

Since the change in total cost (Δy) of $12 000 and production activity (Δx) of 6000 units are known, we are solving for b:

$$b = \Delta y \div \Delta x$$

$$\$2.00 = \$12\,000 \div 6000$$

The value for b can now be substituted into the $y = a + bx$ formula using the high or low levels of production activity to estimate the total fixed cost per month (i.e. $a = y - bx$):

High production activity of 85 000 units

$$a = \$180\,000 - (\$2.00 \times 85\,000 \text{ units})$$

$$a = \$10\,000$$

Low production activity of 79 000 units

$$a = \$168\,000 - (\$2.00 \times 79\,000 \text{ units})$$

$$a = \$10\,000$$

If two other pairs of data points, say July and December, were selected, the estimated total fixed cost a and variable cost per unit produced b will be the same if the assumptions of the relevant range are not compromised. If costs are affected by inflation, then part of the change in total costs (i.e. y) is unrelated to changes in activity. As there is only potentially a six-month difference in when costs are incurred (i.e. 1 July versus 31 December), inflation is unlikely to have any significant effect on the estimated values for a and b. However, if the time series used for estimating the behaviour of costs encompasses several years of monthly observations, estimates of a and b maybe significantly impacted by inflation, changes in process technologies, learning and experience curve effects.

A more sophisticated method of cost estimation is regression analysis. The linear regression model involves making a number of observations from past cost behaviour and statistically analysing the data to produce a line of best fit.

Even more sophisticated regression analysis techniques such as multiple regression, which takes account of more than one independent variable, and curvilinear regression can be used.

The use of past data to determine future costs and the way in which they will behave is problematic. The following briefly summarises some of the problems.

- *Relevant range of activity.*
  As previously mentioned, little confidence can be placed in cost estimates beyond the range of activity from which the data has been derived. It is dangerous to extrapolate cost trends well beyond previously experienced levels of output.
- *The number of observations.*
  It is important in statistical analysis to incorporate many observations of output and cost levels in making accurate predictions of future cost behaviour. The greater the number of observations used, the higher the accuracy of the estimate and the better the prediction.
- *Changes in prices.*
  Past costs may not reflect current price levels and they will bias the estimates downwards. Therefore, there may be a need to adjust the dollar value of historical costs to current levels (e.g. use a relevant price index to inflate the lower values of historical costs).
- *Changes in technology.*
  Only observations taken from current production operations should be included in the analysis. Costs of work practices using plant and equipment that is no longer used, for example, will be irrelevant to future decisions.

- *Incorporation of past inefficiencies.*
  If operations were performed in an inefficient manner in the past and cost estimates are derived from this past period, the costs will incorporate inefficiencies.

Along with the development of more sophisticated techniques, there is increasing use of industrial engineering methods to predict future costs. Using time and motion studies, input and output analysis, and production control productivity surveys, it is possible to relatively accurately specify the relationship between labour time, machine time, materials consumption and physical output. These techniques look to future physical levels of resources and then convert them into monetary values instead of using past costs as being the basis for estimating future costs.

STOP AND THINK 4

Classify the following cost items as fixed, variable or a mix of fixed and variable.

a   power to operate a drill

b   an engine in a car

c   advertising

d   sales commissions

e   fuel for a forklift

f   depreciation on a boat

g   amalgam used by a dentist

h   forms used to file insurance claims

i   printing and postage for advertising circulars

COST VERSUS EXPENSE

In our examination of financial accounting, costs were classified as being either expired (i.e. an expense) or unexpired (i.e. an asset). Consistent with financial accounting, cost can be defined as the economic sacrifice of economic resources (e.g. cash, inventories and the use of plant and equipment) to acquire a future economic benefit in the form of products (or services). Costs may be classified in different ways so as to facilitate the decisions of managers.

As previously discussed, costs are calculated for a variety of purposes. One significant purpose is determining the cost of a product (or service) supplied. In the case of manufactured products, the costing system identifies the costs incurred in converting raw materials into finished goods. As noted at the beginning of the chapter, product costing is important for many reasons. Knowledge of product cost enables the firm to make decisions about the selling prices to set for each product, to identify areas where cost improvement must be made if the product is to be profitable when the market sets the selling price, and to value unsold inventory for external reporting purposes at the end of each accounting period. As discussed in chapters 16 and 17, product cost is also important in considering whether a product range should be broadened or contracted, or if a new product line should be introduced.

For a firm that manufactures a range of flavoured milk products, cost are those outlays giving rise to the creation of a future economic benefit (e.g. the raw milk to be used in manufacturing a flavoured milk product). As these costs provide future economic benefits, they are carried forward as part of work in progress inventories (where raw milk has yet to be fully processed) or finished goods inventory (where flavoured milk has been mixed and packaged and is stored in a coolroom awaiting sale). In a manufacturing firm, the outlays that are considered to be 'inventoriable' are materials, manufacturing labour and manufacturing overhead.

On the other hand, expenses are generally referred to as expired costs (i.e. the outlays provide no future economic benefit). Typical examples of outlays that immediately become expenses are those expenditures that relate to selling and distribution (e.g. advertising, sales office salaries and commissions, and freight outwards), general and administrative activities (e.g. administration salaries, depreciation on administration office equipment, rates and taxes on the administration office buildings) or financial (bad and doubtful debts and interest expense). These expenses are also known as period expenses as they only provide a readily measurable benefit to the period in which they were incurred.

A *cost object* can be a product, service, customer, process or any other object about which management requires cost information. For example, a cost object could be:

- *A product or service*
  The costs of producing a particular product or service (e.g. the cost of manufacturing flavoured milk).
- *A project or program*
  The costs of undertaking a particular project or program (e.g. for assessing the feasibility of a new production technology to use in the manufacture of flavoured milk).
- *An operation or an activity*
  The costs involved in performing a particular operation or activity (e.g. mixing machine set-up for a change in the flavour of the flavoured milk product).
- *A department or division*
  The costs of running a department or a division (e.g. the cost of the work performed in the flavoured milk batching department).

5 LEARNING OBJECTIVE

Explain the cost assignment process

Dwphotos/Shutterstock.com

14.6

KEY CONCEPT

COST OBJECT

A cost object can be a product, service, customer, process, activity or any object for which costs are to be measured and assigned.

An activity is a basic unit of work such as billing a customer, paying an invoice or approving a loan. An activity describes the process of doing something and so it always includes an action verb followed by a noun; for example, 'setting up machinery' where 'setting up' is the action verb and 'machinery' is the noun or name.

14.7

KEY CONCEPT

ACTIVITY

An activity is a cost object and involves an action verb and an object. It is the doing of something, such as invoicing a customer or setting up equipment ready for production.

6 LEARNING OBJECTIVE

Explain the difference between direct and indirect costs

Direct and indirect manufacturing costs

How does a business allocate costs to a cost object? Some costs can be easily allocated to a cost object; for example, the cost of an engine for a newly assembled vehicle. Other costs are far more difficult to allocate; for example, the electricity costs of the automotive plant where vehicles are assembled. Costs are either directly or indirectly related to a cost object.

- *Direct costs*
  A direct cost is a cost that can be readily and economically identified with a given cost objective (e.g. a product or production department). Examples of direct cost include the cost of raw milk used in manufacturing a flavoured milk product (where the cost object is the product) and the salary of the packaging department's supervisor (where the department is the cost object).

- *Indirect costs*
  An indirect cost is a cost that cannot be readily and economically identified with a given cost objective. The salary of a packaging department supervisor would be an indirect cost if a coffee-flavoured milk product is the cost object. Other examples of an indirect manufacturing cost include raw material incidental but not directly traceable to individual products (e.g. the crates used to distribute flavoured milk products to retail outlets).

The higher the proportion of costs that can be traced and attached to a cost object, the greater will be the accuracy of the cost assignment process. It is possible for the same cost to be direct for one cost object and indirect for another. For example, if the cost object is an automotive assembly facility, electricity would be a direct cost for the assembly plant. However, if the cost object is the vehicles assembled in the facility, the electricity would be an indirect cost. At times, the identification of a cost as direct is determined by the benefit obtained from having a higher level of precision in the direct versus indirect classification. For some costs (e.g. assembly materials such as rivets or glue), the cost of identifying the cost as direct outweighs any benefit that might be obtained. Thus, some costs that are direct in their relationship to the cost object might be treated as being indirect.

KEY CONCEPT

DIRECT AND INDIRECT COSTS

A direct cost is one that is easily traceable, and thus attributable, to a cost object. Indirect costs (also known as overhead costs) are those that cannot be easily and conveniently identified with a particular cost object.

Provided the management accounting system (MAS) is able to supply the necessary information, the allocation of direct costs to a cost object is relatively straightforward. The most common direct costs are direct labour and direct material costs in a manufacturing business. These costs are sometimes referred to as prime costs. In practice, there are a number of different types of costing systems that are contingent on the type of technology used in the production process and the type of product being produced. Traditionally, the systems are classified into two categories: job costing and process costing. At this stage of your studies, it is not necessary to examine the two main types of manufacturing systems in detail, but a brief description will be useful. Job-costing systems are used when the costs of each unit of production, or batch of units, can be identified at any time in the manufacturing cycle. For example, job costing is relevant for the construction industry (e.g. houses), vehicles and aircraft. In contrast, in a system of process costing, individual products cannot be identified until the manufacturing process is complete. A number of similar products are manufactured at the same time within the process. Costs are accumulated on a process or departmental basis and are then divided by the number of units produced to obtain an average unit cost. In such cases, product costs represent the average unit costs of production. Examples of areas where process costing applies include the brewing of beer, the refining of petroleum and the processing of chemical products.

Sometimes it is more convenient to classify a cost as indirect, even though it is possible to identify it directly with a product. Consider, for example, the labour costs of a supervisor who is responsible for a group of employees working on various products. An elaborate system would have to be set up to record the time spent supervising each employee and then to relate this time (and thus costs) to particular products. In this case it may be considered more cost-effective and convenient simply to classify supervision costs as indirect.

STOP AND THINK 5
Define direct and indirect costs.

Costing systems and the implication for costs

All firms require the provision of relevant management accounting information. Knowledge of resource use and the outputs generated by the firm is important to managers whether they work for manufacturing, merchandising or service firms in either the public or private sectors. However, given the nature of some organisational activities (predominantly in the service sector), the development and use of management accounting information is more easily understood in the context of manufacturing firms.

A manufacturing firm is one that acquires raw materials for further processing, which emerge in a form suitable for sale. The processing activity may involve a number of different production stages (e.g. for Australian Dairies – pasteurisation, mixing and packaging). Figure 14.10 provides a simplified version of the flavoured milk manufacturing cycle.

Costs are meaningless unless they are tied to a cost objective. Cost objectives are also themselves meaningless unless they relate to the specific decision-making needs of a manager. As noted, an important cost objective is the cost of a manufactured product. The costs of manufacturing a product are usually classified into three types:

* *Raw materials cost*
  The cost of raw materials transformed by the production process into finished products. Where raw material can be readily traced to the product being manufactured (e.g. the raw milk in a flavoured milk product), the cost is known as a direct materials cost. Where the raw material is 'immaterial' or cannot be readily traced to the product being produced (e.g. the lubricants for the flavoured milk

FIGURE 14.10 THE FLAVOURED MILK PRODUCTION CYCLE

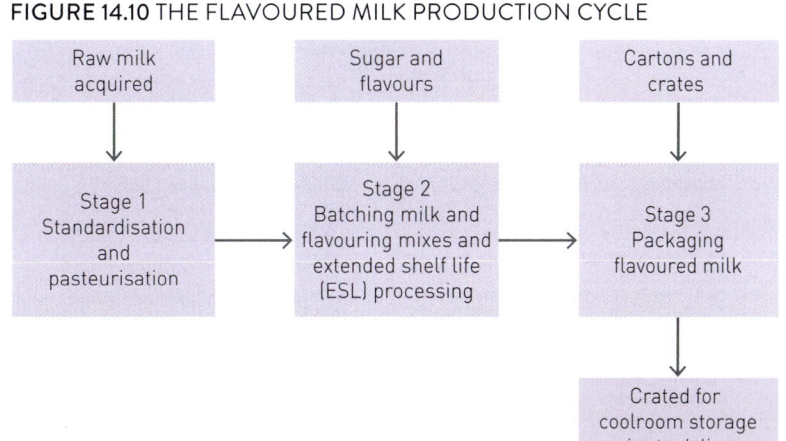

packaging equipment), the cost is referred to as an indirect materials cost. Indirect materials costs are typically classified as being part of indirect manufacturing (overhead) cost.

- *Labour cost*
  The cost of labour employed in transforming raw materials into a finished product. Where the labour cost can be readily traced to the product being manufactured (e.g. the standardisation and pasteurisation of raw milk), the cost is known as a direct labour cost. Where the labour is 'immaterial' or cannot be readily traced to the product being produced (e.g. the quality inspection of flavoured milk products), the cost is referred to as an indirect labour cost. Indirect labour costs are classified as being part of indirect manufacturing (overhead) cost.

- *Indirect manufacturing (overhead) cost*
  All other costs incidental to the manufacture of the finished product (e.g. depreciation, insurance and maintenance on plant and equipment, utility costs for power and water) and indirect materials and indirect labour.

Figure 14.11 illustrates the flow of costs from the introduction of raw materials to include the conversion costs (i.e. indirect manufacturing [overhead] cost and manufacturing labour) to the cost of finished products.

Figure 14.12 Flavoured milk product costs are costs that have been carried forward as part of inventory and eventually become an expense at the point they are sold (i.e. the asset *Finished Goods* inventory becomes the expense *Cost of Goods Sold*).

FIGURE 14.11 FLAVOURED MILK PRODUCT COSTS

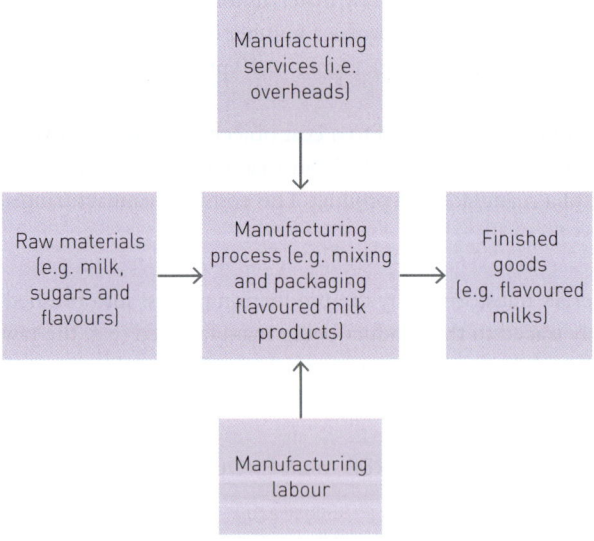

FIGURE 14.12 FLAVOURED MILK PRODUCT AND PERIOD COSTS

Costs to carry forward as inventory:	Outlays to expense in period concerned:
• Raw materials	• Cost of goods sold
• Work in progress*	• Selling and distribution
• Finished Goods*	• General and administrative
	• Financial
* Includes raw materials, labour and indirect manufacturing overhead.	

Product and period costs

Product costs include all the costs that are attached to a product; the costs that are included depend on whether the entity uses an absorption-costing or variable-costing approach. Products are not restricted to the output of manufacturing firms. While a vehicle is a product for an automotive assembler manufacturer, a variable-rate home loan is a financial product for a bank.

Any costs not categorised as product costs are normally classified as period costs. This means such costs are expensed to the statement of comprehensive income in the period they are incurred. Product costs are recognised as an expense in the statement of comprehensive income only when the product is sold.

Prior to sale, the cost of products is shown as an asset (either as work in progress or finished goods) in the balance sheet, thereby indicating that these items have some future benefit to the business. The principle adopted here is the concept of accruals. Period costs, in contrast, are seen as costs that relate to the current period. Therefore, they are viewed as costs that cannot justifiably be carried forward to future periods because they do not represent future benefits, or the future benefits are so uncertain as to defy reliable measurement. Thus, period costs are recognised in the statement of comprehensive income in the period they are incurred. As will be seen below, the distinction between product and period is important in the valuation of inventory and the determination of profit.

We examine the effect of this categorisation of costs in further detail later in this chapter, when we analyse the differences between the variable and absorption-costing methods.

Worked example 14.2 illustrates whether a consumption of economic resources is an 'inventoriable' cost or a period expense.

14.2 WORKED EXAMPLE

Australian Dairies is the largest producer and distributor of frozen and chilled dairy foods in Australasia. In the last year, the following outlays were made.

NO.	ITEM	FUTURE BENEFIT?	INVENTORIABLE COST	PERIOD EXPENSE
1	Sales display equipment depreciation	No		Yes
2	Raw milk used	Yes	Yes	
3	Manufacturing power and lighting	Yes	Yes	
4	Administration office salaries	No		Yes
5	Discount allowed on accounts receivable	No		Yes
6	Raw milk cartage inwards	Yes	Yes	
7	Administration equipment depreciation	No		Yes
8	Cost of flavoured milk sold	No		Yes
9	Packaging department wages	Yes	Yes	

NO.	ITEM	FUTURE BENEFIT?	INVENTORIABLE COST	PERIOD EXPENSE
10	Depreciation on ESL equipment	Yes	Yes	
11	Bad and doubtful debts	No		Yes
12	Administration staff superannuation	No		
13	Magazine and television advertising	No		Yes
14	Discount received on accounts payable	No		Yes
15	Budgeted insurance on packaging equipment	Yes	Future	

Having identified what items are 'inventoriable', the costs can then be classified as being raw materials, manufacturing labour, or manufacturing overhead:

- Raw material costs: raw milk cartage inwards and milk used
- Manufacturing labour: packaging department wages
- Manufacturing overhead: manufacturing power and lighting, depreciation on ESL equipment and insurance on packaging equipment.

STOP AND THINK 6
Explain product and period costs.

Past and future manufacturing costs

Costs may be also be classified on the basis of their time orientation, as past or future costs. While a more detailed examination of past and future costs will be deferred until Chapter 16, it is useful to briefly identify the time orientation of costs.

- *Past*

  A past cost is a cost that has already been incurred and cannot be changed. Examples of past costs include the cost of raw milk used in the manufacture of a coffee-flavoured milk product and the salary paid to the packaging department's supervisor.

- *Future*

  A future cost is one that has yet to be incurred and, subject to certain conditions being satisfied, may be changed as a result of decisions taken by managers. An example of a future cost is the budgeted salary to be paid to the packaging department's supervisor. (Note that it may not be possible to change the salary of the packaging department's supervisor in the short term as the firm's enterprise bargaining agreement may govern the conditions under which the supervisor is employed.)

In summary, a cost can be classified on a number by dimensions: behaviour (fixed or variable), type (materials, labour or overhead), identification with a cost object (direct or indirect) and orientation to time (past or future). Review Worked example 14.3 and identify the characteristics of each cost.

14.3

WORKED EXAMPLE

Australian Dairies incurs the following costs. Determine what cost classifications apply for each cost. Assume that the object is the cost of a flavoured milk product (e.g. iced coffee).

Note that the above classifications are indicative of the typical classifications of costs. A case may be made for an alternative classification of costs (e.g. the superannuation contributions paid by Australian Dairies for packaging employees could be classified as a direct labour cost).

NO.	ITEM	TYPE OF COST	BEHAVIOUR OF COST	TIME ORIENTATION	TRACEABILITY OF COST
1	Budgeted packaging department wages	Direct labour	Variable	Future	Direct
2	Straight-line depreciation on dairy laboratory PC	Overhead	Fixed	Past	Indirect
3	Dairy power and lighting used	Overhead	Variable	Past	Indirect
4	Raw milk used	Direct materials	Variable	Past	Direct
5	Estimated rates and taxes on dairy	Overhead	Fixed	Future	Indirect
6	Cartage inwards paid	Direct materials	Variable	Past	Direct
7	Dairy manager's salary paid	Overhead	Fixed	Past	Indirect
8	Depreciation on warehouse pallets using straight line	Overhead	Fixed	Past	Indirect
9	Packaging department wages	Direct labour	Variable	Past	Direct
10	Budgeted depreciation on ESL equipment using accelerated depreciation method	Overhead	Fixed	Future	Indirect
11	Raw milk purchases budget	Direct materials	Variable	Future	Direct
12	Dairy telephone bill paid	Overhead	Variable	Past	Indirect
13	Packaging employee superannuation contributions paid	Overhead	Variable	Past	Indirect
14	Discount received on bulk purchase of milk flavourings	Direct materials	Variable	Past	Direct
15	Budgeted insurance on packaging plant	Overhead	Fixed	Future	Indirect

At this point, it should be emphasised that costs are equally as important for the managers of service-providing organisations as they are for a manufacturing firm. For for-profit service-providing firms to survive in the long term, services must be priced at a level that recovers all costs and makes a profit. For example, an insurance broker will need to identify the costs of selling different types of policies, such as car insurance and life assurance, in order to determine the profitability of the different types of policies written. This information will influence the type and mix of policies that the broker may wish to offer to prospective clients. Similarly, a bank needs to determine the costs of its various financial products for it to know which product is the most profitable. A not-for-profit or public-sector organisation must not only know costs in order to manage them, but also to maximise the value realised from the services provided. Service costing describes the form of MAS used by service providers to measure and report costs for a cost object (e.g. cost per patient treatment provided by a hospital's outpatient clinic).

Not surprisingly, a product-costing system is a key element of a manufacturing firm's MAS. For the purposes of our analysis in this chapter, we will focus on manufacturing firms.

COSTING SYSTEMS AND ACCOUNTING FOR OVERHEAD

As will be discussed below, different types of costing systems are developed to meet the particular decision-making needs of managers. However, a common problem requiring resolution across all types of costing systems is the accounting for indirect costs. Before addressing the issue of accounting for overhead in more detail, three different approaches for costing products can be used: actual, normal and standard costing.

- *Actual cost*
  Actual costs incurred for materials, labour and overhead are recorded. As many overhead costs are paid as a single lump sum (e.g. insurance premiums and rates and taxes), they are not incurred uniformly throughout the financial year. Thus, where a manufacturing firm breaks a year into shorter control periods (e.g. 13 by 4 weeks long), the products manufactured in different control periods will absorb differing amounts of manufacturing overhead cost. As some periods will be burdened with a disproportionate share of overhead costs, the use of actual costing will result in potentially significant fluctuations in the cost of a product depending on when the product was manufactured.
- *Normal cost*
  Actual costs for materials and labour are used, but manufacturing overheads are applied based on predetermined manufacturing overhead cost rates. The use of predetermined overhead rates usually creates over- or under-applied manufacturing overhead costs (an overhead cost variance), which must be disposed of at year's end. The advantage of this approach is that manufacturing overheads are spread uniformly over all units produced during a year, as opposed to being charged against the units manufactured when the manufacturing overhead costs were incurred. Normal costing prevents large fluctuations in unit product costs due to the timing of overhead outlays, as would occur under an actual cost system.
- *Standard cost*
  Standard quantities and prices are used to calculate product cost. The differences between actual and standard costs are recorded as variances to be disposed of at period end. As the use of standard costing is beyond the scope of this text, it will not be addressed any further.

A firm must elect to develop product costs using one of these three approaches.

KEY CONCEPT

14.9

NORMAL COSTING

Using normal costing, the cost of a cost object is determined using the actual costs for direct costs and a predetermined rate for the allocation of overhead costs.

COSTING METHODS: ABSORPTION AND VARIABLE COSTING

For a manufacturing firm, the costs incurred in producing and selling a product consist of production costs and other costs such as administration, selling and distribution expenses. The production costs are either direct or indirect costs. The costs to be included in a cost object for internal management accounting purposes will depend on the wishes of management. The two most common cost methods are described as absorption costing (sometimes called full costing) and variable costing (sometimes erroneously called direct costing). Absorption costing allocates all the direct and indirect costs of production to a product while variable costing only allocates the variable costs of production to a product.

For external reporting purposes, absorption costing must be used to comply with accounting standards, but for internal purposes either method can be used.

Absorption (full) costing

The costs to be included under the absorption costing method might include all costs or just some, such as production costs. The scope and style of absorption costing adopted depend upon the purpose for which products are costed and the preferences of management. As previously emphasised, the accounting information reported for management purposes is not regulated by external requirements such as the *Corporations Act* or accounting standards. Management is free to adopt definitions and use accounting data at its discretion in meeting managers' own decision-making needs.

For the purposes of our analysis, we will adopt a definition of absorption costing that includes only production costs. This is the definition of absorption costing conventionally used for the purpose of valuing finished inventories and work in progress, as was discussed in Chapter 8. In the context of inventory valuation, it is argued that it is only appropriate to include those costs that are incurred prior to the sale of the inventory. Normally, these costs will only consist of those related to production.

KEY CONCEPT 14.10

ABSORPTION COSTING

Absorption costing allocates the direct and indirect costs of production to the cost object.

KEY CONCEPT 14.11

VARIABLE COSTING

Variable costing allocates only the variable costs of production to the cost object. A cost is variable if it changes in response to changes in the level of activities.

STOP AND THINK 7

Explain the absorption product costing model.

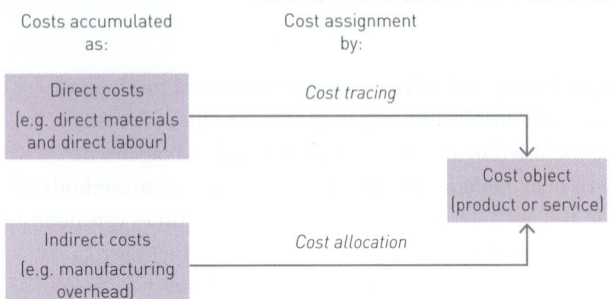

FIGURE 14.13 COST ALLOCATION AND COST TRACING

As noted, the cost of a product comprises three cost elements: direct materials, direct labour and manufacturing overhead costs. In the case of direct materials and direct labour, the costs are traced to the product. However, as shown in Exhibit 14.13, in the case of manufacturing overhead costs, they must be allocated to the product.

9 **LEARNING OBJECTIVE**

Identify the stages that are involved in determining the allocation of overheads to products

Absorbing overheads

We have already mentioned that a system has to be devised to link costs to individual products. This process is relatively straightforward for direct costs since they can be reasonably identified with a specific product. For example, when materials are obtained from inventory, their cost is recorded against the product and accounted for as a cost of the product. The complexity arises when we have to share overhead costs with products. The objective is to share them out equitably. This is important for profit-making firms as they need to be able to price each product (or service) to ensure the price is competitive and generates an adequate profit. Therefore, the method adopted should take into account the amount of indirect services and related overhead costs used to support the manufacture of products. The term used for the process of sharing out overhead costs to products is 'absorption of overheads'.

The choice of the allocation base to use in allocating indirect manufacturing costs is constrained by the cost-benefit test. The collection of financial and activity data and the education of managers about the allocation method employed (and the associated behavioural consequences) are costly, and some allocation bases are more expensive to use than others. Thus, each cost allocation method must be evaluated in terms of the net benefit provided. For example, while the cause-and-effect basis of allocating indirect manufacturing costs may provide the most accurate charging of those indirect manufacturing costs, management may choose to use a less complex method as the cause-and-effect basis fails the cost-benefit test.

The two main systems that can be used to allocate overhead costs are the traditional volume-based and activity-based costing (ABC) systems. We will initially examine the absorption of overheads using the traditional volume-based costing system before concluding with ABC.

Traditional volume-based costing systems

A traditional volume-based costing (TVBC) system classifies all costs as either variable or fixed in relation to changes in the volume or units produced. Variable costs are those that vary with usage or activity, while fixed costs do not. Under a TVBC system, the main drivers used to assign the overhead costs to products are volume-based, such as direct labour hours or machine hours. We illustrate the process of allocating overhead costs in a TVBC system. Much of the process described here also applies to ABC systems.

Production overhead costs are incurred by cost centres that support the production activity. A goods inwards department, whose function it is to ensure that goods and materials received from suppliers are of the standard and quantity ordered, is a typical example of a service cost centre in a manufacturing firm. The overhead costs of both the production and service cost centres must be absorbed into the product to establish the full cost of products.

At this stage it is appropriate to summarise the stages in the absorption of overheads. Figure 14.14 shows the three stages in this process.

FIGURE 14.14 STAGES IN THE ABSORPTION OF OVERHEADS

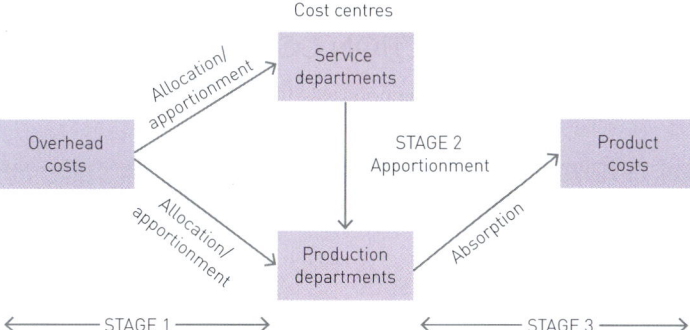

STAGE 1

The first stage in the absorption of overhead costs is to identify and collect overhead costs associated with both production and service cost centres. Some costs will be relatively easy to allocate to particular cost centres. The word 'allocated', in the context of product costing, means that the cost can be directly traced to a cost centre. For example, a product design office that provides a service to a number of different production cost centres would be classified as a service cost centre. The salaries of design engineers can be identified with the centre by recording the salary payment from the payroll against the cost centre. In contrast, the cost of heating and lighting consumed by the product design office may not be so easy to establish. Unless each area of a production facility is separately metered, the cost of heating and lighting would be billed to the whole facility, of which the product design office is only one of many occupying cost centres. In such cases, because the cost is difficult, if not impossible, to accurately relate to any one cost centre, a method of apportioning these costs on a fair and equitable basis must be used.

The term 'apportioning' describes the sharing out of overhead costs that cannot be directly traced to a cost centre. For a TVBC system, a reasonable method of apportioning heat and lighting costs would relate the benefit (heating and lighting) enjoyed by the product design office on the basis of the area occupied by the office. For example, if the total cost of heating and lighting a 30 000m² square metre manufacturing facility is $150 000 and the area used by the drawing office is measured as 500m², the cost apportioned to the product design office would be

$$\$150\,000 \times (30\,000m^2 \div 500m^2) = \$2500$$

STAGE 2

When all the overhead costs – allocated and apportioned – have been established for each service cost centre, it is then necessary to charge these costs to the production cost centres that have drawn upon those services. Once again, some method of apportionment is required. The reason for this is that service cost centres usually service multiple production cost centres and the costs of the service are unlikely to be readily identified with any individual centre. Using the example of the product design office, it is likely that the services supplied by this office spread over a number of production cost centres and it would not be possible to accurately identify the cost of this service with any one production department. In these circumstances, a method of apportionment has to be adopted that fairly charges the service cost to the production cost centres. Before moving to stage 3, Worked example 14.4 will be used to illustrate the allocation and apportionment of costs to production cost centres.

WORKED EXAMPLE

CHARGING COSTS TO PRODUCTION COST CENTRES

Australian Dairies has four cost centres: Production Cost Centres A and B and Service Cost Centres X and Y.

ITEM	BASIS	TOTAL AMOUNT	PRODUCTION COST CENTRES		SERVICE COST CENTRES	
			A	B	X	Y
		$000	$000	$000	$000	$000
Indirect materials	Allocated	200	80	40	50	30
Indirect labour	Allocated	300	140	60	40	60
Electricity	Machine hours	220	100	120	–	–
Rent and rates	Area	100	20	50	20	10
Insurance	Book value	80	30	20	30	–
Total overheads		900	370	290	140	100
Service X to production	Number of employees		50	90	(140)	
Service Y to production	Direct labour hours		80	20		(100)
Total overheads		900	500	400	–	–
Data used for apportioning overheads						
Item	*Quantity*					
Machine hours	1 100 000		500 000	600 000	–	–
Area	30 000m2		6000	15 000	6000	3000
Book value of non-current assets	$960 000		$360	$240	$360	–
No. of employees	7000		2500	4500		
Direct labour hours	2 000 000		700 000	1 300 000	–	–

As shown above, Worked example 14.4 demonstrates the allocation and apportionment of overhead costs to production cost centres. Various overhead costs items are initially identified and shown under total amount. The costs are then allocated or apportioned to production and service cost centres. Because indirect labour and materials can be directly identified with each cost centre, these costs are allocated to them. Of the total amount of $200 000 for the indirect materials consumed, $80 000 has been directly traced to Production Cost Centre A. In contrast, the costs related to power, rent and rates and insurance cannot be directly traced to any cost centre. Therefore, they are apportioned to the centres using a basis that equitably reflects the benefits that each centre has enjoyed. For example, in the case of the power costs, the number of machine hours consumed by each cost centre would be an equitable basis for apportionment. The information relating to the use of machine hours shows that only the two production cost centres made use of the machinery. Of the total of 1 100 000 machine hours, 500 000 were consumed by Production Cost Centre A and 600 000 hours by Cost Centre B. The cost of electricity for each of these centres is then calculated with reference to the consumption by the two departments as follows:

PRODUCTION COST CENTRE	
Cost Centre A 500 000 hours ÷ 1 100 000 hours × $220 000 =	$100 000
Cost Centre B 600 000 hours ÷ 1 100 000 hours × $220 000 =	$120 000
Total cost of electricity	$220 000

Therefore, the apportioned charge to Production Cost Centre A is $100 000 and that to Cost Centre B is $120 000. Similar calculations, using different assumptions, are made to establish the apportioned charge to the cost centres for rent and rates, and insurance.

After allocating and apportioning overheads to the production and service cost centres, the next stage is to apportion service centre costs to production cost centres. The basis of apportionment chosen in the case of Service Cost Centre X is the number of employees in each production cost centre. The number of direct labour hours worked by the employees in the production cost centres is the basis of apportionment used for Service Cost Centre Y. As previously mentioned, the basis of apportionment should reflect the benefits enjoyed by the consuming production cost centres. For example, it might be that Service Cost Centre X is the works canteen. If so, the number of employees in each production cost centre might be a reasonable basis for calculating the amount of use made of this facility by production cost centre employees. The calculation of the apportioned charge to production cost centres is similar to the calculation for apportioning electricity costs. Thus, in the case of Service Cost Centre X, the calculation will be as follows:

PRODUCTION COST CENTRE	
Cost Centre A (2500 ÷ 7000) × $140 000 =	$50 000
Cost Centre B (4500 ÷ 7000) × $140 000 =	$90 000
Total cost of service cost centre X	$140 000

It can be seen that the whole of the costs of service centre X are now apportioned to the two production cost centres. Similar calculations will be made to apportion the cost of Service Cost Centre Y to the two production cost centres. Finally, the overhead costs are aggregated for each of the two production cost centres and are shown as the final Total overheads.

STAGE 3

As has been mentioned, the production cost centres are where the manufacturing activity takes place. Units of products physically pass through these cost centres in the course of the manufacturing cycle. As the products pass through the centre, a proportion of the overhead cost is charged to the product (or absorbed into the product). The objective here is to charge overheads to units of production on some equitable basis. Normally, an absorption rate is used for this purpose. The absorption rate is determined by the following formula:

$$\frac{\text{Total overheads of a production cost centre}}{\text{Level of activity}}$$

We discussed how the numerator in this formula is determined in Stage 2, above. The denominator, the activity level, is chosen with reference to the types of products passing through each production cost centre and the main activities of the centre. For example, if the products passing through a production cost centre are homogeneous – that is, similar in construction – the appropriate activity to be chosen is likely to be the number of units processed in the production centre. The activity in these circumstances is the units of production and since the benefits enjoyed by each unit from the expenditure of overheads should be equal or very similar, units should be an equitable basis for absorbing overheads. In Worked example 14.4, if it was estimated that 100 000 units were to be processed during the year by Production Cost Centre A, and assuming the products were homogeneous, the absorption rate would be $500 000 ÷ 100 000$ units $= \$5.00$ per unit. This rate would then be applied to each unit of production worked on in the cost centre and would represent a reasonable and appropriate share of the overhead cost to be allocated to each product.

In contrast, if the products are not homogeneous, it is necessary to choose an activity measure that corresponds more closely with the overhead expenditure of each production cost centre. For example, if the overhead expenditure incurred in a production cost centre mainly supports the direct labour function, the measure chosen should be based on this activity. In these circumstances, the number of direct hours would be a suitable measure.

In practice, in a traditional volume-based cost management system, the most common activity measures used to absorb overheads into product costs are:

- direct labour hours (DLH)
- direct labour costs ($DL)
- machine hours (MH)
- cost of direct materials ($DM).

The following shows the calculation of the absorption rate with reference to the data given in Worked example 14.4 for Production Cost Centre A, assuming that the number of machine hours is the appropriate activity measure.

$$\frac{\text{Total overheads of cost centre A}}{\text{Level of activity}} = \frac{\$500\ 000}{500\ 000\ \text{MH}}$$

Therefore, the absorption rate is $1 per machine hour. This rate is applied to each product that passes through Cost Centre A. For example, if a 10-unit batch of a product that passes through Cost Centre A uses 40 MH in the manufacturing time, the overhead allocated to the 10-unit product batch will be:

$$40\ \text{MH} \times \$1\ \text{per MH} = \$40$$

10 LEARNING OBJECTIVE

Explain what is meant by predetermined overhead absorption rates

Predetermined overhead absorption rates

In practice, overhead absorption rates are normally determined annually, before the actual cost is incurred. Thus, the two elements of the above formula are estimates. That is, the total overheads of each production cost centre and the level of activity chosen are based on estimates rather than actual numbers.

There are two main reasons why normal costing is used in preference to actual costing. First, some overhead costs are not known until some time after they have been incurred. For example, electricity costs are normally billed to consumers on a bimonthly basis. Therefore, a manufacturing firm would have to wait two months before it could identify what this overhead cost, and only then could it charge the cost to products that may have already been manufactured and sold. Clearly, such a delay in determining costs would mean that management would receive out-of-date information. Second, some overhead costs, such as heating costs, are seasonal. Seasonal variations can distort the costing of products. For example, if a product is manufactured in summer, the cost of heating absorbed into the product cost is likely to be zero. On the other hand, if the product was manufactured in winter, the cost would include a charge for heating. Therefore, the cost of a product can depend upon when it was produced. It can be argued that such circumstances distort the costing of products and a firm would have to set up complex costing systems to reflect seasonal variations.

The use of estimates in determining the overhead absorption rate creates problems. Because of forecast errors in the estimates used to calculate the predetermined overhead allocation rate, often the actual overhead cost incurred during a period will not equal the overheads that have been absorbed into product costs. The amount of overheads absorbed during a period will be the same as the cost actually incurred only if the actual overhead cost of the production cost centre is equal to the estimated cost (the numerator in the formula) and the actual level of activity is equal to the estimated activity level (the denominator in the formula). Normally, any difference between the total overheads absorbed and the actual overheads incurred during a period is directly charged to the statement of comprehensive income for that period. These differences in costs are not allocated or apportioned to products, but are classified as a period cost. It is generally seen as impractical and too costly to identify the differences for individual products, but large differences should be investigated.

STOP AND THINK 8

Explain why it is necessary to use estimates in determining an absorption rate for overheads.

Worked example 14.5 illustrates the process of absorbing overheads into units of production where the actual overhead cost is different from the original estimates on which the absorption rate was based.

WORKED EXAMPLE

ABSORBING DIFFERENCES IN OVERHEAD COSTS

The following are estimates relating to the manufacture of a number of similar products for the forthcoming year:

Estimated units to be produced during the year	100 000
Estimated overhead cost during the year	$150 000

Therefore, the overhead absorption rate is calculated thus:

$$\frac{\$150\,000}{100\,000 \text{ units}} = \$1.50 \text{ per unit}$$

If the actual number of units produced during the year was 110 000, the charge to products passing through the cost centre is 110 000 units × $1.50 (the absorption rate) = $165 000.

However, the total overhead cost actually incurred during the year was $176 000. So, the difference between actual total overhead cost and what was absorbed during the year is $176 000 − $165 000 = $11 000. This $11 000 is charged to the statement of comprehensive income as an **under-recovery of overhead** during the year; it is classified as a period cost because it is not identified with any of the units of production manufactured during the year.

11 LEARNING OBJECTIVE

Explain the difference between traditional volume-based and activity-based costing methods

12 LEARNING OBJECTIVE

Explain the terms activity, cost pool and cost driver as used in activity-based costing

Activity-based costing systems

Activity-based costing seeks to capture the change in manufacturing technology by apportioning overhead costs to products on a more realistic basis that takes into account the type of activity and the number of transactions driving the cost. For cost-management purposes, ABC, with its focus on managing activities, can lead to sustainable cost reductions being achieved.

The application of ABC involves the following two stages.

Stage 1: Identify significant activities and assign overhead costs to each activity. This is called an **activity cost** pool.

Stage 2: Identify **cost drivers** and allocate the cost from each activity pool to each cost object.

THE IDENTIFICATION AND CLASSIFICATION OF ACTIVITIES AND COST DRIVERS

14.12

KEY CONCEPT

ACTIVITY COST POOL

Under the ABC system, the costs of an activity are accumulated in an activity cost pool.

Costs are grouped according to what drives them or causes them to increase. These cost drivers are then used as the bases upon which overhead costs are absorbed into the cost object.

Key concept 14.7 defines an activity as one that involves an action verb and an object. It is the doing of something, such as invoicing a customer or setting up equipment ready for production.

In many organisational settings where multiple products or services are manufactured or supplied, numerous activities are carried out and it would be impractical or economically infeasible for a cost rate to be struck for each individual activity that is undertaken. Grouping activities into related categories decreases the number of **cost pools** and rates to be used, simplifies the task of computing product costs and reduces ABC system complexity. For activities to be grouped together, they should:
- have a common objective or purpose (e.g. activities relate to the same process)
- be performed at the same or similar activity level (e.g. batch)
- use the same **activity driver** for assigning costs to individual products, service lines or other cost objects with minimal variation in costs allocated.

Having identified the most cost-effective grouping of activities, they can then be classified according to the level at which they occur. A four-level **activity hierarchy** is typically identified: (i) unit, (ii) batch, (iii) product (or customer), and (iv) facility.

Unit-level activities are those activities that are performed for every unit of output (e.g. materials used, machine or assembly hours). As production activity increases, so too do unit-level activities (e.g. machine hours). Thus, differences in per-unit product costs are driven by the differences in the activity requirements per unit of product manufactured (e.g. each unit of Product X requires two machine hours, Product Y requires three machine hours and Product Z requires five machine hours). Not surprisingly, unit-level **activity cost analysis** achieves the same assignment of costs as the TVBC product-costing system does.

Batch-level activities are activities performed for a batch (say 50 units) of a product. Examples of batch-level activities include production line set-ups, moving materials or parts around the factory, order taking and processing, production scheduling, inspecting, and procurement where a just-in-time inventory system is used. Thus, every time a batch is processed, batch-level activities will be triggered. As batch-level costs are independent of the number of units produced, differences in batch-level costs per unit are driven by the differences in the size of the batch manufactured (e.g. Product X is produced in batches of 20 units, Product Y is produced in batches of 30 units and Product Z is produced in batches of 50). Differences in production batch sizes typically occur in firms where a standard high-volume product is made in long and regularly repeated production runs and other products are manufactured to customer specification in small and sometimes one-off production runs.

Product-level activities are those activities that are performed for the benefit of a product line and not for the individual unit or batch produced. They are performed less routinely than unit- or batch-level activities and include engineering design, engineering changes which maintain or update the product specifications, special testing and product certification if the product is regulated or licensed (e.g. pharmaceuticals or telephones), rework, procurement if raw materials are placed into storage, market research and marketing. While product-level costs can be traced to an individual product line, they are independent of the number of units or batches produced. Thus, differences in product-level activities typically occur when products have differing attributes or characteristics to others. As Product X is a well-established product sold in a mature market, it should have fewer product-level activities being performed than a new Product P, which is being sold in a highly competitive market and the exact formulation of the product is still being refined through in-market product testing.

Facility-level activities are those activities that sustain the whole production plant rather than benefit any particular product unit, batch or line. Facility-level activities include the cost of manufacturing facility space and general utility costs (e.g. heating, lighting and cooling). As these costs sustain the whole manufacturing facility and are independent of the number of units, batches or products manufactured, it has been argued that they should never be allocated to individual products but be written off as a period expense. On the other hand, as all costs must eventually be covered and despite the arbitrariness of the allocation methodology employed, many firms still choose to allocate facility-level costs to products using either unit, batch or product-level activities.

STOP AND THINK 9

Select an organisation that you are familiar with (e.g. a university). Identify an example of a support activity undertaken in that organisation and explain the type of costs incurred in carrying out that activity and the driver of the costs incurred.

In an ABC system, costs are assigned to cost objects using both unit- and non-unit-based activity drivers. For example, costs could be allocated to inspecting products on the basis of the number of units (unit-based) or number of inspections (activity-based). We now will examine Worked example 14.6, where a simple application of ABC is presented and the resultant product costs are compared to the calculation obtained from using TVBC.

WORKED EXAMPLE

ONYX LTD – ABC VERSUS TBC

Onyx Ltd manufactures two products, X and Y. The manufacturing process for the two products is very similar. Information about the product data for these two products for last year is provided below:

DETAILS	X	Y
Units produced	5000	7000
Direct labour hours (DLH) per unit	1 DLH	2 DLH

DETAILS	X	Y
Labour cost per DLH	$20	$20
Direct material cost per unit	$40	$20
Number of set-ups	10 set-ups	40 set-ups
Number of orders	15 orders	60 orders
Machine hours (MH) per unit manufactured	3 MH	1 MH

An examination of manufacturing overhead costs reveals the following breakdown of costs by type:

MANUFACTURING OVERHEAD COSTS:	$
Cost of setting up	19 900
Cost of handling orders	45 000
Costs relating to machine activity	220 000
Total overhead costs	284 900

Onyx wishes to determine the cost per unit in respect of manufacturing overhead costs, using:

1. a TVBC accounting system allocating manufacturing overhead costs on the basis of MH to products X and Y

2. an ABC accounting system using suitable cost drivers to trace manufacturing overheads to products X and Y.

1 TRADITIONAL VOLUME-BASED COSTING SYSTEM

Denominator activity: Machine hours

In the past, many TVBC systems have used DLH as the basis, or denominator activity, for allocating manufacturing overheads. However, as $220 000 of the overhead costs incurred by Onyx Ltd relate to machine activity, none if any appears to be in support of direct labour activity. That is, a significant proportion of manufacturing overhead costs are not driven by direct labour activity. Using DLH as the basis for apportioning overhead costs in these circumstances would distort the costs apportioned to individual products. This is because more DLH are worked on Y than on X.

Thus, the first step is to calculate the total number of MH:

PRODUCT	TOTAL MH
X (5 000 units × 3 hours)	15 000
Y (7 000 units × 1 hour)	7000
Total	22 000

The second step is to calculate an overhead cost per MH.

As total overhead costs are $284 900 and total denominator activity is 22 000 MH, the overhead absorption rate is:

$$= \$284\,900 \div 22\,000 \text{ MH}$$

$$= \$12.95 \text{ per MH}$$

The third step is to calculate the manufacturing overhead absorbed into each unit of products X and Y:

X: 3 hours × $12.95 = $38.85

Y: 1 hour × $12.95 = $12.95

Finally, we are now able to determine the total cost per unit for products X and Y using the TVBC system.

COST ELEMENT	X	Y
Prime costs		
Direct materials	$40.00	$20.00
Direct labour	$20.00	$40.00
Total prime costs	$60.00	$60.00
Manufacturing overheads	$38.85	$12.95
Total unit cost	$98.85	$72.95

2 ACTIVITY-BASED COSTING

The appropriate cost drivers in this example are those that relate to the way in which manufacturing overhead costs are incurred. Manufacturing overhead costs are those relating to machine activity, setting up and handling orders. The main driver of set-up costs is the number of set-ups and this is a non-unit activity measure. 'To set-up machinery' is an activity and involves doing something.

The first step is to identify the cost pools, the cost drivers and the cost pool rates. Then manufacturing overhead costs, based on the cost drivers, will be absorbed into the two products.

MANUFACTURING OVERHEAD COST POOLS	POOL COSTS AND COST DRIVER CALCULATIONS	COST POOL RATE
Machining costs	$220 000 ÷ 22 000 hours	$10 per machine hour
Set-up driven costs	$19 900 ÷ 50 set-ups	$398 per set-up
Order driven costs	$45 000 ÷ 75 orders	$600 per order

We can now determine the product costs for products X and Y as shown below:

MANUFACTURING OVER-HEAD COST POOLS	POOL RATE	PRODUCT X		PRODUCT Y	
		ACTIVITY	TOTAL	ACTIVITY	TOTAL
Machine costs	$10 per MH	15 000	$150 000	7000	$70 000
Set-up costs	$398 per set-up	10	$3 980	40	$15 920
Order costs	$600 per order	15	$9 000	60	$36 000
Total overheads			$162 980		$121 920
Number of units produced			5000		7000
Total manufacturing overheads			$32.60		$17.42
Direct material			$40.00		$20.00
Direct labour			$20.00		$40.00
Total unit cost			$92.60		$77.42

As the prime costs of direct materials and labour are unaffected by the choice of product costing system, the following table only compares the manufacturing overhead cost per unit calculated using the TVBC accounting system with MH and ABC:

PRODUCT COSTING SYSTEM	PRODUCT X	PRODUCT Y
Traditional volume-based	$38.85	$12.95
ABC	$32.60	$17.42
Difference	$6.25	($4.47)

COMMENTARY

The following conclusions can be drawn regarding the effect of the different product costing systems upon the determination of overhead cost per unit of products X and Y for Onyx Ltd:

- TVBC (using machine-hour basis). Although this basis for absorbing overheads clearly takes account of the main cost driver, machine-related costs, it ignores other cost drivers associated with manufacturing overheads, namely handling and set-up costs.

- ABC. A more realistic basis for absorbing costs because it takes into account all three significant overhead cost drivers. Thus, ABC suggests that the TVBC system over-costs product X by $6.25 per unit and under-costs product Y by $4.47 per unit.

The difference in costs under traditional volume-based and activity-based systems could have an impact on the selling prices of products X and Y or alternatively influence the mix of products that are to be manufactured based on an incorrect determination of the most 'profitable' product. For example, if Onyx's pricing policy was cost plus 25 per cent then the selling prices for products X and Y under the two systems would be:

DETAILS	PRODUCT X			PRODUCT Y		
Costing system	TVBC	ABC	Difference	TVBC	ABC	Difference
Total cost per unit	$98.85	$92.60	($6.25)	$72.95	$77.42	($4.47)
Mark-up on cost per unit @ 25%	$24.71	$23.15	($1.56)	$18.24	$19.36	($1.12)
Selling price per unit	$123.56	$115.75	($7.81)	$91.19	$96.78	($5.59)

As a result, Onyx would be over pricing product X and under pricing product Y when the ABC prices are compared to the traditional volume-based system prices. Companies that have moved to ABC have found that, with the better knowledge about costs it provides, they are able to determine more appropriate selling prices for their products.

STOP AND THINK 10

Explain what problems might occur if a firm has a significant error in how overheads are allocated to cost objects.

In summary, as illustrated by Worked example 14.6, the following steps are taken when employing an ABC product costing system:

Step 1: Identify major activities. For example, machining, production runs and orders.

Step 2: Collect the overhead costs in a cost pool for each major activity.

Step 3: Determine the cost drivers for each activity. For example, in Worked example 14.6, the economically plausible cost drivers were used as follows:

- machining – cost per machine hour
- production runs – cost per set-up
- number of orders – cost per order.

Step 4: Trace the cost of the activities to the cost object using the cost drivers as a measure of the demand on the services provided by each cost pool (e.g. for the set-up cost pool, the number of set-ups or productions runs).

STOP AND THINK 11

Explain the term 'activity-based costing'.

14.1

CASE STUDY

ACTIVITY-BASED FUNDING FOR AUSTRALIAN HOSPITALS

As identified in the introduction to this chapter, the delivery of healthcare services has become a significant financial burden for many governments at both national and state levels. For example, over the past decade, the annual spend by Australian state governments on health services has increased by approximately 9 per cent while growth in state revenues has been at a more sedate 6 per cent per annum. It has been forecast that, at the current level of spending on health services, by 2045-46 most state governments would find their entire budgets consumed by health costs. Not surprisingly, government has sought to develop initiatives that deliver quality health outcomes but at a lower cost.

While not all forms of health care are identical and actual treatments and outcomes are influenced by many factors, including physician preferences and patient comorbidities, there is sufficient commonality as to suggest that a standard or benchmark cost could be established for many procedures. For example, procedures such as hip and knee replacements, appendectomies and cholecystectomies have become fairly routinised operations with well-established post-operative health management protocols in place. Thus, earlier models for funding health care sought to identify a standard cost for a bundle of related health services identified as a diagnosis related group (DRG).

Since the late 1980s federal and state governments have endeavoured to shift funding for healthcare providers, such as public hospitals, from a block funding model to one based on the type of health service provided and the mix and number of patients treated (a form of activity-based funding or ABF). Given that funding for a specified procedure (e.g. a hip replacement) would be at a set price, a hospital would have strong financial incentives for ensuring that patients were discharged as promptly as possible (i.e. as soon as they were well enough to leave).

Despite the long history of using DRGs and ABF in Australia, there was no coordinated framework for determining how much a particular procedure should be funded for. This meant that different prices were paid to similar types of hospitals for exactly the same medical procedure. Thus, in August 2011 the Council of Australian Governments (COAG) agreed to establish ABF as the primary funding methodology for Australian public hospitals. While primarily being used as a mechanism for bringing jurisdictional and regional consistency and transparency to the funding of hospital-provided health services, ABF is also intended to drive continuous improvement within the healthcare sector and deliver superior value for money.

13 LEARNING OBJECTIVE

Explain how time-driven activity-based costing (TDABC) provides a simpler and less costly activity-based method of allocating indirect costs

AN ALTERNATIVE TO ABC, THE TIME-DRIVEN ABC MODEL

Given the significant cost associated with initially introducing and then operating an ABC system, it should not be surprising that many small firms will find that these costs outweigh the benefits. Thus, only those sufficiently large firms and/or those with operational characteristics where the traditional costing model yields inaccurate product cost data (e.g. a higher proportion of overhead to be allocated and significant diversity in product range and production volumes) might find the benefits of ABC will exceed the costs of adoption. While not directly testing this proposition, survey evidence collected over the last 20 years suggests that of all respondents, the adoption rate for ABC is no more than 25 per cent. However, when looking just at large multi-product manufacturing firms, ABC adoption rates are typically more than half of respondents.

In spite of the benefits that it purportedly brings, the global adoption of ABC has been significantly less than expected. Kaplan and Anderson (2007) developed a refined approach to ABC that they refer to as time-driven activity-based costing (TDABC). Kaplan and Anderson (2007, p. 8) suggest that as TDABC is a simpler, cheaper and far more powerful approach to allocating overheads, many of the difficulties plaguing the adoption of ABC have been overcome.

Kaplan and Anderson (2007) provide a very detailed analysis and illustration of the TDABC approach. In essence, the TDABC approach entails two steps:

*   Identify all relevant organisational resources and calculate the total cost and capacity of each resource. For example, a relevant organisational resource for a manufacturing firm might be the order-filling function and the costs would include all human resources, supplies, occupancy and IT costs, and the capacity would be the total time that order-processing personnel have available for the provision of that particular function. Typically, capacity is measured in minutes and a capacity cost rate is simply the total resource cost (i.e. the numerator dollar value) divided by the total available capacity (i.e. the denominator activity measured in units of time, say minutes). Note that capacity is measured in terms of available capacity and not actual capacity. Available capacity is measured as the total capacity provided by a resource adjusted for paid time devoted to staff development and training activities, meetings and other similar types of activity. Thus, where actual time is less than available capacity, idle time will be identified and the 'cost' of this unused capacity brought to management attention. This might encourage a firm's management to either downsize capacity so as to reduce the total resource cost incurred or identify other value adding products that could make use of this otherwise idle capacity.
*   For each unique type of activity carried out by the organisational resource, the time taken to perform the activity is estimated. For example, order-filling personnel might be engaged in filling different types of orders that vary in terms of the quantity, value and fragility of the product to be shipped as well as the method of shipment. Filling an order for a low-volume, high-value, fragile product that

is to be express delivered to customer A would be more time-consuming than for a bulk order for low-value sturdy products that are to be delivered through regular delivery service to customer B. A TDABC system would allocate a greater amount of order-filling cost to the more time-consuming order placed by customer A.

As only two parameters are required by a TDABC model (i.e. the number of units of time consumed by the activities related to the cost object and the cost per unit of time) it can be readily developed, implemented and updated in comparison to the traditional ABC. Thus, it could be suggested that TDABC solves the problems of ABC without losing the benefits it provides. Worked example 14.7 provides a simple illustration of TDABC.

14.7

WORKED EXAMPLE

TDABC AND DESPATCH DEPARTMENT COSTS

In an attempt to have a better understanding of the cost of operating its despatch department, Perth Fine China has decided to introduce a TDABC system. Annual net departmental costs total $300 000 and the equivalent of three full-time employees work an average of five eight-hour days per week for 50 weeks per year, giving a total of 6000 hours total order-filling capacity time. However, after allowing for paid breaks, training and professional development activities and regular and ad hoc meetings, the available time in the order-filling department is only 5000 hours (or 300 000 minutes).

The capacity cost rate for the despatch department is calculated using two variables: (i) the total operating cost of the resource ($300 000), and (ii) the available capacity time (300 000 minutes). The capacity cost rate for the despatch department is calculated as follows:

$$\$1 \text{ per minute} = \$300\,000 \div 300\,000 \text{ minutes}$$

As the orders to be filled by Perth Fine China vary in terms of size (i.e. number of items packed), destination and method of shipment and the fragility of china packed, the following time equation has been developed for the different types of orders filled by the despatch department:

$$\text{Time to fill an order (in minutes)} = a + [(0.25 \times X1) \times X2] + (5 \times X3)$$

Where:

 $a = 10$ minutes order-filling time irrespective of order filling variations.

 $X1$ = number of items to be shipped.

 $X2$ = fragility of items to be packed: Yes = 1, weighting of 2; No, weighting of 1.

 $X3$ = method of shipment: standard delivery = 1, express delivery 2.

Perth China has an order for of 40 fragile items to be despatched to the customer via express delivery.

The first step is to calculate the time expected for the despatch department to ship this order. Inserting the shipment-related factors (i.e. order size, fragility and shipment method) into the formula yields the following estimated time:

Time to fill order	= 10 minutes	+	[(0.25 minutes × 40) × 2]	+	(5 minutes × 2)
	= 10 minutes	+	20 minutes	+	10 minutes
	= 40 minutes				

The second step is to calculate the cost of this order being shipped by the despatch department where the order-filling cost is $1 per minute:

$$\text{Despatch department cost} = \$1 \text{ per minute} \times 40 \text{ minutes for filling order}$$
$$= \$40$$

Despite the theoretical simplicity of TDABC, there is minimal empirical evidence as to how useful it is in providing management with decision-relevant information. Most published papers to date are either practical explanations of how it works, such as Worked example 14.7, or case study-type recounts of TDABC applications that are more ad hoc in nature than providing a systematic body of evidence in support of the costing method.

Presenting cost information for management purposes: manufacturing statements

In chapters 1 to 11 we dealt with financial accounting and the preparation of financial statements. The financial accounting system collects information to assist with the preparation of these statements. Management accounting is very much concerned with the collection of cost information and the assignment of such costs to objects. Accordingly, the MAS assists managers in allocating costs to various cost objects for decision-making purposes. The more accurate the cost-assignment process, the better the decisions that management will make about selling prices and sales mix for multi-product firms. In addition, the better the choices about prices and sales mix, the more viable the business and the higher the future profits.

We will now consider how to calculate the cost of goods placed into production, work in progress and finished goods. The calculation of these costs is necessary for determining the value of inventory to be carried as a current asset in the balance sheet and for calculating the periodic profit earned.

Costs are accumulated in three ways: (i) the cost of raw materials acquired that have yet to be used, (ii) the costs placed into production (i.e. direct materials, direct labour and manufacturing overhead) that relate to unfinished production and (iii) the cost of completed goods that are awaiting sale. Figure 14.15 illustrates how the costs associated with the above inventory accounts are calculated.

FIGURE 14.15 COST FLOWS AND THREE TYPES OF INVENTORY

Manufacturing costs for the period =	Cost of goods manufactured =	Cost of goods sold for the period =
• Direct materials + Direct labour + Manufacturing overhead	• Opening work-in-progress + Manufacturing costs - Ending work-in-process	• Opening finished goods + Cost of goods manufactured - Ending finished goods

Worked example 14.8 will demonstrate how the following costs have been determined: (i) the cost of raw materials issued to production, (ii) the cost of manufacturing costs introduced for the period, (iii) the cost of work in progress, (iv) the cost of finished goods, and (v) the cost of sales. For simplicity, it will be assumed that the actual costing approach is employed.

14.8

WORKED EXAMPLE

Australian Dairies provides the following cost and activity data for the month ended 30 June.

Inventories on hand as at 1 June:	
Raw materials	$50 000
Work in progress	$200 000
Finished goods	$400 000
Costs incurred during June:	
Raw material purchased	$210 000
Dairy payroll	$150 000
Other manufacturing overheads	$80 000
Inventories on hand as at 30 June:	
Raw materials	$90 000
Work in progress	$250 000
Finished goods	$300 000
Other expenses incurred during June:	
Warehousing and order-filling costs	$100 000
Selling and product promotion expense	$120 000
Corporate administrative expense	$150 000
Sales revenue for June:	$1 200 000

Analysis of the raw materials issued to production reveal that $20 000 was indirect materials and 20 per cent of the factory payroll was indirect labour.

i. Raw materials issued to production during the month ending 30 June:

Opening raw materials (1 June)	$50 000
Materials purchased during June	$210 000
Materials available for use	$260 000
Less Closing raw materials (30 June)	$90 000
Materials issued to production	$170 000
Less Indirect materials	$20 000
Direct materials issued to production during June	$150 000

ii. Factory payroll the month ending 30 June

Total payroll for month ending 30 June	$150 000
less Indirect labour (20%)	$30 000
Direct labour incurred during June	$120 000

iii. Manufacturing overhead for the month ending 30 June

Indirect materials	$20 000
Indirect labour	$30 000
Other manufacturing overhead	$80 000
Total manufacturing overhead for June	$130 000

iv. Cost of goods sold during the month ending 30 June

Opening work in progress (1 June)		$200 000
Manufacturing costs introduced during June		
Direct materials	$150 000	
Direct labour	$120 000	
Manufacturing overhead	$130 000	$400 000
Total costs in production during June		$600 000
Less closing work in progress 30 June		$250 000
Finished goods completed during June		$350 000

v. Cost of goods sold during the month ending 30 June

Opening finished goods (1 June)	$400 000
Finished goods completed during June	$350 000
Goods available for sale during June	$750 000
Less Closing finished goods (30 June)	$300 000
Cost of goods sold during June	$450 000

Having determined the above costs, the profit or loss for Australian Dairies can be calculated.

Sales revenue		$1 200 000
Cost of sales during June		
Cost of goods sold	$450 000	
Warehousing and order-filling costs	$100 000	$550 000
Gross margin		$650 000
Less Operating expenses		
Selling and product promotion expense	$120 000	
Corporate administrative expense	$150 000	$270 000
Net operating profit for the month ending 30 June		$380 000

Variable costing versus absorption costing

As noted, the cost of a product consists of three elements: direct materials, direct labour and manufacturing overheads. Before the introduction of machine-based methods of production, direct material and labour costs comprised the major part of product cost. However, over time, the cost profile of many products changed with manufacturing overheads (e.g. depreciation and running costs on plant and equipment) becoming a significant cost element. This trend continued with the introduction of automated manufacturing technologies. For some products, direct labour now constitutes less than 10 per cent of total product cost.

Whereas in the past production costs were mainly variable, automation required significant investments in fixed manufacturing capacity which resulted in increasing levels of fixed manufacturing overheads. As these overhead costs are incidental to the manufacturing process, product costs not only comprise the prime costs of direct materials and labour, but also fixed manufacturing overheads. Thus, we have the absorption (or full) product costing model where all manufacturing costs (direct materials, direct labour and manufacturing overheads) are treated as part of the cost of production (and are inventoried in work in process and finished goods) and non-manufacturing expenses (e.g. selling and distribution, administration and financial) are written off in the period incurred.

The logic underlying the absorption (or full) product costing model is intuitively appealing and it is the method of costing required for external reporting purposes. However, while the absorption product costing model might be sound for external reporting purposes, the relevance of fixed costs for decisions about production volumes and pricing decisions is questionable. In particular, as will be discussed in chapters 17 and 18, fixed manufacturing overheads are not relevant for certain management decisions (e.g. the price charged for products manufactured from otherwise idle production capacity). Thus, alternative ways for measuring and presenting cost data for internal reporting purposes are required. One alternative model is variable costing, where the only costs included in product cost are variable manufacturing costs: direct materials and labour and variable manufacturing overhead. Variable costing treats fixed manufacturing overheads as a period expense to be written off in the period incurred (in the same fashion as selling and distribution, administration and financial expenses). Thus, as variable costing does not include fixed manufacturing overheads in product cost for internal decision-making purposes, these costs are never inventoried. While the impact on internally reported profit measures is influenced by the period-to-period changes in inventory levels for work in progress and finished goods, variable costing ensures that, unlike absorption costing, fixed manufacturing overheads can never be 'sold' to inventory simply because periodic production volumes have been greater than actual sales volumes. We can summarise the differences between the absorption and variable costing methods as outlined below.

- When sales equal production (that is, when there is no movement in inventory) variable and absorption costing will yield the same profit. The amount of fixed manufacturing costs charged to the statement of comprehensive income is the same.
- When production exceeds sales (that is, when inventories are increasing) absorption costing shows a higher profit than variable costing does. Under absorption costing, a portion of the fixed manufacturing costs is charged to inventories and thereby deferred to future periods.
- When sales exceed production, absorption costing shows a lower profit than variable costing does. This is because the fixed manufacturing costs included in the inventories are charged to the period in which the inventories are sold.
- In the long run, the profit figures disclosed by the two methods must even out because sales cannot continuously exceed production, nor can production continuously exceed sales.

The differences in profits derived from the application of the two methods can be reconciled by the following arithmetical expression:
- Difference in profits = fixed manufacturing overhead absorption rate × the movement in inventories during a period.

For decision-making purposes, the absorption and variable methods of costing both have their virtues and the method that is preferred is dependent on the decision management is to make. For example, in the case of relevant costs and decisions involving future costs and benefits, the arguments in favour of variable costing as the preferred method are well documented (as will be discussed in chapters 17 and 18). However, the preference is not so clear when other applications are considered. The preferred method depends on individual judgments regarding the strengths and weaknesses of the two methods.

SUMMARY

LEARNING OBJECTIVE 1

IDENTIFY REASONS WHY MANAGEMENT NEED RELIABLE INFORMATION ABOUT THE COSTS OF GOODS AND SERVICES THEY PROVIDE TO CUSTOMERS

The information is needed to aid planning, control costs, value inventories, aid price setting and to help ascertain the relative profitability of product and services.

LEARNING OBJECTIVE 2

EXPLAIN THE DIFFERENCE BETWEEN VARIABLE AND FIXED COSTS

A cost is fixed if it does not change in response to changes in the level of activity within the relevant range of activity. A variable cost is the same per unit of activity within the relevant range of activity. Total variable costs increase or decrease in direct proportion to the increase or decrease in activity level whether being measured on productivity or sales output.

LEARNING OBJECTIVE 3

EXPLAIN WHAT IS MEANT BY A LINEAR COST FUNCTION

A linear cost function is a straight-line cost function that can be shown mathematically as $y = a + bx$. Within this mathematical expression, y is the total cost to be predicted, a is a constant (the total fixed cost), b is the cost that will be the same for each unit of activity (variable cost) and x is the number of units measured in units of output or sales.

LEARNING OBJECTIVE 4

IDENTIFY WHAT IS MEANT BY THE RELEVANT RANGE OF ACTIVITY

The relevant range of activity is the levels of activity that a firm has experienced in past periods. In this range, it is assumed that the relationship between the independent and dependent variables will be similar in a following period.

LEARNING OBJECTIVE 5

EXPLAIN THE COST ASSIGNMENT PROCESS

A cost object is any item management requires cost information for and can be a product, service, activity or customer process. Costs will be either direct or indirect, and the way costs are assigned depends on their nature.

LEARNING OBJECTIVE 6

EXPLAIN THE DIFFERENCE BETWEEN DIRECT AND INDIRECT COSTS

A direct cost is one that is easily traceable (with an acceptable level of accuracy) to a cost object (e.g. bottles used in a bottling factory). Indirect costs (also known as overhead costs) are those that cannot be easily and conveniently identified with a particular object (e.g. electricity charges).

LEARNING OBJECTIVE 7

IDENTIFY WHAT IS MEANT BY PRODUCT AND PERIOD COSTS

Product costs are those costs that can be allocated to a product (e.g. direct materials and labour). All other costs incurred during a period are period costs and are expensed in that period (e.g. marketing and administration expenses).

LEARNING OBJECTIVE 8

EXPLAIN THE ABSORPTION AND VARIABLE COSTING METHODS

For product-costing purposes, absorption or full costing incorporates both variable and fixed manufacturing costs whereas variable costing only allocates variable manufacturing costs.

LEARNING OBJECTIVE 9

IDENTIFY THE STAGES THAT ARE INVOLVED IN DETERMINING THE ALLOCATION OF OVERHEADS TO PRODUCTS

» *Stage 1.* Overhead costs are identified and collected from production and service cost centres. A design department is an example of a service cost centre. These costs are apportioned to production departments using a predetermined formula. For example, electricity costs could be apportioned based on the space occupied.

» *Stage 2.* Once production and service department costs have been identified and collected, service department costs are allocated to production departments on some basis. For example, the percentage of space occupied by production departments could determine the percentage of electricity costs allocated to each production cost centre.

» *Stage 3.* The allocation of overheads to a single product is achieved by dividing a production cost centre's total overhead by the number of products manufactured. The resulting amount can then be applied as the overhead component of the total cost of each product.

LEARNING OBJECTIVE 10

EXPLAIN WHAT IS MEANT BY PREDETERMINED OVERHEAD ABSORPTION RATES

Many overhead costs are estimates of future expenditure. There are two main reasons for estimating costs. First, many costs are known after the event (e.g. electricity charges are billed bimonthly in arrears). Second, costs vary over time (e.g. air conditioning). Because budgets are usually set annually in advance, these costs are budgeted and set at a constant rate over the year so that any seasonal influence on product cost is eliminated.

LEARNING OBJECTIVE 11

EXPLAIN THE DIFFERENCE BETWEEN TRADITIONAL VOLUME-BASED AND ACTIVITY-BASED COSTING METHODS

» The traditional volume-based activity costing method allocates overhead costs to product (or services) using volume-related measures of activity, such as machine hours, direct labour hours or units. However, for firms supplying multiple products (or services) that significantly vary in the production processes employed, the use of traditional volume-based costing methods can result in low volume and under-allocation of the true amount of overhead costs incurred for complex-to-produce products or services. Similarly, high volume and simple-to-manufacture products are more likely to be over-allocated their share of overhead costs incurred. On the other hand, the activity-based costing method recognises that overhead costs are driven by activities other than those directly measured by volume-based measures, such as machine hours or direct labour hours. For a multi-product manufacturing firm, activities, such as materials handling and movement, production set-up and inspections, may be unrelated to the number of machine hours or direct labour hours used in producing each of the firm's products. In such settings, as activity-based costing uses cost pools to allocate overheads to individual products on the basis of each product's consumption of the activities provided by each pool, a more accurate allocation of overheads will result. Thus, low-volume and complex-to-manufacture products will typically be allocated a higher and more accurate share of overhead costs incurred using activity-based costing than if the traditional volume-based costing method was employed.

LEARNING OBJECTIVE 12

EXPLAIN THE TERMS 'ACTIVITY', 'COST POOL' AND 'COST DRIVER' AS USED IN ACTIVITY-BASED COSTING

Activity is what the organisation does (e.g. process customer orders). Cost pool is the aggregation of related indirect or overhead costs for the purposes of assigning costs to a cost object (e.g. the total costs incurred by the customer order department in processing customer orders). A cost driver is the activity factor that causes a change in the cost incurred for that activity (e.g. the number of customer orders processed would influence the costs incurred in the customer order department).

LEARNING OBJECTIVE 13

EXPLAIN HOW TIME-DRIVEN ACTIVITY-BASED COSTING (TDABC) PROVIDES A SIMPLER AND LESS COSTLY ACTIVITY-BASED METHOD OF ALLOCATING INDIRECT COSTS

As only two parameters are required by a TDABC model (i.e. the number of units of time consumed by the activities related to the cost object and the cost per unit of time), TDABC is more readily developed, implemented and updated in comparison to the traditional ABC. Thus, it should not only be simpler to install and operate, it should be cheaper as well.

REVIEW QUESTIONS

1   Explain why it is important to determine product or service cost.

2   It is often assumed that there is only one independent variable in cost behaviour. Explain the nature of independent variables and why this assumption is necessary.

3   What is the difference between a linear fixed cost and a curvilinear variable cost? Give examples, other than those given in the text.

4   What are some of the problems with using past activity and cost data to predict future cost behaviour?

5   Give examples of expenditure in a manufacturing firm that would be classified as direct costs and indirect costs.

6   What are period costs?

7   Discuss the advantages and disadvantages of using variable costing for product costing.

8   Define and briefly explain what is meant by each of the following terms:

    i   activity

    ii   cost pool

    iii cost driver.

9   TVBC methods have been criticised on the grounds that they provide misleading information when fixed manufacturing overheads account for a significant proportion of product cost. Explain how ABC might yield more meaningful product cost information.

10 Under what circumstances would you expect that ABC would provide superior product cost information than obtained from a TVBC system?

11 'ABC is only really useful for costing manufactured products. Thus, ABC is of no use to service-providing organisations.' Critically evaluate this statement using an example of a service-providing industry (e.g. higher education, banking or retailing) to support your view.

12 What factors should a manager of a medium-sized multi-product manufacturing firm consider before deciding to implement a 'traditional' ABC product costing model? In what way might time-driven activity-based costing (TDABC) be a suitable alternative to the traditional ABC model?

PROBLEMS FOR DISCUSSION AND ANALYSIS

1 ABC Limited incurs the following costs at the following levels of activity. Determine what the cost behaviour classification is for the three cost items and calculate the cost per unit of activity.

ACTIVITY LEVEL (UNITS)	COST A	COST B	COST C
5000	$30 000	$20 000	$8 000
5500	$30 000	$22 000	$8 500
6000	$30 000	$24 000	$9 000
6500	$30 000	$26 000	$9 500
7000	$30 000	$28 000	$10 000
7500	$30 000	$30 000	$10 500

2 If a manager is paid a bonus based on the profit he/she has earned, what might be the problems, in the short run, of using absorption costing?

3 Discuss how the use of variable costing may ignore the impact of fixed costs.

4 JBQ Ltd produces electronic mapping devices for luxury cars and uses a normal costing system. The following data is available for the current year:

BUDGETED:	
Overhead	$900 000
Machine hours	37 500
Direct labour hours	120 000
ACTUAL:	
Units produced	150 000
Overhead	$893 250
Prime (direct) costs	$1 350 000
Machine hours	37 575
Direct labour hours	117 000

Overhead is applied on the basis of direct labour hours.

Required

a What is the predetermined overhead rate?

b What is the applied overhead for the current year?

c Was overhead over-applied or under-applied during the current year, and by how much?

d What is the cost per unit for the current year?

5   Barclay Ltd uses a predetermined overhead rate in applying overheads to product costs, using direct labour costs for Cost Centre X and machine hours for Cost Centre Y. The details of the forecasts for next year are as follows:

	X	Y
Direct labour costs	$100 000	$35 000
Production overheads	$140 000	$150 000
Direct labour hours	16 000	5 000
Machine hours	1 000	20 000

Required

a   Calculate the predetermined overhead rate for Cost Centres X and Y.

b   BNH is one of the products manufactured by Barclay. The manufacturing process involves both cost centres X and Y. The following data relates to the resources that were used in the manufacture of the product during the current year. Determine the total production cost for product BNH, using absorption costing.

	X	Y
Direct materials	$20 000	$40 000
Direct labour	$32 000	$21 000
Direct labour hours	4 000	3 000
Machine hours	1 000	13 000

c   Assuming that product BNH consists of 20 000 units, what is the per unit cost of BNH?

d   At the end of the year, it was found that actual production overhead costs amounted to $160 000 in Cost Centre X and $138 000 in Cost Centre Y. The total direct labour cost in Cost Centre X was $144 200, and 18 000 machine hours were used in Cost Centre Y during the year. Calculate the over- or under-absorbed overhead for each cost centre.

6   Agent Orange Ltd operates a factory with two production departments, P1 and P2, and one service department, S1. Estimates of factory overhead for the year commencing 1 January were as follows:

	$	$
Fixed overhead		
Factory rates		7 500
Insurance (buildings)		5 200
Maintenance		14 600
Depreciation (equipment)		32 800
Variable overhead		
Electricity		12 000
Indirect labour		

	$	$
P1	18 000	
P2	23 500	
S1	<u>44 000</u>	85 500
Indirect materials		
P1	10 000	
P2	13 000	
S1	<u>8 000</u>	31 000

Other information available is as follows:

	DEPARTMENT		
	P1	P2	S1
Floor space (m²)	800	1 400	400
Value of equipment	$180 000	$100 000	$48 000
Machine hours	4 400	1 200	500
Direct labour hours	8 800	12 500	–
Allocation basis – S1	60%	40%	

Required

a Prepare overhead application rates for Department P1 based on machine hours and for Department P2 based on direct labour hours.

b Calculate a single plant-wide overhead application rate based on direct labour hours.

7 Briefly respond to each of the following comments. Indicate how management accounting information can assist managers in doing their jobs.

a *Division manager*: 'Our accountants perform a valuable function in providing information to the shareholders about the performance of our company, but my task is to manage this division and I can't see how they can assist me in this task.'

b *Café proprietor*: 'I agree that management accounting is valuable in a manufacturing firm, but I manage a cafe. How can it help my business?'

c *Local council recreation manager*: 'Management accounting may be significant in a for-profit entity, but my task is to provide community services, without the goal of making a profit. Why should I be concerned with costs?'

d *Project supervisor*: 'I carefully analyse my project's performance on a regular basis and reprimand my staff whenever we spend too much money and let them know they must perform better.'

e *Sales senior manager*: 'Pricing a product is like throwing darts at a dartboard. Pick the numbers out of the air and hope the product sells and the company makes a profit if this happens.'

f *Civil engineering graduate*: 'I have a real desire to be in charge of and responsible for the building of bridges, airports and massive dams. Why do I need to know about management accounting?'

8   Benzfor Ltd manufactures cars. The following data covers the months of April, May and June.

	APRIL	MAY	JUNE
Car production			
Opening inventory	0	100	250
Production	600	800	650
Sales	500	650	350
Variable costs			
Manufacturing costs per car	10 000	10 000	10 000
Marketing and administration	1 000	1 000	1 000
Fixed costs			
Manufacturing	500 000	500 000	500 000
Administration, etc.	85 000	90 000	85 000

The retail price for each car is $27 000.

Required

Prepare a statement of comprehensive income for the three months using absorption costing.

Note to instructors: The following problems are considered more suitable for use in MBA courses. However, undergraduate courses may also find them useful.

9   The managers of Absent Ltd have been studying the results for the first three years of this company and are concerned about the figures. They think of profits as being directly related to the volume of sales, and find it confusing that for one year the reported sales are higher than those of the previous year but the reported net profit is lower.

The following figures apply to the years under consideration.

	YEAR BEFORE LAST	LAST YEAR	CURRENT YEAR
Actual sales (units)	36 000	50 000	60 000
Actual production (units)	58 000	35 000	53 000

In each of the three years, the estimated production volume was 45 000 units and the estimated fixed overheads were $67 500.

The selling price was $4.00 per unit and variable costs were $1.50 per unit for the three years.

Actual costs were equal to estimated costs in all years. Selling and administrative expenses for each year were $10 000. The company had no opening inventory. The management accountant had difficulty explaining to the managers that fluctuations in profits resulted from differences between the volume of sales and the volume of production within an accounting period, together with the system of product valuation used.

Required

a   Prepare statements of comprehensive income for Absent Ltd using absorption costing for each of the three years.

b   Briefly explain how the statements of comprehensive income prepared using variable costing would differ from the absorption costing statements prepared for requirement (a).

c   Which costing method would you recommend be used to aid the management accountant's explanation.

10   Drawrod Ltd has three manufacturing cost centres: Punching, Stamping and Assembly. In addition, the company has two service cost centres: Maintenance and Inspection. The following table gives Drawrod's estimated production overhead expenses for the year to 31 December:

	$	$
Indirect materials		
Punching	12 000	
Stamping	14 000	
Assembly	10 000	
Maintenance	8 000	
Inspection	4 000	48 000
Indirect labour		
Punching	24 000	
Stamping	30 000	
Assembly	14 000	
Maintenance	36 000	
Inspection	10 000	114 000
Other overhead expenses		
Electricity	56 000	
Rent	128 000	
Rates	32 000	
Insurance of buildings	32 000	
Insurance of machines	40 000	
Depreciation of machines	40 000	328 000
Total		490 000

The following figures are additional estimates relating to Drawrod's manufacturing for the year ended 31 December.

	AREA OCCUPIED (M²)	WORKING HOURS	BOOK VALUE OF MACHINES	MACHINE HOURS	NUMBER OF EMPLOYEES
Punching	18 000	52 500	$200 000	51 200	180
Stamping	12 000	45 000	$140 000	64 000	150
Assembly	24 000	30 000	$60 000	44 800	240
Maintenance	3 000	15 000	–	–	30
Inspection	3 000	7 500	–	–	60
Total	60 000	150 000	$400 000	160 000	660

The costs of the service cost centres are to be apportioned as follows:

	MAINTENANCE %	INSPECTION %
Punching	40	20
Stamping	30	30
Assembly	30	50
	100	100

The company's bases for the absorption of overheads are as follows:

- Punching: machine hours
- Stamping: machine hours
- Assembly: working hours

Required

a Calculate the absorption rates for the Punching, Stamping and Assembly cost centres (to the nearest cent).

b With reference to the system applied to Drawrod Ltd, specify and explain the factors that need to be considered in determining whether to use a single factory-wide overhead absorption rate for all factory overheads or a separate rate for each manufacturing cost centre.

11 Metway reported it had implemented an ABC system and it intended to use the information about profitable and less profitable customers, as generated by the ABC system, as part of its customer relationship management system. How would it use such information?

12 Howard Ltd provides a wide range of web-based resources for different education markets (e.g. schools and universities). Some resources are simple to produce, market and sell in high volumes, while others are highly customised one-off product.

a Explain why ABC might provide more useful cost information than Howard's existing traditional volume-based costing (TVBC) model.

b Explain how ABC might be more influential in shaping the internal software development and external marketing strategies of Howard Limited than its existing TVBC system.

13 Formula 500 Cars Ltd manufactured the metal frames of a small racing car called the Formula 500. It produced two different models, and the costs of direct material and direct labour for each model in February this year were:

	MODEL ABC	MODEL XYZ
Direct materials	$200 000	$250 000
Direct labour	$400 000	$450 000

Formula 500 uses an activity-based costing system to allocate the overhead costs. The following details are available about cost drivers:

ACTIVITY	COST DRIVER
Welding	Number of welds (W)
Assembly	Number of direct labour hours (DLH)
Inspection	Time to inspect (IH)

The following schedule shows the projected costs and the amount of each cost driver for the year ending 31 December:

	ESTIMATED COSTS	ESTIMATED COST DRIVER
Welding	$1 000 000	800 000 welds
Assembly	$800 000	400 000 DLH
Inspection	$500 000	20 000 IH
	$2 300 000	

During February, the actual amounts for each cost driver were:

	A	Z
Number of welds	30 000	40 000
Direct labour hours	15 000	20 000
Hours of inspection	600	1 000

Required

a Calculate the total costs for model ABC and model XYZ for February.

b Calculate the cost per car for each model if, during February, 1500 of ABC and 1630 of XYZ were produced.

c If actual overhead for February was $190 000, determine if the factory overhead was under- or over-applied in February. How does the company report this under- or over-application of overhead?

14 JayDees Boats Ltd builds custom-designed company boats. The company uses an activity-based costing system for determining the costs of each boat it produces. The following activities and cost drivers apply to the construction of boats.

ACTIVITY	COST DRIVER
Construction	Direct labour hours (DLH)
Inspection	Time to inspect (TTI)
Testing	Time to test (TTT)

At the beginning of the current year, the following estimates were made for each activity and cost driver.

	ESTIMATED COSTS FOR YEAR $	ESTIMATED COST DRIVER HOURS
Construction	3 000 000	100 000 (DLH)
Inspection	1 000 000	20 000 (TTI)
Testing	500 000	8000 (TTT)
	4 500 000	

During March this year, the actual direct materials and amounts for each cost driver for two boats – Mustang and Jaguar – were:

	MUSTANG	JAGUAR
Direct materials	$160 000	$120 000
Direct labour hours	4 000	6 000
Inspection time	800	1 200
Testing time	200	300

Required

a Determine the total cost for Mustang and Jaguar.

b If the actual overhead for March was $440 000, was the overhead under- or over-applied in March?

15 ChemWise is engaged in the production of chemicals for industrial use. One plant specialises in the production of chemicals used in the nickel industry. Two compounds are produced: compound Y-5 and compound Z-9. Compound Y-5 was originally developed by ChemWise chemists and played a key role in the extraction of nickel from low-grade ore. The patent for compound Y-5 has expired, and competition in this market has become fierce. Compound Y-5 produced the highest volume of activity, and for many years was the only chemical compound the plant produced. Six years ago, Z-9 was added. Compound Z-9 was more difficult to manufacture and required special handling and set-ups. For the first four years after the addition of the new product, profits increased. In the last two years the plant has faced intense competition, and its sales of Y-5 have declined. In fact, the plant reported a small loss in the most recent accounting period. The plant manager is convinced that competing producers have been guilty of selling Y-5 below the cost to produce it – perhaps with the objective of increasing their share of the market.

ChemWise has concerns about the future of the plant and its products, and has hired independent consultants to investigate its production costs and relative efficiency. After a four-month review, the consulting group has provided the following information on the plant's production activities and costs associated with the two products:

	Y-5	Z-9
Production (kilograms)	1 000 000	200 000
Selling price	$15.93	$12.00
Overhead per unit*	$6.41	$2.89
Prime (direct) cost per kilogram	$4.27	$3.13
Number of production runs	100	200
Receiving orders	400	1 000
Machine hours	125 000	60 000
Direct labour hours	250 000	22 500
Engineering hours	5 000	5 000
Material handling (number of moves)	500	400

* Calculated using a plant-wide rate based on direct labour hours, which is the current way of assigning the plant's overhead to its products.

The consulting group has recommended switching the overhead assignment to an activity-based approach. It maintains that an activity-based costing assignment is more accurate and will provide higher-quality information for decision making. To assist with this recommendation, the plant's activities have been grouped into similar sets based on common processes, activity levels and consumption ratios. The costs of these activity pools are as follows:

MANUFACTURING OVERHEAD COST POOL*	$
Set-up costs	240 000
Machine costs	1 750 000
Receiving costs	2 100 000
Engineering costs	2 000 000
Material-handling costs	900 000
Total	6 990 000

* The pools are named for the major activities found within them. All overhead costs within each pool can be assigned using a single driver (based on the major activity after which the pool is named).

Required

a Confirm the manufacturing overhead cost per unit reported by the consulting group using direct labour hours to assign overhead. Compute the per-unit gross margin for each product.

b Recompute the unit cost of each product using activity-based costing. Calculate the per-unit gross margin for each product.

c Should the company change its emphasis from the high-volume product to the low-volume product? Comment on the validity of the plant manager's concern that competitors are selling Y-5 below its cost of production.

d Explain the apparent lack of competition for Z-9. Also, comment on the fact that customers are prepared to accept a 25 per cent increase in price for this compound.

e What steps would you take given the information provided by the activity-based unit costs?

(Adapted from D. Hansen and M. Mowen, Management Accounting, *6th edn, South-Western, Mason, OH, Problem 4-21, p. 152.)*

ETHICS CASE STUDY

Digital Electronics Ltd manufactures specialised scientific instruments to customer specifications. It has contracts with government departments that are on a cost-plus basis. Under this arrangement, the costs are defined as those costs that can be directly traced to the instruments supplied, plus overheads based on a predetermined overhead rate, using an appropriate application base. Digital's other customers are in the non-government sector and selling prices are fixed.

During February, the company worked on two main contracts: one with the Department of Defence and the other with the Sarich Corporation. The two contracts were quite different, with the contract for the Department of Defence requiring a large number of direct labour hours, while the contract for Sarich was the reverse.

The financial controller of the company has recommended to the general manager of Digital that the most appropriate base for the allocation of overheads is machine hours. However, the general manager has decided in favour of using direct labour hours to allocate overheads to both contracts.

Discuss

a Why do you think the general manager has chosen direct labour hours for the allocation of overheads instead of the machine hours recommended by the financial controller?

b The ethical issues involved in this case: should the financial controller take any further action?

SUGGESTED ANSWERS TO STOP AND THINK EXERCISES IN THE CHAPTER

1 It is assumed that variable costs are the same per unit of activity; therefore, the variable costs will move in proportion to activity levels (i.e. in a linear fashion). In reality, variable costs do not strictly behave in this manner. For example, firms will often receive quantity discounts when they purchase large quantities of goods for manufacture or resale. In such cases, the cost per unit of material will not solely depend upon the activity but will also be influenced by the quantity of inputs purchased. As a result, variable costs will not behave in a linear fashion and will tend to follow a downward sloping curvilinear function. On the other hand, for some types of costs (e.g. utilities including power and water), the variable cost per unit consumed increases at higher levels of consumption. In this case, the variable portion of the cost will tend to follow an upward sloping curvilinear function.

A fixed cost is assumed to be constant over all levels of output. Once again, in reality these costs tend not to be strictly linear. Fixed costs will often only be fixed over a limited range of output, and will tend to behave in a stepped rather than linear function.

2 A linear fixed cost is one that remains constant for all levels of activity. A stepped fixed cost is constant for certain levels of activity but steps up to a new figure once a certain level of activity is exceeded; for example, annual supervisory salaries would be fixed for a specified level of supervision (e.g. 10 subordinates working an hour hour shift) but will increase if an extra 8-hour shift was to be worked.

3 The relevant range of activity refers to the level of activity that the firm has experienced in past periods. The significance of this range is that cost behaviour – the relationship between the dependent and independent variables – can be established with a certain amount of confidence. This is because the firm has previously experienced cost behaviour in this range and can observe the relationship between cost and activity levels. This information is useful in predicting future costs for decision-making purposes. As past cost behaviour is not known outside of this range, it can be more difficult to predict.

4 a variable
   b fixed
   c variable
   d variable
   e variable
   f fixed
   g variable
   h variable
   i variable

5 A direct cost is one that is traceable and is readily identifiable with a product. Indirect costs, also known as overhead costs, cannot be easily and conveniently identified with a particular product.

6 Product costs are those costs that can be allocated to a product. As in our discussion of inventory in Chapter 8, we use the principle that product costs are all the costs that are reasonable and have, by necessity, been incurred to get a product to a condition and location ready for sale. All other costs incurred during a period are period costs.

7 Absorption costing means that it has been determined that the costs of a product include all variable and fixed manufacturing costs.

8 There are two main reasons why estimates are used in determining absorption rates.

First, some overhead costs are only known some months after they have been incurred. For example, as water consumption charges may be billed to customers biannually, a firm would have to wait six months before they could determine this charge – which is not timely for management purposes.

Second, a number of overhead costs are seasonal (e.g. for heating and lighting). Seasonal variations can distort the costing of products. For example, if a product is manufactured in the summer, it is likely that heating costs would be minimal. Thus, the cost of a product could be dependent upon when the product was manufactured. It is argued that such variations may distort the costing of products and also require complex systems to reflect these seasonal variations.

9   As suggested, we could choose a university as being an organisation that we are all familiar with. A support activity might be the reader services of the library where you are now reading this answer. The cost of reader services would primarily relate to the cost of library staff and other related expenditures (e.g. information technology, accommodation and utility costs and other services). The driver of the costs incurred in reader services would be the number of student enquiries made with perhaps some allowance for the complexity of each enquiry.

10 If a firm has a significant error in how overheads are allocated to cost objects, such as a product, it may find that it is setting prices that are either too high or too low. In the case of the former, the firm is not able to compete with rivals and could be expected to lose market share. Alternatively, if prices are set too low, not only might the firm find itself left with a bigger market share but the prices set fail to generate an acceptable profit margin. If prices are set by the market than the firm, a significant error in how overheads are allocated to products might lead to an incorrect determination of the profitability of different products. In noting having an accurate measure of product profitability, flawed decisions are more likely made as to which products are to be promoted.

11 Activity-based costing (ABC) is a system of costing where the costs are allocated to a cost object based on an activity measure. Therefore, this is the major influence on the costs incurred by various cost objects.

CENGAGENOW

Go to http:\\login.cengagebrain.com to link to CengageNOW resources, including online crosswords, animated examples and flashcards featuring the key concepts of cost behaviour and cost-volume-profit analysis.

BUDGETS

15

LEARNING OBJECTIVES

At the end of this chapter, you should be able to:

1. discuss some of the reasons for producing budgets
2. explain what is meant by the budget process
3. explain the stages and parties that are typically involved in the budget process
4. identify the factors that influence the choice of the budget period
5. summarise what is normally included in the master budget
6. outline the role of sales and production budgets, and the relationship between them
7. calculate budgets for materials in units and in monetary terms
8. calculate cost budgets for materials per unit manufactured and sold, and for labour
9. explain why, in addition to the cost budgets for materials and labour, it may also be important to construct budgets for overheads.

INTRODUCTION

In Chapter 12, the stages of the planning and control process were identified. The third stage, making operating decisions, focused on the use of resources and the individual decisions necessary to use them consistently within the overall objectives of an organisation. It was also stated that, in this stage, the decisions would be translated into a short-term plan, a budget, defined as 'a plan of action expressed in monetary terms'. In this chapter, we examine the purpose of budgets, the budgeting process and the preparation of budgets.

A budget must match the organisation's needs. In Chapter 12 we mentioned the application of contingency theory to all accounting information systems. The major contingency factors identified were technology, the commercial environment and the structure of the organisation. These factors affect the type of budget that is used by an organisation. For example, in a retail organisation the budget mainly deals with the level of consumer sales and the purchase of goods necessary to satisfy these sales. In contrast, the budget of a manufacturing firm focuses on the sales of products and the production activity necessary to meet these sales. There are some similarities between the two types of budget, and there is a common basis for preparing the budgets of different types of organisation. In this chapter we concentrate on the relativity sophisticated budgets of large manufacturing organisations.

1 LEARNING OBJECTIVE

Discuss some of the reasons for producing budgets

THE PURPOSES OF BUDGETS

The purpose of a budget depends on the type of organisation; the following are common to most organisations.

The ThirdMan/Shutterstock.com

ENCOURAGE PLANNING

The introduction of budgets within an organisation forces management to look ahead and set short-term targets. By looking to the future, management can anticipate potential problems. For example, the identification of shortages of cash at particular times during a budget period provides management with the opportunity to address these shortages, such as by negotiating an overdraft facility with the organisation's bank.

COORDINATE FUNCTIONS WITHIN AN ORGANISATION

The preparation of budgets tends to increase the coordination between departments and units within an organisation because it requires the integration of the individual plans of managers. Managers are obliged to consider the relationships between various departments. For example, to ensure during the budget period that the needs of manufacturing in terms of material requirements are satisfied, it is important for procurement to ensure that inventories (or stocks) are maintained to the optimal level.

A FORM OF COMMUNICATION

A budget is often a useful means by which senior management can formally communicate objectives and strategies for the forthcoming budget period. This function is periodically reinforced through a control mechanism that reviews actual performance against the budget during the budget period (this is described later in the chapter). The extent to which lower-level managers are involved in establishing a budget communicates important information about the philosophy of senior management (also discussed later).

PROVIDE A BASIS FOR RESPONSIBILITY ACCOUNTING

Individual managers are identified with their budget centres and are made responsible for achieving budgeted targets. These targets are in terms of expenditure, income and output considered to be within the manager's control. Responsibility accounting was outlined in Chapter 13. Within the context of budgets, responsibility accounting represents an important feature of the delegation of responsibility within an organisation.

> **15.1 KEY CONCEPT**
>
> ## RESPONSIBILITY ACCOUNTING
>
> Responsibility accounting is where an entity is structured into strategic business units and the performance of these units is measured in financial and non-financial terms.

PROVIDE A BASIS FOR A CONTROL MECHANISM

The budget provides a basis for comparing actual performance with a plan and identifying any deviation from that plan. The identification of these deviations gives management the opportunity to take corrective action so that such deviations are eliminated. When budgets are used as a control mechanism, it is described as budgetary control.

AUTHORISE EXPENDITURE

The budget can act as a formal authorisation of future expenditure from senior management to the individuals who are responsible for the expenditure. If an item of expenditure is contained in a budget that has been approved by the top management of the organisation, it implies that the item has been approved, and generally no further authorisation is required.

MOTIVATE EMPLOYEES

The budget can be used as a target to motivate employees to reach certain levels of attainment. For example, if, during one budget period, a sales representative achieves sales of products to the value of $30 000, management might in the next period set a target of $40 000, believing, rightly or wrongly, that this new target will motivate the sales representative to exceed the level achieved in the previous period.

Budgets mean different things to different people within an organisation. For example, a budget that is introduced by management with the aim of monitoring production costs might be perceived by production managers as a device to monitor their performance. Budgets have the potential to lead to much misunderstanding, frustration and friction within an organisation.

Positive behaviour flows from budgets when the goals of the entity and the individual are aligned so that there is goal congruence (as discussed in Chapter 13). In these cases, the manager is motivated to achieve the budget's goals. Negative or *dysfunctional* behaviour flows from budgets when the goals of the individual and the organisation are not aligned.

There is an ethical aspect to dysfunctional behaviour as it involves managers taking actions such as deliberately understating sales targets or overstating costs in order to easily achieve the budget that is set for them. This process of padding the budget (sometimes referred to as budgetary slack) is one of the many dysfunctional behavioural aspects to budgeting that can have a negative impact on organisational performance.

STOP AND THINK 1

What is a budget? What are the main reasons for an organisation introducing budgets?

THE BUDGET PROCESS

The following analysis focuses on the main features of the budget process for a manufacturing firm. The products that are manufactured and sold in a budget period are determined via operating decisions, as previously described in Chapter 12. Operating decisions are made throughout an organisation and not only will production be tasked with making these decisions, but so too will be support functions relating to procurement, marketing, sales and distribution, and corporate services such as administration and finance. Each of these functions also requires access to resources, both financial and personnel.

15.2 KEY CONCEPT

THE BUDGET PROCESS

The phrase 'the budget process' refers to the sequence of operations necessary to produce a budget for a particular organisation. The sequence of operations depends upon the type of organisation and its perceived requirements for planning and control.

At the beginning of the budget process, consideration is collectively given to proposed operating decisions of the organisation's functions, and the interrelationships between the functions described. At this stage, the resource implications of proposed decisions are analysed so as to determine the extent to which they will draw upon the functions described above.

From this analysis, guidelines are formulated for the preparation of the budget. The guidelines identify the overall levels of activity and the organisation's policies on performance criteria, such as productivity. At this stage, the only people involved in the process are the organisation's senior management. They include those who have overall responsibility for the sales and production activities and those who are responsible for ensuring that the activities are coordinated; for example, an accountant who has responsibility for the coordination of the accounting information input, often referred to as the budget accountant. Thus, the vitally important management task of coordinating the various interrelated aspects of decision making begins with the budgeting process.

For example, in a manufacturing organisation the main task of coordination is concerned with the overall policy about sales and production volumes. The coordination of these activities involves ensuring that the level of production is sufficient to meet the sales demand for products plus any required inventory of finished goods. For example, assuming there is no opening inventory of finished goods available, if the sales demand for a product is 150 units and the desired closing inventory of finished goods is 30 units, 180 units will have to be manufactured in the budget period to meet the sales and inventory requirements. The functions such as marketing and finance necessary to support these levels of output are also considered at this stage. In addition, management's policies on desired levels of performance (or targets) for the budget period are also formulated.

When the output levels and associated policies have been determined by top management, they must be communicated to the preparers of budgets, along with the guidelines. Budgets are prepared for the individual responsibility centres, which have been defined by the organisation's hierarchy. These centres are managed by personnel who are responsible for particular functions within the organisation, such as generating sales, manufacturing products, and supporting the sales and production functions.

Whilst there is some debate on the extent to which managers responsible for departments that spend and generate income should be involved in the preparation of their own budgets, they usually have some influence. The extent of influence varies from organisation to organisation and depends on top management style. For example, the senior management of some organisations might impose rules on subordinates without consultation or discussion. Where a manager is solely responsible for the preparation of the budget, it is likely to be biased in favour of the manager. However, this bias is not in the best interests of the organisation as a whole. For example, a manager who is responsible for the sales of a particular product range might set budget targets that can easily be attained, thereby gaining the favour of superiors.

However, it is likely that a responsibility centre manager will possess greater knowledge and understanding of the operation of the centre than any other manager within the organisation, and this knowledge is important in the formulation of budgets. Thus, there is a strong case for some involvement by a responsibility centre's manager in the preparation of the centre's budget. Typically, in the budgeting process of an organisation, individual budgets for each responsibility centre are the subject of negotiation before being approved and implemented by the organisation. The parties to the negotiations include the manager of the responsibility centre, the preparer of the budget (if not the manager) and the manager's superior. The accountant who is responsible for budgets within the organisation often acts as an intermediary. In large organisations, the negotiation process has several stages as the budget moves up the organisational hierarchy for higher managerial approval.

Participative budgeting occurs when lower-level managers are involved in the budget process rather than having the budget imposed from above. Figure 15.1 shows a two-way flow in the establishment of the budget. This process will vary across organisations. In some organisations, the flow will be one-way, down from the board, while in others there will be participation by lower-level managers in the process. In some organisations, lower-level managers will appear to be involved in the process but, ultimately, top-level managers make the decisions. This process of only appearing to involve lower-level managers is referred to as pseudo-participation and can be as damaging as having no subordinate manager participation at all.

3 **LEARNING OBJECTIVE**

Explain the stages and parties that are typically involved in the budget process

FIGURE 15.1 PARTICIPATIVE PROCESS OF NEGOTIATION AND ESTABLISHMENT OF A BUDGET

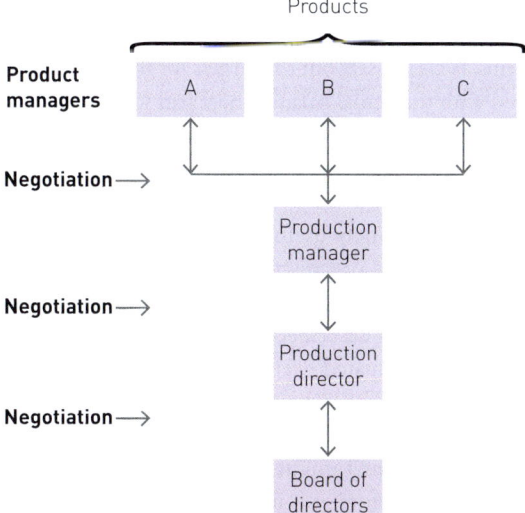

KEY CONCEPT

PARTICIPATIVE BUDGETING

Participative budgeting is where lower-level managers are involved in the process of establishing the budget.

Figure 15.1 also illustrates a typical hierarchy for the production management of an organisation and the stages of negotiation of the production budget for three groups of products. First, the production budgets (costs and output levels) are determined for products A, B and C. It has been assumed that a product manager is individually responsible for the manufacturing of each product. As mentioned, it is likely that each product manager will prepare his or her own budget – or at least have some influence over its content. When budgets have been prepared, the first stage in negotiation takes place between each individual product manager and the production manager who has overall responsibility for this range of products. After agreement has been reached on individual budgets, the combined budgets for the product range are then negotiated with a more senior manager who oversees and is responsible for the overall manufacturing operations of the organisation. The negotiation of the production budget can flow upwards to the board of directors where the budget will be given its final approval.

At each stage of the negotiation process, bargains are struck between the managers responsible for the budget and their immediate superiors. The negotiations between managers in the hierarchy of an organisation represent a bargaining process where the individual goals of managers are formulated for a forthcoming budget period. Ethics case 2 provides an interesting take on the practical and ethical consequences of this negotiation process upon an organisation's use of budgets as a tool for planning and controlling its future activities.

The board has the final decision on the budget. This process involves ensuring that all the budgets are consistent with each other; for example, that the required material inventory levels are sufficient to meet the production requirements throughout the year. When all the individual budgets have been finalised and approved at this level, they are summarised into what is commonly referred to as the master budget. The master budget is usually in the form of a budgeted statement of comprehensive income and a balance sheet for the budget period. Such financial statements are identified as being prospective financial statements and they may be supplied to external stakeholders such as a bank in support of loan applications. The information in the master budget is, in effect, a summary of all the individual budgets, and it represents the overall plan for an organisation in quantitative terms. It clearly sets out the targets for the organisation in an easily understandable form and can later be compared with the actual balance sheet and statement of comprehensive income.

After final approval at board level, budgets are passed down the organisation to the respective responsibility centre managers and it is these managers who are tasked with carrying out the plans contained within each individual budget.

Plans in the form of budgets are extremely useful to an organisation, as demonstrated by the purposes identified earlier. Importantly, they compel organisations to look ahead and thereby anticipate any particular problems that might arise in the future.

The nature of budgeting that has been described so far is static, in the sense that the planning process is based upon certain assumptions and anticipated events that will occur in the forthcoming budget period. However, in reality, the business environment is dynamic and events might not turn out as anticipated in the budget. Some deviations from the budget might be so extreme as to be harmful to the organisation. For example, the cost of producing a product might be greater than anticipated when the budget was prepared, and losses might be made. Therefore, it is important that the actual events in a budget period are monitored against a budget flexed to actual activity so that corrective action can be initiated to alleviate any undesirable situations.

When undesirable deviations from the budget are caused by events that are within the organisation's control, action can be taken to ensure that such deviations do not occur in the future. In contrast, events beyond the control of the organisation, such as a downturn in the economy, could mean that the organisation has to reconsider its plans. Typically, this results in organisation's 'trimming' its operations to lower levels of activity, or diversifying into other markets. The point to note is that undesirable situations can be averted if an efficient system of control is imposed, and if the actual and budgeted performances are frequently compared.

STOP AND THINK 2

What kind of human behaviour problems might one expect if budget goals have no flexibility and are set at such a high level to be almost unattainable under normal operational conditions?

THE BUDGET PERIOD

4 LEARNING OBJECTIVE

Identify the factors that influence the choice of the budget period

The budget period normally employed by organisations is one year, which coincides with the periodic reporting requirements for general-purpose financial reports (GPFR) required by the *Corporations Act*. Most public companies, for example, are required to annually publish GPFR in conformity with approved accounting standards. There is usually a link between the information in the budgets and GPFR: an organisation's budget normally provides an ex ante (or forecast) estimate of the planned total sales for the period while the GPFR show the ex post (or actual) sales achieved for that budget period. Generally, and depending on the needs of the particular organisation and the state of the economy, the budget for the year is broken down into quarterly, monthly, four-weekly and weekly periods for control purposes. An organisation that operates in a very competitive market will want to monitor performance on a frequent basis to ensure it is maintaining its competitive position, as reflected in actual income, costs and outputs.

PREPARATION OF THE MASTER BUDGET

5 LEARNING OBJECTIVE

Summarise what is normally included in the master budget

The master budget clearly sets out the objectives and targets for the forthcoming budget period and provides a basis for coordinating individual functional budgets. In a medium-sized or large manufacturing organisation, these functional budgets usually consist of sales, production, administration, distribution and cash budgets. Sales and production budgets are discussed in the next section.

15.4 KEY CONCEPT

THE MASTER BUDGET

The master budget usually consists of the budgeted statement of comprehensive income and the balance sheet, which represents a summary of the individual functional budgets of the organisation as a whole.

Frequently, for small organisations, the statement of comprehensive income, the balance sheet and the cash budget are sufficient for the manager's needs. The information contained in these three budgeted statements provides a reasonable base from which to analyse the forthcoming period. In particular, a number of ratios and indicators can be derived, such as those relating to profitability, liquidity and financing. The use of these ratios and indicators was discussed in Chapter 10.

In Worked example 15.1 we consider the preparation of a statement of comprehensive income, a balance sheet and cash budget for a small business that is just commencing.

WORKED EXAMPLE

SIVRAJ LTD

Sivraj Ltd was formed on 1 July with a share capital of $40 000. Of this, $24 000 was immediately invested in non-current assets, leaving $16 000 cash over to fund the company's working capital requirements.

It is estimated that the non-current assets have a 10-year life and will have no residual value. Sivraj has decided to depreciate these assets using the straight-line method of depreciation. Therefore, the annual depreciation charge will be $24 000 ÷ 10 years = $2400, or, in monthly terms, $2400 ÷ 12 months = $200.

Business plans have been formulated for the first six months of operations. The cash budget for these plans is set out below.

Sales for the six months are estimated to be $600 000. However, Sivraj operates in a seasonal market and will also be allowing some of its customers to take credit. The company anticipates the following cash receipts from sales over the next six months:

	CASH RECEIPTS $
July	40 000
August	50 000
September	50 000
October	70 000
November	120 000
December	170 000
	500 000

From this breakdown of the anticipated cash received over the six-month period, it is apparent that at the end of the period there will be money owing from customers (that is, accounts receivable) of $600 000 – $500 000 = $100 000.

Materials required to meet the demand for sales are estimated to be $240 000. To allow Sivraj to maintain sufficient inventory on hand to ensure against any shortages, $260 000 worth of materials will be purchased during the period. Because of the production cycle, and the credit that Sivraj will obtain from its suppliers, the pattern and amount paid to suppliers will be as follows:

	PAYMENT TO SUPPLIERS FOR MATERIALS $
July	60 000
August	60 000
September	20 000
October	20 000
November	20 000
December	20 000
	200 000

At the end of the six-month period, the company has purchased materials costing $260 000 but has paid only $200 000 for them; thus it owes (that is, has accounts payable) of $60 000 at the end of December.

The estimated labour cost that will be incurred over the six months will be $170 000. In addition, Sivraj anticipates that overheads (excluding depreciation) of $138 000 will also be incurred during this period. Overheads and wages will be paid evenly over the six-month period apart from wages for December, which are $20 000. Also, $10 000 in taxes will be paid in December. Any cash deficits are to be financed by a bank overdraft. While interest will be payable on any cash drawn down from the overdraft facility, we will assume that such payments will be ignored for the purposes of focusing on the given forecast cash flows.

To ensure that sufficient cash resources are available, the company wishes to calculate a cash budget (forecast) on a monthly basis, as well as a budgeted statement of comprehensive income for the period and a balance sheet at the end of the period.

We will begin by constructing the three budgeted statements from the information given. This will be followed by a commentary concerning the usefulness of these statements to management. The cash budget will be considered first.

SIVRAJ LTD
CASH BUDGET FOR SIX MONTHS ENDING 31 DECEMBER

	JULY $	AUGUST $	SEPTEMBER $	OCTOBER $	NOVEMBER $	DECEMBER $	TOTAL FOR 6 MONTHS $
Cash inflows:							
Share capital	40 000						40 000
Sales receipts	40 000	50 000	50 000	70 000	120 000	170 000	500 000
Total cash inflows	80 000	50 000	50 000	70 000	120 000	170 000	540 00
Cash outflows:							
Materials	60 000	60 000	20 000	20 000	20 000	20 000	200 000
Wages	30 000	30 000	30 000	30 000	30 000	20 000	170 000
Taxation	0	0	0	0	0	10 000	10 000
Overheads	23 000	23 000	23 000	23 000	23 000	23 000	138 000
Non-current assets	24 000						24 000
Total cash outflows	137 000	113 000	73 000	73 000	73 000	73 000	542 000
Net cash flow	(57 000)	(63 000)	(23 000)	(3 000)	47 000	97 000	2 000
Balance brought forward		(57 000)	(120 000)	(143 000)	(146 000)	(99 000)	0
Balance carried forward	(57 000)	(120 000)	(143 000)	(146 000)	(99 000)	(2 000)	(2 000)

It can be seen from the cash budget for Sivraj Ltd that the inflows and outflows of cash are recorded in the budget statement when the cash is actually received or paid. There are a few main points to remember when constructing a cash budget:

- The dates of receipt and payment of cash and purchases are relevant; allowance must be made for any credit period given or received. For Sivraj Ltd, the relevant sales figures are when the cash is actually received and not when the sales are earned in the period.

- Provisions should be excluded as they do not affect cash flows. For example, depreciation on non-current assets is excluded because the cash flow associated with non-current assets occurs when the asset is purchased.

- Any inflows of capital, and outflows, such as drawings, payment of tax and dividends, must be included. In the example of Sivraj Ltd, the only relevant item of this nature is the capital that was initially injected into the business when it was formed.

- The format of the cash budget is similar to the worksheets that were introduced in Chapter 7. In the case of cash budgets, the column headings relate to the time period chosen for the budget. In this example, the requirement is monthly for six months to the 31 December. The company could have chosen weeks, for example. In such a case, there would be a column for each week of the six-month period. The time dimension depends upon the decision-making needs of the organisation's managers.

Unlike the cash budget, Sivraj Ltd's statement of comprehensive income is constructed by applying the concept of accrual accounting rather than cash flow accounting. Thus, the material cost is the cost of materials included in the sales rather than the cash paid for the materials. The depreciation charge for the six months is calculated by multiplying by six the monthly charge of $200.

SIVRAJ LTD
STATEMENT OF COMPREHENSIVE INCOME FOR THE SIX MONTHS ENDING 31 DECEMBER

	$	$
Sales		600 000
Cost of sales:		
Materials	240 000	
Wages	170 000	410 000
Gross profit		190 000
Depreciation	1200	
Overheads	138 000	139 200
Profit before tax		50 800
Tax		10 000
Profit after tax		40 800
Other comprehensive income		0
Total comprehensive income for the year		40 800

Again, Sivraj Ltd's balance sheet, like the statement of comprehensive income, is prepared on an accrual basis of accounting. After the statement, we briefly explain how the value of some of the assets and liabilities has been derived.

SIVRAJ LTD
BALANCE SHEET AS AT 31 DECEMBER

	$	$
Assets		
Current assets		
Inventory	20 000	
Accounts receivable	100 000	
Total current assets		120 000
Non-current assets		
Machinery (at cost)	24 000	
Less Accumulated depreciation	(1200)	
Total non-current assets		22 800
Total assets		142 800
Liabilities		
Current liabilities		
Bank overdraft	2000	
Accounts payable	60 000	
Total current liabilities		62 000
Net assets		80 800
Equity		
Share capital		40 000
Profit and loss		40 800
Total equity		80 800

The inventory balance on hand as at 31 December represents the difference between materials purchased ($260 000) and materials consumed in the sales during the six-month period ($240 000). Accounts receivable of $100 000 is the difference between the sales for the period and cash received. The sum of $60 000 for Accounts payable is the difference between the materials purchased ($260 000) and the cash paid over the six months ($200 000). The bank overdraft is derived from the cash budget, and is the balance at 31 December.

From a brief glance at these three budgeted statements for Sivraj Ltd, their usefulness for planning should be apparent. For example, it is predicted that although the company anticipates making an apparently healthy profit of $40 800 for the six months ending 31 December, there will be large deficits of cash during this period. The problem for Sivraj Ltd is the pattern of cash payments and receipts. High material costs are incurred in the first two months, as well as the payment for the non-current assets. In contrast, sales, the major source of cash, are greater in the latter part of the period. Identifying this situation prior to business activity commencing is extremely useful because action can be taken to reduce these cash deficits while trying to obtain any additional funding that might be required. It might be possible to get receipts from sales in earlier, either by limiting the credit given to customers or by encouraging customers to pay more promptly by offering discounts for prompt payment. This would result in cash being received earlier and reduce the monthly cash deficit.

By identifying cash shortages at this stage, Sivraj Ltd is also in a better position to finance any deficits. The bank would look more favourably on an application for an overdraft after having some insight into the future profitability of the company. This situation can be contrasted with the likely negative attitude of a bank when an application for funding is made after a business has unexpectedly gone into debt. Another alternative action to relieve the cash shortage is to raise additional equity capital to fund the cash deficits of the business.

In the analysis of the budgets of Sivraj Ltd, our main concern has been, not surprisingly, the cash deficits. If Sivraj Ltd had cash surpluses rather than deficits during the budget period, this information would also be useful to the business. By identifying surpluses at this early stage, the company would be in a better position to plan the investment of such funds (e.g. in short-term deposits) to maximise the amount of interest it could earn on otherwise surplus funds.

As mentioned, a number of other characteristics of the business can be analysed through the use of ratio analysis. In general, the major benefit of budgets of this nature to an organisation such as Sivraj Ltd is that events can be anticipated and action taken in the best interests of the company.

As discussed in Chapter 12, external funding organisations always require budgeted information from businesses, similar to that produced for Sivraj Ltd, before agreeing to lend money. This is particularly the case when small businesses, such as Sivraj Ltd, apply for bank finance.

SIVRAJ LTD
CASH BUDGET VARIANCE REPORT FOR THE MONTH OF JULY

	JULY BUDGET $	JULY ACTUAL $	VARIANCE $
Cash inflows:			
Share capital	40 000	40 000	0
Sales receipts	40 000	42 000	2 000(F)
Total cash inflows	80 000	82 000	2 000(F)
Cash outflows:			
Materials	60 000	65 000	5 000(U)
Wages	30 000	35 000	5 000(U)
Taxation	0	0	0
Overheads	23 000	24 000	1 000(U)
Non-current assets	24 000	20 000	4 000(F)
Total cash outflows	137 000	144 000	7 000(U)
Net cash flow	(57 000)	(62 000)	5 000(U)
Balance brought forward			
Balance carried forward	(57 000)	(62 000)	

Note: F = favourable; U = unfavourable

An examination of the cash budget variance report shows management that:

- Cash receipts were $2000 better than expected which may indicate higher sales
- Materials and wages costs are both $5000 higher than expected and represent potential areas of concern. Are wages costs higher because of unplanned changes in pay rates or because overtime has been worked? Both these increases in costs may require management to review prices.
- $4000 less spent on acquiring non-current assets, which may mean a better price has been obtained from the suppliers of the non-current assets or fewer assets were purchased.

CASE STUDY

SINK OR SWIM WITH CASH FLOW

ALLAN MCALISTER

Of all the elements of business and functions of business, cash flow is one of the most vital. Profit, of course, is important and I have written often of the necessity to analyse profit to assess it against budget and to use as many controls as possible to protect it. The most significant aspect about cash flow is that a problem can occur overnight whereas the profit analysis is an ongoing situation, which only really raises its head at the end of the financial year.

Bikeriderlondon/Shutterstock.com

The best method to control cash flow is to budget income and expenditure in, say, three-monthly periods. List the estimated income over the next three months and estimate purchases and expenses over the same period. This can be done on a weekly, monthly or quarterly basis. The actual income and outgoings should then be listed and placed against the budgeted elements for the same period. Variations should be noted immediately and trigger an investigation as to why.

It might be that a price increase has occurred on a bought-in product and this will show up on the actual against the budgeted comparison. The important thing is to know what has caused this variance and then alterations to the forward quarterly cash flow budget can be made to reflect this change. It's important to consider what effect this will have on overall annual budgeted result.

For example, your analysis may show that you are facing a cash flow problem in a few weeks. It is far better to advise the bank manager of this as far ahead as possible rather than have the bank ring you on a given day to advise that your account is over the limit. Comparing actual to what you have budgeted also reveals things are getting out of hand and that predicted profit is not going to be achievable.

The cash flow comparison to budget is yet another way of controlling your business and enables you to instigate action immediately. It is also of vital importance since the reduction in cash flowing in can curtail business progress. A reduction in cash can, of course, have devastating effects since a business lives on its source of finance more than profitability.

Accordingly, estimate your income and expenses, set down a budget for them and plot the actuals against them progressively. Such a program gives important protection in running your business and will protect and improve your profitability.

* Allan McAlister is a volunteer member of the non-profit Small Business Mentoring Service and has spent 21 years as a Fellow of Australia's Certified Practicing Accountants. He has had a distinguished career in the hotel, liquor and gaming industries and from 1985–1995 was president of the Collingwood Football Club.

COMMENTARY

The above article discusses the importance of cash to a business. Cash budgets are useful to help manage cash flow and allow businesses to plan to invest surplus cash at the best rates or, when cash is required, arrange borrowings at the cheapest rates. Budgets assist a business to plan where it is heading in the future and the use of budgets can help a business to get where it intends to go. It is important that the cash flows are regularly monitored.

STOP AND THINK 3

What is a master budget?

STOP AND THINK 4

Describe the main differences in the budgeting process for a small retail business and a large manufacturing business.

6 **LEARNING OBJECTIVE**

Outline the role of sales and production budgets, and the relationship between them

SALES AND PRODUCTION BUDGETS

The sales and production budgets prepared for manufacturing firms reflect the respective targets for these functions in the forthcoming budget period. Since these functions involve cash payments and receipts, they are also the source for the overall cash budget. As previously mentioned, the summation of these budgets is embodied within prospective financial statements in the form of the statement of comprehensive income, the balance sheet and the cash flow statement.

In Worked example 15.2, we will concentrate on the sales and production budgets. We also emphasise the importance of coordinating these different functions within an organisation – in particular in determining the production output level required to support the sales volume and desired inventory levels.

WORKED EXAMPLE

NADIA LTD

Nadia Ltd has gathered the following data about future sales and production requirements for the year ending 31 December:

ESTIMATED SALES

PRODUCT	UNITS	PRICE ($)	OPENING INVENTORY 1 JANUARY	DESIRED CLOSING INVENTORY 31 DECEMBER
			UNITS	UNITS
A	20 000	55	8000	10 000
B	50 000	50	15 000	14 000
C	30 000	65	6000	6000

MATERIALS USED IN MANUFACTURE

ITEM NO.	UNIT	AMOUNT PER UNIT		
		A	B	C
54	component	3	–	5
32	metres	2	1	3
44	kilograms	–	2	–

ESTIMATED PURCHASE PRICE OF MATERIALS

ITEM NO.	PRICE
54	$3 per component
32	$2 per metre
44	$4 per kilogram

LEVELS OF INVENTORY MATERIALS

ITEM NO.	OPENING INVENTORY 1 JANUARY	CLOSING INVENTORY 31 DECEMBER
54	21 000 components	25 000 components
32	17 000 m	23 000 m
44	8000 kg	10 000 kg

LABOUR REQUIREMENTS

PRODUCT	HOURS PER UNIT	RATE PER HOUR $
A	4	7
B	5	5
C	5	6

Fixed manufacturing and non-manufacturing overheads are estimated at $500 000 per year. For internal management purposes, Nadia Ltd adopts a variable costing system. Therefore, all overheads are treated as a period charge (see Chapter 14).

In this example, we presumed that the sales demand, in terms of volume, is the constraining factor. Thus, the production volume will be dependent upon the sales demand.

The management of Nadia Ltd requires the following budgetary information for the forthcoming budget period:

a. sales budget in monetary terms

b. production budget in units

c. materials-purchased budget in units

d. materials-purchased budget in monetary terms

e. materials cost per unit manufactured and sold

f. the total labour hours worked during the period and the cost, plus the labour cost per unit manufactured and sold

g. the unit contribution for each product

h. the profit and loss for the budget period

i. the value of closing finished inventory at the end of the budget period.

Sales budget in monetary terms

We have been given the price per unit and the volume of units that it is estimated will be sold. To calculate the total sales revenue generated from these sales, we multiply these two variables.

PRODUCT	UNIT × PRICE ($)	SALES REVENUE ($000)
A	20 000 × 55	1100
B	50 000 × 50	2500
C	30 000 × 65	1950
Total		5550

Production budget in units

The production level during the budget period must not only satisfy the sales demand but must ensure that the inventory levels are sufficient for the period. In the case of Nadia Ltd, the opening and closing inventory levels have been estimated, and we have been given the sales demand. From this information, with the help of a simple equation, we can determine the production level to satisfy this demand.

The equation we use, sometimes referred to as the inventory formula, is as follows (measured in units):

$$production + opening\ inventory = sales + closing\ inventory$$

It states that the units produced during the budget period plus what is in inventory at the beginning of this period are equal to the units to be sold plus the units required as inventory at the end of the period.

For our purposes, as there is only one unknown quantity (production), we need to rearrange the equation as follows:

$$sales + closing\ inventory - opening\ inventory = production$$

Applying this equation to the figures for Nadia Ltd, measured in units, we obtain the following:

PRODUCT	SALES (UNITS)	+	CLOSING INVENTORY (UNITS)	−	OPENING INVENTORY (UNITS)	=	PRODUCTION (UNITS)
A	20 000	+	10 000	−	8000	=	22 000
B	50 000	+	14 000	−	15 000	=	49 000
C	30 000	+	6000	−	6000	=	30 000

Materials-purchased budget, measured in units

Three types of materials described by item numbers 54, 32 and 44 are used in the production of A, B and C.

	MATERIALS REQUIRED PER UNIT OF PRODUCT AND IN TOTAL						
	PRODUCT A (UNITS)		PRODUCT B (UNITS)		PRODUCT C (UNITS)		ALL 3 PRODUCTS
MATERIALS							
Production (units)	22 000		49 000		30 000		Total
Raw material requirements	Per unit	Total	Per unit	Total	Per unit	Total	
No. 54	3	66 000	–	0	5	150 000	216 000
No. 32	2	44 000	1	49 000	3	90 000	183 000
No. 44	-	0	2	98 000	-	0	98 000

Before determining how many units of inventory will need to be purchased in the period, we must first calculate the number of units of inventory necessary to satisfy production requirements.

The purchase of materials that are required for the forthcoming budget period can now be calculated using a similar equation to that used in determining required production levels:

$$\text{purchases} + \text{opening inventory} = \text{production} + \text{closing inventory}$$

Purchases in this equation are measured in terms of material units; for example, components in the case of item no. 54.

The equation states that the materials required for production during the period and closing inventory at the end of the period will be met from the purchase of materials and the inventory that is available at the beginning of the period.

In this example, we are told the opening and closing inventory requirements and we have calculated the materials required for production. Therefore, three of the four variables in the equation are known to us, and by rearranging the equation we can calculate the purchases figure:

$$\text{production} + \text{closing inventory} - \text{opening inventory} = \text{purchases}$$

Applying this equation to the information that has been given for the three inventory numbers, we obtain the following:

ITEM NO.	PRODUCTION	+	CLOSING INVENTORY	−	OPENING INVENTORY	=	PURCHASES
54	216 000 components	+	25 000 components	−	21 000 components	=	220 000 components
32	183 000 metres	+	23 000 metres	−	17 000 metres	=	189 000 metres
44	98 000 kilograms	+	10 000 kilograms	−	8000 kilograms	=	100 000 kilograms

It should be remembered that the above purchases figures represent the units for the respective materials; thus, for example, in the case of item no. 54 the purchases requirement will be 220 000 components.

Materials purchased in monetary terms

The calculation of purchases, measured in monetary terms, is straightforward. We multiply the purchases, in terms of units, by the cost per unit that was given at the beginning of the example:

ITEM NO.	PURCHASES (UNITS)	COST PER UNIT ($)	TOTAL COST ($)
54	220 000	3	660 000
32	189 000	2	378 000
44	100 000	4	400 000
			1 438 000

Materials cost per unit manufactured and sold

This information might be required by management to determine the profitability of each of the products sold and for inventory valuation purposes. All the relevant information regarding this calculation has been given and it just remains for us to perform the calculation. For each unit of product, we need to multiply the cost per unit of material by the amount of the material required to manufacture each product.

ITEM NO.	COST PER UNIT OF ITEM ($)	COST ($) PER UNIT OF PRODUCT					
		PRODUCT A		PRODUCT B		PRODUCT C	
		Input	Cost	Input	Cost	Input	Cost
54	3	3	$9	–	$0	5	$15
32	2	2	$4	1	$2	3	$6
44	4	–	$0	2	$8	–	$0
	Material cost per unit sold		13		10		21

Labour

Management needs to know the total labour worked in the period, the total cost, and the cost of labour per unit of goods manufactured and sold.

We begin by computing the labour cost per unit of goods manufactured and sold. This information will provide management with data that is useful to assess profitability, and for inventory valuation purposes. The arithmetic for the calculation is simple – to obtain the total labour cost per unit we multiply the hours per unit by the rate per hour.

PRODUCT	HOURS PER UNIT	RATE PER HOUR	TOTAL LABOUR COST PER UNIT
		$	$
A	4	7	28
B	5	5	25
C	5	6	30

For calculation of the total labour hours, the production units are multiplied by the hours per unit. If we then multiply the total labour by the rate per unit, we can determine the total cost. It is important to appreciate why production units are used in these calculations rather than sales units. The reason is that the objective here is to determine how many hours were actually worked and the cost of those hours during the year. If sales units were used, we would be establishing the total hours that have been consumed in producing the sales. If there are changes between the opening and closing levels of finished inventory, the units produced will not equal the sales units sold. This was the case for products A and B, as can be seen when we determined the production levels for these two products earlier. In contrast, for product C the beginning and finished inventory levels are the same. Therefore, the production and sales units for product C are forecast to be the same; that is, 30 000 units.

PRODUCT	PRODUCTION UNITS	LABOUR HOURS		RATE ($) PER HOUR	TOTAL COST ($)
		PER UNIT	TOTAL		
A	22 000	4	88 000	7	616 000
B	49 000	5	245 000	5	1 225 000
C	30 000	5	150 000	6	900 000
			483 000		2 741 000

Unit contribution of each product

We will used the concept of contribution margin in chapters 17 and 18 in relation to cost-volume-profit analysis. The contribution per unit is equal to the sales price per unit, less variable costs per unit. The only variable costs in this example are materials and labour. These variable costs were determined earlier. Thus, the contribution per unit for these three products will be as follows:

	A		B		C	
	$	$	$	$	$	$
Sales price		55		50		65
Less Variable costs						
Material	13		10		21	
Labour	28	41	25	35	30	51
Contribution per unit		14		15		14

Profit or loss for the budget period

On the basis of information that we have been provided with thus far, we can determine the total contribution margin for the three products and then deduct the total manufacturing and non-manufacturing overhead cost to arrive at a forecast profit for the year ending 31 December:

PRODUCT	CONTRIBUTION PER UNIT ($)	UNITS SOLD	$
A	14	20 000	280 000
B	15	50 000	750 000
C	14	30 000	420 000
Total manufacturing contribution margin			1 450 000
Less Overheads			500 000
Profit			950 000

As will be discussed below, this information can then be incorporated into the prospective statement of comprehensive income. However, before considering the preparation of this financial statement, we will look at the valuation of inventories: for the cost of goods sold and the finished goods inventory.

Value of cost of goods sold and the finished goods inventory at the end of the budget period

Under the variable costing regime, inventory is valued at variable cost. From the information already obtained, we know the variable costs of each product and we multiply this cost by the number of units of sold to determine the cost of goods sold and the finished goods inventory as at 31 December.

PRODUCT	VARIABLE COST ($)	COST OF GOODS SOLD		FINISHED INVENTORY	
		UNITS SOLD	TOTAL $	UNITS UNSOLD	TOTAL $
A	41	20 000	820 000	10 000	410 000
B	35	50 000	1 750 000	14 000	490 000
C	51	30 000	1 530 000	6000	306 000
Total inventory values			4 100 000		1 206 000

The uses of sales and production budgets

Budgets, such as those presented for Nadia Ltd, act as a source of information in the construction of the projected statement of comprehensive income, the balance sheet and the cash budget. To explore the preparation of the projected financial statements for Nadia Ltd, we will use some additional information to explore how the previous calculations assist with the preparation of these statements.

PROJECTED FINANCIAL STATEMENTS

The primary purpose of budgeting is to facilitate the implementation of a firm's strategic and operational decisions. As a primary business purpose is to provide a return on the investment made by different external stakeholders in the firm (e.g. shareholders, lenders, suppliers and employees), the development of projected financial statements provides a forward-looking view of how the firm's financial performance and position might appear to these stakeholders. As discussed in Chapter 12, external stakeholders do have an interest in receiving management accounting information, however, a firm's managers would be most reluctant to release projected financial statements given that they are based upon managerial assumptions that are not readily verifiable. Since there is a high likelihood of forecast error having an unintended effect on the information contained in projected financial statements, more conservative forecast assumptions would be a consequence of managers being compelled to release these statements to external stakeholders. So conservative might these assumptions become that the budgets upon which the projected statements are prepared will no longer be as useful for managerial planning and control purposes. Nevertheless, projected financial statements can assist the decisions made by managers through:

- Providing insight on the effect of budgets on the firm's future financial performance and position, and whether expected outcomes from particular courses of action would be acceptable
- Identifying future financing needs and presenting the impact of different funding sources (e.g. debt versus equity raisings) on the capital structure (or gearing) of the firm.

15.3

WORKED EXAMPLE

NADIA LTD

The following information has been developed from the accounting records of Nadia Ltd as at 1 January and the budget papers for the year ending 31 December:

BALANCE SHEET	ACTUAL BALANCE AS AT 1 JANUARY	FORECAST BALANCE AS AT 31 DECEMBER
Cash at bank	$142 000	Not given
Accounts receivable	$450 000	$515 000
Inventories		
Raw materials	$129 000	$161 000
Finished goods	$1 159 000	$1 206 000
Non-current assets (at net book value)	$3 520 000	$3 600 000
Total assets	$5 400 000	Not given
Accounts payable	$117 000	$105 000
Wages payable	$29 000	$20 000
Dividend payable	$200 000	$220 000
Income tax payable	$180 000	Not given
Loan Payable (6 per cent per annum)	$250 000	$0

BALANCE SHEET	ACTUAL BALANCE AS AT 1 JANUARY	FORECAST BALANCE AS AT 31 DECEMBER
8% debentures payable (due 2020)	$1 500 000	$1 500 000
Total liabilities	$2 276 000	Not given
Net assets	$3 124 000	Not given
Shareholders' equity		
Contributed capital	$2 500 000	$2 800 000
Retained profits	$624 000	Not given
Total equity	$3 124 000	Not given

During the year ending 31 December, the following events are expected to occur:

- A further cash equity injection for $300 000 is expected to be raised during November.
- On 31 December, the loan payable will be paid out in full along with the annual interest expense incurred for the year.
- New plant and equipment is to be purchased during May for $200 000 cash. The purchase of the new equipment is expected to increase the total annual depreciation expense to $120 000. This depreciation charge is the only non-cash expense included in the fixed manufacturing and non-manufacturing overhead costs of $500 000.
- Due to the granting of credit early last year to a customer who has since been declared bankrupt, the outstanding debt of $35 000 is now expected to be written off in full as irrecoverable during January.
- Interest owing on the long-term 8 per cent debentures will be paid at the year's end.
- Dividends that had been declared out of the prior year's profit are expected to be paid on 21 February.
- Taxes for the current year's profit will be payable in February of the next year at the rate of 30 per cent.

Before preparing the projected financial statements, the amounts received from credit sales and payments to suppliers, employees and lenders need to be calculated.

The equation from Chapter 7 we use for cash receipts from customers, sometimes referred to as the receivables formula, is as follows (measured in $):

$$\text{Sales} + \text{opening receivables} = \text{cash collected from receivables} + \text{closing receivables} + \text{bad debts written off}$$

It states that the sales for the budget period plus what is in receivables at the beginning of this period are equal to the cash collected from receivables plus the receivables at the end of the period + bad debts written off.

For our purposes, as there is only one unknown dollar amount (cash collected from receivables), we need to rearrange the equation as follows:

$$(\text{Sales} + \text{opening receivables}) - (\text{closing receivables} + \text{bad debts written off}) = \text{cash collected from receivables}$$

$$(\$5\,550\,000 + \$450\,000) - (\$515\,000 + \$35\,000) = \$5\,450\,000.$$

The equation from Chapter 7 we use for cash payments to suppliers and employees, sometimes referred to as the payables formula, is as follows (measured in $):

> Purchases (or expense) + opening payables = cash paid to suppliers and employees + closing payables

It states that the purchases (or expense) for the budget period plus what is in payables at the beginning of this period are equal to the cash paid to suppliers and employees plus the payables at the end of the period.

For our purposes, as there is only one unknown dollar amount (payments made to each of suppliers and employees), we need to rearrange the equation as follows:

> (Purchases or expense + opening payables) − closing payables = cash paid to suppliers and employees.

Thus, the budgeted payments to suppliers would be estimated as follows:

> ($1 438 000 + $117 000) − $105 000 = $1 450 000.

Payments to employees would be calculated as follows:

> ($2 741 000 + $29 000) − $20 000 = $2 750 000.

Other cash payments that need to be accounted for are as follows:

- Manufacturing and non-manufacturing overheads $380 000. Total expense of $500 000 included a non-cash depreciation expense of $120 000.
- Dividends payable declared from last year's profits of $200 000 as at 1 January will be paid in February.
- The 6 per cent loan payable of $250 000 is to be paid back along with the annual interest expense of $15 000 (i.e. $250 000 × 6% = $15 000). Total paid = $265 000.
- Interest on the 8 per cent debentures of $1 500 000 will be paid in December. Total paid = $120 000 (i.e. $1 500 000 × 8% = $120 000).
- Income tax owing from last year's profit of $210 000 will be paid in February of this year. Total paid = $210 000. Note: the taxes payable for the current year's profits are yet to be calculated and will be paid in February of next year.

NADIA LTD
PROJECTED STATEMENT OF COMPREHENSIVE INCOME FOR THE YEAR ENDING 31 DECEMBER

	$	$
Sales		5 550 000
Less Cost of goods sold		4 100 000
Manufacturing contribution margin		1 450 000
Less Operating expenses		
Manufacturing and non-manufacturing overheads	500 000	
Bad debts written off	35 000	
Loan payable interest expense	15 000	
Debentures payable interest expense	120 000	670 000
Net profit before tax		780 000
Less Income tax expense (@ 30%)		234 000
Net profit after tax		546 000

We will now prepare the projected financial statements for the year ending 31 December.

NADIA LTD

PROJECTED BALANCE SHEET AS AT 31 DECEMBER

	$	$
Current assets		
Cash at bank	347 000	
Accounts receivable	515 000	
Inventories		
Raw materials	161 000	
Finished goods	1 206 000	2 229 000
Non-current assets (at net book value)		3 600 000
Total assets		5 829 000
Current liabilities		
Accounts payable	105 000	
Wages payable	20 000	
Dividend payable	220 000	
Income tax payable	234 000	579 000
Non-current liabilities		
8% debentures payable (due 2020)		1 500 000
Total liabilities		2 079 000
Net assets		3 750 000
Shareholders' equity		
Contributed capital		2 800 000
Retained profits [A]		950 000
Total equity		3 750 000

[A] Retained profits as at 31 December of $950 000 is the sum of the opening retained earnings ($624 000) plus the budgeted profit for the year ($546 000) less the dividends that have been declared and paid next year ($220 000).

NADIA LTD

PROJECTED CASH FLOW STATEMENT FOR THE YEAR ENDING 31 DECEMBER

	$	$
Operating cash flows		
Cash receipts from customers	5 450 000	
Payments to suppliers and employees [A]	(4 580 000)	
Interest expense paid [B]	(135 000)	
Taxes paid	(180 000)	
Net operating cash inflows		555 000
Investing cash flows		
Payment for property, plant and equipment	(200 000)	
Net investing cash outflows		(200 000)
Financing cash outflows		
Proceeds from share issue	300 000	
Dividends paid	(200 000)	
Repayment of loan payable	(250 000)	
Financing cash outflows		(150 000)

	$	$
Net increase in cash and cash equivalents		205 000
Cash and cash equivalents as at 1 January		142 000
Cash and cash equivalents as at 31 December		347 000

A Payments to suppliers and employees of $4 580 000 is the sum of payments for purchases ($1 450 000), employee wages and salaries ($2 750 000) and manufacturing and non-manufacturing overheads ($380 000).

B Payments for interest expense of $135 000 is the sum of payments for interest paid on the loan payable ($15 000) and the 8 per cent debentures ($120 000). Although interest payments can be classified as a financing cash outflow, Nadia Ltd treats interest payments as an operating cash flow consistent with past practice.

Budget figures at a corporate level are disaggregated to provide budgets for individual responsibility centres, enabling the lower-level responsibility centre managers to clearly identify that part of the organisation's plans for which they are accountable.

The budgets and projected financial statements prepared for Nadia Ltd are not suitable for all manufacturing firms, but the example illustrates the main principles in the preparation of budgets for most organisations.

STOP AND THINK 5

Why should preparers of the production budget liaise with the preparers of the sales budget?

9 **LEARNING OBJECTIVE**

Explain why, in addition to the cost budgets for materials and labour, it may also be important to construct budgets for overheads

BUDGETING FOR OVERHEAD EXPENDITURE

In Worked example 15.2, Nadia Ltd's overheads were given as one figure; that is, $500 000 per year. Normally, as mentioned in the earlier section on the budgeting process, organisations also prepare detailed budgets for overhead expenditure. These represent the planned costs associated with supporting the manufacturing function, such as machine maintenance, administration and sales. As new technology and automation are introduced into the manufacturing environment, overhead costs are growing as a proportion of the total cost of operations. Organisations should be placing more emphasis on the planning and control of such costs, but many of the systems that are in use have not been designed to cope with this change in the method of manufacturing. There is considerable debate at present about the methods of costing and budgeting that should be introduced to monitor overhead costs. These issues were addressed in our discussion of ABC in Chapter 14.

STOP AND THINK 6

What is the purpose of the cash budget and how does it differ from the projected cash flow statement?

SUMMARY

LEARNING OBJECTIVE 1

DISCUSS SOME OF THE REASONS FOR PRODUCING BUDGETS

There are a number of reasons why businesses produce a budget or budgets. Some of these reasons are:

» to encourage planning
» to provide a control mechanism
» as authorisation for expenditure
» to motivate employees
» as a form of communication
» to provide a basis for responsibility accounting.

LEARNING OBJECTIVE 2

EXPLAIN WHAT IS MEANT BY THE BUDGET PROCESS

The budget process is the sequence of operations necessary to produce a budget for a particular organisation. The operations depend upon the type of organisation and its perceived requirements for planning and control.

LEARNING OBJECTIVE 3

EXPLAIN THE STAGES AND PARTIES THAT ARE TYPICALLY INVOLVED IN THE BUDGET PROCESS

At the beginning of the budget process, consideration is given to operating decisions which involve all levels of the production cycle; for example, the manufacturing area. This can involve procurement, production, marketing, sales, and so on. It is important that all levels of lower management are involved and consulted in this process.

LEARNING OBJECTIVE 4

IDENTIFY THE FACTORS THAT INFLUENCE THE CHOICE OF THE BUDGET PERIOD

The time frame of a budget is normally one year. The reason for this period is that most public entities are required by law to publish annual accounts. However, depending on the information that is required by an entity, the budget period can be split into whatever period is required for good decision making.

LEARNING OBJECTIVE 5

SUMMARISE WHAT IS NORMALLY INCLUDED IN THE MASTER BUDGET

The master budget normally consists of the budgeted statement of comprehensive income and the balance sheet, and represents a summary of the individual functional budgets of the organisation as a whole.

LEARNING OBJECTIVE 6

OUTLINE THE ROLE OF SALES AND PRODUCTION BUDGETS, AND THE RELATIONSHIP BETWEEN THEM

The production budget prepares a production schedule to meet inventory needs, and the sales department's projected sales. It is important that there is communication between the sales and production departments so that production does not fall short of expected sales (or exceed them by too much) otherwise the business incurs the costs of lost sales or storage, and the potential loss from obsolescence.

SUMMARY

LEARNING OBJECTIVE 7

CALCULATE BUDGETS FOR MATERIALS PURCHASED IN UNITS AND IN MONETARY TERMS

Budgets for materials purchased in units are a useful indicator of inventory levels. This is necessary for production activities to be effectively undertaken. The calculation of materials purchased in monetary terms is required for the cash budget.

LEARNING OBJECTIVE 8

CALCULATE COST BUDGETS FOR MATERIALS PER UNIT MANUFACTURED AND SOLD, AND FOR LABOUR

This information might be required by management in order for it to determine the profitability of products sold, and for inventory valuation purposes.

Both materials and labour budgets are important. In relation to materials, budgets show if prices have increased or if there is wastage in the manufacturing process. In relation to labour, budgets ensure that there is not an abnormal amount of overtime worked or that labour efficiency is below what was budgeted.

LEARNING OBJECTIVE 9

EXPLAIN WHY, IN ADDITION TO THE COST BUDGETS FOR MATERIALS AND LABOUR, IT MAY ALSO BE IMPORTANT TO CONSTRUCT BUDGETS FOR OVERHEADS

The importance of overhead budgets is to keep track of planned overhead costs that support items such as supervision, administration and advertising, to name a few.

REVIEW QUESTIONS

1 Discuss the stages and parties that are typically involved in the budget process.
2 Explain how budgets mean different things to different people within an organisation, giving reasons.
3 Why should all senior personnel participate in formulating and submitting budget estimates?
4 Discuss the interrelationships between the sales budget and the production budget in a manufacturing organisation.
5 Explain, giving examples, the main advantages of identifying cash surpluses and deficits in a cash budget.
6 What determines the budget time period?
7 What is a master budget? Describe its role in relation to other budgets.

PROBLEMS FOR DISCUSSION AND ANALYSIS

1 What points need to be considered before preparing a budget?
2 Some companies, such as Volvo, no longer prepare budgets. What are the main advantages and disadvantages of using a budget?
3 Projected sales for each of the first three months of operations for AKP Ltd are as follows:

	$
March	480 000
April	590 000
May	505 000

The company expects to sell 10 per cent of its merchandise for cash. Of sales on account, 60 per cent are expected to be collected in the month of the sale, 30 per cent in the month following the sale, and the remainder in the second month following the sale.

Required

Prepare a schedule indicating cash collections from sales for March, April and May.

4 Jenny Smith, a university student, decided that she needed to prepare a cash budget on her personal finances for the months March to June inclusive. From the following information, prepare a cash budget for Jenny for each month and comment on her cash position:

	$
Cash balance at 1 March	2637
Paid guild fees, 7 March	250
Rent paid on the 1st of the month in advance	750
Monthly food bill	600
Electricity quarterly account paid, 15 May	89
Average spent monthly on entertainment	130
Part-time monthly earnings, paid on 15th of each month	850
Paid deposit on 15 June for travel during vacation	500
Purchased ticket on 10 May to Foo Fighters concert	125

5 With reference to Sivraj Ltd (Worked example 15.1), prepare a statement of comprehensive income and a balance sheet from the data, using worksheets.

6 CJH Ltd is preparing its annual budget. The following data is available:

PRODUCT	ESTIMATED SALES (UNITS)	OPENING INVENTORY (UNITS)	CLOSING INVENTORY (UNITS)
X	18	8	10
Y	50	15	15
Z	30	6	6

MATERIAL	COST PER UNIT ($)	UNITS OF MATERIAL USED PER UNIT OF PRODUCT X	Y	Z	OPENING INVENTORY (UNITS)	CLOSING INVENTORY (UNITS)
A	3	3	–	5	21	25
B	2	2	1	3	17	23
C	4	–	2	1	10	15

a   Prepare the production budget in units.

b   Give the total budgeted cost of materials used in the production of X, Y and Z.

c   Give the total cost of materials A, B and C purchased.

7   Buzzbub is preparing its quarterly production budget and the following forecast information is available:

PRODUCT	ESTIMATED SALES (UNITS)	OPENING INVENTORY (UNITS)	CLOSING INVENTORY (UNITS)
P	276	12	33
Q	33	7	6
R	99	12	15

MATERIAL	COST PER UNIT ($)	UNITS OF MATERIAL USED PER UNIT OF PRODUCT			OPENING INVENTORY (UNITS)	CLOSING INVENTORY (UNITS)
		P	Q	R		
F	76	0.5	2	–	22	8
G	8	–	3	7	102	45

Required

a   Prepare the production budget in units.

b   Give the total cost of materials used in the production of P, Q and R.

c   Give the total cost of materials purchased.

8   Kanga Meat Pie Company produces two types of pie: chicken and fish. The monthly sales budget is for sales of 20 000 chicken pies and 12 000 fish pies. Pies are snap-frozen after manufacture. For this month, opening inventory is 2000 chicken pies and 1500 fish pies. Kanga wishes to budget for a closing inventory of 20 per cent of production.

DIRECT MATERIALS	CHICKEN PIES (GRAMS)	FISH PIES (GRAMS)
Pastry	500	750
Chicken	100	–
Fish	–	150
Vegetables	400	600

The following information is available for each material:

	PASTRY	CHICKEN	FISH	VEGETABLES
Opening inventory	745 kg	100 kg	50 kg	125 kg
Estimated closing inventory	600 kg	100 kg	90 kg	200 kg
Price per kilogram	$2.00	$7.00	$10.00	$0.90

Required

a Prepare the (material) purchases budget for the month.

b Prepare the production budget for the month.

9 The finance manager of Art & Craft Direct Ltd has provided the following information:

	MATERIALS USED IN MANUFACTURE			
	ENAMEL ($)	PAINT ($)	PORCELAIN ($)	TOTAL ($)
Total purchases budgeted for June	28 580	5340	96 400	130 320
Estimated inventory, 1 June	1250	2400	4540	8190
Desired inventory, 30 June	2000	2150	5000	9150

	DIRECT LABOUR COST		
	KILN DEPARTMENT	DECORATING DEPARTMENT	TOTAL
Total budgeted for June	$36 500	$105 800	$142 300

	FINISHED GOODS INVENTORIES ($)				WORK IN PROGRESS INVENTORIES ($)
	DISH	BOWL	FIGURINE	TOTAL	
Estimated, 1 June	4180	3270	2580	10 030	2900
Desired, 30 June	3250	3940	3100	10 290	1350

BUDGETED FACTORY OVERHEAD COSTS FOR JUNE

	$
Indirect factory wages	45 800
Depreciation of plant and equipment	14 600
Power and lighting	5300
Indirect materials	3400
Total	69 100

Required

Use the information provided to prepare a budget for the cost of sales section of the statement of comprehensive income for June.

10 The owner of a business that sells fitness equipment for use in homes has requested a forecast of sales from her two salespeople for the next three months. She is trying to prepare a cash budget

for the first quarter of next financial year. The two sales representatives provide the following sales forecasts:

	JOE'S ESTIMATES $	DEBBIE'S ESTIMATES $
July	100 000	90 000
August	150 000	200 000
September	170 000	300 000
October	160 000	400 000

The following details are available:

- Inventory costs average 70 per cent of sales. Purchases are enough to cover the next month's sales and all purchases are paid in the month of purchase.
- All sales are on account. Most customers pay the total within one month of the sale. Accounts receivable as at 30 June are forecast to be $80 000.
- Fixed expenses are $30 000 per month and variable expenses are 1 per cent of sales. All operating expenses are paid in the month in which they are incurred.
- The company is expected to have cash in bank of $5000 as at 1 July. The owner wants a minimum balance of cash on hand of $5000 at the end of every month commencing from 1 July.

Required

a   Prepare two cash budgets for July to September for the estimates provided by Joe and Debbie.

b   Discuss what the owner should do in view of the differing sales estimates from Joe and Debbie.

11 The financial controller of BBQ Essentials requests estimates of sales, production and other operating data from the various administrative units every month. Selected information concerning sales and production for May is summarised as follows:

	ESTIMATED SALES FOR MAY	
SALES TERRITORY	BASIC BACKYARD MODEL PER UNIT	DELUXE MASTER MODEL PER UNIT
Sydney	3500 units @ $550	1800 units @ $1300
Hobart	2800 units @ $500	1500 units @ $1200
Perth	4000 units @ $600	2900 units @ $1500

	ESTIMATED INVENTORIES AT 1 MAY	DESIRED INVENTORIES AT 31 MAY	ANTICIPATED PURCHASE PRICE
Direct materials:			
Grates	1000 units	800 units	$15 per unit
Stainless steel	2500 kg	1900 kg	$3 per kg
Burner sub assemblies	600 units	800 units	$72 per unit

	ESTIMATED INVENTORIES AT 1 MAY	DESIRED INVENTORIES AT 31 MAY	ANTICIPATED PURCHASE PRICE
Shelves	400 units	480 units	$7 per unit
Finished products:			
Basic model	1500 units	1200 units	
Deluxe model	400 units	500 units	

	DIRECT MATERIALS USED IN PRODUCTION	
	BASIC MODEL PER UNIT OF PRODUCT	DELUXE MODEL PER UNIT OF PRODUCT
Grates	2 units	6 units
Stainless steel	25 kg	65 kg
Burner sub assemblies	1 unit	4 units
Shelves	2 units	3 units

	DIRECT LABOUR REQUIREMENTS	
DEPARTMENT	BASIC MODEL PER HOUR	DELUXE MODEL PER HOUR
Prefabrication	0.50 hours @ $12	0.60 hours @ $12
Forming	0.75 hours @ $10	1.50 hours @ $10
Assembly	1.50 hours @ $9	2.50 hours @ $9

Required

a Prepare a sales budget for May.

b Prepare a production budget for May.

c Prepare a direct materials purchases budget for May.

d Prepare a direct labour cost budget for May.

Note to instructors: The following problems are considered more suitable for use in MBA courses. However, undergraduate courses may also find them useful.

12 Borough Equipment Ltd produces two products, A and B, for sale to electrical wholesalers. The following information relates to the six months ending 31 December:

PRODUCT	BUDGETED SALES (UNITS)	PRICE PER UNIT ($)	BUDGETED INVENTORY (UNITS) 1 JULY	BUDGETED INVENTORY (UNITS) 31 DECEMBER
A	16 200	14.35	5100	8100
B	11 800	12.20	2600	6600

COMPONENTS BOUGHT IN AND USED IN MANUFACTURE:

COMPONENT	AMOUNT USED PER UNIT OF PRODUCT		PRICE ($)	EXPECTED INVENTORY 1 JULY (UNITS)	EXPECTED INVENTORY 31 DECEMBER (UNITS)
	A	B			
X	5	3	0.68	38 000	46 000
Y	2	4	0.24	13 500	19 500

LABOUR:

PRODUCT	HOURS PER UNIT	RATE PER HOUR ($)
A	2	4.50
B	1	4.00

Overheads for the six months are expected to be $25 000. The company uses a variable costing system and treats overheads as a period cost.

a Prepare the following:

    i   sales budget

    ii production budget

    iii purchases budget in terms of components

    iv purchases budget in dollars

    v total labour hours and cost for the period

    vi contribution per unit

    vii profit and loss for the period.

b Comment on the usefulness of the budgets for planning, decision making and control.

13 Alan Blue is considering going into business by opening a supermarket. Suitable premises have been found. Before granting him overdraft and lending facilities, his local bank has asked him to draw up a cash budget for the first three months of trading.

    Alan has $100 000 of his own money, which he is willing to invest in the business. The premises will have to be leased one month before opening, and inventory and staff need to be on hand two weeks prior to trading. The following information is relevant:

- Expected sales for each of the first three months of trading are: $75 000, $90 000 and $110 000.

- Costs: staff costs, $1500 per week; rent, including rates, $2000 per week, payable one month in advance; utilities, $500 per week, payable a month in arrears; insurance, $10 000, payable a year in advance; administration, $200 per week; equipment, $45 000, to be bought when the premises are first rented and to be depreciated, straight-line, over 10 years with no residual value.

- Alan is allowing a 25 per cent mark-up on all goods sold. Because he is a newly established business, all suppliers are insisting on being paid within seven days. Inventory is ordered three weeks before it is required and there is a weekly delivery. It is assumed that sales are even throughout the four-week period.

- The bank is prepared, if the cash budget indicates that there has been successful trading, to grant overdraft facilities to a maximum of $10 000, with interest set at 0.5 per cent per week. Further, the bank is prepared to grant a long-term loan of $50 000 with an interest rate of 12 per cent per annum, with interest to be paid quarterly (every 13 weeks). The long-term loan, if required, must be taken in full regardless of whether all the $50 000 is needed.
- Alan further estimates that his weekly turnover in 12 months time will be $175 000.

Required

a   Prepare a cash budget that covers all the operations until the end of the last week of the budget period.

b   Given that the forecasts are reasonable, will the business be successful?

c   Given that the turnover will increase, what other costs would you expect to increase?

14   The manager of a sports store wants to expand the size of her shop by renting the vacant premises next door. She approaches her bank with the following projections for the six months from 1 July:

STATEMENT OF COMPREHENSIVE INCOME

	$	$
Sales		400 000
Inventory costs		225 000
Profit before expenses		175 000
Purchase of shelves, counters, etc.	80 000	
Salaries and dividends	60 000	140 000
Profit after expenses		35 000
Other comprehensive income		0
Total comprehensive income for the year		35 000

CASH IN AND CASH OUT

	$	$
Cash collections		400 000
Expenditures:		
Depreciation	30 000	
Six months' rent prepaid in June	6000	
Cost of sales	185 000	
Repayment of note and interest	60 000	
Salaries and dividends	60 000	341 000
Difference		59 000

BALANCE SHEET

DEBITS	$
Cash	20 000
Furniture and fixtures	150 000
Total	170 000

CREDITS	
Accounts payable	50 000
Capital	40 000
Accumulated profits	80 000
Total	170 000

Required

The manager has asked you for your opinion about these projections. What advice would you give her?

15 Faraday Ltd is a wholesaler. The management has been extremely worried about the entity's cash position over the last few years. In January, they sought your advice and asked you to prepare a cash budget for the forthcoming months of April, May and June. In addition, they asked you to write a report on the cash position over this period, and, in particular, to identify ways in which it could be improved.

The following data is made available to you regarding the entity's operations.

- Estimated sales for the six months to 30 June are as follows:

MONTH	CREDIT SALES $	CASH SALES $
January	122 000	12 900
February	137 000	14 500
March	142 000	17 700
April	148 000	20 100
May	134 000	15 000
June	126 000	12 600

Cash is received immediately on cash sales. The entity allows customers one month's credit on sales other than those for cash.

- Purchases of goods for resale are made on credit. The entity receives two months' credit on these purchases. The purchases for the six months to 30 June are on the next page:

MONTH	$
January	62 000
February	58 000
March	71 000
April	80 000
May	54 000
June	48 000

- An inventory check at the end of last year has revealed that $45 000 of inventory, valued at cost, is considered obsolete. The entity is currently negotiating the sale of this inventory for $9500 and expects payment during May.
- Faraday's manufacturing overheads are estimated to be $12 000 per month. This includes a charge for depreciation of $2000 per month. The company takes one month to pay these expenses.
- Selling and distribution expenses are estimated to be $50 400 a year and are incurred evenly over the year. One month's credit is taken.
- In June, Faraday anticipates paying $3880 tax to the Australian Taxation Office.
- Faraday has agreed to purchase new inventory-handling equipment. The cost of $105 200 is payable in two equal instalments in April and May.
- Faraday expects to be able to buy adjacent property (costing $150 000) in June to expand its operations.
- Faraday is currently negotiating a marketing campaign with an advertising agency. The cost will be $6300 in May and $7700 in June. Payments will be made in cash.
- It is estimated that the cash balance at 1 April will be $16 000.

ETHICS CASE STUDY 1

Jetco Ltd manufactures and sells Tyrus, an automatic vacuum cleaner for swimming pools. Jetco employs 10 salespeople and pays them a commission of $50 for each Tyrus they sell. In addition, if they meet the annual budgeted sales figure of 1000 units, they receive an annual bonus of $10 000.

Sue Clean is one of the sales staff and a close friend of Roger Pool, the accountant for Jetco. One day over lunch, Sue confides in Roger about a problem that is hurting Jetco's profits. She explains that the sales target of 1000 is quite easy for the sales staff to achieve. Once achieved, there is no further financial incentive to increase sales in that year as the bonus is fixed at $10 000. Therefore, many sales staff commit customers to buy at the beginning of the following year, which may mean a delay on the delivery of the vacuum cleaners of four to eight weeks. This means that these sales are recorded next year and the salesperson is well on the way to achieving next year's target.

Discuss

a the problems for Jetco as a result of the strategies of the salespeople
b what Roger should do with this information. Should he tell management or keep it confidential as Sue requested? If management discovered that he knew of this practice and did not say anything, he could lose his job. However, if he does say something then Sue could lose her job, and Roger could lose a friend.

ETHICS CASE STUDY 2

Aussie Fries is a large Australian Securities Exchange (ASX) listed company with nine operating business divisions. Anna Karckie, the newly appointed Chief Executive Officer (CEO) of Aussie Limited, is reviewing various internal management reports about the planned performance of the company for the next two years. She is concerned by what she sees in these reports as all financial targets are achieved without exception. She recollects a comment about corporate budgeting and performance management made by Michael Jensen over a decade ago. In respect to budgeting, Jensen (2001, p. 95) offered the following opinion:

> Corporate budgeting is a joke, and everyone knows it. It consumes a huge amount of executives' time, forcing them into endless rounds of dull meetings and tense negotiations. It encourages managers to lie and cheat, lowballing targets and inflating results, and it penalizes them for telling the truth. It turns business decisions into elaborate exercises in gaming. It sets colleague against colleague, creating distrust and ill will. And it distorts incentives, motivating people to act in ways that run counter to the best interests of their companies.
>
> Source: Jensen, Michael C. (2001) 'Corporate Budgeting Is Broken - Let's Fix It', *Harvard Business Review*, Volume 79 Issue 10, November, pp. 94–101.

Apart from your normal duties, you provide advice to the Chief Executive Officer (CEO) of Aussie Fries on matters where she requires independent and thoughtful comment. In case she needs to do an impromptu presentation to the company's board of directors about the issue of budgeting as practiced in the company, she passes the above quotation to you. She indicates that she would like you to prepare a short background briefing paper summarising your views about the view on budgeting given by Jensen and how it might relate to the budgeting practices of Aussie Fries in general and each of the nine operating divisions in particular.

In getting your ideas together in preparing the background briefing paper, you appreciate that the CEO expects you to critically evaluate the quotation made by Michael Jensen in terms of what appears to be the past and current budgeting practices in the company. Where necessary, she also expects that you will refer to other relevant examples of budget practices of which you have personal experience to support and illustrate your response. You also believe that she will want you to address the challenges Aussie Fries faces in linking managerial compensation to business performance and the impact of these challenges on the use of budgets for both planning and control purposes. You remember that all divisional managers have a significant at-risk fixed annual cash bonus of $25 000 awarded on meeting a minimum return on investment (ROI) of 15 per cent per annum.

Your task is to prepare a first draft of this short background briefing paper.

SUGGESTED ANSWERS TO STOP AND THINK EXERCISES IN THE CHAPTER

1   A budget is a defined plan of action expressed in monetary terms. However, it should be stressed that different types of organisations will require different types of budgets to enable them to function effectively. The budget must match the organisation's circumstances; for example, units of production in a production budget.

The following are the main reasons that organisations introduce budgets:

» Budgets compel management to look ahead and set short-term targets. By looking ahead, management are then in a good position to anticipate potential problems.

» The introduction of budgets encourages greater coordination of the functions within the organisation. For example, a production budget can only be constructed with knowledge of the forthcoming period's sales and desired stock levels.

» Budgets may be introduced to force management to formally communicate their objectives and strategies in the forthcoming periods. Communications between staff are also enhanced in the organisation when budgets are compared periodically with actual expenditure. Discussions through this control mechanism will invariably occur regarding future actions.

» Budgets provide a basis for identifying those responsible for differing functions within an organisation and provide a basis for measuring their performance.

» If an organisation wishes to implement control mechanisms, the budget is an important part of these mechanisms. In such cases, budgets will act as a benchmark that can be compared with the actual performance of managers and operatives.

» Budgets may be introduced as a medium through which expenditure is authorised. If expenditure is contained within a budget, it implies that it has been approved by top management and no further approval is required.

» Another reason for introducing budgets in an organisation may be to motivate employees. In this sense, the budget is once again being primarily used as a target to motivate employees to reach certain levels of attainment.

2   If budget goals have no flexibility and are set too high, employees will become demotivated, which can result in poor quality work, absenteeism and so on.

3   The master budget will normally represent a summary of the individual functional budgets of the organisation as a whole. It conventionally consists of a budgeted statement of comprehensive income and a balance sheet.

4   In the case of a small retail business, the main emphasis of the budget will be on consumer sales and, in particular, the changing pattern of sales. Attention will also be given to ensuring that there are sufficient purchases to meet the demand of customers. Typically, in a manufacturing business, the budgets will be more complex due to the production process itself being complex. The emphasis here will be on the sales budget, and the production planning necessary to meet the sales budgets. The production plan will normally include functional budgets concerning direct and indirect labour, materials and bought-in parts, machining resources, stocks and overheads.

5   It is important that there is communication between sales and production departments so that production levels do not fall short of expected sales, or exceed them by too much. If there is no communication, the business may incur the costs of lost sales or storage and potential stock losses from the obsolescence of unsold inventory.

6   The cash budget helps a business to plan when to invest excess cash at the highest rates and, when necessary, to borrow cash at the cheapest rates. It also allows a business to decide when it may have the cash resources to embark on equipment upgrades. If a business is not able to pay its bills it can be forced into making arrangements with lenders that are very restrictive or ultimately into liquidation. Thus, the cash budget is a critical component of a master budget. In terms of the differences between the cash budget and the projected cash flow statement, if the definition of cash (and cash equivalents) is common, both financial documents will reveal the same net change in cash position during the budget period. However, where the two differ is that the cash budget classifies forecast cash flows during the budget period as being receipts or payments whereas the

projected cash flow statement classifies the cash flows as being one of operating, investing or financing. Cash inflows (or receipts) and cash outflows (or payments) appear in each of the three cash flow statement classifications with a net operating cash flow for operating, investing and financing cash flows being either a net inflow or outflow.

CENGAGENOW

Go to http:\\login.cengagebrain.com to link to CengageNOW, your online study tool. First take the Pre-Test for this chapter to get your Personalised Study Plan, and then:

» revise your understanding of the key terms related to budgets by completing the online crossword
» review the key concepts with online flashcards
» follow animated examples on the relationship between sales and production budgets.

After you have completed the activities in your Personalised Study Plan take the Post-Test to determine what concepts you have mastered and what you still need work on.

COST-VOLUME-PROFIT ANALYSIS

INTRODUCTION

1 LEARNING OBJECTIVE

Identify what is meant by cost-volume-profit analysis

Profit maximisation is assumed to be the primary business goal of most firms. This would be the case whether the firm is a small owner-managed business or a large listed company where the goals of the managers are aligned with those of the company's shareholders.

This chapter focuses on decisions that managers take for improving the short-run profitability of the firm. Since a firm's short-term profitability is affected by the interaction of production and sales volumes, revenues and costs, useful decision-relevant information can be obtained from cost-volume-profit (CVP) analysis. CVP analysis examines the interrelationships between cost, volume and profit at different levels of activity. Apart from making decisions about volume and pricing, this type of analysis is useful for making special decisions about whether to accept customer orders that are priced below the full cost of a product or if a department or business unit ought to be shut down. The latter application of CVP analysis will be covered in Chapter 17.

Given the strategic decision-making focus of this text, management accounting systems (MAS) must supply managers with relevant and reliable information about not only past but also future costs and revenues and the ways in which these vary at different levels of activity. In order to use this information effectively, managers should understand how costs are determined. In Chapter 14 we introduced some basic cost concepts, such as direct and indirect costs, and looked at a very simple product costing system. We then broadened our appreciation of the need for more complex MAS for determining the cost of products in a multi-product firm.

Implicit in our discussion is an assumption that a manager using CVP analysis has control over costs, revenues, production output and sales volumes. By definition, control over such factors suggests that the manager is, at a minimum, held responsible for the performance of a profit centre. Thus, when information about costs and revenues is utilised in CVP analysis, it is provided in a way that clearly indicates what the manager has effective decision-making control over. By focusing on controllable factors, the manager is able to model the results of various profit-increasing options relating to changes in selling prices, costs, and manufacturing and sales volumes. However, this is not to suggest that a manager can ignore the factors they cannot control. For example, many fixed overhead costs cannot be controlled by a manager because they cannot be readily changed in the short term or another manager is responsible for the cost incurred (e.g. corporate overheads), however, they still need to be covered if the firm is to make a profit. Thus, when making a decision about varying the pricing, cost and or volumes of products that a manager has control over, the contribution made by these products to covering non-controllable costs must be taken into account.

CVP analysis is used to calculate three key measures:

* Contribution margin (CM)

  The contribution margin describes the amount of sales (in units or dollars) that contributes to covering fixed costs and profit.

* Break-even point (BEP)

  Break-even is the point (in units or dollars) where total revenue equals total cost.

* Desired profit

  Acknowledging that profit is the primary business goal, the desired profit is calculated working backwards to determine the amount of sales (in units and dollars) required to generate a desired profit target.

With this information, we are able to model the results of a variety of possible options regarding changes in sales price, volume sold and changed expenditure in relation to variable or fixed costs. For example, if all the fixed costs for a period have already been covered by previous sales, a reduced sales price that is above the variable cost may still be beneficial to the organisation. While CVP analysis has some assumptions that may limit its usefulness, it is a helpful starting point for considering sales and relevant production and purchasing estimates.

CVP ANALYSIS

Organisations are constantly faced with decisions relating to the products and services they sell, for example:

- Should we change the selling price, and if so what would be the effect on profit?
- How many units must be sold to break even?
- How many units must be sold to achieve a specified target profit?
- Should more money be spent on advertising?

The cost data used in CVP analysis is derived from the prediction of future costs, discussed in Chapter 14.

KEY CONCEPT

16.1

CVP ANALYSIS

CVP analysis is a tool used by a firm's managers to help them make decisions by examining the interrelationships between cost, volume and profits.

BREAK-EVEN: THE GENERAL PRINCIPLES OF CVP ANALYSIS

Break-even analysis is an alternative application of variable costing and is often referred to as CVP analysis. By using variable costing techniques, it is possible to ascertain the contribution per unit. The total contribution from all sales during a period is then compared with the fixed costs for that period; any excess (or deficiency) of contribution over fixed costs represents the profit (or loss) for the period.

A firm's managers not only want to know the profit that would be made if budgeted production and sales for the year are achieved, but also the level of activity at which there is neither profit nor loss and the amount by which actual sales can fall below budgeted sales without a loss being incurred.

The underlying assumptions of CVP analysis

FIGURE 16.1 THE SALES REVENUE INCREASES IN DIRECT PROPORTION TO SALES OUTPUT

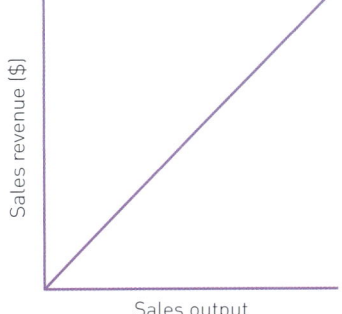

It is normally assumed in CVP analysis that sales revenues, like costs, behave in a linear fashion for varying output levels. That is, the sales price per unit sold is the same for all levels of output. Figure 16.1 illustrates a sales revenue function; the vertical axis represents the total sales revenue and the horizontal axis is the sales output levels.

It can be seen that the sales revenue function increases in direct proportion to sales output. This is because the selling price is the same for every unit that is sold.

The sales function is similar to the cost functions considered in Chapter 14. Only the one independent variable, sales volume, is considered for revenue. Total costs comprise the sum of total fixed and variable costs. The only additional variables required for CVP analysis are sales price and profit, being the difference between total sales revenue and total costs.

The basic principle behind CVP analysis is if one extra unit is produced, then the costs that vary with production will increase. Therefore, the costs that vary with changes in activity need to be identified (i.e. variable costs). The variable manufacturing cost per unit of a product comprises: direct materials, direct labour and variable manufacturing overheads, such as the cost of power consumed. On the other hand, overheads such as rent, rates and heating will remain the same even if an extra unit is produced. They are fixed and, within the relevant range, are not immediately influenced by changing levels of production.

THE CONTRIBUTION MARGIN METHOD

2 LEARNING OBJECTIVE

Explain and apply the contribution margin approach to measuring break-even sales levels and other sales levels for required profits

The contribution margin is the difference between sales value and the variable cost of sales. For example, if an item has a variable cost of $10 a unit, and is sold for $12 a unit, each sale generates a contribution margin of $2. This contribution will go towards covering the fixed overheads of the business, and once these have been covered, the excess is profit. If the business has fixed overheads of $10 000 a year, the first 5000 units sold will generate enough contribution to pay the fixed overheads of the year, and any further sales contribute $2 a unit clear profit. In any business, the total contribution from all sales during a period can be compared with the fixed costs for that period; any excess of contribution over fixed costs (or of fixed costs over contribution) represents the profit (or loss) for the period.

Thus, algebraically, the contribution margin (C) is equal to the sales price per unit (SP), less the variable cost (VC) per unit; that is:

$$C = S - VC$$

16.2 KEY CONCEPT

CONTRIBUTION MARGIN

The contribution margin is sales revenue less all variable expenses.

The contribution margin is a very important concept and is widely used by managers when making short-term decisions. For example, as the major costs of hotel and airline companies are fixed, the contribution margin is an important concept for making decisions about the pricing of hotel rooms or airline tickets and the use of otherwise idle capacity. Airline companies prefer to operate flights when an aircraft is close to full capacity. As the depreciation of an aircraft will not be any less if it flies with only 50 per cent capacity when compared to 100 per cent capacity, the airline would want to ensure that all otherwise empty seats are filled with passengers who make a contribution towards covering the fixed cost of operating the plane. Similarly, as the major expense for a hotel is the depreciation of the building, a hotel company would want high occupancy rates every night to generate a contribution towards covering the fixed cost of operating the hotel. Airline and hotel companies use complex pricing structures, with varying levels of discount, so as to ensure that no seat or hotel room remains empty. Provided a positive contribution is made across these different pricing strategies, profit will be enhanced. We will examine these ideas in more detail in Chapter 17.

The break-even point (BEP) can be calculated arithmetically. The number of units that must be sold in order for the organisation to break even is equal to the total fixed costs divided by the contribution margin per unit. This is because the contribution required to break even must be an amount that exactly equals the total amount of fixed costs.

$$\text{Break-even point (BEP) Units to be sold} = \frac{\text{Total fixed costs}}{\text{Contribution margin per unit}}$$

WORKED EXAMPLE

16.1

THE BREAK-EVEN POINT

Lucky Limited provides the following revenue and cost data:

- Expected sales 120 000 units at $10 $1 200 000
- Variable cost $6 per unit
- Fixed costs $360 000

REQUIRED:

Compute the BEP.

The contribution per unit is	=	$10 – $6
	=	$4
BEP	=	$360 000/$4
	=	90 000 units
In sales revenue, the BEP	=	(90 000)($10)
	=	$900 000

Sales above $900 000 will result in profit of $4 for each unit of additional sales and sales below $900 000 will result in a loss equivalent to (90 000 units – actual units sold) × ($4).

		SALES	
	89 999 units	90 000 units	90 001 units
	$	$	$
Revenue	899 990	900 000	900 010
Less Variable costs	539 994	540 000	540 006
Contribution margin	359 996	360 000	360 004
Less Fixed costs	360 000	360 000	360 000
Profit/(loss)	(4)	0	4

STOP AND THINK 1

Define the term 'break-even point'.

16.3

KEY CONCEPT

CONTRIBUTION MARGIN RATIO

The contribution margin ratio is the contribution margin divided by sales revenue. This shows the proportion of each sales dollar available to cover fixed costs and contribute to profit.

The contribution margin ratio

An alternative way of calculating the BEP to give an answer in terms of sales revenue is as follows:

$$\text{Sales revenue at BEP} = \frac{\text{Total fixed costs}}{\text{CM ratio}}$$

The contribution margin ratio is also sometimes called a profit/volume or P/V ratio. In Worked example 16.1, the contribution margin ratio is 40 per cent (i.e. $4 ÷ $10). Therefore, the break-even is where sales revenue = $900 000 (i.e. fixed costs of $360 000 ÷ 0.40). At a price of $10 per unit, break-even sales are 90 000 units.

The contribution margin ratio is a measure of how much contribution is earned from each $1.00 of sales. The contribution margin ratio of 40 per cent in Worked example 16.1 means that for every $1.00 of sales, a contribution of $0.40 is earned.

16.2

WORKED EXAMPLE

CONTRIBUTION MARGIN RATIO AND BREAKEVEN SALES REVENUE

The contribution margin ratio of Product Keewee is 20 per cent. EnZ Ltd, the manufacturer of Product Keewee, wishes to make a contribution of $1 000 000 towards fixed costs.

REQUIRED:

BEP (in sales revenue)	=	$\dfrac{\text{Total required contribution margin to cover fixed costs}}{\text{Contribution margin ratio}}$
	=	$\dfrac{\$10000000}{20\%}$
	=	$5 000 000
BEP (in sales units)	=	$\dfrac{\$5000000}{\$10}$
	=	500 000 units

		SALES	
	499 999 units	500 000 units	500 001 units
	$	$	$
Sales revenue (100%)	4 999 990	5 000 000	5 000 010
Less Variable costs (@ 80% of sales)	3 999 992	4 000 000	4 000 008
Contribution margin (@ 20% of sales)	999 998	1 000 000	1 000 002

- What is the total sales revenue to be generated from Product Keewee to achieve contribution of $1 000 000 towards fixed costs?
- How many units would be required if the selling price for Product Keewee is $10 per unit?

STOP AND THINK 2

Define the term 'contribution margin' and how it is measured for use in CVP analysis.

THE MARGIN OF SAFETY

In budgeting, the margin of safety is a measure by which the budgeted volume of sales is compared with the volume of sales required to break even. It is the difference in units between the budgeted sales volume and the break-even sales volume and it is sometimes expressed as a percentage of the budgeted sales volume. It may also be expressed as the difference between the budgeted sales revenue and break-even sales revenue, expressed as a percentage of the budgeted sales revenue.

3 LEARNING OBJECTIVE

Explain and calculate the margin of safety

16.3

WORKED EXAMPLE

MARGIN OF SAFETY

Mo-aye Ltd makes and sells a product that has a variable cost of $30 and which sells for $40. Budgeted fixed costs are $700 000 and budgeted sales are 80 000 units.

- Calculate the BEP.
- Calculate the margin of safety.
- Comment on the information revealed by the margin of safety.

a. *BEP*

BEP (in units to be sold)	=	Total fixed costs / Contribution margin per unit
	=	$700 000 / ($40 − $30)
	=	70 000 units

b. *Margin of safety*

Margin of safety	=	Budgeted sales - breakeven sales / Budgeted sales
	=	80 000 − 70 000 / 80 000
	=	12.5% of budgeted sales

c. *The margin of safety indicates to management that actual sales can fall short of budget by 10 000 units or 12.5 per cent before the BEP is reached and no profit is earned.*

BREAK-EVEN ANALYSIS MODELS

Before we look at the construction of the break-even analysis models, we need to establish the assumptions upon which break-even analysis is based. These assumptions include the following:

- It is assumed that fixed costs are the same in total and variable costs are the same per unit at all levels of output. As discussed in Chapter 14, this assumption is highly questionable for many firms.

- It is assumed that selling prices will be constant at all levels of activity. This may not be true, especially at high volumes of output where prices have to be reduced to stimulate higher sales volumes.
- Production and sales are assumed to be the same. Therefore, the consequences of any increase in inventory levels (when production exceeds sales) or de-stocking (when sales exceed production) are ignored.

Although these assumptions limit the extent to which break-even analysis reflects reality, it can still be used in deriving the formulae to explain how costs and revenues behave.

The total revenue formula

We assume that the selling price is constant at all levels of activity. Therefore, total revenue is equal to the selling price per unit multiplied by the quantity sold.

This can be written as $TR = Px$ where:

TR = total revenue

SP = selling price per unit

x = sales volume or quantity sold

The total cost formula

Total costs typically comprise fixed costs and variable costs. Since fixed costs are assumed to be the same in total and variable costs per unit remain the same whatever the level of output, the following equation can be written as $TC = FC + VCx$ where:

TC = total costs

FC = total fixed costs

VC = variable cost per unit

x = quantity sold

The total profit formula

Total profit (TP) is the difference between total revenue and total cost and this is:

$p = TR - TC$

$p = TR - TC$

$= xSP - (FC + xVC)$

$= x(SP - VC) - FC$

The total contribution formula

The contribution margin per unit (K) is the difference between the selling price per unit and the variable cost per unit. This can be written as $K = (SP - VC)$ where:

$$K = \text{contribution per unit}$$

The formula for total contribution, TK, is therefore:

$$TK = x(SP - VC)$$

A comparison of the formulae for total contribution and total profit reveals that the difference between them is, obviously, FC, the total fixed costs.

What happens at the BEP?

Having established the formulae necessary to solve any break-even analysis problem, consider what happens to the formulae at the BEP.

At the BEP, neither profit nor loss occurs and so p = 0.

We know that p = TR − TC.

If TP = 0 then 0 = TR − TC and so TC = TR, that is, total revenue equals total costs.

If TR = SPx and TC = FC + VCx,

at the BEP, SPx = FC + VCx and so x(SP − VC) = FC

Remember that TK = x(SP − VC) and so, at the BEP, TK = FC.

16.4

WORKED EXAMPLE

USING THE BREAK-EVEN FORMULAE

The budgeted annual output of a factory is 240 000 units. The fixed overheads amount to $200 000 and the variable costs are $1.00 a unit. The selling price is $2.00 a unit.

- Calculate the budgeted profit.
- Ascertain the BEP.
- Determine the margin of safety in units and as a percentage of budgeted sales revenue.

a. *Budgeted profit*

	$
Sales (240 000 units @ $2)	480 000
Less Variable costs (240 000 units @ $1)	240 000
Contribution margin (240 000 units @ $1)	240 000
Less Total fixed costs	200 000
Total profit	40 000

b. *BEP*

FC   = $200 000
VC   = $1.00
SP   = $2.00
BEQ = breakeven quantity

    At the breakeven point

TK   = FC
but TK   = x(SP − VC)
and so
x(SP − VC) = FC

    Substituting the values given

x($2 − $1)   = $200 000
so
BEQ   = $200 000 ÷ $1.00
            = 200 000

c. *Margin of safety*

In units	$= 240\,000 - 200\,000$ units
	$= 40\,000$ units
% $ sales	$= \$80\,000$ of revenue
	$= \$80\,000 \div \$480\,000$
	$= 16.67\%$ of budgeted revenue

STOP AND THINK 3

What is the margin of safety?

4 LEARNING OBJECTIVE

Explain what is meant by a break-even chart

THE BREAK-EVEN CHART

A useful method of illustrating the relationships between cost, volume and profit is a **break-even chart**, which is also known as a CVP chart. The relationship between these variables is plotted on a graph. The cost and sales revenue functions, which in previous illustrations have been shown separately, are now included together in the break-even chart.

FIGURE 16.2 THE BREAK-EVEN CHART FOR BOYCOTT INDUSTRIES

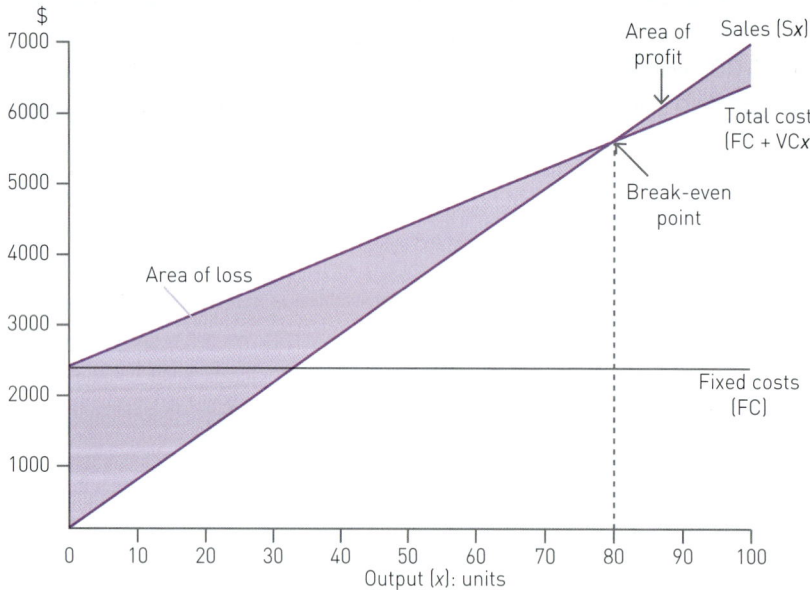

Figure 16.2 shows the break-even chart for Boycott Industries. You will notice that in the construction of this chart the variable costs are plotted above the fixed costs, resulting in a total cost function that rises from the intercept at $2400 and increases at the rate of $40 per unit. Another way of constructing

the total cost function in break-even charts will be illustrated later. The main advantage the chart provides to management is that the BEP and the areas of loss and profit can be identified clearly and quickly. Referring to the chart enables management to establish the effect of varying output levels that it examines and to determine the impact of volume changes upon business profitability.

16.1 CASE STUDY

AKARA EYES EXPANDED OUTPUT
BY NANCHANOK WONGSAMUTH

Thailand's largest gold miner, Akara Mining, expects to increase its production capacity by 2.7 million tonnes next year, raising its revenue to 5 billion baht, after this year's revenue fell short of estimates by 40 per cent due to the floods, says CEO Pakorn Sukhum.

The floods, which have disrupted logistics and mining attempts, have also delayed plans to construct a second processing plant with a production capacity of 2.7 million tonnes of ore per year. The 4-billion-baht plant will be funded partly by bank loans of 3 billion baht. Akara has production capacity of 2.3 million tonnes. Mr Pakorn said construction should be finalised by April or May next year.

The company estimates gold production this year to total 60 000–70 000 ounces, short of its target of 100 000 ounces. It attributed some of the blame to the closure of some pits because communities complained about environmental effects, said Mr Pakorn. But gold prices this year averaged US$1500 per ounce, which has helped balance out the low production volume, he said. 'If [the gold price] drops to $1400–1500, it would be very bad for us,' he said, adding the break-even point is $1100.

Nanchanok Wongsamuth, *Bangkok Post*, 22 December 2011

The above article discusses gold production for Akara Mining and states that it expects the production of gold may be between 60 000 and 70 000 ounces this year. If the price of gold falls to US$1100 per ounce the company will only break even. Hence, the price of gold is a key factor in decisions about level of production for Akara Mining. The greater the price above $1100, the higher the company's profits. If the price fell below $1100, and management was of the opinion it was likely to remain below this price for some time, managers would assess whether the mine should suspend production until the price rose above $1100.

Figure 16.3 is another version of the break-even chart, in which the total cost function is constructed by first plotting the variable costs and then adding the total fixed costs parallel to the total variable cost line. By constructing the total cost function in this way, we can identify the impact of the contribution margin on profitability; being the difference between the sales revenue and variable cost functions, as shown on the chart.

FIGURE 16.3 THE BREAK-EVEN CHART FOR BOYCOTT INDUSTRIES, SHOWING THE CONTRIBUTION MARGIN

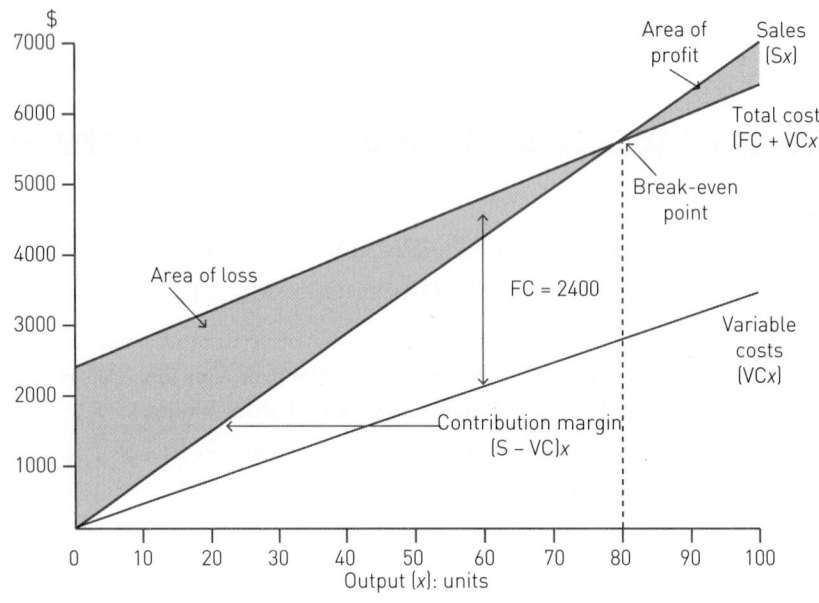

CASE STUDY

AMEX SOUNDS LTD

Amex Sounds Ltd is a company that specialises in the sale of domestic electronic sound equipment. The company purchases goods from manufacturers and sells them to the retail trade. A high proportion of the goods it sells is manufactured abroad and imported. Since starting five years ago, the organisation has been very successful, in terms of sales and profit growth. The managing director has recently been offered an exclusive contract to sell a DVD player that is manufactured in South Korea. Although this player has been sold successfully in the USA, it has yet to be sold in the Australasian market.

The company is currently assessing whether or not to enter into the contract. The following information relates to the estimated costs and revenues of the contract.

A market survey has been completed with the help of a market consultant. At a price of $40 per player, the estimated sales in the first year would be 9500 players. This is considered to be the most realistic price and volume level for the forthcoming year, taking account of competition.

The procurement cost of each recorder will be $19.50. This includes the cost of packaging and shipment. The contract specifies that this price will be fixed for one year from the contract date. Variable costs, other than the cost of the player, are estimated to be $3.00 per player sold.

The company is currently trading from a rented warehouse in Sydney. However, there is very little space for further expansion. After considering location and cost, it is decided that a warehouse in Parramatta will be rented and used exclusively for the sale of these recorders, if the contract is accepted. Parramatta has been chosen primarily because the cost of renting premises there is lower than in the inner city and a pool of potential warehouse employees is readily available. The rent for the warehouse will be $46 000 per annum and it is estimated that salaries will be $65 000 per year. Other fixed costs are anticipated to be $15 000.

The following table summarises the costs per unit that will be incurred in selling the DVD player.

	COSTS
	$
Variable costs per unit	
Purchase price of DVD players	19.50
Other variable costs	3.00
Total variable costs per unit	22.50
Fixed costs (per year)	
Rent of warehouse	46 000
Salaries	65 000
Other fixed costs	15 000
Total annual fixed costs	126 000

When deciding whether or not to accept this contract, CVP analysis will be a useful aid. We begin by determining the profit for the estimated sales of 9500, first rearranging the equation used earlier:

p = TR – TC

Where:

TR = total revenue [$40 × 9500 units]

SP = selling price per unit [$40.00]

x = sales volume or quantity sold [9500 units]

TC = FC + VCx

TC = total costs [$126 000 + ($22.50 × 9500)]

FC = total fixed costs [$126 000]

VC = variable cost per unit [$22.50]

p = TR – TC

= xSP – (FC + xVC)

= x(SP – VC) – FC

= 9500 × ($40.00 – $22.50) – $126 000

= $166 250 – $126 000

= $40 250

To determine the number of units which need to be sold to break even, p = 0. Thus, using the formula for calculating the BEP gives:

SPx = VCx + FC + p

40.00x$ = 22.50x$ + $126 000 + $0

17.50x$ = $126 000

x = $126 000 ÷ $17.50

x = 7200 units

The difference between the BEP and the estimated sales in terms of units is $9500 - 7200 = 2300$ units. This would give Amex Sounds a margin of safety in percentage terms of approximately 24 per cent (i.e. $2300 \div 9500 \times 100$).

Clearly, the information derived from our analysis is useful in the assessment of this contract. In particular, the determination of the break-even point gives the managers of Amex Sounds a basis from which to evaluate the risk associated with the contract. Knowledge that there is a margin of safety of 2300 units will be useful in this assessment.

We now extend our analysis to consider advertising. It will be assumed that costs and revenues listed earlier remain constant with the exception of any effect associated with advertising.

The company consults an advertising firm regarding the sales of the players. Two separate strategies are proposed.

1. Expenditure on advertising of $21 000 will increase the sales volume in the year to 10 300 units.

2. Expenditure of $28 000 will increase the sales volume in the year to 11 500 units.

These two strategies will be considered separately and compared with the original analysis above, taking into account the profit and break-even levels.

1 Advertising costs $21 000, sales volume 10 300 units

The advertising costs are classified as fixed costs; therefore, fixed costs will now be $126 000 + $21 000 = $147 000. Using the equation, we can determine the profit:

$$p = x(SP - VC) - FC$$
$$p = [10\,300 \times (\$40.00 - \$22.50)] - [\$126\,000 + \$21\,000]$$
$$p = \$180\,250 - \$147\,000$$
$$p = \$33\,250$$

The BEP in sales units is given by:

$$BEQ_x = FC \div CM \text{ per unit}$$
$$= \$147\,000 \div \$17.50$$
$$= 8400 \text{ units}$$

This proposal, we can safely say, will not be attractive to Amex Sounds because profits are $40 250 - $33 250 = $7000 lower than the original proposal, and the risk is greater because the break-even point is higher by $8400 - 7200 = 1200$ units.

2 Advertising costs $28 000, sales volume 11 500 units

Fixed costs increase to $126 000 + $28 000 = $154 000.

$$p = [11\,500 \times (\$40.00 - \$22.50)] - [\$126\,000 + \$28\,000]$$
$$p = \$201\,250 - \$154\,000$$
$$p = \$47\,250$$

The BEP in sales units is:

$$BEQ_x = FC \div CM \text{ per unit}$$
$$= \$154\,000 \div \$17.50$$
$$= 8800 \text{ units}$$

In this case, the decision as to whether to use advertising is somewhat more complex. First, the profit will increase by $7000 (i.e. $47 250 - $40 250), which presumably will be attractive to Amex Sounds. However, the risk (measured in terms of break-even analysis) is greater, because the break-even point has risen from 7200 to 8800 units.

The analysis of these advertising strategies, in terms of profit and break-even points, is clearly useful in determining whether Amex Sounds should use advertising. However, it is important to appreciate that this is only some the information needed to evaluate such a proposal. For example, it is also necessary to consider the effect on cash flow. It is likely that Amex Sounds will require additional funds to support an advertising campaign and this should be taken into account.

The choice of employing a linear or a non-linear function to represent sales in the CVP analysis, once again, depends on the costs and benefits of the information.

In the example of the application of CVP analysis, we examined a one-product firm – Boycott Industries. In reality, most firms produce more than one type of product. There are particular problems associated with the application of CVP analysis in multi-product firms.

In many cases, there are interdependencies between the production and demand of two or more of the firm's products. For example, the demand for one product, such as butter, might be affected by the demand for another product, such as margarine. In these cases, it is necessary to examine the CVP relationships together. This will not cause a problem if the sales mix (the proportion of sales volumes of the interdependent products) and the profit margins are the same. If the sales mix changes, the overall volume targets might be achieved, but the effects on profits will depend on whether the product of higher or lower margin dominates the mix.

Not all costs are fixed or variable. Some costs are *mixed costs*, having both a fixed and a variable component. For example, a computer sales representative might be paid $1000 a month plus $100 for each computer sold.

Fixed costs represent another problem in the application of CVP analysis in multi-product firms. If the fixed cost can be identified with particular products, there is no cause for concern. But if fixed costs are of a general nature, for example, corporate head office expenses, they will have to be apportioned or allocated on some fairly arbitrary basis. This could be misleading and lead to inaccurate CVP-related decisions.

If one or more of the resources available to a firm is scarce, there will be a constraint on the potential total sales output. The problem is how the resources should be allocated among the products. This depends on how effectively each product uses the resource. Chapter 17 will examine this problem in more detail.

LIMITATIONS OF CVP ANALYSIS

5 LEARNING OBJECTIVE

Discuss the limitations of using a linear cost assumption in CVP analysis

The CVP model that has been examined and illustrated in this chapter has been assumed to be linear. The assumptions and limitations of a linear cost function were covered in the discussion of cost behaviour in Chapter 14, and these are relevant to the CVP model.

It is assumed that at all levels of output the total fixed costs are the same and variable costs are the same per unit. This assumption is rarely valid in practice. Total fixed costs will change if output falls or increases substantially (most fixed costs are step costs). The variable cost per unit will decrease where economies of scale are realised at higher output volumes, and the variable cost per unit will also eventually rise where diseconomies of scale begin to appear at yet higher volumes of output (for example the extra cost of labour overtime).

It is important to remember that although CVP analysis is based on the assumption that total fixed costs and the variable cost per unit are constant, this is only correct within a normal range or relevant range of output. It is generally assumed that both the budgeted output and also the break-even point of sales lie within a given relevant range.

As it is assumed that the sales price will remain constant for all levels of activity, sales are also assumed to be a linear function. Empirical evidence suggests that this is unlikely for the majority of products and services. A more realistic sales function would be represented by a curvilinear pattern. Yet although the assumption of a linear function seems to be too simplistic, there is evidence that within the relevant range of activity, the sales function – like cost – does approximate to a linear pattern.

In spite of its limitations, CVP analysis is a useful technique for managers in planning sales prices, determining the desired sales mix and short-term profitability.

- There are two other significant limitations of CVP analysis. Production and sales are assumed to be the same. Therefore, the consequences of any increase in inventory levels (when production volumes exceed sales) or de-stocking (when sales volumes exceed production levels) are ignored.
- Uncertainty in the estimates of total fixed costs and unit variable costs is often ignored in CVP analysis, and some costs (for example mixed costs and step costs) are not always easily categorised or partitioned into fixed and variable components.

Although CVP analysis should be used with a full awareness of its limitations, it can usefully be applied to provide simple and quick estimates of break-even volumes or profitability given variations in sales price, sales mix, variable and fixed costs and sales volumes, within a relevant range of output/sales volumes.

SUMMARY

LEARNING OBJECTIVE 1

IDENTIFY WHAT IS MEANT BY COST-VOLUME-PROFIT ANALYSIS

CVP analysis is a technique that is used by organisations to assist them in making decisions by examining the interrelationships between cost, volume and profit.

LEARNING OBJECTIVE 2

EXPLAIN AND APPLY THE CONTRIBUTION MARGIN APPROACH TO MEASURING BREAK-EVEN SALES LEVELS AND OTHER SALES LEVELS FOR REQUIRED PROFITS

The contribution margin is the sales revenue less all variable costs. Provided that the variable costs are less than the sales revenue, then there is a contribution towards reducing the cost of the fixed overheads. By using this approach, the break-even point can be calculated — along with a profit figure that is required above break-even.

LEARNING OBJECTIVE 3

EXPLAIN AND CALCULATE THE MARGIN OF SAFETY

The margin of safety is the excess of budgeted (or actual) sales revenue over break-even sales. The margin of safety can also be measured as the excess of budgeted (or actual) units sold over break-even sales in units.

LEARNING OBJECTIVE 4

EXPLAIN WHAT IS MEANT BY A BREAK-EVEN CHART

Break-even is a point in CVP analysis where costs are equal to revenues; therefore, at this level of activity, there is no loss or profit.

LEARNING OBJECTIVE 5

DISCUSS THE LIMITATIONS OF USING A LINEAR COST ASSUMPTION IN CVP ANALYSIS

CVP analysis is a useful tool, however there are certain problems associated with its use. They are as follows:

» There is an assumption that all costs and revenues are linear. For example, costs may increase in order to gain extra sales (advertising) or fixed costs could change and follow a stepped path.

» It is assumed that we are dealing with a single-product firm. Where a firm produces more than one product, allocating costs can be a problem.

» Not all costs are fixed or variable, some may be mixed; for example, sales staff being paid a wage and a bonus on sales.

» In a multi-product firm, fixed costs may be difficult to allocate; for example, the heating of premises. A suitable allocation method will need to be found.

REVIEW QUESTIONS

1 What are the problems associated with CVP analysis in a multi-product firm?

2 Explain why the contribution margin produces profit when an entity sells goods above the break-even point.

3   Suppose a firm with a contribution margin ratio of 0.3 increased advertising expenses by $10 000 and found sales increased by $30 000. Why is this simple problem an important one?

4   If the fixed costs associated with a product increase while variable costs and the selling price per unit remain constant, briefly explain what will happen to:

  a   contribution margin

  b   breakeven point.

5   In undertaking CVP analysis, several important assumptions must be made. Identify and briefly explain two such important assumptions.

6   Why is it useful to prepare a CVP chart when illustrating the impact of changing volumes on revenues, costs and profits?

7   How can CVP analysis assist a firm to make decisions about next year's selling prices, production volumes and promotional expenditures?

8   Manufacturing firms that utilise advanced manufacturing technologies typically have a higher proportion of their cost structure comprised of fixed costs. Briefly discuss what this might mean in terms of contribution margin per unit sold, the break-even point in unit sold and the margin of safety.

9   What is meant by the term 'sales mix' and why is it important in determining the break-even point in a multi-function firm?

10 Happy Ltd sells products X, Y, and Z. The budgeted sales mix for the three products is 50 per cent of X, 30 per cent of Y and 20 per cent for Z. The budgeted contribution margins per unit are $2.00 for X, $2.50 for Y, and $3.25 per unit for Z. Annual total fixed costs are budgeted to be $720 000. How many units of products X, Y and Z would Happy Limited sell at the budgeted break-even point?

11 Activity-based costing (ABC) is said to give a better understanding of the true cost behaviour of many manufacturing overheads. For example, many fixed manufacturing costs previously perceived as being fixed vary according to the number of batch- or product-sustaining level activities undertaken. How might ABC influence management's use of CVP analysis?

12 Chaos Ltd distributes products into markets with a downward sloping demand curve. The budget for next year is forecasting that the company will be lucky to break even. At a recent meeting of the corporate executive, it was suggested that Chaos Ltd ought to increase the selling prices of its products in an attempt to lower the break-even point and decrease the likelihood of a loss being incurred. Critically evaluate this suggestion.

13 Identify and briefly discuss the limitations of CVP analysis for making short-term managerial decisions.

PROBLEMS FOR DISCUSSION AND ANALYSIS

1   In the table below, fill in the blank spaces.

	SALES	VARIABLE COSTS	FIXED COSTS	TOTAL COSTS	PROFIT	CONTRIBUTION
	$	$	$	$	$	$
a	2 000	1 400		2 000		
b	3 000		600		1 000	
c		1 000		1 600	2 400	
d	4 000		600		400	

2 In the table below, fill in the blank spaces.

	SALES	VARIABLE COSTS	FIXED COSTS	TOTAL COSTS	PROFIT	CONTRIBUTION
	$	$	$	$	$	$
a	7 249	1436		7250		
b	3 642		1 028		738	
c		8 321		8 321	932	
d	634		236		83	

3 With a sales figure of $500 000, Fidget Ltd reaches the break-even point for widget sales. Fixed costs are $200 000.

   a What is the contribution margin?

   b If variable costs are $6 per widget, what is the selling price?

   c If 55 000 widgets are sold, calculate the profit/loss.

4 Remember Enterprises manufactures miniature digital diaries. Variable costs are $30 per diary, the price is $45, and fixed costs are $90 000.

   Required

      a What is the contribution margin for one diary?

      b How many diaries must Remember Enterprises sell to break even?

      c If Remember Enterprises sells 6300 diaries, what is the net profit?

5 Mr Potter sells various pottery items at local markets. His fixed expenses (depreciation on the kiln, utilities, tools and portable selling booth) are $5000 per year. The average price for a piece of pottery is $5.50, and the average variable cost (e.g. clay, paints, glazes and price tags) is $3.50 per item.

   Required

      a How many pieces of pottery must Mr Potter sell to cover his expenses?

      b If Mr Potter wants to earn $7000 profit, how many pieces of pottery must he sell? Prepare a statement of comprehensive income (using variable costing) to verify your answer.

6 Hayley and Peter Brush have started their own business, Cleaner Homes, which offers cleaning services for households. The Brushes have fixed expenses of $4000 per month for office rent, advertising and a receptionist. Variable expenses for the cleaners' wages and cleaning supplies are $22 per job. Cleaner Homes charges $42 for the average job.

   Required

      a How many jobs must Cleaner Homes average each month to break even?

      b What is the net profit for Cleaner Homes in a month with 240 jobs? With 190 jobs?

      c Suppose that Cleaner Homes decides to increase the price to $45 per job. What is the new break-even point in the number of jobs per month?

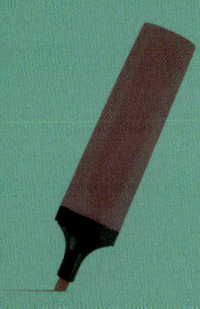

7   Clean-it Pty Ltd makes washing machines, and with its existing plant capacity the maximum production possible is 1000 units per year. Fixed costs are estimated at $36 000 per annum and the selling price of each machine is $240. Sales for the next year are expected to drop to 800 units. The cost of each washing machine is calculated as follows: direct material cost, $40; direct labour cost, 10 hours at $8 per hour.

a   Calculate (i) the break-even point (ii) the maximum profit and (iii) the profit at an estimated sales level of 800 units.

b   Costs alter by the following proportions:
    • direct materials increase by 20 per cent
    • fixed costs come down by $12 000
    • direct labour costs increase by $2 per hour.
    What will be (i) the new break-even point and (ii) the new profit at the estimated sales level of 800 units?

8   The Green Finger Co. is considering an investment in a new compost bin. The equipment is expected to generate additional annual sales of 4000 units at $21 per unit. The cost of the equipment is $160 000 and it is expected to have a 10-year life and zero residual value. Selling expenses related to the new product are expected to be 2 per cent of sales revenue. The variable costs to manufacture the compost bin are shown below:

COST PER UNIT	$
Direct labour	5.00
Direct materials	8.25
Variable factory overhead	1.50
Total variable cost per unit	14.75

Determine

a   the break-even sales per year in units for the new investment

b   the expected profit each year from the investment

c   whether the company should proceed with the investment. Give reasons for your recommendation.

9   You are in charge of organising a conference for a group of accounting academics. You have obtained the following details:

	$
Rental of conference venue	300
Speakers' costs	500
Notebooks and pens	100
Cost of lunch and morning and afternoon teas (per person)	30

The conference fee for the 45 academics is $50 per person.

Required

a How many academics would have to attend at $50 per person for the conference to break even?

b If 60 academics attend at $50 per person, what is the expected profit?

c The committee believes that $250 spent on promotion would attract a total of 80 academics. Should they spend this if they want to keep the fee at $50 per person?

10 The Threadbare Clothing Company has to decide whether to produce trousers or skirts. The manager knows that the demand for trousers is 1200 per month at a selling price of $45 each and the demand for skirts is 800 at $60 each. Costs of production are as follows:

	TROUSERS	SKIRTS
Monthly rent	$550.00	$550.00
Material per unit	$15.00	$21.00
Labour hours per unit	1.25	0.75
Selling costs per unit	$0.25	$0.30
Administration costs	$1 000.00	$1 000.00
Labour rate per hour	$8.50	$8.50
Depreciation on plant	$120.00	$120.00

Required

Advise Threadbare's management as to whether it is more profitable to produce trousers or skirts, giving the break-even points for each product, and the level of profit or loss in each case.

11 Cords Pty Ltd manufactures a style of corduroy jeans that it sold last year at $36 a pair. The cost specifications for these jeans were as follows:

VARIABLE COST PER PAIR OF JEANS	$
Materials	13
Labour	7
Fixed overheads per month	52 800

Cords Pty Ltd made a profit of $22 080 each month.

Required

a How many pairs of jeans did Cords Pty Ltd sell each month?

b Cords Pty Ltd is now planning next year's operations. The sales director is proposing to boost sales by reducing the selling price to $34 and spending an additional $6000 per month on advertising. She estimates that these actions will enable the company to sell 5800 pairs of jeans each month.

c Evaluate the sales director's proposals, taking into account the expected impact on profits and the break-even point. State any assumptions you need to make.

d If the managing director of Cords Pty Ltd was to require that next year's profit shows a 15 per cent increase over last year's performance, how many pairs of jeans would have to be sold each month, assuming that (i) the sales director's policies were adopted and (ii) that they were not?

12 The Incr-Edible Pie Company Ltd has the following revenue and cost functions for next year:

Total revenues = $30x

Total costs = $150 000 + 20x

where x = number of units

Required

a Prepare a break-even chart for the Incr-Edible Pie Company. Label the vertical axis in $50 000 amounts and the horizontal axis in 5000-unit amounts.

b What is the break-even point in units and dollars?

c Prove your answer in (b) by calculating the profits at the break-even level.

13 DEF Ltd produces stereos and sells these for $250 each. The company can produce a maximum of 5000 units per year. Variable costs are $185 per unit and fixed costs are $250 000 per year, regardless of production.

a Calculate the break-even point.

b What is the profit for the company if it sells 5000 units?

c The company believes it can sell more units if it leases additional equipment. The lease costs are $200 000 a year and the company has to give one year's notice to cancel the lease. Because of the increased production capacity, variable costs are reduced to $175 per unit. If the maximum number of units the company can produce and sell with the new equipment is 8100, should the company lease the new equipment?

d If there is a recession in the audio industry and the company can now sell only 4000 units at $240, should the company cease producing stereos? Give reasons for your answer. (Assume it did not lease additional equipment.)

14 Daly Limited has determined the number of units of Product Y that it would have to sell in order to break even. However, Greg, the CEO of the company, would like to attain a 30 per cent profit on sales of Product Y.

Required

a Explain how break-even analysis can be used to determine the number of units of Product Y that Daly Limited would have to sell to attain a 30 per cent profit on sales.

b If variable cost per unit increases as a percentage of the sales price, how would that affect the number of units of Product Y that Daly Limited would have to sell in order to break even and why?

c Identify and briefly discuss the limitations of CVP analysis that Greg should be aware of when making decisions about the costs, pricing and volumes of Product Y produced and sold.

Note to instructors: the following problems are considered more suitable for use in MBA courses. However, undergraduate courses may also find them useful.

15 The Gigantic DVD Store sells three categories of DVDs relating to sport, drama and comedy. Unit selling prices and variable costs for each category are as follows:

	SPORT	DRAMA	COMEDY
	$	$	$
Selling price	100	70	200
Variable cost	60	50	100

The fixed costs at Gigantic are $90 000 per year and this amount is subject to income tax at the rate of 40 per cent. The company aims to make after-tax profits of $27 000 per year. The current unit sales mix is as follows:

	% OF TOTAL
Sport	40
Drama	50
Comedy	10

Required

Calculate each of the following for the current sales mix:

a   the break-even, in units, for each category

b   the average unit contribution margin

c   the break-even unit sales volume in total, and for each category

d   the unit sales volume required to earn the desired after-tax profits in total and for each category.

16 This year, Ashfield Ltd sold 8000 car alarms at $90 each. The following details are available.

	VARIABLE COSTS PER UNIT	TOTAL FIXED COSTS
Production	$50	$100 000
Selling	$10	$80 000
	$60	$180 000

Ashfield can reduce its variable production costs by $10 per unit if it invests $100 000 in new equipment.

Required

a   Calculate the break-even point in units for the original and revised set of figures.

b   Calculate the profit using the original and revised set of figures for sales of 8000 units.

c   What are the sales, in units, when the profit is the same for both the original and revised set of figures?

d   If the company reduced its selling price by $10 per unit, expected sales would increase to 15 000 units. Should the company reduce its selling price under either alternative?

17 Golden Bakeries Ltd has three major product lines: bread rolls, donuts and fudge cakes. For the year ended 31 December, Golden Bakeries Ltd achieved the following sales volumes:

	BREAD ROLLS	DONUTS	FUDGE CAKES	TOTAL
Sales in kilograms	400 000	100 000	100 000	600 000

The incomplete statement of comprehensive income for the year ended 31 December, prepared by product line using absorption costing, is shown below.

GOLDEN BAKERIES LTD
STATEMENT OF COMPREHENSIVE INCOME FOR THE YEAR ENDING 31 DECEMBER

	BREAD ROLLS	DONUTS	FUDGE CAKES	TOTAL
	$000	$000	$000	$000
Revenue from sales	2 000	800	400	3 200
Cost of sales				
Direct materials	660	320	200	1 180
Direct labour	180	80	40	300
Factory overhead	216	96	48	360
Less Total cost of sales	1 056	496	288	1 840
Gross profit	944	304	112	1 360
Operating expenses				
Selling expenses				
Advertising	100	60	40	200
Commissions	100	80	40	220
Salaries	60	40	20	120
Total selling expenses	260	180	100	540
Administration expenses				
Royalties	100	40	30	170
Salaries	120	50	30	200
Total administration expenses	220	90	60	370
Less Total operating expenses	480	270	160	910
Net profit before tax	464	34	(48)	450

The following additional information is available:

a Advertising is considered necessary by management, despite the fact that no direct correlation between the level of sales and the amount spent on advertising has been demonstrated. As a result, an annual advertising strategy is developed for each product line. Each product is advertised separately.

b Sales commissions are paid to the salespeople at the rate of 5 per cent on the bread rolls and 10 per cent on the donuts and fudge cakes.

c Royalties for the recipes for each product are required. These are an annual payment for each product.

d Salary costs are related to the company's overall activities rather than to any product line. Sales and administrative staff spend time and effort on each product line, and on the company as a whole. Managers estimate the amount of time spent on each product and these estimates are used to allocate the cost of salaries and wages.

e Cost of sales information:

Common facilities are used to produce all three products. The company's inventories of raw materials and finished goods are similar from year to year. The inventories as at 31 December this and last year were essentially the same.

The factory overhead costs for the current year ending 31 December were as follows:

	$
Variable indirect labour and supplies	30 000
Variable employee benefits	60 000
Supervisory salaries	70 000
Plant occupancy costs	200 000
Total	360 000

Factory overhead was applied to products at the rate of 120 per cent of direct labour dollars. There was no over- or under-applied overhead for the year.

Required

The financial controller of Golden Bakeries has recommended that the company do a cost-volume-profit analysis of its operations. The company has also asked that you first prepare a revised statement of comprehensive income that utilises a product contribution margin format that will be useful in CVP analysis. The statement should show the contribution margin for each product line and the net profit (before taxes) for the company as a whole.

ETHICS CASE STUDY

Dave Johnston is analysing a request from a special customer for an order of 1000 electric kettles. The customer has proposed that he will pay an amount per unit based on the contribution margin plus 20 per cent. The customer is in Hong Kong and he wants the goods before Christmas and the date is 12 December.

The other details of the proposal are:

1 The customer is to pay all freight costs.

2 Dave's company is to make a $5000 payment to a friend of the customer who works in the customs area in Hong Kong so that the kettles can be cleared through customs before Christmas.

The relevant data for the kettles is as follows:

Variable unit manufacturing costs	$25
Variable unit selling and administrative costs	$12
Selling price	$50

Dave's boss has explained that the customer is a very important one and, as the order will lead to the plant operating at full capacity, workers will be able to earn a little extra for Christmas by working overtime.

Discuss

a the accounting and ethical issues in this case

b whether Dave should accept the terms proposed for the special order.

SUGGESTED ANSWERS TO STOP AND THINK EXERCISES IN THE CHAPTER

1 The BEP is the point where costs are exactly covered by income and there is no profit or loss.

2 The contribution margin is the difference between total revenue and total variable costs (irrespective of whether they are manufacturing or non-manufacturing costs). The contribution margin can be measured as a percentage of sales, dollars per unit or total dollars. The contribution margin per unit usually is the best approach to use in CVP analysis questions.

3 The margin of safety is the excess of budgeted (or actual) sales revenue over break-even sales. The margin of safety can also be measured as the excess of budgeted (or actual) units sold over break-even sales in units.

CENGAGENOW

Go to http:\\login.cengagebrain.com to link to CengageNOW resources, including online crosswords, animated examples and flashcards featuring the key concepts of CVP analysis.

17

ACCOUNTING FOR DECISION MAKING: WITH AND WITHOUT RESOURCE CONSTRAINTS

Daniela Pelazza/Shutterstock.com

LEARNING OBJECTIVES

At the end of this chapter, you should be able to:

1 explain what is meant by the term 'sunk costs'
2 explain what is meant by differential (incremental) costs
3 identify what is meant by avoidable and unavoidable costs
4 discuss the concept of opportunity costs and its role in decision making
5 explain the costs and benefits that are relevant to specific decisions
6 explain and apply the contribution margin approach to decision making in cases where there are no resource constraints
7 apply the contribution margin approach to decisions concerning whether to close unprofitable departments, business units or divisions

8 explain what is meant by decision making with constraints
9 illustrate the use of the contribution margin approach in relation to decisions with one scarce resource
10 evaluate problems of whether a firm should make or buy a product or a service in cases where there is (i) spare capacity and (ii) no spare capacity
11 discuss the role of qualitative factors in making decisions where constraints are present.

INTRODUCTION

Management needs to make decisions about future business opportunities to ensure that the firm's objectives are met. Many of these decisions relate to the short term and are expressed in financial terms in the firm's budget (see Chapter 15). Management is also required to make decisions of a more immediate nature, which relate to opportunities that were not anticipated at the planning stage. To ignore profitable opportunities because they have not been specifically included in the budget would be irresponsible in a dynamic business environment. These decisions can be categorised as below.

DECISIONS WHERE THERE ARE NO RESOURCE CONSTRAINTS

In these circumstances, firms are free to make a decision, knowing that it will not affect other opportunities. For instance, the introduction of a new product might not affect, in any way, the demand and production levels of other products. These decisions can also be described as 'accept or reject' decisions.

DECISIONS WHERE THERE ARE RESOURCE CONSTRAINTS

This situation occurs when a firm experiences a shortage of physical resources; for example, a particular type of material. In such cases, the firm cannot accept all potentially desirable opportunities. To decide which opportunity to choose, it will be necessary to implement a priority (ranking) system.

MUTUALLY EXCLUSIVE DECISIONS

These are decisions where the acceptance of one opportunity means that others will be rejected. For instance, when management has to decide whether to make or buy a component to be embodied within one of the firm's products, the decision to make eliminates the option to buy. Mutually exclusive decisions include situations both with or without resource constraints.

In the case of decisions where there are resource constraints, we will consider situations where there is only one scarce resource. Decision making when there are two or more scarce resources is beyond the scope of this text. The same principles apply, but with two or more scarce resources, more complex mathematical skills using linear programming are required.

The conventional assumption for short-term decisions is that they affect the business for a period of one year. It is also assumed that the values of cash inflows and outflows throughout the year are of an equivalent value. In reality, this is naive as as all individuals and businesses prefer to receive, for example, cash today rather than in 11 months time. For analytical clarity, it is convenient to make this assumption, because of the complexities that arise when we take account of the time value of money in the decision-making process.

In our analysis of short-term decisions, we will initially assume that only quantitative factors are relevant. However, in reality qualitative factors can be influential in the decision-making process. We conclude our examination of short-term decision making by considering the nature of qualitative factors and looking at some examples in which they influence the decision.

COSTS AND BENEFITS RELEVANT TO DECISION MAKING

Decisions relate to the future, and the purpose of decision making is to select courses of action that satisfy the objective of the business. There is no opportunity to alter the past, although past experience might help us in making future decisions. For example, the observation of past cost behaviour might help to determine future levels of cost.

Relevant costs and benefits can therefore be defined as those costs and benefits that result from making a specific decision. A more precise definition will be established after we have examined the underlying principles of relevant costs and benefits and considered some examples of the application of these principles.

The relevant costs for decision making are different from those used in accrual accounting. This is not surprising because the principles of traditional costing (e.g. overhead absorption methods) evolved from the need to report historical events, rather than to determine future costs and benefits. A number of methods adopted by accountants to account for decisions about the future are derived from economic theory and you may have some familiarity with these.

We now consider the principles underlying relevant costs for decision making and the application of these principles to specific types of decisions. The differences between the application of relevant costs and traditional costing methods will also be discussed.

Future and sunk (past) costs

1 LEARNING OBJECTIVE

Explain what is meant by the term 'sunk costs'

Costs of a historical nature, which are normally referred to as sunk costs, are incurred as a result of a past decision and cannot be changed. Therefore, sunk costs are irrelevant to future decisions and should be ignored.

17.1

KEY CONCEPT

SUNK COSTS

Sunk costs, or past costs, can be easily identified in that they have either been paid for, or the entity has already committed itself and cannot avoid making such payment in the future.

17.1

WORKED EXAMPLE

DISPOSAL OF AN OBSOLETE MACHINE

A business has an obsolete machine that was purchased and paid for two years ago for $90 000. The net book value (NBV) of the machine before it became obsolete, as shown in the accounts of the business, is $72 000. The alternatives now available to the business are:

- to make alterations to the machine at an estimated cost of $20 000 and then sell it for $40 000
- to sell it for scrap, at an estimated selling price of $15 000.

The net book value of $72 000 represents the original cost of purchasing the machine less the accumulated depreciation (charge for depreciation over the two-year period). The original cost of $90 000 is the result of a past decision: it was incurred two years ago and therefore is a sunk cost. Similarly, the NBV of $72 000 is equally as irrelevant. It is irrelevant to the future decision concerning whether to alter the machine and sell it, or to sell it for scrap. The depreciation is also based on the original cost of the machine and is accordingly irrelevant for this future decision. The only relevant costs and benefits in this example are those related to the future. We can analyse these as follows.

	ALTER	SCRAP
	$	$
Future benefits	40 000	15 000
Future costs	20 000	–
Future income	20 000	15 000

From the analysis of relevant costs and benefits, it can be seen that the business will be $5000 better off by altering the machine and selling it rather than selling it for scrap.

STOP AND THINK 1

In the context of decision making, explain the meaning of a sunk cost.

Differential (incremental) costs

Another important principle in the determination of relevant costs and benefits is that only differential (incremental) costs and benefits are relevant to future decisions. The application of the principles underlying differential costing is illustrated in Case study 17.1, where a business that has spare capacity, or idle manufacturing capacity, is offered a special order. By comparing the costs and benefits associated with the opportunities available to the business, we can identify differential costs and benefits. It is these costs and benefits that are relevant to choosing between competing opportunities.

KEY CONCEPT

DIFFERENTIAL COSTS

Differential (incremental) costs are the differences in costs and benefits between alternative opportunities available to a firm. It follows that when a number of opportunities are being considered, those costs and benefits common to both alternative opportunities are irrelevant to the decision.

17.1

CASE STUDY

KT's Inc. manufactures hats and has a current capacity of 120 000 hats per year. However, it is predicted that sales will be only 90 000 hats in the forthcoming year. A mail-order business offers to buy 20 000 hats at $7.50 each. The acceptance of this special order will not affect regular sales and it will take a year to complete. The managing director is reluctant to accept the order because $7.50 is below the manufactured unit cost of $8 per hat.

The following gives the predicted total profit and the predicted profit per unit, in a traditional costing format, if the order were *not* accepted.

	TOTAL		PER UNIT	
	$	$	$	$
Sales: 90 000 hats at $10 each		900 000		10.00
Less factory expenses:				
Variable	540 000		6.00	
Supervision	90 000		1.00	
Other fixed costs	90 000	720 000	1.00	8.00
Gross profit		180 000		2.00
Selling expenses:				
Variable	22 500		0.25	
Fixed	112 500	135 000	1.25	1.50
Profit		45 000		0.50

The management accountant, with the production and sales manager, is requested to review the costs of taking on the special order. These are their conclusions:

1   The variable costs of production relate to direct labour and materials and these will be incurred at the same rates as for the production of the normal production units.

2   There will be a need for additional supervision. However, it is anticipated that four of the current supervisors can cover this requirement if each of them works overtime for two hours per week. Supervisors are paid $25 per hour and overtime is paid at a premium of $5 per hour. There are 48 working weeks in the year. Therefore, the additional costs are:

2 hours × $30 per hour × 48 weeks × 4 supervisors = $11 520

3   Other fixed costs are factory rent and the depreciation of plant. It is anticipated that these will remain the same if the order is accepted.

❯

4   If the contract is accepted, there will be a need to hire an additional machine, costing $10 000.

5   The variable sales cost relates to sales commissions, and this cost will not be incurred on the special order.

6   The fixed sales expenses relate to the administering of sales. These costs will remain the same, except that a part-time clerk will be required to help with the additional workload if the special order is accepted. The salary will be $6000 per year.

Using the differential costing approach, we can compare the total profit for the year for KT's Inc. if the order is accepted or rejected:

	ACCEPT	REJECT	DIFFERENTIAL COST AND REVENUE
	$	$	$
Sales	1 050 000	900 000	150 000
Factory expenses:			
Variable costs	660 000	540 000	120 000
Supervision	101 520	90 000	11 520
Other fixed costs	90 000	90 000	–
Hire of plant	10 000	–	10 000
	861 520	720 000	141 520
Sales expenses:			
Variable costs	22 500	22 500	–
Fixed costs	118 500	112 500	6 000
Total costs	1 002 520	855 000	147 520
Profit	47 480	45 000	2 480

COMMENTARY

From the differential analysis, it can be seen that KT's Inc. will be $2480 better off if the special order is accepted. Also, it can be observed that a number of the costs are irrelevant in the decision analysis. That is, they are the same whether or not the order is accepted: for example, other fixed costs are $90 000 for both the 'accept' and the 'reject' decisions.

The analysis of data could have been simplified by considering only the differential costs and revenues related to the special order. If the differential analysis of costs and revenues results in a profit, then, from a purely quantitative perspective, the order should be accepted. In this case the profit is minimal and is only about 5 per cent of total profit. Hence qualitative factors such as the impact on other customers will more than likely dominate the decision.

3 LEARNING OBJECTIVE

Identify what is meant by avoidable and unavoidable costs

Avoidable and unavoidable costs

There is an alternative way of determining whether a cost is relevant or irrelevant in decisions, such as the special order for the hats illustrated in Case study 17.1. Instead of using the differential analysis, we ask the question: would a cost be avoided if the company did not proceed with the special order? If the answer is yes, the cost is relevant and should be included. For example, consider this question with regard to the cost of plant hire for the special order in Case study 17.1: will the cost of plant hire be avoided if the company does not proceed with the order? The answer is yes. The cost is relevant to the decision because it will only be incurred if the order is accepted. A cost is described as unavoidable if it will be incurred regardless of the decision to accept or reject; that is, the cost is irrelevant to the decision.

STOP AND THINK 2

In the context of decision making, explain the meaning of avoidable and unavoidable costs.

Opportunity costs

4 **LEARNING OBJECTIVE**

The economists' concept of opportunity cost has been adopted by accountants for decision-making purposes. This concept relates to the cost of using resources for alternative opportunities.

Discuss the concept of opportunity costs and its role in decision making

17.3 KEY CONCEPT

OPPORTUNITY COST

The opportunity cost of a resource is normally defined as the maximum benefit which could be obtained from that resource if it were used for some other purpose. If a firm uses a resource for alternative A rather than B, the opportunity cost is the potential benefits that are forgone by not using the resource for alternative B. Therefore, the potential benefits that are forgone – the opportunity cost – are a relevant cost in the decision to accept alternative A.

The following is an example of the concept of opportunity costs. Jeff Jones, a qualified accountant, is a sole practitioner. He works 40 hours per week and charges clients $40 per hour. Jeff is already overworked and will not work any extra hours. A circus offers Jeff $2000 per week to become a clown. In the decision to become a clown, Jeff must consider the benefits he would forgo from closing his accounting practice; that is, $40 × 40 hours = $1600 per week. This is the opportunity cost of Jeff becoming a clown. Assuming that Jeff is concerned only with financial rewards, he will accept the offer to become a clown because he will be $400 per week better off.

Governments are often confronted with issues around opportunity costs. The decision to spend many hundreds of millions of dollars on a potentially world-class sporting stadium will be opposed by some on the grounds that the money could be better spent on health and education.

Replacement costs

If a resource was originally purchased for some purpose other than the option currently under consideration, the relevant cost of using that resource is its replacement cost. This cost has come about as a direct result of the decision to use the resource for a purpose not originally intended and the need to replace it. The following example will help you to understand the application of this principle.

Easy Done Ltd has been approached by a customer who would like a special job done. The job would require the use of 500 kg of material Z. Material Z is used by Easy Done Ltd for a variety of purposes.

Currently, the company holds 1000 kg in inventory that was purchased one month ago for $6 per kilogram. Since then, the price per kilogram has increased to $8 per kilogram. If 500 kg were used on this special job it would need to be replaced to meet the production requirements of other jobs.

The relevant cost of using material Z on this special job is the replacement cost, 500 kg × $8 = $4000. This is because the material will need to be replaced as a result of its use, and the replacement will cost $4000. This cost has arisen as a direct result of accepting the special order and, therefore, it is relevant to the decision. It should be noted that the original cost of $6 per kilogram is irrelevant to the decision as it relates to a past decision and has already been incurred (that is, it is a sunk cost).

STOP AND THINK 3

Explain the meaning of opportunity cost.

Comparison with traditional costing methods

Case study 17.2 illustrates the application of the principles of relevant costs compared with traditional costing methods.

17.2

CASE STUDY

NO PROBLEM LTD

No Problem Ltd (NPL) is considering whether to accept the offer of a contract to undertake some reconstruction work at a price of $73 000. The work can begin immediately and will take about one year to complete. NPL's accountant has submitted the following statement (see page 571).

NPL management doubt whether it is advisable to incur the inevitable risks involved for such a small profit margin. On making further enquiries, the following information becomes available:

1. Material A was bought two years ago for $7000. It would cost $8000 at today's prices. If not used on this contract, it could be sold for $6500. There is no alternative use for this material and no expected future use.

2. Material B was ordered for another job but will be used on this job if the contract is accepted. The cost to purchase more material B for the other job will now cost $9000.

3. NPL has a minimum wage agreement with employees, as a result of which direct wages of $21 000 will be incurred whether the contract is undertaken or not. If not employed on this contract, these employees could be used to do much-needed maintenance work, which would otherwise be done by an outside contractor at an already quoted cost of $18 500.

	COSTS $	BENEFITS $
Contract price		73 000
Less Costs		
Cost of work already incurred in drawing up detailed costings		4 700
Materials		
A	7 000	
B	8 000	15 000
Labour		
Direct	21 000	
Indirect	12 000	33 000
Machinery		
Depreciation on machines owned	4 000	
Hire of special equipment	5 000	9 000
Manufacturing overheads		10 500
Total cost		72 200
Expected profit		800

4 The indirect labour is the wage of a supervisor who will have to be recruited to supervise the contract. A suitable person is ready to take up this appointment.

5 The machine, which is already owned, is six years old. The final depreciation charge for writing off the balance of the asset is $4000. There is no alternative use for the machine, and due to the high cost associated with dismantling and removing the machine, it has a negligible scrap value.

6 The manufacturing overhead absorption rate is 50 per cent of direct labour. Manufacturing overheads are expected to rise by $4000 if the contract is accepted.

With reference to this information, and the principles of relevant costs, we will consider how each individual cost item should be accounted for in making the decision to accept or reject the proposed contract:

1 *Material A*: As the $7000 originally paid for the material is a sunk cost, it is irrelevant. We are told that the current replacement cost is $8000. However, NPL would only obtain $6500 if it was sold; that is, the net realisable value. This is the benefit NPL forgoes (the opportunity cost) by using the material on this contract. Thus, $6500 is the relevant cost.

2 *Material B*: As this material has already been ordered, NPL is committed to pay the supplier for this material. Thus, $8000 can also be considered a sunk cost and be irrelevant . The only alternative for material B is to use it on the other job. If so, NPL would have to purchase more material at a cost of $9000. This is the opportunity cost of using the material B on this contract.

3 *Direct labour*: These employees will be paid whether the contract is accepted or not. Therefore, this cost is unavoidable and irrelevant. However, if they were not employed on this contract NPL would save $18 500 that would otherwise be payable to the outside maintenance contractor. Therefore, the $18 500 is a relevant cost as this is the opportunity cost of using the employees on the contract.

4 *Indirect labour*: The cost of $12 000 for employing the supervisor is an incremental cost as it will only be incurred if the contract is accepted. Therefore, it is relevant to the contract.

5 *Depreciation on the machine owned*: As the cost of depreciation relates to a past cost (i.e. a sunk cost), it is irrelevant to the decision. A relevant benefit is the machine's scrap value. However, as this is negligible, it is ignored.

6 *Hire of special equipment*: As the cost of $5000 will only be incurred if the contract is accepted, it is an incremental cost and is relevant to the decision.

7 *Manufacturing overheads*: The only relevant cost is the increase in overheads of $4000 if the contract is accepted. This cost is incremental, hence it is relevant to the decision. All the other costs related to manufacturing overheads are unavoidable (and irrelevant).

8 *Cost of work already incurred in drawing up costings*: This cost ($4700, detailed at the beginning of the schedule) is irrelevant to the contract: it is a sunk cost and should be excluded.

We are now in a position to draw up an amended statement of costs for the contract.

	RELEVANT COSTS	RELEVANT BENEFITS
	$	$
Contract price		73 000
Less Costs		
Materials		
A	6 500	
B	9 000	15 500
Labour		
Direct	18 500	
Indirect	12 000	30 500
Hire of special equipment		5 000
Overheads		4 000
Total costs		55 000
Expected profits		18 000

COMMENTARY

When considering only relevant costs, the contract is more attractive to NPL. In the original schedule of costs and revenues, which were based on traditional costing methods, the expected profit was only $800 compared with $18 000. It should be stressed that the higher profits yielded from the analysis of relevant costs and benefits compared with the traditional analysis is not always the rule. The result depends on the particular circumstances of the firm making such a decision.

5 LEARNING OBJECTIVE

Explain the costs and benefits that are relevant to specific decisions

The principles underlying the relevance of costs and benefits to decisions described and illustrated in Case study 17.2 focus on costs rather than income. However, the same principles apply to income. Only the income that will be generated as a result of the decision is relevant to the decision and should be brought into the decision model. Relevant benefits, by their nature, relate to the future. All benefits that have been received, or are due to be received from a prior commitment, are irrelevant to future decisions.

The meaning of relevance

Earlier in this chapter relevant costs and benefits were defined, in general terms, as the costs and benefits resulting from a specific decision. We derive a more precise definition.

17.4 KEY CONCEPT

RELEVANT COSTS AND BENEFITS

Relevant costs and benefits are those that relate to the future. They are additional costs incurred and income earned as a result of a decision.

Costs that are relevant to a decision might also be:

» the cost of replacing a resource that was originally purchased for another purpose
» the opportunity cost of using a resource that could be used for an alternative purpose.

There are also costs and income incurred or generated by a firm that are irrelevant to a decision; that is, those that are not affected by a decision. It is important to identify these costs and benefits so that we can eliminate them from our analysis.

Unfortunately, some firms ignore the principles of relevant costs and benefits in making future decisions. This distorts decision making and results in poor decisions being made.

STOP AND THINK 4

Depreciation is an important concept in the determination of profit. Discuss why it is classified as an irrelevant cost in decision making.

FIXED AND VARIABLE COSTS AND THE CONTRIBUTION APPROACH

The concept of contribution margin was introduced in Chapter 16. The contribution margin is the difference between sales revenue and variable costs. This concept is also relevant to decisions taken in the context of relevant costs and decision making.

It is normally assumed that costs behave in a linear fashion: total fixed costs remain constant for all volumes and total variable costs vary in direct proportion to volume. Often, fixed costs are unavoidable and are not relevant to decisions as they remain the same whatever decision is taken. When there are no scarce resources and the sales revenue exceeds the relevant variable costs, a decision to accept should be made. This rule applies to several types of decisions.

A word of caution: there are some situations when costs do not behave in a linear fashion, so variations in unit variable costs or in total fixed costs might occur. For example, the cost of new machinery that is specifically purchased for a future contract is classified as a fixed cost, but it is relevant to the contract because it can be avoided. When fixed costs are directly attributable to opportunities, they are relevant to the decision to accept or reject. However, unless you are given a clear indication to the contrary, you should always assume that costs behave in a linear fashion. This assumption was also adopted in Chapter 16.

The contribution approach can be applied to a number of types of decisions that management must take when running a business. Worked examples 17.2 and 17.3 illustrate this with respect to the range of products a firm has, and closing an unprofitable part of the business.

6 LEARNING OBJECTIVE

Explain and apply the contribution margin approach to decision making in cases where there are no resource constraints

The range of products

A firm's managers are confronted with a number of opportunities each year and have to decide which to include in their plans. In Worked example 17.2, the products are independent of each other. We can derive a simple rule from this example: if a product makes a positive contribution, it is worth considering for acceptance in the firm's production schedule. The fixed costs have been apportioned to products. This is the convention under absorption costing described in Chapter 14, where overheads are absorbed into products using predetermined rates based on budgeted overhead costs and activity. Normally, overhead costs are unavoidable and are not relevant, as in this example. Overhead costs are relevant only if they are incremental in nature.

WORKED EXAMPLE

PRODUCTS 1, 2 AND 3

A business has the opportunity to manufacture and sell three products, named 1, 2 and 3, in the forthcoming year. Here is a draft summary of the profit or loss on the products:

		1	2	3	TOTAL
		$	$	$	$
Sales		30 000	20 000	150 000	200 000
Variable costs		21 400	13 200	101 400	136 000
Fixed costs		3 400	7 400	33 200	44 000
Total costs		24 800	20 600	134 600	180 000
Profit (loss)		5 200	(600)	15 400	20 000

The fixed costs of $44 000 represent overhead costs which have been apportioned to the products and will remain the same regardless of whether all or only some of the products are sold during the year.

Because of the loss shown by product 2, the management proposes to eliminate that product from its range.

The business would be making a profit of $20 000 if all three products were manufactured and sold. However, if only 1 and 3 were sold, as management suggests, the profit would be reduced.

		1	3	TOTAL
		$	$	$
Sales		30 000	150 000	180 000
Variable costs		21 400	101 400	122 800
Contribution		8 600	48 600	57 200
Fixed costs				44 000
Profit				13 200

This reduction in profit is because product 2 makes a contribution of $6800 ($20 000 – $13 200) and the fixed costs remain unchanged at $44 000, regardless of whether or not products 1, 2 or 3 are manufactured and sold.

Closing an unprofitable section

Apply the contribution margin approach to decisions concerning whether to close unprofitable departments, business units or divisions

In dynamic business environments, firms need to regularly appraise the economic viability of departments, business units and divisions. Although a decision regarding whether or not to close a department, business unit or division is very different from that involved in the determination of the range of products to be manufactured and sold, the same principles of relevance are adopted.

In practice, invariably there are a number of costs that are allocated to departments that are outside their control and relate to overheads incurred by the firm as a whole. A typical example is corporate head office expenses, which relate to the administration of the business. As these types of costs are unavoidable, they are irrelevant.

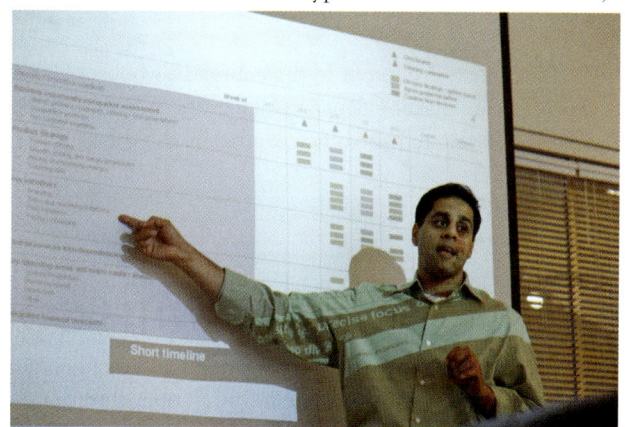

The rule to be applied in such decisions is that if a department makes a positive contribution (i.e. income exceeds variable costs), the department should remain open, and vice versa. However, when there are fixed costs that are directly attributable to a department, and they are avoidable, the rule can be amended as follows: if the income generated by a department exceeds the costs directly attributable to that department, it should remain open, and vice versa. Worked example 17.3 illustrates such a decision.

WORKED EXAMPLE

17.3

ALPHA, BETA AND GAMMA DEPARTMENTS

The following are the costs and income of three departments, Alpha, Beta and Gamma, summarised in a traditional costing format:

	ALPHA	BETA	GAMMA	TOTAL
	$000	$000	$000	$000
Sales	80	40	60	180
Department costs	24	15	46	85
Apportioned costs	20	10	20	50
Total costs	44	25	66	135
Profit (loss)	36	15	(6)	45

The apportioned costs of $50 000 in total are unavoidable and relate to corporate head office overheads.

From the way the data is presented, it could be argued that Gamma should be closed because it makes a loss of $6000. Currently, the total profit of all departments is $45 000. However, if Gamma were to be closed, the profit would decrease.

| | ALPHA | BETA | TOTAL |
	$000	$000	$000
Sales	80	40	120
Less Department costs	24	15	39
Departmental profit	56	25	81
Less Apportioned costs			50
Profit			31

The reduction in profit to the entity as a whole of $14 000 is due to the closure of Gamma, which, in fact, makes a departmental profit of $14 000 ($60 000 – $46 000) which contributes to covering corporate head office overheads and the firm's overall profit. Thus, department Gamma should remain open.

DECISION MAKING WITH CONSTRAINTS

8 LEARNING OBJECTIVE

Explain what is meant by decision making with constraints

In situations where there are no constraints and fixed costs are unavoidable (that is, irrelevant) we have come to the following conclusion: all opportunities should be accepted if they make a positive contribution to covering fixed costs and profits.

However, if the availability of one or more resources is restricted, a firm will be unable to accept every opportunity that yields a positive contribution. Therefore, it is necessary to formulate a decision-making rule that account for resource constraints.

Before considering the process used to determine optimum outputs, it is appropriate to examine the nature of constraints that a firm might experience in the context of its operations.

Traditionally, the only constraints that are considered relate to shortages of manufacturing resources, such as particular types of materials, labour skills and the capacity of the manufacturing facility. However, firms in the service sector can also face such constraints that limit their earning capacity. For example, because of the shortage of qualified accounting staff, an accounting practice may face a constraint in the number of audit clients it can accept. Nevertheless, it is important to note that the principles to be applied when there are constraints are the same for both manufacturing and service sector firms.

The constraints described relate to the short term and can invariably be eliminated in the long term. For example, a business has the opportunity to manufacture and sell two products, A and B, both of which yield a positive contribution per unit. However, due to a shortage of skilled machine operators, the firm cannot satisfy the demand for these products. Clearly, this constraint is only a short-term phenomenon as the business could start training machine operators so that there will not be a shortage in the longer term. However, in the short term this remains a constraint on production volumes and the firm's profitability.

KEY CONCEPT

17.5

DECISION MAKING WITH CONSTRAINTS: OBJECTIVES

When there are resource constraints, the objective to be applied is establish the optimum output within the constraints that maximise the contribution margin and, thus, profits.

THE CONTRIBUTION APPROACH WITH ONE SCARCE RESOURCE

9 LEARNING OBJECTIVE

Illustrate the use of the contribution margin approach in relation to decisions with one scarce resource

In determining the optimum output, the analysis takes account only of quantitative factors. Qualitative factors can often influence a final decision: for example, unprofitable products might be included in a product range in order to retain customer loyalty for all of the products sold by the firm. This should always be borne in mind when making such decisions.

To determine the optimum output with one constraint we must first determine the contribution, then establish the contribution per unit of the constraint for all those opportunities that yield a positive contribution. For example, say product A yields a positive contribution of $16 per unit and takes four labour hours to produce. Assuming that labour is the only effective production constraint, then the contribution per labour hour in producing product A is $16 ÷ 4 hours = $4 per labour hour. This provides crucial information about the efficiency of the use of the constrained resource in terms of contribution and, thus, profitability.

The next stage is to rank these opportunities, preferring those that yield the highest contribution per constraint. If, for example, product B only generates a positive contribution per labour hour of $3, product A will be ranked higher, in the absence of other factors, because it yields $1 more in contribution margin per labour hour. The optimum plan can then be derived within the total resources available. In the example above, this will be total labour hours available to the firm for a defined period.

Case study 17.3 illustrates the stages of this process.

CASE STUDY 17.3

TROY LTD

The directors of Troy Ltd are drawing up the production plan for the forthcoming year. There are five products that are under consideration: A, B, C, D and E. The following statement regarding the contribution per unit of these opportunities has been prepared by the company's accountant:

	A	B	C	D	E
	$	$	$	$	$
Selling price	100	240	480	130	220
Variable costs					
Materials	70	30	20	30	20
Labour	40	70	100	20	50
Total variable costs	110	100	120	50	70
Contribution per unit	(10)	140	360	80	150
Estimated demand in units	800	700	800	600	400
Labour hours per unit	4	7	10	2	5

For convenience of calculation, we will assume that all labour is paid at the rate of $10 per hour. The total of fixed costs for the year is estimated to be $49 900 and will vary with the range of products actually produced and sold.

Labour is scarce, and it is expected that only 7000 hours will be available next year.

We begin our analysis to determine the optimum production schedule, within the labour constraint confronted by Troy Ltd, by accepting all opportunities that yield a positive contribution and rejecting those that yield a negative contribution margin. All of the opportunities with the exception of product A yield a positive contribution margin. Thus, at this stage, product A, which has a negative contribution margin, can be eliminated from the company's future range of products.

Before continuing, it is wise to check whether the labour constraint of 7000 hours is a constraint on the company's activities. We do this by calculating the total labour hours required to meet the demand for the four products yielding positive contribution margins. We begin with product B and then products C, D and E in alphabetical order until the labour hour constraint is exceeded.

| PRODUCT | DEMAND (UNITS) | LABOUR HOURS | | |
		PER UNIT	TOTAL	CUMULATIVE
B	700	7	4 900	4 900
C	800	10	8 000	12 900

It can be seen from the cumulative labour hours column that, if we satisfied the demand of only products B and C, the company would exceed the labour hours it has available (that is, 7000 hours). Thus, we can conclude that labour hours are a constraint on the company's level of production and that the firm will be unable to accept all opportunities available to it.

We can now calculate, for the four remaining opportunities, the contribution per labour hour by dividing the labour hours per unit into the contribution per unit and ranking the opportunities in order of the highest contribution per labour hour.

	B	C	D	E
Contribution	$140 ÷ 7 hours	$360 ÷ 10 hours	$80 ÷ 2 hours	$150 ÷ 5 hours
Per labour hour	= $20	= $36	= $40	= $30
Ranking	4	2	1	3

Product D is ranked first because it yields the highest contribution per labour hour ($40), followed by product C with a contribution of $36 per hour, and then products E (with $30) and B ($20). This priority ranking can now be applied to determine the products that will be included in the profit maximising production schedule and establish the total contribution that is generated by this schedule.

| RANKING | PRODUCT | DEMAND UNITS | LABOUR HOURS | | CONTRIBUTION PER UNIT | |
			PER UNIT	TOTAL	PER UNIT	TOTAL
1	D	600	2	1 200	$80	48 000
2	C	580	10	5 800	$360	208 800
				7 000		256 800

❯

Within the labour constraint of 7000 labour hours, the company can satisfy the total demand for the first ranked product D, leaving $7000 - 1200 = 5800$ hours available for the production of other products. Product C is the second ranked product in terms of contribution margin per direct labour hour. While the total demand for C is estimated to be 800 units and would require a total of 8000 labour hours (i.e. 800 units ✕ 10 hours per unit = 8000 hours), only 5800 labour hours remain available. Therefore, due to the shortage of labour, the company will be restricted to producing only 580 units of product C (i.e. 5800 ÷ 10 = 580 units). Products B and E must be excluded from the production schedule as there are no more labour hours available.

This is the optimal production schedule because it takes into account two important variables: contribution margin and the scarce resource, labour hours. If the production schedule had been based on a priority ranking scheme that only took account of the contribution margin per unit and ignored the impact of the labour constraint, the ranking order in terms of the highest contribution per unit would be as follows:

PRODUCT	CONTRIBUTION MARGIN PER UNIT	RANKING
C	$360	1
E	$150	2
B	$140	3
D	$80	4

The total contribution that would be yielded from this ranking order would have been as follows:

PRODUCT	DEMAND UNITS	LABOUR HOURS PER UNIT	LABOUR HOURS TOTAL	CONTRIBUTION PER UNIT	CONTRIBUTION TOTAL
C	700	10	7 000	$360	$252 200

It can be seen that, following this approach, only product C, which was ranked first using the ranking order based on the highest contribution per unit, would be produced and sold by the company. This is because the maximum demand for product C is 800 units and, because of the restriction on labour hours available, only 700 units can be produced (that is, 10 hours × 700 units = 7000 hours). The important point to recognise is that the contribution of $252 200 generated from this ranking order is less than the contribution ($256 800) from using the ranking based on contribution per labour hour described above.

COMMENTARY

The comparison of profitability using two approaches clearly shows that if a firm is to maximise its profits when there are resource constraints, these constraints must be taken into account in making a decision about the use of the constrained resource.

KEY CONCEPT

DECISION MAKING WITH CONSTRAINTS: RULE

All products should be ranked in terms of the contribution margin per unit of resource constraint. The decision rule is to choose to sell products with the highest positive contribution margin per unit of resource constraint until demand for the product is exhausted and/or the scarce resource is depleted.

10 LEARNING OBJECTIVE

Evaluate problems of whether firms should make or buy a product or a service in cases where there is (i) spare capacity and (ii) no spare capacity

MAKE OR BUY DECISIONS

An example of a **make or buy decision** is whether a firm should design and develop its own computer programs, or whether an external software house should be hired to do the work.

The make option provides the firm's managers with more direct control over the computer software design and development work. However, external contractors often have specialist skills and expertise. As with most decisions considered in this chapter, make or buy decisions should not be made on the basis of cost alone. Qualitative factors do count and will be considered in more depth at the end of this chapter.

KEY CONCEPT

MAKE OR BUY DECISIONS

A make or buy decision is one where a business chooses between making a product or carrying out a service using its own resources, or paying for another firm to do so.

We begin our analysis by first examining whether it is more beneficial to make or buy a product or service when the firm has spare capacity. We then consider the situation when capacity is restricted because of a shortage in a required input resource.

Where there is spare capacity

We assume that a firm is not working to full capacity and it has sufficient resources available to make products or components it requires, without affecting the manufacture of any other products. Case study 17.4 illustrates the principles that should be applied to make and buy decisions in these circumstances.

CASE STUDY

LEIGH LTD

Leigh Ltd is a company that is trying to decide if it should make or buy three components: Bot, Lot and Tot. The respective costs are as follows:

	BOT	LOT	TOT
Production units	1 000	2 000	4 000
	$	$	$
Variable costs per unit:			
Materials	4	5	2
Labour	10	12	5
Total variable cost	14	17	7

The fixed costs per annum that are directly attributable (avoidable costs) to the manufacture of the components and are apportioned (unavoidable costs) to components are as follows:

	$
Avoidable costs:	
Bot	1 000
Lot	5 000
Tot	13 000
Apportioned fixed costs	30 000
	49 000

A subcontractor has offered to supply units of Bot, Lot and Tot for $12, $21 and $10 respectively. The relevant costs to be taken into account in this decision are the differential costs associated with making and with buying. For this decision, the differential costs are the differences in unit variable costs and the directly attributable fixed costs. The following is a summary of the relevant costs:

	BOT	LOT	TOT
Variable cost per unit, making	$14	$17	$7
Cost per unit, buying	$12	$21	$10
Additional cost per unit of buying	($2)	$4	$3
Production units per annum	1 000	2 000	4 000
Additional total variable cost of buying	($2 000)	$8 000	$12 000
Fixed costs saved by buying	$1 000	$5 000	$13 000
Additional total cost of buying	($3 000)	$3 000	($1 000)

COMMENTARY

The firm would save $3000 per annum by subcontracting out the manufacture of component Bot. This is because the variable cost per unit to make the component is greater than the purchase price. Similarly, the firm would save $1000 per annum by subcontracting out component Tot. This is due to the saving of $13 000 of fixed costs directly attributable to making the component more than offsets the incremental variable cost of buying Tot. In the case of component Lot, the firm will be $3000 better off by continuing to make this component.

It should also be noted that apportioned fixed costs are irrelevant to this decision as they are unavoidable.

In such decisions there are normally other considerations. For example, if components Bot and Tot are to be purchased from a subcontractor, it is likely that the firm will have spare capacity which may have some economic value (e.g. the now vacant space could be profitably let to an outside party). This additional profit should be included as a relevant factor in making components as the profit will be forgone if the company continues to make all three components itself. The rental income forgone from continuing to make, rather than buy, is an opportunity cost.

Inevitably there will be qualitative factors that should be taken into account. Leigh Ltd, for example, might be concerned about the quality of the subcontractor's work. This factor might lead the organisation to favour making components Bot and Tot, although, in cost terms, this policy would be unprofitable.

Where there is no spare capacity

A business might be confronted with a decision about whether to make or buy a component when it is currently working at full capacity. To make the component, it will be necessary for the business to stop or restrict its current production output. In such cases, the cost of making the component must include not only the costs directly attributed to making it but also the contribution forgone from the production that has been displaced by the decision to make the component.

Case study 17.5 illustrates make or buy decisions when capacity is restricted.

17.5

CASE STUDY

KELLEE LTD

Kellee Ltd is in the process of deciding whether to make or buy a component of one of the products it manufactures and sells. Labour is in short supply and the factory is currently working at full capacity. The following are the estimated costs per unit to make the component. (The assumption that labour is paid $20 per hour is made for convenience of calculation.)

	COST PER UNIT
	$
Direct labour (5 hours @ $20 per hour)	100
Direct material	75
Fixed overheads	25
Total cost per unit	200

As the fixed overhead costs are apportioned to the product and are unavoidable, whether or not the component is made, this cost is irrelevant to the decision. All the other costs are directly attributable to the cost of producing the component and are therefore relevant. As a result of this, the relevant cost associated with making the component is $175.

The alternative is to buy in the component from another entity. The cost of buying the component is $190 per unit.

If labour were not in short supply, the business would make the component rather than buy it because the relevant costs of making ($175) are less than the purchase price of buying ($190).

However, in view of the labour shortage, we must consider the contribution that is forgone because of the decision to make. To do so, we must account for the contribution generated from the current production activity that is to be restricted if we decide to make the component.

The following data relates to the income and cost per unit associated with a product that is to be displaced by producing (making) the component:

	PER UNIT DATA	
	$	$
Selling price		102
Less Costs		
Direct labour (3 hours @ $20 per hour)	60	
Direct material	<u>24</u>	<u>84</u>
Contribution per unit		<u>18</u>

The contribution per unit is added to the relevant cost to make the component of $175 to yield a total cost to make the component of $193, which is $3 higher than the buy option.

COMMENTARY

The inclusion of the contribution lost if the component is made internally, because it is relevant to the decision to make the component, has resulted in a cost of $193 for making the component. This marginally exceeds the buying price of $190; thus, purely on financial grounds the decision should be to buy rather than to make. As discussed below, a considered analysis of relevant qualitative factors may lead to a decision to continue make the component in-house.

QUALITATIVE FACTORS

In our analysis of the decisions made in this chapter, all have been made on the basis of financial criteria. Often, qualitative factors can be very influential in making such decisions. Indeed, opportunities that would be rejected on purely quantitative or financial criteria may be accepted due to other, strategically significant qualitative reasons.

Qualitative factors are those factors that cannot be quantified in terms of revenues, costs and profit. They might stem from either non-financial objectives or factors which could be expressed in monetary terms but as there is insufficient information to generate a reliable estimate, they have not been quantified.

The nature of these qualitative factors will vary with individual circumstances. The following are some examples of qualitative factors that might influence decisions.

Customers

The inclusion or exclusion of a product from the range offered or the quality of the product and after-sales service may affect the demand for the product and customer loyalty. For example, the exclusion of one product from a range because it is uneconomic to produce and sell could affect the demand for the firm's other products. In a multi-product firm, the products manufactured can often be interdependent and this interdependence must be considered when making a decision to eliminate one or more products.

Employees

Decisions involving the closure of part of a business, or relocation, or changes in work procedures, require acceptance by employees. If the changes are poorly implemented, problems between employees and management could lead to spillover effects in terms of morale, less efficient work practices and ultimately lower profits.

11 LEARNING OBJECTIVE

Discuss the role of qualitative factors in making decisions where constraints are present

Competitors

In a competitive market, decisions by one business to enhance its competitive position might result in retaliation by competitors (i.e. a price war). For example, a decision to reduce selling prices in order to acquire a greater market share will not be successful if all competitors take similar action (as has occurred in the tobacco and beverage products industries).

A firm might decide to produce an unprofitable product or offer a service at a loss because it would otherwise leave the market to its competitors which then use their stronger market presence to attack the firm in the market it retained. Also, the firm might need to consider the demand for its remaining products as a consequence of the leakage of existing customers who can no longer purchase from the firm one of the products they require.

Legal constraints

An opportunity is sometimes rejected because of doubts about pending legislation. The decision to open a hotel, for example, might be influenced by draft legislation on safety requirements that could result in additional costs which are too difficult to reliably estimate.

Suppliers

A business might rely on maintaining a good relationship with a particular supplier for the prompt delivery of supplies. Some decisions might detrimentally affect that relationship.

STOP AND THINK 5

Qualitative factors can often be influential in the decision-making process. Describe the nature of qualitative factors and give three examples that might influence a company's decision to make a component rather than buy it from another firm.

SUMMARY

LEARNING OBJECTIVE 1

EXPLAIN WHAT IS MEANT BY THE TERM 'SUNK COSTS'

Sunk costs are those costs that have been paid or are owed and committed to be paid by a firm. They are irrelevant for future decision making.

LEARNING OBJECTIVE 2

EXPLAIN WHAT IS MEANT BY DIFFERENTIAL (INCREMENTAL) COSTS

Differential costs are the differences in costs and benefits between alternative opportunities available to a firm. When a number of opportunities are being considered, costs and benefits that are common to these alternative opportunities are irrelevant to the decision.

LEARNING OBJECTIVE 3

IDENTIFY WHAT IS MEANT BY AVOIDABLE AND UNAVOIDABLE COSTS

An avoidable cost is one that will not have to be paid if a firm does not proceed with a decision. An unavoidable cost is one that will be incurred regardless of whether the firm decides to accept or reject a proposal.

LEARNING OBJECTIVE 4

DISCUSS THE CONCEPT OF OPPORTUNITY COSTS AND ITS ROLE IN DECISION MAKING

The opportunity cost of a resource is normally defined as the maximum benefits which could be obtained from that resource if it were used for some alternative purpose. If the benefits from Project A are $400 and the potential benefits from Project B are $600, the opportunity cost that is given up by accepting Project B over Project A is $400.

LEARNING OBJECTIVE 5

EXPLAIN THE COSTS AND BENEFITS THAT ARE RELEVANT TO SPECIFIC DECISIONS

Relevant costs and benefits are those costs and benefits that relate to the future. They are the incremental costs incurred and income earned as the result of a decision being made.

LEARNING OBJECTIVE 6

EXPLAIN AND APPLY THE CONTRIBUTION MARGIN APPROACH TO DECISION MAKING IN CASES WHERE THERE ARE NO RESOURCE CONSTRAINTS

Assuming a linear cost and sales function, where there are no restraints on available resources, a firm will accept all proposals that produce a positive contribution margin.

LEARNING OBJECTIVE 7

APPLY THE CONTRIBUTION MARGIN APPROACH TO DECISIONS CONCERNING WHETHER TO CLOSE UNPROFITABLE DEPARTMENTS, BUSINESS UNITS OR DIVISIONS

Normally, within the contribution margin approach, if a proposal's income exceeds variable costs, it should proceed. However, some fixed costs (e.g. supervisory salaries) are allocated based on a predetermined basis. These allocated costs may need to be taken into account when making a decision to close an unprofitable department, business unit or division depending upon whether or not they could be avoided.

When fixed costs are directly attributable to a proposal and are avoidable, the approach should be: where income exceeds all costs directly attributable to a purportedly unprofitable department, business unit or division, it should be kept open.

LEARNING OBJECTIVE 8

EXPLAIN WHAT IS MEANT BY DECISION MAKING WITH CONSTRAINTS

When there are resource constraints, the objective should be to establish the optimum output within the constraints in order to maximise the contribution margin and, thereby, profits. These resource constraints could be labour, materials or available machinery.

LEARNING OBJECTIVE 9

ILLUSTRATE THE USE OF THE CONTRIBUTION MARGIN APPROACH IN RELATION TO DECISIONS WITH ONE SCARCE RESOURCE

To determine the optimum output with one constraint, we first determine the contribution margin. Second, we establish the contribution per unit of the constraint for all those opportunities that yield a positive contribution. Third, we rank them according to the contribution per unit of the constraint, with the highest ranked project being the one that yields the highest contribution margin per unit of the constraint.

LEARNING OBJECTIVE 10

EVALUATE PROBLEMS OF WHETHER FIRMS SHOULD MAKE OR BUY A PRODUCT OR A SERVICE IN CASES WHERE THERE IS (I) SPARE CAPACITY AND (II) NO SPARE CAPACITY

The make or buy decision is one that is made by a firm when it chooses between using its own resources or purchasing a product, component or service from an external supplier. If there is spare capacity, the firm only needs to look at its variable and directly attributable fixed costs, plus any opportunity costs in relation to the spare capacity that could be available for other profitable purposes (e.g. renting unused space to others), before making a decision. If there is no otherwise spare capacity, the firm needs to look at its variable and directly attributable fixed costs plus the contributed loss from the product or service that has been displaced.

LEARNING OBJECTIVE 11

DISCUSS THE ROLE OF QUALITATIVE FACTORS IN MAKING DECISIONS WHERE CONSTRAINTS ARE PRESENT

Some decisions that need to be made may override the financial criteria involved and focus on other issues such as good customer relations, giving exceptional after-sale service, environmental issues and conditions for employees (especially where changes are to occur in the workplace). There are many more qualitative factors and, in evaluating a financial decision, these factors may very well be the ones that change the decision outcome from what had been determined solely on the basis of quantified data.

REVIEW QUESTIONS

1 Discuss the reasons why accrual accounting methods are not appropriate for decisions concerning the future.

2 In the majority of cases, fixed costs are irrelevant in decision making, but on some occasions they are relevant. Describe the circumstances when fixed costs are relevant to future decisions.

3 Explain why a shortage of resources in an organisation is a short-term phenomenon.

4   In some circumstances, the opportunity cost of a resource might be higher than the resource's purchase price. Explain why this might be the case.

PROBLEMS FOR DISCUSSION AND ANALYSIS

1   Calculators Ltd manufactures and sells pocket calculators. The price of these calculators is $22. The company's current output is 40 000 units per month, which represents 90 per cent of its productive capacity. Kodix, a chain-store customer which specialises in selling electronic goods, offers to buy 2000 calculators as a special order at $16 each. The calculators would be sold under the name of Kodix.

   The total costs per month are $800 000, of which $192 000 are fixed costs.

   a   Advise Calculators Ltd on whether it should accept the special order.

   b   Would your advice change if Kodix wanted 5000 calculators?

2   Sprinks Ltd produces three products: A, B and C. The following is an estimate of costs and revenues for the forthcoming year:

	A	B	C
	$	$	$
Sales	32 000	50 000	45 000
Total cost	36 000	38 000	34 000
Net profit (loss)	(4 000)	12 000	11 000

   The total cost of each product comprises one-third fixed costs and two-thirds variable costs. Fixed costs are constant whatever the volume of sales. The managing director argues that because product A makes a loss, production of it should be discontinued.

   Comment on the managing director's argument.

3   Agro Company has been producing 10 000 units of part 7021 for its products. The unit cost for the part is as follows:

	$
Direct materials	5
Direct labour	10
Variable manufacturing overhead	6
Fixed manufacturing overhead	8
Total	29

   Agro can purchase 10 000 units of part 7021 for $25 each. If the part is purchased, Agro can make another product and provide a contribution margin of $10 000. If the part is purchased, 75 per cent of the fixed manufacturing overhead costs will still be incurred.

Required

Should Agro make or buy the part?

4 Advance Ltd manufactures two solar-powered frisbees – Wild One and Bold One. The company has only a limited supply of skilled labour, which is essential in the production process.

The following information is available:

	WILD ONE	BOLD ONE
Contribution margin per unit	$15	$18
Hours to produce one unit	3	4

» Anticipated sales exceed capacity for both products.
» Total labour hours available: 12 000 hours.

Required

Determine which product should be produced.

5 XYZ Ltd manufactures two products. On average, it sells 40 000 units of product 1 and 60 000 units of product 2 each year. This year the company has a restricted advertising budget of $50 000, which is only enough to effectively promote one of its products. The marketing department estimates that average sales of product 1 will increase by 20 per cent if it is advertised, while product 2's average sales will increase by 15 per cent if it is advertised.

The following data is provided:

	1	2
	PER UNIT	PER UNIT
Selling price	$20	$30
Variable cost	$10	$14
Total fixed costs of $800 000. Allocated to each product line in proportion to direct labour hours	$5	$10
Production time (in direct labour hours)	2	4

Required

a Assuming unlimited direct labour hours, which product should it advertise?
b If there were only 336 000 direct labour hours, would you change your decision?

6 The MNO Company manufactures gas cylinders for use in campervans and caravans. The costs per cylinder are as follows.

	$
Direct materials per unit	5.30
Direct labour per unit	4.20
Variable overhead per unit	0.35
Fixed overhead (per month)	125 000

MNO manufactures and sells 20 000 cylinders per month and has the capacity, without increasing overhead costs, to manufacture 25 000.

Fixed costs are allocated on the basis of cylinders manufactured.

Avco Ltd has offered to purchase 6000 cylinders for $72 000. This is a one-off order and will not be repeated.

a Should MNO accept the order? Why or why not?

b What problems might the company face if it accepts the order?

7 Gallop Corporation Ltd has two divisions: production and assembly. The cost per unit that is charged by the production division to the assembly division is set to increase from $12 to $15, which is the same price as customers pay when they purchase directly from the production division. The manager of the assembly division is extremely upset and has expressed his intentions to buy the units from an outside supplier at a cost of $12 per unit.

The following data relates to the production division:

Units produced	100 000
Variable production costs per unit	$10
Indirect fixed costs allocated to the production division	$200 000
Normal profit per unit with production division	$3

The assembly division normally purchases 50 000 units from the production division.

Required

a What is the impact on Gallop Corporation's overall profit if the assembly division purchases units from outside suppliers?

b Discuss the implications of this decision for (i) the shareholders of Gallop, (ii) the management of Gallop Corporation, and (iii) the heads of the production and assembly divisions who each have an annual cash bonus linked to a controllable profit measure based on divisional contribution margins.

8 At present, Coyle Ltd manufactures all the components that go into making up its finished products. A components supplier has offered to fulfil the company's requirements in relation to two components, the BC100 (at $7.75 each) and the BC200 (at $2.00 each).

If the company buys in components, the capacity that is presently utilised for these components would be unused. The company currently manufactures 50 000 units of each component and the current costs of production are as follows:

	BC100	BC200
	$	$
Materials	2.50	1.00
Labour	3.00	1.25
Fixed overheads	3.50	1.75
Total cost per unit	9.00	4.00

a   On a quantitative basis, should the company continue to manufacture BC100 and BC200 or should it buy in one or both of the components?

b   Discuss the qualitative factors which are likely to influence this decision.

9   Mikel Ltd manufactures components for bicycles. At the moment, sales are 100 000 units at $10 per unit. Fixed costs are $500 000 and variable costs are $5.50 per unit.

If Mikel stopped production, it would still have long-term fixed costs of $100 000.

a   Should Mikel stop production? If not, what steps could the company consider to improve profit?

b   Mikel has been offered a contract by Bell Ltd to supply 150 000 units at $9.00 per unit. Assuming Mikel has the capacity to produce these units at the same variable and fixed costs, should it accept the order?

10 Philco is a manufacturer of portable analogue radios. The costs per radio, for a production run of 20 000 units, are as follows:

	$
Direct materials	27.00
Direct labour	13.00
Variable overhead	6.00
Fixed overhead	10.00

Fixed overhead is applied on a per-unit basis.

Dorro Ltd has offered to supply the circuit board with components for $20.00 per unit. This would result in a saving of $10.00 in direct materials, $3.00 in direct labour and $4.00 in variable overhead. There would be no saving in fixed overhead. If Philco was to accept this offer, it would then have the capacity to manufacture 10 000 micro radios. The cost per unit for the micro radios are as follows:

	$
Direct materials	4.00
Direct labour	3.00
Fixed overhead	2.00

The fixed overhead for the micro radios is in addition to the existing fixed overhead already incurred on analogue radios. The micro radio is expected to sell for $10.10 per unit.

Should Philco accept Dorro Ltd's offer, assuming that all production is sold?

11 TVS Ltd manufactures a range of digital flat-screen television sets. At present, the company is able to sell only 80 per cent of the plant's capacity of its 20-centimetre digital sets. These sets are sold to retailers for $200 per unit. With the present production, TVS sells 100 000 sets, and has total fixed costs of $7 500 000 and variable costs of $100 per unit.

a What is the present profit?

b If TVS reduced its price to retailers to $185 it believes it would operate at 100 per cent capacity. Should TVS take this step?

c Low Price Stores Ltd has offered to purchase 20 000 sets at $175. If TVS accepted this offer, the variable costs on the additional sets would be $95 because there would be no marketing costs. Given that TVS is operating at 80 per cent capacity, which of the three options produces the maximum profit:

    i   the present profit

    ii reduce the selling price to $185

    iii retain existing price of $200 and accept special offer conditions and sell 20 000 sets to Low Price Stores.

12 Pigeon Ltd proposes a production plan for this year, aiming to maximise profits. The following details are available:

	A	B	C	D	E	F
Labour hours per unit	6.4	7	4	9	5	12
Machine hours per unit	3	2	1	3	1	8
Maximum demand	2500	1200	700	1100	900	2900
	$	$	$	$	$	$
Selling price	20	28	8	36	16	40
Costs:						
Direct materials	4	4	1.2	2.4	2.8	1.6
Direct labour	4	6	2.4	8.8	3.6	3.2
Fixed overhead	4	6	2.4	8.8	3.6	3.2
Total cost	12	16	6.0	20.0	10.0	8.0
Profit	8	12	2.0	16.0	6.0	32.0

Total fixed overhead, which is estimated to cost $10 000 irrespective of what is produced and sold, is applied at 100 per cent of direct labour cost.

A maximum of 64 000 direct labour hours is expected to be available.

Calculate the optimal profit-maximising production schedule and explain the reasons for your choice.

13 Tredways Shoe Company produces three different types of shoes. The condensed results for the company for the past year are as follows:

	SCOUT	TROUPER	HOUND DOG
	$	$	$
Sales	250 000	150 000	320 000
Cost of goods sold	210 000	155 000	250 000
Gross profit	40 000	(5 000)	70 000
Operating expenses	55 000	20 000	35 000
Net profit	(15 000)	(25 000)	35 000

The CEO believes Tredways should stop making Scouts and Troupers. However, before making a final decision she asks to be provided with more details about the cost items. These details are presented below.

	SCOUT	TROUPER	HOUND DOG
	$	$	$
Cost of goods sold			
Variable manufacturing costs	125 000	100 000	170 000
Fixed manufacturing costs	85 000	55 000	80 000
Operating costs			
Variable	35 000	13 000	20 000
Fixed	20 000	7 000	15 000

Required

Is the CEO correct? Should the information that is provided lead to the company stopping the manufacture of Scouts and Troupers? What additional information would you need before making a final recommendation?

Note to instructors: The following problems are considered more suitable for use in MBA courses. However, undergraduate courses may also find them useful.

14 You have recently been appointed as a consultant to the Murphy Manufacturing Company. The management of the company has prepared a report showing certain data concerning

the two products Mox and Tox. The following information has been extracted from this report:

	MOX	TOX
Monthly sales in units	1 000	2 000
	$	$
Selling price	3.00	1.50
Costs		
Direct materials	0.80	0.50
Direct labour	1.00	0.20
Fixed overheads	1.40	0.50
Total cost	3.20	1.20
Profit (loss)	(0.20)	0.30

In view of the poor results shown by Mox, the following changes have been proposed by management:

Abandon the production of Mox and buy in 1000 units per month for $2800. The quality is identical and selling price will remain unchanged.

Use the spare capacity to make Cox. It is estimated that 1000 units could be sold at $1 each. Material costs are $0.40 per unit and labour costs $0.20.

All overheads are fixed and are not expected to change from the present cost of $2000 per month. No inventories are held.

a Comment on the suitability of management's approach to assessing product profitability, as illustrated in the report, and indicate any ways in which you think it could be improved.

b Prepare a monthly statement of comprehensive income for the present program and the proposed new program. Do the proposed changes appear to be profitable? Explain the reasons for your answer.

15 Burco Ltd produces and sells two products: X and Y. During the last year, 700 hours were worked and the operating results were as follows:

	X	Y	TOTAL
Units sold	1000	1000	2 000
	$	$	$
Sales	10 000	20 000	30 000
Variable costs:			
Labour	2 000	5 000	7 000
Materials	5 500	9 000	14 500
Total variable costs	7 500	14 000	21 500
Contribution margin	2 500	6 000	8 500
Fixed costs			6 000
Net profit			2 500

All variable costs are a linear function of output. The material used for X is quite different from that used for Y, but both can be produced with the same labour force.

Five units of X can be made in one labour hour, while only two units of Y can be made in one labour hour. Labour hours are expected to be limited to 800 next year.

Information about the market for X and Y for the next year is set out below:

	X	Y
Maximum quantity that can be sold (units)	1100	1200
Minimum quantity that must be sold to retain market (units)	600	800

a Assuming that plant capacity is fully used, what is the optimum mix of X and Y?

b Assuming that the price of material for Y decreases by 20 per cent, what is the optimal mix of X and Y? Assume no change in the price of X or Y.

c Assuming that the cost of labour increases by 20 per cent, that prices can be put up by only 10 per cent without affecting sales limits and that the number of labour hours available is reduced to 600, what is the optimal mix of X and Y?

d What is the net profit in each of these three cases?

e Discuss the limitations of your analysis.

16 Eatinatural Ltd specialises in the manufacture and sale of health foods. The company has just completed market research on a new type of organic toothpaste called Abrasive. The budget, derived from the market research for one year's production and sales, was presented to the board by the marketing manager as follows:

ABRASIVE TOOTHPASTE

	$	$
Cost of production (100 000 kg)		
Labour		
Direct wages	250 000	
Supervisory	<u>150 000</u>	400 000
Raw materials		
Ingredient X	85 000	
Ingredient Y	35 000	
Ingredient P	45 000	
Ingredient Z	<u>5 000</u>	170 000
Other variable costs		50 000
Fixed overheads (60% of direct labour)		150 000
Research and development		<u>100 000</u>

	$	$
Total costs		870 000
Sales (100 000 kg at $8.00 per kg)		800 000
Loss		(70 000)

The board of directors is disappointed with this budget in view of the research and development costs of $20 000 that have already been incurred and the need to make use of the spare capacity in the factory. Fred Sharpe, the managing director, suggests bringing in a consultant to examine the costs of the new product.

The following additional information is available:

a It would be possible to transfer 60 per cent of the direct labour requirement from another department within the company. The monthly contribution of this department ($25 000) subject to the introduction of a special machine into the department at an annual hire cost of $20 000, would fall by only 20 per cent of its current level as a result of the reduction in the labour force. The remainder of the direct labour requirement would have to be recruited. It is anticipated that their wages will be the same as the workers transferred from the other department. In addition, it is estimated that the costs of recruitment – for example, advertising – will be $15 000.

b Two supervisors would be required at a cost of $75 000 each per year. One would be recruited; the other, Reg Raven, would remain at work instead of retiring. The company will pay him a pension of $25 000 per year on his retirement.

c Inventories of ingredient X are currently available for a whole year's production of Abrasive, and are valued at their original cost. The price of this ingredient is subject to dramatic variations, and the current market price is double the original cost. It could be resold at the market price less 10 per cent selling expenses, or retained for use later in another new product to be manufactured by the company, by which time it is expected that the market price will have fallen by about 25 per cent.

d Ingredient Y's price has been very stable and it is used for other products currently manufactured and sold by the company. There are no inventories available for the production of Abrasive.

e Ingredient P is another commodity with a fairly static price. Half of the annual requirement is in inventory and the other half will have to be purchased during the year at an estimated cost of $22 500. The materials in inventory could be resold for $20 000 less 10 per cent selling expenses, or could be used to produce another product, after some further processing. This processing, which would take 2000 hours in the Mixing Department, where labour is paid $12 per hour, would save the company additional purchasing costs of $25 000. The Mixing Department only has sufficient idle capacity to do this amount of work.

f Ingredient Z was bought well in advance and is in inventory. It has no alternative use. Fred Sharpe is beginning to regret the decision to buy this ingredient in advance because it will deteriorate in store and might become dangerous before the end of the budget period. It cannot be sold and it will cost the company $5000 to dispose of it if it is not used to produce Abrasive.

g The other variable costs can all be avoided if the contract is not accepted.

h Fixed overheads for the company are expected to increase by $20 000 per year as a result of manufacturing and selling Abrasive.

Required

As the consultant employed by the company, you are requested to re-examine this statement, taking account of the additional information, and recommend any necessary action. Clearly state any assumptions that you make.

17   As the personal assistant to your company's managing director, you have been requested to prepare a confidential report on the possible closure of the Hobart factory and the centralisation of all activities within the Perth facility. Two major reasons appear to be behind the request for the report: an expected increase in rent of $15 000, and the express wish of the managing director's daughter (who is married to the Hobart manager) to return to Perth.

Due to the nature of the report, information for the decision is difficult to obtain. However, the following data is available from corporate budgets for the ensuing year:

a   The annual fixed costs of the Hobart operations are, at present, $85 000. This figure comprises the $50 000 salary of the Hobart manager (who will be transferred back to Perth), rent at $25 000 and the $10 000 salary of a part-time clerical officer whose services would be dispensed with upon the closure of the Hobart factory.

b   Variable costs at the Hobart factory are $125 000.

c   The sale of plant and other assets in Hobart will be sufficient to pay the termination of all Hobart staff, including the part-time clerical officer.

d   Additional space in Perth may be rented in steps of $10 000 per 10 000 units manufactured.

e   A common price policy has established the price for product B52, the sole product produced by the company, at $10.00 per unit. Budgeted figures call for 25 000 units to be produced at Hobart and 40 000 units to be produced at Perth. There are no inventories.

f   Additional staff in Perth would need to be hired to meet the extra workload resulting from the closure of the Hobart factory. This cost is expected to be $17 500. The cost to service the Hobart market from Perth would be $1.10 per unit in addition to the variable costs.

g   Variable costs at Perth have been budgeted at $160 000.

h   The Hobart factory has been allocated $45 000 of the head office costs.

i   A local manufacturer in Hobart can make and supply a version of product B52 to the Hobart region and is willing to do so with a royalty of $2.00 per unit being paid to your company.

Required

In your report, list the alternatives that are available to your company, including a full and complete cost justification to support your recommendation. What factors should be considered besides the cost factor? List such qualitative factors in your report.

ETHICS CASE STUDY 1

Orbital Machines Ltd is a company that has been manufacturing a revolutionary new engine for motor vehicles for 10 years. It employs 1000 workers, and the economy of Winjarra is completely dependent on Orbital Machines.

On 10 July, the company won a major contract with the Aussie Motor Company to provide orbital engines for all its cars from 1 January next year. In order to meet the production requirements, the company would need to make a significant investment in additional manufacturing equipment and employ more workers.

The costs of operating in Winjarra have increased because of higher rates and taxes, as well as the wages that will have to be offered in order to recruit the required skills in an increasingly tight labour market. The company would be reluctant to invest significant funds if increases in costs are likely to continue to be a problem.

The company has received an approach from the mayor of Binjarra, a small city 500 kilometres from Winjarra. As Binjarra's mayor would like Orbital to move its entire operation to her city, she has offered the following incentives:

1   A large parcel of land with no rates and taxes to be levied for five years.
2   A workforce where the average labour costs are 25 per cent lower than in Winjarra.
    In return, Orbital can only employ local residents.

This move would allow Orbital to avoid the cost pressures it currently faces in Winjarra. This, in turn, would allow it to compete more effectively in foreign markets.

Discuss

a   who are the stakeholders in this decision
b   the quantitative and qualitative factors that are relevant to this decision
c   whether there are any ethical issues for the management of Orbital Machines to consider.

ETHICS CASE STUDY 2

Forpark Ltd is planning to add slides to the cubby houses it produces. Joe Clark, the accountant of Forpark, has just completed an analysis to see if the company should make or buy the slides. His analysis shows that, based on the written quotations received from two suppliers of the slides, the company should purchase the slides.

The manager of Forpark agrees with Clark and they issue instructions to the purchasing department that orders should be placed for the slides, as long as the price is not greater than $35 per unit.

A couple of days later, Clark is informed by the purchasing department that both suppliers have increased their price to $40 per unit. He discusses the situation with the manager and they decide that Forpark should now manufacture the slides. Clark thinks it is odd that both suppliers have increased their prices to the same figure.

Later in the week, Joe Clark is approached by his secretary, Jane Brown. Jane informs him that a friend of hers, who works for one of the suppliers of the slides, has told her about an agreement reached between the two suppliers of the slides. Essentially, the two suppliers have agreed to raise the price of their slides to $40 per unit. Jane does not want her friend to get into trouble for disclosing this type of confidential information, but at the same time she thought she ought to tell Joe.

Discuss

a   What Joe should do with the information received from Jane, remembering his responsibilities to the accounting profession, to his company and to Jane?
b   Who is affected by the scheme to manipulate tenders in this manner?

SUGGESTED ANSWERS TO STOP AND THINK EXERCISES IN THE CHAPTER

1. Sunk costs are costs of a historical nature. Therefore, they have been incurred as a result of a past decision. It follows that these costs are irrelevant to future decisions. Sunk costs can be easily identified because they either have been paid or are subject to legally binding contracts, which means the firm is committed to paying for these contracts in the future.

2. An avoidable cost is a cost that can be avoided if an opportunity is not taken up. These costs are relevant as they are directly attributable to the decision to take up an opportunity. In contrast, an unavoidable cost is one that is going to be incurred regardless of whether the decision in relation to a particular proposal is accepted or rejected. Unavoidable costs are irrelevant in decision making.

3. An opportunity cost is defined as the maximum benefit that could be obtained from a resource if it were used for some alternative purpose other than the opportunity under consideration. Therefore, the opportunity costs of resources are relevant costs in decision making.

4. The cost associated with the depreciation of an asset is based on the historic cost of that asset. Therefore, the historic cost of an asset is the result of a past decision, which means it is a sunk cost and irrelevant to the decision to be made. It follows that the cost of depreciation, which is based on the asset's historic cost, is also a sunk cost and is also irrelevant.

5. Qualitative factors are not capable of being quantified in terms of costs and revenue. They may stem either from non-financial objectives or from factors that might be able to be quantified in monetary terms, but because there is insufficient information to make reliable estimates, they have not been quantified. The nature of qualitative factors in any decision-making task will vary with the circumstances that are related to the opportunities being considered.

   Examples of qualitative factors in the make or buy decision:

   » *Quality*. If a firm makes a component rather than buying it from an external party, it has greater control over the quality of the component. For example, the firm can implement its own quality and inspection policies and amend these as seen fit. Although this factor may be difficult to assess in monetary terms, it may be highly influential in the make or buy decision.

   » *Reliability of supplies*. It is likely that a firm will have greater control over the reliability of supplies if it makes a component rather than buys it in from another firm. For example, the cost of buying a component externally may be less than the cost of making the component. However, the potential supplier may have a poor industrial relations history that could periodically jeopardise the reliability of supply. This may be a significant factor in the decision to make or buy.

   » *After-sales service*. When a firm sells a product that has a component purchased externally, it may find it difficult to service the product if the component is the cause of a malfunction. After-sales service may be influential in the firm's ability to sell the product. Thus, the make or buy decision will also be influenced by this factor.

CENGAGENOW

Go to http:\\login.cengagebrain.com to link to CengageNOW, your online study tool. First take the Pre-Test for this chapter to get your Personalised Study Plan, and then:

» revise your understanding of the key terms related to accounting for decision making by completing the online crossword
» review key definitions through extended online definition links
» review the key concepts with online flashcards.

After you have completed the activities in your Personalised Study Plan take the Post-Test to determine what concepts you have mastered and what you still need work on.

CAPITAL INVESTMENT DECISIONS

LEARNING OBJECTIVES

At the end of this chapter, you should be able to:

1 explain the importance of well-made strategic capital investment decisions to the growing of business value

2 explain the characteristics of capital investment decisions as they differ from other managerial decisions

3 identify the multi-period dimension and the importance of life-cycle analysis to the evaluation of proposed capital investments

4 outline the seven steps to a capital investment decision

5 explain and apply the concept of accounting rate of return (ARR) and the payback period method, and evaluate their usefulness in making capital investment decisions

6 explain and apply the internal rate of return (IRR) and net present value (NPV) methods in carrying out the discounted cash flow (DCF) analysis of proposed capital investments

7 compare IRR and NPV methods of DCF analysis, appreciate the differences in their underlying assumptions and explain why they may provide contrary recommendations

8 discuss how mutually exclusive investments are dealt with

9 explain the importance of qualitative factors to a capital investment decision

10 explain the significance of risk to capital investment decisions and identify the use of inappropriate adjustments for dealing with that risk

11 explain how sensitivity analysis is used to deal with uncertainty and focuses managerial attention on those critical variables that have significance for a capital investment decision

12 explain the value of post-implementation audits as a tool for managing existing and any future project requiring a capital investment

13 explain what is meant by project abandonment and its implications for the making of a capital investment decision.

INTRODUCTION

Before we start our discussion of capital investment decisions, it is important that you are able to understand and solve some basic financial mathematics problems. The following Stop and think exercise is intended to assess your capacity to solve three basic financial mathematics questions. If you are not able to complete the exercises then you should refer to 'An introduction to financial mathematics', which can be found online at www.cengagebrain.com.

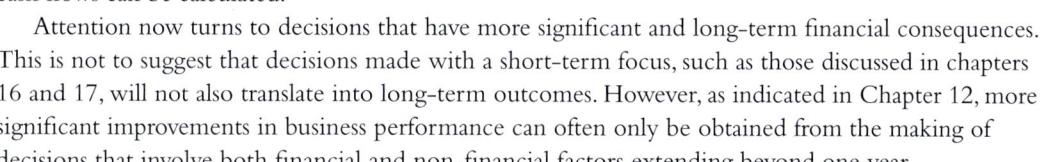

STOP AND THINK 1

a   Calculate the simple interest on $1245 at 5.6 per cent per annum from 1 June to 15 December.

b   How long will it take $100 to accumulate to $200 at 6 per cent per annum?

c   A family buys a house for $120 000. It sells its old house for $70 000 and uses this as a deposit. It borrows the balance at 7 per cent per annum compound interest. What amount, payable at the end of each year, would pay off the loan over 10 years?

The online Appendix 'Exploring the time value of money concept' provides an alternative approach to developing your understanding of the time value of money concept and how the present value of future cash flows can be calculated.

Attention now turns to decisions that have more significant and long-term financial consequences. This is not to suggest that decisions made with a short-term focus, such as those discussed in chapters 16 and 17, will not also translate into long-term outcomes. However, as indicated in Chapter 12, more significant improvements in business performance can often only be obtained from the making of decisions that involve both financial and non-financial factors extending beyond one year.

As discussed in Chapter 12, to grow or sustain a business, strategic decisions about existing or new products and/or existing or new markets need to be made. The challenge for a firm's managers is to decide how much needs to be invested in support of each feasible strategic initiative and how that investment is to be funded.

In Chapter 12 it was noted that most strategic decisions entail some form of change to what the business is currently engaged in. For example, strategic decisions might be to increase the scale of exiting business activities, to expand the scope of business activities to related or unrelated activities and/or to change the way in which business activities are undertaken. Alternatively, as some business activities might be viewed as limiting the firm's profitability, other types of strategic decisions might be to no longer engage in existing business activities. Case Study 18.1 outlines some of the recent strategic decisions taken by Woolworths.

1   LEARNING OBJECTIVE

Explain the importance of well-made strategic capital investment decisions to the growing of business value

18.1 CASE STUDY

Woolworths has made many strategic decisions that impact on both the scale and scope of its business activities and how they are undertaken. For example:

»   The investment in new supermarket outlets

»   The establishment of the Masters Home Improvement chain

»   The development of digital platforms to provide customers with an online channel as an alternative to the traditional bricks-and-mortar supermarket retailing model

»   The divestment of Woolworths' investments in a wholesaling joint venture in India in October and Dick Smith Electronics (DSE) in November 2012

» The decision to spin off company-owned retail properties into the Shopping Centres Australasia (SCA) Property Group.

COMMENTARY

Each of these examples is a significant strategic decision made by Woolworths.

» With new residential developments being continually released to accommodate Australia's growing population, Woolworths must invest in new retailing outlets if it is to maintain its competitive position within the Australasian grocery industry. Although Woolworths may not immediately establish a presence in all newly developed suburbs, a decision to not proceed will only occur after the company has fully evaluated the competitive advantage obtained by rival retailers (e.g. Coles or Aldi) if they were to be the first to enter emerging market locations.

» Wesfarmers-owned Bunnings dominates the Australian hardware and home improvements industry and delivers significant returns to its parent. With annual hardware and home improvements turnover in Australia forecast to be in excess of $42 billion by 2014, the decision by Woolworths to establish Masters, in partnership with the United States–based Lowes home improvement chain, is intended to capture a share of this growing market.

» Apart from investing in information technology enabling its customers to buy groceries, liquor and home improvement products online, Woolworths also acquired other firms, such as Cellarmasters and EziBuy, which already had an established online retailing presence in liquor, apparel and home wares.

» Woolworths sought to establish a presence in the Australasian electronics consumer market with its acquisition of DSE and in India with an electronics wholesaling joint venture. Unfortunately, DSE failed to generate the returns expected by Woolworths and, in November 2012, it sold the electronics business to Anchorage Capital for just $20 million. The sale of Woolworths' consumer electronics division resulted in the company suffering an initial loss on disposal of $420 million. This loss was subsequently reduced when an additional $74 million was paid to pre-emptively buy out Woolworths' remaining interest in any proceeds that would be realised by Anchorage on a subsequent sale of Dick Smith.

» With the Global Financial Crisis (GFC) of September 2008, private sector investment in new shopping centres in Australasia fell. Given the need for Woolworths to continually open new retail outlets, it was obliged to commission and build its own portfolio of retail properties which grew to approximately $1.27 billion. By late 2012, an independent market valuation ascribed a value of approximately $1.406 billion to Woolworths' retail property portfolio, a significant investment in non-current assets. Since Woolworths believed that its primary purpose was to be Australia's leading retailer, it viewed its ownership of a retail property portfolio as not being a core business activity for the company to be engaged in. Thus, the spinning off of Woolworths-owned retail properties into the SCA Property Group was seen to offer benefits to: not only allowing the firm to focus on core retailing activities, but the receipt of $850 million in cash also allowed it to reduce high-cost debt and to generate an increased return on equity (ROE). Furthermore, the in specie allocation of stapled units in the SCA trust to Woolworths' shareholders provided many with a tax-free distribution.

2 LEARNING OBJECTIVE

Explain the characteristics of capital investment decisions as they differ from other managerial decisions

In deciding to make strategic decisions such as those above, Woolworths' managers had to address many issues and questions. For example, deciding to enter the Australasian hardware and home improvement market required the firm to establish how it wanted to build a presence in the sector (e.g. acquire existing retailers or establish a new start-up business)? Having identified that it would establish a new business, how many Masters retail outlets were to be opened, when and where? What would be the product offer in each store, what was the range of products to be stocked and what pricing policy was to be implemented for the products sold? From what sources were products and services be procured?

What stocking levels would be required to meet customer needs? How would the business be promoted and what market share would be required to achieve a profitable outcome? What is the skill set and experience that would be required of employees and what would the customer service staff head count be in each store? This list of questions is not intended to provide a comprehensive coverage of the issues that demanded the attention of Woolworths' managers as they contemplated setting up the Masters Home Improvement business. However, and not surprisingly, questions such as these illustrate that whatever answers were found, they all affected the flow of economic resources into and out of Woolworths.

In this chapter we examine decisions involving the commitment of significant sums of money over an extended period of time. This is an important decision-making area for management. Capital investment decisions are difficult because they involve cash flows over time, and the time value of money must be incorporated into the decision. There is also the problem of determining the relevant future cash flows associated with an asset that may have an expected life of a number of years. At its simplest level, management must make decisions such as whether to purchase machine X or Y, or whether to invest money in project A or B. The techniques that can be used to inform these decisions will be presented in this chapter.

> ## 18.1 KEY CONCEPT
>
> ### CAPITAL INVESTMENT AS A PROJECT
>
> Capital investment decisions focus on the multi-period financial consequences of investing funds in non-current assets or other options that are intended to assist a firm achieve its business goals. As such, the making of an investment decision entails a logical sequence of tasks that are planned, bounded by time, financial and human resources and have desired outcomes or 'deliverables' to be realised.

CAPITAL INVESTMENTS AND LIFE CYCLE ISSUES

3 LEARNING OBJECTIVE

Identify the multi-period dimension and the importance of life-cycle analysis to the evaluation of proposed capital investments

As will be demonstrated with the worked examples in this chapter, a decision to accept or reject a proposed capital investment typically focuses on the initial acquisition cost of the investment. However, equally as significant are the cost implications of activities related to the operation and maintenance of the implemented investment decision. Just as trade-offs can be made in terms of a project's critical success factors, the initial spending for a proposed capital investment might be increased due to the savings that will flow from lower operating and maintenance costs.

The application of life-cycle costing to capital investment projects first emerged in the 1970s, when it became apparent that insufficient attention was being paid to the cost implications of operating and maintaining planned investments. In essence, a life-cycle costing analysis of a proposed capital investment takes into account the total cost of a non-current asset during its useful life. Thus, the life-cycle costs of a capital asset can be grouped into three broad categories:
- initial costs of acquisition
- operating costs
- disposal costs.

How the capital asset is to be acquired will influence what is to be included in the initial cost of the asset. As discussed in Chapter 8, the cost of a purchased non-current asset would include the purchase price paid to the supplier along with the costs of installing and commissioning the asset, stocking of required spares, purchase of maintenance equipment and the recruitment and training of operational and support staff (e.g. maintenance personnel). For non-current assets that are constructed in-house, the acquisition cost would include the expenditure on research and development, documentation of design specifications, manufacturing the asset, quality control and testing, design modifications, and the recruitment and training of operational and support staff.

Operating costs for an item of capital investment include not just its operating and maintenance costs, but also the cost of indirect materials, tools, support services such as materials handling, quality control, energy, training provided to newly recruited staff and so on. Operating costs should also include the opportunity costs that result from:

- lost production during manufacturing down time attributable to scheduled preventive maintenance or unscheduled repairs due to machine failure
- poor performance where the manufacturing equipment has produced poor-quality output that cannot be disposed of for a profit
- low utilisation where the manufacturing equipment has failed to meet original specifications and it is unable to produce the output it was initially expected to deliver.

Disposal costs can be significant for some non-current assets such as a heavy-industry manufacturing facility or an offshore oil and gas platform. As such assets may need to be demolished or dismantled and removed before the site occupied can be made good for other purposes or returned to its original natural state, the disposal task can be both complex and costly. While the cost associated with the disposal of a non-current asset can be offset by any proceeds realised from disposal, invariably such offsets are trivial.

To optimise life-cycle costs for a capital asset, it is necessary to:

- identify the capacity (or quantity of output) and cost of the capital investment required
- account for other life-cycle costs, in addition to purchase cost, for each option
- optimise the trade-off between acquisition costs, commissioning costs, operating costs, maintenance costs, disposal costs and so on over the useful life for each proposed investment option.

If a firm is trying to select which of two alternative items of plant and equipment to buy, it should not make the decision solely on the basis of which one has the lowest purchase cost. Such a decision is similar to a buy-now, pay-later approach where the cheaper plant and equipment ultimately cost more to operate and maintain, and yield much less on eventual disposal. For example, a firm is choosing between two ICT projects: X and Y. Project X costs significantly more, but is known to be more reliable than project Y. This means that with the greater reliability of project X, its expected capacity utilisation will be greater. Thus, when making the choice between projects X and Y, a manager should recognise that the lower purchase cost of project Y comes with a cost of potentially lower capacity utilisation.

18.2

CASE STUDY

The big four Australian banks rely heavily upon their information technology (IT) investments to deliver financial services to their customers. However, two different approaches can be discerned in the approaches taken by the Big Four banks to such IT investments:

» The Commonwealth Bank (CBA) and NAB have each committed to spending in excess of $1 billion on upgrading their core IT systems. By 2016, NAB's IT investment is expected to exceed $2.5 billion.

» Westpac and the ANZ Bank are investing more heavily in customer-facing systems than they are in upgrading their core IT systems.

COMMENTARY

It has been reported that the core operating systems of Westpac and the ANZ are up to 40 years old and may be less reliable than the IT assets of the CBA and NAB. However, the IT investment strategies of both Westpac and the ANZ Bank appear to suggest that, although they are not spending as much as on upgrading core operating systems as the CBA and NAB, they believe that improved customer service can still be delivered through the use of more up-to-date customer-facing platforms and applications. Thus, they believe that their IT investment will more than offset any potential problems flowing from the use of less up-to-date core operating systems.

On the other hand, the CBA's and NAB's IT investments are intended to improve core operating system scale and reliability, delivering for each bank greater capacity and reduced out-of-pocket and opportunity costs (e.g. non-scheduled down time events are eliminated). Furthermore, a comprehensive system-wide upgrade is likely to be cheaper in the long run than a staged investment project where new systems have to be integrated or grafted onto existing and potentially out-of-date systems.

18.2 KEY CONCEPT

LIFE-CYCLE COSTING AND CAPITAL INVESTMENT DECISIONS

Life-cycle costing identifies all costs associated with a proposed capital investment from the initiation of the proposed capital investment through to the end of the useful life of the implemented investment.

THE CAPITAL INVESTMENT DECISION-MAKING PROCESS

Well-managed capital investment projects will proceed through a systematic and logical process. For example, the steps for making a capital investment decision could proceed as illustrated in Figure 18.1.

4 LEARNING OBJECTIVE

Outline the seven steps to a capital investment decision

FIGURE 18.1 MAKING A CAPITAL INVESTMENT DECISION: A PHASED APPROACH

Gap analysis need for investment	Conceptual scoping study	Pre-feasibility study	Feasibility study	Investment decision	Investment implementation	Post-investment evaluation
Identify need for action based on gap in desired business performance	Identify potential strategic options for closing the gap in business performance	Identify strategic initiatives that could potentially be developed into feasible projects	Investigate and evaluate the projects that best fit the firm's strategic priorities	Select project with attention to the definition of project delivery KPIs in terms of quality, scope, timetable and cost	Implement project with periodic review, as required, of actual against targeted project delivery performance	Evaluate project with intent of remedying implementation failures and informing future investment decisions

Woolworths: To deliver sustainable, profitable future growth that maximises shareholder value

Regulatory activity and industry dynamics limiting future growth potential in Australian grocery business	Options for Woolworths to expand business activities beyond Australian grocery industry explored	Strategic initiatives include off-shore grocery retailing (e.g. Hong Kong) or new retailing sector (e.g. home improvements)	Evaluate off-shore grocery retailing or new retailing options in terms of profitable, future growth creating opportunities	Select Masters Home Improvement joint venture with Lowes and refine business case parameters	Roll out Masters Home Improvement business, monitoring project KPIs (e.g. store openings, stocking, pricing, staffing)	Masters Home Improvement roll-out evaluated with existing business issues addressed, as required, and planned investments amended

The following material now considers how proposed capital investments are assessed using two traditional methods of evaluation and two discounted cash flow (DCF) methods.

> **18.3** **KEY CONCEPT**
>
> ## CAPITAL INVESTMENTS AS A DECISION-MAKING PROCESS
>
> A capital investment decision-making process can follow a logical sequence including the identification of a need for investment, the gathering and evaluation of information about feasible investment opportunities, the selection and implementation of a preferred investment option and the post-implementation assessment of actual investment performance.

5 **LEARNING OBJECTIVE**

Explain and apply the concept of accounting rate of return (ARR) and the payback period method, and evaluate their usefulness in making capital investment decisions

Traditional methods of capital investment evaluation

We begin the analysis of capital investment decisions by examining two traditional methods that have been used to evaluate capital projects:

- accounting rate of return (ARR)
- payback period.

ACCOUNTING RATE OF RETURN (ARR)

Prior to the use of the discounted cash flow techniques that are discussed later in this chapter, the accounting rate of return (ARR) method was widely used by firms when evaluating proposed capital investments. As mentioned above, ARR was an attractive measure to use because of its simplicity, the use of the familiar accounting terms 'net profit' and 'book value of investment', and its similarity to the return on investment (ROI) ratio, another widely used financial statement analysis metric.

The ARR can be calculated in many ways. While the measure of profit used in the numerator can be readily identified with little discussion, the denominator for the investment base may be measured using net or gross book for opening, closing or average values. As the profit measure is used to reflect the return earned on assets during a period, it has been argued that the investment base should also be measured in a similar fashion (i.e. the average net book value for the period). Alternatively, the use of gross values has been supported on the grounds that it is from the initial capital investment that profits after depreciation and tax are generated. Although different definitions of the investment base could be used to calculate a proposed investment's ARR, our consideration will be limited to just two: average net book value of the investment (Formula 1) and gross initial investment value (Formula 2). Key concept 18.4 illustrates two formulas for calculating ARR.

> **18.4** **KEY CONCEPT**
>
> ## ACCOUNTING RATE OF RETURN (ARR)
>
> Formula 1
>
> $$ARR\% = \frac{\text{Net profit after tax}}{\text{Average net book value of investment}} \times 100\%$$
>
> Formula 2
>
> $$ARR\% = \frac{\text{Net profit after tax}}{\text{Gross initial value of investment}} \times 100\%$$

As will be illustrated with Worked example 18.1, the ARR using Formula 1 will be higher than that using Formula 2. Provided the same formula is used to evaluate competing projects, a consistent approach will be achieved. The net profit in the formula is after depreciation and tax expenses.

18.1

WORKED EXAMPLE

PROJECTS ALPHA AND BETA

The following details relate to two mutually exclusive projects: Alpha and Beta. The initial cost of each project is $150 000, generate three years of net profits after depreciation and tax, and both have a zero residual value on disposal.

	YEAR 1	YEAR 2	YEAR 3	THREE-YEAR AVERAGE
	$	$	$	$
Net profit (after depreciation and tax)				
Alpha	40 000	60 000	80 000	60 000
Beta	60 000	60 000	60 000	60 000
Book values				
1 January	150 000	100 000	50 000	–
31 December	100 000	50 000	0	–
Average book values	125 000	75 000	25 000	75 000

Average book values = (1 January value + 31 December value)/2

FORMULA 1	YEAR 1	YEAR 2	YEAR 3	THREE YEAR AVERAGE
$\dfrac{\text{NET PROFIT AFTER DEPRECIATION \& TAX}}{\text{AVERAGE NET BOOK VALUE}} \times 100\%$				
Project Alpha	$\dfrac{\$40\,000}{\$125\,000}$	$\dfrac{\$60\,000}{\$75\,000}$	$\dfrac{\$80\,000}{\$25\,000}$	$\dfrac{\$60\,000}{\$75\,000}$
	32.00%	80.00%	320.00%	80.00%
Project Beta	$\dfrac{\$60\,000}{\$125\,000}$	$\dfrac{\$60\,000}{\$75\,000}$	$\dfrac{\$60\,000}{\$25\,000}$	$\dfrac{\$60\,000}{\$75\,000}$
	48.00%	80.00%	240.00%	80.00%

What can be observed from the use of Formula 1? Firstly, as the investment base declines in value with the passage of time, Formula 1 reports an increase in the ARR. Secondly, while both projects yield a similar ARR when measured using the three-year average, as Project Beta is forecast to generate one and a half times the net profit after depreciation and tax in Year 1 than for Project Alpha, it is expected deliver an ARR 50 per cent greater than the alternative investment.

❯

Using Formula 1, which project would be selected? The decision criterion for ARR is to accept projects with a **rate of return** that is higher than some minimum desired rate of return. If the projects are competing or mutually exclusive, the project with the highest rate of return would be recommended, subject to it achieving the minimum desired rate of return. Were the three-year average ARR to be used, projects Alpha and Beta appear equally desirable. However, if the manager who is to evaluate each investment option has his or her annual bonus compensation based in part on the use of financial metrics (e.g. ARR), he/she is more likely to have a short-term time horizon when recommending a project. As Beta returns more net profit after depreciation and tax in Year 1 and yields a higher ARR than Alpha, it would be preferred.

FORMULA 2	YEAR 1	YEAR 2	YEAR 3	THREE-YEAR AVERAGE
$\dfrac{\text{NET PROFIT AFTER DEPRECIATION \& TAX}}{\text{GROSS INITIAL INVESTMENT VALUE}} \times 100\%$				
Project Alpha	$\dfrac{\$40\,000}{\$150\,000}$	$\dfrac{\$60\,000}{\$150\,000}$	$\dfrac{\$80\,000}{\$150\,000}$	$\dfrac{\$60\,000}{\$150\,000}$
	26.67%	40.00%	53.33%	40.00%
Project Beta	$\dfrac{\$60\,000}{\$150\,000}$	$\dfrac{\$60\,000}{\$150\,000}$	$\dfrac{\$60\,000}{\$150\,000}$	$\dfrac{\$60\,000}{\$150\,000}$
	40.00%	40.00%	40.00%	40.00%

As before, if the three-year average were to be used in Formula 2, both projects would be expected to achieve the same ARR. However, if Formula 2 were to be used on an annual basis, as the investment base remains constant over each of the three years, changes in the annual ARR simply reflect the year-to-year variation in the forecast net profit after depreciation and tax. Thus, since Project Beta is forecast to generate 50 per cent more net profit after depreciation and tax in Year 1 than Project Alpha, it reports an ARR again 50 per cent greater than the alternative investment. If the manager who is to recommend which project should be implemented has a short-term time horizon, Beta would be the preferred investment.

ADVANTAGES OF ARR

The main advantages of using ARR to evaluate capital investment projects are:
- it is simple to calculate and easy to understand.
- it is familiar to managers, investors and other external users of financial statements, who use profit and returns on assets (i.e. ROI) to assess the performance of management.

DISADVANTAGES OF ARR

The disadvantages from using ARR to evaluate capital investment projects are:
- it applies the same weighting to profits in all periods and ignores the time value of money.
- alternative definitions of the investment base (i.e. gross or net book and opening, closing and average values) may generate different rates of return and lead to different recommendations being made
- it uses accounting measures based on accrual accounting and not cash flows. While accounting measures are important in assessing managerial performance, cash flows are important in investment evaluations, for it is the cash flows that are used to pay employee remuneration, amounts owing to the suppliers of goods and services on credit, and so on.

PAYBACK PERIOD

Another traditional method used to assist in decisions about capital investments is the payback period. An important issue when considering any long-term investment is how long it will take for the initial investment to be recouped. Investments are made with a view to profit, but an important component of this view to profit is the desire to avoid a loss. The payback period is the period of time within which recovery of the initial investment is expected. Other things being equal, if two competing investments offered similar expected benefits, the one with a shorter payback period would be preferred. Where the payback period method differs from the ARR is that it uses net cash flow after tax in place of net profit after depreciation and tax.

The payback period is used as a measure of risk: the longer the payback period, the greater the level of uncertainty surrounding future profits and underlying cash flows and the higher the risk of the project. This is a crude measure of risk and other more sophisticated techniques, such as sensitivity analysis, are available to assess risk. Nevertheless, the payback period continues to be used in conjunction with other techniques of investment analysis, including the discounted cash flow methods that are to be discussed later in this chapter.

18.5 KEY CONCEPT

PAYBACK PERIOD FOR EQUAL CASH INFLOWS

The payback period is calculated by dividing the initial investment by the net cash inflow.

If the annual net cash flows are constant over the useful life of the investment, the payback can be found by dividing the initial investment cost by the annual net cash flow. If project Y costs $150 000 and will returns net cash inflows of $50 000 per annum for four years, it will have a payback period calculated as follows:

$$
\text{Payback period} = \frac{\text{Initial investment}}{\text{Annual net cash inflow}}
$$

$$
= \frac{\$150\,000}{\$50\,000}
$$

$$
= 3 \text{ years}
$$

If a project is forecast to generate non-uniform or uneven annual net cash flows for five years, as shown below, each year's cash inflows must be summed until the cumulative cash flows equal the initial investment. Project Z, an alternative mutually exclusive investment option to project Y, also has an initial investment cost of $150 000 at T_0 and generates non-uniform or uneven annual net cash flows for five years as shown below. What would be project Z's payback period?

	T_0	Year 1	Year 2	Year 3	Year 4	Year 5
Cash inflows		$30 000	$40 000	$50 000	$60 000	$70 000
Cumulative cash inflows		$30 000	$70 000	$120 000	$180 000	$250 000
Investment recovered	($150 000)	($120 000)	($80 000)	($30 000)	$30 000	$100 000

If cash flows are assumed to occur uniformly within each year, project Z would achieve the payback period halfway through Year 4. As project Y has a quicker payback period than project Z, it would be preferred by a manager with a short-term time horizon. Worked example 18.2 will review the calculation of the payback period for two mutually exclusive investment options.

Assuming cash inflows are evenly spread throughout the year for both projects, the payback period for Alpha is a little over 18 months. On the other hand, Beta has a slightly quicker payback period of less than 16 months.

WORKED EXAMPLE

PROJECTS ALPHA AND BETA

The following details relate to two mutually exclusive projects: Alpha and Beta. The initial cost of each project is $150 000, generate three years of net cash flows after tax with zero residual value on disposal.

PROJECT	T_0	YEAR 1	YEAR 2	YEAR 3
Alpha	($150 000)	$90 000	$110 000	$130 000
Beta	($150 000)	$110 000	$110 000	$110 000

PROJECT ALPHA	T_0	YEAR 1	YEAR 2	YEAR 3
Cash inflows		$90 000	$110 000	$130 000
Cumulative cash inflows		$90 000	$200 000	$330 000
Investment recovered	($150 000)	($60 000)	$50 000	$180 000

Payback period 1 year and 6.55 months

PROJECT BETA	T_0	YEAR 1	YEAR 2	YEAR 3
Cash inflows		$110 000	$110 000	$110 000
Cumulative cash inflows		$110 000	$220 000	$330 000
Investment recovered	($150 000)	($40 000)	$70 000	$180 000

Payback period 1 year and 3.66 months

The decision criterion for the payback method would be to set a minimum period and accept only projects with a payback below this minimum. For mutually exclusive investments where only one project is required, the one with the lowest payback period would be selected, provided this was less than the minimum period. Thus, when reviewing the payback periods for projects Z and Y and Alpha and Beta, the payback period method would favour project Y over project Z and Beta over Alpha. Project Z is expected to generate significantly higher cash inflows than project Y, but as these occur after the payback period they are not taken into account. Hence, choosing to ignore cash flows after the payback period is a significant deficiency of the payback method.

ADVANTAGES OF THE PAYBACK PERIOD

The advantages of using the payback period to support of decisions about capital investments are:
- it is easy to understand.
- it provides some, albeit imperfect, assessment of risk.
- it is a simple and well-understood method. Managers are well aware that the payback period means the time required to recoup the initial investment.

DISADVANTAGES OF THE PAYBACK PERIOD

The disadvantages of the payback period method are:
- it does not take into consideration a project's cash flows after the payback period. Therefore, less profitable investments may be selected if the payback period was used in isolation.
- it ignores the time value of money and treats all cash flows as equal, irrespective of the year in which they occur. This problem can be overcome by using the discounted payback period, in which cash

flows are discounted to reflect the time value of money. However, since cash flows after the discounted payback periods are still ignored, the benefit of future cash inflows beyond payback is still not recognised.

DISCOUNTED CASH-FLOW TECHNIQUES

6 LEARNING OBJECTIVE

Explain and apply the internal rate of return (IRR) and net present value (NPV) methods in carrying out the discounted cash flow (DCF) analysis of proposed capital investments

The most common methods for evaluating capital investment proposals involve the use of discounted cash-flow techniques. The two main methods are:

- internal rate of return
- net present value.

Both methods focus on cash flows, rather than accounting profit, and recognise that the use of money has a cost. The alternative to buying a productive asset would be investing the money, which would then be compounded. With capital investments, cash is invested now with the hope of receiving a greater amount in the future from increased cash flows from the sales of goods and services, reduced operating cash flows or a combination of both.

In discussing the discounted cash-flow techniques, we use will concepts from financial mathematics such as the present value of $1 per period. Remember, the concepts of financial mathematics are explained in material available at the website for this book. (The online Appendix Exploring the time value of money concept can be reviewed for a simple illustration of some of the principles underlying the time value of money.)

INTERNAL RATE OF RETURN (IRR)

To overcome the problems associated with the traditional methods used to evaluate capital investment projects, the internal rate of return (IRR) method was developed and is now widely used in business. We have already discussed various rates of return in Chapter 10, and earlier in this chapter we examined the accounting rate of return (ARR).

The IRR differs from the ARR in that it uses cash flows and adjusts for the fact that $1.00 to be received (or paid) today is worth more than $1.00 received (or paid) in one year's time. The IRR is that rate of return which equates the present value of the expected cash inflows with the present value of the expected cash outflows. It is not, therefore, the same as the ARR, and is regarded as a superior method.

18.6 KEY CONCEPT

INTERNAL RATE OF RETURN

The internal rate of return (IRR) is the rate of return which discounts the cash flows of a project so that the present value of cash inflows equals the present value of cash outflows.

To calculate the IRR, the following formula is used. We have to solve for in the formula:

$$OCC = \frac{NCF^1}{(1+R)^1} + \frac{NCF^2}{(1+R)^2} + \frac{NCF^3}{(1+R)^3} + \cdots \frac{NCF^n}{(1+R)^n}$$

where

OCC = Original cash cost

NCF^1 = net cash flow at the end of Year 1, and so on

R = r or cost of capital ÷ 100

n = number of periods

PV = net present value

When the net cash flows remain the same each year, the formula becomes:

$$OCC = NCF \times \left[\frac{1}{(1+R)^1} + \frac{1}{(1+R)^2} + \cdots \frac{1}{(1+R)^n}\right]$$

$$OCC = NCF \times PVF(IRR, n)$$

where

$$PVF = present\ value\ factor$$

dotshock/Shutterstock.com

18.3 WORKED EXAMPLE

IRR ON A MACHINE GENERATING UNIFORM CASH INFLOWS

An amount of $180 000 was outlaid on a machine which is expected to return cash inflows of $60 120 per year for five years. After five years, the machine is expected to be worthless. Calculate the internal rate of return on the machine.

The investment of $180 000 produces a benefit of $60 120 a year for five years. Therefore $OCC = \$180\,000$, $NCF = \$60\,120$ and $n = 5$ and r is unknown.

$$OCC = NCF \times PVF(IRR,n)$$
$$\$180\,000 = \$60\,120 \times PVF(IRR, 5)$$
$$PVF(IRR,5) = \$180\,000 \div \$60\,120$$
$$= 2.9906$$

In Table 4 of Appendix 2, we can look along the $n = 5$ row until we find the PVF closest to 2.9906. The 20 per cent column for five years reports the present value factor for an **annuity** in arrears of 2.9906. Hence, the IRR is 20 per cent.

This approach is possible only when the cash inflows each year are equal (see annuity due and annuity in arrears in the glossary). In practice, this is not likely to be the case. Determining the IRR when net cash flows vary from year to year is more complicated. Consider the following worked example.

18.4

WORKED EXAMPLE

IRR ON A PROJECT GENERATING NON-UNIFORM CASH INFLOWS

A project with an initial cost of $500 000 was forecast to generate the following cash flows:

T_0	YEAR 1	YEAR 2	YEAR 3	YEAR 4
($500 000)	$100 000	$150 000	$230 000	$280 000

What is the IRR for this project?

To solve for the IRR, we want to find the value of R which will make OCC equal to $500 000. If OCC = ($500 000), NCF1 = $100 000, NCF2 = $150 000, and so on then:

$$(\$500\,000) = \frac{\$100\,000}{(1+R)^1} + \frac{\$150\,000}{(1+R)^2} + \frac{\$230\,000}{(1+R)^3} + \frac{\$280\,000}{(1+R)^4}$$

Solving such an equation algebraically would be too difficult for most. An alternative approach is to use trial and error. We pick a value for 'r' and substitute into the right-hand side of the equation to calculate a present value of the future cash flows.

Assume IRR = 20 per cent, so R = 0.20.

$$PV = \frac{\$100\,000}{(1+0.20)^1} + \frac{\$150\,000}{(1+0.20)^2} + \frac{\$230\,000}{(1+0.20)^3} + \frac{\$280\,000}{(1+0.20)^4}$$

$$\sim \$459\,663 = \sim \$83\,333 + \sim \$104\,167 + \sim \$133\,102 + \sim \$135\,031$$

Since the present value of the four years of cash inflows is only $455 663, it is some $44 367 below the $500 000 cost of the investment. As noted above, a higher present value occurs when a lower interest rate is used, so perhaps the interest rate of 15% could be used.

Now assume IRR = 15 per cent, so R = 0.15.

$$PV = \frac{\$100\,000}{(1+0.15)^1} + \frac{\$150\,000}{(1+0.15)^2} + \frac{\$230\,000}{(1+0.15)^3} + \frac{\$280\,000}{(1+0.15)^4}$$

$$\sim \$511\,698 = \sim \$86\,956 + \sim \$113\,422 + \sim \$151\,229 + \sim \$160\,091$$

As the present value of the four years of cash inflows is now $511 698, it is some $11 698 above the $500 000 cost of the investment. As noted above, a lower present value will occurs when a higher interest rate is used, so perhaps the interest rate of 16% could be used.

Finally, assume IRR = 16 per cent, so R = 0.16.

$$PV = \frac{\$100\,000}{(1+0.16)^1} + \frac{\$150\,000}{(1+0.16)^2} + \frac{\$230\,000}{(1+0.16)^3} + \frac{\$280\,000}{(1+0.16)^4}$$

$$\sim \$500\,000 = \sim \$86\,207 + \sim \$114\,474 + \sim \$147\,351 + \sim \$154\,642$$

As the present value of the future cash inflows approximates the $500 000 cost of the investment, the IRR is approximately 16 per cent.

The trial-and-error approach can be a laborious and time-consuming method to use for calculating the IRR. However, Excel's IRR formula and financial mathematics calculators can make the task of determining IRR a matter of simply entering the key variables of initial cost and the time series of future cash inflows.

The decision criterion for IRR is to accept projects that offer an IRR above a certain minimum desired rate of return. This rate of return is often called the cost of capital, which is the rate of return that equates the present value of a firm's expected future cash flows to the firm's value. For mutually exclusive investments, the project with the highest IRR is accepted, provided the IRR is above the minimum.

Advantages of IRR

The advantages of the IRR method of project evaluation are:

- it uses the concept of a rate of return and this concept is familiar to many managers. As managers have a propensity to making decisions using concepts with which they are familiar, IRR is a metric that they can relate to. Note that this was also one of the advantages of using the ARR.
- it does not treat cash received in different years as equal and thus incorporates the time value of money. It is essential that cash flows received or paid in different periods are not treated equally.
- it uses cash flows and not accrual accounting profit figures. It is the cash inflows from a project that will be required to pay the cash outflows incurred in investing in the project.

Disadvantages of IRR

The disadvantages of the IRR method are:

- some types of investment can have more than one IRR, and in some cases no IRR. These types of investment are often described as non-conventional. A conventional investment is one in which an initial cash outflow occurs at the beginning of year 1 and then a series of net cash inflows occur at the end of the years that follow. A non-conventional investment is one in which further net cash outflows occur during the life of the investment such that the net cash flows might be positive in two or three years, negative in the next year before returning to positive net cash flows in the remaining years of the project. The more sign changes that occur for a project, the greater the number of IRR measures that complicate the managerial decision-making process.
- for competing investments, where the selection of one means the rejection of the others, the IRR can provide a ranking of investments different from the net present value. In effect, using IRR means that a project that will not maximise the firm's value (which is one of the main objectives of a firm) could be ranked ahead of a project that would do so.
- it is dependent on the accuracy of the estimates of future cash flows. Consequently, the less reliable the estimates, the less reliable will be the calculated IRR.

NET PRESENT VALUE (NPV)

The second discounted cash-flow technique is the net present value (NPV) method. Unlike the IRR, which expresses a result in a percentage, the NPV expresses the result in dollars. The NPV is determined by calculating the present value of all cash inflows and outflows at a certain rate and then adding the two together to arrive at either a positive or a negative result. A positive NPV suggests that the project should be accepted, while a negative NPV suggests that the project should be rejected.

KEY CONCEPT

18.7

NET PRESENT VALUE

The NPV is the figure that results from discounting all the cash flows of a project at the minimum rate of return and summing the resultant present values.

18.5

WORKED EXAMPLE

NPV ON INVESTMENT

An investment of $100 000 is expected to yield a company $60 000 net cash inflows at the end of each year for two years, after which time it will be worthless. The company requires a rate of return of 10 per cent on such investments. To determine the NPV, we must calculate the present value at 10 per cent of a cash inflow of $60 000 each year for the next two years.

The outflow occurs immediately, so the value in today's dollars (T_0) is $100 000. As the inflows occur at the end of each of the next two years, the present value is calculated by using either the formula we used above or Table 2 in Appendix 2:

$$PV = \frac{\$60\,000}{(1+0.10)^1} + \frac{\$60\,000}{(1+0.10)^2}$$

$$\sim \$104\,132 = \sim \$54\,545 + \sim \$49\,587$$

As the NPV is a positive value of $4132 (i.e. $4132 = $104 132 – $100 000), the decision would be to accept the project, even though the amount is only small and management would need to consider other factors including those risks that are associated with the investment. How certain are the cash inflows? Are there alternative and potentially more profitable uses for the money? What is the opportunity cost of investing in this project?

How did we arrive at the figure of 10 per cent as the discount rate? This is often called the cost of capital, which is defined in Key concept 18.8. While it is beyond the scope of this book to fully discuss how this rate is determined, a simple example will be presented to illustrate the mechanics of calculating a firm's weighted average cost of capital.

18.6

WORKED EXAMPLE

CALCULATING THE WEIGHTED AVERAGE COST OF CAPITAL (WACC)

K Limited is a listed firm with a current capital structure believed to be optimal for the industry it operates in. The debt ratio is 40 per cent and the average cost of debt after tax is 7 per cent per annum. Based on the firm's market returns, it is estimated that the cost of equity capital is 12 per cent per annum. What is the WACC of K Limited?

Noting that the debt ratio is 40 per cent, then equity must be 60 per cent. To calculate the weighted average cost of capital, the proportion that debt and equity contribute to the total capital funding of the firm is multiplied by the relevant cost of capital. This can be presented as:

$$R_{WACC} = (D\% \times R_D) + (E\% \times R_E)$$

Where

R_{WACC} = weighted average cost of capital

$D\%$ = debt ratio

R_D = after-tax cost of debt

$E\%$ = equity ratio

R_E = cost of equity

$$10.00\% = (40\% \times 7.00\%) + (60\% \times 12.00\%)$$
$$10.00\% = 2.80\% \qquad + 7.20\%$$

However the weighted average cost of capital is calculated, a positive NPV for a capital investment will result in an increase in the overall value of the firm and should be accepted.

KEY CONCEPT

COST OF CAPITAL

The cost of capital is the rate of return that equates the present value of a firm's expected future cash flows to the value of the firm.

WORKED EXAMPLE

CALCULATING THE NPV WITH A 10 PER CENT WACC

Using the data from Worked example 18.5 we will assume that the project that had an investment cost of $500 000 has a minimum desired rate of return of 10 per cent. What is the project's NPV?

Firstly, what are the relevant cash flows?

T_0	YEAR 1	YEAR 2	YEAR 3	YEAR 4
($500 000)	$100 000	$150 000	$230 000	$280 000

The NPV can be calculated with a 10 per cent cost of capital as follows:

$$NPV = (\$500\,000) - \frac{[\$100\,000 + \$150\,000 \quad \$230\,000 + \$280\,000]}{(1+0.10)^1 \quad (1+0.10)^2 \quad 1+0.10)^3 \quad (1+0.10)^4}$$

$$\$78\,922 = (\$500\,000) - [\ \$90\,909 + \$123\,967 \quad \$172\,802 + \$191\,244\ ]$$

We know that the IRR for this proposed project was 16 per cent, and since it is a conventional investment, the NPV should be positive – as indeed it is. This means that by using the IRR and NPV methods, we arrive at the same decision to accept this particular project. However, as stated earlier, the two methods can give conflicting results for projects with non-conventional cash flows and in the ranking of mutually exclusive projects. Therefore, the decision rule for NPV is to accept all projects with a positive NPV except mutually exclusive projects; for mutually exclusive projects, choose the project with the highest positive NPV.

Advantages of NPV

The main advantages of the NPV method of project evaluation are:
- it incorporates the time value of money into the evaluation of a proposed capital investment and so does not treat as equal cash flows received or paid in different years
- once cash flows have been discounted at the minimum rate of return, they can be added together to arrive at an amount in present-day dollars
- for mutually exclusive projects, it gives a ranking superior to IRR (as will be explained in the next section)

- it uses cash flows, not accrual-based profit numbers, and is a more sophisticated and less arbitrary approach to investment evaluation.

Disadvantages of NPV

The disadvantages of the NPV method are:
- if the calculation of the minimum rate of return is not accurate, then the NPV will be less reliable as a decision criteria
- because it is dependent on the accuracy of the estimates of future cash flows, the less reliable the estimates, the less reliable the NPV.

STOP AND THINK 2

Bluejet Ctd is looking at a capital expenditure proposal that involves an investment of $78 345 and annual net cash flows of $15 250 for each of the eight years of the useful life of the project. There is a zero scrap value.

a   What is the internal rate of return?

b   What is the net present value if the cost of capital is 11 per cent?

c   What is the payback period?

STOP AND THINK 3

Waugh Electronics Ltd is thinking of buying, at a cost of $25 093, some new quality control equipment that is expected to save $5000 in cash operating costs. Its estimated useful life is 10 years, and it will have a zero disposal value. Calculate:

a   the internal rate of return

b   the net present value if the cost of capital is 10 per cent

c   the payback period.

COMPARISON OF IRR AND NPV

The graph in Figure 18.2 shows the relationship between NPV and IRR. Remember that:

$$NPV = \ OCC \ - \ \frac{NCF^1}{(1+R)^1} + \frac{NCF^2}{(1+R)^2} + \frac{NCF^3}{(1+R)^3} + \dots \frac{NCF^n}{(1+R)^n}$$

7 LEARNING OBJECTIVE

Compare IRR and NPV methods of DCF analysis, appreciate the differences in their underlying assumptions and explain why they may provide contrary recommendations

FIGURE 18.2 PROJECT EVALUATION WITH IRR AND NPV

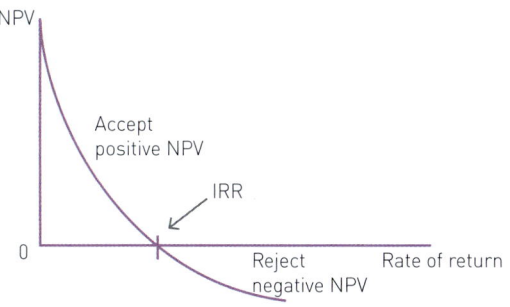

The NPV will be at its maximum value when the rate of return, r, is zero. This is the intercept on the vertical axis and will be a positive value if the sum of the net cash flows exceeds the original cost.

As R becomes larger, each term of $NCF1/(1+R)1 + NCF2/(1+R)^2$ and so on, becomes smaller.

Hence, the NPV decreases as r increases, in a curve as shown. At some stage, the NPV becomes zero. At this point:

$$NPV = 0 = OCC - \frac{NCF^1}{(1+R)^1} + \frac{NCF^2}{(1+R)^2} + \frac{NCF^3}{(1+R)^3} + \cdots \frac{NCF^n}{(1+R)^n}$$

The above expression for determining that NPV is zero is similar to the formula we used to find the IRR. Hence, the intercept on the horizontal axis is also the IRR.

Do the IRR and NPV methods give the same answer for decision-making purposes? Unfortunately they do not! The answer will depend on whether the investments are *independent* (that is, the acceptance or rejection of one project has no effect on whether or not other projects could be implemented) or *mutually exclusive* (that is, if one project is selected, the other is automatically rejected). It will also depend on whether the cash flows associated with the project are what are described as conventional (i.e. cash outflow, followed by cash inflows) or unconventional (i.e. changing signs for annual cash flows: Y_1 = cash inflow, Y_2 = cash inflow, Y_3 = cash outflow, Y_4 = cash inflow). We only illustrate mutually exclusive projects in this book.

8 LEARNING OBJECTIVE

Discuss how mutually exclusive investments are dealt with

MUTUALLY EXCLUSIVE INVESTMENTS

Independent conventional cash-flow projects are ranked the same using both the NPV and IRR methods. For mutually exclusive projects, the IRR and NPV methods can give different rankings and therefore lead to different decisions, as illustrated in Worked example 18.8.

WORKED EXAMPLE 18.8

PROJECTS A AND B

Two mutually exclusive projects have the following cash flows:

PROJECT	INVESTMENT COST	NET CASH FLOW (NCF) RECEIVED ENDING				
	T_0	YEAR 1	YEAR 2	YEAR 3	YEAR 4	YEAR 5
A	($45 000)	$13 500	$13 500	$13 500	$13 500	$13 500
B	($30 000)	$9 150	$9 150	$9 150	$9 150	$9 150

Which project should be chosen? Assuming a minimum rate of 10 per cent per annum, the NPV and the IRR for both projects can be calculated. The answers are summarised and ranked in Table 18.1, opposite.

Firstly, we will calculate the IRR for each project.

IRR: Project A

$$OCC = NCF \times PVF(IRR,n)$$
$$\$45\,000 = \$13\,500 \times PVF(IRR,5)$$
$$3.3333 = PVF(IRR,5)$$

Looking across row n = 5 in Table 4 in Appendix 2, you will see that the PVF for 15 per cent is 3.3521. Hence, for project A with a predicted PVF of 3.3333, the IRR is slightly more than 15 per cent. Using Excel's IRR formula yields a more accurate answer of 15.24 per cent.

IRR: Project B

$$OCC = NCF \times PVF(IRR,n)$$

$$\$30\,000 = \$9150 \times PVF(IRR,5)$$

$$3.2787 = PVF(IRR,5)$$

Looking once again across row $n = 5$, you will see that the PVF for 15 per cent is 3.3521 and as PVF for project B of 3.2787 is slightly lower than the PVF for project A, the actual IRR must be greater than that of A. An educated guess might suggest that project B has an IRR of about 16 per cent. Again Excel's IRR formula gives a more accurate IRR measure for project B of 15.94 per cent.

Having calculated each project's IRR, the NPV for each project will now be determined.

NPV: Project A

$$NPV = -OCC + NCF \times PVF(10,5)$$

$$NPV = -\$45\,000 + (\$13\,500 \times 3.7907)$$

$$= \$6174.45$$

NPV: Project B

$$NPV = -\$30\,000 + (\$9150 \times 3.7907)$$

$$= \$4684.91$$

Using these results, we can rank the projects as shown in Table 18.1.

TABLE 18.1 SUMMARY OF IRR AND NPV RESULTS AND RANKINGS FOR PROJECTS A AND B

PROJECT	IRR		NPV	
	METRIC VALUE	RANK	METRIC VALUE	RANK
A	15.24%	2	$6174.45	1
B	15.94%	1	$4684.91	2

Table 18.1 shows that the IRR method ranks B the best while the NPV method ranks A the best. Which project should be chosen? We could answer the question by looking at the return on the extra dollars invested in project A.

The differences in net cash flow for projects A and B are shown in Table 18.2:

TABLE 18.2

PROJECT	T_0	YEAR 1	YEAR 2	YEAR 3	YEAR 4	YEAR 5
A – B	–$15 000	$4350	$4350	$4350	$4350	$4350

IRR: Incremental of project A over project B

$$OCC = NCF \times PVF(IRR,n)$$

$$\$15\,000 = \$4350 \times PVF(IRR,5)$$

$$3.4483 = PVF(IRR,5)$$

From Table 4 in Appendix 2, we can see that the IRR is between 12 per cent and 15 per cent. Excel's IRR formula determines that the incremental cash flows of project A over project B generates an IRR of 13.82 per cent.

As the extra investment in project A (i.e. the incremental IRR of 13.82 per cent) provides a rate of return higher than the minimum rate of return, project A should be accepted above project B. This conclusion confirms the recommendation given if the NPV method was used. To sum up, project A should be chosen because it returns more dollars to the company and increases the overall value of the investing firm.

COMPARISON OF IRR AND NPV RANKINGS

The difference in the ranking of projects under the IRR and NPV methods arises because of the assumption on the reinvestment rates for cash flows received during the life of the project. IRR assumes reinvestment of intermediate cash flows at the IRR of the project, while NPV assumes reinvestment at the minimum rate of return. This is illustrated in Worked example 18.9.

18.9

WORKED EXAMPLE

PROJECTS P AND Q

Projects P and Q are mutually exclusive projects with an initial investment cost of $200 000. Both projects will generate two years of positive net cash inflows, as shown below, and these are to be discounted with a 10 per cent cost of capital.

TABLE 18.3 SUMMARY OF NET CASH FLOWS, IRR AND NPV RESULTS FOR PROJECTS P AND Q

PROJECT	NET CASH FLOWS			DCF METRICS	
	T_0	YEAR 1	YEAR 2	IRR	NPV
P	−$200 000	$20 000	$364 000	40%	$119 008
Q	−$200 000	$200 000	$150 000	50%	$105 785

As a self-study exercise, you might like to check that the DCF metrics reported in Table 18.3 are correct.

Note that a minimum rate of return of 10 per cent was assumed. The IRRs were calculated using the trial-and-error method. The NPVs were calculated using Appendix 2 Table 2.

Analysis of reinvestment assumptions are presented in Table 18.4.

TABLE 18.4 SUMMARY OF NET CASH FLOWS AND REINVESTMENT OF YEAR 1 NET CASH INFLOW USING PROJECT IRR AND 10 PER CENT COST OF CAPITAL

DCF METHOD	PROJECT AND YEAR OF CASH FLOW	NET CASH FLOWS	REINVESTMENT RATE	PRESENT VALUE
IRR	Project P			
	Year 1 reinvested in Year 2	$20 000	1.4000	$28 000
	Year 2	$364 000	1.0000	$364 000
	Total			$392 000
	Project Q			
	Year 1 reinvested in Year 2	$200 000	1.5000	$300 000
	Year 2	$150 000	1.0000	$150 000
	Total			$450 000
NPV	Project P			
	Year 1 reinvested at 10% in Year 2	$20 000	1.1000	$22 000
	Year 2	$364 000	1.0000	$364 000
	Total			$386 000

❯

DCF METHOD	PROJECT AND YEAR OF CASH FLOW	NET CASH FLOWS	REINVESTMENT RATE	PRESENT VALUE
	Project Q			
	Year 1 reinvested at 10% in Year 2	$200 000	1.1000	$220 000
	Year 2	$150 000	1.0000	$150 000
	Total			$370 000

The above analysis illustrates that the IRR reinvestment assumption results in project Q with a total value of $450 000 ranking above project's P total value of $392 000. The NPV assumption results in the ranking being reversed as project P has a total value of $386 000 which is greater than project Q's total value of $370 000.

If we wish to evaluate the two projects, then reinvestment should be considered at the minimum rate of return. To do otherwise, prejudges the use of available funds for other projects. A firm should be able to reinvest funds at a return that is at least equal to its minimum rate of return for all projects.

The recommended rule to use is the NPV rule, although supporters of the IRR method argue that using the incremental IRR can overcome all the problems with mutually exclusive projects.

In December 2011, it was reported that Telstra had agreed to provide NBN Co with access to the telco's 'infrastructure and to move its customers to the NBN for payments over the next 30 years with a net present value of $11 billion' (McDulling, 2011, p. 35). This is an example of the importance of the use of net present value.

18.9

KEY CONCEPT

DECISION RULE

The net present value (NPV) method is the recommended method for evaluating capital investment decisions.

QUALITATIVE FACTORS AND CAPITAL INVESTMENT DECISIONS

9 LEARNING OBJECTIVE

Explain the importance of qualitative factors to a capital investment decision

The techniques outlined in this chapter provide important quantitative information to assist managers to make very significant and important capital investment decisions. However, managers should also buttress their analysis of quantitative data with the benefit of qualitative factors before making a final decision.

Qualitative factors include considering the impact of the decision on:
* employees, in terms of the impact of a proposed capital investment on future work opportunities and remuneration levels
* other parts of the business, where a proposed capital investment may impact on how the activities in other parts of the business are undertaken
* the environment, particularly in terms of the emission of greenhouse gases or the production of waste

- future business opportunities, where the planned investment might create future business growth opportunities
- the image of the company, where the investment may result in changed customer and community perceptions towards the company.

Finally, managers must decide if the risk is too high, even if there is a positive NPV. In short, the financial details are only part of the puzzle; managers must bring together all the pieces of the puzzle to make the final decision.

KEY CONCEPT

QUALITATIVE FACTORS

Qualitative factors are significant capital investment project activities or outcomes not readily expressed in quantitative terms.

10 LEARNING OBJECTIVE

Explain the significance of risk to capital investment decisions and identify the use of inappropriate conservative adjustments for dealing with that risk

CONSERVATISM AS A MEANS FOR DEALING WITH CAPITAL INVESTMENT UNCERTAINTY

At a basic level, the investment decision may simply be about the replacement of existing manufacturing plant and equipment with new manufacturing technology (e.g. automated machinery). More complex investment decisions could be in respect to more intangible capital assets in the form of product and process research and development activities or in advanced ICT systems. The cost of making such product or process investments is justified on the basis of the future economic benefits expected to be realised in the form of increased market share in either existing or new markets, and cycle time, quality and cost efficiencies that are forecast to be delivered from improved product and manufacturing process design and performance.

However, many of the benefits from such investments are difficult to quantify and, given the significant resources that often must be committed to implementing them (e.g. for advanced manufacturing systems or new management ICT systems), managers tends to adopt a conservative approach to making these types of investment decision. This conservatism appears in a number of forms:
- shortening payback time periods
- using cost of capital rates that are higher than the true weighted average cost of capital
- making overly optimistic assessments of the financial consequences of retaining the status quo
- making excessive adjustments for risk
- choking feasible investment opportunities by placing upper limits on the capital spending powers of divisional managers.

KEY CONCEPT

Sound capital investment decisions rely on robust estimates of costs and benefits, the application of discounted cash flow analysis where arbitrary adjustments for risk are avoided, and a final decision made in the context of material intangible factors that are not so readily quantified.

DEALING WITH UNCERTAINTY AND THE ROLE OF SENSITIVITY ANALYSIS

In general, risky projects are those whose future cash flows, and hence project returns, are likely to be variable. The greater the variability in projected cash flows, the greater the risk. The problem of risk is more acute with capital investment decisions than other decisions for the following reasons:

- estimates of capital expenditure might be for up to several years ahead, such as for major ICT projects, and all too often with long-term projects, actual costs escalate well above budget as the work progresses
- estimates of benefits will be for up to several years ahead, sometimes 10, 15 or 20 years ahead or even longer, and such long-term estimates can, at best, be no more than an approximation.

11 LEARNING OBJECTIVE

Explain how sensitivity analysis is used to deal with uncertainty and focuses managerial attention on those critical variables that have significance for a capital investment decision

Why are projects risky?

A decision about whether or not to go ahead with a proposed capital investment is based on expectations about the future. As we have seen, decisions to accept or reject a proposed capital investment are based in part on forecasts of net cash flows that are expected to arise following a particular course of action. However, these forecasts are made on the basis of what is expected to happen given the present state of knowledge, and the future is, by definition, uncertain. Actual cash flows are almost certain to differ from prior expectations. It is this uncertainty about a project's future income and costs that gives rise to business risk in general and investment decision making in particular.

Using sensitivity analysis

Sensitivity analysis is one method of analysing the risk surrounding a capital investment decision and enables an assessment to be made of how responsive the proposed project's NPV is to changes in the variables that are used to calculate that NPV. The NPV could depend on a number of uncertain independent variables. These main variables would include the following:

- estimated selling prices
- estimated sales volumes
- estimated cost of capital
- estimated initial costs
- estimated operating costs
- estimated financial benefits.

THE MARGIN-OF-ERROR APPROACH

The margin-of-error approach to sensitivity analysis is to calculate a proposed project's NPV under alternative assumptions to determine how sensitive it is to changing conditions. Thus, an indication is provided of those variables to which the NPV is most sensitive (critical variables) and the extent to which those variables may change before an otherwise acceptable investment returns a negative NPV. Therefore, sensitivity analysis provides an indication of why a project might fail. Once these critical variables have been identified, a manager can review them to assess whether or not there is a strong possibility of the conditions that result in a negative NPV actually occurring. Management should also pay particular attention to controlling those variables to which the NPV is particularly sensitive, once the decision has been taken to accept the investment.

12 **LEARNING OBJECTIVE**

Explain the value of post-implementation audits as a tool for managing existing and any future project requiring a capital investment

POST-IMPLEMENTATION AUDIT

A post-implementation (or post-completion) audit is a review of the net cash flows from a project either after it has reached the end of its life, or at some point subsequent to its being implemented. In as far as possible, the actual cash flows of the implemented investment should be measured and compared with the estimates contained in the original capital investment business case. Where possible, the manager responsible for the project should be asked to explain any significant variances.

Why carry out a post-implementation audit?

As the funds associated with an implemented capital investment project have already been spent, a post-implementation audit cannot reverse the original decision to commit those funds. However, a post-implementation audit does provide value in terms of the discipline it might bring to the making of capital investment decisions. For example:

- if a manager asks for and gets approval for a proposed capital investment project, and knows that in due course the project will be subject to a post-implementation audit, the manager may be more likely to pay greater care to the estimation of project benefits and costs than if a post-implementation audit was not scheduled to be undertaken. Thus, the scheduling of a post-implementation audit will motivate managers to be more diligent in extracting the benefits promised from an implemented project.

- if the post-implementation audit takes place before the life of the project ends, and if it finds that the benefits have been less than expected because of management inefficiency, steps can be taken to improve efficiency and earn greater benefits over the remaining life of the project. Alternatively, the post-implementation audit may highlight those projects that should be discontinued.

- a post-implementation audit can help to identify managers who have been good performers and those who have been less so. This information would not only be helpful in identifying the pool of managers from which future senior executives will be recruited, but also to allow the firm to select who will manage the implementation of future capital investment projects.

- a post-implementation audit might identify weaknesses in the forecasting and estimating techniques used to evaluate projects, and so should help to improve the discipline and quality of forecasting for future investment decisions.

- areas where improvements should have been made in past capital investment decisions are revealed by a post-implementation audit, which should help to achieve better results in general from future capital investment decisions.

- original estimates may be more realistic if managers are aware that they will be monitored. However, post-implementation audits should never be unfairly critical. Capital investment decisions involve risk, and it will often be the case that actual results do not come up to expectation through no fault of the manager responsible for the project. If post-implementation audits are overly critical, management initiative would be discouraged. A cautious risk-avoiding attitude could develop among managers with the result that otherwise acceptable capital investment projects are never recommended.

Which capital investment projects should be audited?

As it may be too expensive to audit all implemented capital investment projects, managers may need to select a sample for a post-completion audit. The selection will depend on the probability that the audit of any particular project will produce benefits, which can be difficult to determine.

Generally size is likely to be the best guide as to which projects should be audited. However, managers should *perceive* that *every* capital expenditure project has a chance of being the subject of a detailed post-implementation audit. A reasonable guideline might be to audit all projects above a certain size, and a random selection of smaller projects.

A post-implementation audit does not need to focus on all aspects of an implemented capital investment, but should concentrate on those aspects that have been identified as particularly sensitive or critical to the success of a project. The most important point to remember is that post-implementation audits can be very time-consuming and costly and so careful consideration should be given to the cost-benefit trade-off arising from undertaking a post-implementation audit.

When should projects be audited?

If the post-implementation audit is carried out too soon, the information gathered may not be complete and faulty conclusions reached. On the other hand, if the post-implementation audit is too late then management action will be delayed and the usefulness of the information is greatly reduced. While there is no correct answer to the question of when to audit, in practice most companies perform a post-implementation audit approximately one year after a capital investment project has been completed.

Problems with post-implementation audits

The main problems associated with undertaking a post-implementation audit are:
- a long-term capital investment project can have many uncontrollable factors, such as environmental or regulatory changes. Since such factors are outside management control, there may be little to gain by identifying the resulting variances.
- the task identifying the actual costs and benefits of any particular implemented capital investment project may be difficult. This means that it may not be possible to disentangle a project's specific net cash flows from those of the business as a whole.
- post-implementation audits can be a costly and time-consuming exercise.
- applied punitively, a post-implementation audit may lead to managers becoming overly cautious and unnecessarily risk averse.
- the strategic effects of a capital investment project may take years to materialise and it may in fact never be possible to properly and fully identify or quantify them.

Despite the growth in popularity of post-implementation audits, alternative control processes are possible. For example:
- teams could be set up to manage a project from beginning to end, control being used before the project is started and during its life, rather than being deferred until, or some point just prior to, the end of the project's useful life.
- more managerial attention could be devoted to the careful evaluation of proposed capital investments rather than checking completed projects.

KEY CONCEPT

POST-IMPLEMENTATION AUDITS

Through comparing actual capital investment performance with the costs and benefits planned at the time of the original decision, a post-implementation audit provides managers with feedback about significance variances that may be eliminated or reduced through the taking of corrective action or matters that require greater attention in the making of future capital investment decisions.

PROJECT ABANDONMENT

In an ideal world the outcome of a project would be known with certainty but, of course, real life is not like that and so outcomes are always uncertain. One way in which the uncertainty facing the decision maker impacts on investment decisions is in project abandonment. A project needs to be abandoned if it becomes apparent that the net expected proceeds from abandonment are greater than the net expected proceeds from continuing the project. In an ideal world with no uncertainty, a manager should know in advance if such a situation was going to occur.

In general, a capital investment will have to be abandoned because revised estimates of future revenues and costs do not correspond to those originally used in making the investment decision. These revisions might be consistent with the data available when the original investment decision was made. If so, the possibility of project abandonment would have been known from the outset and project abandonment would have been one of the possible outcomes. Alternatively, the revisions to future revenues and costs might be completely different to the data upon which the decision was based. In such circumstances, project abandonment would not have been a possible outcome envisaged when making the initial capital investment decision.

A significant behavioural issue associated with capital investment projects is where managers have been subject to escalation commitment. That is, despite clear and unequivocal information suggesting that an in-process implementation of a capital investment ought to be discontinued, managers continue to support the continuation of the project. Part of the reasoning for such economic irrationality is that a firm's managers focus on what has been invested to date (i.e. the sunk costs of the money already spent) and are reluctant to let go of this 'money.' The consequence of such escalation commitment is that good money (i.e. further capital spending) is thrown away in the pursuit of a capital investment project that ought to have been abandoned or significantly scaled back.

KEY CONCEPT

PROJECT ABANDONMENT

Implemented capital investment projects with finite useful lives will eventually need to be abandoned. The costs associated with winding up or abandoning an implemented capital investment project may have some relevance to the making of the original investment decision.

SUMMARY

LEARNING OBJECTIVE 1

EXPLAIN THE IMPORTANCE OF WELL-MADE STRATEGIC CAPITAL INVESTMENT DECISIONS TO THE GROWING OF BUSINESS VALUE

Strategic capital investment decisions are the long-term financial aspects of the strategic decisions made by a firm's managers. As strategy is about change, most firms will have any number of strategic options to consider in seeking to maintain, if not enhance, their competitive position. Each strategic option will not only vary in terms of its initial cost but also in terms of the amount, duration and timing of the future economic benefits it is anticipated to generate. Thus, well-made strategic investment decisions are the result of a thorough and robust identification, analysis and evaluation of a firm's strategic options with the option ultimately selected and implemented being the one that provides the greatest addition to business value.

LEARNING OBJECTIVE 2

EXPLAIN THE CHARACTERISTICS OF CAPITAL INVESTMENT DECISIONS AS THEY DIFFER FROM OTHER MANAGERIAL DECISIONS

While not all capital investment decisions are the same, many differ from other types of management decisions in terms of their scale and the duration of the economic consequences of the decision made. For example, capital investment decisions can involve a high initial capital investment and a long period over which the future economic benefits are to be realised (e.g. Woolworths' decision to set up the Masters Home Improvement business unit). Other management decisions (e.g. a decision to decrease a product's selling price by 2 per cent) may have no initial 'cost' and relatively short-term financial impacts. Furthermore, while historical data might help to inform capital investment decisions, the investment decision is based on management's forward-looking estimates of costs and benefits. Since the future is never 100 per cent certain, a capital investment decision may be more risky than other types of management decisions and if poorly made can, given the scale of the investment, result in business value being destroyed.

LEARNING OBJECTIVE 3

IDENTIFY THE MULTI-PERIOD DIMENSION AND THE IMPORTANCE OF LIFE-CYCLE ANALYSIS TO THE EVALUATION OF PROPOSED CAPITAL INVESTMENTS

By definition, capital investment decisions involve multiple periods ranging from two or three years up to and beyond 40 years. Furthermore, most capital investments (e.g. a new automated manufacturing facility) encompass three stages: installation and commissioning, operation and disposal. The costs incurred and benefits realised in each stage will vary and will be impacted by decisions made about the other two stages. For example, building an automated manufacturing facility in a particular form and location might be more costly in terms of installation but deliver significant reductions in operational costs such as labour and transportation logistics. Similarly, the decision to construct a facility in a particular location (e.g. a floating liquid natural gas processing platform) will have implications for the cost of removing the facility at the end of its useful life. Thus, sound capital investment decisions rely on management having a sound understanding of the whole-of-life costs and benefits of each investment option and the trade-offs that can be made between each.

SUMMARY

LEARNING OBJECTIVE 4

OUTLINE THE SEVEN STEPS TO A CAPITAL INVESTMENT DECISION

The seven steps for a capital investment decisions are:

1   identify a need for action based on a gap in the desired business performance

2   identify potential strategic options for closing the gap in business performance

3   identify strategic initiatives that could be potentially developed into feasible projects

4   investigate and evaluate the projects that best fit the firm's strategic priorities

5   select a project to implement with attention to the definition of project delivery KPIs in terms of quality, scope, timetable and cost

6   implement project with periodic review, as required, of actual against targeted project delivery performance

7   evaluate the implemented project with the intent of remedying implementation failures and informing future investment decisions.

LEARNING OBJECTIVE 5

EXPLAIN AND APPLY THE CONCEPT OF ACCOUNTING RATE OF RETURN (ARR) AND THE PAYBACK PERIOD METHOD, AND EVALUATE THEIR USEFULNESS IN MAKING CAPITAL INVESTMENT DECISIONS

The accounting rate of return is a simple method of calculating return based on net profit or book value. It is not widely used due to its failure to account for the time value of money.

The payback period concept focuses on the time it takes for the cost of the initial investment to be recouped. It is simple to use and provides a low-level assessment of risk. Like the ARR method, it ignores the time value of money. This problem can be overcome by using the discounted payback period, in which cash flows are discounted to reflect the time value of money. However, any subsequent cash flows generated beyond the discounted payback period are still ignored.

LEARNING OBJECTIVE 6

EXPLAIN AND APPLY THE INTERNAL RATE OF RETURN (IRR) AND NET PRESENT VALUE (NPV) METHODS IN CARRYING OUT THE DISCOUNTED CASH FLOW (DCF) ANALYSIS OF PROPOSED CAPITAL INVESTMENTS

The NPV method uses the present value of future dollars received against the future value of cash outflows. Discounted cash flows can be added and, for mutually exclusive projects, the NPV method is superior to the IRR method.

The IRR method uses the present value of future dollars received against the present value of cash outflows in determining an investment proposal's internal rate of return. The IRR method in identifying the rate of return that gives a zero present value (i.e. the present value of all inflows and outflows are equal), provides a measure of a project's acceptability against a specified (or hurdle) rate of return. Where the IRR of a proposed capital investment is higher (or lower) than the hurdle rate, the investment decision would be to accept (or reject) the proposal. Problems can occur when it is possible to have more than one IRR for a given project, and it can rank investments differently from the NPV method.

Note: All methods mentioned above rely on the estimates of future returns.

COMPARE IRR AND NPV METHODS OF DCF ANALYSIS, APPRECIATE THE DIFFERENCES IN THEIR UNDERLYING ASSUMPTIONS AND EXPLAIN WHY THEY MAY PROVIDE CONTRARY RECOMMENDATIONS

The NPV method assumes that the future cash flows can be discounted to a present value using the firm's weighted average cost of capital and that the choice of mutually exclusive benefit-generating investment proposals is based on the highest net present value, or for some types of investment decisions, the lowest net present cost (NPC). On the other hand, the IRR in identifying an investment proposal's internal rate of return assumes that future cash flows are reinvested at that rate, and this may not be the case. Where a proposed investment has an IRR higher than the hurdle rate, it could be accepted. However, a proposed investment might have a higher internal rate of return but a lower NPV than other mutually exclusive projects. In this case, a conflict between the two decision rules occurs and contrary recommendations could be made. In situations such as these, the NPV decision rule dominates and the proposed investment with the highest NPV should be implemented.

DISCUSS HOW MUTUALLY EXCLUSIVE INVESTMENTS ARE DEALT WITH

Mutually exclusive investments occur when two or more projects are being evaluated but only one can be implemented (i.e. the selection of one investment proposal automatically means that other competing projects cannot be implemented). Business value is maximised when the mutually exclusive investment proposal with the highest NPV (or lowest NPC) is selected.

EXPLAIN THE IMPORTANCE OF QUALITATIVE FACTORS TO A CAPITAL INVESTMENT DECISION

Based on a quantitative analysis of a proposed capital investment, a project may have a marginally positive NPV that, absent any alternative investment proposals, could be recommended for adoption. However, difficult-to-quantify factors might be of some significance to the investment decision and, once taken into account, might suggest that a marginally acceptable project ought to be rejected. For example, a decision to outsource to an external supplier might appear to be financially acceptable based on DCF analysis but, because of its negative impact on customer satisfaction, employee morale and the loss of potentially strategic capabilities, might be rejected. While such impacts may ultimately be measured in financial terms, initially management's consideration of these factors might be more qualitatively based.

EXPLAIN THE SIGNIFICANCE OF RISK TO CAPITAL INVESTMENT DECISIONS AND IDENTIFY THE USE OF INAPPROPRIATE CONSERVATIVE ADJUSTMENTS FOR DEALING WITH THAT RISK

As capital investment decisions are based on forward-looking assumptions about 'states of the world' (e.g. political and macro-economic conditions) and estimates of future cash inflows and outflows, they are susceptible to measurement error. Thus, a decision based on a particular set of assumptions and forecasts might be found to be in error as actual cash flows fail to match those that were predicted to occur. Given the potential losses that might result from accepting an investment proposal that should, with the benefit of hindsight, not have been accepted, management will make use of conservative adjustments for dealing with that risk including:

1   shortening payback time periods

2   using cost of capital rates that are higher than the true weighted average cost of capital

3 making overly optimistic assessments of the financial consequences of retaining the status quo

4 forecasting future cash flows on a certainty equivalent basis where estimates of likely net cash flows are adjusted by assuming inflows will be less than 100 per cent of likely cash inflows (e.g. 70 per cent) and cash outflows are assumed to be more than 100 per cent of likely cash outflows (e.g. 120 per cent)

5 choking feasible investment opportunities by placing upper limits on the capital spending powers of divisional managers.

LEARNING OBJECTIVE 11

EXPLAIN HOW SENSITIVITY ANALYSIS IS USED TO DEAL WITH UNCERTAINTY AND FOCUSES MANAGERIAL ATTENTION ON THOSE CRITICAL VARIABLES THAT HAVE SIGNIFICANCE FOR A CAPITAL INVESTMENT DECISION.

Sensitivity analysis is a method for analysing the risk surrounding a capital investment decision and enables an assessment to be made of the responsiveness of a proposed project's NPV to changes in the variables that are used to calculate that NPV. A proposed capital investment's NPV could depend on a number of critical variables including: estimated selling prices, estimated sales volumes, estimated cost of capital, estimated initial costs, estimated operating costs and estimated financial benefits. While a change in most variables for an otherwise positive NPV capital investment proposal might lead to a change to a negative NPV, some variables could be more significant than others. For example, a 2 per cent decrease in sales volume as opposed to a 50 per cent increase in the cost of an investment might be sufficient to change a project's NPV from positive to negative. Given the greater likelihood of a 2 per cent reduction in selling prices occurring, management would devote greater attention to ensuring that forecast sales revenues are reliably estimated.

LEARNING OBJECTIVE 12

EXPLAIN THE VALUE OF POST-IMPLEMENTATION AUDITS AS A TOOL FOR MANAGING EXISTING AND ANY FUTURE PROJECT REQUIRING A CAPITAL INVESTMENT

Post-implementation audits provide an ex post assessment of an implemented capital investment decision. Two benefits flow from post-implementation audits:

1 For the project that is the focus of the post-implementation audit, management might be able to identify the reasons for the investment not achieving expected net economic benefits and then be able to initiate corrective action for closing the gap between intended and current outcomes.

2 For future capital investment proposals, management can learn from the mistakes made in the project that is being subjected to a post-implementation audit. After completing a post-implementation audit, management might come to better understand the impact of inappropriate assumptions or statistical models on the forecasting of future cash flows and the initial decision made. This better understanding will benefit future capital investment decisions as greater attention will be given to the use of more robust assumptions and forecasting models when evaluating alternative proposals.

LEARNING OBJECTIVE 13

EXPLAIN WHAT IS MEANT BY PROJECT ABANDONMENT AND ITS IMPLICATIONS FOR THE MAKING OF A CAPITAL INVESTMENT DECISION

Many capital investment projects have finite useful lives that are often less than their economic or physical lives. For example, manufacturing plant and equipment might have an operational life of

10 years but, because of technological innovation or physical wear and tear, be less efficient than the equipment used by rival firms. Abandonment occurs when the economic case for retaining and using an existing asset is no longer justified and it should be replaced. As with any new capital investment proposal, the timing of a decision to 'abandon' an existing asset (i.e. project) and replace it with an alternative investment is guided by the use of DCF analysis. A common example of such abandonment decisions is the disposal of motor vehicles every two or three years or 50 000 kilometres, whichever occurs first. Although a motor vehicle will have an economic or physical life greater than three years or 50 000 kilometres, these are the optimal points, in NPV terms, identified by a firm for a vehicle to be replaced.

REVIEW QUESTIONS

Note: You may need to refer to 'An introduction to financial mathematics', which can be accessed through www.cengagebrain.com, and also to Appendix 2,: 'Present and future value factor tables', to answer the following questions.

1   Find the simple interest on $900 at 4.5 per cent per annum from 1 April to 16 May.

2   If the following amounts are invested at compound interest, what will they amount to at the end of the following periods?
    a $1000 invested at 5 per cent for five years.
    b $200 invested at 10 per cent for 15 years.

3   If the following amounts are invested at compound interest, what will they amount to at the end of the following periods?
    a $1250 at 6.5 per cent per annum for six years, interest compounded annually.
    b $6500 at 7.75 per cent per annum for four years, interest compounded semi-annually.

4   If the cost of funds is 10 per cent, what is the present value of:
    a $1000 to be received in three years' time
    b $1500 to be received in 10 years' time?

5   How long will it take $125 to accumulate to $330 at 10 per cent per annum with interest compounded quarterly? Give your answer to the nearest quarter.

6   At a given annual compound rate of interest, $1000 amounts to $2100 after seven years. What is the interest rate?

7   A machine costing $100 000 has a life of 10 years and no salvage value. It will require annual maintenance expenditure of $10 000 but will save labour costs totalling $25 000 per annum. What rate of return can be expected from this machine?

8   An investment costs $75 and pays $100 after a period of 10 years. What is the effective annual compound interest rate?

9   At a given annual compound rate of interest, $1000 amounts to $1500 in 10 years. What will it amount to after six years?

10 What annual rate of interest must be earned for deposits of $400 at the start of the year for 10 years, and deposits of $1000 for the following five years, to accumulate a sum of $20 000 at the end of 15 years?

11 What is the purchase price of a house that can be bought for $4000 cash plus $400 at the end of each year for 20 years? (Interest is assumed to be 6 per cent per annum compounded).

12 If I deposit $100 in the bank now, $100 regularly at 12-month intervals for the next five years and $200 regularly at 12-month intervals for the following 10 years, what is:

   a   the accumulated value at the end of the 15 years

   b   the present value of the payments? (Assume 5 per cent per annum compounding interest).

13 What annual rate of interest must be earned for deposits of $500 at the start of each year to accumulate to $10 000 in 15 years?

14 A company pays $1000 each year into a bank sinking fund earning 6 per cent per annum compound interest. After five payments, the rate of interest granted by the bank on the fund is reduced to 4 per cent. The company, therefore, decides to increase its future deposits to $1200. What amount is in the fund after 15 payments altogether have been made?

15 A loan of $81 000 is to be repaid by 10 equal annual instalments of principal and interest which is at the rate of 5 per cent per annum.

   a   What is the annual instalment?

   b   Draw up a schedule showing the amount of principal and the amount of interest contained in each instalment, and the principal still outstanding after each payment.

   c   As a check, calculate, independently, the amount outstanding after the fourth and seventh payments.

16 What amount payable in 10 years' time would be equivalent to $500 payable in five years' time plus $1000 payable in 15 years' time? (Assume 6 per cent per annum compound interest.)

17 A person owes $1000 payable in three years' time and $1000 payable in 13 years' time, and would like to settle the debt by making a $2000 payment. If interest is 5 per cent per annum compound, when should the payment be made?

18 A $200 refrigerator is sold 'on easy terms'. These terms are:

   a   no deposit

   b   simple interest of 10 per cent

   c   monthly repayments over two years.

      Given such terms, what is the true rate of compound interest which the customer is paying?

19 What is the payback method and explain how it is used to rank competing investment proposals that only differ in terms of the amount and duration of future cash inflows. What are the strengths and weaknesses of the payback method?

20 A manager said to a company's shareholder, 'When it comes to the time value of money, there are two things to remember, it is my time and your money.' Is this what is meant by the time value of money concept?

21 NPV and IRR are two DCF methods for analysing a proposed capital investment. Briefly explain how each method can be used to make a capital investment decision and the strengths and weaknesses of each.

22 'When using DCF analysis to make an investment decision, many overheads, including depreciation, are irrelevant.' Critically evaluate this statement and comment on the extent that overheads, including depreciation, are relevant or irrelevant to an investment decision.

23 Two mutually exclusive capital investment proposals have been evaluated using DCF analysis and the difference between their NPVs is marginal. Briefly explain how a consideration of strategic or qualitative factors might influence the evaluation of the two proposals.

24 Explain how sensitivity analysis contributes to better-informed capital investment decision making.

25 Discuss why a firm may choose to undertake a post-implementation audit and the factors that determine when and which implemented projects are to be audited.

26 Many contemporary capital investment proposals can have a significant information and communication technology (ICT) component. What are the difficulties associated with identifying and measuring the variables to be accounted for when using DCF analysis for evaluating proposals with a high ICT component? What impact could qualitative factors have on the evaluation of such proposals?

PROBLEMS FOR DISCUSSION AND ANALYSIS

1 What is the present value of an *annuity* with payments of $1000 per year for five years if money is worth 12 per cent per annum compounded quarterly?

2 A car is priced to sell for $27 000 cash, or a $6000 deposit and six bimonthly payments of $4200. What is the implied interest rate in the deferred payment option?

3 A car yard is offering special terms of no repayments for two years. A down payment of $5000 is required, followed by six half-yearly payments of $2000 starting at the end of two years. If the cash value of the car is $11 000, what is the implied interest rate? (*Note:* interest is calculated from the date of purchase.)

4 Bloggs Ltd has to replace its widget-making machine in five years. The company estimates the new machine will cost $30 000. It wishes to provide for this machine by putting aside a regular annual amount in a reserve. Natbank has offered the company two options:

a Deposit five equal amounts at the beginning of each year to earn 5 per cent compound interest.

b Deposit five equal amounts at the beginning of each year to earn an increasing compound interest rate of 2.5 per cent for the first year and increasing by 1 per cent each year after that.

Which option allows the company to put the least annual amount into a reserve, and what is that annual amount?

5 The Fidget Co. is proposing to spend $91 280 on a seven-year project whose estimated net cash flows are $20 000 for each of the seven years.

a Calculate the net present value using a rate of 15 per cent (use the table of present values in Appendix 2).

b Based on the analysis prepared in (a), is the rate of return:

  i more than 15 per cent

  ii 15 per cent

  iii less than 15 per cent?

    Briefly explain your response.

c Calculate the internal rate of return.

6 The following details are available for three projects:

CASH FLOW ($)

PROJECT	YEAR 0 ($)	YEAR 1 ($)	YEAR 2 ($)	YEAR 3 ($)	YEAR 4 ($)	YEAR 5 ($)
1	−5000	500	500	500	500	5500
2	−5000	1319	1319	1319	1319	1319
3	−5000	–	–	–	–	8053

a   Calculate the net present value of each of these projects, and then rank them. Use discount rates of 5, 10 and 15 per cent.

b   Calculate the internal rate of return for each of the projects and then rank them.

7   Use the data below to calculate:

a   the accounting rate of return

b   the payback period

c   the internal rate of return

d   the net present value.

How would your answers differ if the net cash inflows were as shown below?

Project cost	$20 000
Estimated life	5 years
Estimated salvage value	$2 000
Annual net cash inflow	$6 000
Required rate of return	10%

	$
Year 1	6 000
Year 2	7 000
Year 3	12 000
Year 4	3 000
Year 5	10 000

8   AKP Fashion Designers are considering two investment projects. The estimated net cash flows from each project are as follows:

YEAR	PLANT EXPANSION ($)	RETAIL STORE EXPANSION ($)
1	100 000	150 000
2	130 000	120 000
3	150 000	110 000
4	130 000	110 000
5	170 000	190 000
Total	680 000	680 000

Each project requires an investment of $380 000. A rate of 20 per cent has been selected for the net present value analysis.

Required

a Compute the following for each project:

   i   cash payback period

   ii net present value.

b Prepare a brief report advising management on the relative merits of each of the two projects.

9 Jenny and Bill Smith wish to buy a property costing $100 000. They have a $20 000 deposit. Bankpac offers them the following alternatives:

a a fixed interest rate of 7.5 per cent with the interest being charged on the first day of the month each year, commencing with the first day of the loan.

b a fixed interest rate of 8.5 per cent with the interest being charged from the last day of each month. The loan is to commence from the first day of the month.

   If Jenny and Bill want to pay off their loan in 10 years, which loan requires the least outlay of money? Show workings.

10 Silver Corporation is evaluating five investment opportunities. The company's cost of capital is 15 per cent. No investment is accepted if the payback period is greater than three years. The company will only accept a maximum of two investment projects. The following investments are being considered.

INVESTMENT	INITIAL COST ($)	EXPECTED RETURNS ($)
A	130 000	40 000 per year for 5 years
B	60 000	30 000 per year for 6 years
C	40 000	12 000 per year for 10 years
D	25 000	9000 per year for 6 years
E	15 000	4500 per year for 3 years

Required

a Which projects would be accepted using the NPV and payback methods to screen investments?

b Discuss the benefits of using the payback method together with NPV or IRR.

Note to instructors: The following problems are considered more suitable for use in MBA courses. However, undergraduate courses may also find them useful.

11 Reflex Ltd is considering the purchase of a new punch machine to produce coins. The machine would cost $11 000 cash. A service maintenance contract on the machine is essential and would cost an extra $100 per month. The expected life of the machine is four years and the expected salvage value is $200. The new machine will save $350 per month in labour costs and $40 per month in materials costs. The old machine would be sold for its book value of $500. The cost of capital for Reflex is 15 per cent. The tax rate is 40 per cent, which means depreciation tax savings of $1080 each year.

Required

Calculate:

a   the payback period

b   the net present value.

12 The Porter Group is considering allocating a limited amount of capital investment funds among four proposals. The amount of proposed investment, estimated income from operations, and net cash flow for each proposal is as follows:

	INVESTMENT ($)	YEAR	INCOME FROM OPERATIONS ($)	NET CASH FLOW ($)
Proposal A:	600 000	1	40 000	160 000
		2	40 000	160 000
		3	40 000	160 000
		4	0	120 000
		5	0	120 000
Proposal B:	520 000	1	96 000	200 000
		2	56 000	160 000
		3	56 000	160 000
		4	56 000	160 000
		5	48 000	152 000
Proposal C:	180 000	1	44 000	80 000
		2	24 000	60 000
		3	24 000	60 000
		4	24 000	60 000
		5	22 500	58 500
Proposal D:	250 000	1	50 000	100 000
		2	50 000	100 000
		3	(10 000)	40 000
		4	(10 000)	40 000
		5	(10 000)	40 000

The company's capital rationing policy requires a maximum cash payback period of three years. In addition, a minimum average accounting rate of return of 10 per cent is required on all projects. If the preceding standards are met, the net present value method and present value indexes (= total present value of net cash flows divided by amount to be invested) are used to rank the remaining proposals.

Required

a Calculate the cash payback period for each of the four proposals.

b Assuming straight-line depreciation on the investments, and no estimated residual value, calculate the average accounting rate of return for each of the four proposals. Round to one decimal place.

c Using the following format, summarise the results of your calculations in (a) and (b). Indicate which proposals should be accepted for further analysis and which should be rejected.

PROPOSAL	CASH PAYBACK PERIOD	AVERAGE ACCOUNTING RATE OF RETURN	ACCEPT/REJECT
A			
B			
C			
D			

d For the proposals accepted for further analysis in (c), calculate the net present value. Use a rate of 10 per cent. Round to the nearest dollar.

e Calculate the present value index (PVI) for each of the proposals in (d). Round to two decimal places (PVI = total present value of net cash flows divided by amount to be invested).

f Rank the proposals from the most attractive to the least attractive, based on the present values of net cash flows calculated in (d).

g Rank the proposals from the most attractive to the least attractive, based on the present value indexes calculated in (e).

h Based upon the analyses, comment on the relative attractiveness of the proposals ranked in (f) and (g).

(Adapted from C.S. Warren, J.M. Reeve and P.E. Fess, *Accounting*, 20th edn, South-Western, Mason, OH, 2002, Problem 24-6A, p. 1009).

ETHICS CASE STUDY

Newark Ltd is planning to build a new manufacturing plant. Jenny Frame is the person appointed to head the task force responsible for preparing an analysis of the options available to Newark. Frame's team completes a detailed analysis of three possible types of manufacturing facilities.

1 *Option 1* This is the lowest-cost option but it has a higher risk of employee injuries and a greater risk of environmental damage from toxic gases arising from poor venting.

2 *Option 2* This has a higher cost than option 1 but reduces the risk of injury to employees. It still has the potential for environmental damage.

3 *Option 3* This is the highest-cost option but provides the greatest safety to workers and offers the least danger to the environment.

Jenny submits the results of the analysis to her boss and he thanks her for the fantastic job that she and her team have done. He will make special mention of her efforts in her job evaluation report this year.

Jenny is pleased with her boss's response, but a week later she is disturbed after coming across a copy of a report from her boss to the board. The report focuses on the costs associated with each option and does not mention the risks to the workers and the environment.

Jenny is unsure of what she should do. She could speak to her boss and risk losing the favourable job evaluation (or even her job). Alternatively, she could pretend she never saw the report. She is uncertain as to where her responsibilities end. She is, however, also worried about how she would feel if someone were to be hurt as a result of the company selecting option 1.

Discuss

Discuss Jenny's responsibilities after you have identified them. Suggest a possible course of action.

SUGGESTED ANSWERS TO STOP AND THINK EXERCISES IN THE CHAPTER

1 **a** Simple interest $= \$1245 \times 5.6\% \times \dfrac{198}{365}$

$= \$37.82$

b We are looking for a future value factor of 2 ($200 ÷ $100) at 6 per cent in Table 1 of Appendix 2. At different years we see:

For life $= 11$, factor $= 1.89\,829$

For life $= 12$, factor $= 2.01\,219$

Therefore, it is close to 12 years (11 years 11 months) before an annuity accumulates from $100 to $200.

c Amount borrowed $= \$50\,000$

From Table 4, Appendix 2, the present value (PV) of $1 per annum for 10 years at 7 per cent $= 7.0235$

PV of $1/(7.0235) per annum for 10 years at 7 per cent $= \$1$

PV of $50\,000/7.0235 per annum for 10 years at 7 per cent $= \$50\,000$

Therefore, an amount of $7118.96 (= $50\,000/7.0235 for 10 years at 7 per cent) would repay the loan.

2 **a** IRR

$OC = NCF \times PVF\,(IRR, n)$

$78\,345 = 15\,250 \times PVF\,(IRR, 8)$

$5.13737 = PVF\,(IRR, 8)$

from Appendix 2, Table 4, IRR is approximately 11 per cent.

b NPV

$NPV = -OC + NCF \times PVF\,(8,11)$

$NPV = -78\,345 + 15\,250 \times 5.13737$

(Table 4, Appendix 2)

$= 0$

    c   Pay back = Initial investment/NCF

          $NCF = \dfrac{\$78\,345}{\$15\,250}$

          = 5.137 years

3 **a** IRR

      OC = NCF x PVF (IRR, n)

      25 093 = 5000 x PVF (IRR, 10)

      5.0186 = PVF (IRR, 10)

      From Table 4, Appendix 2, IRR = 15 per cent.

    b NPV

      NPV = –OC + NCF x PVF (10,10)

      NPV = –25 093 + 5000 x 6.1445

      (Table 4, Appendix 2)

      = $5629.50

    c Pay back = Initial investment /NCF

          $NCF = \dfrac{\$25\,093}{\$55\,000}$

          = 5.0186 years

APPENDIX 1: EXTRACT FROM WOOLWORTHS LIMITED 2013 ANNUAL REPORT

CONSOLIDATED INCOME STATEMENT – WOOLWORTHS LIMITED

To see the full annual report, please visit www.woolworthslimited.com.au and search for the 2013 'Financial Report to Shareholders'.

	NOTE	2013 53 WEEKS $M	2012 52 WEEKS $M
Continuing Operations			
Revenue from the sale of goods	2a	58,516.4	54,777.1
Other operating revenue	2a	157.7	138.9
Total revenue from continuing operations		58,674.1	54,916.0
Cost of sales		(42,912.6)	(40,455.0)
Gross profit from continuing operations		15,761.5	14,461.0
Other revenue	2b	247.6	223.5
Branch expenses		(9,799.8)	(8,777.3)
Administration expenses		(2,614.7)	(2,560.8)
Earnings from continuing operations before interest and tax		3,594.6	3,346.4
Financial expense	3	(410.1)	(316.8)
Financial income	3	30.3	34.6
Net financing costs from continuing operations		(379.8)	(282.2)
Profit from continuing operations before income tax expense		3,214.8	3,064.2
Income tax expense relating to continuing operations	5a	(959.9)	(885.0)
Profit from continuing operations after income tax expense		2,254.9	2,179.2
Discontinued Operations			
Profit/(loss) from discontinued operations	33	9.7	(362.0)
Profit for the period		2,264.6	1,817.2
Profit attributable to:			
Equity holders of Woolworths Limited		2,259.4	1,816.7
Non-controlling interests		5.2	0.5
		2,264.6	1,817.2
Profit attributable to owners of Woolworths Limited relates to:			
Profit from continuing operations		2,249.7	2,178.7
Profit/(loss) from discontinued operations		9.7	(362.0)
		2,259.4	1,816.7
Earnings Per Share (EPS) from continuing and discontinued operations			
Basic EPS (cents per share)	20	182.6	148.7
Diluted EPS (cents per share)	20	181.8	147.9
Weighted average number of shares used in the calculation of basic EPS (million)	20	1,237.4	1,222.0
Earnings Per Share (EPS) from continuing operations			
Basic EPS (cents per share)	20	181.8	178.3
Diluted EPS (cents per share)	20	181.0	177.4

The above consolidated income statement should be read in conjunction with the accompanying notes to the consolidated financial statements

CONSOLIDATED STATEMENT OF COMPREHENSIVE INCOME – WOOLWORTHS LIMITED

	NOTE	2013 53 WEEKS $M	2012 52 WEEKS $M
Net profit from continuing operations		2,254.9	2,179.2
Net profit/(loss) from discontinued operations		9.7	(362.0)
Profit for the period		2,264.6	1,817.2
Other comprehensive income from continuing operations			
Movement in translation of foreign operations taken to equity		197.8	37.8
Movement in the fair value of investments in equity securities		32.9	(16.3)
Movement in the fair value of cash flow hedges		256.4	95.7
Transfer cash flow hedges to the income statement		(231.9)	(175.4)
Actuarial gains/(losses) on defined benefit plans		12.5	(50.8)
Tax effect of items recognised directly to equity		(36.3)	34.2
Other comprehensive income/(loss) for the period (net of tax) from continuing operations		231.4	(74.8)
Other comprehensive income from discontinued operations			
Movement in translation of foreign operations taken to equity		0.3	(0.8)
Movement in the fair value of cash flow hedges		0.4	(0.3)
Tax effect of items recognised directly to equity		(0.1)	0.2
Other comprehensive income/(loss) for the period (net of tax) from discontinued operations		0.6	(0.9)
Total comprehensive income from continuing operations		2,486.3	2,104.4
Total comprehensive income/(loss) from discontinued operations		10.3	(362.9)
Total comprehensive income for the period		2,496.6	1,741.5
Total comprehensive income from continuing operations attributable to:			
Equity holders of Woolworths Limited		2,481.1	2,103.9
Non-controlling interests		5.2	0.5
Total comprehensive income for the period from continuing operations		2,486.3	2,104.4
Total comprehensive income/(loss) from discontinued operations attributable to:			
Equity holders of Woolworths Limited		10.3	(362.9)
Total comprehensive income/(loss) for the period from discontinued operations		10.3	(362.9)

Woolworths Limited Annual Report 2013 page 103

CONSOLIDATED STATEMENT OF COMPREHENSIVE INCOME – WOOLWORTHS LIMITED

INCOME TAX ON OTHER COMPREHENSIVE INCOME/(LOSS) FROM CONTINUING OPERATIONS FOR THE PERIOD ENDED 30 JUNE 2013	BEFORE TAX $M	TAX (EXPENSE)/ BENEFIT $M	NET OF TAX $M
Movement in translation of foreign operations taken to equity	197.8	(25.1)	172.7
Movement in the fair value of investments in equity securities	32.9	–	32.9
Movement in the fair value of cash flow hedges	256.4	(76.9)	179.5
Transfer cash flow hedges to the income statement	(231.9)	69.5	(162.4)
Actuarial gains on defined benefit plans	12.5	(3.8)	8.7
Total of items recognised in other comprehensive income	**267.7**	**(36.3)**	**231.4**

INCOME TAX ON OTHER COMPREHENSIVE (LOSS)/INCOME FROM CONTINUING OPERATIONS FOR THE PERIOD ENDED 24 JUNE 2012	BEFORE TAX $M	TAX (EXPENSE)/ BENEFIT $M	NET OF TAX $M
Movement in translation of foreign operations taken to equity	37.8	(4.9)	32.9
Movement in the fair value of investments in equity securities	(16.3)	–	(16.3)
Movement in the fair value of cash flow hedges	95.7	(28.7)	67.0
Transfer cash flow hedges to the income statement	(175.4)	52.6	(122.8)
Actuarial losses on defined benefit plans	(50.8)	15.2	(35.6)
Total of items recognised in other comprehensive income	**(109.0)**	**34.2**	**(74.8)**

INCOME TAX ON OTHER COMPREHENSIVE INCOME/(LOSS) FROM DISCONTINUED OPERATIONS FOR THE PERIOD ENDED 30 JUNE 2013	BEFORE TAX $M	TAX (EXPENSE) $M	NET OF TAX $M
Movement in translation of foreign operations taken to equity	0.3	–	0.3
Movement in the fair value of cash flow hedges	0.4	(0.1)	0.3
Total of items recognised in other comprehensive income	**0.7**	**(0.1)**	**0.6**

INCOME TAX ON OTHER COMPREHENSIVE (LOSS)/INCOME FROM DISCONTINUED OPERATIONS FOR THE PERIOD ENDED 24 JUNE 2012	BEFORE TAX $M	TAX BENEFIT $M	NET OF TAX $M
Movement in translation of foreign operations taken to equity	(0.8)	0.1	(0.7)
Movement in the fair value of cash flow hedges	(0.3)	0.1	(0.2)
Total of items recognised in other comprehensive income	**(1.1)**	**0.2**	**(0.9)**

The above consolidated statement of comprehensive income should be read in conjunction with the accompanying notes to the consolidated financial statements

CONSOLIDATED BALANCE SHEET – WOOLWORTHS LIMITED

	NOTE	2013 $M	2012 $M
Current assets			
Cash and cash equivalents		849.2	833.4
Trade and other receivables	8	968.6	869.9
Inventories		4,205.4	3,698.3
Other financial assets	9	54.2	23.8
		6,077.4	5,425.4
Assets classified as held for sale	33	148.7	376.7
Total current assets		6,226.1	5,802.1
Non-current assets			
Trade and other receivables	8	16.6	24.5
Other financial assets	9	358.7	238.8
Property, plant and equipment	10	9,246.1	9,589.0
Intangible assets	11	5,784.3	5,282.0
Deferred tax assets	5d	618.4	644.7
Total non-current assets		16,024.1	15,779.0
Total assets		22,250.2	21,581.1
Current liabilities			
Trade and other payables	12	5,390.3	5,242.2
Borrowings	14	169.4	54.4
Current tax liabilities	5c	193.2	221.5
Other financial liabilities	13	145.9	107.4
Provisions	16	967.2	939.8
		6,866.0	6,565.3
Liabilities directly associated with assets classified as held for sale	33	–	200.9
Total current liabilities		6,866.0	6,766.2
Non-current liabilities			
Borrowings	14	4,282.5	4,695.3
Other financial liabilities	13	992.6	887.2
Provisions	16	549.2	527.3
Other		259.4	258.8
Total non-current liabilities		6,083.7	6,368.6
Total liabilities		12,949.7	13,134.8
Net assets		9,300.5	8,446.3
Equity			
Issued capital	17	4,522.7	4,336.6
Shares held in trust	17	(180.5)	(60.7)
Reserves	18	25.1	(243.9)
Retained earnings	19	4,661.1	4,163.4
		9,028.4	8,195.4
Amounts recognised directly in equity relating to assets classified as held for sale	33	–	(7.2)
Equity attributable to the members of Woolworths Limited		9,028.4	8,188.2
Non-controlling interests		272.1	258.1
Total equity		9,300.5	8,446.3

The above consolidated balance sheet should be read in conjunction with the accompanying notes to the consolidated financial statements

CONSOLIDATED CASH FLOW STATEMENT – WOOLWORTHS LIMITED

	2013 53 WEEKS $M	2012 52 WEEKS $M
Cash Flows from Operating Activities		
Receipts from customers	63,789.8	61,545.6
Receipts from vendors and tenants	47.0	50.9
Payments to suppliers and employees	(59,685.1)	(57,412.0)
Interest and costs of finance paid	(476.7)	(396.1)
Interest received	22.2	26.8
Income tax paid	(977.3)	(941.4)
Net cash provided by operating activities	2,719.9	2,873.8
Cash Flows from Investing Activities		
Proceeds from the sale of property, plant and equipment	100.3	199.5
Proceeds from the sale of property to the Shopping Centres Australasia Property Group	802.8	–
Payments for property, plant and equipment – property development	(767.4)	(1,165.8)
Advances/(repayments) of property related receivables	14.8	(1.1)
Payments for property, plant and equipment (excluding property development)	(1,136.0)	(968.7)
Payments for intangible assets	(66.7)	(6.2)
Proceeds from the sale of subsidiaries	105.8	–
Payments for the purchase of businesses	(235.4)	(145.2)
Payments for the purchase of investments	(28.0)	(0.6)
Dividends received	8.1	7.8
Net cash used in investing activities	(1,201.7)	(2,080.3)
Cash Flows from Financing Activities		
Proceeds from the issue of equity securities	188.1	120.9
Proceeds from the issue of equity securities in subsidiary to non-controlling interest	230.0	203.0
Proceeds from external borrowings	5,974.5	12,361.9
Repayment of external borrowings	(6,501.8)	(12,830.8)
Dividends paid	(1,396.7)	(1,317.2)
Dividends paid to non-controlling interests	(20.1)	(15.6)
Repayment of employee share plan loans	5.6	8.6
Net cash used in financing activities	(1,520.4)	(1,469.2)
Net decrease in cash and cash equivalents held	(2.2)	(675.7)
Effects of exchange rate changes on foreign currency held	6.2	1.3
Cash and cash equivalents at the beginning of the period	845.2	1,519.6
Cash and cash equivalents at the end of the period	849.2	845.2
Non-cash financing and investing activities		
In accordance with the Company's Dividend Reinvestment Plan (DRP) 12% (2012: 13%) of the dividend paid was reinvested in the shares of the Company		
Dividends (Note 6)	1,597.5	1,516.8
Issuance of shares under the DRP	(198.6)	(199.6)
Dividends paid on Treasury shares	(2.2)	–
Net cash outflow	1,396.7	1,317.2

The above consolidated cash flow statement should be read in conjunction with the accompanying notes to the consolidated financial statements

RECONCILIATION OF NET CASH PROVIDED BY OPERATING ACTIVITIES TO PROFIT AFTER INCOME TAX EXPENSE	2013 53 WEEKS $M	2012 52 WEEKS $M
Profit after income tax expense	**2,264.6**	1,817.2
Depreciation and amortisation	965.5	895.9
Foreign exchange losses/(gains)	13.3	(0.8)
Employee benefits expense – share based payments	34.9	39.8
Loss on disposal and write off of property, plant and equipment	9.7	10.2
Borrowing costs capitalised	(77.4)	(90.1)
Amortisation of borrowing costs	6.4	8.1
Consumer Electronics restructuring provision	–	393.1
Profit from sale of subsidiaries	(9.9)	–
Dividends received	(8.1)	(7.8)
Other	(7.5)	5.4
Decrease/(increase) in deferred tax asset	1.8	(104.7)
(Decrease)/increase in current tax liability	(17.2)	19.1
Increase in trade and other receivables	(61.8)	(107.3)
Increase in inventories	(550.3)	(297.3)
Increase in trade payables	59.7	14.7
Increase in sundry payables and provisions	96.2	278.3
Net cash provided by operating activities	**2,719.9**	2,873.8

Acquisition of businesses

Details of the aggregate cash outflow relating to the acquisition of businesses and the aggregate assets and liabilities of those businesses as at the date of acquisition were as follows:

- property, plant and equipment	29.8	49.8
- inventories	30.6	10.0
- liquor and gaming licences and other intangible assets	158.5	40.1
- cash	3.2	0.3
- receivables	10.9	7.8
- deferred tax (liability)/asset	(0.9)	0.3
- accounts payable	(20.0)	(4.8)
- provisions	(5.0)	(1.1)
- other liabilities	(7.2)	–
Net assets acquired	**199.9**	102.4
Minority interest share of acquired business	(7.2)	–
Goodwill on acquisition	45.9	42.1
Fair value of net assets acquired	**238.6**	144.5

Analysed as follows:

Consideration

- cash paid	238.6	144.5
Total consideration	**238.6**	144.5
Cash paid	238.6	144.5
Add: deferred consideration paid	–	1.0
Less: cash balances acquired	(3.2)	(0.3)
Cash consideration paid	**235.4**	145.2

Details of acquisitions are shown at Note 30.

Reconciliation of cash and cash equivalents

For the purposes of the consolidated cash flow statement, cash and cash equivalents includes cash at bank and on hand, net of outstanding bank overdrafts. Cash at the end of the financial period as shown in the consolidated cash flow statement is reconciled to the related items in the consolidated balance sheet as follows:

	2013 $M	2012 $M
Cash at bank and on hand from continuing operations	849.2	833.4
Cash at bank and on hand from discontinued operations	–	11.8
Balance per consolidated cash flow statement	**849.2**	845.2

CONSOLIDATED STATEMENT OF CHANGES IN EQUITY – WOOLWORTHS LIMITED

FOR THE YEAR ENDED 30 JUNE 2013	ISSUED CAPITAL $M	SHARES HELD IN TRUST $M	HEDGING RESERVE $M	FOREIGN CURRENCY TRANSLATION RESERVE $M	REMUNERATION RESERVE $M
Balance at 25 June 2012	4,336.6	(60.7)	(52.8)	(349.0)	246.2
Profit after income tax expense	–	–	–	–	–
Other comprehensive income for the period (net of tax)	–	–	17.4	173.0	–
Total comprehensive income for the period (net of tax)	–	–	17.4	173.0	–
Dividends paid	–	–	–	–	–
Dividends paid – treasury shares	–	–	–	–	–
Issue of shares as a result of options exercised under employee long term incentive plans	188.1	–	–	–	–
Issue of shares as a result of the dividend reinvestment plan	198.6	–	–	–	–
Issue of shares under the employee share plan and long term incentive plans	–	26.0	–	–	(14.4)
Issue of shares to non-controlling interests	–	–	–	–	–
Equity settled share based payments expense	–	–	–	–	34.9
Tax provision impact of share based payments	–	–	–	–	23.9
Sale of businesses	–	–	(0.2)	8.7	–
Reclassification of non-controlling interests for recognition of financial liability	–	–	–	–	–
In-specie distribution to Woolworths Limited shareholders	(340.3)	–	–	–	–
Shares issued to/(acquired by) the Woolworths Employee Share Trust	145.8	(145.8)	–	–	–
Other	(6.1)	–	–	–	–
Balance at 30 June 2013	4,522.7	(180.5)	(35.6)	(167.3)	290.6

FOR THE YEAR ENDED 24 JUNE 2012	ISSUED CAPITAL $M	SHARES HELD IN TRUST $M	HEDGING RESERVE $M	FOREIGN CURRENCY TRANSLATION RESERVE $M	REMUNERATION RESERVE $M
Balance at 27 June 2011	3,988.6	(56.1)	3.2	(381.2)	220.4
Profit after income tax expense	–	–	–	–	–
Other comprehensive income for the period (net of tax)	–	–	(56.0)	32.2	–
Total comprehensive income for the period (net of tax)	–	–	(56.0)	32.2	–
Dividends paid	–	–	–	–	–
Issue of shares as a result of options exercised under employee long term incentive plans	120.9	–	–	–	–
Issue of shares as a result of the dividend reinvestment plan	199.6	–	–	–	–
Issue of shares under the employee share plan and long term incentive plans	–	29.8	–	–	(14.1)
Issue of shares to non-controlling interests	–	–	–	–	–
Equity settled share based payments expense	–	–	–	–	39.8
Tax provision impact of share based payments	–	–	–	–	0.1
Reclassification of non-controlling interests for recognition of financial liability	–	–	–	–	–
Shares issued to/(acquired by) the Woolworths Employee Share Trust	34.4	(34.4)	–	–	–
Other	(6.9)	–	–	–	–
Balance at 24 June 2012	4,336.6	(60.7)	(52.8)	(349.0)	246.2

The above consolidated statement of changes in equity should be read in conjunction with the accompanying notes to the consolidated financial statements

ASSET REVALUATION RESERVE $M	EQUITY INSTRUMENT RESERVE $M	RETAINED PROFITS $M	EQUITY ATTRIBUTABLE TO MEMBERS OF WOOLWORTHS LIMITED $M	NON-CONTROLLING INTERESTS $M	TOTAL EQUITY $M
16.4	(111.9)	4,163.4	8,188.2	258.1	8,446.3
–	–	2,259.4	2,259.4	5.2	2,264.6
–	32.9	8.7	232.0	–	232.0
–	32.9	2,268.1	2,491.4	5.2	2,496.6
–	–	(1,597.5)	(1,597.5)	(20.1)	(1,617.6)
–	–	2.2	2.2	–	2.2
–	–	–	188.1	–	188.1
–	–	–	198.6	–	198.6
–	–	–	11.6	–	11.6
–	–	–	–	230.0	230.0
–	–	–	34.9	–	34.9
–	–	–	23.9	–	23.9
–	–	–	8.5	–	8.5
–	–	–	–	(197.3)	(197.3)
–	–	(176.1)	(516.4)	–	(516.4)
–	–	–	–	–	–
–	–	1.0	(5.1)	(3.8)	(8.9)
16.4	(79.0)	4,661.1	9,028.4	272.1	9,300.5

ASSET REVALUATION RESERVE $M	EQUITY INSTRUMENT RESERVE $M	RETAINED PROFITS $M	EQUITY ATTRIBUTABLE TO MEMBERS OF WOOLWORTHS LIMITED $M	NON-CONTROLLING INTERESTS $M	TOTAL EQUITY $M
16.4	(95.6)	3,897.5	7,593.2	252.6	7,845.8
–	–	1,816.7	1,816.7	0.5	1,817.2
–	(16.3)	(35.6)	(75.7)	–	(75.7)
–	(16.3)	1,781.1	1,741.0	0.5	1,741.5
–	–	(1,516.8)	(1,516.8)	(15.6)	(1,532.4)
–	–	–	120.9	–	120.9
–	–	–	199.6	–	199.6
–	–	–	15.7	–	15.7
–	–	–	–	110.0	110.0
–	–	–	39.8	–	39.8
–	–	–	0.1	–	0.1
–	–	–	–	(89.1)	(89.1)
–	–	–	–	–	–
–	–	1.6	(5.3)	(0.3)	(5.6)
16.4	(111.9)	4,163.4	8,188.2	258.1	8,446.3

NOTES TO THE CONSOLIDATED FINANCIAL STATEMENTS

1 SIGNIFICANT ACCOUNTING POLICIES

Woolworths Limited (the 'Company') is a company domiciled in Australia. The Financial Report of the Company for the 53 weeks ended 30 June 2013 comprises the Company and its subsidiaries (together referred to as the 'consolidated entity' or 'Group'). The comparative period was for the 52 weeks ended 24 June 2012.

The Financial Report was authorised for issue by the Directors on 27 September 2013.

(A) STATEMENT OF COMPLIANCE

This Financial Report is a general purpose financial report which has been prepared in accordance with the *Corporations Act 2001*, Accounting Standards and Interpretations, and complies with other requirements of the law.

The Financial Report represents the consolidated financial statements of the Group. For the purposes of preparing the consolidated financial statements, the Company is a for-profit entity.

Accounting Standards include Australian equivalents to International Financial Reporting Standards ('A-IFRS'). Compliance with A-IFRS ensures that the financial statements and notes of the consolidated entity comply with International Financial Reporting Standards ('IFRS').

(B) BASIS OF PREPARATION

The Financial Report is presented in Australian dollars.

The Financial Report has been prepared on the historical cost basis except for available-for-sale financial assets, derivative financial instruments, financial assets valued through other comprehensive income and other financial liabilities that are measured at revalued amounts or fair values, as explained in the accounting policies below.

The accounting policies set out below have been applied consistently to all periods presented in these financial statements.

The comparative income statement and statement of comprehensive income has been re-presented as if an operation discontinued during the current period had been discontinued from the start of the comparative period (see Note 33).

The Company is of a kind referred to in ASIC Class Order 98/100, dated 10 July 1998 and in accordance with the Class Order, amounts in the Financial Report have been rounded off to the nearest million dollars, unless otherwise stated.

New and amended standards adopted by the Group

In the current period, the consolidated entity has adopted all of the new and revised Standards and Interpretations issued by the Australian Accounting Standards Board (the 'AASB') that are relevant to its operations and effective for annual reporting periods beginning on or after 25 June 2012. These include:

- AASB 1054 *'Australian Additional Disclosures'* and AASB 2011-1 *'Amendments to Australian Accounting Standards arising from Trans-Tasman Convergence Project'*;
- AASB 2010-6 *'Amendments to Australian Accounting Standards – Disclosures on Transfers of Financial Assets'*; and
- AASB 2010-8 *'Amendments to Australian Accounting Standards – Deferred Tax: Recovery of Underlying Assets'*

The adoption of these new and revised accounting standards has not resulted in any significant impact on the financial results, as the standards and amendments are primarily concerned with disclosures.

In previous financial periods, the Group early adopted AASB 9 *Financial Instruments (December 2009)*, including AASB 2009-11 *Amendments to Australian Accounting Standards arising from AASB 9*, AASB 9 *Financial Instruments (December 2010)* and AASB 2010-7 *Amendments to Australian Accounting Standards arising from AASB 9 (December 2009)*. AASB 9 provides an option to designate and measure an investment in equity instruments at fair value, with changes recognised in other comprehensive income and only dividends being recognised in profit or loss. The Group elected to apply this option. The application of this standard affected accounting for the investments in The Warehouse Group Limited and Australian Leisure and Entertainment Property Management Limited (the 'ALE Property Group'), both of which have been designated as fair value through other comprehensive income. These changes have been adopted retrospectively with no impact on retained earnings in the current or previous financial years.

Issued standards and interpretations not early adopted

The following standards and Amendments to Standards were available for early adoption and were applicable to the consolidated entity but have not been applied in these financial statements:

- AASB 1053 *'Application of Tiers of Accounting Standards'* and AASB 2010-2 *'Amendments to Australian Accounting Standards arising from Reduced Disclosure Requirements'*. Woolworths Limited is listed on the Australian Stock Exchange and is not eligible to adopt the new Australian Accounting Standards – Reduced Disclosure Requirements. Applies to annual reporting periods beginning on or after 1 July 2013;
- AASB 13 *'Fair Value Measurement'* and AASB 2011-8 *'Amendments to Australian Accounting Standards arising from AASB 13'*. This standard establishes a single source of guidance for fair value measurements and disclosures about fair value measurements. The directors anticipate that the application of the new Standard may result in more extensive disclosures in the financial statements. Applies to annual reporting periods beginning on or after 1 January 2013;
- AASB 119 *'Employee Benefits' (2011)* and AASB 2011-10 *'Amendments to Australian Accounting Standards arising from AASB 119' (2011)*. This standard changes the accounting for defined benefit plans and termination benefits. The most

significant change relates to the accounting for changes in defined benefit obligations and plan assets. The directors anticipate that the application of the new Standard will decrease the defined benefit obligation liability by $7.9 million. Applies to annual reporting periods beginning on or after 1 January 2013;

- AASB 2011-4 'Amendments to Australian Accounting Standards to Remove Individual Key Management Personnel Disclosure Requirements'. Applies to annual reporting periods beginning on or after 1 July 2013;
- AASB 2011-9 'Amendments to Australian Accounting Standards – Presentation of Items of Other Comprehensive Income'. Applies to annual reporting periods beginning on or after 1 July 2012;
- AASB 2012-2 'Amendments to Australian Accounting Standards – Disclosures – Offsetting Financial Assets and Financial Liabilities'. Applies to annual reporting periods beginning on or after 1 January 2013;
- AASB 2012-3 'Amendments to Australian Accounting Standards – Offsetting Financial Assets and Financial Liabilities'. Applies to annual reporting periods beginning on or after 1 January 2014;
- AASB 2012-5 'Amendments to Australian Accounting Standards arising from Annual Improvements 2009–2011 Cycle'. Applies to annual reporting periods beginning on or after 1 January 2013; and
- AASB 2012-10 'Amendments to Australian Accounting Standards – Transition Guidance and Other Amendments'. Applies to annual reporting periods beginning on or after 1 January 2013.

In August 2011, a package of six Standards on consolidation, joint arrangements, associates and disclosures was issued, including AASB 10, AASB 11, AASB 12, AASB 127 (2011), AASB 128 (2011) and AASB 2011-7. These six Standards are effective for annual reporting periods beginning on or after 1 January 2013. These Standards were available for early adoption and were applicable to the consolidated entity but have not been applied in these financial statements. Key requirements of these six Standards are described below.

- AASB 10 'Consolidated Financial Statements'. This standard includes a new definition of control. A review of the current accounting treatment for non wholly owned subsidiaries has been performed. This standard is not expected to have a significant impact on amounts reported in the consolidated financial statements;
- AASB 11 'Joint Arrangements'. This standard deals with how a joint arrangement of which two or more parties have joint control should be classified and changes the accounting for jointly controlled entities. This standard is not expected to have a significant impact on amounts reported in the consolidated financial statements;

- AASB 12 'Disclosure of Interests in Other Entities'. This is a disclosure standard and is applicable to entities that have interests in subsidiaries, joint arrangements, associates and/or unconsolidated structured entities. In general, the disclosure requirements in AASB 12 are more extensive than those in the current standards. The application of this standard will result in more extensive disclosures in the consolidated financial statements;
- AASB 127 'Separate Financial Statements' (2011). This standard is amended by the issuance of AASB 10;
- AASB 128 'Investments in Associates and Joint Ventures' (2011). This standard is amended by the issuance of AASB 10; and
- AASB 2011-7 'Amendments to Australian Accounting Standards arising from the Consolidation and Joint Arrangements standards'.

Critical accounting estimates

The preparation of a Financial Report in conformity with Australian Accounting Standards requires management to make judgements, estimates and assumptions that affect the application of policies and reported amounts of assets and liabilities, income and expenses. The estimates and associated assumptions are based on historical experience and various other factors that are believed to be reasonable under the circumstances, the results of which form the basis of making the judgements about carrying values of assets and liabilities that are not readily apparent from other sources. Actual results may differ from these estimates.

Management, together with the Audit, Risk Management and Compliance Committee, determines the development, selection and disclosure of the consolidated entity's critical accounting policies and estimates and the application of these policies and estimates.

The estimates and judgements that have a risk of causing a significant adjustment to the carrying amounts of assets and liabilities within the next financial year are included in the following notes:

- Note 1(G) and 1(I) – Estimation of useful lives of assets
- Note 10 and 11 – Impairment of tangible and intangible assets
- Note 1(Q) and 16 – Self-insured risks provisions
- Note 1(R) and 26 – Put options over non-controlling interests
- Note 1(P) and 23 – Employee benefits provisions, share based payments and defined benefits obligations.

The estimates and underlying assumptions are reviewed on an ongoing basis. Revisions to accounting estimates and underlying assumptions are recognised in the period in which the estimate is revised if the revision affects only that period; or in the period and future periods if the revision affects both current and future periods.

NOTES TO THE CONSOLIDATED FINANCIAL STATEMENTS

1 SIGNIFICANT ACCOUNTING POLICIES CONTINUED

(C) BASIS FOR CONSOLIDATION
(i) Subsidiaries
These consolidated financial statements incorporate the assets and liabilities of all subsidiaries of Woolworths Limited ('the Company') as at 30 June 2013 and the results of all subsidiaries for the period then ended.

Subsidiaries are entities controlled by the Company. Control exists when the Company has the power, directly or indirectly, to govern the financial and operating policies of an entity so as to obtain benefits from its activities. In assessing control, potential voting rights that presently are exercisable or convertible are taken into account. The financial statements of subsidiaries are included in the Financial Report from the date that control commences until the date that control ceases.

Non-controlling interests in the equity and results of subsidiaries are shown as a separate item in the consolidated Financial Report.

(ii) Transactions eliminated on consolidation
Intra-group balances and transactions and any unrealised gains and losses or income and expenses arising from intra-group transactions, are eliminated in preparing the consolidated Financial Report.

(D) FOREIGN CURRENCY
Transactions in foreign currencies are translated at the foreign exchange rate ruling at the date of the transaction. Monetary assets and liabilities denominated in foreign currencies are translated to Australian dollars at the foreign exchange rate ruling at the balance sheet date. Non-monetary assets and liabilities that are measured in terms of historical cost in a foreign currency are translated using the exchange rate at the date of the transaction.

Exchange differences are recognised in the profit or loss in the period in which they arise except that:
- exchange differences on transactions entered into in order to hedge certain foreign currency risks are reported initially in the hedging reserve to the extent the hedge is effective (refer Note 1(F)); and
- exchange differences on monetary items receivable from or payable to a foreign operation for which settlement is neither planned nor likely to occur, and which form part of the net investment in a foreign operation, are recognised in the foreign currency translation reserve and recognised in profit or loss on disposal of the net investment.

Financial statements of foreign operations
The assets and liabilities of foreign operations, including goodwill and fair value adjustments arising on consolidation, are translated to Australian dollars at foreign exchange rates ruling at the balance sheet date. Revenue and expense items are translated at the average exchange rates for the period. Exchange differences arising on translation of foreign operations, if any, are recognised in the foreign currency translation reserve and recognised in consolidated profit and loss on disposal of the foreign operation.

(E) DERIVATIVE FINANCIAL INSTRUMENTS
The consolidated entity uses derivative financial instruments to hedge its exposure to foreign exchange and interest rate risks arising from operational, financing and investment activities. In accordance with its treasury policy, the consolidated entity does not hold or issue derivative financial instruments for trading purposes. However, derivatives that do not qualify for hedge accounting are accounted for as trading instruments.

Derivative financial instruments are recognised initially at fair value on the date a derivative contract is entered into. Subsequent to initial recognition, derivative financial instruments are stated at fair value. The gain or loss on remeasurement to fair value is recognised immediately in profit or loss unless the derivatives qualify for hedge accounting, whereby the timing of the recognition of any resultant gain or loss depends on the nature of the hedge relationship (refer Note 1(F)).

The fair value of interest rate swaps is the estimated amount that the consolidated entity would receive or pay to terminate the swap at the balance sheet date, taking into account current interest rates and the time to maturity.

The fair value of forward exchange contracts is their quoted market price at the balance sheet date, being the present value of the quoted forward price.

(F) HEDGING
(i) Cash flow hedge
A cash flow hedge is a hedge of an exposure to uncertain future cash flows. A cash flow hedge results in the uncertain future cash flows being hedged back into fixed amounts. Woolworths' cash flow hedges include:
- Interest rate swap contracts that convert floating interest rate payments on borrowings into fixed amounts;
- Cross currency interest rate swaps that convert foreign currency denominated principal and interest rate payments on offshore loans into fixed Australian dollar amounts; and
- Forward foreign exchange contracts that convert foreign currency denominated payments to offshore suppliers and income of offshore subsidiaries into Australian dollar amounts.

Where a derivative financial instrument is designated as a hedge of the variability in cash flows of a recognised asset or liability, or a highly probable forecasted transaction, the effective part of any gain or loss on the derivative financial instrument is recognised directly in equity.

When the forecast transaction subsequently results in the recognition of a non-financial asset or non-financial liability, the associated cumulative gain or loss is removed from equity and included in the initial cost or other carrying amount of the non-financial asset or liability. If a hedge of a forecasted transaction subsequently results in the recognition of a financial asset or a financial liability, then the associated gains and losses that were recognised directly in equity are reclassified into profit or loss in the same period or periods during which the asset acquired or liability assumed affects profit or loss (i.e. when interest income or expense is recognised).

The ineffective part of any derivative designated as a hedge is recognised immediately in the consolidated income statement.

When a hedging instrument expires or is sold, terminated or exercised, or the entity revokes designation of the hedge relationship but the hedged forecast transaction still is expected to occur, the cumulative gain or loss at that point remains in equity and is recognised in accordance with the above policy when the transaction occurs. If the hedged transaction is no longer expected to take place, then the cumulative unrealised gain or loss recognised in equity is recognised immediately in the consolidated income statement.

Gains or losses removed from equity during the period in relation to interest rate hedge instruments are recognised within 'net financing costs' in the consolidated income statement.

(ii) Fair value hedge
A fair value hedge is a hedge of a fair value (i.e. 'mark-to-market') exposure arising on a recognised balance sheet asset or liability. A fair value hedge results in the fair value exposure being offset.

Changes in the fair value of derivatives that are designated and qualify as fair value hedges are recorded in profit or loss immediately, together with any changes in the fair value of the hedged asset or liability that is attributable to the hedged risk.

Hedge accounting is discontinued when the hedge instrument expires or is sold, terminated, exercised, or no longer qualifies for hedge accounting. The adjustment to the carrying amount of the hedged item arising from the hedged risk is amortised to profit or loss from that date.

(iii)Hedge of monetary assets and liabilities
When a derivative financial instrument is used to hedge economically the foreign exchange exposure of a recognised monetary asset or liability, hedge accounting is not applied and any gain or loss on the hedging instrument is recognised in the consolidated income statement.

(G) PROPERTY, PLANT AND EQUIPMENT
Freehold land, warehouse, retail, development and other properties are held at the lower of cost less accumulated depreciation and recoverable value (refer Note 1(M)).

Borrowing, holding and development costs on property under development are capitalised until completion of the development.

Land and buildings held for sale are classified as current assets and are valued at the lower of cost and fair value less costs to sell and are not depreciated.

Items of plant and equipment are stated at cost less accumulated depreciation (see below) and impairment losses (refer Note 1(M)).

The cost of self-constructed assets includes the cost of materials, direct labour and an appropriate proportion of overheads. The cost of self-constructed assets and acquired assets includes estimates of the costs of dismantling and removing the items and restoring the site on which they are located where it is probable that such costs will be incurred and changes in the measurement of existing liabilities recognised for these costs resulting from changes in the timing or outflow of resources required to settle the obligation or from changes in the discount rate.

Property that is being constructed or developed for future use is classified as development properties and stated at the lower of cost less accumulated depreciation and recoverable value (refer Note 1(M)) until construction or development is complete.

Where parts of an item of property, plant and equipment have different useful lives, they are accounted for as separate items of property, plant and equipment.

(i) Leased assets
Leases whereby the consolidated entity assumes substantially all of the risks and rewards of ownership are classified as finance leases. Property acquired by way of a finance lease is stated at an amount equal to the lower of its fair value and the present value of the minimum lease payments at inception of the lease, less accumulated depreciation (see below) and impairment losses (refer Note 1(M)). Lease payments are accounted for as described in Note 1(T).

(ii) Depreciation
(a) Buildings, plant and equipment
Buildings and plant comprising lifts, air conditioning, fire protection systems and other installations are depreciated on a straight-line basis over the estimated useful life of the asset to the consolidated entity. Estimates of remaining useful lives are made on a regular basis for all assets.

The expected useful lives are as follows:

	2013	2012
Buildings	**25–40 years**	25–40 years
Plant and equipment*	**3-10 years**	3-10 years

* Some immaterial assets have a useful life of greater than 10 years

(b) Leasehold improvements
The cost of leasehold improvements is amortised over the remaining period of the individual leases or the estimated useful life of the improvement to the consolidated entity, whichever is the shorter. Leasehold improvements held at the reporting date are amortised over a maximum period of 20 years for retail properties and 40 years for hotels.

NOTES TO THE CONSOLIDATED FINANCIAL STATEMENTS

1 SIGNIFICANT ACCOUNTING POLICIES CONTINUED

(c) Plant and equipment

Plant, equipment and shop fittings (including application software) are depreciated on a straight-line basis over the estimated useful life of the asset to the consolidated entity. Estimates of remaining useful lives are made on a regular basis for all assets.

The expected useful lives are as follows:

	2013	2012
Plant and equipment*	2.5-10 years	2.5-10 years

Some immaterial assets have a useful life of greater than 10 years

(d) Proceeds from sale of assets

The gross proceeds of asset sales are recognised at the date that an unconditional contract of sale is exchanged with the purchaser. The net gain/(net loss) is recorded in other income/(other expenses).

(H) GOODWILL

Business combinations prior to 27 June 2004

As part of its transition to A-IFRS, the consolidated entity elected to restate only those business combinations that occurred on or after 27 June 2004. In respect of business combinations prior to 27 June 2004, goodwill is included on the basis of its deemed cost, which represents the amount recorded under previous Australian GAAP.

Business combinations since 27 June 2004

All business combinations are accounted for by applying the purchase method. Entities and businesses acquired are accounted for using the cost method of accounting, whereby fair values are assigned to all the identifiable underlying assets acquired and liabilities assumed, including contingent liabilities, at the date of acquisition.

Goodwill represents the difference between the cost of the acquisition and the fair value of the net identifiable assets acquired. Goodwill is not amortised, but tested for impairment annually and whenever an indication of impairment exists (refer Note 1(M)). Goodwill is stated at cost less any accumulated impairment losses. Goodwill is allocated to cash-generating units. Any impairment is recognised directly in the consolidated income statement and is not subsequently reversed.

(I) OTHER INTANGIBLES

(i) Brand names

Brand names recognised by the consolidated entity generally have an indefinite useful life and are not amortised. Each period, the useful life of this asset is reviewed to determine whether events and circumstances continue to support an indefinite useful life assessment for the asset. Such assets are tested for impairment in accordance with the policy stated in Note 1(M).

(ii) Liquor licences

Liquor licences are valued at cost. Liquor licences are considered to have an indefinite useful life. As a consequence, no amortisation is charged. They are tested for impairment annually and whenever an indication of impairment exists. Any impairment is recognised immediately in profit or loss.

(iii) Gaming licences

Gaming licences are valued at cost. Gaming licences are considered to have an indefinite useful life. As a consequence, no amortisation is charged. They are tested for impairment annually and whenever an indication of impairment exists. Any impairment is recognised immediately in profit or loss.

(iv) Gaming entitlements

Gaming entitlements acquired pursuant to the Victorian Gaming Regulations effective August 2012 are valued at cost. Gaming entitlements are amortised on a straight-line basis over the life of the entitlement, which is 10 years.

(v) Research and development

Expenditure on research activities, undertaken with the prospect of gaining new technical knowledge and understanding, is recognised in the profit and loss as an expense as incurred.

Expenditure on development activities, whereby research findings are applied to a plan or design for the production of new or substantially improved products and processes, is capitalised if the product or process is technically and commercially feasible and the consolidated entity has sufficient resources to complete development. The expenditure capitalised includes the cost of materials, direct labour and an appropriate proportion of overheads.

Other development expenditure is recognised in the income statement as an expense as incurred. Capitalised development expenditure is stated at cost less accumulated amortisation and impairment losses (refer Note 1(M)).

(vi) Other intangible assets

Other intangible assets that are acquired by the consolidated entity are valued at cost less accumulated amortisation and accumulated impairment losses. If the assets are considered to have an indefinite useful life, no amortisation is charged. If the assets have a finite useful life, amortisation is charged.

Expenditure on internally generated goodwill and brand names is recognised in profit or loss as an expense as incurred.

(J) FINANCIAL ASSETS

Financial assets valued through other comprehensive income

The consolidated entity's investments in equity securities are designated as financial assets valued through other comprehensive income. The investments are initially measured at fair value net of transaction costs.

Subsequent to initial recognition, the equity investments are measured at fair value with any change recorded through the equity instrument reserve. Dividend income is recognised in profit or loss in accordance with *AASB 118 Revenue*. This treatment has been selected as the equity investments in the Warehouse Group Limited and the Australian Leisure and Entertainment Property Management Limited ('ALE Property Group') are deemed to be strategic equity investments.

Trade and other receivables

Trade and other receivables are stated at their cost less impairment losses (refer Note 1(M)).

(K) INVENTORIES

Inventories are valued at the lower of cost or net realisable value.

Cost includes all purchase related rebates, settlement discounts and other costs incurred to bring inventory to its present condition and location for sale.

Net realisable value is the estimated selling price in the ordinary course of business, less the estimated costs of completion and selling expenses.

Where inventory systems do not provide appropriate item level information, the retail method technique is adopted in order to measure cost.

(L) CASH AND CASH EQUIVALENTS

Cash and cash equivalents comprise cash balances and call deposits with an original maturity of three months or less. Bank overdrafts that are repayable on demand and form an integral part of the consolidated entity's cash management are included as a component of cash and cash equivalents for the purpose of the consolidated cash flow statement.

(M) IMPAIRMENT

The carrying amounts of the consolidated entity's tangible assets, excluding inventories (refer Note 1(K)) and deferred tax assets (refer Note 1 (V)), are reviewed at each reporting date to determine whether there is any indication of impairment. If any such indication exists, the asset's recoverable amount is estimated (refer below).

For goodwill and other intangible assets that have an indefinite useful life and intangible assets that are not yet available for use, the recoverable amount is estimated annually and whenever there is an impairment indicator.

An impairment loss is recognised whenever the carrying amount of an asset or its cash generating unit ('CGU') exceeds its recoverable amount. Impairment losses are recognised in the income statement unless the asset has previously been revalued, in which case the impairment loss is recognised as a reversal to the extent of that previous revaluation with any excess recognised through the consolidated income statement.

(i) Calculation of recoverable amount

The recoverable amount of the consolidated entity's investments in held-to-maturity securities and receivables is calculated as the present value of estimated future cash flows, discounted at the original effective interest rate (that is, the effective interest rate computed at initial recognition of these financial assets).

Receivables with a short duration are not discounted.

Impairment of receivables is not recognised until objective evidence is available that a loss event has occurred. Significant receivables are individually assessed for impairment.

Impairment testing of significant receivables that are not assessed as impaired individually is performed by placing them into portfolios of significant receivables with similar risk profiles and undertaking a collective assessment of impairment.

Non-significant receivables are not individually assessed. Instead, impairment testing is performed by placing non-significant receivables in portfolios of similar risk profiles, based on objective evidence from historical experience adjusted for any effects of conditions existing at each balance date.

The recoverable amount of other assets is the greater of their fair value less costs to sell and value in use. In assessing value in use, the estimated future cash flows are discounted to their present value using a pre-tax discount rate that reflects current market assessments of the time value of money and the risks specific to the asset. For an asset that does not generate largely independent cash inflows, the recoverable amount is determined for the cash-generating unit to which the asset belongs.

Impairment losses recognised in respect of a CGU will be allocated first to reduce the carrying amount of any goodwill allocated to the CGU and then to reduce the carrying amount of the other assets in the unit on a pro-rata basis to their carrying amounts.

(ii) Reversals of impairment

An impairment loss in respect of a held-to-maturity security or receivable is reversed if the subsequent increase in recoverable amount can be related objectively to an event occurring after the impairment loss was recognised.

An impairment loss in respect of goodwill is not reversed. In respect of other assets, an impairment loss is reversed if there has been a change in the estimates used to determine the recoverable amount.

An impairment loss is reversed only to the extent that the asset's carrying amount does not exceed the carrying amount that would have been determined, net of depreciation or amortisation, if no impairment loss had been recognised.

(N) CAPITAL

(i) Debt and equity instruments

Debt and equity instruments are classified as either liabilities or equity in accordance with the substance of the contractual arrangement.

(ii) Transaction costs on the issue of equity instruments

Transaction costs arising on the issue of equity instruments are recognised directly in equity as a reduction of the proceeds of the equity instruments to which the costs relate. Transaction costs are the costs that are incurred directly in connection with the issue of those equity instruments and which would not have been incurred had those instruments not been issued.

NOTES TO THE CONSOLIDATED FINANCIAL STATEMENTS

1 SIGNIFICANT ACCOUNTING POLICIES CONTINUED

(iii) Interest and dividends

Interest and dividends are classified as expenses or as distributions of profit consistent with the balance sheet classification of the related debt or equity instruments or component parts of compound instruments.

(O) BORROWINGS

Borrowings are recognised initially at fair value less attributable transaction costs. Subsequent to initial recognition, borrowings are stated at amortised cost with any difference between cost and redemption value recognised in the consolidated income statement over the period of the borrowings.

Borrowing costs directly attributable to qualifying assets are capitalised as part of the cost of those assets.

(P) EMPLOYEE BENEFITS

The Company sponsors a Superannuation Plan (the 'Plan') that provides accumulation type benefits to permanent salaried employees and their dependants on retirement, total disablement or death. Defined benefits have been preserved for members of certain former superannuation funds sponsored by the Company, which are now provided for in the Plan.

The Company's commitment in respect of accumulation benefits under the Plan is limited to making the specified contributions in accordance with the Rules of the Plan and/or any statutory obligations.

(i) Defined contribution plans

Obligations for contributions to defined contribution superannuation plans are recognised as an expense in the income statement as incurred.

(ii) Defined benefit plans

Woolworths is the employer sponsor of a defined benefit superannuation fund. Under A-IFRS, the employer sponsor is required to recognise a liability (or asset) where the present value of the defined benefit obligation, adjusted for unrecognised past service cost, exceeds (is less than) the fair value of the underlying net assets of the fund (hereinafter referred to as the 'defined benefit obligation').

The consolidated entity's net obligation in respect of defined benefit plans is calculated separately for each plan by estimating the amount of future benefit that employees have earned in return for their service in the current and prior periods. That benefit is discounted to determine its present value.

The discount rate is the yield at the balance sheet date on Government bonds that have maturity dates approximating the terms of the consolidated entity's obligations. The calculation is performed by a qualified actuary using the projected unit credit method.

When the benefits of a plan are improved, the portion of the increased benefit relating to past service by employees is recognised as an expense in the income statement on a straight-line basis over the average period until the benefits become vested. To the extent that the benefits vest immediately, the expense is recognised immediately in the consolidated income statement.

All movements in the defined benefit obligation are recognised in the consolidated income statement except actuarial gains and losses. All actuarial gains and losses as at 28 June 2004, the date of transition to A-IFRS, were recognised. Actuarial gains and losses that arise subsequent to 28 June 2004 are recognised in full in retained earnings in the period in which they occur and are presented in the consolidated statement of comprehensive income.

When the calculation results in plan assets exceeding liabilities to the consolidated entity, the recognised asset is limited to the net total of any unrecognised actuarial losses and past service costs and the present value of any future refunds from the plan or reductions in future contributions to the plan.

(iii) Long-term service benefits

The consolidated entity's net obligation in respect of long-term service benefits, other than pension plans, is the amount of future benefit that employees have earned in return for their service in the current and prior periods. The obligation is calculated using expected future increases in wage and salary rates including related on-costs and expected settlement dates and is discounted using the rates attached to Government bonds at the balance sheet date which have maturity dates approximating the terms of the consolidated entity's obligations.

(iv) Share based payment transactions

Equity settled share based payments form part of the remuneration of employees (including executives) of the consolidated entity.

The consolidated entity recognises the fair value at the grant date of equity settled share based payments (such as options or performance rights) as an employee benefit expense proportionally over the vesting period with a corresponding increase in equity. Fair value is measured at grant date using a Monte-Carlo simulation option pricing model performed by an independent valuer which takes into account market based performance conditions. The fair value per instrument is multiplied by the number of instruments expected to vest based on achievement of non-market based performance conditions (e.g. service conditions) to determine the total cost. This total cost is recognised as an employee benefit expense proportionally over the vesting period during which the employees become unconditionally entitled to the instruments.

On vesting and over the vesting period the amount recognised as an employee benefit expense will be adjusted to reflect the actual number of options that vest except where forfeiture is due to failure to achieve market based performance conditions.

The consolidated entity operated an Employee Share Plan (ESP) whereby it provided interest-free loans to selected employees to purchase shares in the Company. All shares acquired under the ESP are held by a wholly owned subsidiary of Woolworths as trustee of the share plan trust. Dividends paid by Woolworths are used to repay the loan (after payment of a portion of the dividend to the employee to cover any tax liabilities).

The loans are limited recourse and if the employee elects not to repay the loan, the underlying shares are sold to recover the outstanding loan balance. These have been accounted for as an in-substance option in the financial statements of the consolidated entity.

This plan was last offered in May 2003 with loans maturing in May 2013. It is not intended to re-open this plan to further offers.

(v) Wages and salaries and related employee benefits
Provision is made for benefits accruing to employees in respect of wages and salaries, annual leave, long service leave and sick leave when it is probable that settlement will be required and they are capable of being reliably measured. Provisions made in respect of employee benefits expected to be settled within 12 months are recognised and are measured at their nominal values using the remuneration rate expected to apply at the time of settlement.

Provisions made in respect of employee benefits which are not expected to be settled within 12 months are recognised and measured as the present value of expected future payments to be made in respect of services provided by employees up to period end. Consideration is given to expected future wage and salary levels, experience of employee departures and periods of service.

(Q) PROVISIONS
A provision is recognised in the consolidated balance sheet when the consolidated entity has a present legal or constructive obligation as a result of a past event and it is probable that an outflow of economic benefits will be required to settle the obligation.

When some or all of the economic benefits required to settle a provision are expected to be recovered from a third party, the receivable is recognised as an asset if it is virtually certain that recovery will be received and the amount of the receivable can be measured reliably.

The amount recognised as a provision is the best estimate of the consideration required to settle the present obligation at reporting date, taking into account the risks and uncertainties surrounding the obligation. Where a provision is measured using the cash flows estimated to settle the present obligation, its carrying amount is the present value of those cash flows.

(i) Restructuring
Provision for restructuring is recognised when the consolidated entity has developed a detailed formal plan for the restructuring and has either:

- entered into firm contracts to carry out the restructuring; or
- raised a valid expectation in those affected by the restructuring that the restructuring will occur.

(ii) Onerous contracts
A provision for onerous contracts is recognised when the expected benefits to be derived by the consolidated entity from a contract are lower than the unavoidable cost of meeting its obligations under the contract.

(iii) Self-insurance
The consolidated entity provides for self-insured liabilities relating to workers' compensation and public liability claims. The provisions for such liabilities are based on independent actuarial assessments, which consider numbers, amounts and duration of claims, and allow for future inflation and investment returns.

Allowance is included for injuries which occurred before the balance sheet date, but where the claim is expected to be notified after the reporting date.

The provision is discounted using the Government bond rate with a maturity date approximating the term of the consolidated entity's obligation.

(iv) Warranty
The consolidated entity provides for anticipated warranty costs when the underlying products or services are sold. The provision is based upon historical warranty data.

(v) Make good
The consolidated entity has certain operating leases that require the asset to be returned to the lessor in its original condition. These obligations relate to wear and tear on the premises and not dismantling obligations. The operating lease payments do not include an element for repairs/overhauls. A provision for refurbishment costs is recognised over the period of the lease, measured at the expected cost of refurbishment at each reporting date.

(R) FINANCIAL LIABILITIES
(i) Trade and other payables
These amounts represent liabilities for goods and services provided to the consolidated entity which were unpaid at the end of the period. The amounts are unsecured and are usually settled within 45 days of recognition.

(ii) Put options over non-controlling interests
The put options held by non-controlling interests are classified as a financial liability and are measured at fair value. The non-controlling interests continue to have access to voting rights and dividends in the subsidiaries and continue to be attributed a share of profits. Subsequent changes in the financial liability are recorded directly in equity.

(S) REVENUE RECOGNITION
In general, revenue is recognised only when it is probable that the economic benefits comprising the revenue will flow to the entity, the flow can be reliably measured and the entity has transferred the significant risks and rewards of ownership.

In addition to these general criteria, specific revenue recognition criteria apply as follows:

NOTES TO THE CONSOLIDATED FINANCIAL STATEMENTS

1 SIGNIFICANT ACCOUNTING POLICIES CONTINUED

(i) Sales revenue

Sales revenue represents the revenue earned from the provision of products and rendering of services to parties external to the consolidated entity. Sales revenue is only recognised when the significant risks and rewards of ownership of the products, including possession, have passed to the buyer and for services when a right to be compensated has been attained and the stage of completion of the contract can be reliably measured.

Revenue is recognised on a commission only basis where Woolworths acts as an agent rather than a principal in the transaction. Revenue is recognised net of returns.

Revenue from the sale of customer gift cards is recognised when the card is redeemed and the customer purchases goods using the card, or when the gift card reaches its expiry date.

(ii) Rental income

Rental income is recognised on a straight-line basis over the term of the lease.

(iii) Financing income

Interest income is recognised in the consolidated income statement as it accrues, using the effective interest method. Dividend income is recognised in the consolidated income statement on the date the entity's right to receive payment is established, which in the case of quoted securities, is the ex-dividend date.

(T) LEASES

Leases are classified as finance leases whenever the terms of the lease transfer substantially all the risks and rewards of ownership to the lessee. All other leases are classified as operating leases.

(i) Operating lease payments

Payments made under operating leases are recognised in the consolidated income statement on a straight-line basis over the term of the lease.

Fixed rate increases to lease rental payments, excluding contingent or index based rental increases, such as Consumer Price Index, turnover rental and other similar increases, are recognised on a straight-line basis over the lease term. An asset or liability arises for the difference between the amount paid and the lease expense brought to account on a straight-line basis.

Lease incentives received are recognised in the consolidated income statement as an integral part of the total lease expense and spread over the lease term.

(ii) Finance lease payments

Minimum lease payments made under finance leases are apportioned between the finance expense and the reduction of the outstanding liability. The finance expense is allocated to each period during the lease term so as to produce a constant periodic rate of interest on the remaining balance of the liability.

(U) NET FINANCING COSTS

Net financing costs comprise interest payable on borrowings calculated using the effective interest method, interest receivable on funds invested, dividend income, foreign exchange gains and losses and gains and losses on hedging instruments that are recognised in the income statement (refer Note 1(F)).

(V) INCOME TAX

Income tax in the consolidated income statement for the periods presented comprises current and deferred tax. Income tax is recognised in the income statement except to the extent that it relates to items recognised directly in equity, in which case it is recognised in equity. Where it arises from the initial accounting for a business combination, it is taken into account in the determination of goodwill or excess.

Current tax is the expected tax payable on the taxable income for the year, using tax rates enacted or substantively enacted at the balance sheet date and any adjustment to tax payable in respect of previous years. Current tax for current and prior periods is recognised as a liability to the extent it is unpaid.

Deferred tax is provided using the balance sheet method, providing for temporary differences between the carrying amounts of assets and liabilities for financial reporting purposes and the amounts used for taxation purposes. In accordance with *AASB 112 Income Taxes*, the following temporary differences are not provided for: goodwill, the initial recognition of assets or liabilities in a transaction that is not a business combination and that affects neither accounting nor taxable profit, and differences relating to investments in subsidiaries to the extent that they will probably not reverse in the foreseeable future where the consolidated entity is able to control the reversal of the temporary differences.

The amount of deferred tax provided is based on the expected manner of realisation or settlement of the carrying amount of assets and liabilities, using tax rates enacted or substantively enacted at the balance sheet date.

A deferred tax asset is recognised only to the extent that it is probable that future taxable profits will be available against which the deductible temporary differences or unused tax losses and tax offsets can be utilised.

Deferred tax assets are reduced to the extent that it is no longer probable that the related tax benefit will be realised.

Additional income taxes that arise from the distribution of dividends are recognised at the same time as the liability to pay the related dividend.

Deferred tax assets and liabilities are offset when they relate to income taxes levied by the same taxation authority and the consolidated entity intends to settle its current tax assets and liabilities on a net basis.

(W) NON-CURRENT ASSETS (OR DISPOSAL GROUPS) HELD FOR SALE AND DISCONTINUED OPERATIONS

Non-current assets (or disposal groups) are classified as held for sale if their carrying amount will be recovered principally through a sale transaction rather than continuing use and a sale is considered highly probable. They are measured at the lower of their carrying amount and fair value less costs to sell, except for assets such as deferred tax assets, assets arising from employee benefits, financial assets and investment property that are carried at fair value, which are specifically exempt from this requirement.

An impairment loss is recognised for any initial or subsequent write-down of the asset (or disposal group) to fair value less costs to sell. A gain is recognised for any subsequent increases in fair value less costs to sell of an asset (or disposal group), but not in excess of any cumulative impairment loss previously recognised. A gain or loss not previously recognised by the date of the sale of the non-current asset (or disposal group), is recognised at the date of derecognition. Non-current assets (including those that are part of a disposal group) are not depreciated or amortised while they are classified as held for sale. Interest and other expenses attributable to the liabilities of the disposal group classified as held for sale continue to be recognised.

Non-current assets classified as held for sale and the assets of a disposal group classified as held for sale are presented separately from the other assets in the balance sheet. The liabilities of a disposal group classified as held for sale are presented separately from other liabilities in the balance sheet.

A discontinued operation is a component of the entity that has been disposed of or is classified as held for sale and that represents a separate major line of business or geographical area of operations, is part of a single co-ordinated plan to dispose of such a line of business or area of operations, or is a subsidiary acquired exclusively with a view to resale. The results of discontinued operations are presented separately in the income statement.

(X) GOODS AND SERVICES TAX

Revenue, expenses and assets are recognised net of the amount of goods and services tax (GST), except where the amount of GST incurred is not recoverable from the taxation authority. In these circumstances, the GST is recognised as part of the cost of acquisition of the asset or as part of the expense.

Receivables and payables are stated with the amount of GST included. The net amount of GST recoverable from, or payable to, the tax authorities are included as a current asset or liability in the balance sheet.

Cash flows are included in the cash flow statement on a gross basis. The GST components of cash flows arising from investing and financing activities which are recoverable from, or payable to, the tax authorities are classified as operating cash flows.

(Y) OPERATING SEGMENT REPORTING

(i) Business Segments

Segment information is presented in respect of the consolidated entity's reportable segments which were identified on the basis of the consolidated entity's internal reporting on the components of the Group. The identified reportable segments are regularly reviewed by the chief operating decision maker in order to allocate resources to the segment and assess its performance. Inter-segment pricing is determined on an arm's length basis.

These business units offer different products and services and are managed separately because they require different technology and marketing strategies. The Group's six reportable segments related to continuing operations are as follows:

- **Australian Food and Liquor** – procurement of food and liquor and products for resale to customers in Australia
- **New Zealand Supermarkets** – procurement of food and liquor and products for resale to customers in New Zealand
- **Petrol** – procurement of petroleum products for resale to customers in Australia
- **BIG W** – procurement of discount general merchandise products for resale to customers in Australia
- **Hotels** – provision of leisure and hospitality services, including food and alcohol, accommodation, entertainment and gaming
- **Home Improvement** – procurement of home improvement products for resale to customers in Australia.

The Unallocated group consists of the Group's other operating segments that are not separately reportable as well as various support functions, including property and head office costs.

Discontinued operations represents the Consumer Electronics segment, which is the procurement of electronic products for resale in Australia and New Zealand and a wholesale business in India.

(ii) Geographical information

Segment assets are based on the geographical location of the assets. Woolworths Limited operates in Australia, New Zealand, Hong Kong and India. The majority of business operations are in Australia and New Zealand. Woolworths operates in New Zealand following the acquisition of Foodland Supermarkets in 2006. The global sourcing office is located in Hong Kong. Until the sale of the consumer electronics businesses in 2012, Woolworths operated stores based in Australia and New Zealand and had a business venture with TATA in India which operated stores under the Croma brand.

NOTES TO THE CONSOLIDATED FINANCIAL STATEMENTS

1 SIGNIFICANT ACCOUNTING POLICIES CONTINUED

(Z) PARENT ENTITY FINANCIAL INFORMATION

Financial information for the parent entity, Woolworths Limited, disclosed in Note 32 has been prepared on the same basis as the consolidated financial statements, except as set out below:

(i) Investments in subsidiaries

Investments in subsidiaries are accounted for at cost.

(ii) Tax consolidation

The Company and its wholly-owned Australian resident entities have formed a tax-consolidated group with effect from 1 July 2002 and are therefore taxed as a single entity from that date. The head entity within the tax consolidated group is Woolworths Limited.

Tax expense/income, deferred tax assets and deferred tax liabilities arising from temporary differences of the members of the tax consolidated group are recognised by each member of the tax consolidated group where the member would have been able to recognise the deferred tax asset or deferred tax liability on a standalone basis.

The head entity, in conjunction with other members of the tax consolidated group, has entered into a tax funding agreement which sets out the funding obligations of members of the tax consolidated group in respect of income tax amounts. The tax funding arrangements require payments to the head entity equal to the current tax liability assumed by the head entity.

In addition, the head entity is required to make payments equal to the current tax asset assumed by the head entity in circumstances where the subsidiary member would have been entitled to recognise the current tax asset on a standalone basis.

These tax funding arrangements result in the head entity recognising an inter-entity receivable/payable equal in amount to the tax liability/asset assumed. The inter-entity receivable/payable amounts are at call.

In respect of carried forward tax losses brought into the group on consolidation by subsidiary members, the head entity will pay the subsidiary member for such losses when these losses are transferred to the Woolworths Limited tax consolidated group, where the subsidiary member would have been entitled to recognise the benefit of these losses on a standalone basis.

DIRECTORS' DECLARATION

The Directors declare that:

(a) in the Directors' opinion, there are reasonable grounds to believe that the Company will be able to pay its debts as and when they become due and payable;

(b) in the Directors' opinion, the attached financial statements are in compliance with International Financial Reporting Standards, as stated in Note 1 to the financial statements;

(c) in the Directors' opinion, the attached Financial Statements and notes thereto are in accordance with the *Corporations Act 2001*, including compliance with accounting standards and giving a true and fair view of the financial position and performance of the consolidated entity; and

(d) the Directors have been given the declarations required by s.295A of the *Corporations Act 2001*.

At the date of this declaration, the Company is within the class of companies affected by ASIC Class Order 98/1418. The nature of the deed of cross guarantee is such that each company which is party to the deed guarantees to each creditor payment in full of any debt in accordance with the deed of cross guarantee.

In the Directors' opinion, there are reasonable grounds to believe that the Company and the companies to which the ASIC Class Order applies, as detailed in Note 28 and Note 29 to the Financial Statements will, as a group, be able to meet any obligations or liabilities to which they are, or may become, subject by virtue of the deed of cross guarantee.

Signed in accordance with a resolution of the Directors made pursuant to s.295(5) of the *Corporations Act 2001*.

On behalf of the Directors

Ralph Waters
Chairman

27 September 2013

Grant O'Brien
Managing Director and Chief Executive Officer

INDEGENDENT AUDITOR'S REPORT

Deloitte.

Deloitte Touche Tohmatsu
ABN 74 490 121 060

Grosvenor Place
225 George Street
Sydney NSW 2000
PO Box N250 Grosvenor Place
Sydney NSW 1220 Australia

DX: 10307SSE
Tel: +61 (0) 2 9322 7000
Fax: +61 (0) 2 9322 7001
www.deloitte.com.au

Independent Auditor's Report
to the Members of Woolworths Limited

Report on the Financial Report

We have audited the accompanying financial report of Woolworths Limited (the "Company"), which comprises the consolidated balance sheet as at 30 June 2013, the consolidated income statement, the consolidated statement of comprehensive income, the consolidated cash flow statement and the consolidated statement of changes in equity for the 53 weeks ended on that date, notes comprising a summary of significant accounting policies and other explanatory information, and the directors' declaration of the consolidated entity comprising the company and the entities it controlled at the year's end or from time to time during the financial period as set out on pages 102 to 186.

Directors' Responsibility for the Financial Report

The directors of the company are responsible for the preparation of the financial report that gives a true and fair view in accordance with Australian Accounting Standards and the *Corporations Act 2001* and for such internal control as the directors determine is necessary to enable the preparation of the financial report that gives a true and fair view and is free from material misstatement, whether due to fraud or error. In Note 1, the directors also state, in accordance with Accounting Standard AASB 101 *Presentation of Financial Statements*, that the consolidated financial statements comply with International Financial Reporting Standards.

Auditor's Responsibility

Our responsibility is to express an opinion on the financial report based on our audit. We conducted our audit in accordance with Australian Auditing Standards. Those standards require that we comply with relevant ethical requirements relating to audit engagements and plan and perform the audit to obtain reasonable assurance whether the financial report is free from material misstatement.

An audit involves performing procedures to obtain audit evidence about the amounts and disclosures in the financial report. The procedures selected depend on the auditor's judgement, including the assessment of the risks of material misstatement of the financial report, whether due to fraud or error. In making those risk assessments, the auditor considers internal control, relevant to the company's preparation of the financial report that gives a true and fair view, in order to design audit procedures that are appropriate in the circumstances, but not for the purpose of expressing an opinion on the effectiveness of the company's internal control. An audit also includes evaluating the appropriateness of accounting policies used and the reasonableness of accounting estimates made by the directors, as well as evaluating the overall presentation of the financial report.

INDEPENDENT AUDITOR'S REPORT

We believe that the audit evidence we have obtained is sufficient and appropriate to provide a basis for our audit opinion.

Auditor's Independence Declaration

In conducting our audit, we have complied with the independence requirements of the *Corporations Act 2001*. We confirm that the independence declaration required by the *Corporations Act 2001*, which has been given to the directors of Woolworths Limited, would be in the same terms if given to the directors as at the time of this auditor's report.

Opinion

In our opinion:

(a) the financial report of Woolworths Limited is in accordance with the *Corporations Act 2001*, including:

    (i) giving a true and fair view of the consolidated entity's financial position as at 30 June 2013 and of its performance for the period ended on that date; and

    (ii) complying with Australian Accounting Standards and the *Corporations Regulations 2001*; and

(b) the consolidated financial statements also comply with International Financial Reporting Standards as disclosed in Note 1.

Report on the Remuneration Report

We have audited the Remuneration Report included in pages 50 to 76 of the directors' report for the period ended 30 June 2013. The directors of the company are responsible for the preparation and presentation of the Remuneration Report in accordance with section 300A of the *Corporations Act 2001*. Our responsibility is to express an opinion on the Remuneration Report, based on our audit conducted in accordance with Australian Auditing Standards.

Opinion

In our opinion the Remuneration Report of Woolworths Limited for the period ended 30 June 2013, complies with section 300A of the *Corporations Act 2001*.

Deloitte Touche Tohmatsu

DELOITTE TOUCHE TOHMATSU

Andrew Griffiths

A V Griffiths
Partner
Chartered Accountants
Sydney, 27 September 2013

APPENDIX 2: PRESENT AND FUTURE VALUE FACTOR TABLES

TABLE 1 FUTURE VALUE OF $1 = (1 + R)^n$

n	0.25%	0.5%	0.66%	0.75%	1.0%	1.5%	1.75%	2.0%	2.5%	3.0%	3.5%	n
1	1.002 50	1.005 00	1.006 67	1.007 50	1.010 00	1.015 00	1.017 50	1.020 00	1.025 00	1.030 00	1.035 00	1
2	1.005 01	1.010 03	1.013 38	1.015 06	1.020 10	1.030 23	1.035 31	1.040 40	1.050 63	1.060 90	1.071 23	2
3	1.007 52	1.015 08	1.020 13	1.022 67	1.030 30	1.045 68	1.053 42	1.061 21	1.076 89	1.092 73	1.108 72	3
4	1.010 04	1.020 15	1.026 93	1.030 34	1.040 60	1.061 36	1.071 86	1.082 43	1.103 81	1.125 51	1.147 52	4
5	1.012 56	1.025 25	1.033 78	1.038 07	1.051 01	1.077 28	1.090 62	1.104 08	1.131 41	1.159 27	1.187 69	5
6	1.015 09	1.030 38	1.040 67	1.045 85	1.061 52	1.093 44	1.109 70	1.126 16	1.159 69	1.194 05	1.229 26	6
7	1.017 63	1.035 53	1.047 61	1.053 70	1.072 14	1.109 84	1.129 12	1.148 69	1.188 69	1.229 87	1.272 28	7
8	1.020 18	1.040 71	1.054 59	1.061 60	1.082 86	1.126 49	1.148 88	1.171 66	1.218 40	1.266 77	1.316 81	8
9	1.022 73	1.045 91	1.061 63	1.069 56	1.093 69	1.143 39	1.168 99	1.195 09	1.248 86	1.304 77	1.362 90	9
10	1.025 28	1.051 14	1.068 70	1.077 58	1.104 62	1.160 54	1.189 44	1.218 99	1.280 08	1.343 92	1.410 60	10
11	1.027 85	1.056 40	1.075 83	1.085 66	1.115 67	1.177 95	1.210 26	1.243 37	1.312 09	1.384 23	1.459 97	11
12	1.030 42	1.061 68	1.083 00	1.093 81	1.126 83	1.195 62	1.231 44	1.268 24	1.344 89	1.425 76	1.511 07	12
13	1.032 99	1.066 99	1.090 22	1.102 01	1.138 09	1.213 55	1.252 99	1.293 61	1.378 51	1.468 53	1.563 96	13
14	1.035 57	1.072 32	1.097 49	1.110 28	1.149 47	1.231 76	1.274 92	1.319 48	1.412 97	1.512 59	1.618 69	14
15	1.038 16	1.077 68	1.104 80	1.118 60	1.160 97	1.250 23	1.297 23	1.345 87	1.448 30	1.557 97	1.675 35	15
16	1.040 76	1.083 07	1.112 17	1.126 99	1.172 58	1.268 99	1.319 93	1.372 79	1.484 51	1.604 71	1.733 99	16
17	1.043 36	1.088 49	1.119 58	1.135 44	1.184 30	1.288 02	1.343 03	1.400 24	1.521 62	1.652 85	1.794 68	17
18	1.045 97	1.093 93	1.127 05	1.143 96	1.196 15	1.307 34	1.366 53	1.428 25	1.559 66	1.702 43	1.857 49	18
19	1.048 58	1.099 40	1.134 56	1.152 54	1.208 11	1.326 95	1.390 45	1.456 81	1.598 65	1.753 51	1.922 50	19
20	1.051 21	1.104 90	1.142 13	1.161 18	1.220 19	1.346 86	1.414 78	1.485 95	1.638 62	1.806 11	1.989 79	20
21	1.053 83	1.110 42	1.149 74	1.169 89	1.232 39	1.367 06	1.434 54	1.515 67	1.679 58	1.860 29	2.059 43	21
22	1.056 47	1.115 97	1.157 40	1.178 67	1.244 72	1.387 56	1.464 73	1.545 98	1.721 57	1.916 10	2.131 51	22
23	1.059 11	1.121 55	1.165 12	1.187 51	1.257 16	1.408 38	1.490 36	1.576 90	1.764 61	1.973 59	2.206 11	23
24	1.061 76	1.127 16	1.172 89	1.196 41	1.269 73	1.429 50	1.516 44	1.608 44	1.808 73	2.032 79	2.283 33	24
25	1.064 41	1.132 80	1.180 71	1.205 39	1.282 43	1.450 95	1.542 98	1.640 61	1.853 94	2.093 78	2.363 24	25
30	1.077 78	1.161 40	1.220 59	1.251 27	1.347 85	1.563 08	1.682 80	1.811 36	2.097 29	2.427 26	2.806 79	30
35	1.091 32	1.190 73	1.261 82	1.298 90	1.416 60	1.683 88	1.835 29	1.999 89	2.373 21	2.813 86	3.333 59	35
40	1.105 03	1.220 79	1.304 45	1.348 35	1.488 86	1.814 02	2.001 60	2.208 04	2.685 06	3.262 04	3.959 26	40
45	1.118 92	1.251 62	1.348 52	1.399 68	1.564 81	1.954 21	2.182 98	2.437 85	3.037 90	3.781 60	4.702 36	45
50	1.132 97	1.283 23	1.394 07	1.452 96	1.644 63	2.105 24	2.380 79	2.691 59	3.437 11	4.383 91	5.584 93	50
60	1.161 62	1.348 85	1.489 85	1.565 68	1.816 70	2.432 20	2.831 82	3.281 03	4.399 79	5.891 60	7.878 09	60

n	20.0%	15.0%	12.0%	10.0%	8.0%	7.0%	6.0%	5.0%	4.5%	4.0%	n
1	1.200	1.150	1.120 0	1.100 00	1.080 00	1.070 00	1.060 00	1.050 00	1.045 00	1.040 00	1
2	1.440	1.322	1.254 4	1.210 00	1.166 40	1.144 90	1.123 60	1.102 50	1.092 03	1.081 60	2
3	1.728	1.521	1.404 9	1.331 00	1.259 71	1.225 04	1.191 01	1.157 63	1.1417	1.124 86	3
4	2.074	1.749	1.573 5	1.464 10	1.360 48	1.310 79	1.262 47	1.215 51	1.192 52	1.169 86	4
5	2.488	2.011	1.762 0	1.610 51	1.469 32	1.402 55	1.338 22	1.276 28	1.246 18	1.216 65	5
6	2.938	2.313	1.973 8	1.771 56	1.586 87	1.500 73	1.418 51	1.340 10	1.302 26	1.265 32	6
7	3.583	2.660	2.210 7	1.948 72	1.713 82	1.605 78	1.503 63	1.407 10	1.360 86	1.315 93	7
8	4.300	3.059	2.476 0	2.143 59	1.850 93	1.718 18	1.593 84	1.477 46	1.422 10	1.368 57	8
9	5.160	3.518	2.773 1	2.357 95	1.999 00	1.838 45	1.689 47	1.551 33	1.486 10	1.423 31	9
10	6.192	4.046	3.105 8	2.593 74	2.158 92	1.967 15	1.790 84	1.628 89	1.552 97	1.480 24	10
11	7.430	4.652	3.478 5	2.853 12	2.331 63	2.104 85	1.898 29	1.710 34	1.622 85	1.539 45	11
12	8.916	5.350	3.896 0	3.138 43	2.518 17	2.252 19	2.012 19	1.795 86	1.695 88	1.601 03	12
13	10.699	6.153	4.363 5	3.452 27	2.719 62	2.409 84	2.132 92	1.885 65	1.772 20	1.665 07	13
14	12.839	7.076	4.887 1	3.797 50	2.937 19	2.578 53	2.260 90	1.979 93	1.851 94	1.731 68	14
15	15.407	8.137	5.473 6	4.177 25	3.172 16	2.759 03	2.396 55	2.078 93	1.935 28	1.800 94	15
16	18.488	9.358	6.130 3	4.594 97	3.425 94	2.952 16	2.540 35	2.182 87	2.022 37	1.872 98	16
17	22.186	10.761	6.866 1	5.054 47	3.700 01	3.158 81	2.692 77	2.292 02	2.113 38	1.947 90	17
18	26.623	12.375	7.690 0	5.559 92	3.996 01	3.379 93	2.854 33	2.406 62	2.208 48	2.025 82	18
19	31.945	14.232	8.612 8	6.115 91	4.315 70	3.616 52	3.025 59	2.526 95	2.307 86	2.106 85	19
20	38.338	16.367	9.646 3	6.727 50	4.660 95	3.869 68	3.207 13	2.653 30	2.411 71	2.191 12	20
21	46.005	18.821	10.803 8	7.400 25	5.033 83	4.140 56	3.399 56	2.785 96	2.520 24	2.278 77	21
22	55.206	21.645	12.100 3	8.140 27	5.436 54	4.430 40	3.603 53	2.925 26	2.633 65	2.369 92	22
23	66.247	24.891	13.552 3	8.954 30	5.871 46	4.740 52	3.819 74	3.071 52	2.752 17	2.464 72	23
24	79.497	28.625	15.178 6	9.849 73	6.341 18	5.072 36	4.048 93	3.225 10	2.876 01	2.563 30	24
25	95.396	32.919	17.000 1	10.834 71	6.848 47	5.427 43	4.291 87	3.386 35	3.005 43	2.665 84	25
30	237.376	66.212	29.960 0	17.449 40	10.062 65	7.612 25	5.743 49	4.321 94	3.745 32	3.243 40	30
35	590.668	133.175	52.800 0	28.102 44	14.785 34	10.676 58	7.686 08	5.516 02	4.667 35	3.946 09	35
40	1 469.771	267.862	93.051 0	45.259 26	21.724 52	14.974 45	10.285 71	7.039 99	5.816 36	4.801 02	40
45	3 657.258	538.767	163.987 6	72.890 48	31.920 44	21.002 45	13.764 61	8.985 01	7.248 25	5.841 18	45
50	9 100.427	1 083.652	289.002 1	117.390 85	46.901 61	29.457 02	18.420 15	11.477 40	9.032 64	7.106 68	50
60	56 347.514	4 383.999	897.596 9	304.481 64	101.257 06	57.946 43	32.987 69	18.679 19	14.027 41	10.519 63	60

TABLE 2 PRESENT VALUE OF $1 $= \dfrac{1}{(1+R)^n}$

n	0.25%	0.50%	0.66%	0.75%	1.0%	1.5%	2.0%	2.5%	3.0%	3.5%
1	0.997 51	0.995 02	0.993 38	0.992 56	0.990 09	0.985 22	0.980 39	0.975 60	0.970 87	0.966 18
2	0.995 02	0.990 07	0.986 80	0.985 17	0.980 29	0.970 66	0.961 16	0.951 81	0.942 59	0.933 51
3	0.992 54	0.985 15	0.980 26	0.977 83	0.970 59	0.956 31	0.942 32	0.928 59	0.915 14	0.901 94
4	0.990 06	0.980 25	0.973 77	0.970 55	0.960 98	0.942 18	0.923 84	0.905 95	0.888 48	0.871 44
5	0.987 59	0.975 37	0.967 32	0.963 33	0.951 46	0.928 26	0.905 73	0.883 85	0.862 60	0.841 97
6	0.985 13	0.970 52	0.960 92	0.956 16	0.942 04	0.914 54	0.887 97	0.862 29	0.837 48	0.813 50
7	0.982 67	0.965 69	0.954 55	0.949 07	0.932 71	0.901 02	0.870 56	0.841 26	0.813 09	0.785 99
8	0.980 22	0.960 89	0.948 23	0.941 98	0.923 48	0.887 71	0.853 49	0.820 74	0.789 40	0.759 41
9	0.977 78	0.956 10	0.941 95	0.934 96	0.914 33	0.874 59	0.836 75	0.800 72	0.766 41	0.733 73
10	0.975 34	0.951 35	0.935 71	0.928 00	0.905 28	0.861 66	0.820 34	0.781 19	0.744 09	0.708 91
11	0.972 91	0.946 61	0.929 52	0.921 09	0.896 32	0.848 93	0.804 26	0.762 14	0.722 42	0.684 94
12	0.970 48	0.941 91	0.923 36	0.914 24	0.887 44	0.836 38	0.788 49	0.743 55	0.701 37	0.661 78
13	0.968 06	0.937 22	0.917 25	0.907 43	0.878 66	0.824 02	0.773 03	0.725 42	0.680 95	0.639 40
14	0.965 65	0.932 56	0.911 17	0.900 68	0.869 96	0.811 84	0.757 87	0.707 72	0.661 11	0.617 78
15	0.963 24	0.927 92	0.905 14	0.893 97	0.861 34	0.799 85	0.743 01	0.690 46	0.641 86	0.596 89
16	0.960 84	0.923 30	0.899 14	0.887 32	0.852 82	0.788 03	0.728 44	0.673 62	0.623 16	0.576 70
17	0.958 44	0.918 71	0.893 19	0.880 71	0.844 37	0.776 38	0.714 16	0.657 19	0.605 01	0.557 20
18	0.956 05	0.914 14	0.887 27	0.874 16	0.836 01	0.764 91	0.700 15	0.641 16	0.587 39	0.538 36
19	0.953 67	0.909 59	0.881 40	0.867 65	0.827 73	0.753 60	0.686 43	0.625 52	0.570 28	0.520 15
20	0.951 29	0.905 06	0.875 56	0.861 19	0.819 54	0.742 47	0.672 97	0.610 27	0.553 67	0.502 56
21	0.948 92	0.900 56	0.869 76	0.854 78	0.811 43	0.731 49	0.659 77	0.595 38	0.537 54	0.485 57
22	0.946 55	0.896 08	0.864 00	0.848 42	0.803 39	0.720 68	0.646 83	0.580 86	0.521 89	0.469 15
23	0.944 19	0.891 62	0.858 28	0.842 10	0.795 44	0.710 03	0.634 15	0.566 69	0.506 69	0.453 28
24	0.941 84	0.887 19	0.852 60	0.835 83	0.787 56	0.699 54	0.621 72	0.552 87	0.491 93	0.437 95
25	0.939 49	0.882 77	0.846 95	0.829 61	0.779 76	0.689 20	0.609 53	0.539 39	0.477 60	0.423 14
30	0.927 83	0.861 03	0.819 27	0.799 19	0.741 92	0.639 76	0.552 07	0.476 74	0.411 98	0.356 27
35	0.916 32	0.839 82	0.792 50	0.769 88	0.705 91	0.593 86	0.500 02	0.421 37	0.355 38	0.299 97
40	0.904 95	0.819 14	0.766 61	0.741 65	0.671 65	0.551 26	0.452 89	0.372 43	0.306 55	0.252 57
45	0.893 72	0.798 96	0.741 56	0.714 45	0.639 05	0.511 71	0.410 19	0.329 17	0.264 43	0.212 65
50	0.882 63	0.779 29	0.717 32	0.688 25	0.608 03	0.475 00	0.371 52	0.290 94	0.228 10	0.179 05
60	0.860 87	0.741 37	0.671 21	0.638 70	0.550 45	0.409 30	0.304 78	0.227 28	0.169 73	0.126 93

n	20.0%	15.0%	12.0%	10.0%	8.0%	7.0%	6.0%	5.0%	4.5%	4.0%	n
1	0.833 33	0.869 57	0.892 86	0.909 09	0.925 92	0.934 57	0.943 39	0.952 38	0.956 93	0.961 53	1
2	0.694 44	0.756 14	0.797 19	0.826 45	0.857 33	0.873 43	0.889 99	0.907 02	0.915 72	0.924 55	2
3	0.578 70	0.657 52	0.711 78	0.751 31	0.793 83	0.816 29	0.839 61	0.863 83	0.876 29	0.888 99	3
4	0.482 25	0.571 75	0.635 52	0.683 01	0.735 02	0.762 89	0.792 09	0.822 70	0.838 56	0.854 80	4
5	0.401 88	0.497 18	0.567 43	0.620 92	0.680 58	0.712 98	0.747 25	0.783 52	0.802 45	0.821 92	5
6	0.334 90	0.432 33	0.506 63	0.564 47	0.630 16	0.666 34	0.704 96	0.746 21	0.767 89	0.790 31	6
7	0.279 08	0.375 94	0.452 35	0.513 16	0.583 49	0.622 74	0.665 05	0.710 68	0.734 82	0.759 91	7
8	0.232 57	0.326 90	0.403 88	0.466 51	0.540 26	0.582 00	0.627 41	0.676 83	0.703 18	0.730 69	8
9	0.193 81	0.284 26	0.360 61	0.424 10	0.500 24	0.543 93	0.591 89	0.644 60	0.672 90	0.702 58	9
10	0.161 51	0.247 18	0.321 97	0.385 54	0.463 19	0.508 34	0.558 39	0.613 90	0.643 92	0.675 56	10
11	0.134 59	0.214 94	0.287 48	0.350 49	0.428 88	0.475 09	0.526 78	0.584 67	0.616 19	0.649 58	11
12	0.112 16	0.186 91	0.256 67	0.318 63	0.397 11	0.444 01	0.496 96	0.556 83	0.589 66	0.624 59	12
13	0.093 46	0.162 53	0.229 17	0.289 66	0.367 69	0.414 96	0.468 83	0.530 32	0.564 27	0.600 57	13
14	0.077 89	0.141 33	0.204 62	0.263 33	0.340 46	0.387 81	0.442 30	0.505 06	0.539 97	0.577 47	14
15	0.064 91	0.122 89	0.187 70	0.239 39	0.315 24	0.362 44	0.417 26	0.481 01	0.516 72	0.555 26	15
16	0.054 09	0.106 86	0.163 12	0.217 63	0.219 89	0.338 73	0.393 64	0.458 11	0.494 46	0.533 90	16
17	0.045 07	0.092 93	0.145 64	0.197 84	0.270 26	0.316 57	0.371 36	0.436 29	0.473 17	0.513 37	17
18	0.037 56	0.080 80	0.130 04	0.179 86	0.250 24	0.295 86	0.350 34	0.415 52	0.452 80	0.493 62	18
19	0.031 30	0.070 26	0.116 11	0.163 51	0.231 71	0.276 50	0.330 51	0.395 73	0.433 30	0.474 64	19
20	0.026 08	0.061 10	0.103 67	0.148 64	0.214 54	0.258 41	0.311 80	0.376 88	0.414 64	0.456 38	20
21	0.021 74	0.053 13	0.092 56	0.135 13	0.198 65	0.241 51	0.294 15	0.358 94	0.396 78	0.438 83	21
22	0.018 11	0.046 20	0.082 64	0.122 85	0.183 94	0.225 71	0.277 50	0.341 84	0.379 70	0.421 95	22
23	0.015 09	0.040 17	0.073 79	0.111 68	0.170 31	0.210 94	0.261 79	0.325 57	0.363 35	0.405 72	23
24	0.012 58	0.034 93	0.065 88	0.101 53	0.157 69	0.197 14	0.246 97	0.310 06	0.347 70	0.390 12	24
25	0.010 48	0.030 38	0.058 82	0.092 30	0.146 01	0.184 24	0.232 99	0.295 30	0.332 73	0.375 11	25
30	0.004 21	0.015 10	0.033 38	0.057 31	0.099 37	0.131 36	0.174 11	0.231 37	0.267 00	0.308 31	30
35	0.001 69	0.007 51	0.018 94	0.035 58	0.067 63	0.093 66	0.130 10	0.181 29	0.214 25	0.253 41	35
40	0.000 68	0.003 73	0.010 74	0.022 09	0.046 03	0.066 78	0.097 22	0.142 04	0.171 92	0.208 28	40
45	0.000 27	0.001 86	0.006 10	0.013 72	0.031 32	0.047 61	0.072 65	0.111 29	0.137 96	0.171 19	45
50	0.000 11	0.000 92	0.003 46	0.008 52	0.021 32	0.033 94	0.054 28	0.087 20	0.110 70	0.140 71	50
60	0.000 02	0.000 23	0.001 11	0.003 28	0.009 88	0.017 26	0.030 31	0.053 54	0.071 29	0.095 06	60

TABLE 3 FUTURE VALUE OF $1 PER PERIOD $= \dfrac{(1+R)^n - 1}{R}$

n	0.25%	0.5%	0.66%	0.75%	1.0%	1.5%	2.0%	2.5%	3.0%	3.5%	n
1	1.000 00	1.000 00	1.000 00	1.000 00	1.000 00	1.000 00	1.000 00	1.000 0	1.000 0	1.000 0	1
2	2.002 50	2.005 00	2.006 67	2.007 50	2.010 00	2.015 00	2.020 00	2.025 0	2.030 0	2.035 0	2
3	3.007 51	3.015 03	3.020 04	3.022 56	3.030 10	3.045 23	3.060 40	3.075 6	3.090 9	3.106 2	3
4	4.015 03	4.030 10	4.040 18	4.045 23	4.060 40	4.090 90	4.121 61	4.152 5	4.183 6	4.214 9	4
5	5.025 06	5.050 25	5.067 11	5.075 56	5.101 01	5.152 27	5.204 04	5.256 3	5.309 1	5.362 5	5
6	6.037 63	6.075 50	6.100 89	6.113 63	6.152 02	6.229 55	6.308 12	6.387 7	6.468 4	6.550 2	6
7	7.052 72	7.105 88	7.141 57	7.159 48	7.213 54	7.322 99	7.434 28	7.547 4	7.662 5	7.779 4	7
8	8.070 35	8.141 41	8.189 18	8.213 18	8.285 67	8.432 84	8.582 97	8.736 1	8.892 3	9.051 7	8
9	9.090 53	9.182 12	9.243 77	9.274 78	9.368 53	9.559 33	9.754 63	9.954 5	10.159 1	10.368 5	9
10	10.113 25	10.228 03	10.305 40	10.344 34	10.462 21	10.702 72	10.949 72	11.203 4	11.463 9	11.731 4	10
11	11.138 54	11.279 17	11.374 10	11.421 92	11.566 83	11.863 26	12.168 72	12.483 5	12.807 8	13.142 0	11
12	12.166 38	12.335 56	12.449 93	12.507 59	12.682 50	13.041 21	13.412 09	13.795 6	14.192 0	14.602 0	12
13	13.196 80	13.397 24	13.532 93	13.601 39	13.809 33	14.236 83	14.680 33	15.140 4	15.617 8	16.113 0	13
14	14.229 79	14.464 23	14.623 15	14.703 40	14.947 42	15.450 38	15.973 94	16.519 0	17.086 3	17.677 0	14
15	15.265 37	15.536 55	15.720 63	15.813 68	16.096 90	16.682 14	17.293 42	17.931 9	18.598 9	19.295 7	15
16	16.303 53	16.614 23	16.825 54	16.932 28	17.257 86	17.932 37	18.639 29	19.380 2	20.156 9	20.971 0	16
17	17.344 29	17.697 30	17.937 61	18.059 27	18.430 44	19.201 36	20.012 07	20.864 7	21.761 6	22.705 0	17
18	18.387 65	18.785 79	19.057 19	19.194 72	19.614 75	20.489 38	21.412 31	22.386 3	23.414 4	24.499 7	18
19	19.433 62	19.879 72	20.184 24	20.338 68	20.810 89	21.796 72	22.840 56	23.946 0	25.116 9	26.357 2	19
20	20.482 20	20.979 12	21.318 80	21.491 22	22.019 00	23.123 67	24.297 37	25.544 7	26.870 4	28.279 7	20
21	21.533 41	22.084 01	22.450 93	22.652 40	23.239 19	24.470 52	25.783 32	27.183 3	28.676 5	30.269 5	21
22	22.587 24	23.194 43	23.610 66	23.822 30	24.471 59	25.837 58	27.298 98	28.862 9	30.536 8	32.328 9	22
23	23.643 71	24.310 40	24.768 07	25.000 96	25.716 30	27.225 14	28.844 96	30.584 4	32.452 9	34.460 4	23
24	24.702 82	25.431 96	25.933 19	26.188 47	26.973 46	28.633 52	30.421 86	32.349 0	34.426 5	36.666 5	24
25	25.764 57	26.559 12	27.106 08	27.384 88	28.243 20	30.063 02	32.030 30	34.157 8	36.459 3	38.949 9	25
30	31.113 31	32.280 02	33.088 85	33.502 90	34.784 89	37.538 68	40.568 08	43.902 7	47.575 4	51.622 7	30
35	36.529 24	38.145 38	39.273 73	39.853 81	41.660 28	45.592 09	49.994 48	54.928 2	60.462 1	66.674 0	35
40	42.013 20	44.158 85	45.667 54	46.446 48	48.886 37	54.267 89	60.401 98	67.402 6	75.401 3	84.550 3	40
45	47.566 06	50.324 16	52.277 34	53.290 11	56.481 07	63.614 20	71.892 71	81.516 1	92.719 9	105.781 7	45
50	53.188 68	56.645 16	59.110 42	60.394 26	64.463 18	73.682 83	84.579 40	97.484 3	112.796 9	130.997 9	50
60	64.646 71	69.770 03	73.476 86	76.424 14	81.669 67	96.214 65	114.051 54	135.991 6	163.053 4	196.516 9	60

n	20.0%	15.0%	12.0%	10.0%	8.0%	7.0%	6.0%	5.0%	4.5%	4.0%	n
1	1.00	1.000	1.000	1.000 0	1.000 0	1.000 0	1.000 0	1.000 0	1.000 0	1.000 0	1
2	2.20	2.150	2.120	2.100 0	2.080 0	2.070 0	2.060 0	2.050 0	2.045 0	2.040 0	2
3	3.64	3.472	3.374	3.310 0	3.246 4	3.214 9	3.183 6	3.152 5	3.137 0	3.121 6	3
4	5.36	4.993	4.779	4.641 0	4.506 1	4.439 9	4.374 6	4.310 1	4.278 2	4.246 5	4
5	7.44	6.742	6.353	6.105 1	5.866 6	5.750 7	5.637 1	5.525 6	5.470 7	5.416 3	5
6	9.93	8.754	8.115	7.715 6	7.335 9	7.153 3	6.975 3	6.801 9	6.716 9	6.633 0	6
7	12.92	11.067	10.089	9.487 2	8.922 8	8.654 0	8.393 8	8.142 0	8.019 2	7.898 3	7
8	16.50	13.727	12.300	11.435 9	10.636 6	10.259 8	9.897 5	9.549 1	9.380 0	9.214 2	8
9	20.80	16.786	14.776	13.579 5	12.487 6	11.978 0	11.491 3	11.026 6	10.802 1	10.582 8	9
10	25.96	20.304	17.549	15.937 4	14.486 6	13.816 4	13.180 8	12.577 9	12.288 2	12.006 1	10
11	32.15	24.349	20.655	18.531 2	16.645 5	15.783 6	14.971 6	14.206 8	13.841 2	13.486 4	11
12	39.58	29.002	24.133	21.384 3	18.977 1	17.888 5	16.869 9	15.917 1	15.464 0	15.025 8	12
13	48.50	34.352	28.029	24.522 7	21.495 3	20.140 6	18.882 1	17.713 0	17.150 9	16.626 8	13
14	59.20	40.505	32.393	27.975 0	24.214 9	22.550 5	21.015 1	19.598 6	18.932 1	18.291 9	14
15	72.04	47.580	37.280	31.772 5	27.152 1	25.129 0	23.276 0	21.578 6	20.784 1	20.023 6	15
16	87.44	55.717	42.753	35.949 7	30.324 3	27.888 1	25.672 5	23.657 5	22.719 3	21.824 5	16
17	105.93	65.075	48.884	40.544 7	33.750 2	30.840 2	28.212 9	25.840 4	24.741 7	23.607 5	17
18	128.12	75.836	55.750	45.599 2	37.450 2	33.999 0	30.905 7	28.132 4	26.855 1	25.645 4	18
19	154.74	88.212	63.440	51.159 1	41.446 3	37.379 0	33.760 0	30.539 0	29.063 6	27.671 2	19
20	186.69	102.443	72.052	57.275 0	45.762 0	40.995 5	36.785 6	33.066 0	31.371 4	29.778 1	20
21	225.03	118.810	81.699	64.002 5	50.422 9	44.865 2	39.992 7	35.719 3	33.783 1	31.969 2	21
22	271.03	137.631	92.502	71.402 8	55.456 8	49.005 7	43.392 3	38.505 2	36.303 4	34.248 0	22
23	326.24	159.276	104.603	79.543 0	60.893 3	53.436 1	46.995 8	41.430 5	38.937 0	36.617 9	23
24	392.48	184.167	118.155	88.497 3	66.764 8	58.176 7	50.815 6	44.502 0	41.689 2	39.082 6	24
25	471.98	212.793	133.334	98.347 1	73.105 9	63.249 0	54.864 5	47.727 1	44.565 2	41.645 9	25
30	1181.88	434.744	241.532	164.494 0	113.283 2	94.460 8	79.058 2	66.438 8	61.570 6	56.084 9	30
35	2 948.34	881.168	431.663	271.024 4	172.316 8	138.236 9	111.434 8	90.320 3	81.496 6	73.652 2	35
40	7 343.95	1779.090	767.088	442.592 6	259.056 5	199.635 1	154.762 0	120.799 8	107.030 3	95.025 5	40
45	18 281.31	3 585.128	1 358.224	718.904 8	386.505 6	285.749 3	212.743 5	159.700 2	138.850 0	121.029 4	45
50	45 497.19	7 217.716	2 400.008	1163.908 5	573.770 2	406.528 9	290.335 9	209.348 0	178.503 0	152.667 1	50
60	281 732.57	29 219.992	7 471.641	3 034.816 4	1 253.213 3	813.520 4	533.128 1	353.583 7	289.498 0	237.990 7	60

TABLE 4 PRESENT VALUE OF $1 PER PERIOD $= \dfrac{1 - \dfrac{1}{(1+R)^n}}{R}$

n	0.25%	0.5%	0.66%	0.75%	1.0%	1.5%	2.0%	2.5%	3.0%	3.5%	n
1	0.997 51	0.995 02	0.993 38	0.992 56	0.990 10	0.985 22	0.980 39	0.975 6	0.970 9	0.966 2	1
2	1.992 52	1.985 10	1.980 18	1.977 72	1.970 40	1.955 88	1.941 56	1.927 4	1.913 5	1.899 7	2
3	2.985 06	2.970 25	2.960 44	2.955 56	2.940 99	2.912 20	2.883 88	2.856 0	2.828 6	2.801 6	3
4	3.975 12	3.950 50	3.934 21	3.926 11	3.901 97	3.854 38	3.807 73	3.762 0	3.717 1	3.673 1	4
5	4.962 72	4.925 87	4.901 54	4.889 44	4.853 43	4.782 65	4.713 46	4.645 8	4.579 7	4.515 1	5
6	5.947 85	5.896 38	5.862 45	5.845 60	5.795 48	5.697 19	5.601 43	5.508 1	5.417 2	5.328 6	6
7	6.930 52	6.862 07	6.817 01	6.794 64	6.728 19	6.598 21	6.471 99	6.349 4	6.230 3	6.114 5	7
8	7.910 74	7.822 96	7.765 24	7.736 61	7.651 68	7.485 93	7.325 48	7.170 1	7.019 7	6.874 0	8
9	8.888 52	8.779 06	8.707 19	8.671 58	8.566 02	8.360 52	8.162 24	7.970 9	7.786 1	7.607 7	9
10	9.863 86	9.730 41	9.642 90	9.599 58	9.471 30	9.222 19	8.982 54	8.752 1	8.530 2	8.316 6	10
11	10.836 77	10.677 03	10.572 42	10.520 67	10.367 63	10.071 12	9.786 85	9.514 2	9.252 6	9.001 6	11
12	11.807 25	11.618 93	11.495 78	11.434 91	11.255 08	10.907 51	10.575 34	10.257 8	9.954 0	9.663 3	12
13	12.775 32	12.556 15	12.413 03	12.342 35	12.133 74	11.731 53	11.348 37	10.983 2	10.635 0	10.302 7	13
14	13.740 96	13.488 71	13.324 20	13.243 02	13.003 70	12.543 38	12.106 25	11.690 9	11.296 1	10.920 5	14
15	14.704 20	14.416 62	14.229 34	14.136 99	13.865 05	13.343 23	12.849 26	12.381 4	11.937 9	11.517 4	15
16	15.665 04	15.339 93	15.128 48	15.024 31	14.717 87	14.131 26	13.577 71	13.055 0	12.561 1	12.094 1	16
17	16.623 48	16.258 63	16.021 67	15.905 02	15.562 25	14.907 65	14.291 87	13.712 2	13.166 1	12.651 3	17
18	17.579 53	17.172 77	16.938 94	16.779 18	16.398 27	15.672 56	14.992 03	14.353 4	13.753 5	13.189 7	18
19	18.533 20	18.082 36	17.790 34	17.646 83	17.226 01	16.426 17	15.678 46	14.978 9	14.323 8	13.709 8	19
20	19.484 49	18.987 42	18.665 90	18.508 02	18.045 55	17.168 64	16.351 43	15.589 2	14.877 5	14.212 4	20
21	20.433 40	19.887 98	19.535 66	19.362 80	18.856 98	17.900 14	17.011 21	16.184 5	15.415 0	14.698 0	21
22	21.379 95	20.784 06	20.399 67	20.211 21	19.660 38	18.620 83	17.658 05	16.765 4	15.936 9	15.167 1	22
23	22.324 14	21.675 68	21.257 95	21.053 31	20.455 82	19.330 86	18.292 20	17.332 1	16.443 6	15.620 4	23
24	23.265 98	22.562 87	22.110 54	21.889 15	21.243 39	20.030 41	18.913 93	17.885 0	16.935 5	16.058 4	24
25	24.205 47	23.445 64	22.957 49	22.718 76	22.023 16	20.719 61	19.523 46	18.424 4	17.413 1	16.481 5	25
30	28.867 87	27.794 05	27.108 85	26.775 08	25.807 71	24.015 84	22.396 46	20.930 3	19.600 4	18.392 0	30
35	33.472 43	32.035 37	31.24 55	30.682 66	29.408 58	27.075 60	24.998 62	23.145 2	21.487 2	20.000 7	35
40	38.019 86	36.172 23	35.009 03	34.446 94	32.834 69	29.915 85	27.355 48	25.102 8	23.114 8	21.355 1	40
45	42.510 88	40.207 20	38.766 58	38.073 18	36.094 51	32.552 34	29.490 16	26.833 0	24.518 7	22.495 5	45
50	46.946 17	44.142 79	42.401 34	41.566 45	39.196 12	34.999 69	31.423 61	28.362 3	25.729 8	23.455 6	50
60	55.652 36	51.725 56	49.318 43	48.173 37	44.955 04	39.380 27	34.760 89	30.908 7	27.675 6	24.944 7	60

n	20.0%	15.0%	12.0%	10.0%	8.0%	7.0%	6.0%	5.0%	4.5%	4.0%	n
1	0.8333	0.8695	0.8929	0.9091	0.9259	0.9345	0.9433	0.9524	0.9569	0.9615	1
2	1.5278	1.6257	1.6901	1.7355	1.7832	1.8080	1.8333	1.8594	1.8727	1.8861	2
3	2.1065	2.2832	2.4018	2.4868	2.5770	2.6243	2.6730	2.7232	2.7490	2.7751	3
4	2.5887	2.8549	3.0373	3.1698	3.3121	3.3872	3.4651	3.5460	3.5875	3.6299	4
5	2.9906	3.3521	3.6048	3.7907	3.9927	4.1001	4.2123	4.3295	4.3900	4.4518	5
6	3.3255	3.7844	4.1114	4.3552	4.6228	4.7665	4.9173	5.0757	5.1579	5.2421	6
7	3.6046	4.1604	4.5638	4.8684	5.2063	5.3892	5.5823	5.7864	5.8927	6.0021	7
8	3.8372	4.4873	4.9676	5.3349	5.7466	5.9712	6.2097	6.4632	6.5959	6.7327	8
9	4.0310	4.7715	5.3282	5.7590	6.2468	6.5152	6.8016	7.1078	7.2688	7.4353	9
10	4.1925	5.0187	5.6502	6.1445	6.7100	7.0235	7.3600	7.7217	7.9127	8.1109	10
11	4.3271	5.2337	5.9377	6.4950	7.1389	7.4986	7.8868	8.3064	8.5289	8.7605	11
12	4.4392	5.4206	6.1944	6.8136	7.5360	7.9426	8.3838	8.8633	9.1186	9.3851	12
13	4.5327	5.5831	6.4235	7.1033	7.9037	8.3576	8.8526	9.3936	9.6829	9.9856	13
14	4.6106	5.7244	6.6282	7.3666	8.2442	8.7454	9.2949	9.8986	10.2228	10.5631	14
15	4.6755	5.8473	6.8109	7.6060	8.5594	9.1079	9.7122	10.3797	10.7395	11.1184	15
16	4.7296	5.9542	6.9740	7.8237	8.8513	9.4466	10.1058	10.8378	11.2340	11.6523	16
17	4.7746	6.0471	7.1196	8.0215	9.1216	9.7632	10.4772	11.2741	11.7072	12.1657	17
18	4.8122	6.1279	7.2497	8.2014	9.3718	10.0590	10.8276	11.6896	12.1600	12.6593	18
19	4.8435	6.1982	7.3658	8.3649	9.6035	10.3355	11.1581	12.0853	12.5933	13.1339	19
20	4.8696	6.2593	7.4694	8.5135	9.8181	10.5940	11.4699	12.4622	13.0079	13.5903	20
21	4.8913	6.3124	7.5620	8.6486	10.0168	10.8355	11.7640	12.8212	13.4047	14.0292	21
22	4.9094	6.3586	7.6446	8.7715	10.2007	11.0612	12.0415	13.1630	13.7844	14.4511	22
23	4.9245	6.3988	7.7184	8.8832	10.3710	11.2721	12.3033	13.4886	14.1478	14.8568	23
24	4.9371	6.4337	7.7843	8.9847	10.5287	11.4693	12.5503	13.7986	14.4955	15.2470	24
25	4.9476	6.4641	7.8431	9.0770	10.6747	11.6535	12.7833	14.0939	14.8282	15.6221	25
30	4.9789	6.5659	8.0552	9.4269	11.2577	12.4090	13.7648	15.3725	16.2889	17.2920	30
35	4.9915	6.6166	8.1755	9.6441	11.6545	12.9476	14.4982	16.3742	17.4610	18.6646	35
40	4.9966	6.6417	8.2438	9.7790	11.9246	13.3317	15.0462	17.1591	18.4016	19.7928	40
45	4.9986	6.6542	8.2825	9.8628	12.1084	13.6055	15.4558	17.7741	19.1563	20.7200	45
50	4.9995	6.6605	8.3045	9.9148	12.2334	13.8007	15.7618	18.2559	19.7620	21.4822	50
60	4.9999	6.6651	8.3240	9.9672	12.3766	14.0392	16.1614	18.9293	20.6380	22.6235	60

REFERENCES

1

American Accounting Association. (1966). *A statement of basic accounting theory*.

American Accounting Principles Board. (1970). *Statement no. 4: basic concepts and accounting principles underlying financial statements of business enterprises*. American Institute of Certified Public Accountants.

American Institute of Certified Public Accountants. (1973). *Objectives of financial statements*.

Argyle Diamonds. (2010). *Sustainable development report 2009 and 2010*. www.riotinto.com/documents/ArgyleDiamonds2009and2010SDreport.pdf

Dantes. (2005). *Akzo Nobel*. www.dantes.info/Projectinformation/Glossary/Glossary.html.

Global Reporting Initiative. *G4 sustainability reporting guidelines* available at: www.globalreporting.org/reporting/g4/Pages/default.aspx accessed on February 20, 2014.

Group of 100. (2003). *Sustainability: a guide to triple bottom line reporting*. Group of 100, Melbourne, 12.

Institute of Chartered Accountants of New Zealand. (2002). *Report of the taskforce on sustainable development reporting. October 2002*. ICANZ, Wellington.

Jensen, M., and Meckling, W. (1976) Theory of the firm: managerial behaviour, agency costs and ownership Structure. *Journal of Financial Economics* 3(4), 305–360.

Parker, R. H. (1986). *Macmillan dictionary of accounting*. Macmillan, Sydney.

2

Australian Accounting Standards Board. (2007). *Framework for the preparation and presentation of financial statements*, December.

Australian Accounting Standards Board. (2012). AASB 3 *Business combinations*, December.

Australian Accounting Standards Board. (2012). AASB 10 *Consolidated financial statements* [For for-profits entities] December

Australian Accounting Standards Board. (2012). AASB 101 *Presentation of financial statements* [for for-profit entities], December.

Australian Accounting Standards Board (2013) *Amendments to the Australian conceptual framework*. December

Australian Securities and Investments Commission Act 2001.

Accounting Standards Review Board and Public Sector Accounting Standards Board. (1990). *Statement of accounting concept no. 1 definition of the reporting entity*, August.

The Corporations Law. (1992). Sydney: CCH.

Financial Accounting Standards Board. (1978). *Statement of financial accounting concepts no. 1 Objectives of financial reporting by business enterprises*, November.

International Accounting Standards Board. (2007). *International accounting standard 18 Revenue*, April.

International Accounting Standards Board. (2010). *Framework for the preparation and presentation of financial statements*, April.

International Accounting Standards Board. (2013). *A review of the Conceptual Framework for financial reporting*, July.

Taylor, D. (2011). Hernandez the latest to commit to United with five-year deal. *The Guardian*, 13 October.

3

Albrecht, W.S. (Ed.). (1992). *Ethical issues in the practice of accounting*. South-Western, Mason, OH.

ASX Corporate Governance Council. (2007). *Corporate Governance Principles and Recommendations*, August. Australian Securities Exchange.

Carter, D. A., Simkins, B. J. & Simpson, W. G. (2003). Corporate governance, board diversity, and firm value. *The Financial Review*, 38(1), 33–53.

Dechow, P. M, Sloan, R. G., & Sweeney, A. P. (1996). Causes and consequences of earnings manipulation: An analysis of firms subject to enforcement actions by the SEC. *Contemporary Accounting Research*, 13(1), 1–36.

Finegold, D., Benson, G. S., & Hecht, D. (2007). Corporate boards and company performance: A review of research in light of recent reforms. *Corporate Governance: An International Review*, 15(5), 865–78.

Josephson, M. S. (1992). The need for ethics education in accounting. In Albrecht, W.S. (Ed.), *Ethical issues in the practice of accounting*. South-Western, Mason, OH.

Klein. Economic determinants of audit committee independence. *Accounting Review, April*, 2002, Vol.77(2), p.435(18).

Ramsay, I. (2001). *Independence of Australian company auditors: review of current Australian requirements and proposals for reform*, Commonwealth of Australia, Canberra.

Statsky, W. P. (1985). *West's legal thesaurus/dictionary: a resource for the writer and the computer researcher*. West Publishing Company, St Paul, MN.

Tabor, M. L. (1992). Why I compromised my professional code of ethics. In Albrecht, W.S. (Ed.), *Ethical issues in the practice of accounting*. South-Western, Mason, OH.

4

Hicks, Sir J. (1946). *Value and capital*. Clarendon Press, Oxford.

International Accounting Standards Board. (2010) IFRS 9 *Financial instruments*, October.

International Accounting Standards Board. (2011) IFRS 13 *Fair value measurement*, September.

5

Australian Accounting Standards Board. (2012). *AASB 101 Presentation of financial statements* [for for-profit entities], December.

6

Australian Accounting Standards Board. (2012). *AASB 101 Presentation of financial statements* [for for-profit entities], December.

Dichev, I., Graham, J., Harvey, C., and Rajgopal, S. (2013) Earnings quality: evidence from the field. *Journal of Accounting and Economics*.56 (2-3), 1–33.

International Accounting Standards Board. (2010). *Conceptual framework for the preparation and presentation of financial statements*, April.

7

Australian Accounting Standards Board. (2012). AASB 107 *Statement of cash flows*, December

8

Australian Accounting Standards Board. (2012). *AASB 102 Inventories.* December.

Australian Accounting Standards Board. (2012). *AASB 116 Property, plant and equipment*, September.

Australian Accounting Standards Board. (2012). *AASB 138 Intangible assets (For for-profits entities)*, December.

9

Australian Accounting Standards Board. (2012). AASB 112 Income taxes [for for-profits entities]. December.

Australian Accounting Standards Board. (2012). AASB 117 Leases, September.

Australian Accounting Standards Board. (2012). AASB 137 *Provisions, contingent liabilities and contingent assets*, December.

10

Australian Accounting Standards Board (2012) *AASB 108 Accounting policies, changes in accounting estimates and errors*, December.

12

Emmanuel, C. R., Otley, D. T. & Merchant, K. A. (1990), *Accounting for management control*, 2nd edition, Chapman & Hall, London.

Porter, M.E. (1980), *Competitive strategy*, The Free Press, New York.

—— (1985), *Competitive advantage: creating and sustaining superior performance*, The Free Press, New York.

Shergold, P. (2013) *Service sector reform: a roadmap for community and human services reform*, Department of Human Resources, Melbourne.

13

Coase, R. H. (1937) The Nature of the Firm, *Economica*, November, 386–405.

Hansen, D. & Mowen, M., (2002), *Cost management: accounting and control*, 4th edn, South-Western, Mason, OH.

Hronec, S.M. (1993) *Vital signs, using quality, time and cost performance measurement to chart your company's future*, Amacom, American Management Association, New York.

Kaplan R. S. and Norton D. P. (1992) 'The balanced scorecard: measures that drive performance' *Harvard Business Review*, January-February 71–79.

14

Kaplan, R. S. and Anderson S. R. (2007), The innovation of time-driven activity-based costing, *Cost Management*, March/April, 5–15.

15

Jensen, Michael C. (2001), 'Corporate Budgeting Is Broken - Let's Fix It', *Harvard Business Review*, Volume 79 Issue 10, November, pp. 94–101.

16

Wongsamuth, N. (2011). Akara eyes expanded output. *Bangkok Post*, 22 December.

18

McDulling, J. (2011), Telstra extends NBN deal deadline, *The Australian Financial Review*, 20 December, 35.

GLOSSARY

AASB (Australian Accounting Standards Board)

(Chapter 2) The body responsible for setting accounting standards in Australia.

AASB Accounting Standards

(Chapter 1) The standards issued by the Australian Accounting Standards Board.

absentee owners

(Chapter 2) The shareholders in large businesses.

absorption costing (full costing)

(Chapter 14) The method for determining the cost of inventories by including the appropriate share of both variable and fixed manufacturing costs, the latter usually allocated on the basis of normal operating capacity. While this method is prescribed as the approach to be employed in preparing general-purpose financial statements, a firm may elect to use the variable costing method for internal or managerial decision-making purposes. (AASB 102)

absorption of overheads

(Chapter 14) The term used for the process of sharing out indirect costs to products.

absorption rate

(Chapter 14) An absorption rate is normally used to charge out overheads to units of production on an equitable basis. It is determined by dividing the total overheads of a production cost centre by the level of activity.

account

(Chapter 2) A device used to provide a record of increases and decreases in each item that appears in a firm's financial statements.

accounting

(Chapter 1) The process of identifying, measuring and communicating economic information to permit informed judgement and decisions by users of the information.

accounting profit

(Chapter 9) The amount of profit as determined by the application of Accounting Standards and Concepts.

accounting rate of return (ARR)

(Chapter 18) A method of project evaluation which involves dividing average net profit by either average book value of investment or total initial investment.

accounting system

(Chapter 1) A collection of source documents, records, procedures, management policies and data-processing methods used to convert economic data into useful information.

accrual basis (of accounting)

(Chapters 6) The method of accounting whereby income and expenses are identified with a specific period of time, such as a month or a year, and are recorded as incurred, along with acquired assets, without regard to the date of receipt or payment of cash.

accruals

(Chapter 9) Amounts owing at a point in time, the amounts of which are not known with any certainty.

activity

(Chapter 14) A basic unit of work, an action or an event performed within a firm that results in the consumption of economic resources (e.g. machining of a component).

activity analysis

(Chapter 14) The process of identifying, describing and analysing the activities undertaken by the firm.

activity-based costing (ABC)

(Chapter 14) A costing method which tries to capture the change in technology by apportioning overheads into product costs on a more realistic basis, taking account of the activity and transactions that drive the cost. The focus in ABC is on managing activities instead of costs.

activity costs

(Chapter 14) Costs associated with the performance of a specified activity.

activity driver

(Chapter 14) Factors that measure the use of activities by cost objects (e.g. individual products in a multi-product firm). An activity

driver causes or 'drives' an activity's costs, explains the behaviour of that cost and is used to allocate that cost to identified cost objects.

activity hierarchy

(Chapter 14) A framework for describing different levels of activities that differentially affect the consumption of economic resources (e.g. unit, batch, product and facility sustaining).

ageing analysis

(Chapter 8) An analysis that is prepared by management and examines debts in terms of how old they are in order to reach a decision on the probability of receipt of payment.

agency relationship

(Chapter 1) A contract under which one or more principals engage another person (the agent) to perform some service on their behalf which involves delegating some decision-making authority to the agent.

agency theory

(Chapters 3) A theoretical model describing relationships where one party (i.e. the principal) delegates decision-making powers to another (i.e. the agent), and the mechanisms by which the principal seeks to mitigate the risks of the agent acting only in his/her own interests.

allocated

(Chapter 14) In the context of product costing, a cost that can be directly traced to a cost centre.

allowance for doubtful debts

(Chapter 8) A contra debtors account which shows the estimated total of future bad debts.

amortise

(Chapter 8) To systematically write off a portion or all of an asset over a period of years. This normally applies to intangible assets.

annuity

(Chapter 18) A stream of equal cash flows received or paid over a number of periods.

annuity due

(Chapter 18) A stream of equal cash flows immediately received or paid over a number of periods (e.g. beginning of each year).

annuity in arrears

(Chapter 18) A stream of equal cash flows received or paid in arrears over a number of periods (e.g. end of each year).

apportioning

(Chapter 14) In the context of product costing, this term describes the sharing out of overhead costs that cannot be directly traced to a cost centre.

assets

(Chapters 1) Resources controlled by the entity as a result of past events and from which future economic benefits are expected to flow to the entity. (IASB *Conceptual Framework*, para. 4.4a)

auditing

(Chapter 1) The examination of a company's general-purpose financial statements by an independent external observer (the auditor) to ensure that they present a 'true and fair' representation of the company's financial status. The auditor's findings are presented in the auditor's report.

audit committee

(Chapter 3) A subcommittee of the board of directors, and part of the corporate governance of a company. Its roles depend on the company, but in general it ensures that the financial statements have been reliably prepared and verified.

auditor independence

(Chapter 2) The auditor must be independent of the client for whom the audit is conducted to be able to express a truly objective opinion about the financial statements.

auditor's report

(Chapter 2) A report required by the *Corporations Act 2001*, prepared by an auditor and included with a company's financial statements, stating whether the company's financial statements comply with the requirements of the *Corporations Act*, whether they provide a true and fair view of the state of affairs of the company, and whether they are in accordance with applicable accounting standards.

average cost

(Chapter 8) A method of inventory valuation where an average cost is calculated by dividing the total costs of goods available for sale by the number of units available for sale. Two variations of the average cost method are moving average and weighted average.

avoidable cost

(Chapter 17) A cost that will not have to be paid if the organisation does not proceed with a decision; for example, delivery of a special order. Such a cost is relevant and should be included in the decision.

bad debts

(Chapter 8) Credit sales of a business for which the cash is not collected due to the debtor(s) not paying. Two ways in which this non-payment can be accounted for are by the direct write-off method and the provision for doubtful debts.

balance sheet

(Chapters 1 and 5) A statement that shows all the resources controlled by an entity and all the obligations due by the entity at one point in time.

balanced scorecard

(Chapter 13) A set of measures that give top managers a fast but comprehensive view of the business. The balanced scorecard includes financial measures that tell the results of actions already taken. And it complements the financial measures with operational measures on customer satisfaction, internal processes, and the organisation's innovation and improvement activities – operational measures that are the drivers of future financial performance. (Kaplan, 1992)

bank overdraft

(Chapter 9) A common source of short-term funds whereby a business negotiates with a bank to establish a limit to which the business can write cheques that will be accepted even though there is no money in the account. Normally, an overdraft can be terminated by the bank at short notice.

board of directors

(Chapter 2) The board is an important corporate governance mechanism. Its role is to represent shareholders and create value for shareholders.

break-even chart

(Chapter 16) A method used in CVP analysis which illustrates the relationship between cost, volume and profits by plotting these variables on a graph. The break-even point and areas of profit and loss can clearly and quickly be identified, enabling management to establish the effects of changing one of the variables.

break-even point

(Chapter 16) The sales volume at which income and total costs are equal, with no net profit or loss.

budget

(Chapter 1) A short- and long-term plan of action, expressed in monetary terms, for the future operating activities of a business.

budget period

(Chapter 15) The time frame of the budget – normally one year. The reason for choosing this period relates to the periodic reporting requirements for published accounts regulated by law.

budget process

(Chapter 15) The sequence of operations necessary to produce a budget for a particular organisation. The operations depend upon the type of organisation and its perceived requirements for planning and control.

budgetary control

(Chapter 15) This describes the use of budgets as a control mechanism. For example, actual performance can be compared with the budget to identify any deviations so that management can take corrective action.

business entity principle

(Chapter 5) This states that transactions, assets and liabilities that relate to the entity are accounted for separately. It applies to all types of entities, irrespective of the fact that the entity may not be recognised as a separate legal or taxable entity.

business risk

(Chapter 9) The risk resulting from factors in the uncertain commercial environment affecting the operations of a business. Also referred to as commercial risk, business risk is a function of many variables and differs from industry to industry.

business unit

(Chapter 13)   A division or segment of a firm identified for internal management and reporting purposes.

capital expenditure

(Chapter 18)   A firm's decision about the acquisition or disposal of non-current assets (e.g. property, plant and equipment).

capital structure

(Chapter 18)   A firm's mix of long-term debt and equity financing.

carrying value

(Chapter 8)   The cost of a non-current asset less the total depreciation to date. *See written-down value.*

cash

(Chapter 1)   Cash on hand and cash equivalents.

cash equivalents

(Chapter 7)   Highly liquid investments that are readily convertible to cash on hand which a company or economic entity uses in its cash management function on a day-to-day basis; and borrowings which are integral to the cash management function and which are not subject to a term facility.

cash flows

(Chapter 7)   Cash movements resulting from transactions with parties external to the company (or economic entity).

cash on hand

(Chapter 7)   Notes and coins held, and deposits held at call with a bank or financial institution.

common-size statements

(Chapter 10)   A financial statement in which the amount reported of each item in the statement is stated as a percentage of some specific amount also reported in the statement.

company

(Chapter 2)   An entity incorporated, or taken to be incorporated, under the *Corporations Act* (*Corporations Act*, section 9). It is recognised as a separate legal entity.

competitive strategies

(Chapter 12)   According to Porter, competitive strategies are the strategies a firm pursues for a competitive advantage. A firm may pursue a cost leadership, differentiation or focus strategy. Cost leadership or differentiation strategies are industry-wide strategies. A focus strategy is a market segment strategy and can be split into either a cost leadership or differentiation focus strategy

competitor analysis

(Chapter 12)   Competitor analysis indicates where each competitor is strong and poses a threat to the firm's marketing initiatives or is weak and vulnerable to increased competition. The understanding of the competitive environment obtained from competitor analysis facilitates the formulation of the firm's strategic plan.

compound interest

(Chapter 18)   Interest based on principal plus interest previously earned.

comprehensive income

(Chapter 1)   The sum of profit for the year and other comprehensive income.

conceptual framework

(Chapter 2)   A set of interrelated concepts which define the nature, subject, purpose and broad content of general-purpose financial statements.

conservatism

(Chapter 2)   The concept of conservatism applies to the practice of understatement of income or assets and/or maximum recognition of expenses or liabilities.

consolidated financial statements

(Chapter 2)   The name given to the financial reports prepared on behalf of an economic entity which enable users to examine the performance and financial position of both the parent entity on its own and the combination of the parent entity and the other entities it controls.

contribution margin

(Chapter 16)   Equal to the sales revenue less the variable costs.

contribution margin per unit

(Chapter 16)   Equal to the sales revenue per unit less the variable costs per unit.

contribution margin ratio

(Chapter 16)   A measure of the ratio of total (or per unit) variable costs divided by the total (or per unit) sales revenue.

control

(Chapter 7)   An investor controls an investee when it is exposed, or has rights, to variable returns from its involvement with the investee and has the ability to affect those returns through its power over the investee. (AASB 10)

conversion costs

(Chapter 14)   The cost for labour and overheads that converts inputs in the form of raw materials into outputs such as a finished product.

corporate appraisal

(Chapter 12)   Corporate appraisal is a critical assessment of the strengths, weaknesses, opportunities and threats in relation to those internal and environmental factors that affect a firm. This is sometimes called SWOT analysis and it is undertaken so as to establish the position of the firm prior to the preparation of a long-term plan

corporate governance

(Chapter 3)   Mechanisms such as the board of directors and audit committees which exist to provide some assurance to the absentee owners that the management of a company is accountable for its actions and to minimise agency costs in respect of its management.

corporate social responsibility (CSR)

(Chapter 1)   The mechanisms by which a firm manages those business activities that impact on society (e.g. employment of minorities or the disadvantaged).

correlation

(Chapter 16)   The interdependence between quantitative and qualitative data; the relationship between two or more measurable variables.

cost

(Chapter 14)   The value of economic resources, measured in monetary terms, consumed to achieve an organisational purpose.

cost behaviour

(Chapter 14)   The change that occurs in a total cost with changes in activity levels.

cost-benefit test

(Chapter 12)   A systematic method for comparing the costs and benefits of a proposed decision (e.g. a project or system

to be implemented) where the decision to proceed is guided by the net benefit expected to be realised.

cost centre

(Chapter 14) A business unit, which could be a function, activity or even an item of plant and equipment, which can be held responsible for certain costs.

cost driver

(Chapter 14) The activity base that explains the behaviour of costs. For example, the number of units produced will explain the direct costs incurred in manufacturing a product and it also may explain the behaviour of the indirect costs incurred. However, the behaviour of indirect costs is usually better explained by drivers unrelated to volume (e.g. maintenance hours, number of set-ups, production runs or parts handled, number of products manufactured, etc). A cost driver uses an activity that provides the best explanation of how economic resources are consumed.

cost estimation

(Chapter 14) Relates to methods that are used to measure past (historical) costs at varying activity levels. These costs will then be employed as the basis to predict future costs for decision making.

cost-focus strategy

(Chapter 12) A cost-focus strategy involves selecting a segment of the market and specialising in a product (or products) for that segment. The firm, by specialising in a limited number of products, or by concentrating on a small geographical area, can keep costs to a minimum within that market segment. For example, this type of strategy is often found in the printing, clothes manufacture and car repairs industries.

cost function

(Chapter 14) A graphical representation of the relationship between a dependent cost variable y and an independent cost variable x, where the vertical axis is the dependent cost variable and the horizontal axis is the independent cost variable. Points are plotted on the graph to produce a cost function. The function may be linear or non-linear.

cost leadership strategy

(Chapter 12) The strategy used by a firm where it competes with rival firms (and products) by seeking to be the industry's lowest-cost supplier. A cost leadership strategy can be pursued at a broad or whole-of-industry level or a narrow market niche level. Being competitive on cost provides significant strategic marketing advantages to a firm and these advantages translate into superior profitability.

cost object

(Chapter 14) A product, service, customer, process, activity or any object for which costs are measured and assigned.

cost of the non-current asset

(Chapter 8) Includes: (a) all reasonable and necessary costs incurred to place the asset in a position and condition ready for use; and (b) all costs incurred which enhance the future economic benefits of the asset beyond those initially expected at acquisition.

cost of capital

(Chapter 18) The minimum rate of return required of a project before it is accepted.

cost per unit

(Chapter 14) The value per unit when total costs are divided by the units of product (or service) produced.

cost pool

(Chapter 14) The assignment of individual cost items into a common cost pool having some rational basis for grouping these costs. For example, the allocation of individual cost items into a single cost pool could be justified on the grounds of the costs behaving in the same manner with variations in a relevant activity base (e.g. machine-related overheads) or the costs are trivial and the benefit of separately recording them is outweighed by the costs of doing so.

cost-volume-profit (CVP) analysis

(Chapter 16) A technique used by organisations to help them make decisions by examining the interrelationships between cost, volume and profits.

creditor

(Chapter 1) A person or entity to whom a debt is owed.

current cost

(Chapter 3) The cost of replacing an asset.

curvilinear regression

(Chapter 14) A regression which is not linear.

debentures

(Chapter 9) The term given to a secured transferable loan instrument that can be listed on the stock exchange. Debentures can be secured over specific assets, or by way of a floating charge over all assets.

debtors

(Chapter 8) Also called accounts receivable, debtors arise when a business sells goods or services to a third party on credit terms.

decentralisation

(Chapter 13) The delegation of decision-making power, within prescribed areas and limits, to lower-level managers.

dependent variable

(Chapter 14) In a cost function, the dependent variable is expressed as variable y and is the cost to be predicted – the total cost for an activity.

depreciable amount

(Chapter 8) The historical cost of a depreciable asset, or other revalued amount substituted for historical cost, in the financial report, less, in either case, the net amount expected to be recovered on disposal of the asset at the end of its useful life. (AASB 116)

depreciable asset

(Chapter 8) A non-current asset having a limited useful life. (AASB 116)

depreciation expense

(Chapter 8) An expense recognised systematically for the purpose of allocating the depreciable amount of a depreciable asset over its useful life. (AASB 116)

differential costs (incremental costs)

(Chapter 17) The differences in costs and benefits between alternative opportunities available to an organisation. It follows that when a number of opportunities are being considered, costs and benefits that are common to these alternative opportunities are irrelevant to the decision.

differentiation strategy

(Chapter 12) A differentiation strategy is based on the assumption that competitive advantage can be gained through particular characteristics of a firm's products or brands. The customer is prepared to pay more for this distinguishing characteristic than for the products of other firms. A differentiation strategy can be pursued at a broad (i.e. whole of industry) level or a narrow (i.e. niche or market segment) level.

direct costs

(Chapter 14) A cost that is readily traceable, and thus attributable, to a cost object (e.g. a product).

direct write-off method

(Chapter 8) A method of accounting for bad debts where the amount owing by the debtor is eliminated when it is determined the debtor will not pay. The debtor's balance is reduced and the other side of the transaction is the recognition of an expense.

directors' report

(Chapter 2) A report required by the *Corporations Act*, prepared by a company's directors and included with the company's financial statements, providing information including the directors' names, activities of the company, profit or loss for the year, amount of dividends, review of operations and many other matters in relation to the company.

directors' statement/declaration

(Chapter 2) A statement required by the *Corporations Act*, signed by at least two directors and included with a company's financial statements, outlining whether, in their opinion, the income statement and the balance sheet present a true and fair view, whether the company will be able to pay its debts as they fall due, and whether the financial statements comply with applicable accounting standards.

discounted cash flow (DCF) analysis

(Chapter 18) A technique based on the time value of money concept for evaluating capital investment decisions which recognises the amount, duration, timing and risk of the cash flows estimated to result from an investment decision

discounting

(Chapter 4) Present value of a sum to be received in x period given y interest rate.

dividend cover

(Chapter 10) Number of times the net profit after tax covers the ordinary dividend payment.

double-entry bookkeeping

(Chapter 1) The system developed for recording accounting information based on the concept that every transaction affects two or more components of the balance sheet (accounting) equation.

due process

(Chapter 2) The process designed to allow all interested parties maximum opportunity to comment on proposed accounting standards.

economic consequences

(Chapter 1) The impact of accounting policy changes on the economic position of various parties affected by the change.

economic value

(Chapter 4) The value of the expected earnings from using an item, discounted at an appropriate rate to give a present-day value.

Economic Value Added (EVA)

(Chapter 13) A measure of the residual income after deducting the cost of capital employed. Economic value added (EVA) = after tax profit plus interest − weighted average cost of capital × total capital employed.

efficient markets hypothesis

(Chapter 10) A market is efficient if it reacts immediately and without bias to reflect new information in asset prices.

entity

(Chapter 1) A fictional or notional being, such as a business, club, company or partnership, in respect of which financial transactions occur and accounts are kept.

equity

(Chapter 2) The residual interest in the assets of an entity after deduction of its liabilities. (AASB *Framework*, para. 49)

equity investors

(Chapter 10) The ordinary shareholder in a company, or the owner or partner in a sole proprietorship or partnership.

ethical

(Chapter 3) Behaving in an honest and morally correct manner.

expectation gap

(Chapter 2) The difference between what an auditor is required to do and what is expected by users.

expenses

(Chapter 1) Decreases in economic benefits during the accounting period in the form of outflows or depletions of assets or incurrences of liabilities that result in a decrease in equity, other than those relating to distributions to equity participants. (IASB *Conceptual Framework*, para. 4.25b)

exposure draft

(Chapter 9) A document circulated by the IASB and the AASB to interested groups for comment and amendment before a standard is produced.

factoring

(Chapter 9) The process whereby amounts that are owing by debtors are sold to a collection agency.

fair value

(Chapter 4) The price that would be received to sell an asset or paid to transfer a liability in an orderly transaction between market participants.

FIFO (first in, first out)

(Chapter 8) A method of inventory valuation based on the artificial assumption that the first goods bought are the first ones sold. The inventory held at the end of the period is assumed to be that purchased most recently.

finance lease

(Chapter 9) A lease which effectively transfers from the lessor to the lessee substantially all the risks and benefits

incidental to ownership of the leased property. (AASB 117)

financial accounting

(Chapter 1) That part of an accounting system that tries to meet the needs of various external user groups.

financial risk

(Chapter 9) The risk that a business might not be able to repay borrowed funds or interest as they fall due.

financial statements

(Chapter 1) The means of conveying a concise picture of the profitability and financial position of a business to management and interested outside parties. The most widely used financial statements are the balance sheet, the income statement, the statement of changes in equity and the cash flow statement (plus the notes attached to the statements).

finished goods

(Chapter 8) Goods that have been through the complete production or assembly cycle and are ready for resale to the customer.

five forces model

(Chapter 12) An analytical model developed by Michael Porter to analyse the intensity of competition and profitability in an industry. Porter's five forces comprise: the bargaining power of suppliers, the threat of new entrants, existing industry members, the threat of substitute products and the bargaining power of customers.

fixed assets

(Chapter 5) A term previously in use to describe those assets of an entity which were acquired with the view to be held by the entity, for the purpose of generating income over a number of years. Today, fixed assets are commonly referred to as non-current assets.

fixed charge

(Chapter 9) In relation to a creditor, a fixed charge means that the creditor has a charge against specific assets and normally holds a mortgage or other security over the asset.

fixed costs

(Chapter 14) A cost is fixed if it does not change in response to changes in the level of activity within the relevant range of activity.

floating charge

(Chapter 9) In relation to a creditor, the security over the assets does not relate to a specific asset but to all assets in general.

franked dividends

(Chapter 2) Dividends paid by a company which have been subject to company taxation.

FRC (Financial Reporting Council)

(Chapter 2) Responsible for the priorities, business plan, budget and staffing arrangements of the AASB but not able to influence the AASB's technical deliberations.

full costing (absorption costing)

(Chapter 14) The full cost of a product consists of the direct and indirect costs of production.

gap analysis

(Chapter 12) Gap analysis arises from a projection of current activities into the future to identify if there is a difference between the firm's objectives and the results from the continuation of current activities. Strategies are needed to deal with the differences. Gap analysis identifies the gap (e.g. in sales or profit terms) that has to be closed.

general-purpose financial statements (GPFS)

(Chapter 2) The set of financial statements according to AASB 101 intended to meet the information needs that are common to users who are unable to command the preparation of financial statements so as to satisfy, specifically, all of their needs.

Global Reporting Initiative (GRI)

(Chapter 1) The multi-stakeholder interest group that has taken on the task of developing and having adopted global guidelines for the reporting of organisation sustainability.

goals

(Chapter 12) Goals are the intended long-term outcomes to be achieved by the organisation, usually expressed in a broad and non-quantified form (e.g. to be rated as best in industry). While different organisational stakeholders invariably possess conflicting interests, the collective benefits derived by stakeholders are enhanced as a result

of cooperation. Hence, goals may seek to reinforce collective interests

goal congruence

(Chapter 13) The alignment of organisational goals with the personal and group goals of the individuals within an organisation.

going concern

(Chapter 1) The assumption that a business will continue to operate in the future without any intention to liquidate or to significantly reduce its scale of operations.

goodwill

(Chapter 8) The future benefits from unidentifiable assets.

group

(Chapter 2) The term applied to a parent company and its subsidiaries for which consolidated financial statements are prepared. The group is an economic entity and not a legal entity.

hire-purchase

(Chapter 9) A financial institution buys an asset and hires it to the prospective buyer. Ownership remains with the financial institution until the hirer makes the final payment.

historic cost

(Chapter 4) The cost incurred by an individual or entity in acquiring an item, measured at the time of the originating transaction.

IAS (International Accounting Standards)

(Chapter 2) Standards issued by the IASB prior to January 2002.

IASB (International Accounting Standards Board)

(Chapter 2) The body responsible for the development of International Accounting Standards.

idle capacity

(Chapter 16) The difference between available capacity and the planned usage of that capacity (e.g. with only 80 per cent of 200 000 available machine hours planned to be used, idle capacity = 40 000 machine hours).

IFRS (International Financial Reporting Standards)

(Chapter 2)   Standards issued by the IASB from January 2002. An IFRS includes all new IFRSs, previously issued IASs and interpretations of these standards.

income

(Chapter 2)   Increases in economic benefits during the accounting period in the form of inflows or enhancements of assets or decreases of liabilities that result in increases in equity, other than those relating to contributions from equity participants. (IASB *Conceptual Framework*, para. 4.25a)

income statement

(Chapter 1)   A financial report listing the income, expenses and net profit or net loss of a business (entity) for a time period.

independent variable

(Chapter 14)   In a cost function, the independent variable is expressed as variable x and is the level of activity.

indirect costs (overhead costs)

(Chapter 14)   Costs that cannot be easily and conveniently identified with a particular product.

intangible assets

(Chapter 8)   Non-current assets that lack physical substance and are not used for investment purposes.

integrated reporting

(Chapter 1)   A framework intended to guide the preparation and dissemination of periodic reports about how an organisation's strategy, governance, performance and prospects, in the context of its external environment, lead to the creation of value in the short, medium and long term.

interest

(Chapter 1)   A charge made for the use of money.

interest cover

(Chapter 10)   The number of times net profit before interest and tax covers the interest payment.

internal control

(Chapter 1)   The procedures and processes in place within a business to safeguard all assets including cash.

internal rate of return (IRR)

(Chapter 18)   The rate of return which discounts the cash flows of a project so that the present value of cash inflows equals the present value of cash outflows.

inventories

(Chapter 8)   Goods, other property and services: (a) held for sale in the ordinary course of business; (b) in the process of production for such sale; or (c) in the form of materials or supplies to be consumed in the production process or in the rendering of services. (AASB 102)

investment centre

(Chapter 13)   A business unit where the manager not only has control over the profits of the unit but also has some discretion as to the amount of investment undertaken by the unit.

irrevocable contract

(Chapter 2)   A legal or formal agreement made between two or more people that cannot be changed without incurring significant penalties.

job costing

(Chapter 14)   A method of costing where the cost is determined for units of output that are dissimilar in nature and/or the amount of economic resources used to produce them. Job-order costing is used by manufacturers of unique products such as a shipbuilder, a print shop, a manufacturer of special custom-designed machines, construction projects, etc.

just-in-time management

(Chapter 1)   A management technique designed to lower the costs of holding high levels of stock.

KPIs (key performance indicators)

(Chapter 13)   Measures (financial or non-financial) used to assess the degree of success in achieving certain targets of performance.

lease

(Chapter 9)   A contractual agreement between two parties whereby one party (the lessee) obtains the rights to use an item, such as a machine, in exchange for a series of lease payments to the other party (the lessor).

lenders

(Chapter 1)   Persons or organisations which permit the temporary use of money; for example, in return for payment.

lessee

(Chapter 9)   The person or company obtaining the rights to use leased property.

lessor

(Chapter 9)   The owner of the property which is leased out.

liabilities

(Chapter 2)   A present obligation of the entity arising from past events, the settlement of which is expected to result in an outflow from the entity of resources embodying future economic benefits. (IASB *Conceptual Framework*, para. 4.4b)

LIFO (last in, first out)

(Chapter 8)   A method of inventory valuation based on the assumption that the last goods bought are the first sold. Ending inventory is assumed to consist of the cost of the earliest units purchased.

linear cost function

(Chapter 14)   A linear cost function is a straight-line cost function which can be mathematically expressed as $y = a + bx$ where y is the total cost to be predicted; a is a constant (or fixed cost); b is the cost that will be the same for each unit of activity and, therefore, as the activity varies so will the cost (this cost is known as variable cost); x is the level of activity measured in units of output.

liquidity

(Chapter 1)   The ability of a business to satisfy its short-term obligations. Liquidity refers to the ease with which assets can be converted to cash in the normal course of business.

long-term finance

(Chapter 9)   Finance for periods greater than one year, and often more than 10 years.

make-or-buy decision

(Chapter 17)   The decision made by an organisation which must choose between, on the one hand, making a product or carrying out a service using its own resources, and, on the other hand, paying an external

organisation to make the product or carry out the service for it.

management accounting
(Chapter 1) That part of an accounting system that tries to meet the needs of management and internal users.

management information system (MIS)
(Chapter 12) A system that provides information to managers that is useful for making and evaluating decisions.

margin of safety
(Chapter 16) A measure of the margin by which budgeted (or actual) output exceeds budgeted (or actual) output at the break-even point.

master budget
(Chapter 15) The budgeted income statement and balance sheet, representing a summary of the individual functional budgets of the organisation as a whole.

materiality
(Chapter 2) Broadly, an item can be said to be material if its non-disclosure would cause the accounts to be misleading in some way.

materiality test
(Chapter 2) Assesses whether omission, misstatement or non-disclosure of an item of relevant and reliable information could affect decision making about the allocation of scarce resources by the users of the general-purpose financial reports of an entity.

medium-term finance
(Chapter 9) Not strictly the case, but generally finance for periods of one to 10 years.

mission statement
(Chapter 12) A mission statement serves three functions: it identifies the firm's value system; it indicates the firm's long-term approach to business and its commercial rationale for existing; and it is used as a statement for public relations purposes. A mission statement rarely changes.

multiple regression
(Chapter 14) The regression of a dependent variable on more than one independent or predicted variable.

mutually exclusive projects
(Chapter 18) Where the acceptance of one project results in the rejection of the other project.

net present value
(Chapter 18) The figure that results from discounting all cash flows of a project at a minimum rate of return and summing the resultant present values.

net realisable value
(Chapter 4) The estimated proceeds of sales less, where applicable, all further costs to the stage of completion, and less all costs to be incurred in marketing, selling and distribution to customers. (AASB 102)

non-cancellable lease
(Chapter 2) A contract which cannot be cancelled, allowing a person or entity to use or occupy property in return for rent.

non-current assets
(Chapter 5) All assets other than current assets. (AASB 101)

non-current liabilities
(Chapter 5) Liabilities which are not current liabilities. (AASB 101)

non-financial performance indicators
(Chapter 13) Non-financial performance indicators provides a manager with information in the form of non-financial measures (e.g. kilograms, tonnes or litres, operating performance ratios) of the firm's manufacturing processes and outputs.

non-redeemable preference share
(Chapter 10) Preference shares which cannot be redeemed out of the company's profits or out of the proceeds of a new share issue.

normal costing
(Chapter 14) Where the cost of a product is determined using the actual costs for direct costs and a predetermined rate for the allocation of indirect costs.

objectives
(Chapter 12) Objectives are the specific, quantified and time-bounded expression of organisational goals (e.g. to achieve 45 per cent market share of industry sales by 31 December).

operating cycle
(Chapter 5) The average period between the purchase of merchandise and the conversion of this merchandise back into cash.

operating decisions
(Chapter 12) Decisions that focus on the efficient use of the resources available to a firm in the short term.

operating lease
(Chapter 9) A short-term lease under which most of the risks and rewards associated with ownership of the property remain with the lessor.

opportunity cost
(Chapter 17) The opportunity cost of a resource is normally defined as the maximum benefit which could be obtained from that resource if it were used for some alternative purpose. If a firm uses a resource for alternative A rather than B, it is the potential benefits that are forgone by not using the resource for alternative B that constitute the opportunity cost. The potential benefits forgone, the opportunity cost, are a relevant cost in the decision to accept alternative A. The opportunity cost reflects the cost of the most valuable alternative given up.

ordinary shareholder
(Chapter 9) A person holding a class of shares that have no preferences relative to other classes.

other comprehensive income
(Chapter 6) Items of income and expenses (including reclassification adjustments) that are not recognised in profit or loss as required or permitted by other Australian Accounting Standards. These items are recognised directly in equity.

outcome KPIs
(Chapter 13) The measures of performance of an entity from an external viewpoint.

parent entity
(Chapter 2) One which controls another entity.

partnership
(Chapter 2) The relationship which exists between persons carrying on a business in common with a view to profit. (*Partnership Act* 1891, section 1(1))

payback

(Chapter 18) The time required to recover a proposed project's initial investment.

period costs

(Chapter 14) Costs that relate to the period in question. They are recognised in the income statement in the accounting period when they are incurred and cannot justifiably be carried forward to future periods because they do not represent future benefits, or the future benefits are so uncertain as to defy measurement.

planning and control

(Chapter 12) Planning involves the determination of objectives and the means by which to attain them. The control process is the means of ensuring that the plans are achieved.

post-implementation (post-completion) audit

(Chapter 18) A post-implementation audit is the re-examination of a capital investment project subsequent to its initial acceptance and implementation.

preference shareholder

(Chapter 9) One who holds a class of shares which receive preferential treatment over ordinary shares; for example, preference in dividend distribution.

prepayments

(Chapter 5) Prepayments are payments made in advance for goods and/ or services.

present-day value

(Chapter 4) The value today of a given amount or item.

prime costs

(Chapter 14) The cost for materials and labour that can be directly and readily traced to a product.

principle of duality

(Chapter 5) The basis of the double-entry bookkeeping system on which accounting is based. It states that every transaction has two opposite and equal components.

process costing

(Chapter 14) A method of costing where the cost is determined for units of output that are similar in nature and the total value of economic resources used to produce them can be averaged over all units of output.

product cost

(Chapter 14) The cost of producing an item. When firms manufacture only one product, the process of product costing is straightforward. When firms manufacture more than one product (multi-product firms), the process of product costing can be complex. Two approaches used in determining product costs in multi-product firms are variable costing and absorption costing.

production budget

(Chapter 15) An estimate of the number of units that will be manufactured by an organisation during the budget period.

production cost centre

(Chapter 14) A department where the manufacturing activity physically takes place.

profit

(Chapter 4) The difference between the wealth at the start and at the end of a period, profit is income less expenses. It is a measure of flow that summarises activity over a period.

profit centre

(Chapter 13) A business unit which is accountable for both costs and income.

projected financial statements

(Chapter 15) Projected financial statements are the pro-forma financial statements (i.e. income statement, balance sheet and cash flow statement) prepared for a future budget period. They are primarily prepared for the benefit of an organisation's management in undertaking 'what-if analysis', however, they can also be submitted in support of applications for finance.

qualitative

(Chapter 1) The nature or characteristics of information.

qualitative characteristics of financial information

(Chapter 2) If financial information is to be useful it must be relevant and faithfully represent what it purports to represent. The usefulness of financial information is enhanced if it is comparable, verifiable, timely and understandable. (IASB *Conceptual Framework*, para. QC 4, Chapter 2)

qualitative measures

(Chapter 13) Outcomes that are not usually measured in quantitative terms.

quantitative

(Chapter 1) The amount or size of information.

quantitative measures

(Chapter 13) Outcomes that are measured in numerical terms (e.g. volume, dollars).

rate of return

(Chapter 18) The total income and capital appreciation generated per dollar of funds invested.

realised

(Chapter 5) Convert to cash or a legal claim to cash.

redeemable preference share

(Chapter 9) Preference shares that can be redeemed out of the company's profits or out of the proceeds of a new share issue.

reducing-balance method

(Chapter 8) A method of depreciation that results in a decreasing depreciation charge over the useful life of the depreciable asset. Depreciation expense is calculated for each period through the application of a predetermined depreciation rate to the declining undepreciated cost of the asset, called the written-down value or book value. The following formula, in theory, is used to determine the annual depreciation rate:

$$\text{depreciation rate} = 1 - \sqrt[n]{\frac{r}{C}}$$

where n = estimated useful life (in years), r = estimated residual value, and c = original cost (in dollars). In practice an approximation, such as doubling the straight-line rate, is used.

regression analysis

(Chapter 14) A sophisticated method of cost estimation which involves making a number of observations from past cost behaviour and statistically analysing the data to produce a line of best fit through plotted cost points on a graph. Patterns of behaviour

can be identified from the linear regression model and conclusions drawn about the correlation between cost and the activity being analysed.

relevant range of activity

(Chapter 14)   The levels of activity that a firm has experienced in past periods. It is assumed that in this range the relationship between the independent variables will be similar to that previously experienced.

replacement cost

(Chapter 4)   The amount that would have to be paid at today's prices to purchase an item similar to the existing item. The cost has come about as a direct result of the decision to use a resource for a purpose not originally intended and the need to replace the resource.

reporting entities

(Chapter 2)   Entities (including economic entities) for which there are users who rely on the financial statements as their major source of financial information about the entity. (AASB *Framework*, para 8)

reserves **(Chapter 2)**   Amounts set aside

out of profits and other surpluses which are not designed to meet any liability, contingency, commitment or diminution in value of assets known to exist at the date of the balance sheet. Reserves do not equal cash.

residual income

(Chapter 13)   The net income measured after deducting a charge on the capital employed.

residual value

(Chapter 8)   The residual value of a non-current asset is an estimate of the net amount recoverable on ultimate disposal of the asset when it is no longer viable to use in the business.

responsibility accounting

(Chapter 13)   An approach used to monitor performance whereby personnel in an organisation who incur expenditure and generate income are identified and made responsible for these costs and income.

responsibility centres

(Chapter 13)   The various decision centres throughout an organisation, normally departments or divisions, recognised in the responsibility accounting management

approach. The manager's knowledge of the centre places him or her in an advantageous position within the organisation to ensure that budget targets are achieved.

revenues

(Chapter 2)   Gross inflows of economic benefits during the period arising in the course of the ordinary activities of an entity when those inflows result in increases in equity, other than increases relating to contributions from equity participants. (AASB 118, para. 7)

sales budget

(Chapter 15)   The conversion of the sales forecast for a budget period of an organisation into detailed information concerning the products or services that it is anticipated will be sold.

secured lender

(Chapter 10)   Someone who has a legal charge over the assets of a business and can claim those assets if the business does not repay or service the loan in accordance with the agreement.

sensitivity analysis

(Chapter 18)   A quantitative approach used to assess the effect on a proposed investment project's profitability (e.g. net present value) of changes in independent variables (e.g. investment outlay, cost of capital, revenues and costs) and focuses managerial attention on those variables that are critical to the capital expenditure decision to be made.

service cost centre

(Chapter 13)   Those decision centres that are primarily engaged in servicing the production function, but are not directly involved in the production activity.

short-term finance

(Chapter 9)   Finance for a period of less than one year.

simple interest

(Chapter 18)   Interest based on original principal only.

sole trader

(Chapter 2)   A one-owner business.

solvency

(Chapter 10)   The ability of a business to repay borrowed funds or interest as they fall due. An insolvent firm is unable to meet its commitments.

spare capacity

(Chapter 17)   An organisation which has enough resources available to make another product or component without affecting the production of other products is said to have spare capacity.

standards overload

(Chapter 2)   A problem concerned with the time and costs involved in preparing general-purpose financial reports which must comply with a large number of accounting standards.

statement of cash flows

(Chapter 7)   A financial statement showing the cash inflows and cash outflows for an accounting period.

statement of changes in equity (SOCE)

(Chapter 6)   The purpose of the SOCE is to report all changes to equity that are taken directly to the equity section of the balance sheet, together with the profit or loss for the period. Therefore, this shows the total changes to the equity for the period.

statement of comprehensive income (SOCI)

(Chapter 6)   From 1 January 2009, all entities preparing a general-purpose financial report must prepare a statement of comprehensive income. The statement reports all non-owner changes to equity for an accounting period. It reports items of other comprehensive income that are added/subtracted from profit to produce total comprehensive income.

stewardship

(Chapter 1)   The need to protect a firm's economic resources (normally referred to as assets) from theft, fraud, wastage, and so on.

stock exchange

(Chapter 1)   A market for the buying and selling of stocks and shares in which supply and demand govern price.

straight-line method

(Chapter 8)   A method of depreciation that allocates an equal amount of depreciation to all the periods over the useful life of the depreciable asset. The depreciation charge for each period is determined by dividing the cost of the asset, less the estimate of any residual value at the end of the asset's life, by the useful life of the asset.

strategic decisions

(Chapter 12) Decisions that determine the long-term policies of a firm; necessary if the firm is to meet its objectives.

strategic KPIs

(Chapter 13) The measures of performance that are concerned with how well an entity is achieving its strategies.

strategic plan

(Chapter 12) A strategic plan is a document or statement indicating in some detail the time scale for the strategy, and the resources available for its achievement.

strategic planning

(Chapter 12) The process of deciding upon the objectives of the firm, on changes to those objectives, on the resources to be used to attain those objectives and on the policies that are to govern the acquisition, use and disposition of those resources.

strategy

(Chapter 12) A strategy is a course of action, including the specification of resources required, to achieve a specific objective.

subsidiary

(Chapter 2) An entity which is controlled by a parent entity.

sunk costs (past costs)

(Chapter 17) Costs which have been paid or which are owed by a firm. The firm is committed to paying for them in the future.

SWOT (strengths, weaknesses, opportunities and threats)

(Chapter 12) A framework for critically evaluating organisational resources and capabilities (i.e. strengths and weaknesses) and environmental factors affecting organisational performance (i.e. opportunities and threats).

T account

(Chapter 11) Under the traditional approach to accounting, this was an account format shaped like the letter T. Debits are recorded on the left-hand side and credits on the right-hand side.

taxable income

(Chapter 1) The amount of profit, as determined by the Tax Commissioner, on which the current income tax liability is calculated.

temporary differences

(Chapter 9) The differences between the tax balances and the accounting balances of assets and liabilities.

trade credit

(Chapter 9) The finance that is available from suppliers selling goods on credit.

trend analysis

(Chapter 10) A technique commonly used in financial statement analysis to assess a business's growth prospects.

trial balance

(Chapter 11) The preparation of a statement which lists all the financial accounts and their respective debit or credit balances to ensure the equality of debits and credits made to the accounts.

triple bottom line (TBL) reporting

(Chapter 1) A framework for reporting an organisation's economic, environmental and social performance.

unavoidable cost

(Chapter 17) A cost which will be incurred regardless of whether or not a decision (e.g. the delivery of a special order) is accepted or rejected. Therefore, the cost is irrelevant to the decision.

under-recovery of overhead

(Chapter 14) The difference between the actual overhead cost and the estimate on which the absorption rate is based. The difference is classified as a period cost in the income statement because it is not identified with any of the units of production produced during the year.

units-of-production method

(Chapter 8) A method of depreciation that relates depreciation to use rather than to time. It is appropriate for an asset where usage will materially affect its lifespan. The depreciation charge is determined by dividing the cost of the asset, less the estimate of the asset's residual value, by the estimated number of output units expected from the asset during its estimated useful life. Output units can be expressed in numerous ways; for example, kilometres or operating hours. The result of the calculation is a depreciation rate per output unit which, when multiplied by the number of units used or produced during the period, gives the depreciation expense for a period.

unrealised gain

(Chapter 2) A gain which is yet to be realised by way of a transaction. For example, an increase in the value of an asset represents an unrealised gain until the asset is sold, at which time the gain would be realised.

unrealised loss

(Chapter 2) A loss which is yet to be realised by way of a transaction. For example, a decrease in the value of an asset represents an unrealised loss until the asset is sold, at which time the loss would be realised.

unsecured creditor

(Chapter 10) A creditor that does not have a legal charge on the assets of a business.

useful life

(Chapter 8) For a non-current asset, the time period the asset is expected to be used to produce goods or services.

user group

(Chapter 10) The different classes of people for whom financial statement analysis is being undertaken.

value

(Chapter 1) An item's equivalence in money.

value chain

(Chapter 12) The interlinked chain of activities undertaken by the organisation that transforms inputs into outputs desired by customers and when well-managed, provides a source of competitive advantage. For a manufacturing firm, the value chain includes primary activities such as inbound logistics, manufacturing operations, marketing and sales, outbound distribution logistics and after-sales service. These activities are facilitated by the provision of support services such as procurement, research and development, human resource management and corporate-level activities (e.g. accounting and finance, information technology and legal services).

value chain analysis

(Chapter 12) Value chain analysis examines how a firm's resources are used to create value for customers. It concentrates on the processes of converting inputs into outputs. Traditional costing systems are not

good at identifying the costs involved in creating customer value.

variable costing
(Chapter 14) Only variable production costs are included in variable costing.

variable costs
(Chapter 14) Costs that are the same per unit of activity within the relevant range of activity. Therefore, total variable costs increase and decrease in direct proportion to the increase and decrease in the activity level. The activity level depends upon what is being measured; that is, production output or sales output.

variance
(Chapter 15) The difference, measured in financial and non-financial terms, between budgeted and actual revenues, costs or other factor (e.g. material consumption or machine utilisation).

variance analysis
(Chapter 12) The analytical approach used to identify and investigate the cause of variances with a view to either eliminating or controlling the occurrence of such variances in the future.

wealth
(Chapter 4) A static measure representing a stock at a particular point in time.

weighted average cost of capital
(Chapter 18) A measure of the expected rate of return on a portfolio of a firm's debt and equity securities after adjusting for the tax deductibility of interest on debt.

work in progress
(Chapter 8) Products and services that are at an intermediate stage of completion.

worksheet
(Chapter 5) An arrangement of columns on a sheet of paper, used by accountants to gather and organise the information from which financial statements can be prepared.

written-down historic cost
(Chapter 4) The historic cost after an adjustment for usage (commonly referred to as depreciation).

written-down value
(Chapter 8) The cost of a non-current asset less the total depreciation to date. *See carrying value.*

INDEX